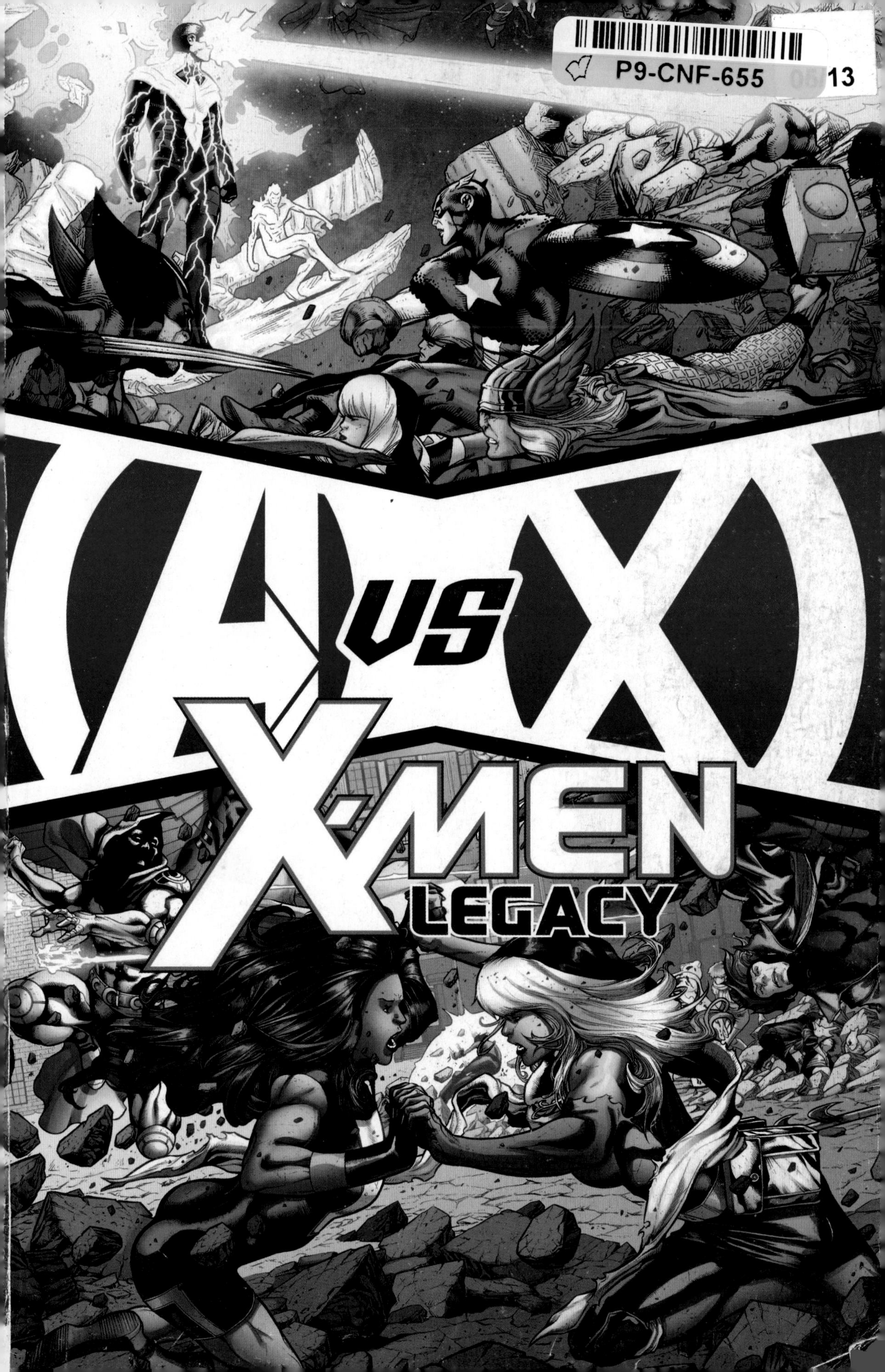
A VS X
X-MEN LEGACY

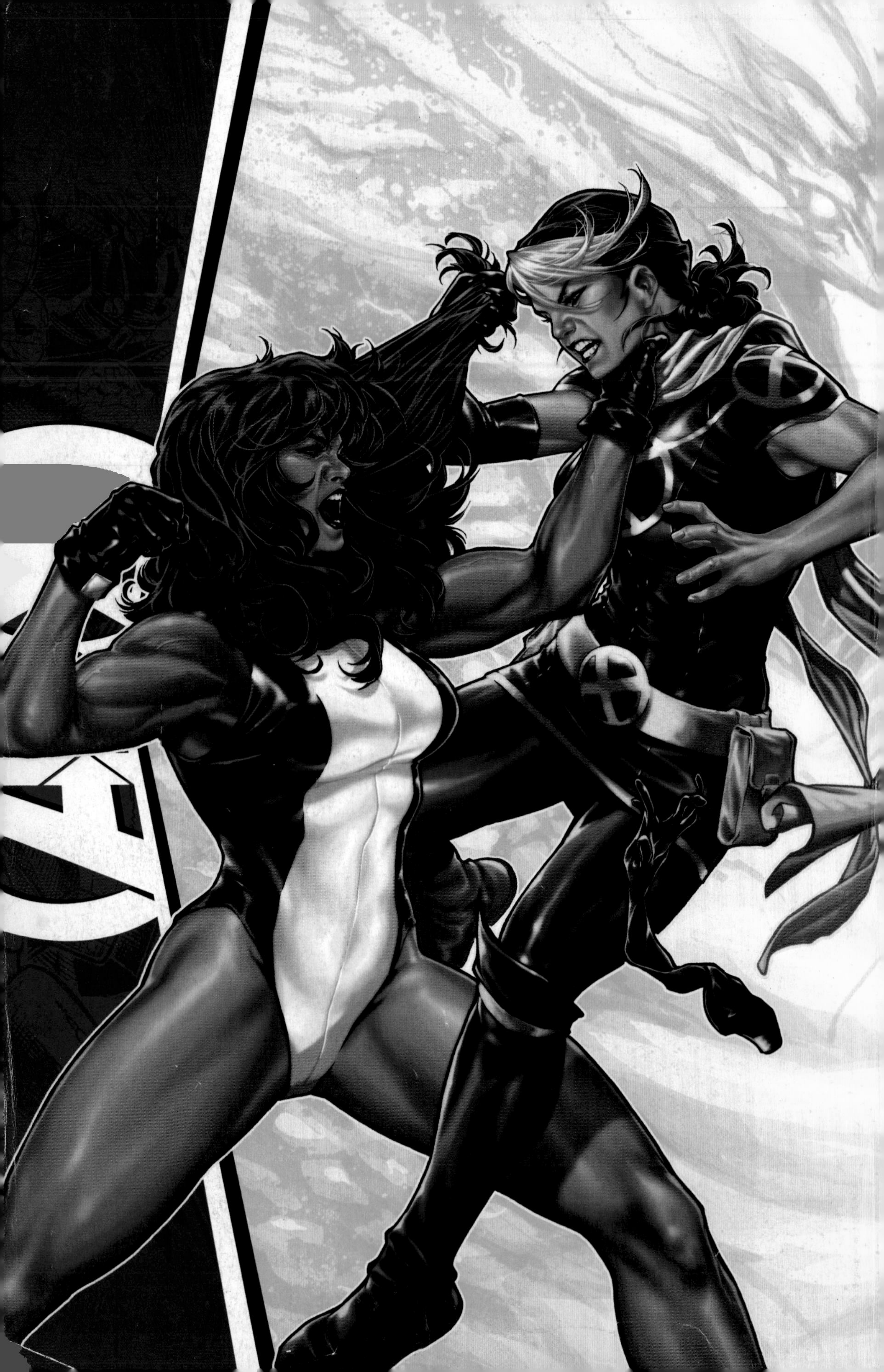

X-MEN LEGACY

WRITER: **CHRISTOS GAGE**

PENCILERS: **RAFA SANDOVAL** (#266-267 & #271-273)

& DAVID BALDEON (#268-270 & #274-275)

INKER: **JORDI TARRAGONA**

COLORISTS: **RACHELLE ROSENBERG** (#266-267 & #271-275)

& BRIAN REBER (#268-270)

LETTERER: **VC'S CORY PETIT**

COVER ART: **MARK BROOKS** (#266, #268-270 & #272-275),

MARK BROOKS & RACHELLE ROSENBERG (#267)

AND **SALVA ESPIN & RACHELLE ROSENBERG** (#271)

ASSISTANT EDITOR: **JORDAN D. WHITE**

EDITOR: **NICK LOWE**

COLLECTION EDITOR: **JENNIFER GRÜNWALD**
ASSISTANT EDITORS: **ALEX STARBUCK & NELSON RIBEIRO**
EDITOR, SPECIAL PROJECTS: **MARK D. BEAZLEY**
SENIOR EDITOR, SPECIAL PROJECTS: **JEFF YOUNGQUIST**
SVP OF PRINT & DIGITAL PUBLISHING SALES: **DAVID GABRIEL**
BOOK DESIGN: **JEFF POWELL**

EDITOR IN CHIEF: **AXEL ALONSO**
CHIEF CREATIVE OFFICER: **JOE QUESADA**
PUBLISHER: **DAN BUCKLEY**
EXECUTIVE PRODUCER: **ALAN FINE**

AVENGERS VS. X-MEN: X-MEN LEGACY. Contains material originally published in magazine form as X-MEN LEGACY #266-275. First printing 2013. ISBN# 978-0-7851-6587-3. Published by MARVEL WORLDWIDE, INC., a subsidiary of MARVEL ENTERTAINMENT, LLC. OFFICE OF PUBLICATION: 135 West 50th Street, New York, NY 10020. Copyright © 2012 and 2013 Marvel Characters, Inc. All rights reserved. All characters featured in this issue and the distinctive names and likenesses thereof, and all related indicia are trademarks of Marvel Characters, Inc. No similarity between any of the names, characters, persons, and/or institutions in this magazine with those of any living or dead person or institution is intended, and any such similarity which may exist is purely coincidental. **Printed in the U.S.A.** ALAN FINE, EVP - Office of the President, Marvel Worldwide, Inc. and EVP & CMO Marvel Characters B.V.; DAN BUCKLEY, Publisher & President - Print, Animation & Digital Divisions; JOE QUESADA, Chief Creative Officer; TOM BREVOORT, SVP of Publishing; DAVID BOGART, SVP of Operations & Procurement, Publishing; RUWAN JAYATILLEKE, SVP & Associate Publisher, Publishing; C.B. CEBULSKI, SVP of Creator & Content Development; DAVID GABRIEL, SVP of Print & Digital Publishing Sales; JIM O'KEEFE, VP of Operations & Logistics; DAN CARR, Executive Director of Publishing Technology; SUSAN CRESPI, Editorial Operations Manager; ALEX MORALES, Publishing Operations Manager; STAN LEE, Chairman Emeritus. For information regarding advertising in Marvel Comics or on Marvel.com, please contact Niza Disla, Director of Marvel Partnerships, at ndisla@marvel.com. For Marvel subscription inquiries, please call 800-217-9158. Manufactured between 2/28/2013 and 3/23/2013 by QUAD/GRAPHICS, VERSAILLES, KY, USA.

10 9 8 7 6 5 4 3 2 1

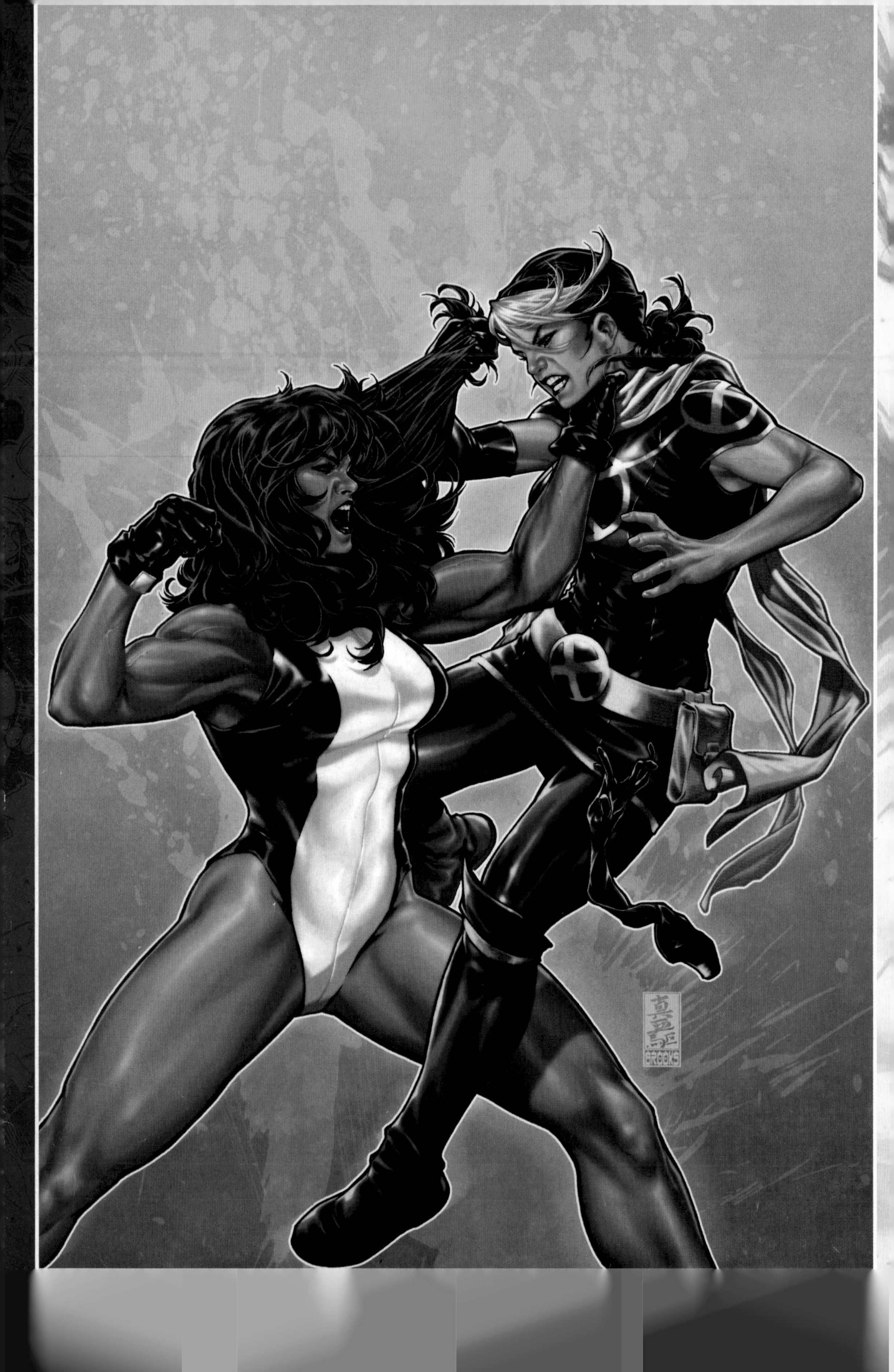
BROOKS

X-MEN LEGACY

Based at the Jean Grey School for Higher Learning, veteran X-Man Rogue leads a group of X-Men in teaching and defending the next generation of mutantkind.

ROGUE

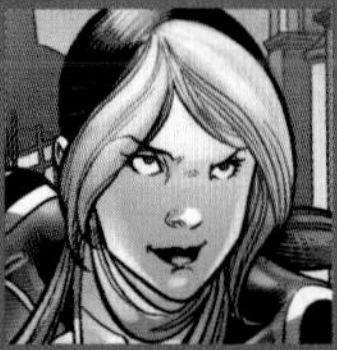

Power Absorption

KITTY PRYDE

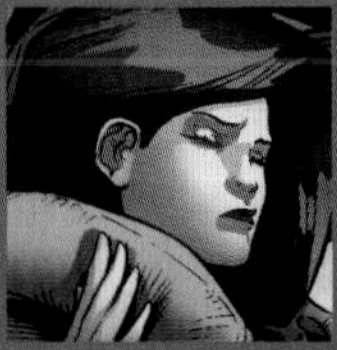

Intangibility

FRENZY

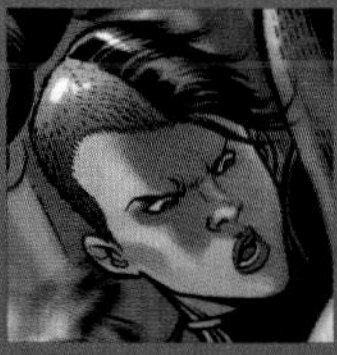

Super-Strength and Durability

CANNONBALL

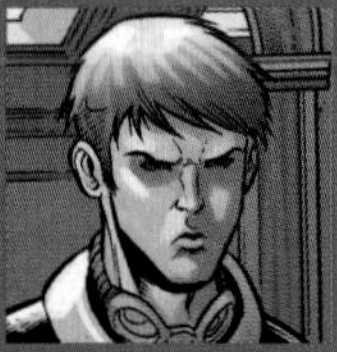

Jet Propulsion

RACHEL GREY

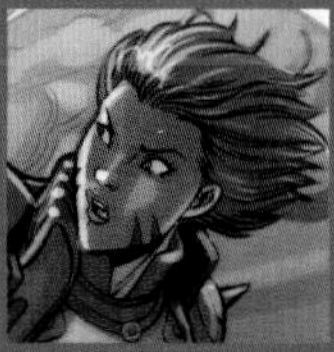

Telepathy; Telekinesis

GAMBIT

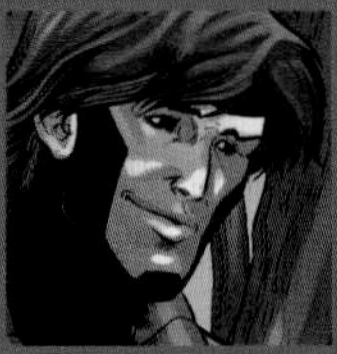

Explosive Energy Projectiles

MIMIC

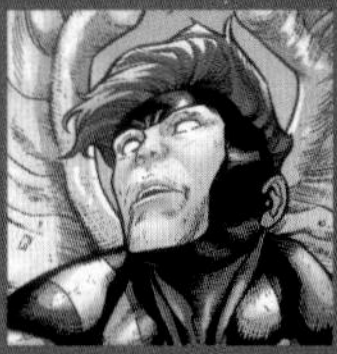

Power Mimicry

HUSK

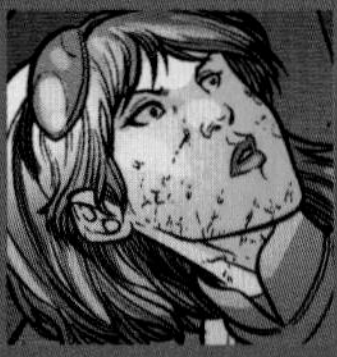

Metamorph

ICEMAN

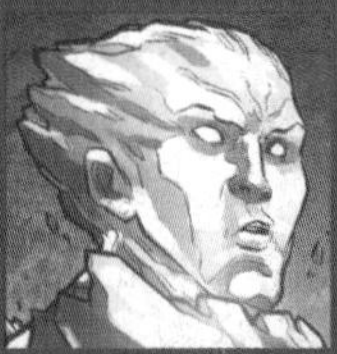

Ice Manipulation

CHAMBER

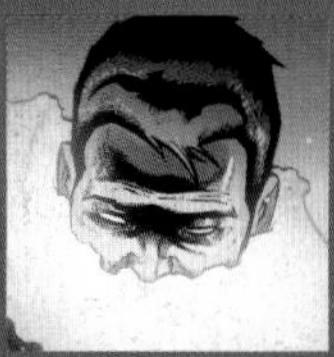

Psionic Energy Blasts

PREVIOUSLY

The Phoenix Force — the cosmic harbinger of rebirth — is headed toward Earth. The human super heroes known as The Avengers believe that it is a destructive force that will lay waste to the planet, while the X-Men believe it is a force of renewal, one that will reignite the dying mutant race. Both groups believe the Phoenix is coming to possess young mutant Hope Summers as its avatar.

While Wolverine joins a team of Avengers on their mission to wrest Hope from the X-Men on Utopia, and Beast takes a team of Avengers into deep space to intercept the firebird before it can reach Earth, Rogue and her team of X-Men are tasked with safeguarding the school. But as they receive news from the front lines, their resolve to remain outside the conflict may be challenged...

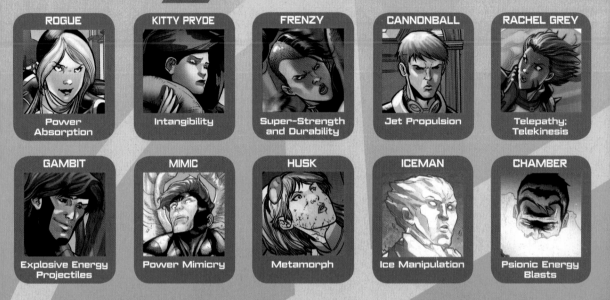

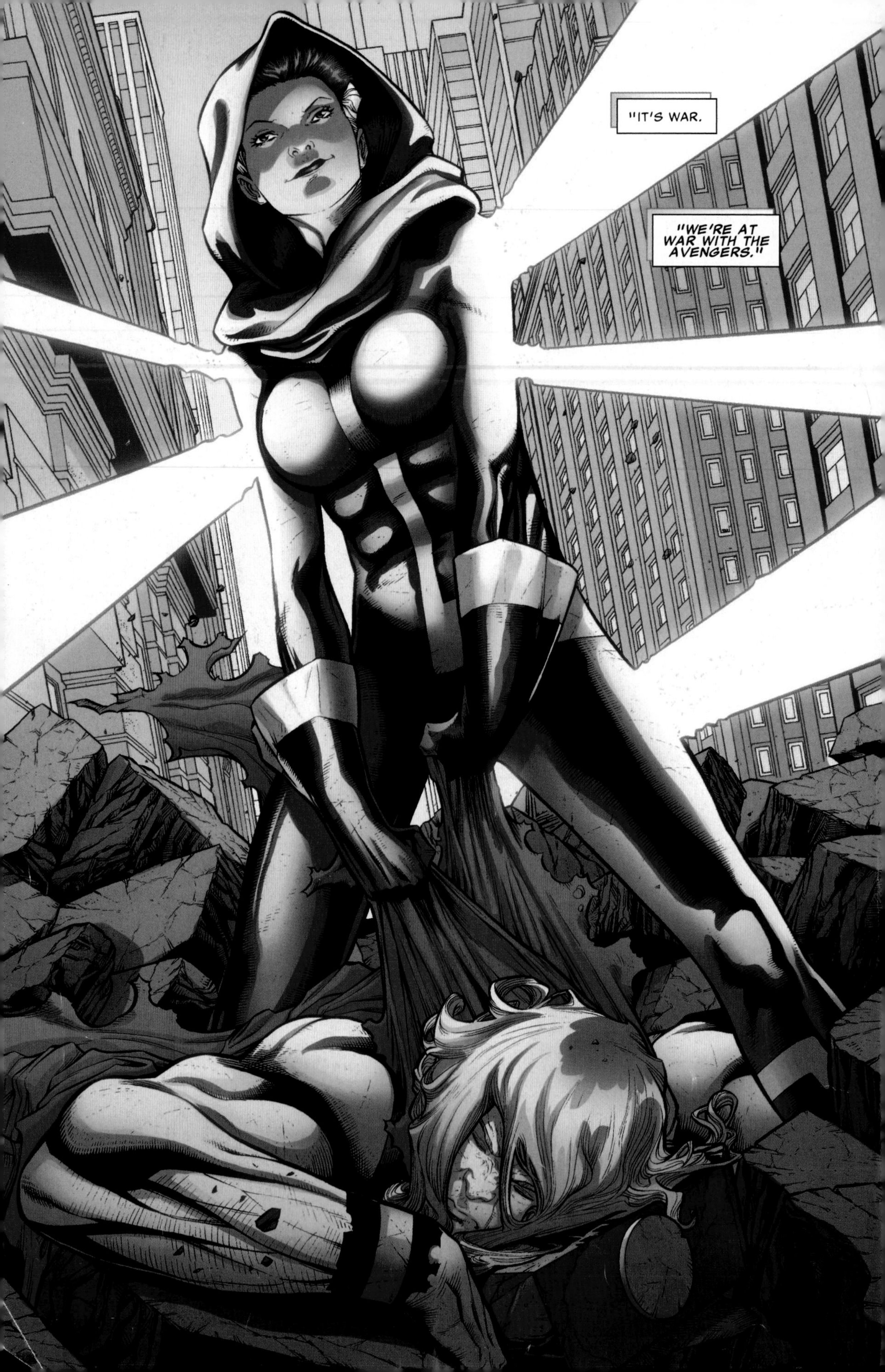
"IT'S WAR.
"WE'RE AT WAR WITH THE AVENGERS."

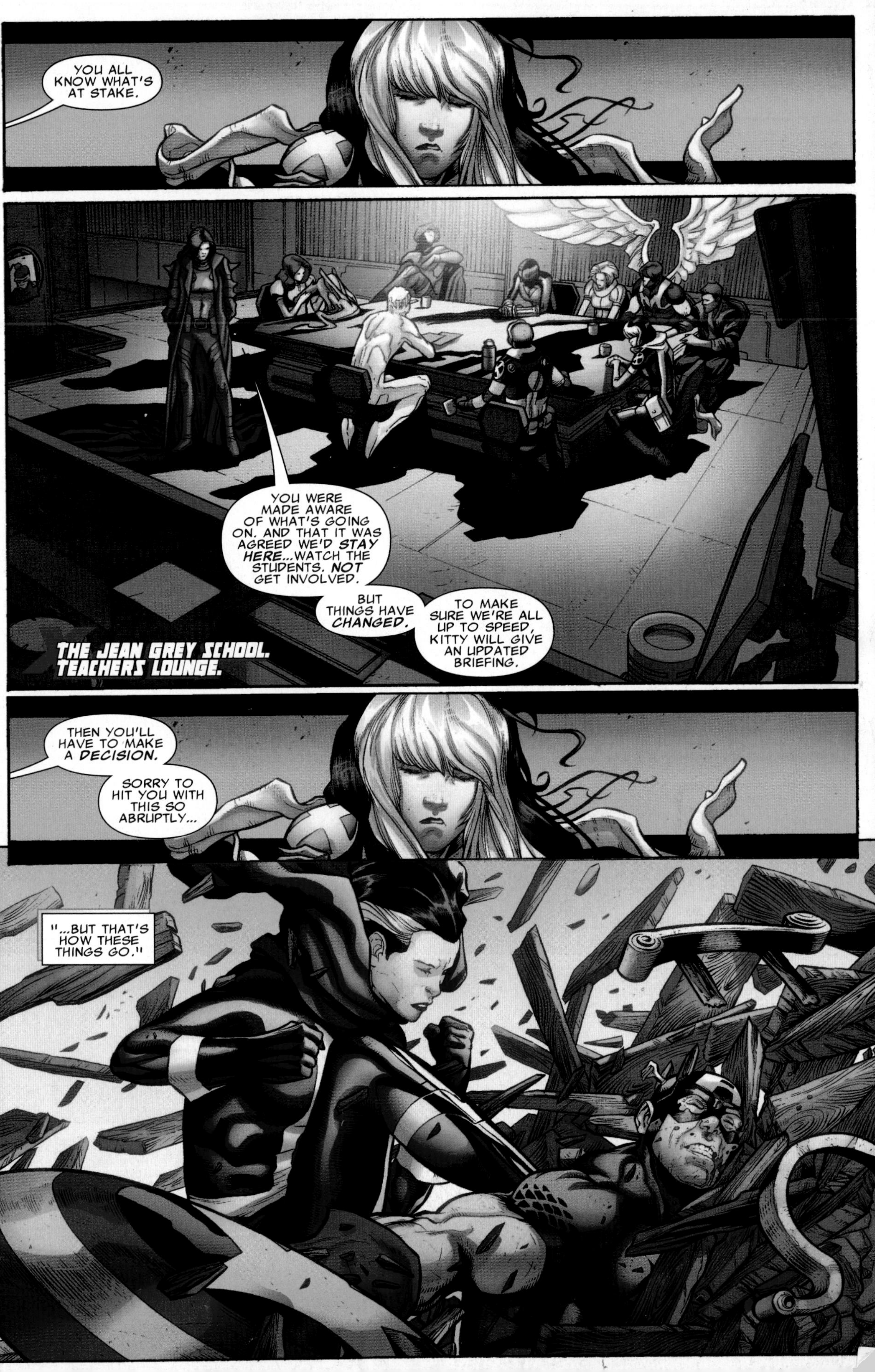
YOU ALL KNOW WHAT'S AT STAKE.
YOU WERE MADE AWARE OF WHAT'S GOING ON. AND THAT IT WAS AGREED WE'D STAY HERE...WATCH THE STUDENTS. NOT GET INVOLVED.
BUT THINGS HAVE CHANGED.
TO MAKE SURE WE'RE ALL UP TO SPEED, KITTY WILL GIVE AN UPDATED BRIEFING.
THE JEAN GREY SCHOOL. TEACHERS LOUNGE.
THEN YOU'LL HAVE TO MAKE A DECISION.
SORRY TO HIT YOU WITH THIS SO ABRUPTLY...
"...BUT THAT'S HOW THESE THINGS GO."

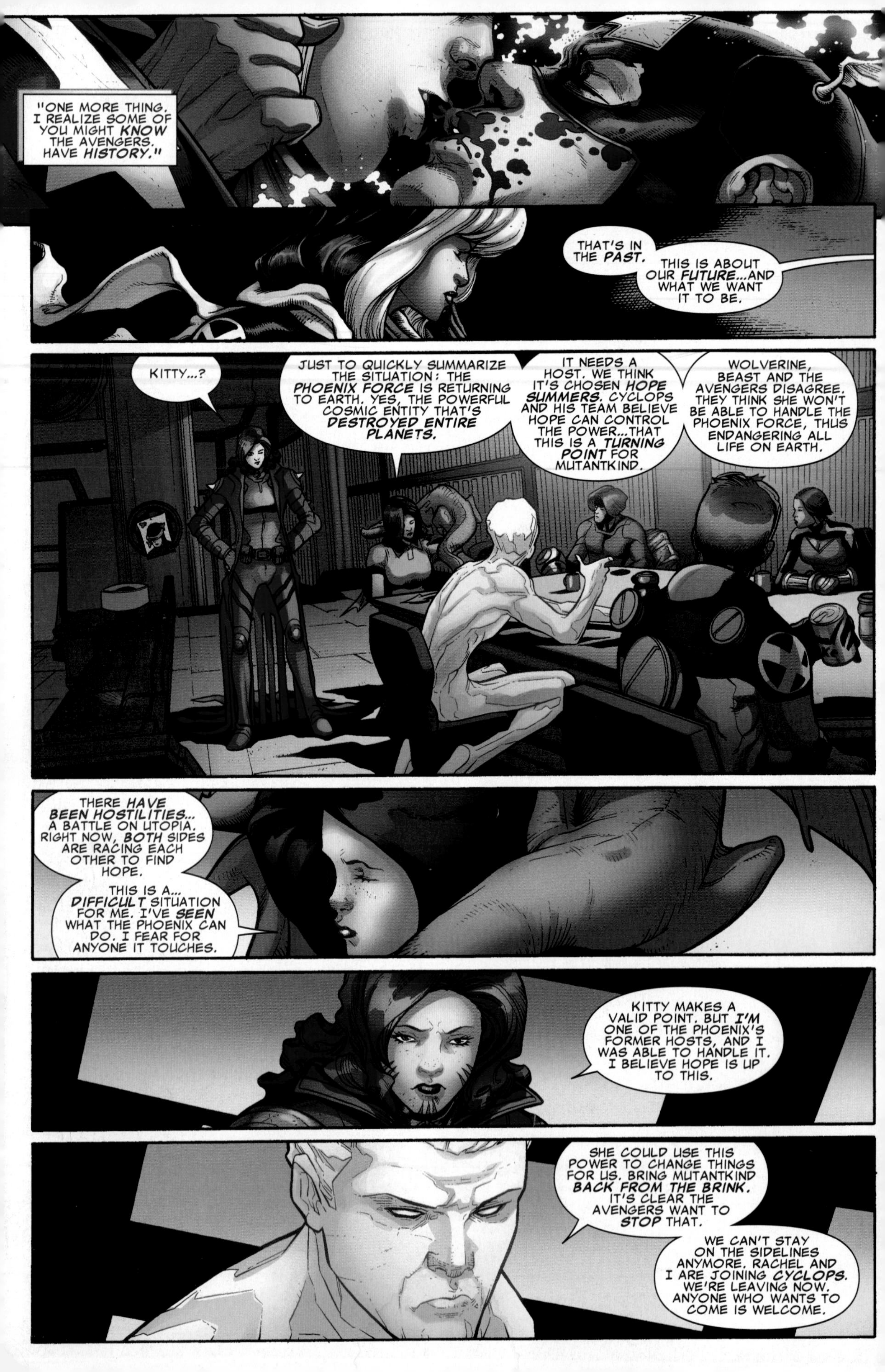
"ONE MORE THING. I REALIZE SOME OF YOU MIGHT KNOW THE AVENGERS. HAVE HISTORY."
THAT'S IN THE PAST.
THIS IS ABOUT OUR FUTURE...AND WHAT WE WANT IT TO BE.
KITTY...?
JUST TO QUICKLY SUMMARIZE THE SITUATION: THE PHOENIX FORCE IS RETURNING TO EARTH. YES, THE POWERFUL COSMIC ENTITY THAT'S DESTROYED ENTIRE PLANETS.
IT NEEDS A HOST. WE THINK IT'S CHOSEN HOPE SUMMERS. CYCLOPS AND HIS TEAM BELIEVE HOPE CAN CONTROL THE POWER...THAT THIS IS A TURNING POINT FOR MUTANTKIND.
WOLVERINE, BEAST AND THE AVENGERS DISAGREE. THEY THINK SHE WON'T BE ABLE TO HANDLE THE PHOENIX FORCE, THUS ENDANGERING ALL LIFE ON EARTH.
THERE HAVE BEEN HOSTILITIES... A BATTLE ON UTOPIA. RIGHT NOW, BOTH SIDES ARE RACING EACH OTHER TO FIND HOPE.
THIS IS A... DIFFICULT SITUATION FOR ME. I'VE SEEN WHAT THE PHOENIX CAN DO. I FEAR FOR ANYONE IT TOUCHES.
KITTY MAKES A VALID POINT. BUT I'M ONE OF THE PHOENIX'S FORMER HOSTS, AND I WAS ABLE TO HANDLE IT. I BELIEVE HOPE IS UP TO THIS.
SHE COULD USE THIS POWER TO CHANGE THINGS FOR US. BRING MUTANTKIND BACK FROM THE BRINK.
IT'S CLEAR THE AVENGERS WANT TO STOP THAT.
WE CAN'T STAY ON THE SIDELINES ANYMORE. RACHEL AND I ARE JOINING CYCLOPS. WE'RE LEAVING NOW. ANYONE WHO WANTS TO COME IS WELCOME.

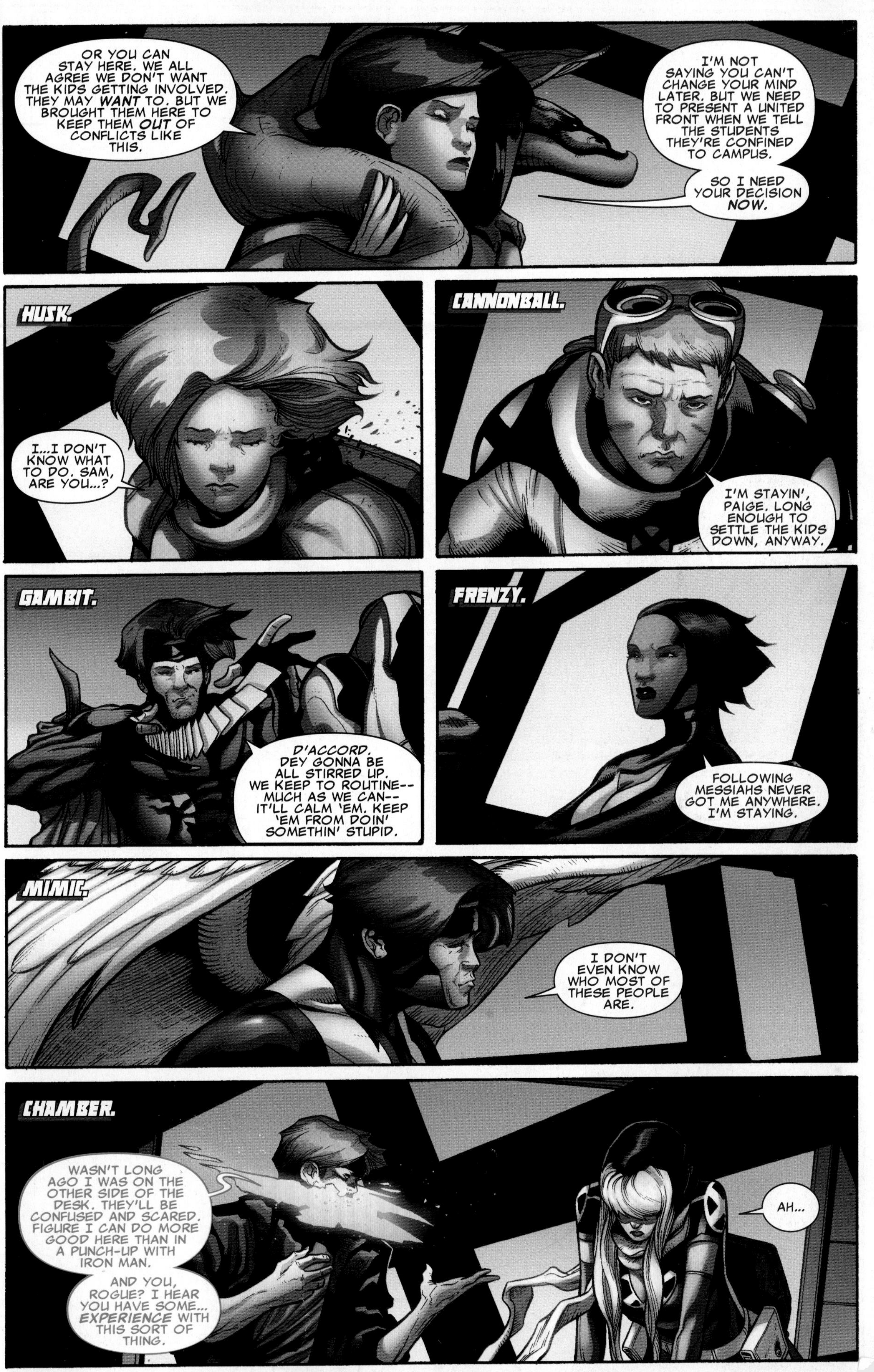
OR YOU CAN STAY HERE. WE ALL AGREE WE DON'T WANT THE KIDS GETTING INVOLVED. THEY MAY WANT TO. BUT WE BROUGHT THEM HERE TO KEEP THEM OUT OF CONFLICTS LIKE THIS.
I'M NOT SAYING YOU CAN'T CHANGE YOUR MIND LATER. BUT WE NEED TO PRESENT A UNITED FRONT WHEN WE TELL THE STUDENTS THEY'RE CONFINED TO CAMPUS.
SO I NEED YOUR DECISION NOW.
HUSK.
I...I DON'T KNOW WHAT TO DO. SAM, ARE YOU...?
CANNONBALL.
I'M STAYIN', PAIGE. LONG ENOUGH TO SETTLE THE KIDS DOWN, ANYWAY.
GAMBIT.
D'ACCORD. DEY GONNA BE ALL STIRRED UP. WE KEEP TO ROUTINE-- MUCH AS WE CAN-- IT'LL CALM 'EM. KEEP 'EM FROM DOIN' SOMETHIN' STUPID.
FRENZY.
FOLLOWING MESSIAHS NEVER GOT ME ANYWHERE. I'M STAYING.
MIMIC.
I DON'T EVEN KNOW WHO MOST OF THESE PEOPLE ARE.
CHAMBER.
WASN'T LONG AGO I WAS ON THE OTHER SIDE OF THE DESK. THEY'LL BE CONFUSED AND SCARED. FIGURE I CAN DO MORE GOOD HERE THAN IN A PUNCH-UP WITH IRON MAN.
AND YOU, ROGUE? I HEAR YOU HAVE SOME... EXPERIENCE WITH THIS SORT OF THING.
AH...

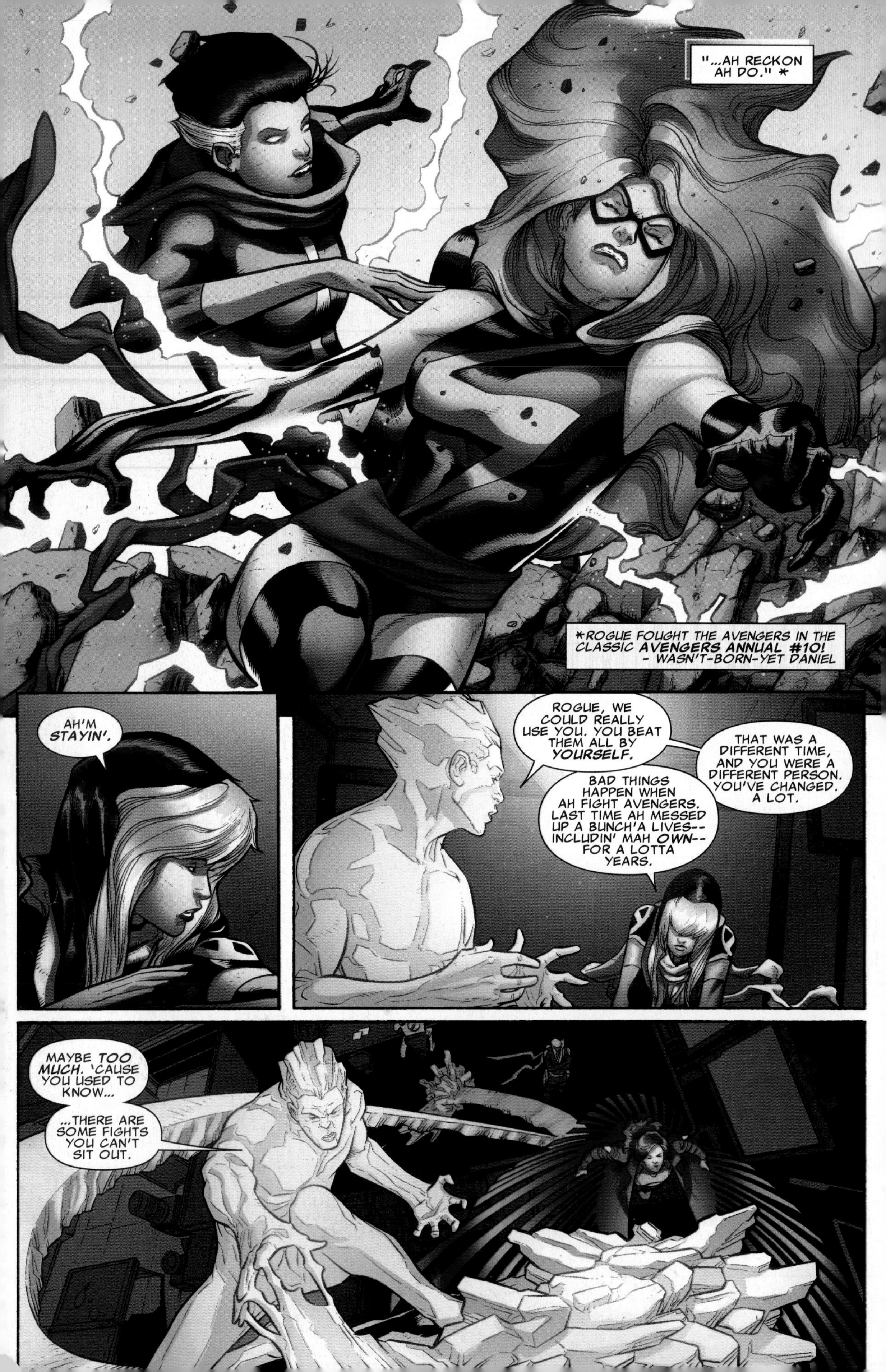
"...AH RECKON AH DO." *
*ROGUE FOUGHT THE AVENGERS IN THE CLASSIC AVENGERS ANNUAL #10! - WASN'T-BORN-YET DANIEL
AH'M STAYIN'.
ROGUE, WE COULD REALLY USE YOU. YOU BEAT THEM ALL BY YOURSELF.
BAD THINGS HAPPEN WHEN AH FIGHT AVENGERS. LAST TIME AH MESSED UP A BUNCH'A LIVES--INCLUDIN' MAH OWN--FOR A LOTTA YEARS.
THAT WAS A DIFFERENT TIME, AND YOU WERE A DIFFERENT PERSON. YOU'VE CHANGED. A LOT.
MAYBE TOO MUCH. 'CAUSE YOU USED TO KNOW...
...THERE ARE SOME FIGHTS YOU CAN'T SIT OUT.

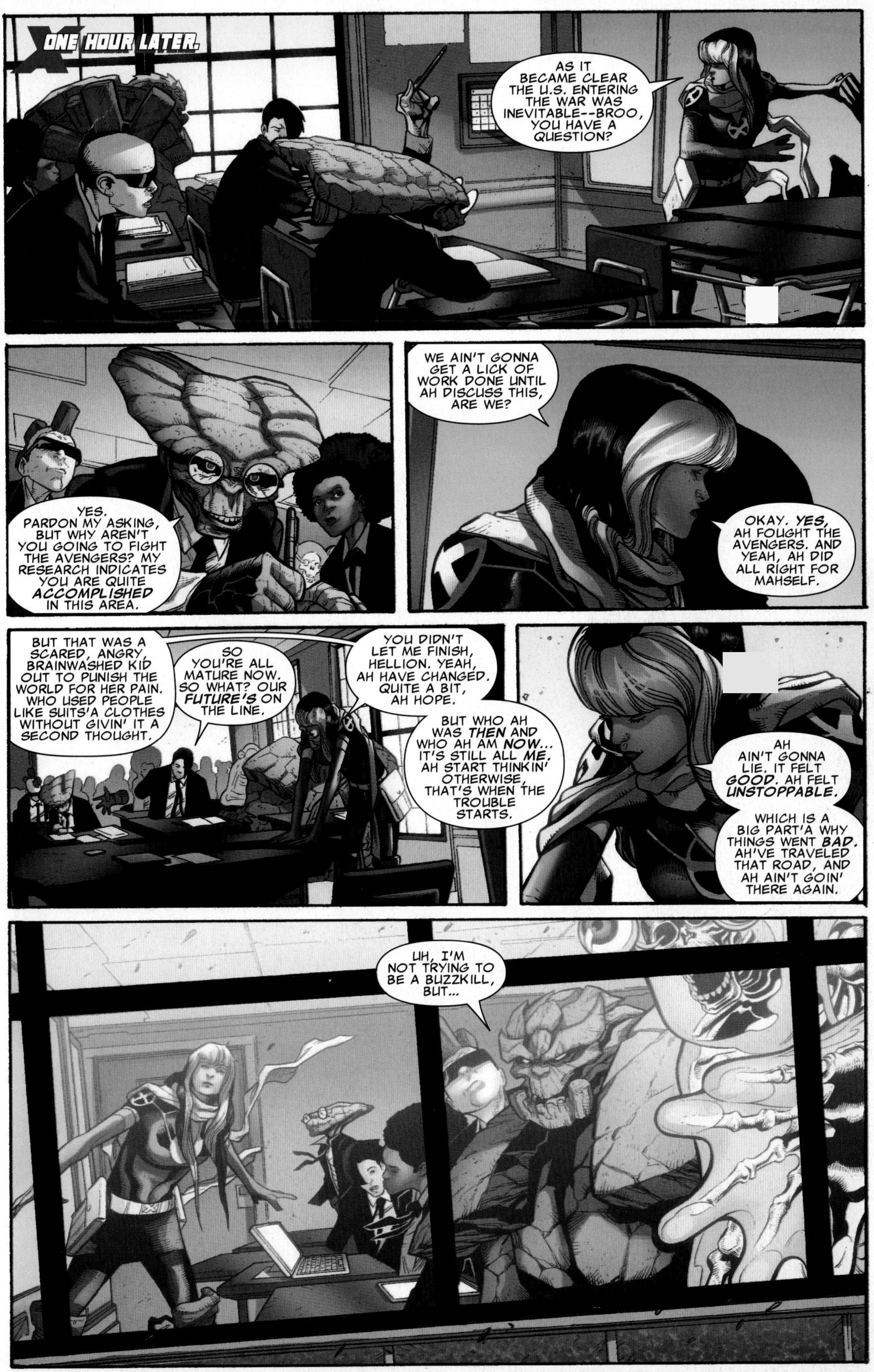
ONE HOUR LATER.
AS IT BECAME CLEAR THE U.S. ENTERING THE WAR WAS INEVITABLE--BROO, YOU HAVE A QUESTION?
YES. PARDON MY ASKING, BUT WHY AREN'T YOU GOING TO FIGHT THE AVENGERS? MY RESEARCH INDICATES YOU ARE QUITE ACCOMPLISHED IN THIS AREA.
WE AIN'T GONNA GET A LICK OF WORK DONE UNTIL AH DISCUSS THIS, ARE WE?
OKAY. YES, AH FOUGHT THE AVENGERS. AND YEAH, AH DID ALL RIGHT FOR MAHSELF.
AH AIN'T GONNA LIE. IT FELT GOOD. AH FELT UNSTOPPABLE.
WHICH IS A BIG PART'A WHY THINGS WENT BAD. AH'VE TRAVELED THAT ROAD, AND AH AIN'T GOIN' THERE AGAIN.
BUT THAT WAS A SCARED, ANGRY, BRAINWASHED KID OUT TO PUNISH THE WORLD FOR HER PAIN. WHO USED PEOPLE LIKE SUITS'A CLOTHES WITHOUT GIVIN' IT A SECOND THOUGHT.
SO YOU'RE ALL MATURE NOW. SO WHAT? OUR FUTURE'S ON THE LINE.
YOU DIDN'T LET ME FINISH, HELLION. YEAH, AH HAVE CHANGED. QUITE A BIT, AH HOPE.
BUT WHO AH WAS THEN AND WHO AH AM NOW... IT'S STILL ALL ME. AH START THINKIN' OTHERWISE, THAT'S WHEN THE TROUBLE STARTS.
UH, I'M NOT TRYING TO BE A BUZZKILL, BUT...

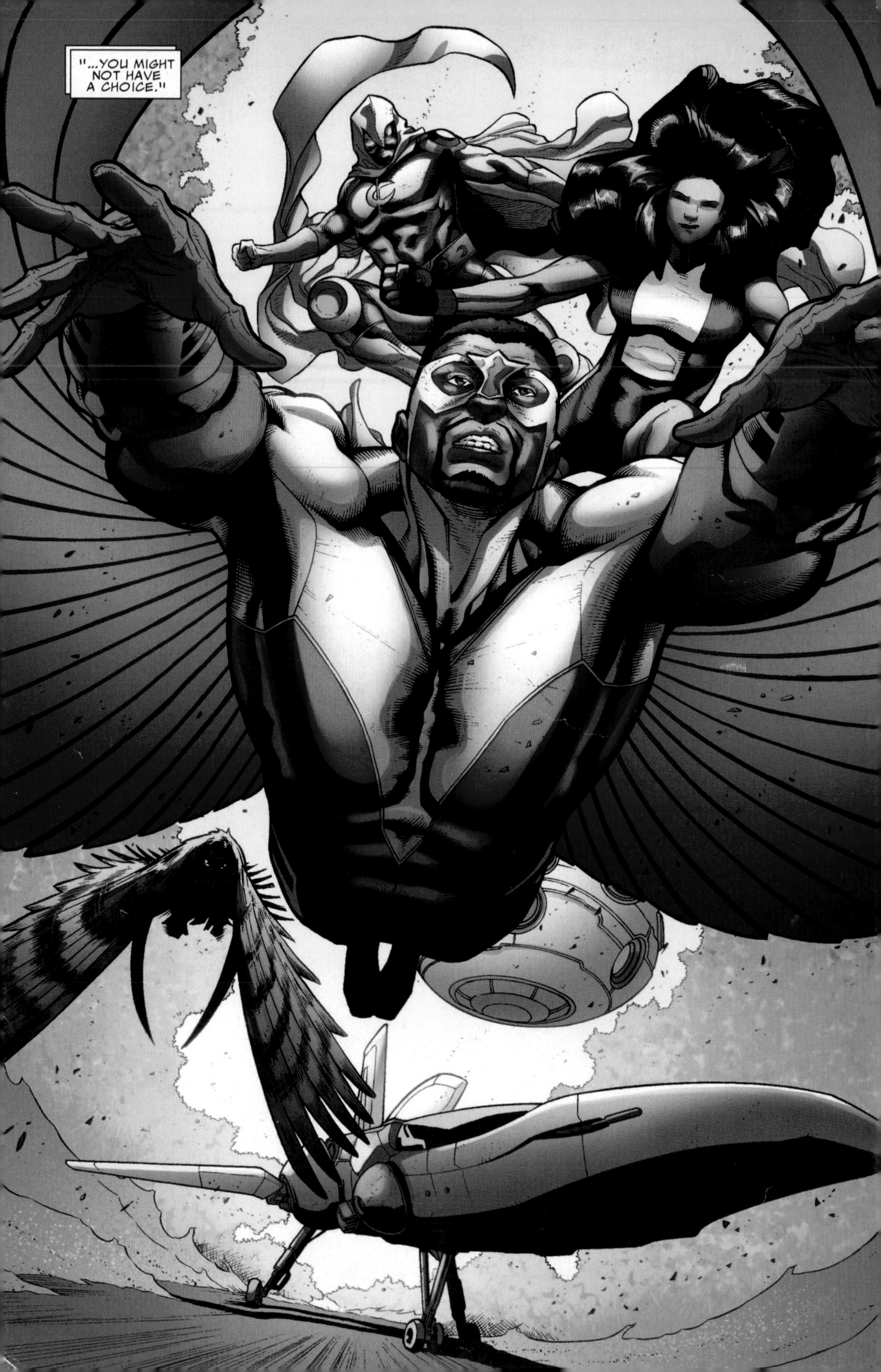
"...YOU MIGHT NOT HAVE A CHOICE."

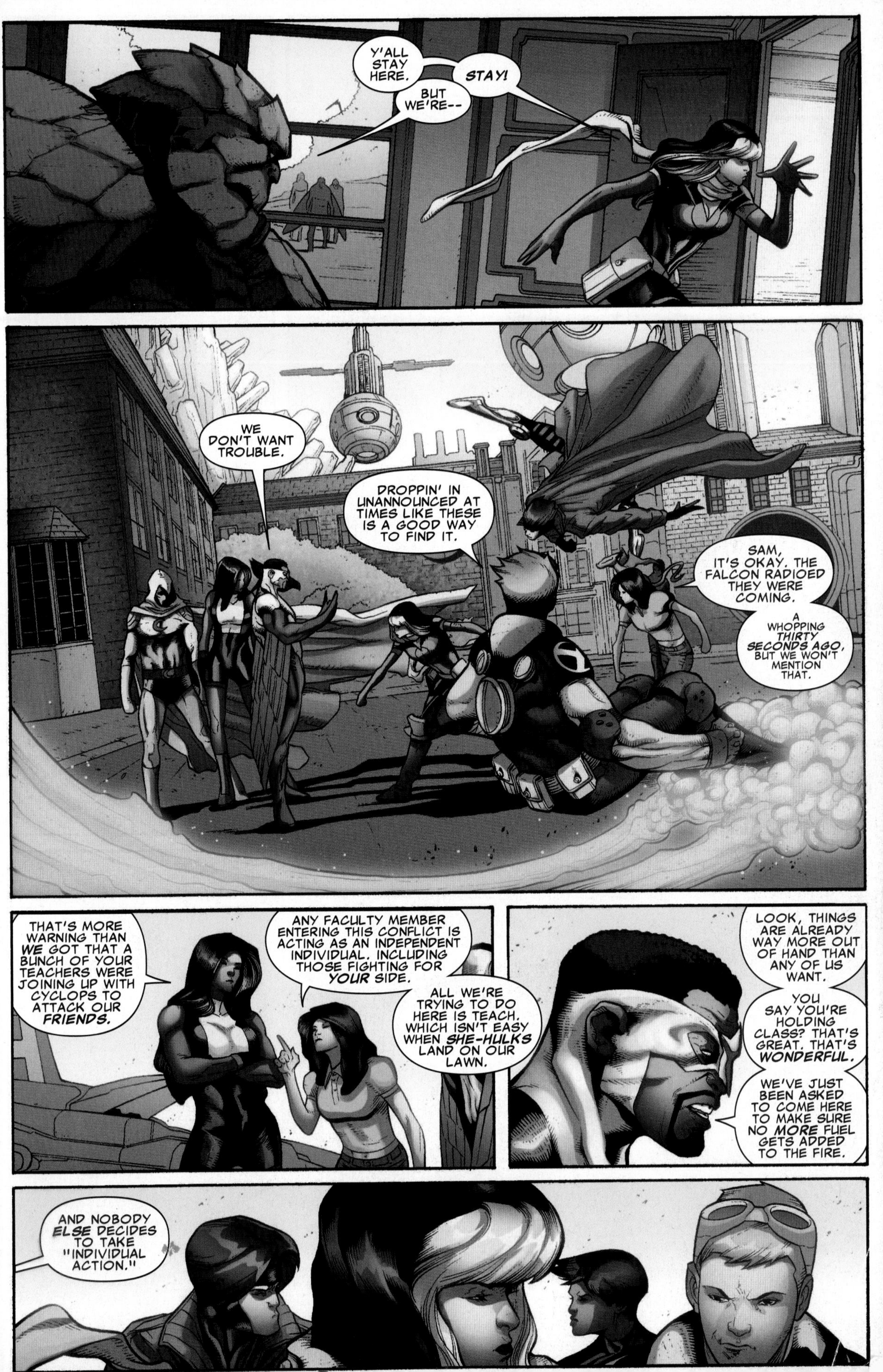
Y'ALL STAY HERE.
BUT WE'RE--
STAY!
WE DON'T WANT TROUBLE.
DROPPIN' IN UNANNOUNCED AT TIMES LIKE THESE IS A GOOD WAY TO FIND IT.
SAM, IT'S OKAY. THE FALCON RADIOED THEY WERE COMING.
A WHOPPING THIRTY SECONDS AGO, BUT WE WON'T MENTION THAT.
THAT'S MORE WARNING THAN WE GOT THAT A BUNCH OF YOUR TEACHERS WERE JOINING UP WITH CYCLOPS TO ATTACK OUR FRIENDS.
ANY FACULTY MEMBER ENTERING THIS CONFLICT IS ACTING AS AN INDEPENDENT INDIVIDUAL. INCLUDING THOSE FIGHTING FOR YOUR SIDE.
ALL WE'RE TRYING TO DO HERE IS TEACH. WHICH ISN'T EASY WHEN SHE-HULKS LAND ON OUR LAWN.
LOOK, THINGS ARE ALREADY WAY MORE OUT OF HAND THAN ANY OF US WANT.
YOU SAY YOU'RE HOLDING CLASS? THAT'S GREAT. THAT'S WONDERFUL.
WE'VE JUST BEEN ASKED TO COME HERE TO MAKE SURE NO MORE FUEL GETS ADDED TO THE FIRE.
AND NOBODY ELSE DECIDES TO TAKE "INDIVIDUAL ACTION."

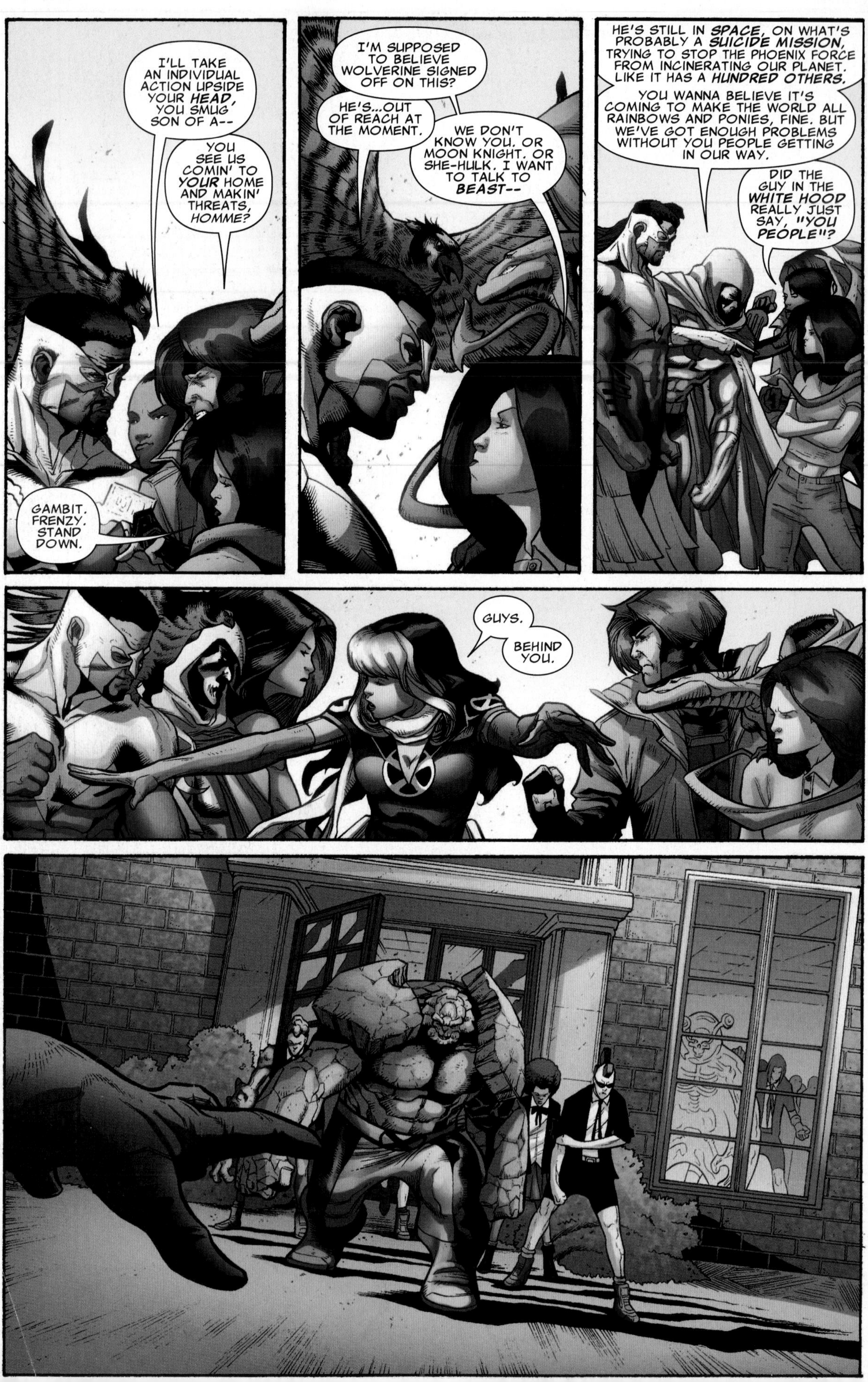

I'LL TAKE AN INDIVIDUAL ACTION UPSIDE YOUR HEAD, YOU SMUG SON OF A--
YOU SEE US COMIN' TO YOUR HOME AND MAKIN' THREATS, HOMME?
GAMBIT. FRENZY. STAND DOWN.
I'M SUPPOSED TO BELIEVE WOLVERINE SIGNED OFF ON THIS?
HE'S...OUT OF REACH AT THE MOMENT.
WE DON'T KNOW YOU. OR MOON KNIGHT. OR SHE-HULK. I WANT TO TALK TO BEAST--
HE'S STILL IN SPACE, ON WHAT'S PROBABLY A SUICIDE MISSION, TRYING TO STOP THE PHOENIX FORCE FROM INCINERATING OUR PLANET. LIKE IT HAS A HUNDRED OTHERS.
YOU WANNA BELIEVE IT'S COMING TO MAKE THE WORLD ALL RAINBOWS AND PONIES, FINE. BUT WE'VE GOT ENOUGH PROBLEMS WITHOUT YOU PEOPLE GETTING IN OUR WAY.
DID THE GUY IN THE WHITE HOOD REALLY JUST SAY, "YOU PEOPLE"?
GUYS.
BEHIND YOU.

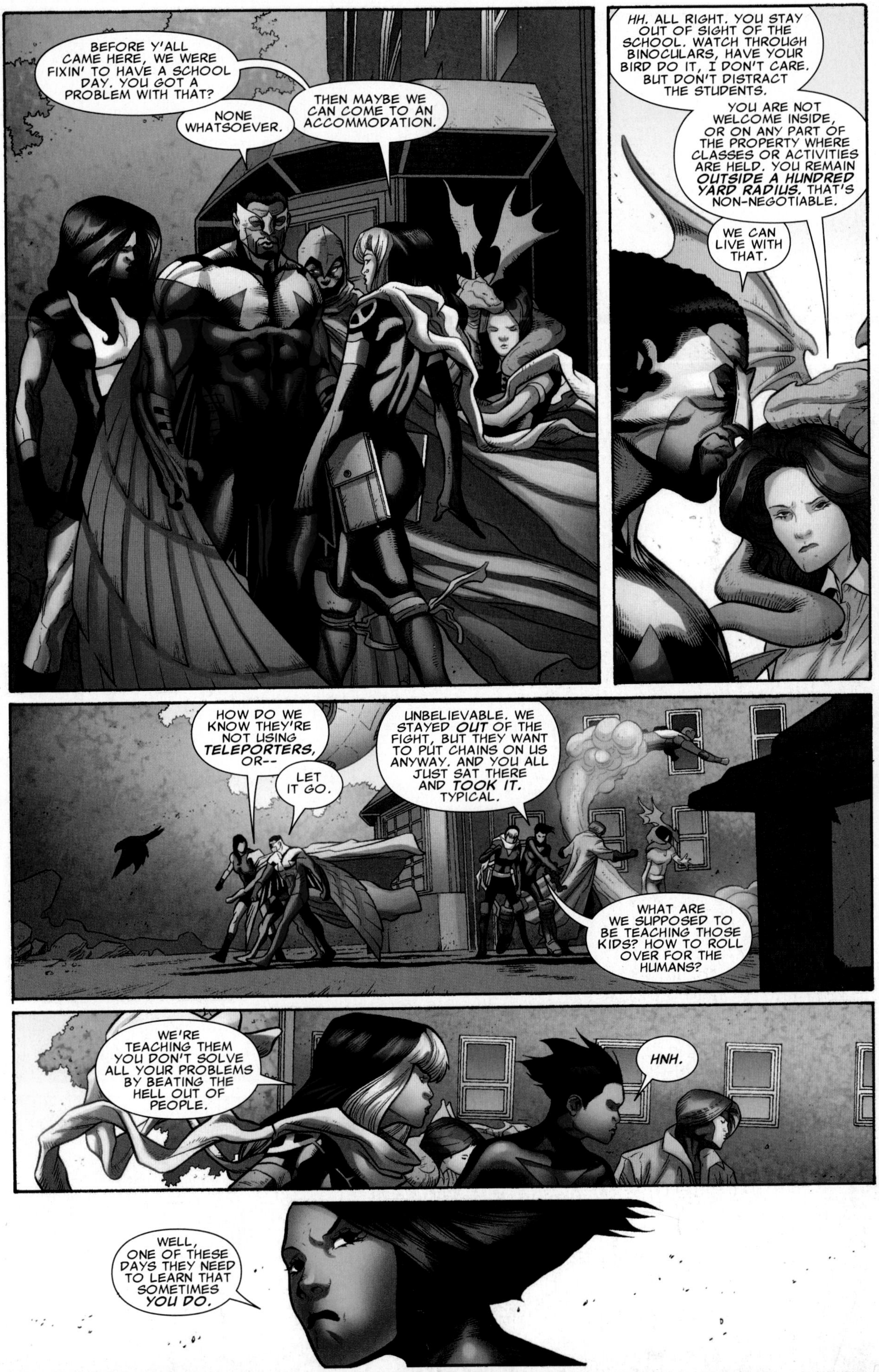
BEFORE Y'ALL CAME HERE, WE WERE FIXIN' TO HAVE A SCHOOL DAY. YOU GOT A PROBLEM WITH THAT?
NONE WHATSOEVER.
THEN MAYBE WE CAN COME TO AN ACCOMMODATION.
HH. ALL RIGHT. YOU STAY OUT OF SIGHT OF THE SCHOOL. WATCH THROUGH BINOCULARS, HAVE YOUR BIRD DO IT, I DON'T CARE. BUT DON'T DISTRACT THE STUDENTS.
YOU ARE NOT WELCOME INSIDE, OR ON ANY PART OF THE PROPERTY WHERE CLASSES OR ACTIVITIES ARE HELD. YOU REMAIN OUTSIDE A HUNDRED YARD RADIUS. THAT'S NON-NEGOTIABLE.
WE CAN LIVE WITH THAT.
HOW DO WE KNOW THEY'RE NOT USING TELEPORTERS, OR--
LET IT GO.
UNBELIEVABLE. WE STAYED OUT OF THE FIGHT, BUT THEY WANT TO PUT CHAINS ON US ANYWAY. AND YOU ALL JUST SAT THERE AND TOOK IT. TYPICAL.
WHAT ARE WE SUPPOSED TO BE TEACHING THOSE KIDS? HOW TO ROLL OVER FOR THE HUMANS?
WE'RE TEACHING THEM YOU DON'T SOLVE ALL YOUR PROBLEMS BY BEATING THE HELL OUT OF PEOPLE.
HNH.
WELL, ONE OF THESE DAYS THEY NEED TO LEARN THAT SOMETIMES YOU DO.

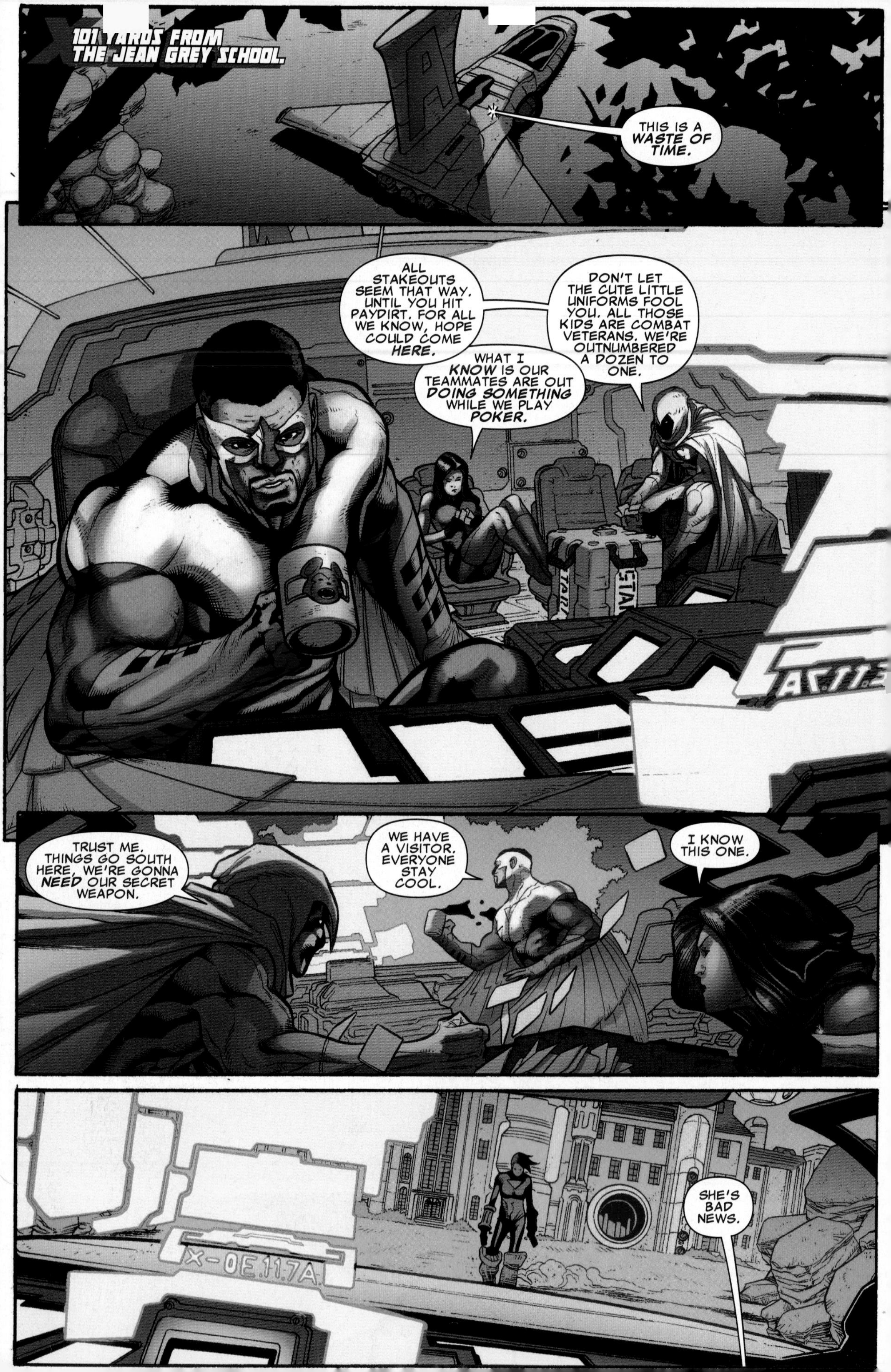
101 YARDS FROM THE JEAN GREY SCHOOL.
THIS IS A WASTE OF TIME.
ALL STAKEOUTS SEEM THAT WAY. UNTIL YOU HIT PAYDIRT. FOR ALL WE KNOW, HOPE COULD COME HERE.
DON'T LET THE CUTE LITTLE UNIFORMS FOOL YOU. ALL THOSE KIDS ARE COMBAT VETERANS. WE'RE OUTNUMBERED A DOZEN TO ONE.
WHAT I KNOW IS OUR TEAMMATES ARE OUT DOING SOMETHING WHILE WE PLAY POKER.
TRUST ME. THINGS GO SOUTH HERE, WE'RE GONNA NEED OUR SECRET WEAPON.
WE HAVE A VISITOR. EVERYONE STAY COOL.
I KNOW THIS ONE.
X-0E.11.7A.
SHE'S BAD NEWS.

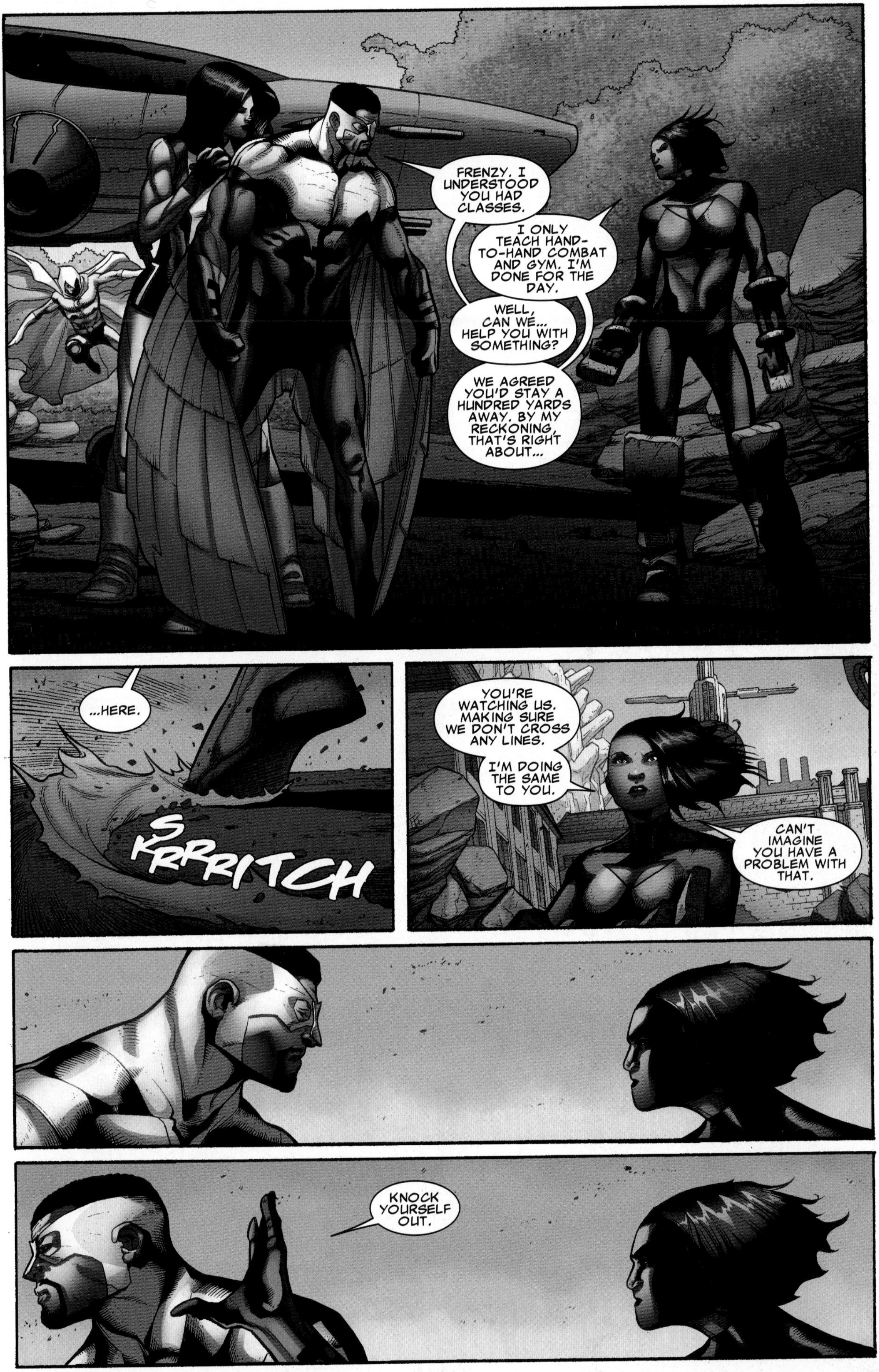
FRENZY. I UNDERSTOOD YOU HAD CLASSES.
I ONLY TEACH HAND-TO-HAND COMBAT AND GYM. I'M DONE FOR THE DAY.
WELL, CAN WE... HELP YOU WITH SOMETHING?
WE AGREED YOU'D STAY A HUNDRED YARDS AWAY. BY MY RECKONING, THAT'S RIGHT ABOUT...
...HERE.
SKRRRITCH
YOU'RE WATCHING US. MAKING SURE WE DON'T CROSS ANY LINES.
I'M DOING THE SAME TO YOU.
CAN'T IMAGINE YOU HAVE A PROBLEM WITH THAT.
KNOCK YOURSELF OUT.

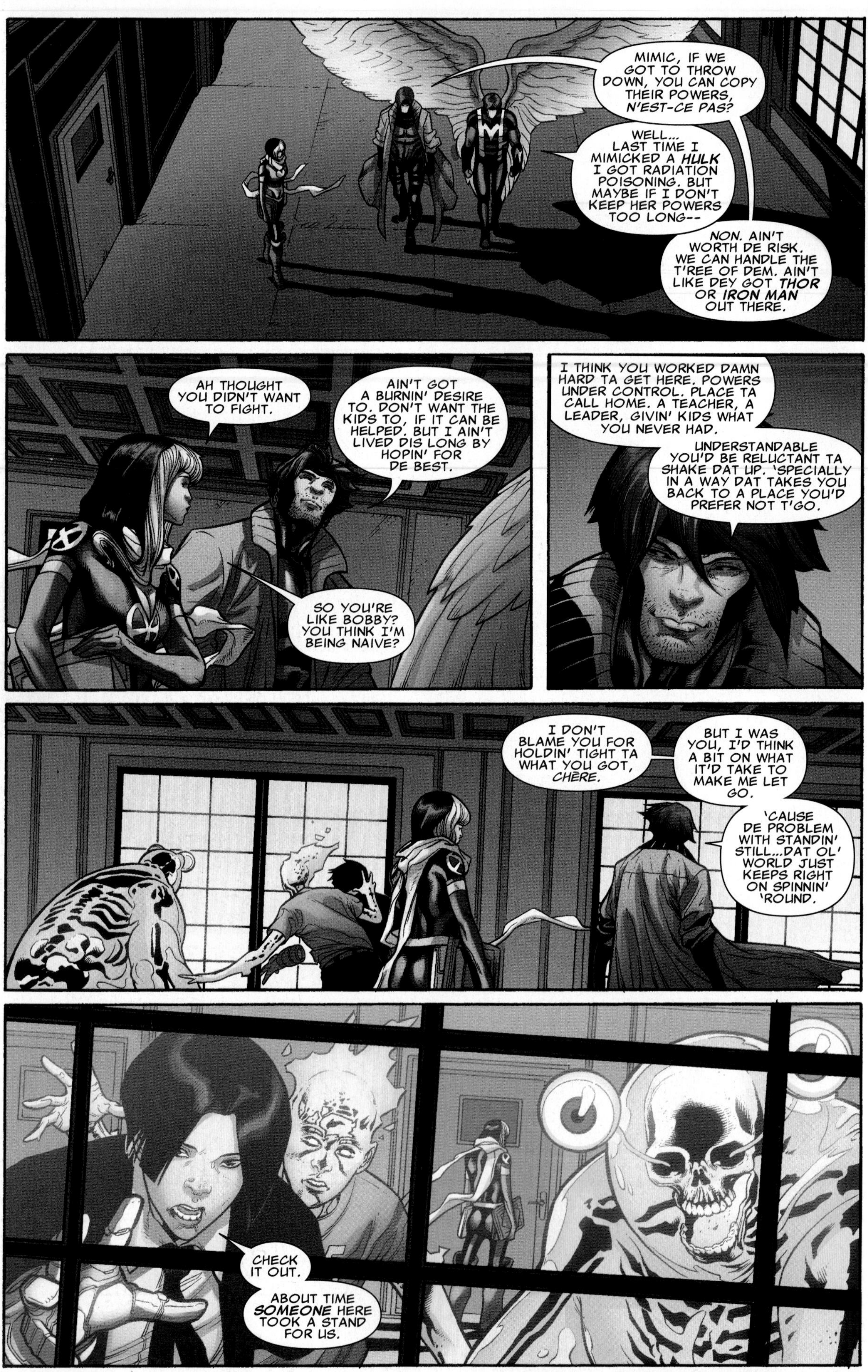
MIMIC, IF WE GOT TO THROW DOWN, YOU CAN COPY THEIR POWERS, N'EST-CE PAS?
WELL... LAST TIME I MIMICKED A HULK I GOT RADIATION POISONING. BUT MAYBE IF I DON'T KEEP HER POWERS TOO LONG--
NON. AIN'T WORTH DE RISK. WE CAN HANDLE THE T'REE OF DEM. AIN'T LIKE DEY GOT THOR OR IRON MAN OUT THERE.
AH THOUGHT YOU DIDN'T WANT TO FIGHT.
AIN'T GOT A BURNIN' DESIRE TO. DON'T WANT THE KIDS TO, IF IT CAN BE HELPED. BUT I AIN'T LIVED DIS LONG BY HOPIN' FOR DE BEST.
SO YOU'RE LIKE BOBBY? YOU THINK I'M BEING NAIVE?
I THINK YOU WORKED DAMN HARD TA GET HERE. POWERS UNDER CONTROL. PLACE TA CALL HOME. A TEACHER, A LEADER, GIVIN' KIDS WHAT YOU NEVER HAD.
UNDERSTANDABLE YOU'D BE RELUCTANT TA SHAKE DAT UP. 'SPECIALLY IN A WAY DAT TAKES YOU BACK TO A PLACE YOU'D PREFER NOT T'GO.
I DON'T BLAME YOU FOR HOLDIN' TIGHT TA WHAT YOU GOT, CHÈRE.
BUT I WAS YOU, I'D THINK A BIT ON WHAT IT'D TAKE TO MAKE ME LET GO.
'CAUSE DE PROBLEM WITH STANDIN' STILL...DAT OL' WORLD JUST KEEPS RIGHT ON SPINNIN' 'ROUND.
CHECK IT OUT.
ABOUT TIME SOMEONE HERE TOOK A STAND FOR US.

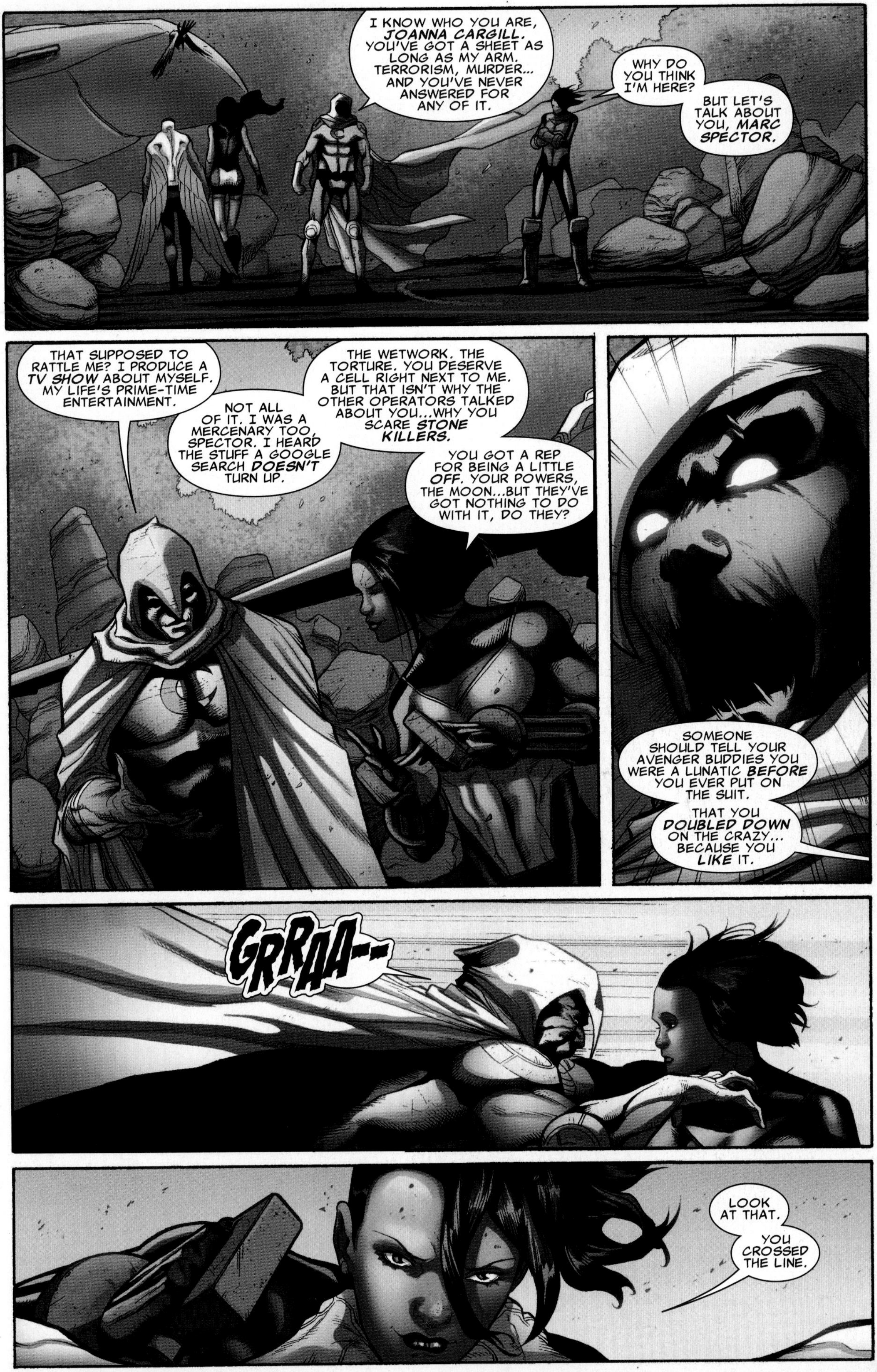

I KNOW WHO YOU ARE, JOANNA CARGILL. YOU'VE GOT A SHEET AS LONG AS MY ARM. TERRORISM, MURDER... AND YOU'VE NEVER ANSWERED FOR ANY OF IT.
WHY DO YOU THINK I'M HERE?
BUT LET'S TALK ABOUT YOU, MARC SPECTOR.
THAT SUPPOSED TO RATTLE ME? I PRODUCE A TV SHOW ABOUT MYSELF. MY LIFE'S PRIME-TIME ENTERTAINMENT.
NOT ALL OF IT. I WAS A MERCENARY TOO, SPECTOR. I HEARD THE STUFF A GOOGLE SEARCH DOESN'T TURN UP.
THE WETWORK. THE TORTURE. YOU DESERVE A CELL RIGHT NEXT TO ME. BUT THAT ISN'T WHY THE OTHER OPERATORS TALKED ABOUT YOU...WHY YOU SCARE STONE KILLERS.
YOU GOT A REP FOR BEING A LITTLE OFF. YOUR POWERS, THE MOON...BUT THEY'VE GOT NOTHING TO DO WITH IT, DO THEY?
SOMEONE SHOULD TELL YOUR AVENGER BUDDIES YOU WERE A LUNATIC BEFORE YOU EVER PUT ON THE SUIT.
THAT YOU DOUBLED DOWN ON THE CRAZY... BECAUSE YOU LIKE IT.
GRRAA--
LOOK AT THAT.
YOU CROSSED THE LINE.

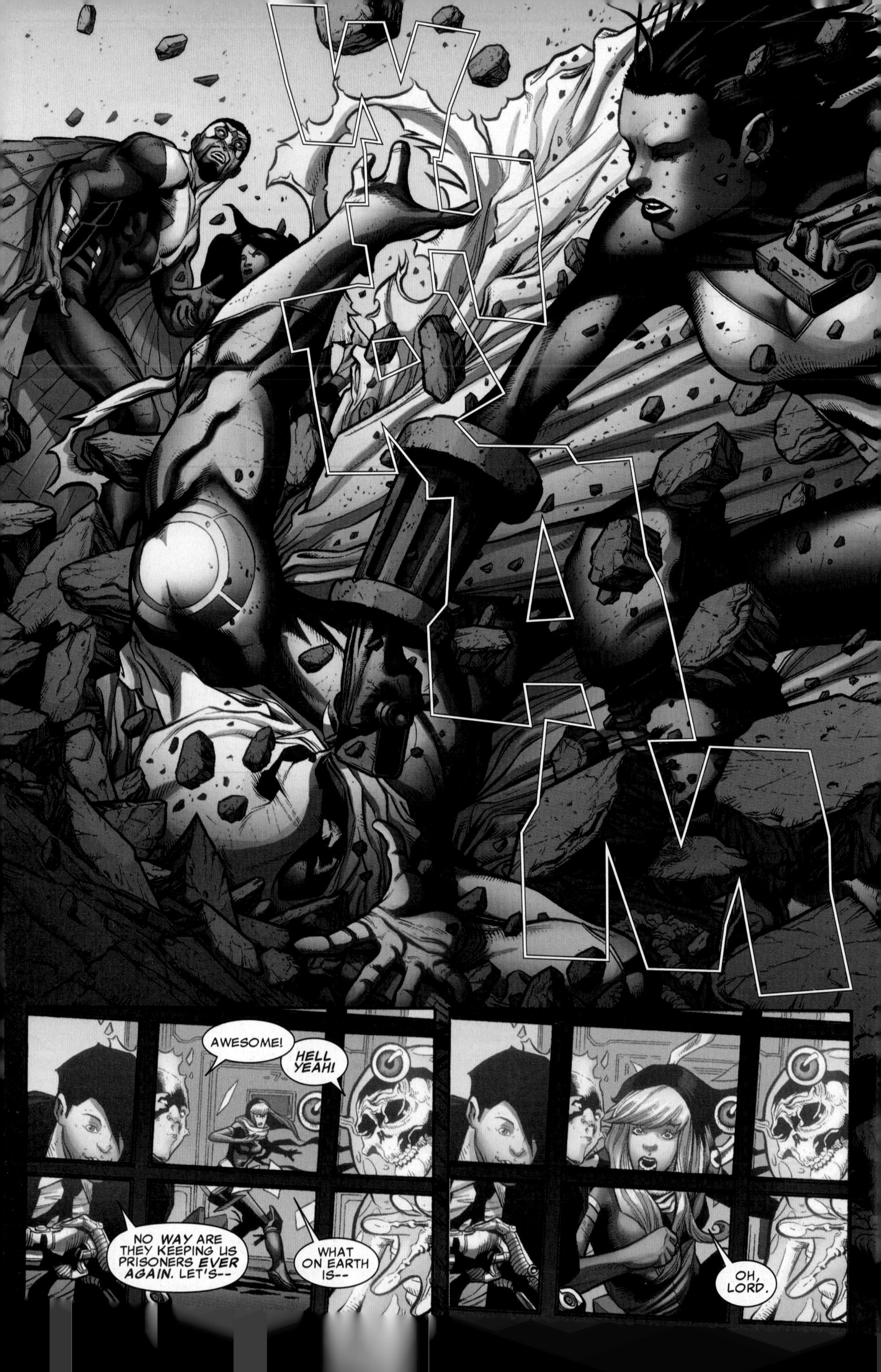
WHAM
AWESOME!
HELL YEAH!
NO WAY ARE THEY KEEPING US PRISONERS EVER AGAIN. LET'S--
WHAT ON EARTH IS--
OH, LORD.

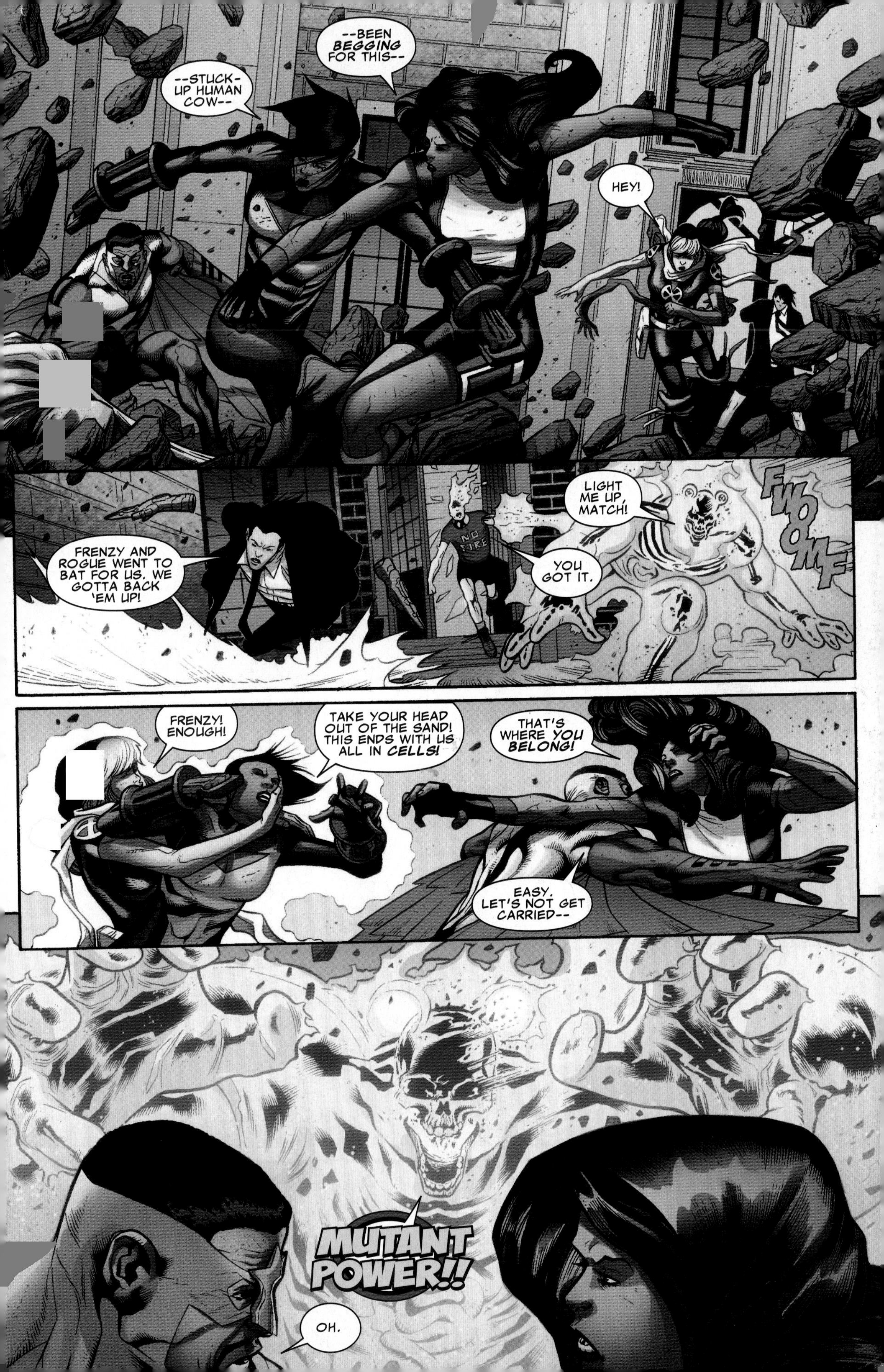
--STUCK-UP HUMAN COW--
--BEEN BEGGING FOR THIS--
HEY!
FRENZY AND ROGUE WENT TO BAT FOR US. WE GOTTA BACK 'EM UP!
LIGHT ME UP, MATCH!
YOU GOT IT.
FWOOMF
FRENZY! ENOUGH!
TAKE YOUR HEAD OUT OF THE SAND! THIS ENDS WITH US ALL IN CELLS!
THAT'S WHERE YOU BELONG!
EASY. LET'S NOT GET CARRIED--
MUTANT POWER!!
OH.

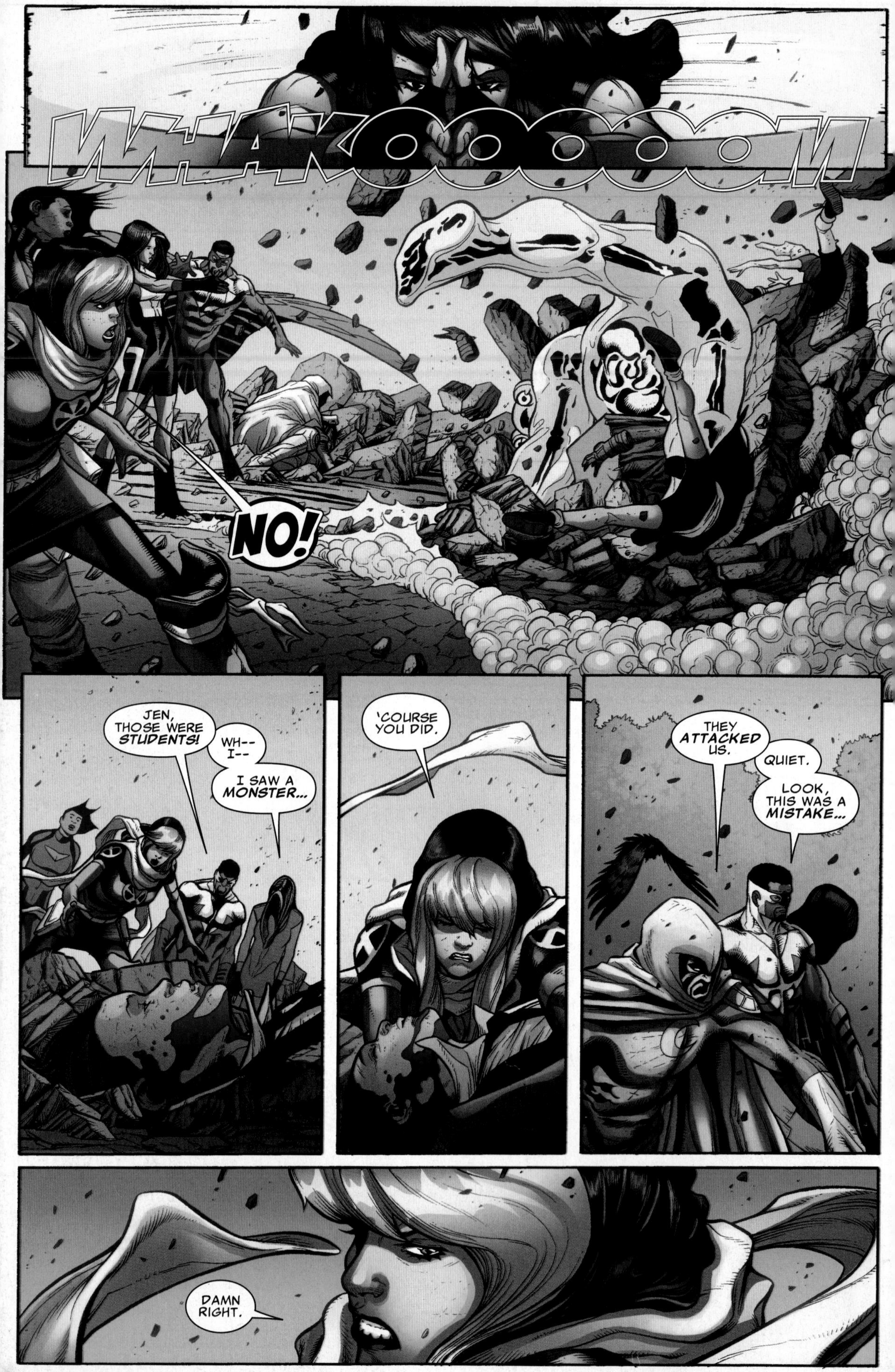
WHAKOOOOOOM
NO!
JEN, THOSE WERE STUDENTS!
WH-- I--
I SAW A MONSTER...
'COURSE YOU DID.
THEY ATTACKED US.
QUIET.
LOOK, THIS WAS A MISTAKE...
DAMN RIGHT.

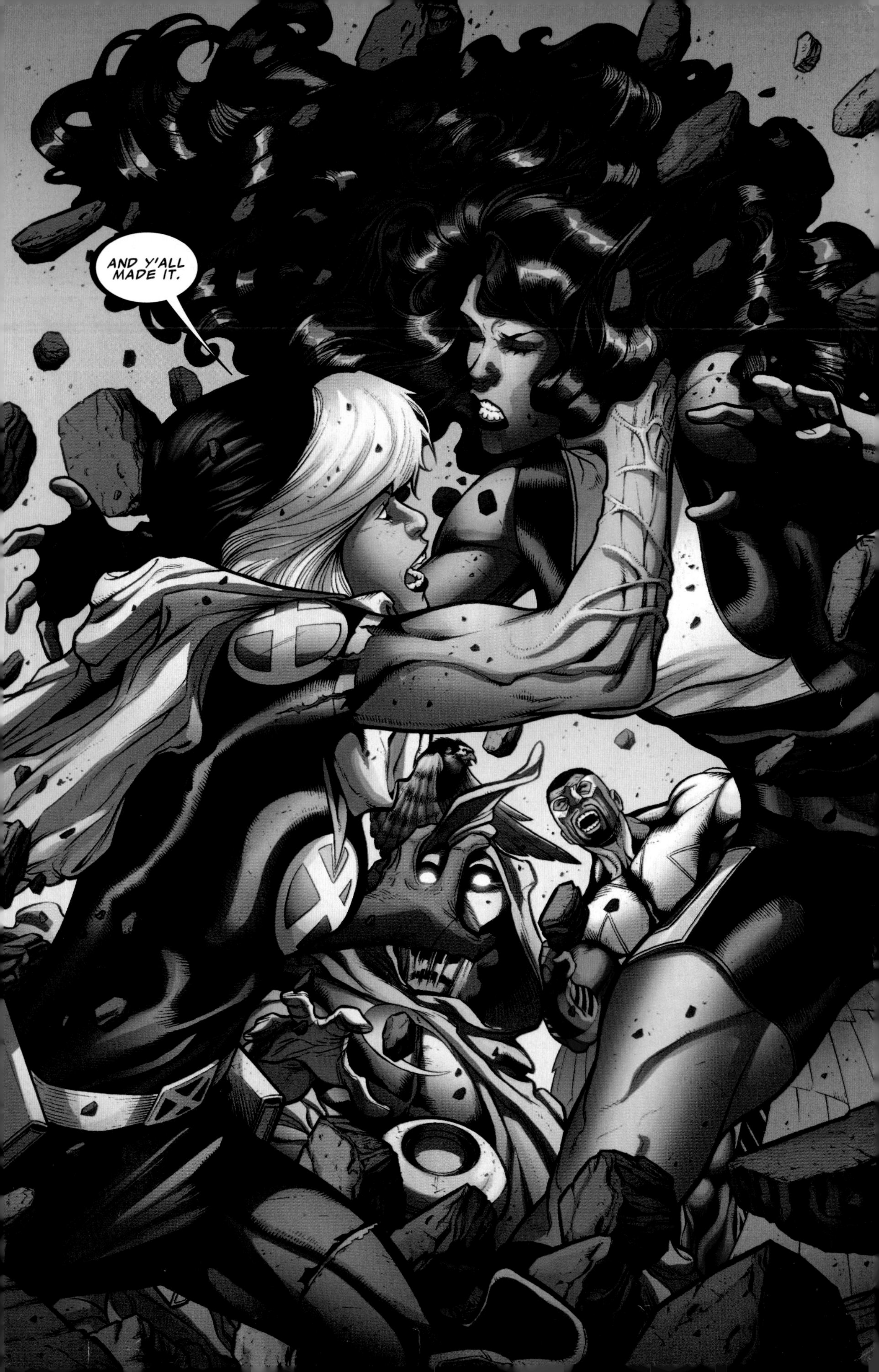
AND Y'ALL MADE IT.

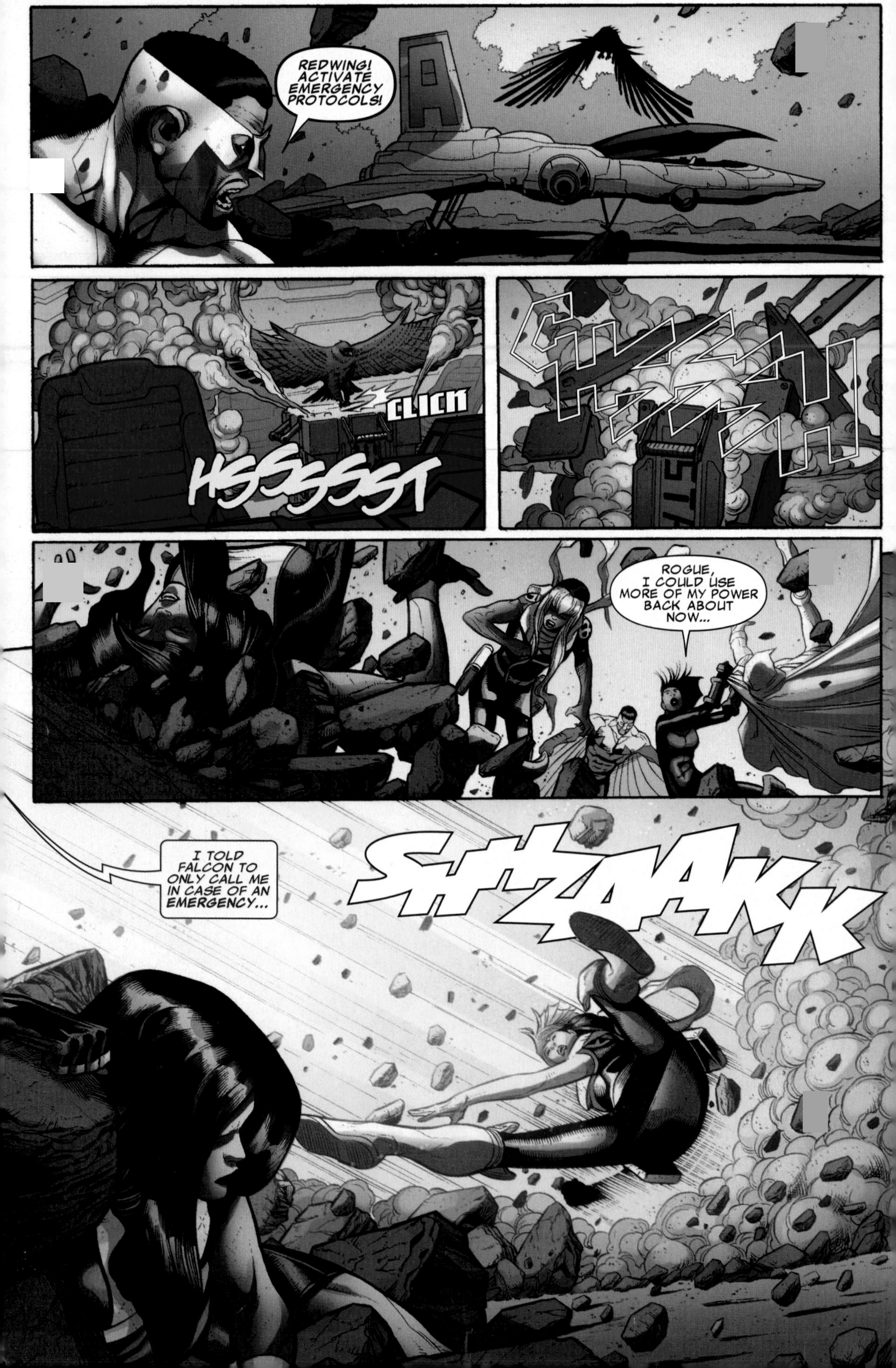
REDWING! ACTIVATE EMERGENCY PROTOCOLS!
CLICK
HSSSSST
ROGUE, I COULD USE MORE OF MY POWER BACK ABOUT NOW...
I TOLD FALCON TO ONLY CALL ME IN CASE OF AN EMERGENCY...
SHZAAKK

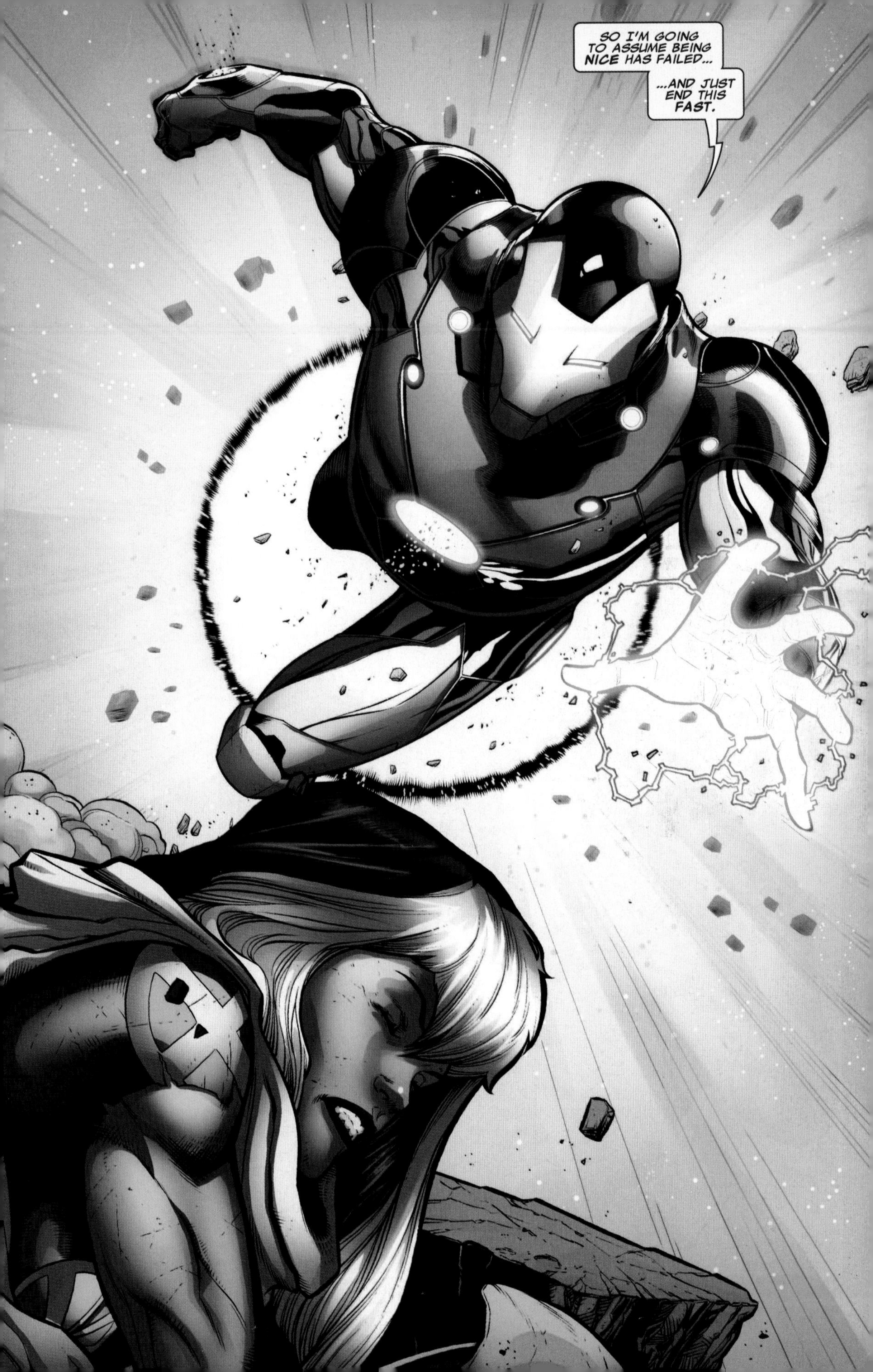
SO I'M GOING TO ASSUME BEING NICE HAS FAILED...
...AND JUST END THIS FAST.

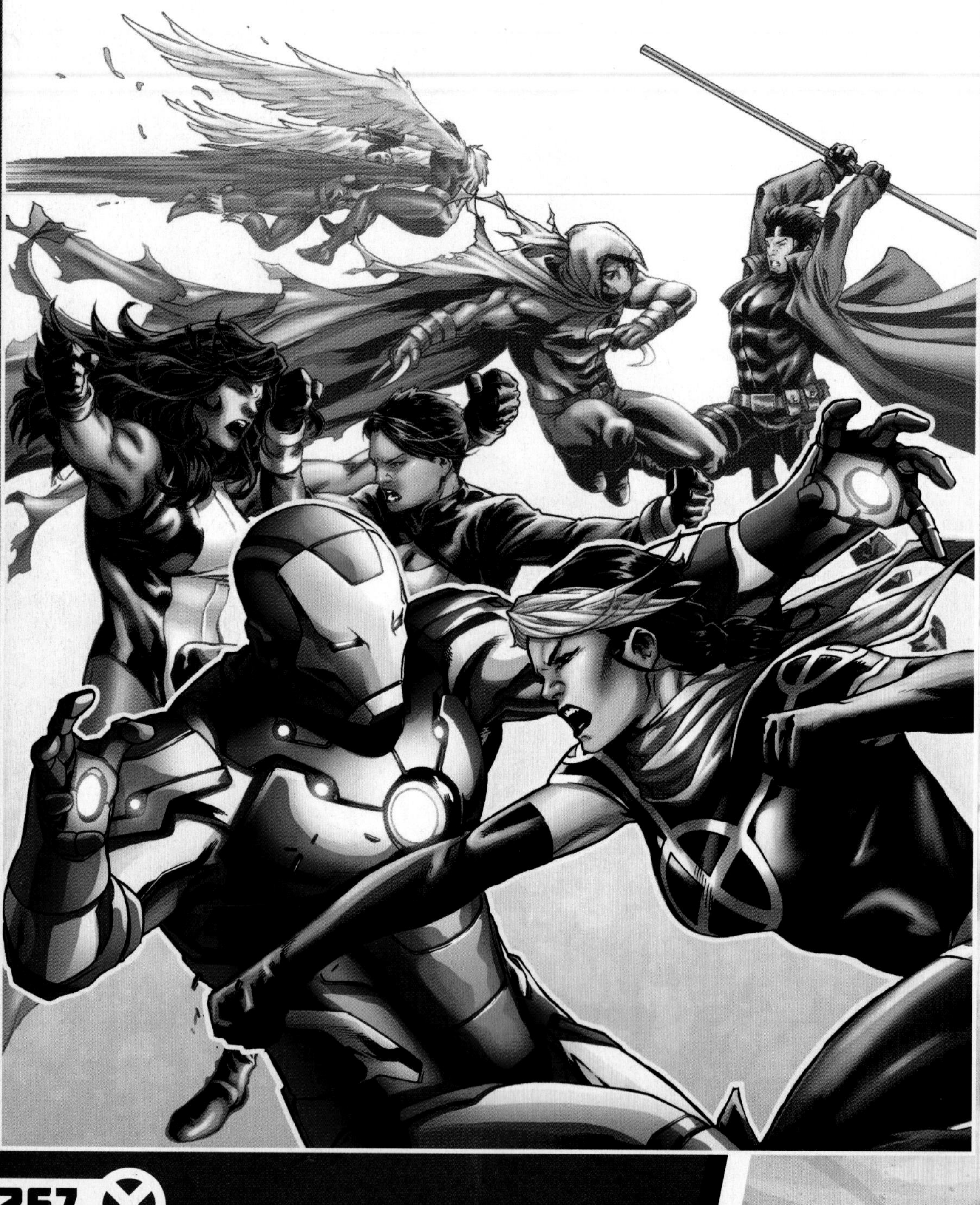

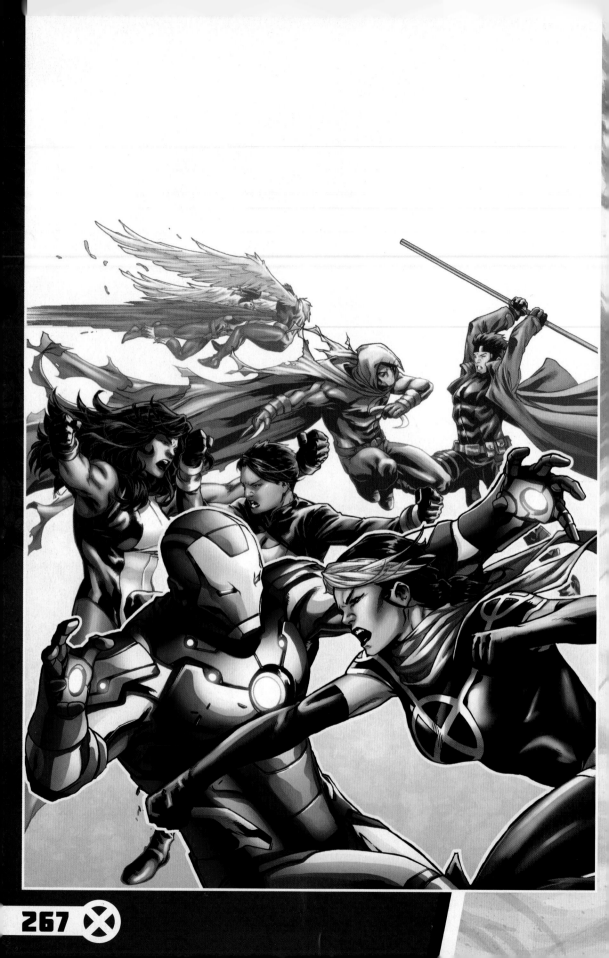

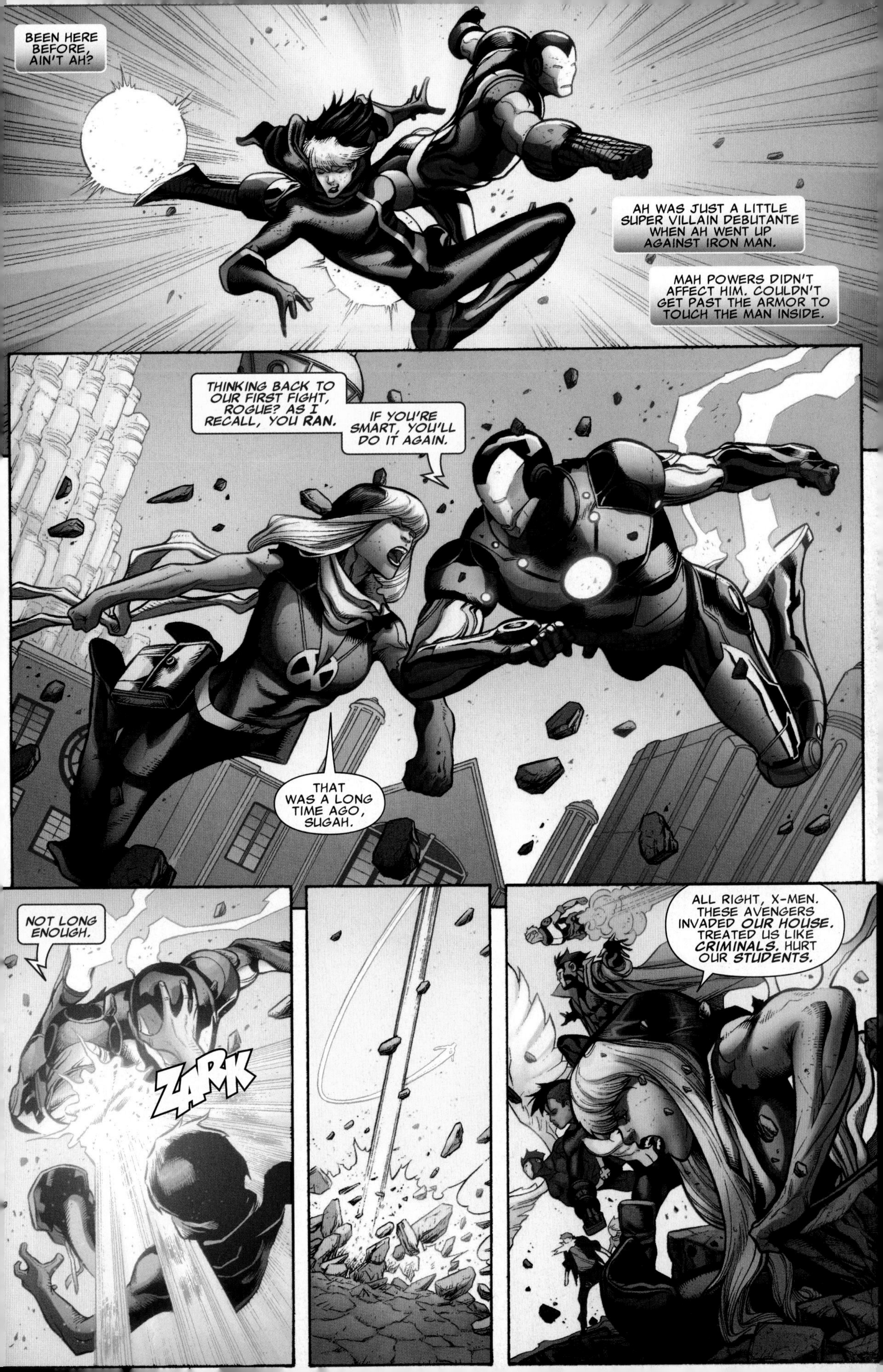
BEEN HERE BEFORE, AIN'T AH?
AH WAS JUST A LITTLE SUPER VILLAIN DEBUTANTE WHEN AH WENT UP AGAINST IRON MAN.
MAH POWERS DIDN'T AFFECT HIM. COULDN'T GET PAST THE ARMOR TO TOUCH THE MAN INSIDE.
THINKING BACK TO OUR FIRST FIGHT, ROGUE? AS I RECALL, YOU RAN.
IF YOU'RE SMART, YOU'LL DO IT AGAIN.
THAT WAS A LONG TIME AGO, SUGAH.
NOT LONG ENOUGH.
ZARK
ALL RIGHT, X-MEN. THESE AVENGERS INVADED OUR HOUSE. TREATED US LIKE CRIMINALS. HURT OUR STUDENTS.

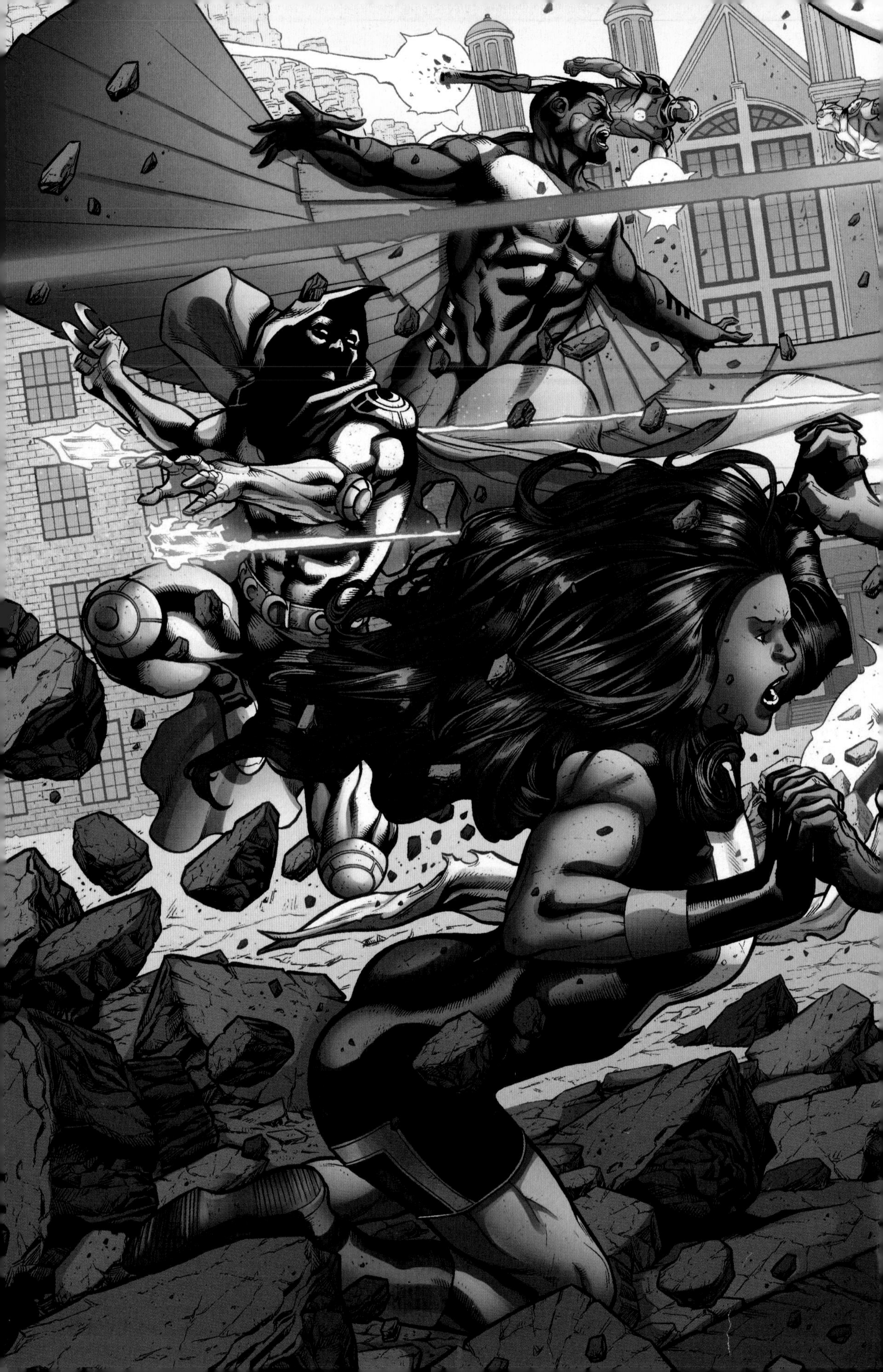

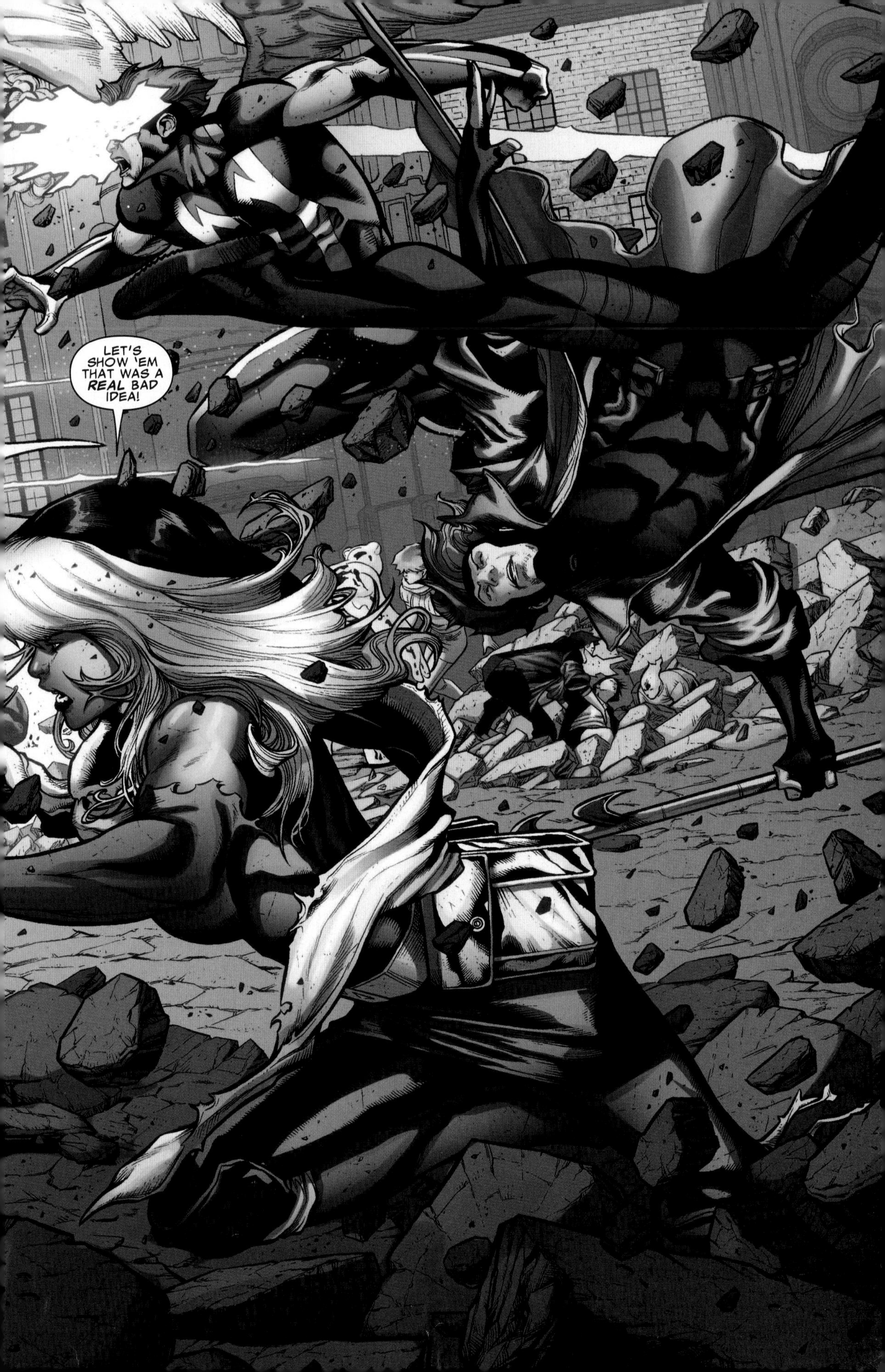
LET'S SHOW 'EM THAT WAS A REAL BAD IDEA!

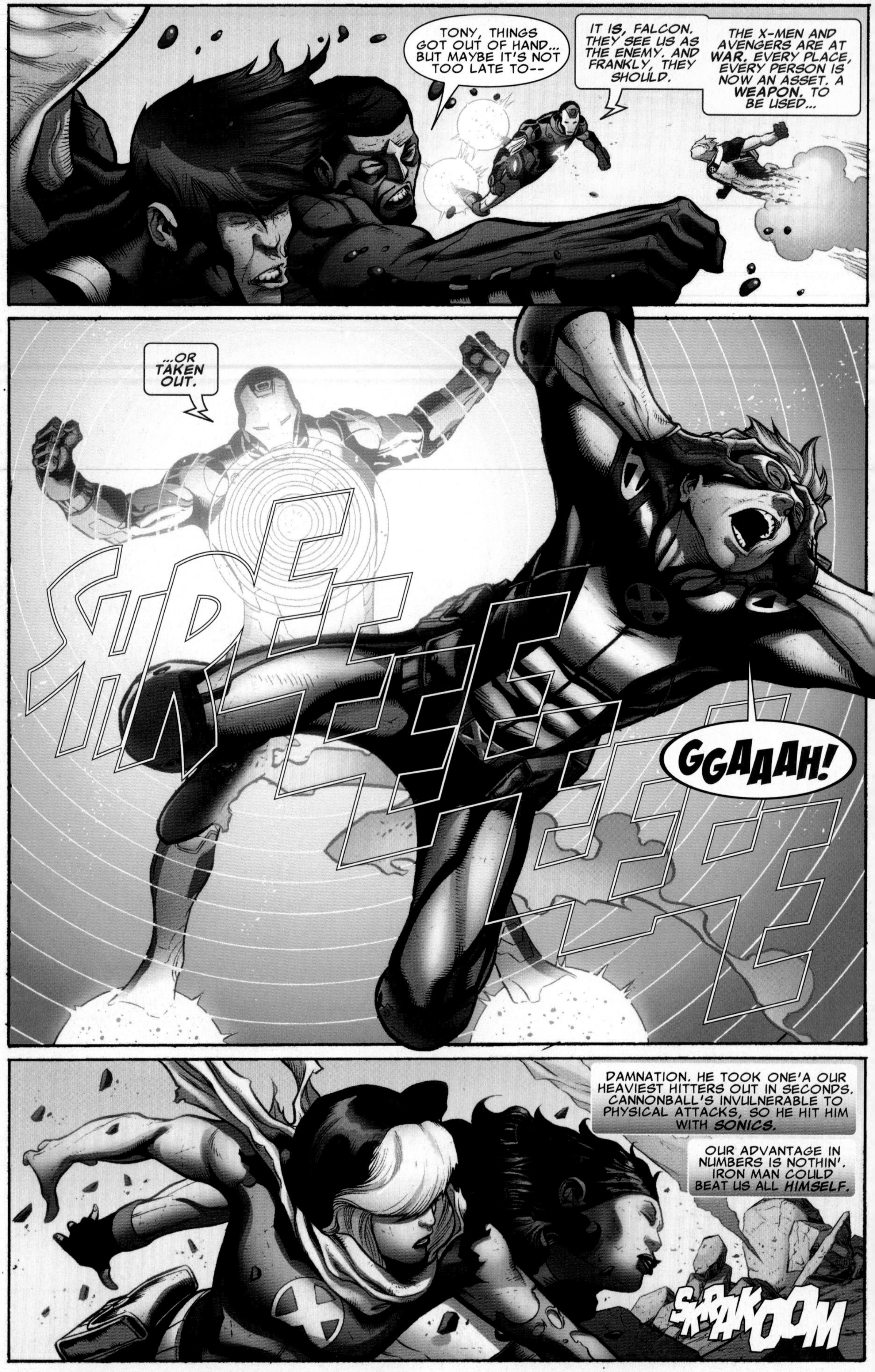
TONY, THINGS GOT OUT OF HAND... BUT MAYBE IT'S NOT TOO LATE TO--
IT IS, FALCON. THEY SEE US AS THE ENEMY. AND FRANKLY, THEY SHOULD.
THE X-MEN AND AVENGERS ARE AT WAR. EVERY PLACE, EVERY PERSON IS NOW AN ASSET. A WEAPON. TO BE USED...
...OR TAKEN OUT.
GGAAAH!
DAMNATION. HE TOOK ONE'A OUR HEAVIEST HITTERS OUT IN SECONDS. CANNONBALL'S INVULNERABLE TO PHYSICAL ATTACKS, SO HE HIT HIM WITH SONICS.
OUR ADVANTAGE IN NUMBERS IS NOTHIN'. IRON MAN COULD BEAT US ALL HIMSELF.
SKRAKOOM

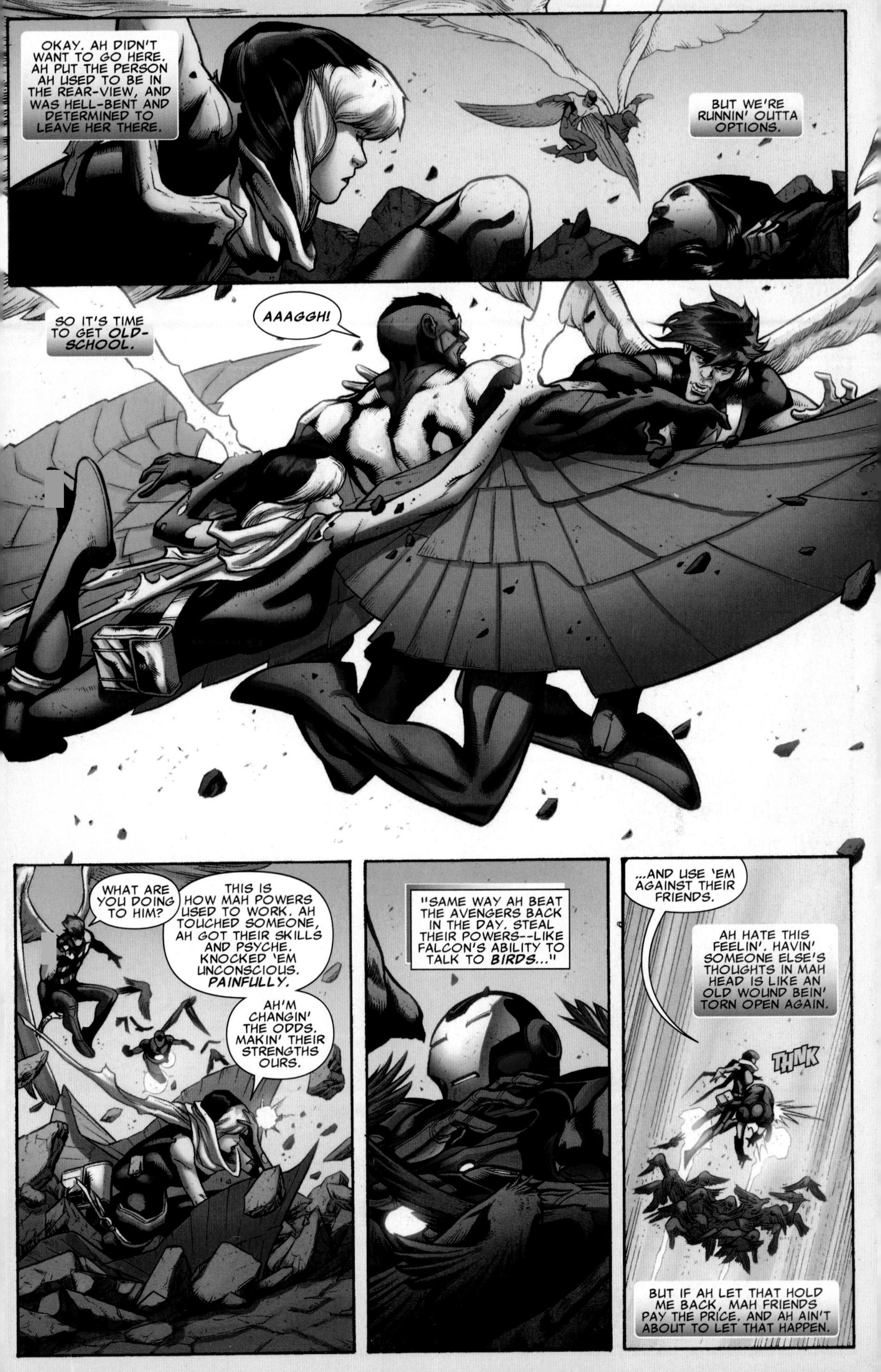
OKAY. AH DIDN'T WANT TO GO HERE. AH PUT THE PERSON AH USED TO BE IN THE REAR-VIEW, AND WAS HELL-BENT AND DETERMINED TO LEAVE HER THERE.
BUT WE'RE RUNNIN' OUTTA OPTIONS.
SO IT'S TIME TO GET OLD-SCHOOL.
AAAGGH!
WHAT ARE YOU DOING TO HIM?
THIS IS HOW MAH POWERS USED TO WORK. AH TOUCHED SOMEONE, AH GOT THEIR SKILLS AND PSYCHE. KNOCKED 'EM UNCONSCIOUS. PAINFULLY.
AH'M CHANGIN' THE ODDS. MAKIN' THEIR STRENGTHS OURS.
"SAME WAY AH BEAT THE AVENGERS BACK IN THE DAY. STEAL THEIR POWERS--LIKE FALCON'S ABILITY TO TALK TO BIRDS..."
...AND USE 'EM AGAINST THEIR FRIENDS.
AH HATE THIS FEELIN'. HAVIN' SOMEONE ELSE'S THOUGHTS IN MAH HEAD IS LIKE AN OLD WOUND BEIN' TORN OPEN AGAIN.
THINK
BUT IF AH LET THAT HOLD ME BACK, MAH FRIENDS PAY THE PRICE. AND AH AIN'T ABOUT TO LET THAT HAPPEN.

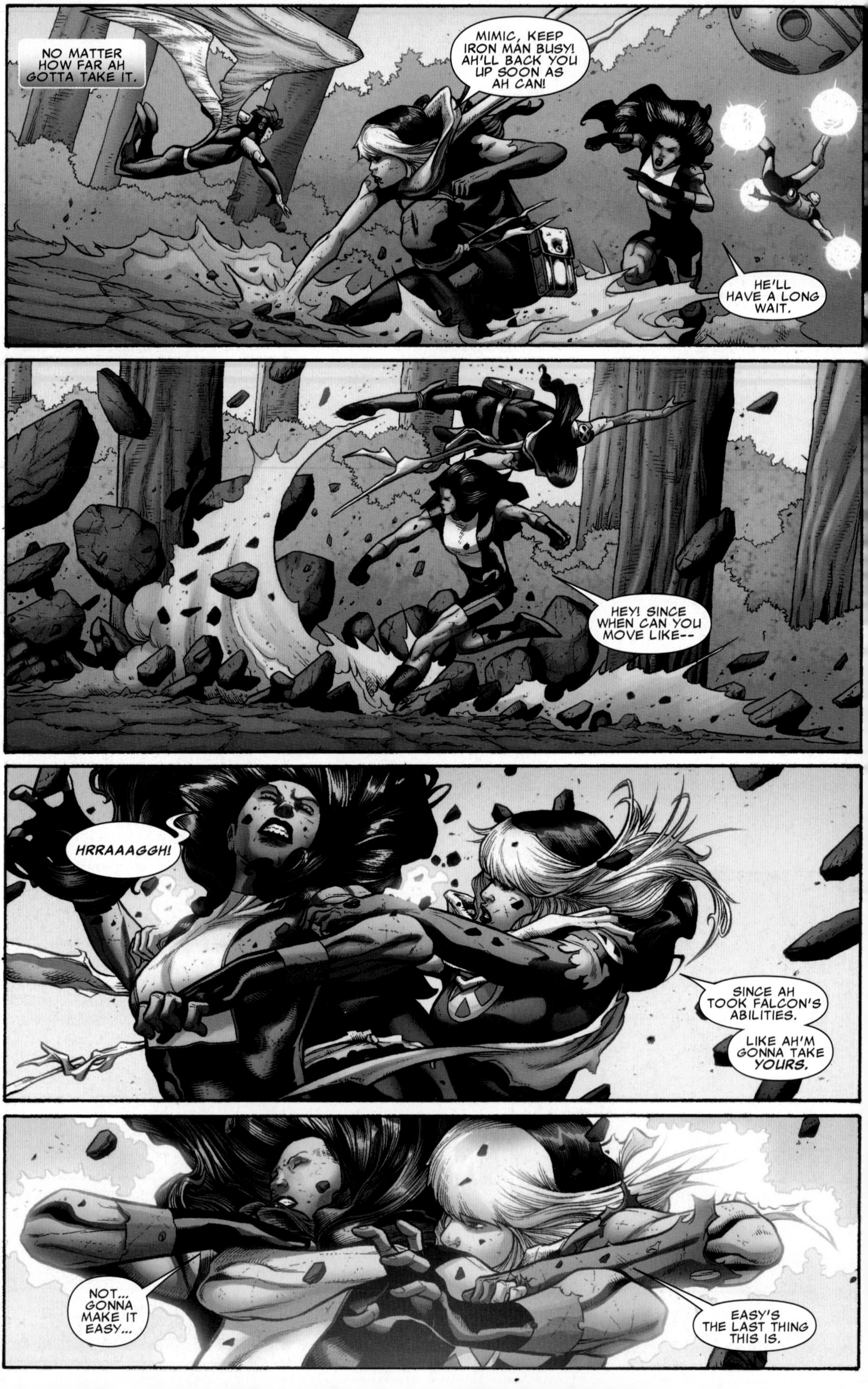
NO MATTER HOW FAR AH GOTTA TAKE IT.
MIMIC, KEEP IRON MAN BUSY! AH'LL BACK YOU UP SOON AS AH CAN!
HE'LL HAVE A LONG WAIT.
HEY! SINCE WHEN CAN YOU MOVE LIKE--
HRRAAAGGH!
SINCE AH TOOK FALCON'S ABILITIES.
LIKE AH'M GONNA TAKE YOURS.
NOT... GONNA MAKE IT EASY...
EASY'S THE LAST THING THIS IS.

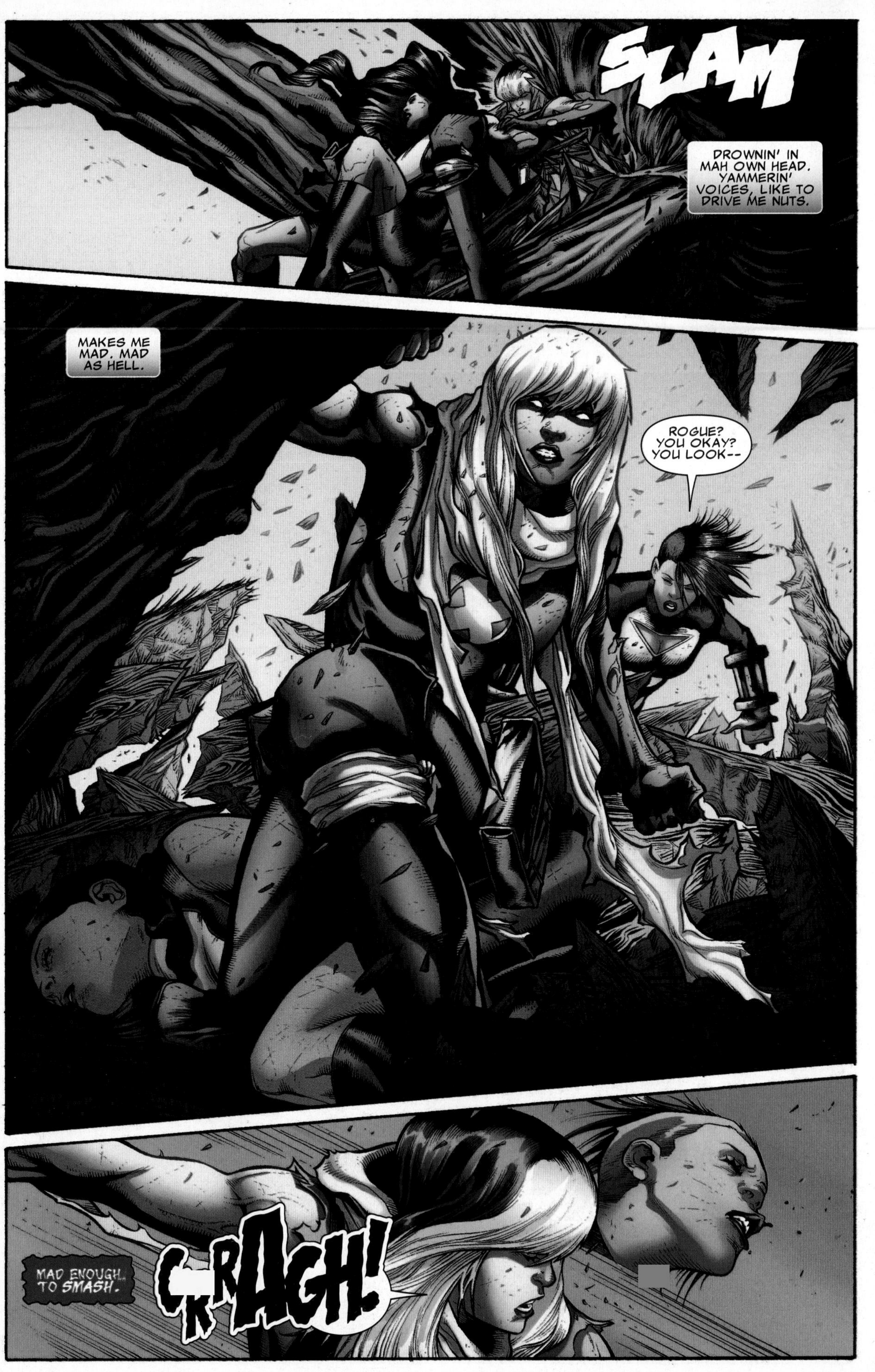
SLAM
DROWNIN' IN MAH OWN HEAD. YAMMERIN' VOICES, LIKE TO DRIVE ME NUTS.
MAKES ME MAD. MAD AS HELL.
ROGUE? YOU OKAY? YOU LOOK--
MAD ENOUGH. TO SMASH.
CKRAGH!

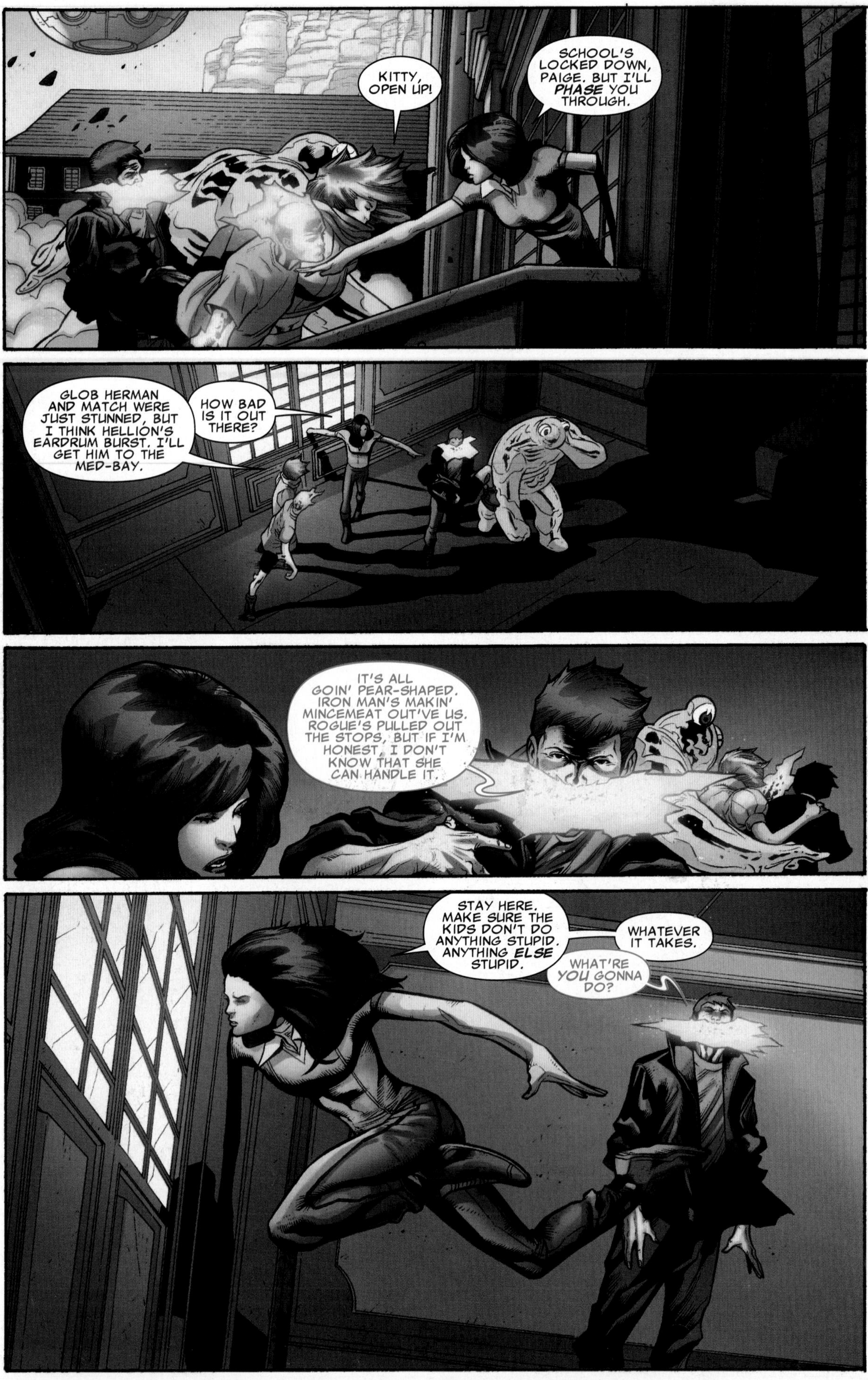
KITTY, OPEN UP!
SCHOOL'S LOCKED DOWN, PAIGE. BUT I'LL PHASE YOU THROUGH.
GLOB HERMAN AND MATCH WERE JUST STUNNED, BUT I THINK HELLION'S EARDRUM BURST. I'LL GET HIM TO THE MED-BAY.
HOW BAD IS IT OUT THERE?
IT'S ALL GOIN' PEAR-SHAPED. IRON MAN'S MAKIN' MINCEMEAT OUT'VE US. ROGUE'S PULLED OUT THE STOPS, BUT IF I'M HONEST, I DON'T KNOW THAT SHE CAN HANDLE IT.
STAY HERE. MAKE SURE THE KIDS DON'T DO ANYTHING STUPID. ANYTHING ELSE STUPID.
WHAT'RE YOU GONNA DO?
WHATEVER IT TAKES.

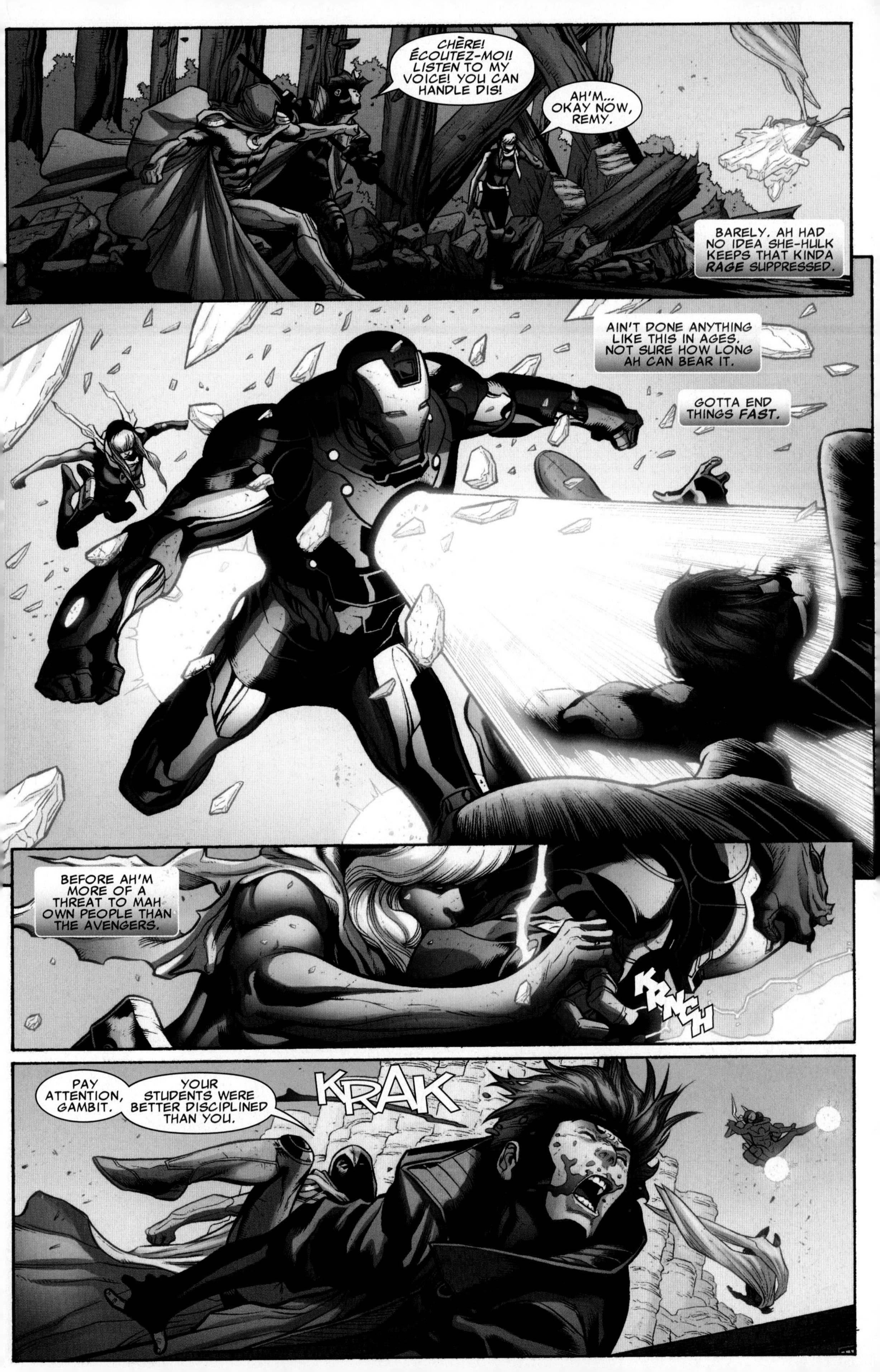
CHÈRE! ÉCOUTEZ-MOI!! LISTEN TO MY VOICE! YOU CAN HANDLE DIS!
AH'M... OKAY NOW, REMY.
BARELY. AH HAD NO IDEA SHE-HULK KEEPS THAT KINDA RAGE SUPPRESSED.
AIN'T DONE ANYTHING LIKE THIS IN AGES. NOT SURE HOW LONG AH CAN BEAR IT.
GOTTA END THINGS FAST.
BEFORE AH'M MORE OF A THREAT TO MAH OWN PEOPLE THAN THE AVENGERS.
KRNCH
KRAK
PAY ATTENTION, GAMBIT.
YOUR STUDENTS WERE BETTER DISCIPLINED THAN YOU.

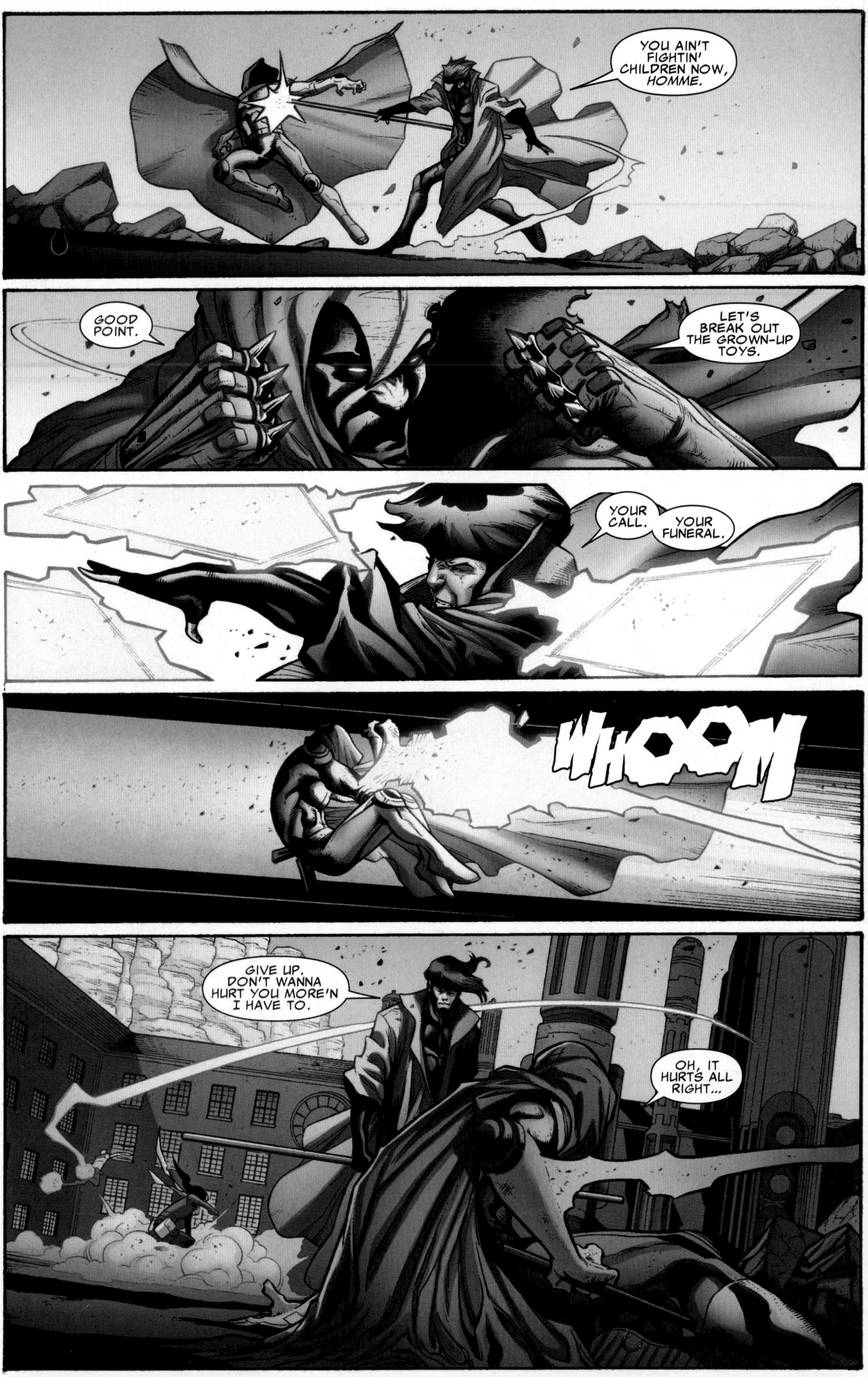
YOU AIN'T FIGHTIN' CHILDREN NOW, HOMME.
GOOD POINT.
LET'S BREAK OUT THE GROWN-UP TOYS.
YOUR CALL.
YOUR FUNERAL.
WHOOM
GIVE UP. DON'T WANNA HURT YOU MORE'N I HAVE TO.
OH, IT HURTS ALL RIGHT...

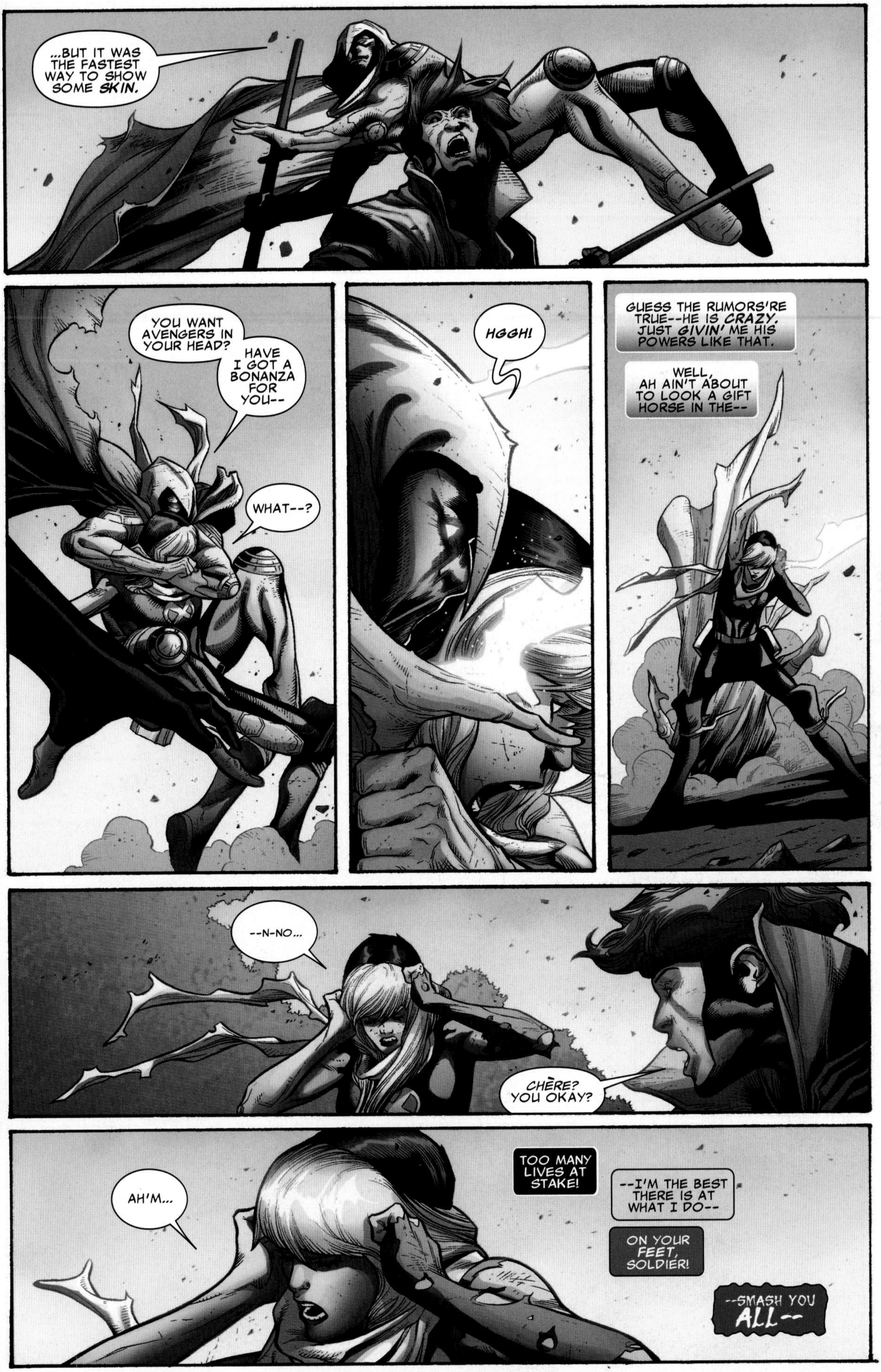
...BUT IT WAS THE FASTEST WAY TO SHOW SOME SKIN.
YOU WANT AVENGERS IN YOUR HEAD?
HAVE I GOT A BONANZA FOR YOU--
WHAT--?
HGGH!
GUESS THE RUMORS'RE TRUE--HE IS CRAZY. JUST GIVIN' ME HIS POWERS LIKE THAT.
WELL, AH AIN'T ABOUT TO LOOK A GIFT HORSE IN THE--
--N-NO...
CHÈRE? YOU OKAY?
AH'M...
TOO MANY LIVES AT STAKE!
--I'M THE BEST THERE IS AT WHAT I DO--
ON YOUR FEET, SOLDIER!
--SMASH YOU ALL--

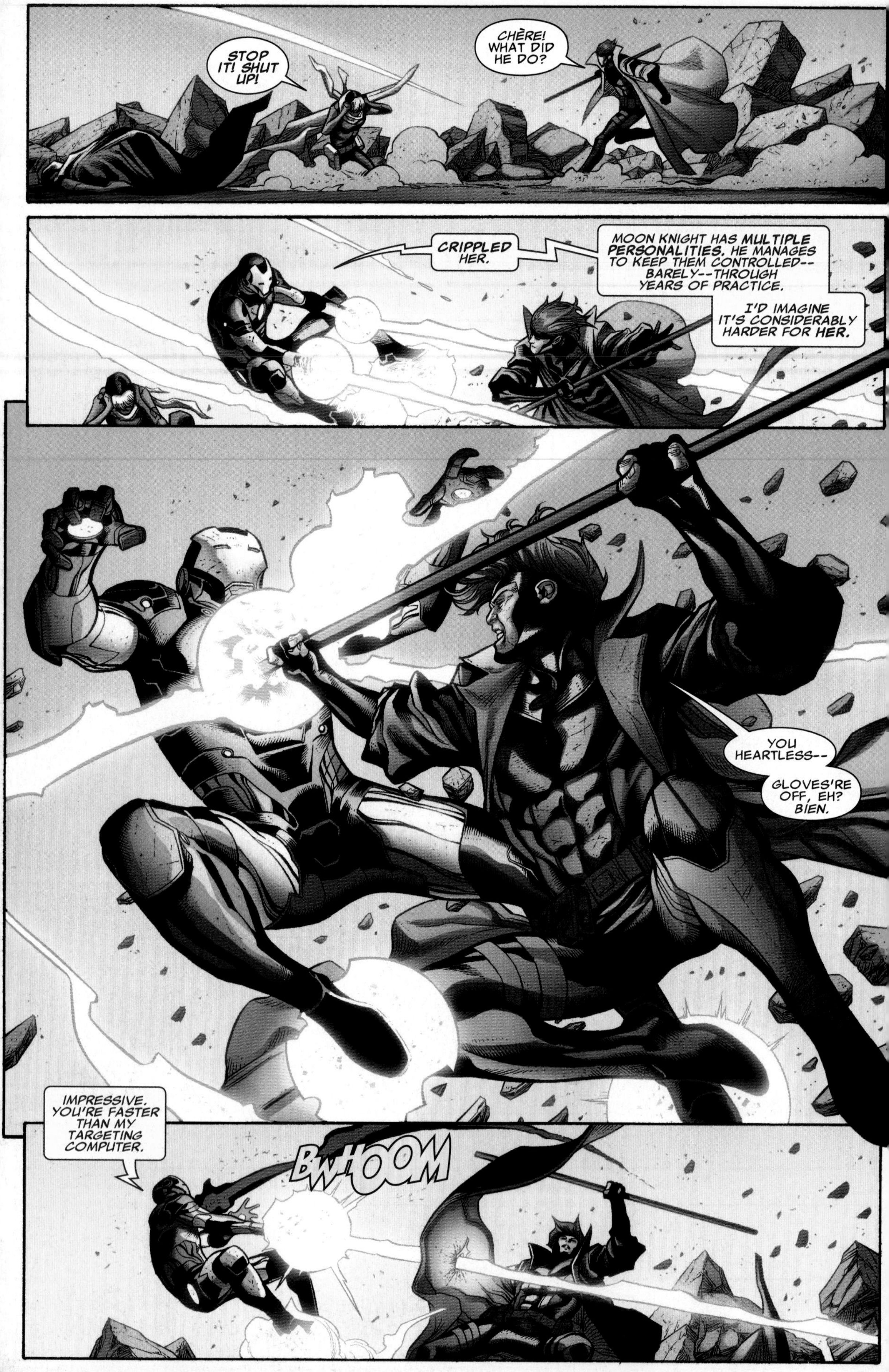

STOP IT! SHUT UP!
CHÈRE! WHAT DID HE DO?
CRIPPLED HER.
MOON KNIGHT HAS MULTIPLE PERSONALITIES. HE MANAGES TO KEEP THEM CONTROLLED-- BARELY--THROUGH YEARS OF PRACTICE.
I'D IMAGINE IT'S CONSIDERABLY HARDER FOR HER.
YOU HEARTLESS--
GLOVES'RE OFF, EH? BIEN.
IMPRESSIVE. YOU'RE FASTER THAN MY TARGETING COMPUTER.
BWHOOM

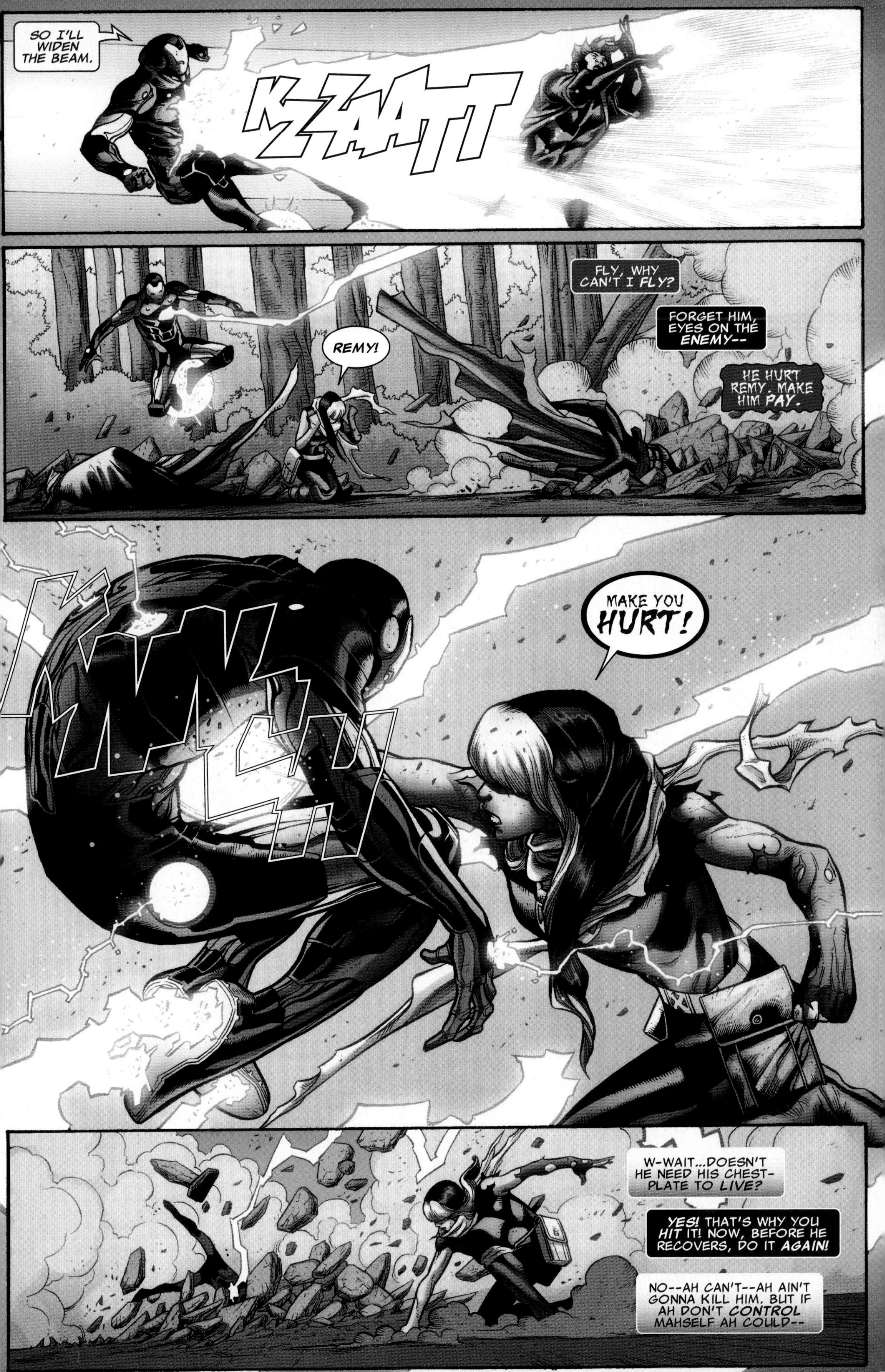
SO I'LL WIDEN THE BEAM.
KZZAATT
FLY, WHY CAN'T I FLY?
FORGET HIM, EYES ON THE ENEMY--
REMY!
HE HURT REMY. MAKE HIM PAY.
MAKE YOU HURT!
W-WAIT...DOESN'T HE NEED HIS CHEST-PLATE TO LIVE?
YES! THAT'S WHY YOU HIT IT! NOW, BEFORE HE RECOVERS, DO IT AGAIN!
NO--AH CAN'T--AH AIN'T GONNA KILL HIM. BUT IF AH DON'T CONTROL MAHSELF AH COULD--

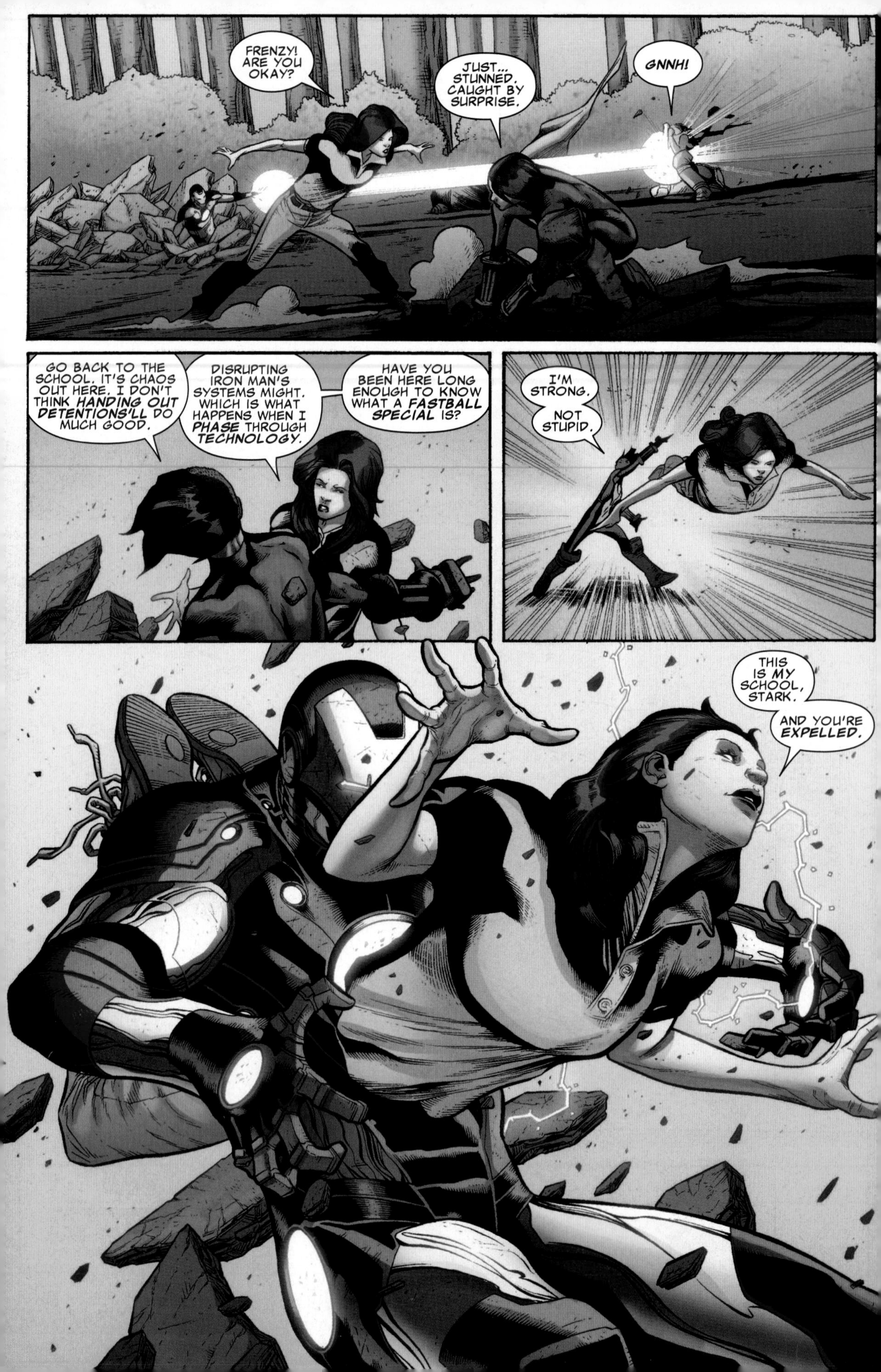

FRENZY! ARE YOU OKAY?
JUST... STUNNED. CAUGHT BY SURPRISE.
GNNH!
GO BACK TO THE SCHOOL. IT'S CHAOS OUT HERE. I DON'T THINK HANDING OUT DETENTIONS'LL DO MUCH GOOD.
DISRUPTING IRON MAN'S SYSTEMS MIGHT. WHICH IS WHAT HAPPENS WHEN I PHASE THROUGH TECHNOLOGY.
HAVE YOU BEEN HERE LONG ENOUGH TO KNOW WHAT A FASTBALL SPECIAL IS?
I'M STRONG.
NOT STUPID.
THIS IS MY SCHOOL, STARK.
AND YOU'RE EXPELLED.

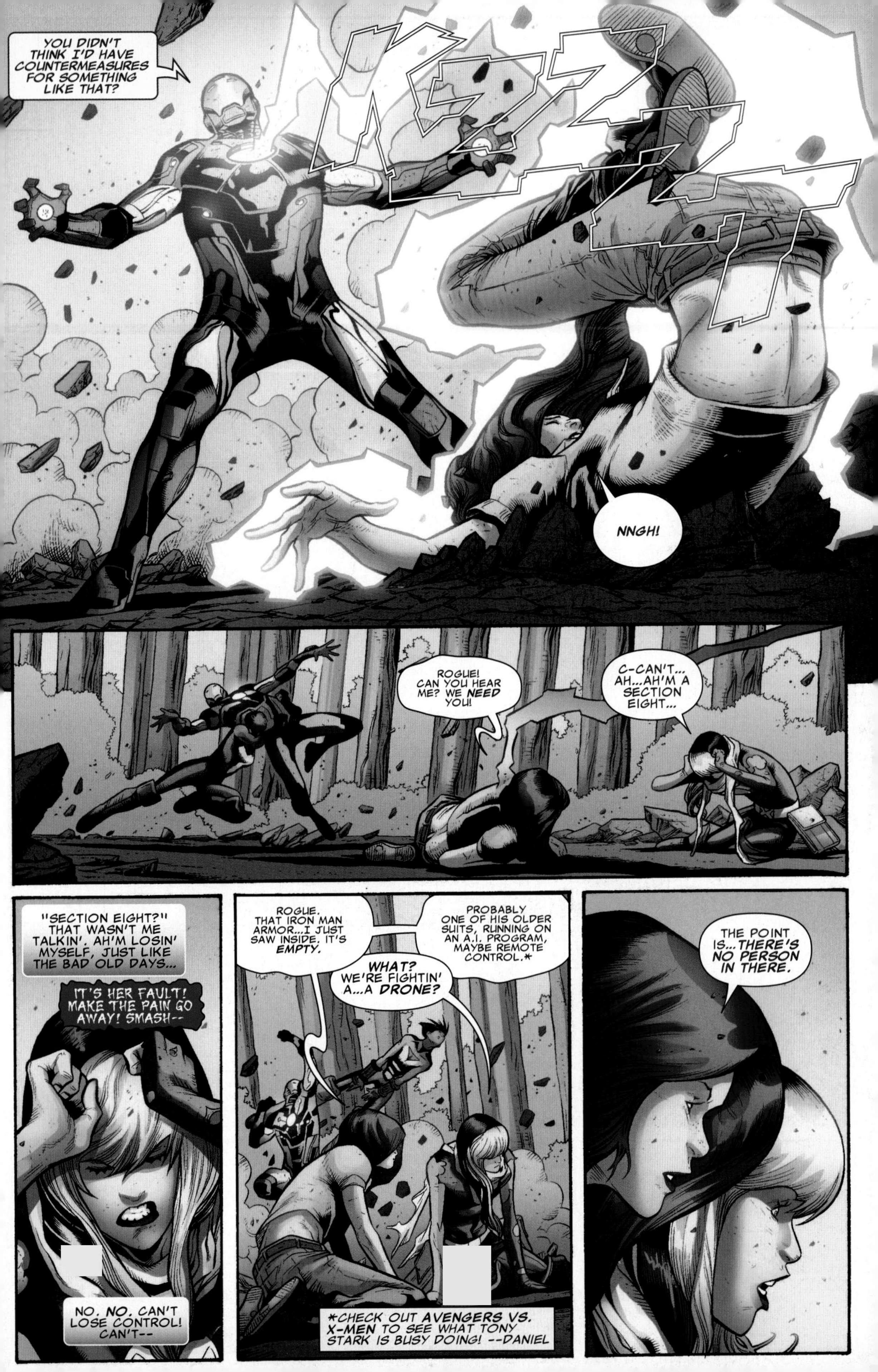
YOU DIDN'T THINK I'D HAVE COUNTERMEASURES FOR SOMETHING LIKE THAT?
NNGH!
ROGUE! CAN YOU HEAR ME? WE NEED YOU!
C-CAN'T... AH...AH'M A SECTION EIGHT...
"SECTION EIGHT?" THAT WASN'T ME TALKIN'. AH'M LOSIN' MYSELF, JUST LIKE THE BAD OLD DAYS...
IT'S HER FAULT! MAKE THE PAIN GO AWAY! SMASH--
NO. NO. CAN'T LOSE CONTROL! CAN'T--
ROGUE. THAT IRON MAN ARMOR...I JUST SAW INSIDE. IT'S EMPTY.
PROBABLY ONE OF HIS OLDER SUITS, RUNNING ON AN A.I. PROGRAM, MAYBE REMOTE CONTROL.*
WHAT? WE'RE FIGHTIN' A...A DRONE?
*CHECK OUT AVENGERS VS. X-MEN TO SEE WHAT TONY STARK IS BUSY DOING! --DANIEL
THE POINT IS...THERE'S NO PERSON IN THERE.

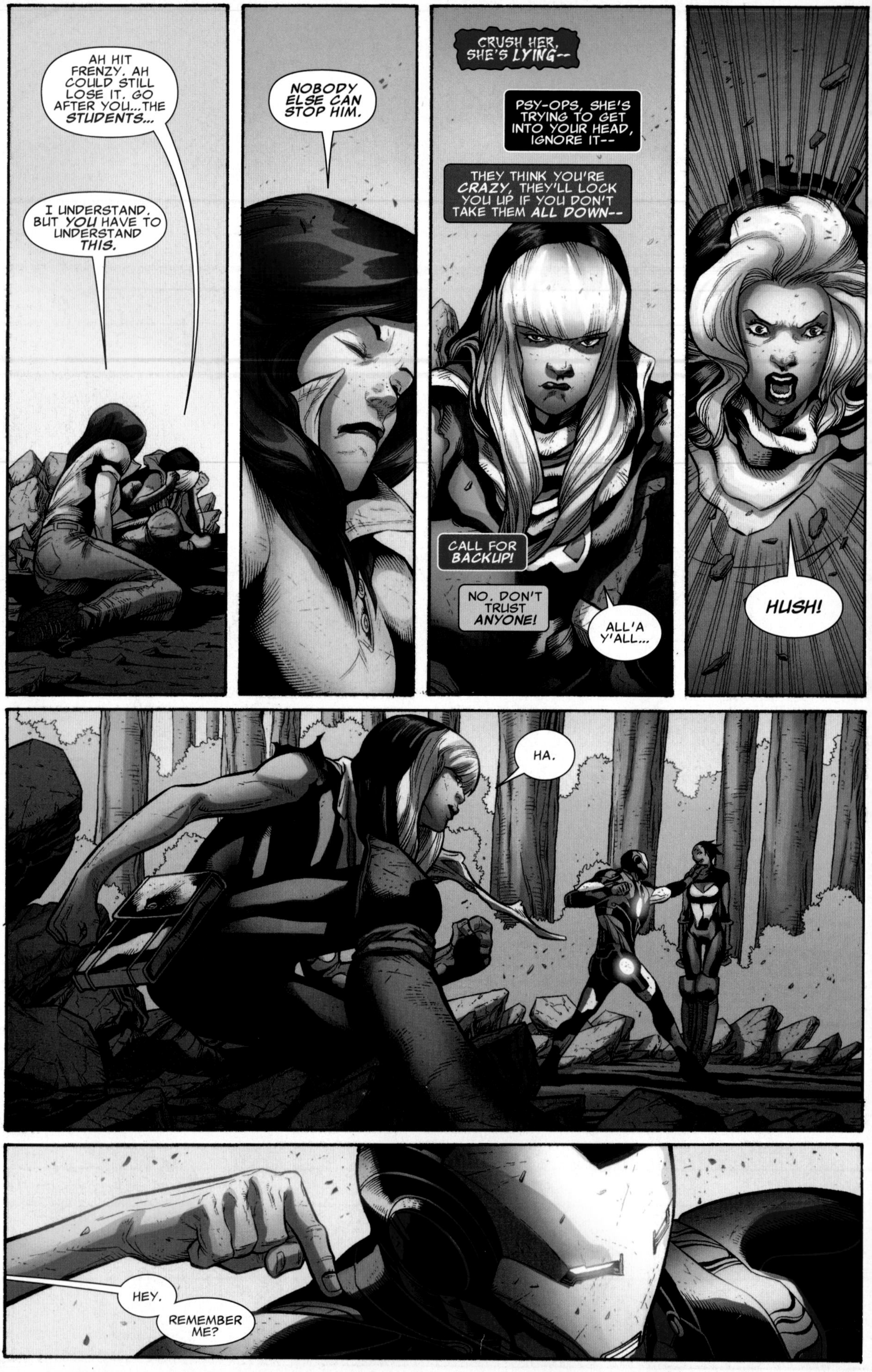

AH HIT FRENZY. AH COULD STILL LOSE IT. GO AFTER YOU...THE STUDENTS...
I UNDERSTAND. BUT YOU HAVE TO UNDERSTAND THIS.
NOBODY ELSE CAN STOP HIM.
CRUSH HER, SHE'S LYING--
PSY-OPS, SHE'S TRYING TO GET INTO YOUR HEAD, IGNORE IT--
THEY THINK YOU'RE CRAZY, THEY'LL LOCK YOU UP IF YOU DON'T TAKE THEM ALL DOWN--
CALL FOR BACKUP!
NO. DON'T TRUST ANYONE!
ALL'A Y'ALL...
HUSH!
HA.
HEY.
REMEMBER ME?

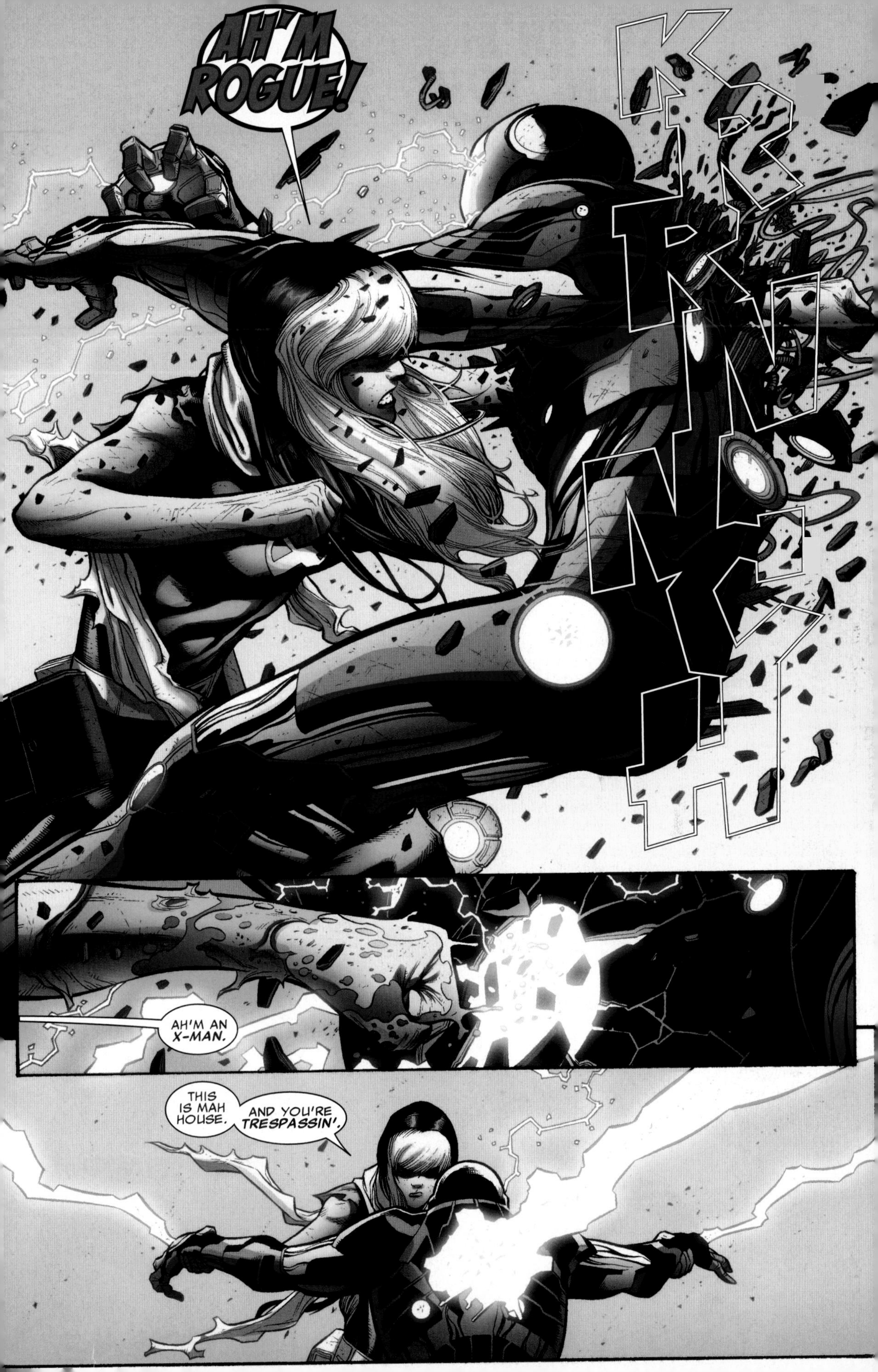
AH'M ROGUE!
KRRNNKKH
AH'M AN X-MAN.
THIS IS MAH HOUSE.
AND YOU'RE TRESPASSIN'.

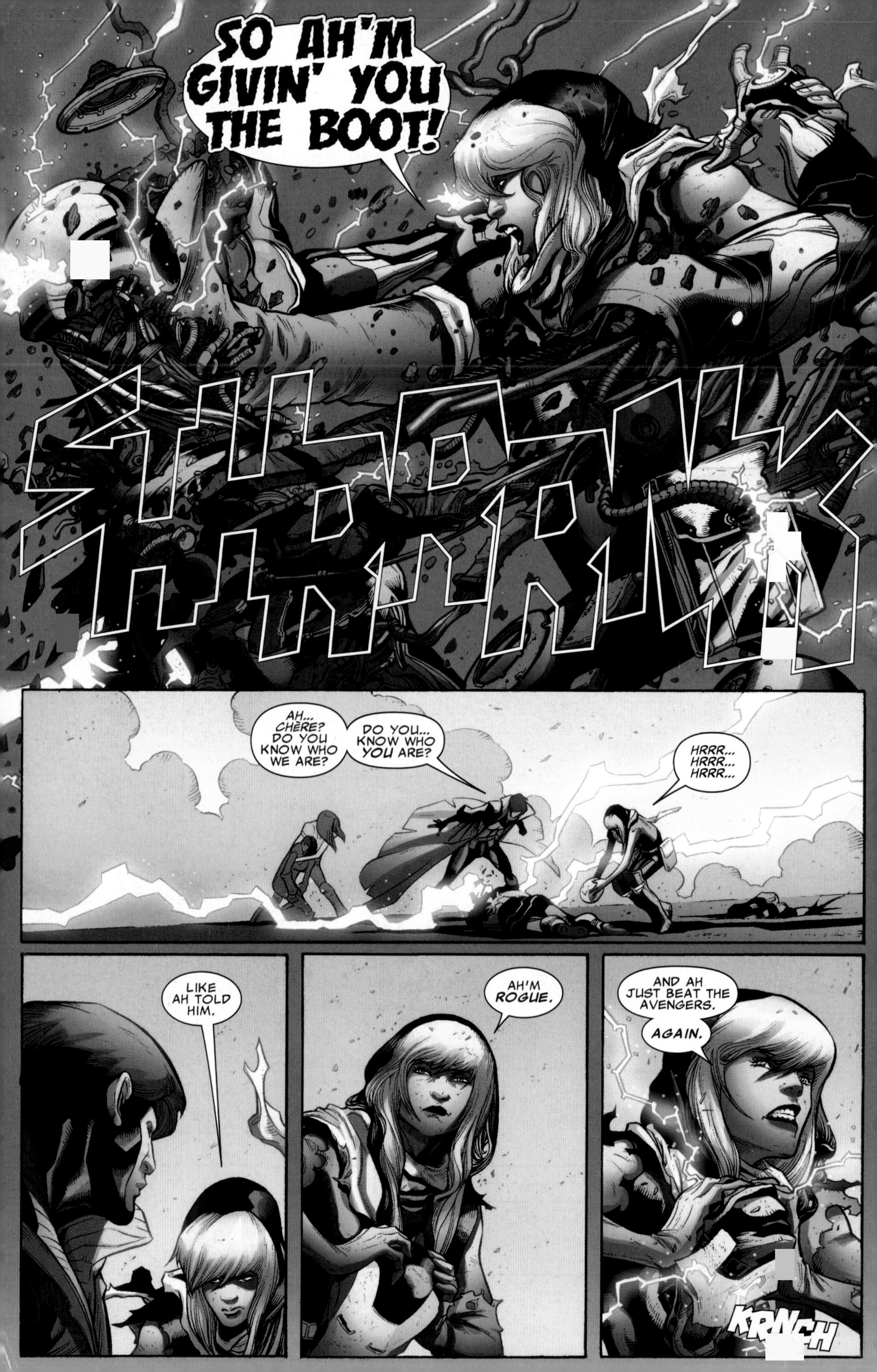
SO AH'M GIVIN' YOU THE BOOT!
AH... CHÈRE? DO YOU KNOW WHO WE ARE?
DO YOU... KNOW WHO YOU ARE?
HRRR... HRRR... HRRR...
LIKE AH TOLD HIM.
AH'M ROGUE.
AND AH JUST BEAT THE AVENGERS.
AGAIN.
KRNCH

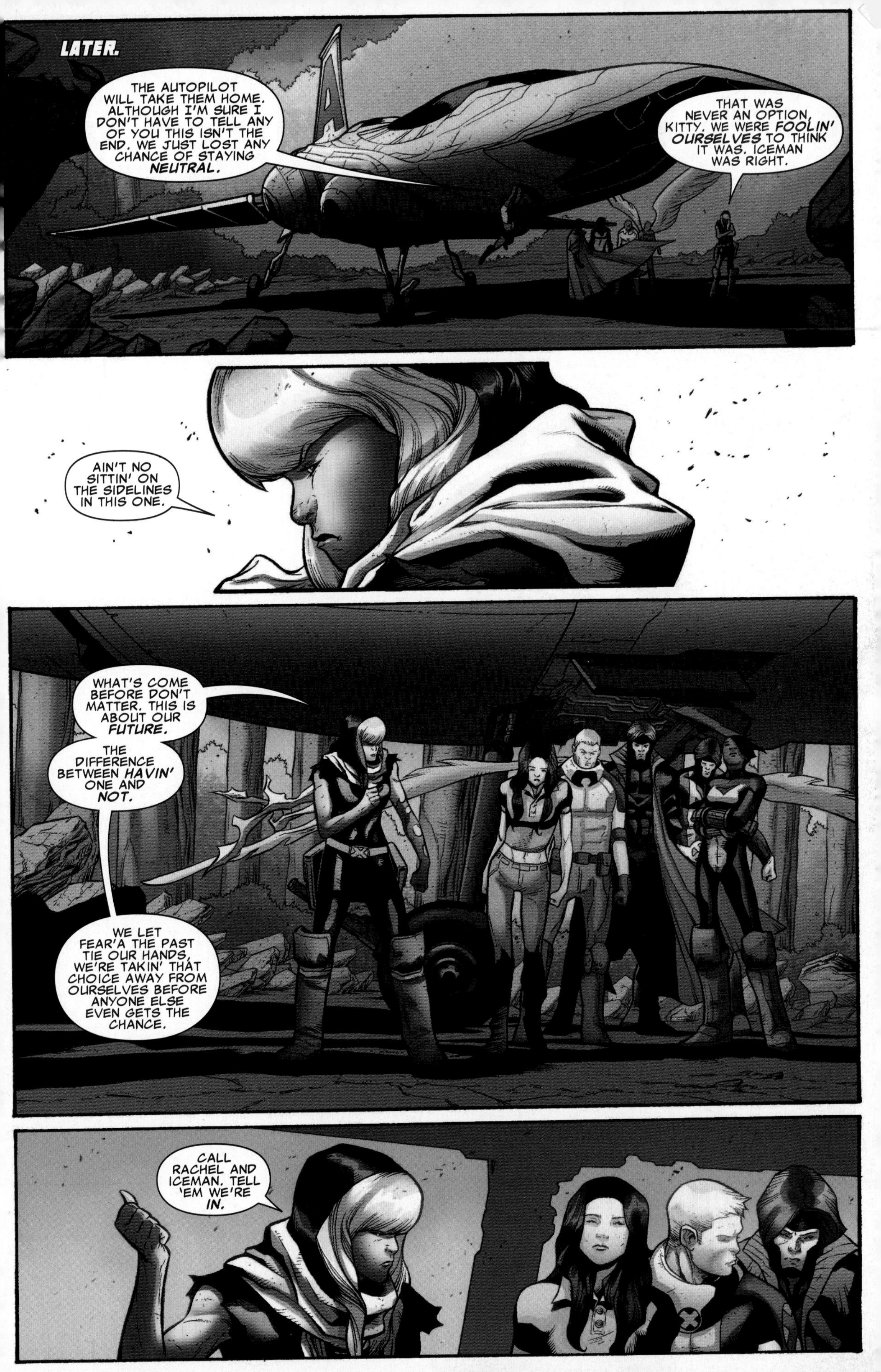
LATER.
THE AUTOPILOT WILL TAKE THEM HOME. ALTHOUGH I'M SURE I DON'T HAVE TO TELL ANY OF YOU THIS ISN'T THE END. WE JUST LOST ANY CHANCE OF STAYING NEUTRAL.
THAT WAS NEVER AN OPTION, KITTY. WE WERE FOOLIN' OURSELVES TO THINK IT WAS. ICEMAN WAS RIGHT.
AIN'T NO SITTIN' ON THE SIDELINES IN THIS ONE.
WHAT'S COME BEFORE DON'T MATTER. THIS IS ABOUT OUR FUTURE.
THE DIFFERENCE BETWEEN HAVIN' ONE AND NOT.
WE LET FEAR'A THE PAST TIE OUR HANDS, WE'RE TAKIN' THAT CHOICE AWAY FROM OURSELVES BEFORE ANYONE ELSE EVEN GETS THE CHANCE.
CALL RACHEL AND ICEMAN. TELL 'EM WE'RE IN.

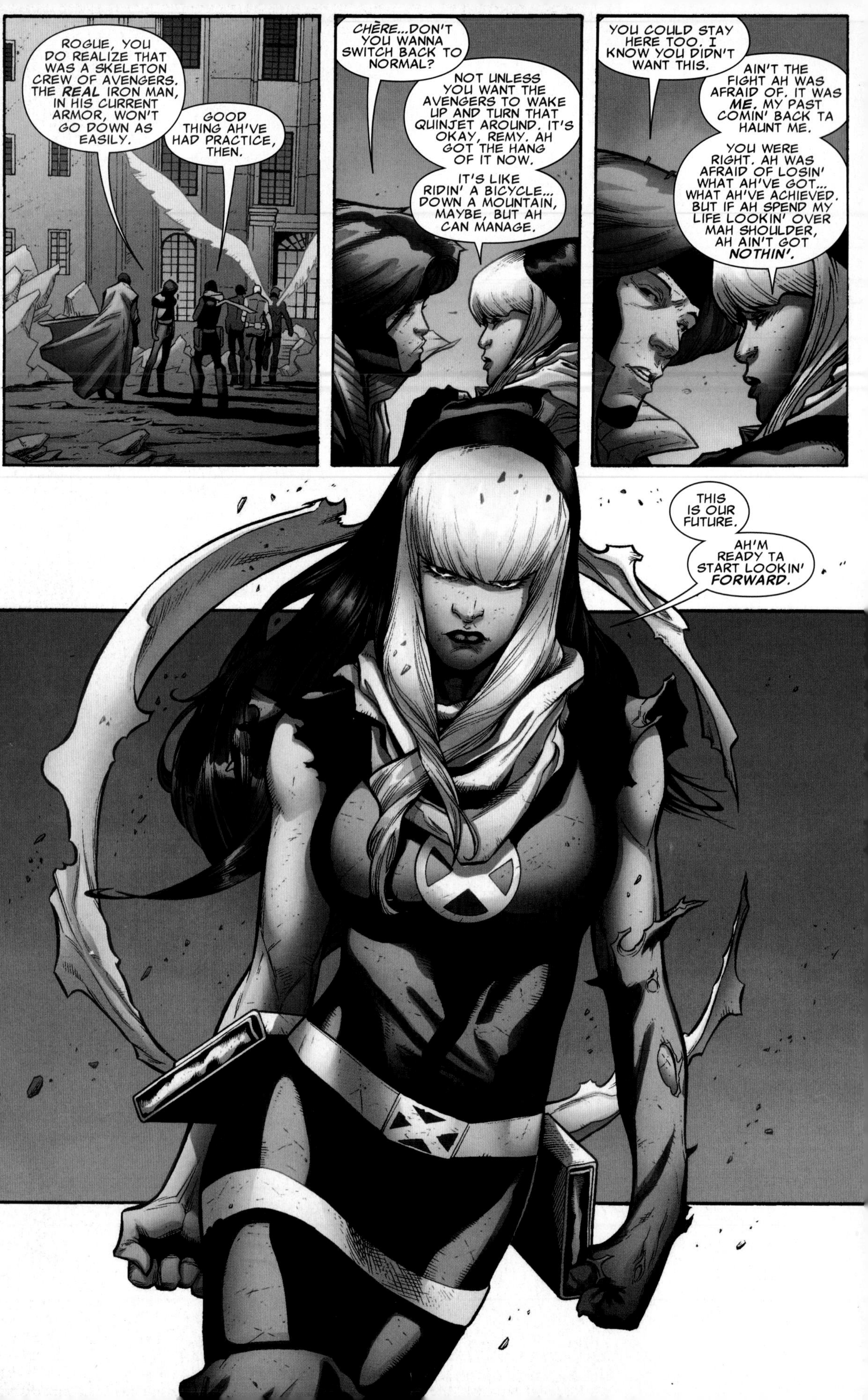
ROGUE, YOU DO REALIZE THAT WAS A SKELETON CREW OF AVENGERS. THE *REAL* IRON MAN, IN HIS CURRENT ARMOR, WON'T GO DOWN AS EASILY.
GOOD THING AH'VE HAD PRACTICE, THEN.
CHÈRE...DON'T YOU WANNA SWITCH BACK TO NORMAL?
NOT UNLESS YOU WANT THE AVENGERS TO WAKE UP AND TURN THAT QUINJET AROUND. IT'S OKAY, REMY. AH GOT THE HANG OF IT NOW.
IT'S LIKE RIDIN' A BICYCLE... DOWN A MOUNTAIN, MAYBE, BUT AH CAN MANAGE.
YOU COULD STAY HERE TOO. I KNOW YOU DIDN'T WANT THIS.
AIN'T THE FIGHT AH WAS AFRAID OF. IT WAS *ME*. MY PAST COMIN' BACK TA HAUNT ME.
YOU WERE RIGHT. AH WAS AFRAID OF LOSIN' WHAT AH'VE GOT... WHAT AH'VE ACHIEVED. BUT IF AH SPEND MY LIFE LOOKIN' OVER MAH SHOULDER, AH AIN'T GOT *NOTHIN'*.
THIS IS OUR FUTURE.
AH'M READY TA START LOOKIN' *FORWARD*.

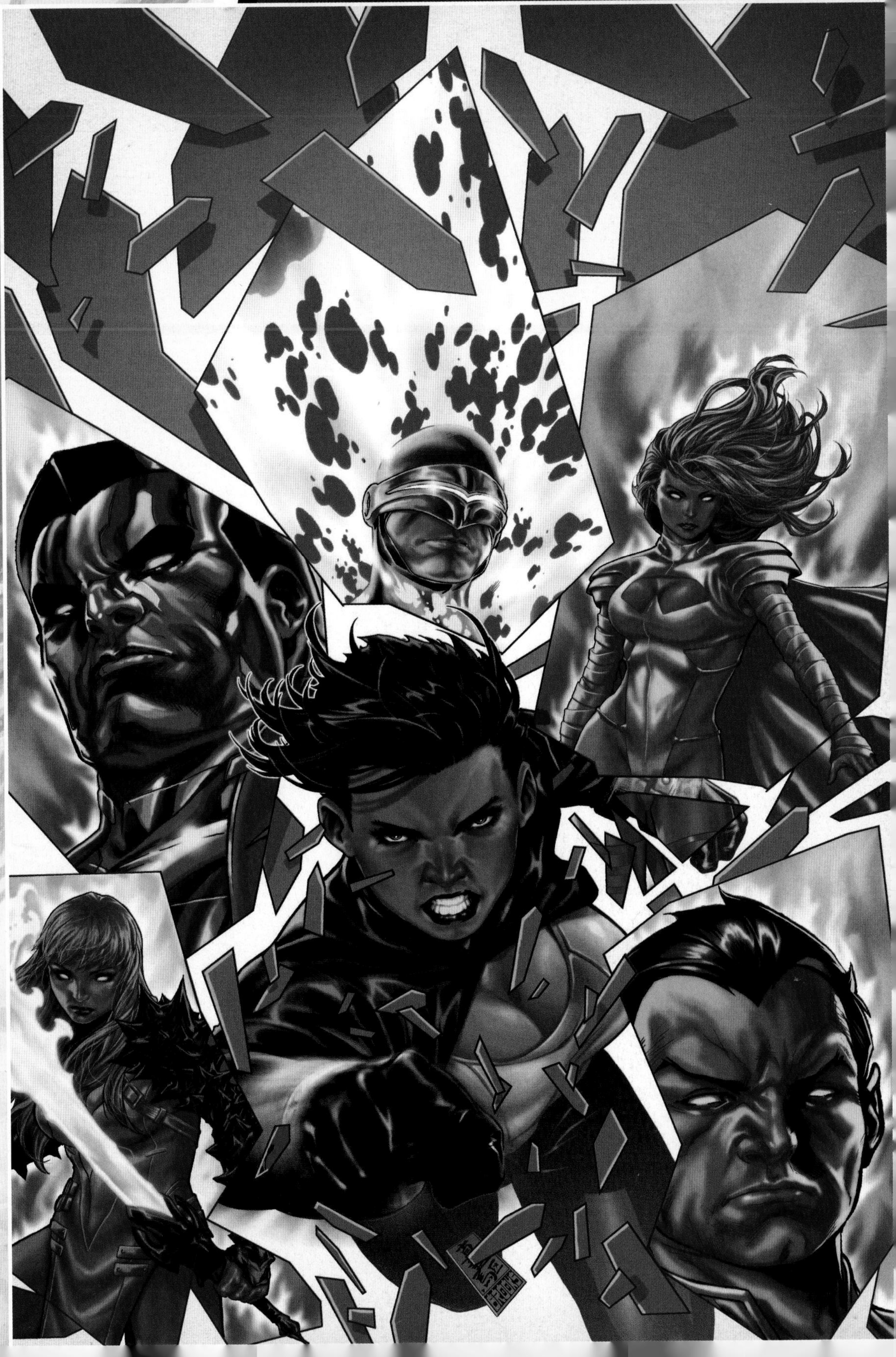

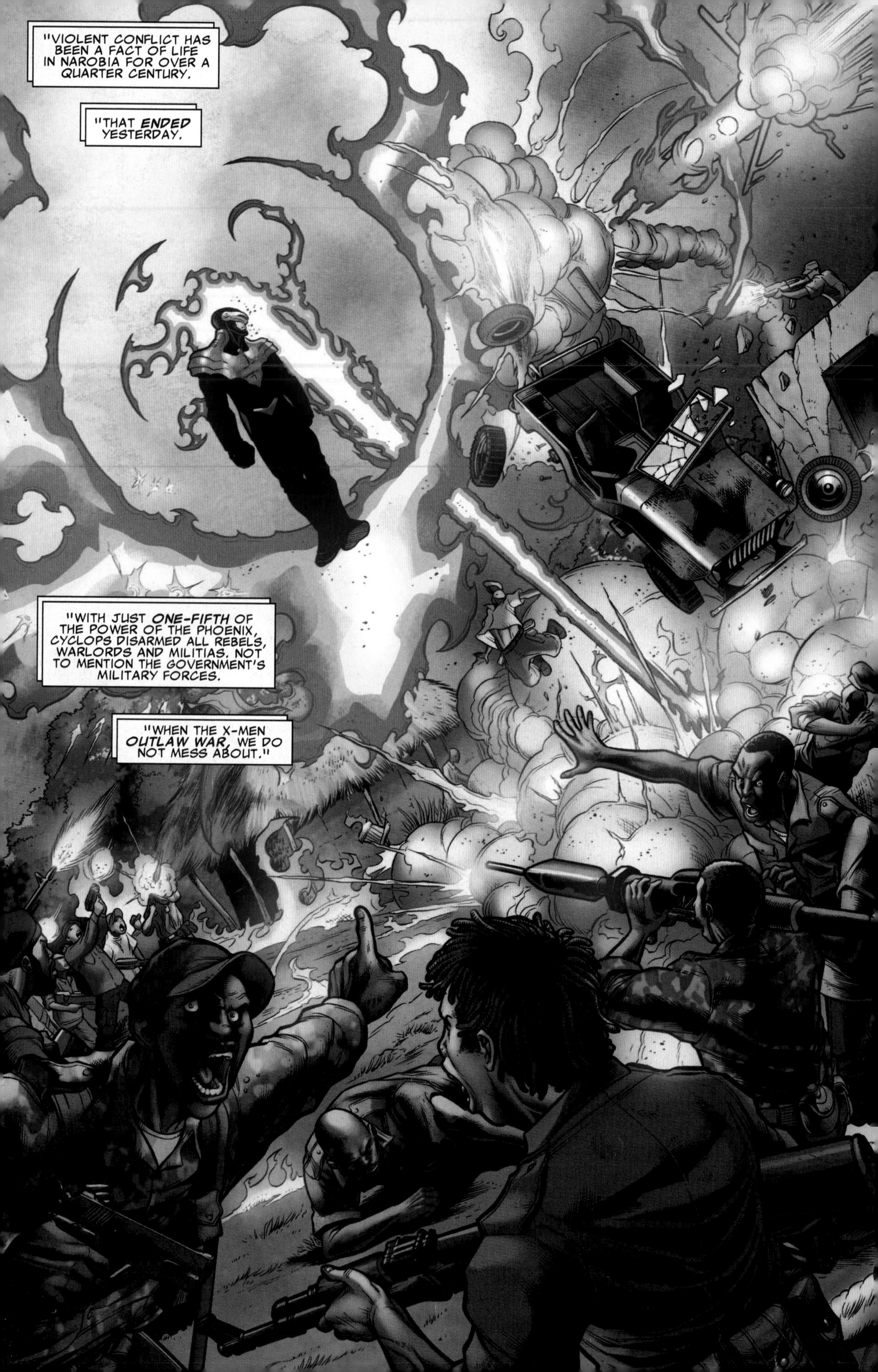
"VIOLENT CONFLICT HAS BEEN A FACT OF LIFE IN NAROBIA FOR OVER A QUARTER CENTURY.
"THAT ENDED YESTERDAY.
"WITH JUST ONE-FIFTH OF THE POWER OF THE PHOENIX, CYCLOPS DISARMED ALL REBELS, WARLORDS AND MILITIAS. NOT TO MENTION THE GOVERNMENT'S MILITARY FORCES.
"WHEN THE X-MEN OUTLAW WAR, WE DO NOT MESS ABOUT."

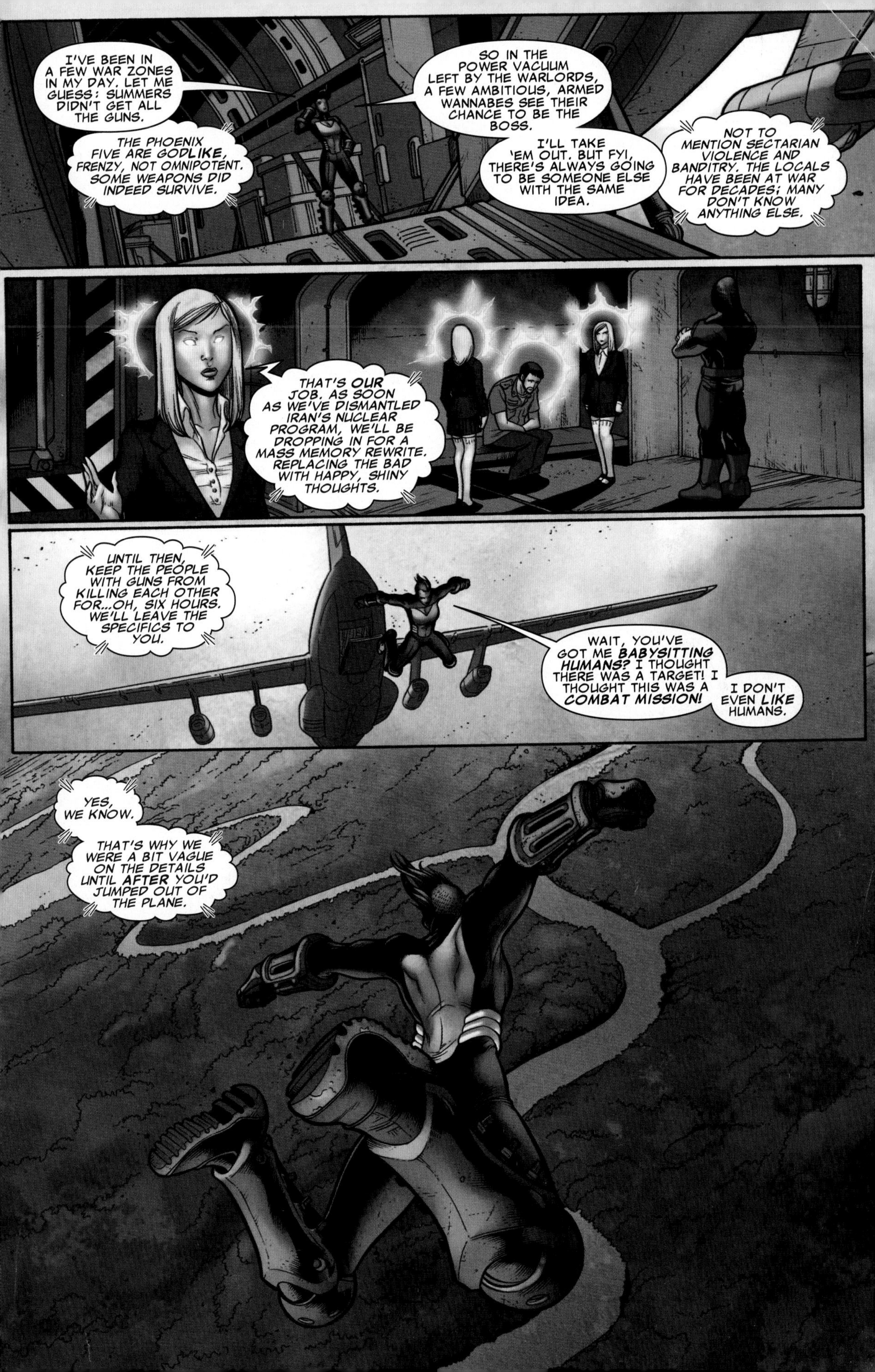
I'VE BEEN IN A FEW WAR ZONES IN MY DAY. LET ME GUESS: SUMMERS DIDN'T GET ALL THE GUNS.
THE PHOENIX FIVE ARE GODLIKE, FRENZY, NOT OMNIPOTENT. SOME WEAPONS DID INDEED SURVIVE.
SO IN THE POWER VACUUM LEFT BY THE WARLORDS, A FEW AMBITIOUS, ARMED WANNABES SEE THEIR CHANCE TO BE THE BOSS.
I'LL TAKE 'EM OUT. BUT FYI, THERE'S ALWAYS GOING TO BE SOMEONE ELSE WITH THE SAME IDEA.
NOT TO MENTION SECTARIAN VIOLENCE AND BANDITRY. THE LOCALS HAVE BEEN AT WAR FOR DECADES; MANY DON'T KNOW ANYTHING ELSE.
THAT'S OUR JOB. AS SOON AS WE'VE DISMANTLED IRAN'S NUCLEAR PROGRAM, WE'LL BE DROPPING IN FOR A MASS MEMORY REWRITE. REPLACING THE BAD WITH HAPPY, SHINY THOUGHTS.
UNTIL THEN, KEEP THE PEOPLE WITH GUNS FROM KILLING EACH OTHER FOR...OH, SIX HOURS. WE'LL LEAVE THE SPECIFICS TO YOU.
WAIT, YOU'VE GOT ME BABYSITTING HUMANS? I THOUGHT THERE WAS A TARGET! I THOUGHT THIS WAS A COMBAT MISSION!
I DON'T EVEN LIKE HUMANS.
YES, WE KNOW.
THAT'S WHY WE WERE A BIT VAGUE ON THE DETAILS UNTIL AFTER YOU'D JUMPED OUT OF THE PLANE.

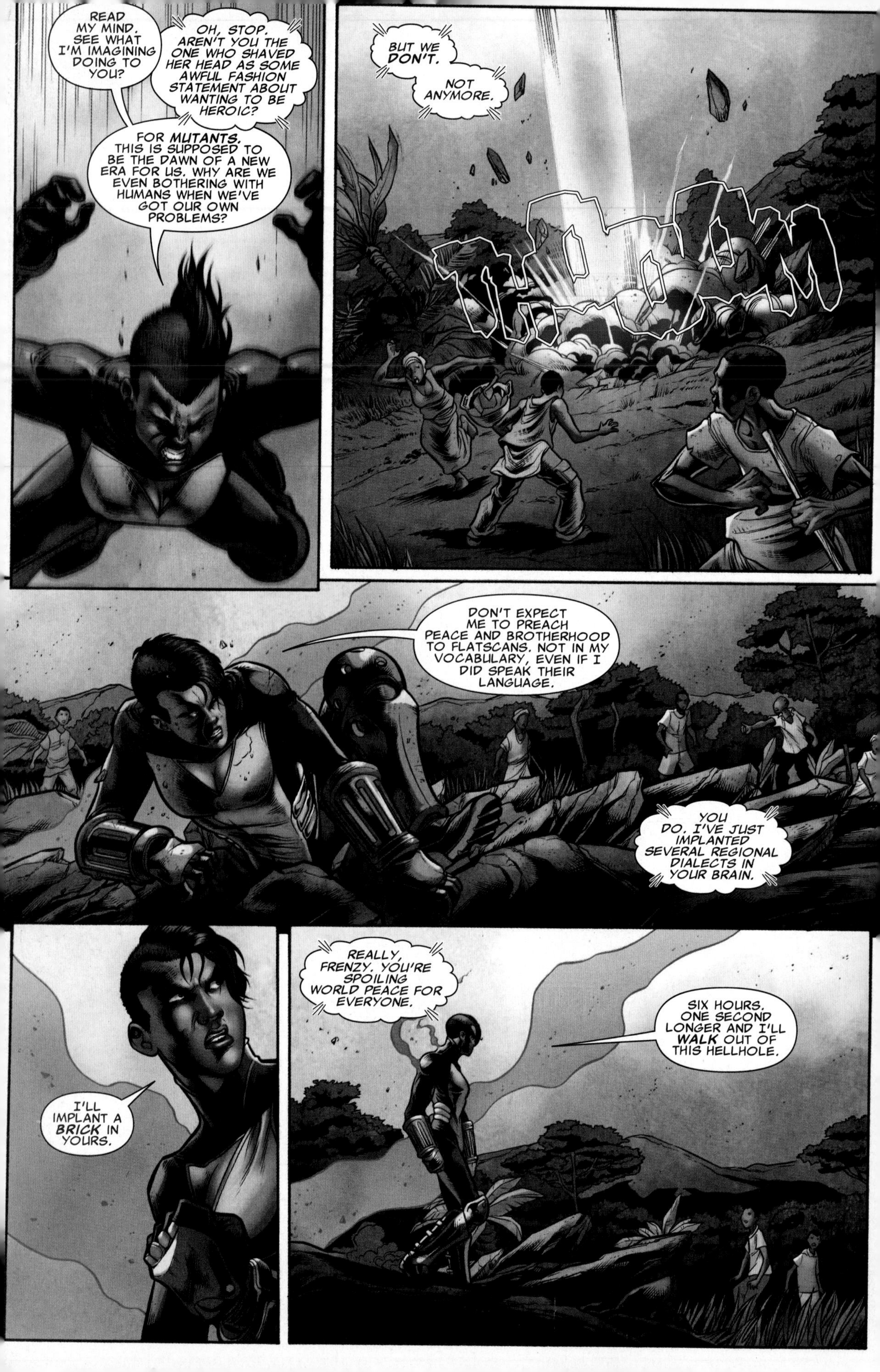
READ MY MIND. SEE WHAT I'M IMAGINING DOING TO YOU?
OH, STOP. AREN'T YOU THE ONE WHO SHAVED HER HEAD AS SOME AWFUL FASHION STATEMENT ABOUT WANTING TO BE HEROIC?
FOR MUTANTS. THIS IS SUPPOSED TO BE THE DAWN OF A NEW ERA FOR US. WHY ARE WE EVEN BOTHERING WITH HUMANS WHEN WE'VE GOT OUR OWN PROBLEMS?
BUT WE DON'T.
NOT ANYMORE.
VOOOOOM
DON'T EXPECT ME TO PREACH PEACE AND BROTHERHOOD TO FLATSCANS. NOT IN MY VOCABULARY, EVEN IF I DID SPEAK THEIR LANGUAGE.
YOU DO. I'VE JUST IMPLANTED SEVERAL REGIONAL DIALECTS IN YOUR BRAIN.
I'LL IMPLANT A BRICK IN YOURS.
REALLY, FRENZY. YOU'RE SPOILING WORLD PEACE FOR EVERYONE.
SIX HOURS. ONE SECOND LONGER AND I'LL WALK OUT OF THIS HELLHOLE.

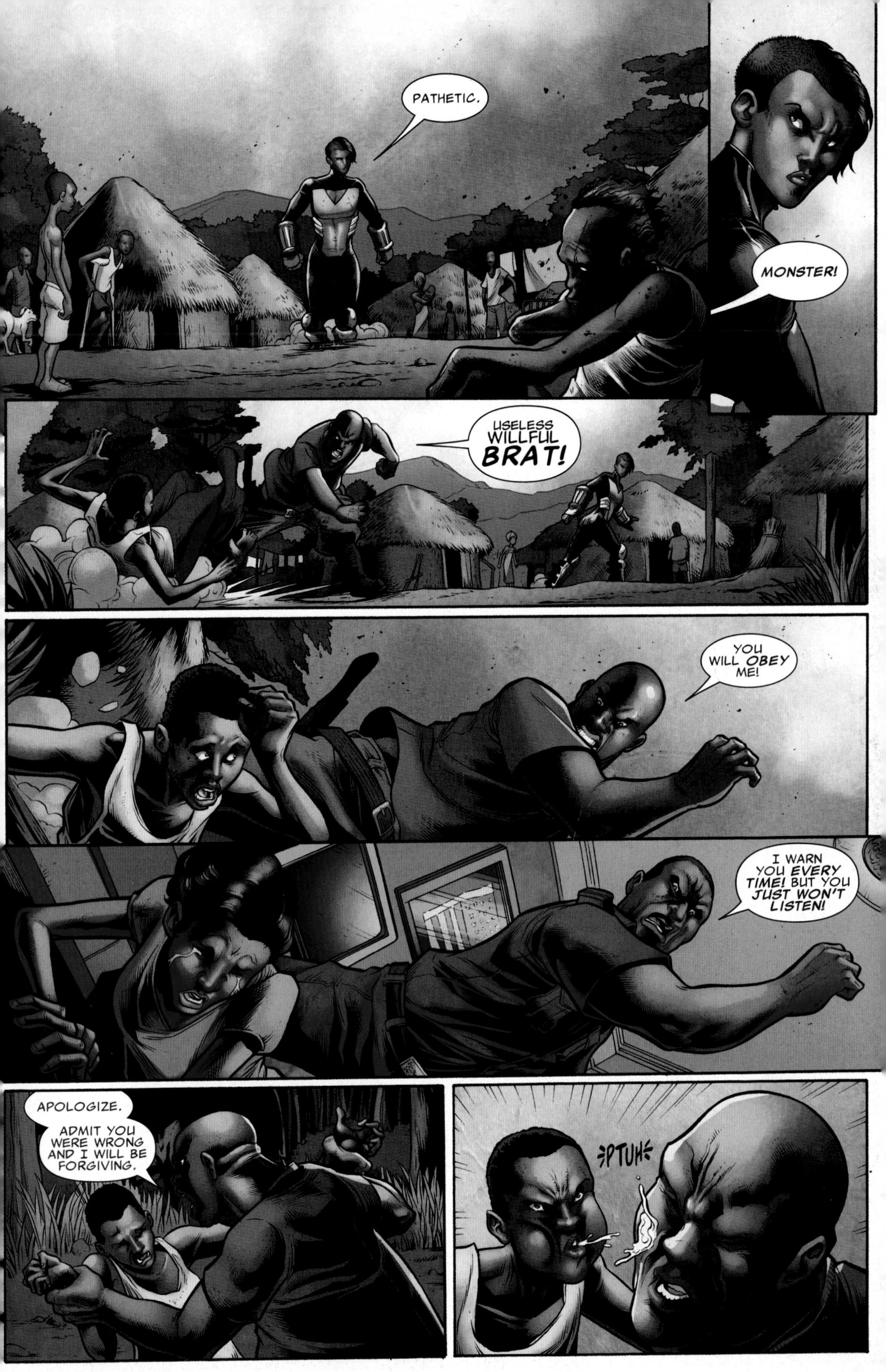
PATHETIC.
MONSTER!
USELESS WILLFUL BRAT!
YOU WILL OBEY ME!
I WARN YOU EVERY TIME! BUT YOU JUST WON'T LISTEN!
APOLOGIZE.
ADMIT YOU WERE WRONG AND I WILL BE FORGIVING.
PTUH

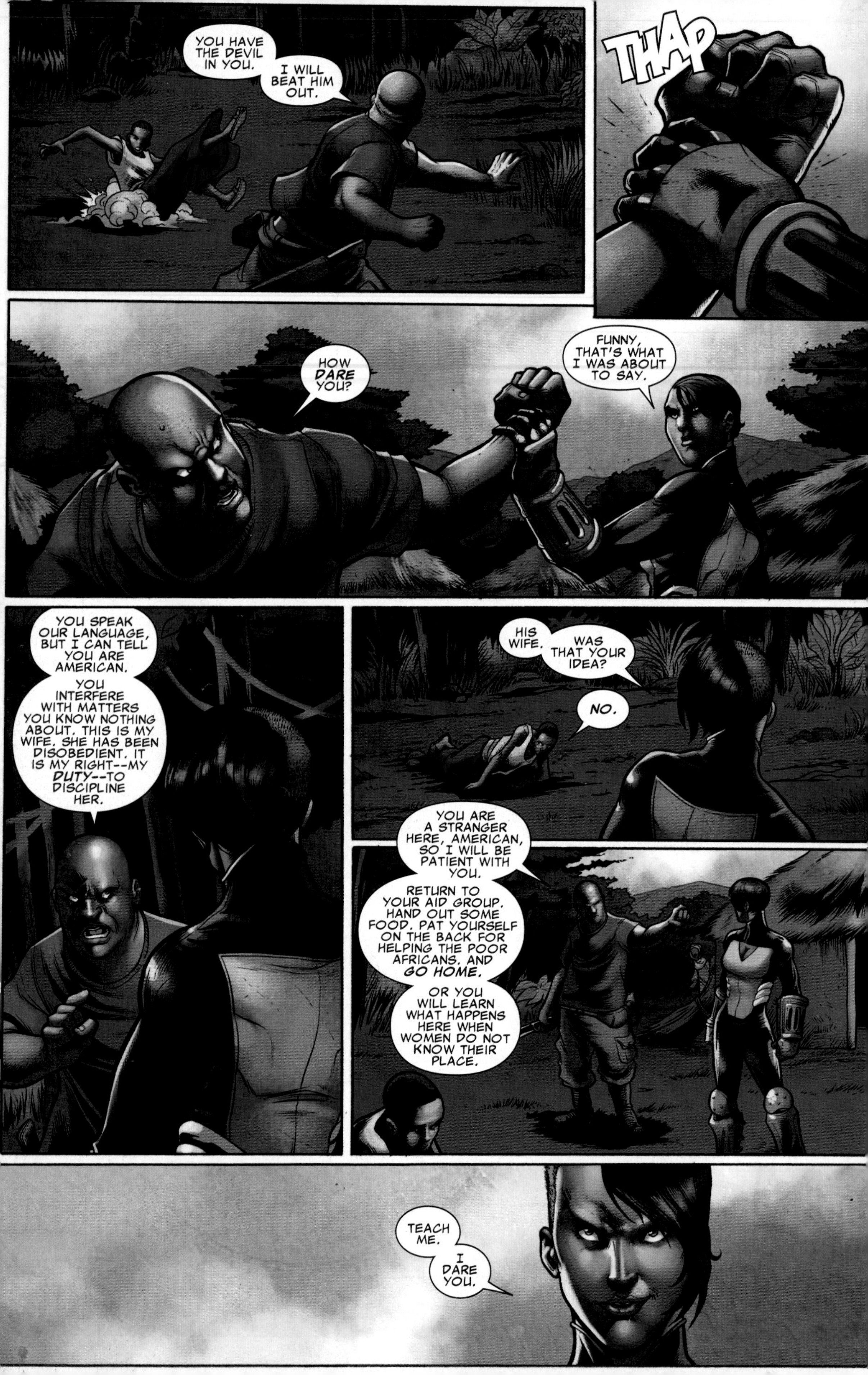
YOU HAVE THE DEVIL IN YOU.
I WILL BEAT HIM OUT.
THAP
HOW DARE YOU?
FUNNY, THAT'S WHAT I WAS ABOUT TO SAY.
YOU SPEAK OUR LANGUAGE, BUT I CAN TELL YOU ARE AMERICAN.
YOU INTERFERE WITH MATTERS YOU KNOW NOTHING ABOUT. THIS IS MY WIFE. SHE HAS BEEN DISOBEDIENT. IT IS MY RIGHT--MY DUTY--TO DISCIPLINE HER.
HIS WIFE.
WAS THAT YOUR IDEA?
NO.
YOU ARE A STRANGER HERE, AMERICAN, SO I WILL BE PATIENT WITH YOU.
RETURN TO YOUR AID GROUP. HAND OUT SOME FOOD. PAT YOURSELF ON THE BACK FOR HELPING THE POOR AFRICANS. AND GO HOME.
OR YOU WILL LEARN WHAT HAPPENS HERE WHEN WOMEN DO NOT KNOW THEIR PLACE.
TEACH ME.
I DARE YOU.

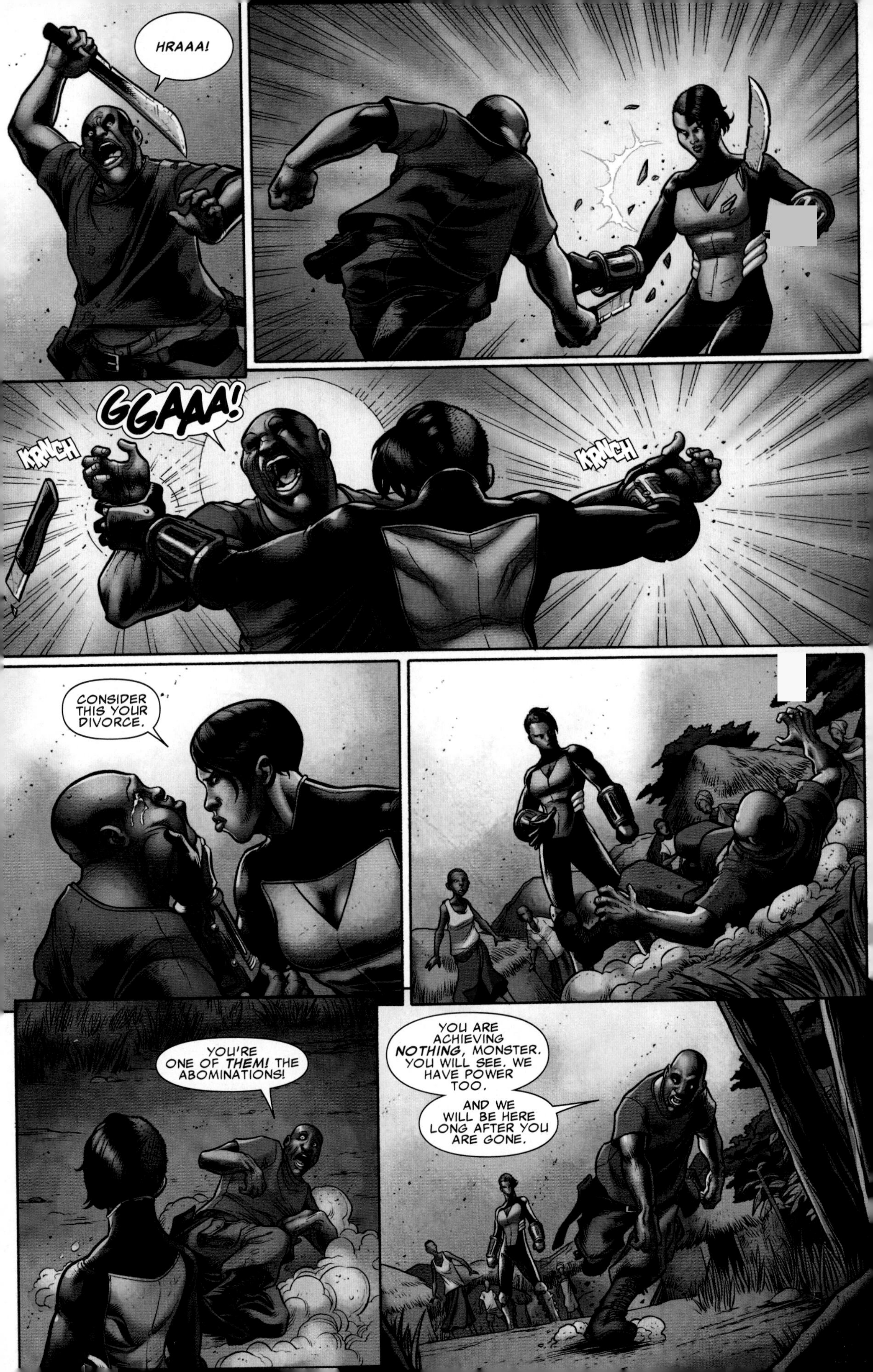
HRAAA!
GGAAAA!
KRNCH
KRNCH
CONSIDER THIS YOUR DIVORCE.
YOU'RE ONE OF THEM! THE ABOMINATIONS!
YOU ARE ACHIEVING NOTHING, MONSTER. YOU WILL SEE. WE HAVE POWER TOO.
AND WE WILL BE HERE LONG AFTER YOU ARE GONE.

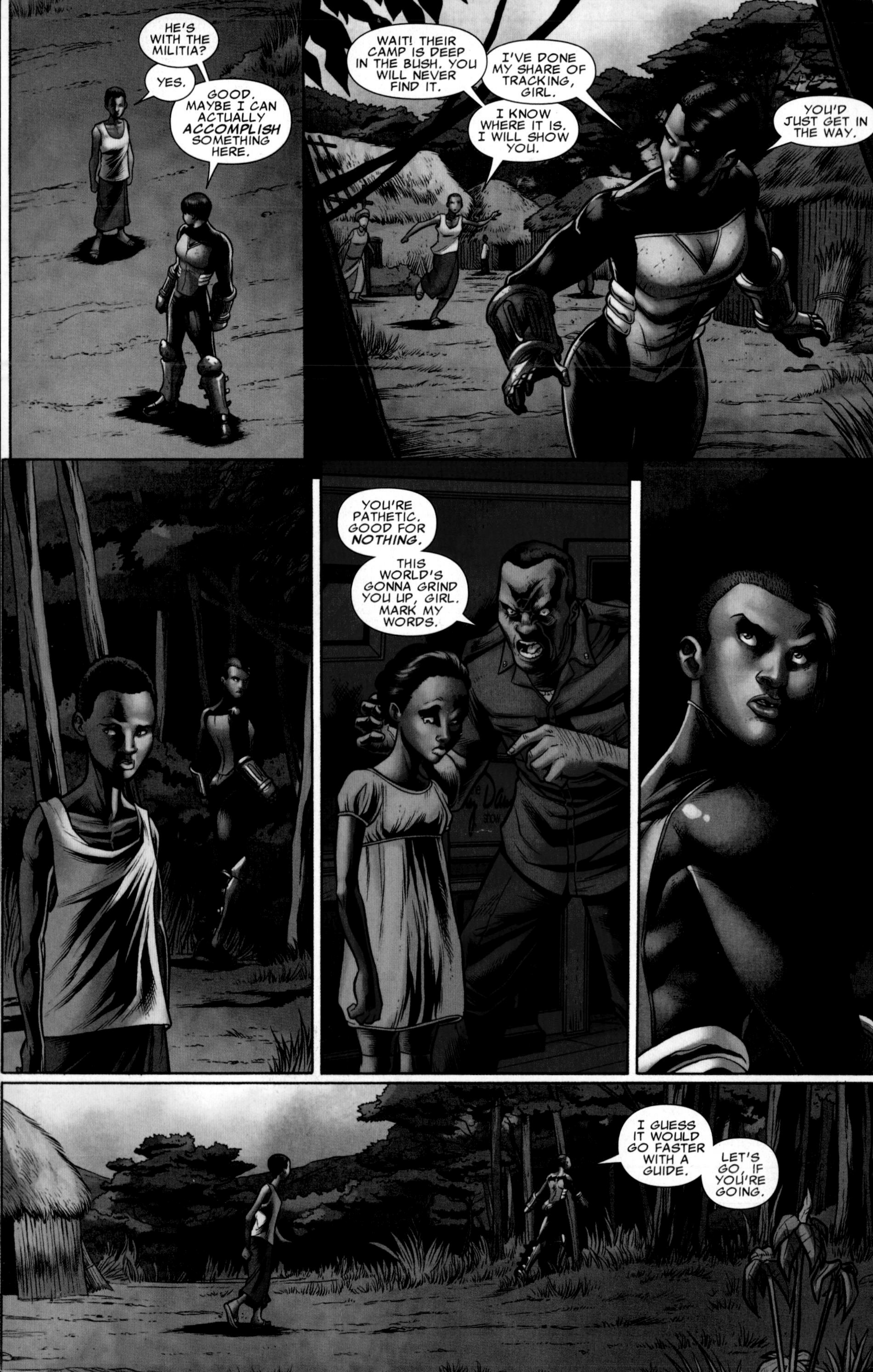
HE'S WITH THE MILITIA?
YES.
GOOD. MAYBE I CAN ACTUALLY ACCOMPLISH SOMETHING HERE.
WAIT! THEIR CAMP IS DEEP IN THE BUSH. YOU WILL NEVER FIND IT.
I'VE DONE MY SHARE OF TRACKING, GIRL.
I KNOW WHERE IT IS. I WILL SHOW YOU.
YOU'D JUST GET IN THE WAY.
YOU'RE PATHETIC. GOOD FOR NOTHING.
THIS WORLD'S GONNA GRIND YOU UP, GIRL. MARK MY WORDS.
I GUESS IT WOULD GO FASTER WITH A GUIDE.
LET'S GO, IF YOU'RE GOING.

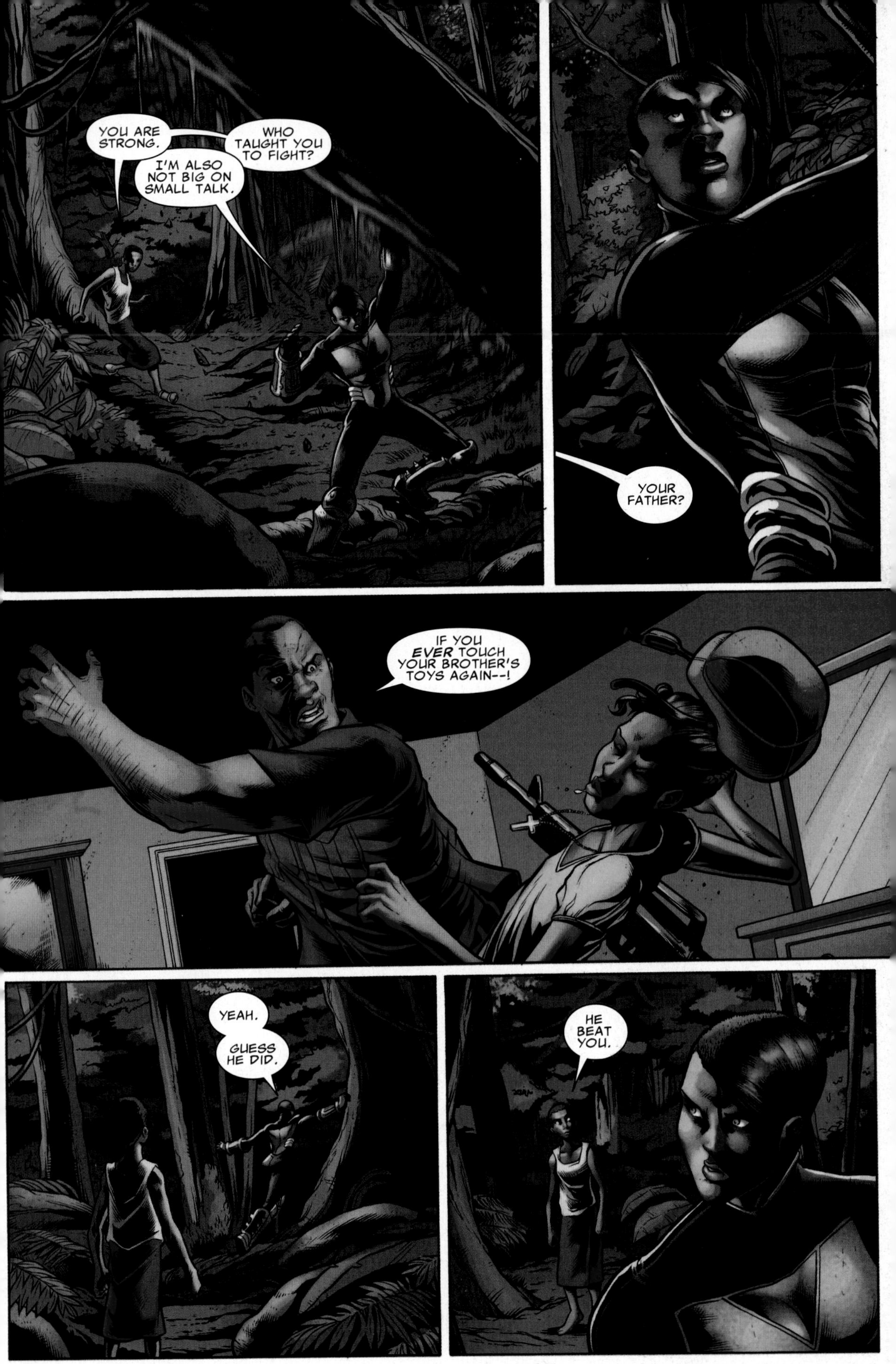
YOU ARE STRONG.
WHO TAUGHT YOU TO FIGHT?
I'M ALSO NOT BIG ON SMALL TALK.
YOUR FATHER?
IF YOU EVER TOUCH YOUR BROTHER'S TOYS AGAIN--!
YEAH.
GUESS HE DID.
HE BEAT YOU.

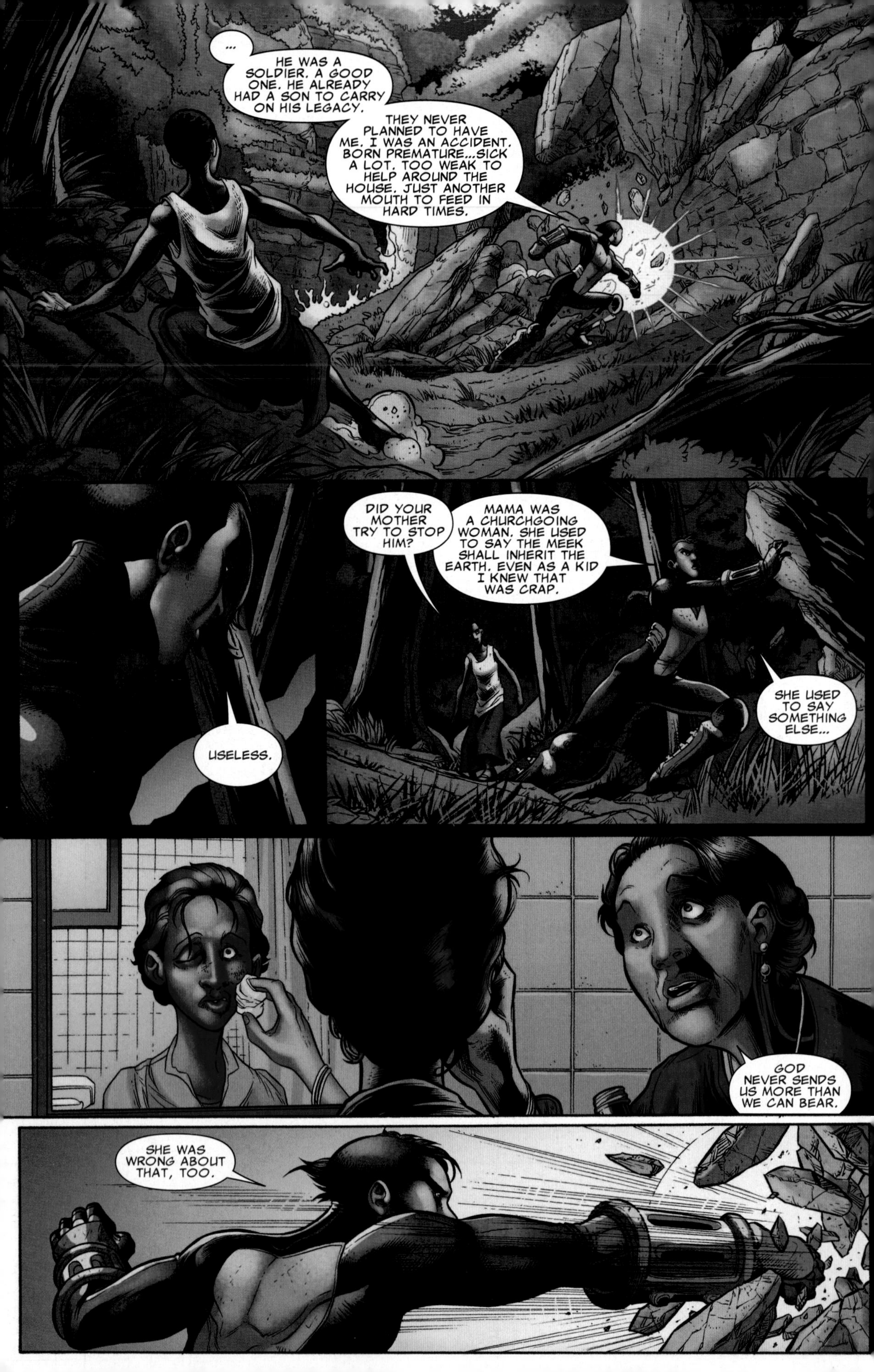
...
HE WAS A SOLDIER. A GOOD ONE. HE ALREADY HAD A SON TO CARRY ON HIS LEGACY.
THEY NEVER PLANNED TO HAVE ME. I WAS AN ACCIDENT. BORN PREMATURE...SICK A LOT. TOO WEAK TO HELP AROUND THE HOUSE. JUST ANOTHER MOUTH TO FEED IN HARD TIMES.
USELESS.
DID YOUR MOTHER TRY TO STOP HIM?
MAMA WAS A CHURCHGOING WOMAN. SHE USED TO SAY THE MEEK SHALL INHERIT THE EARTH. EVEN AS A KID I KNEW THAT WAS CRAP.
SHE USED TO SAY SOMETHING ELSE...
GOD NEVER SENDS US MORE THAN WE CAN BEAR.
SHE WAS WRONG ABOUT THAT, TOO.

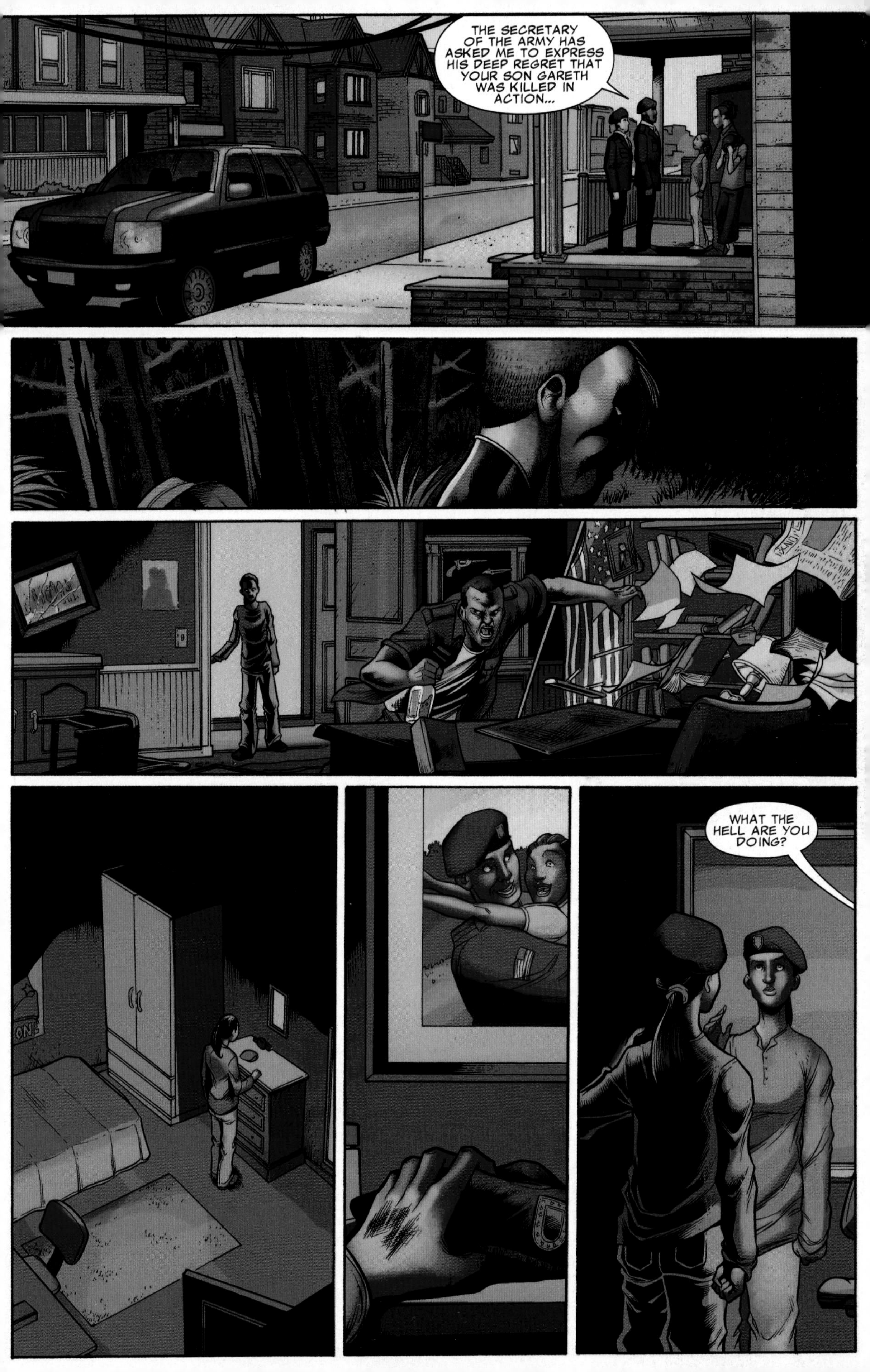
THE SECRETARY OF THE ARMY HAS ASKED ME TO EXPRESS HIS DEEP REGRET THAT YOUR SON GARETH WAS KILLED IN ACTION...
WHAT THE HELL ARE YOU DOING?

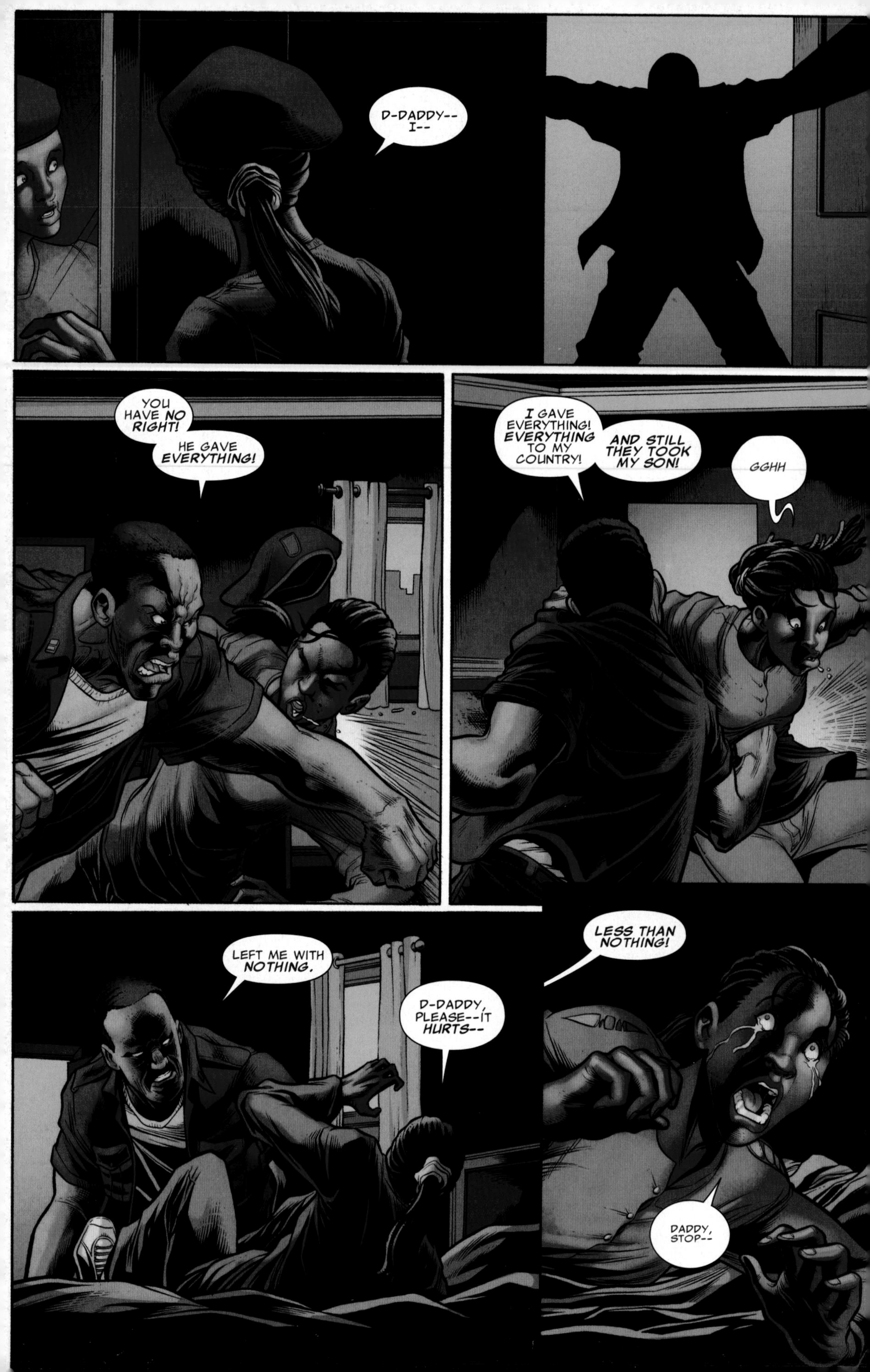
D-DADDY-- I--
YOU HAVE NO RIGHT!
HE GAVE EVERYTHING!
I GAVE EVERYTHING! EVERYTHING TO MY COUNTRY!
AND STILL THEY TOOK MY SON!
GGHH
LEFT ME WITH NOTHING.
D-DADDY, PLEASE--IT HURTS--
LESS THAN NOTHING!
DADDY, STOP--

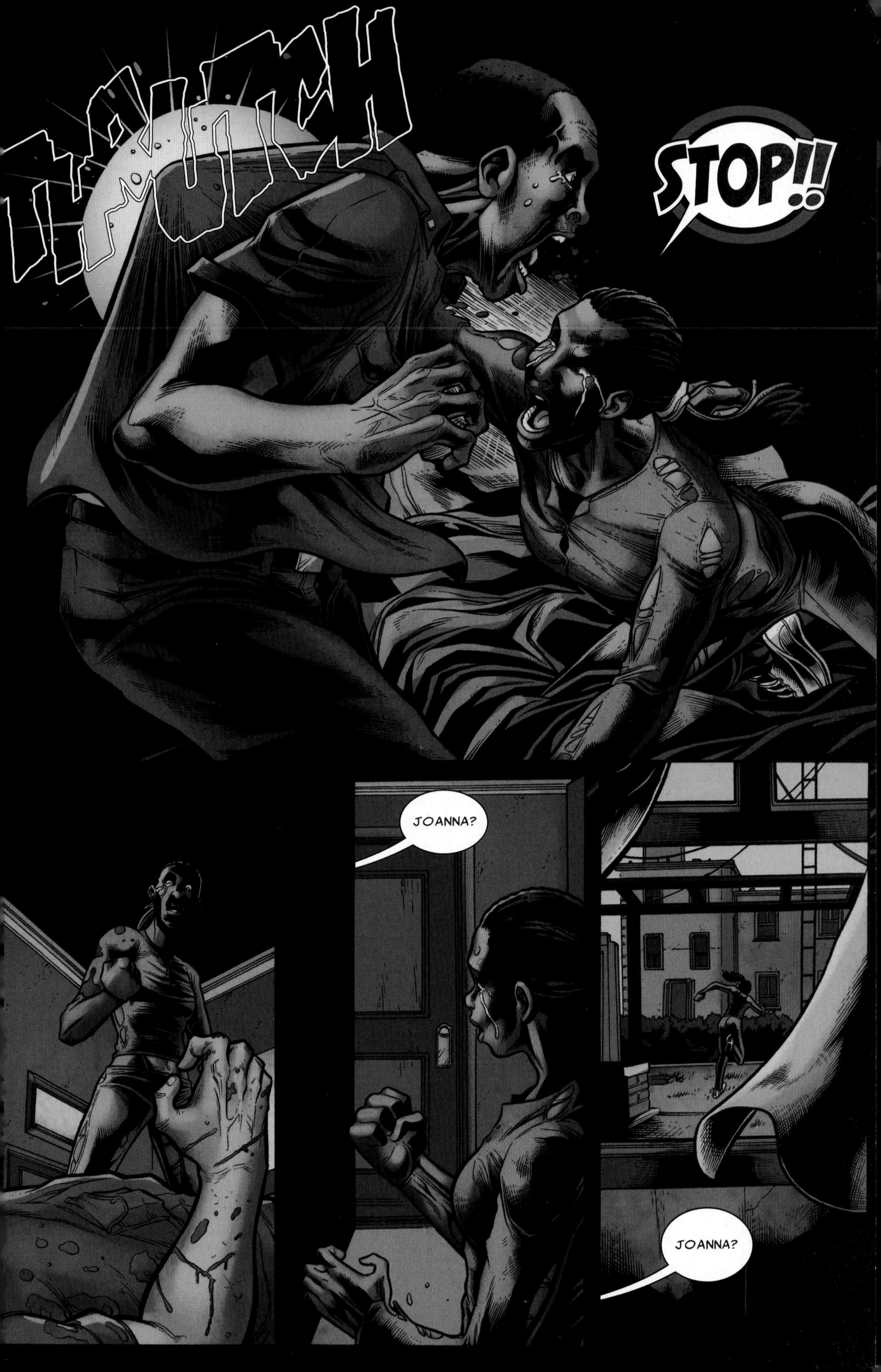
STOP!!
JOANNA?
JOANNA?

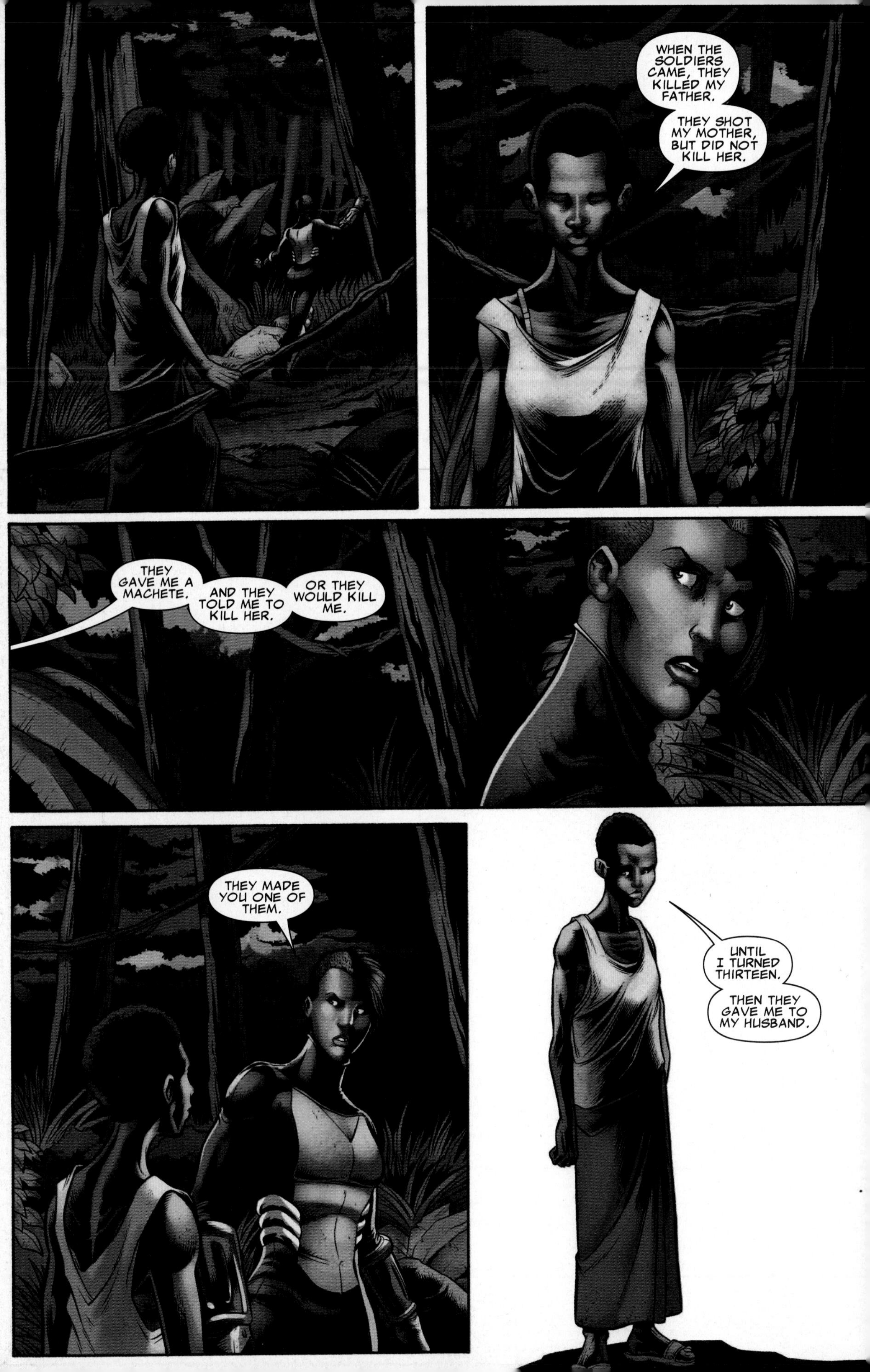
WHEN THE SOLDIERS CAME, THEY KILLED MY FATHER.
THEY SHOT MY MOTHER, BUT DID NOT KILL HER.
THEY GAVE ME A MACHETE.
AND THEY TOLD ME TO KILL HER.
OR THEY WOULD KILL ME.
THEY MADE YOU ONE OF THEM.
UNTIL I TURNED THIRTEEN.
THEN THEY GAVE ME TO MY HUSBAND.

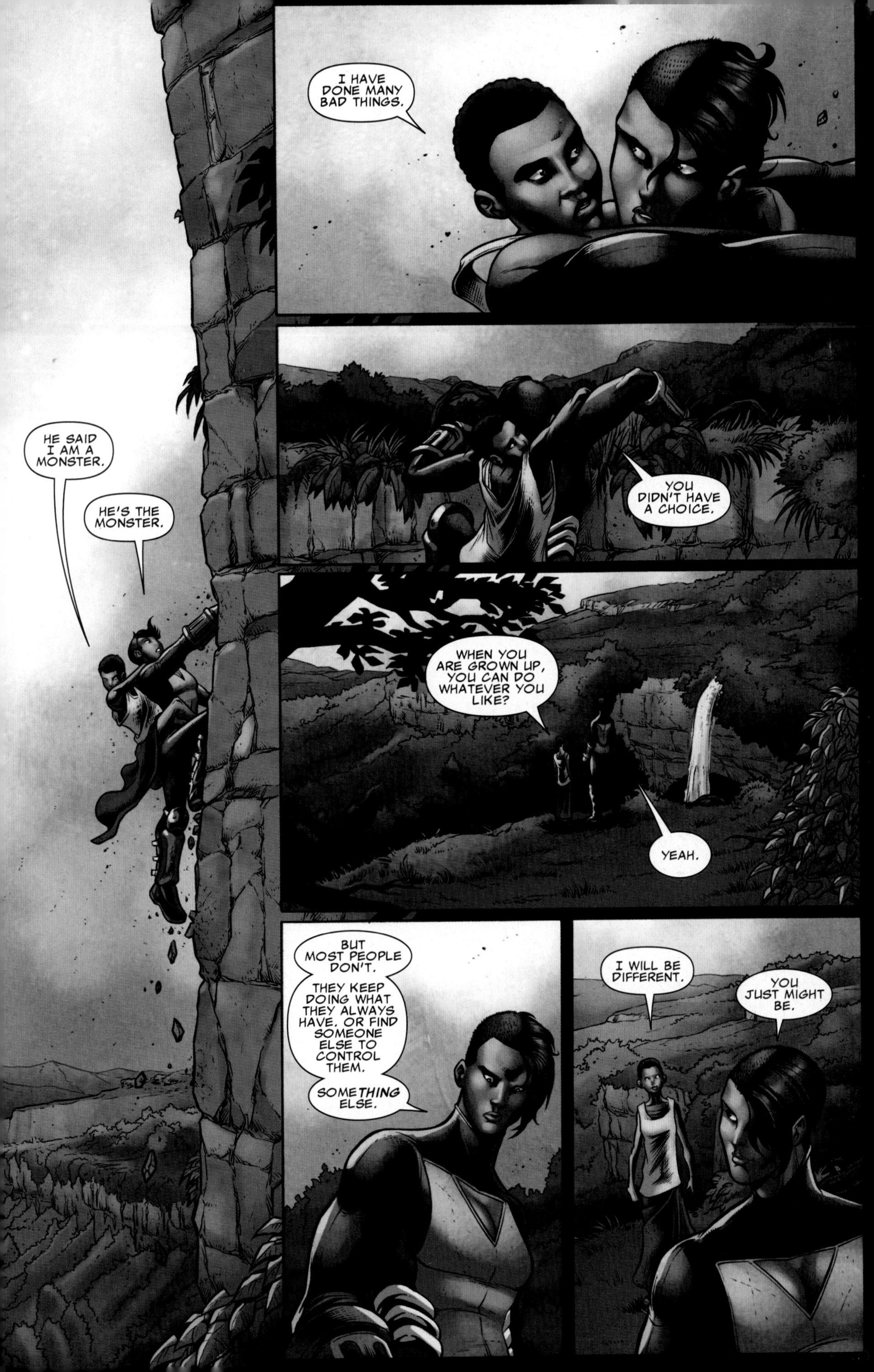
I HAVE DONE MANY BAD THINGS.
HE SAID I AM A MONSTER.
HE'S THE MONSTER.
YOU DIDN'T HAVE A CHOICE.
WHEN YOU ARE GROWN UP, YOU CAN DO WHATEVER YOU LIKE?
YEAH.
BUT MOST PEOPLE DON'T.
THEY KEEP DOING WHAT THEY ALWAYS HAVE, OR FIND SOMEONE ELSE TO CONTROL THEM.
SOME*THING* ELSE.
I WILL BE DIFFERENT.
YOU JUST MIGHT BE.

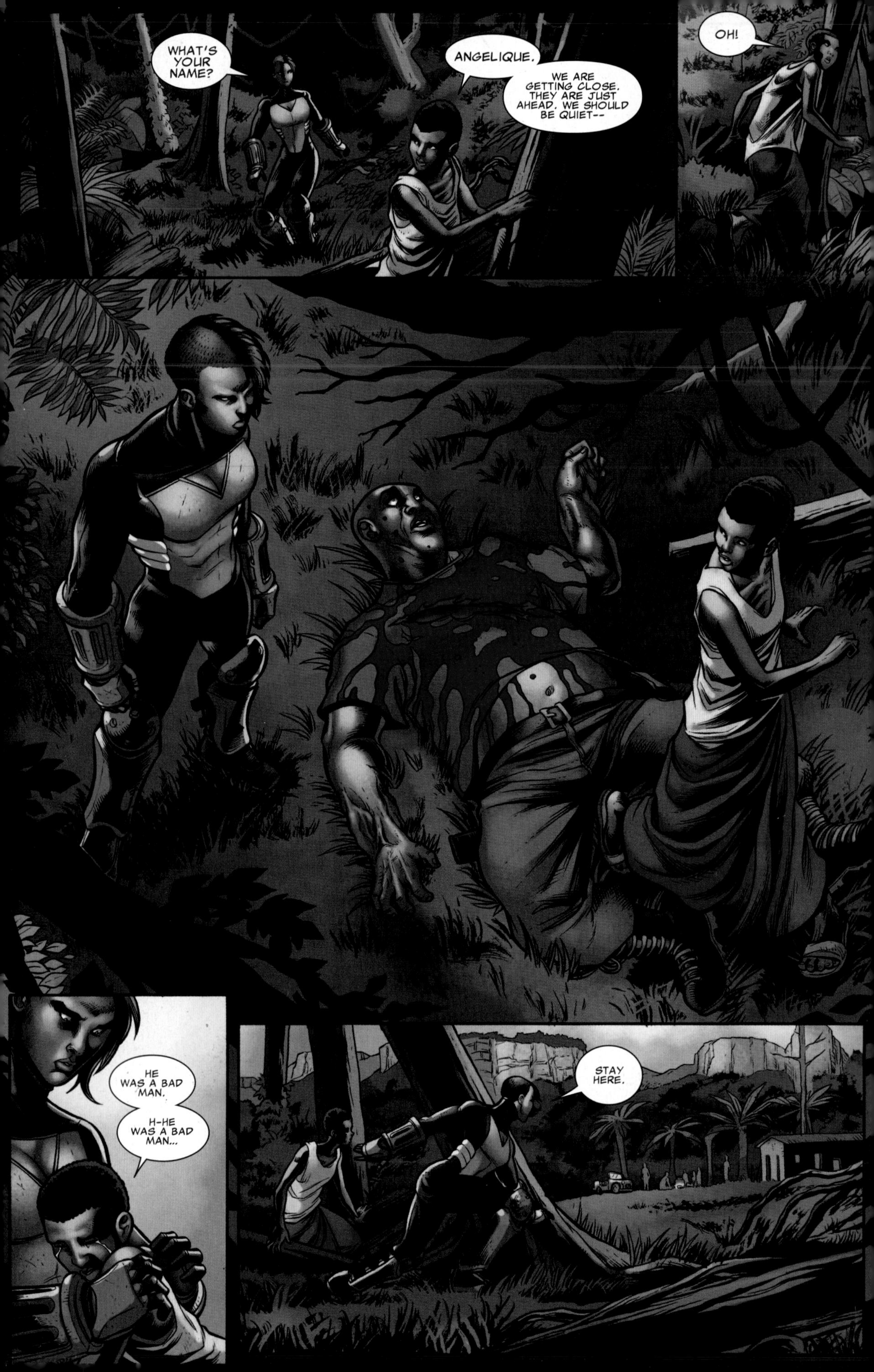
WHAT'S YOUR NAME?
ANGELIQUE.
WE ARE GETTING CLOSE. THEY ARE JUST AHEAD. WE SHOULD BE QUIET--
OH!
HE WAS A BAD MAN.
H-HE WAS A BAD MAN...
STAY HERE.

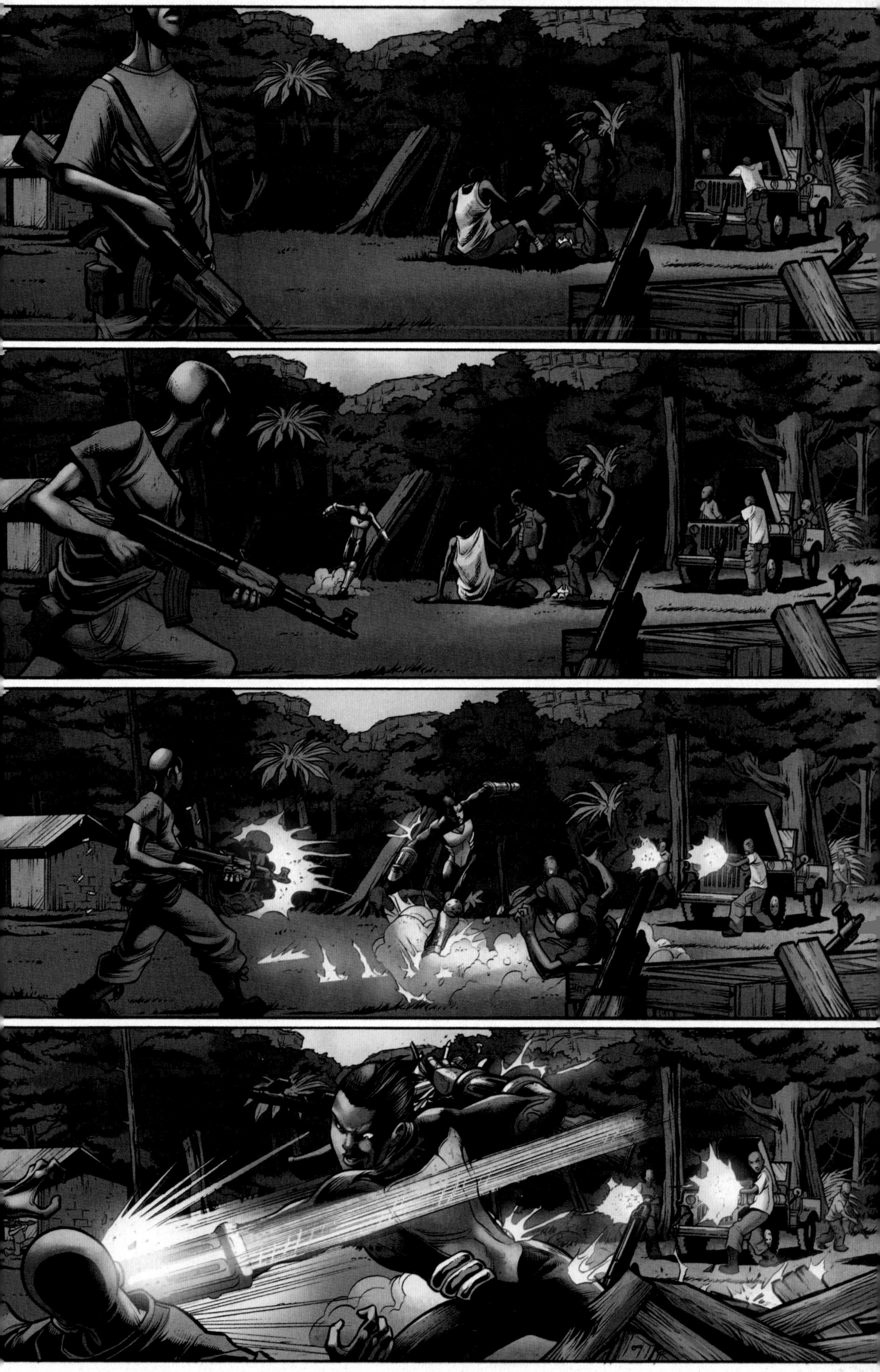

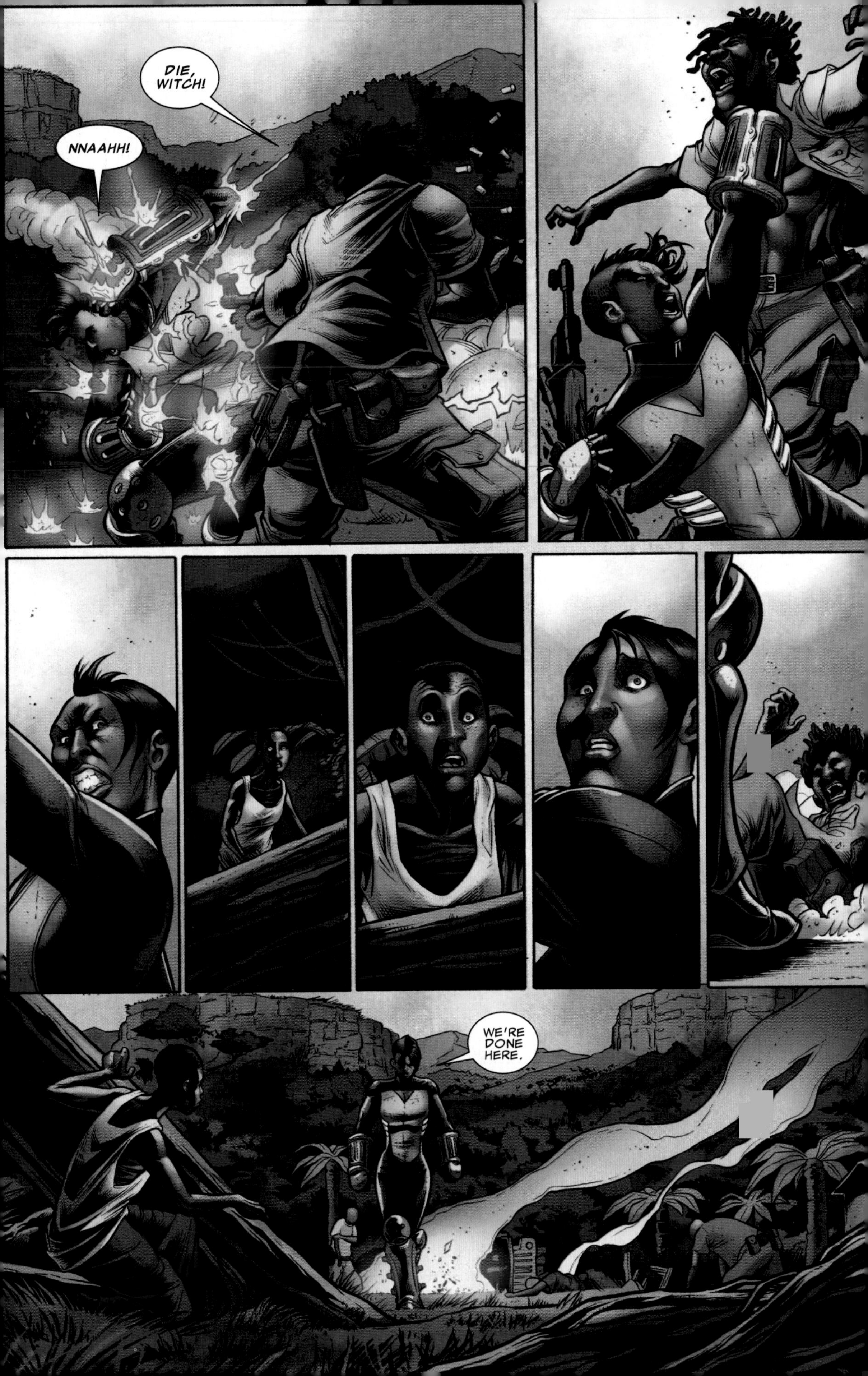
NNAAHH!
DIE, WITCH!
WE'RE DONE HERE.

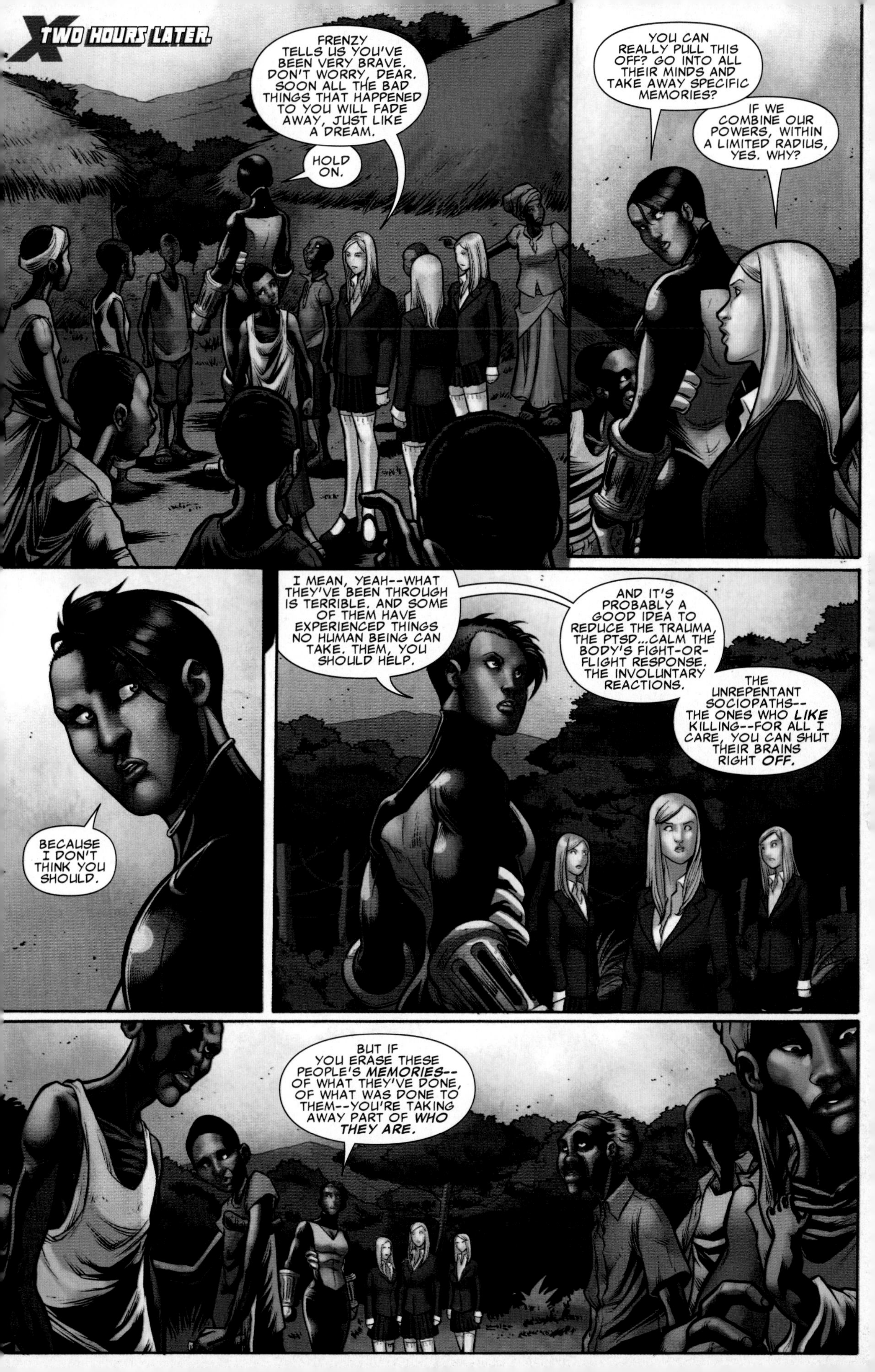
TWO HOURS LATER.
FRENZY TELLS US YOU'VE BEEN VERY BRAVE. DON'T WORRY, DEAR. SOON ALL THE BAD THINGS THAT HAPPENED TO YOU WILL FADE AWAY, JUST LIKE A DREAM.
HOLD ON.
YOU CAN REALLY PULL THIS OFF? GO INTO ALL THEIR MINDS AND TAKE AWAY SPECIFIC MEMORIES?
IF WE COMBINE OUR POWERS, WITHIN A LIMITED RADIUS, YES. WHY?
BECAUSE I DON'T THINK YOU SHOULD.
I MEAN, YEAH--WHAT THEY'VE BEEN THROUGH IS TERRIBLE, AND SOME OF THEM HAVE EXPERIENCED THINGS NO HUMAN BEING CAN TAKE. THEM, YOU SHOULD HELP.
AND IT'S PROBABLY A GOOD IDEA TO REDUCE THE TRAUMA, THE PTSD...CALM THE BODY'S FIGHT-OR-FLIGHT RESPONSE. THE INVOLUNTARY REACTIONS.
THE UNREPENTANT SOCIOPATHS--THE ONES WHO LIKE KILLING--FOR ALL I CARE, YOU CAN SHUT THEIR BRAINS RIGHT OFF.
BUT IF YOU ERASE THESE PEOPLE'S MEMORIES--OF WHAT THEY'VE DONE, OF WHAT WAS DONE TO THEM--YOU'RE TAKING AWAY PART OF WHO THEY ARE.

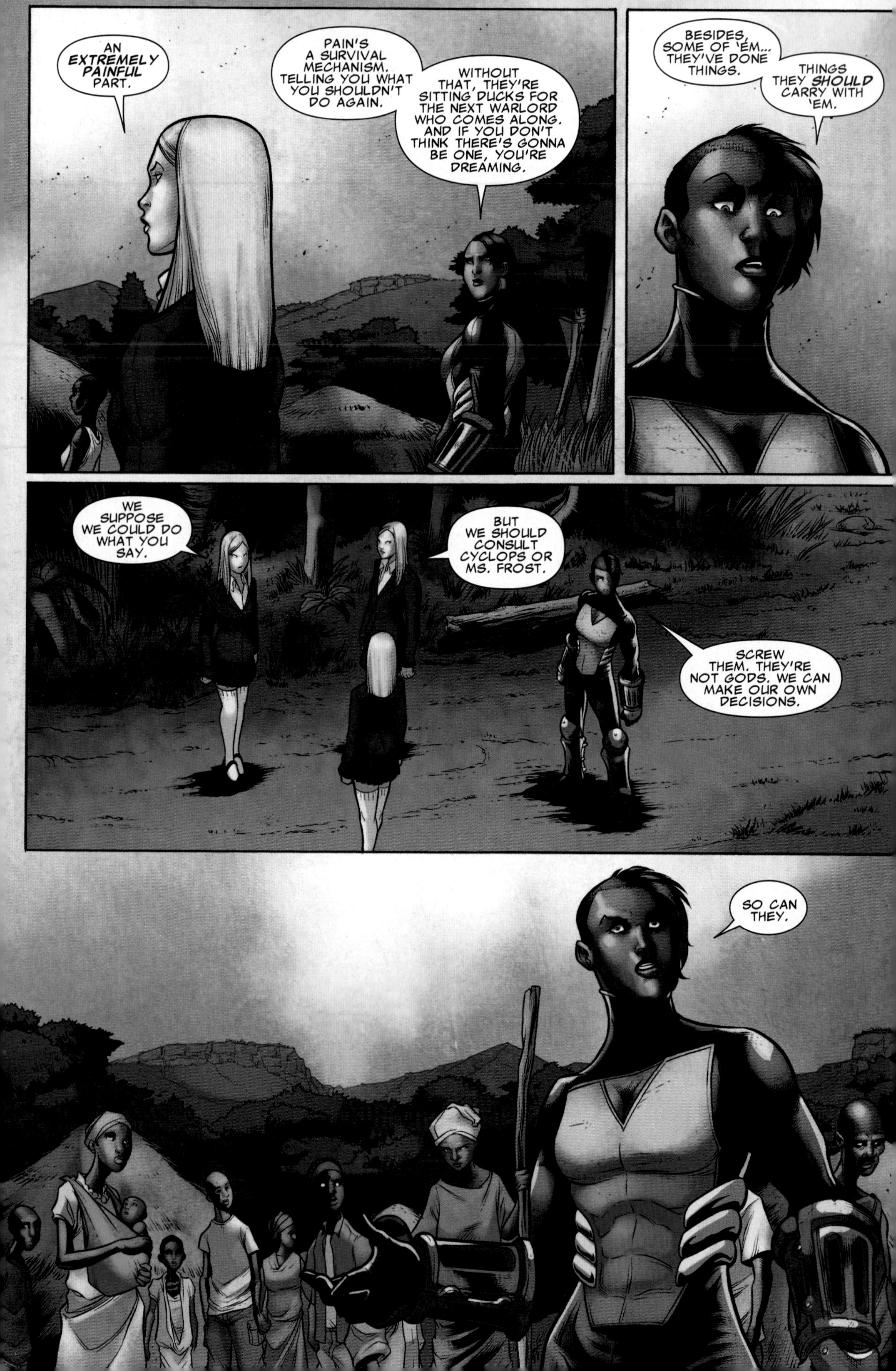
AN EXTREMELY PAINFUL PART.
PAIN'S A SURVIVAL MECHANISM. TELLING YOU WHAT YOU SHOULDN'T DO AGAIN.
WITHOUT THAT, THEY'RE SITTING DUCKS FOR THE NEXT WARLORD WHO COMES ALONG. AND IF YOU DON'T THINK THERE'S GONNA BE ONE, YOU'RE DREAMING.
BESIDES, SOME OF 'EM... THEY'VE DONE THINGS.
THINGS THEY SHOULD CARRY WITH 'EM.
WE SUPPOSE WE COULD DO WHAT YOU SAY.
BUT WE SHOULD CONSULT CYCLOPS OR MS. FROST.
SCREW THEM. THEY'RE NOT GODS. WE CAN MAKE OUR OWN DECISIONS.
SO CAN THEY.

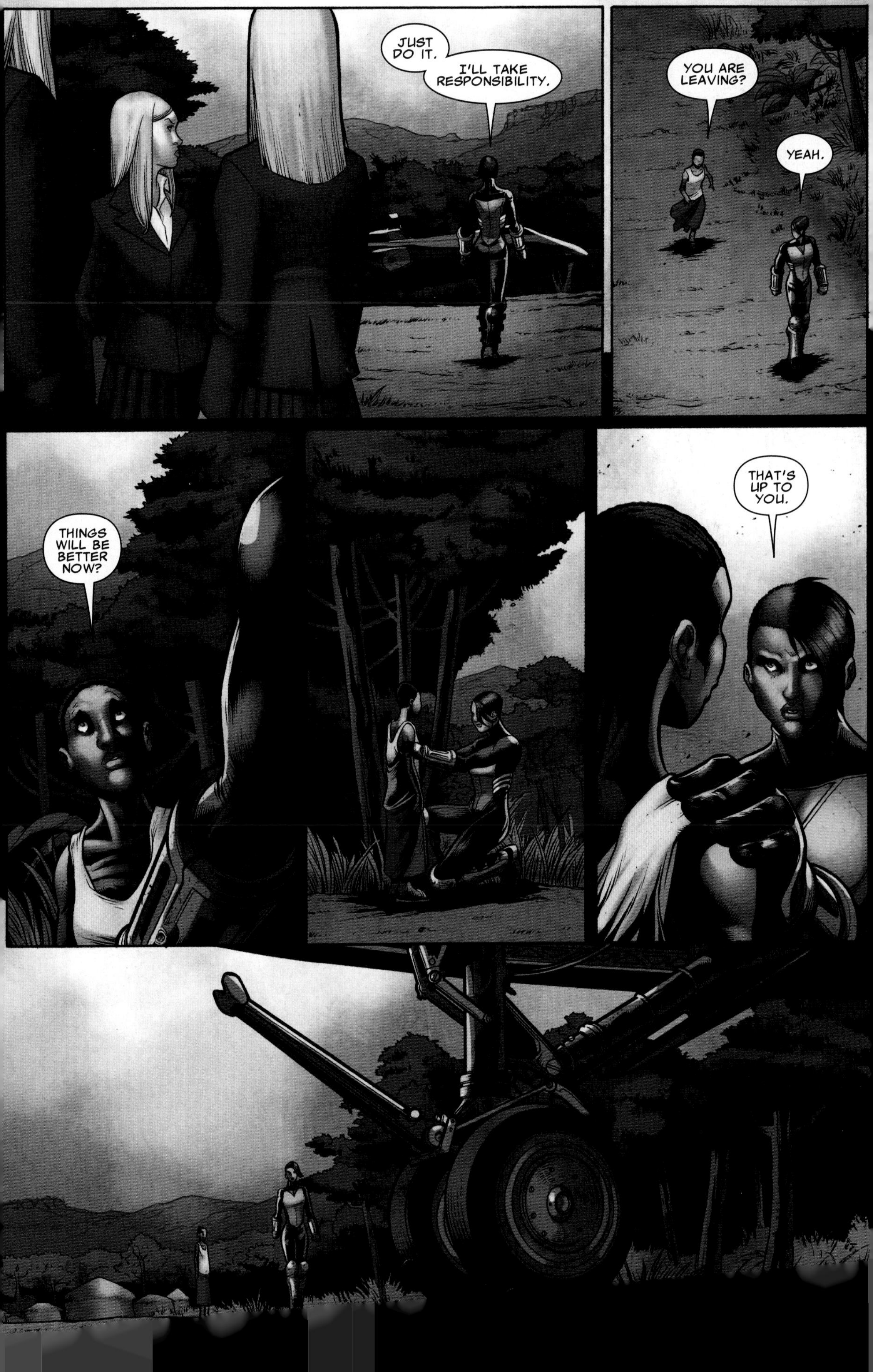
JUST DO IT.
I'LL TAKE RESPONSIBILITY.
YOU ARE LEAVING?
YEAH.
THINGS WILL BE BETTER NOW?
THAT'S UP TO YOU.

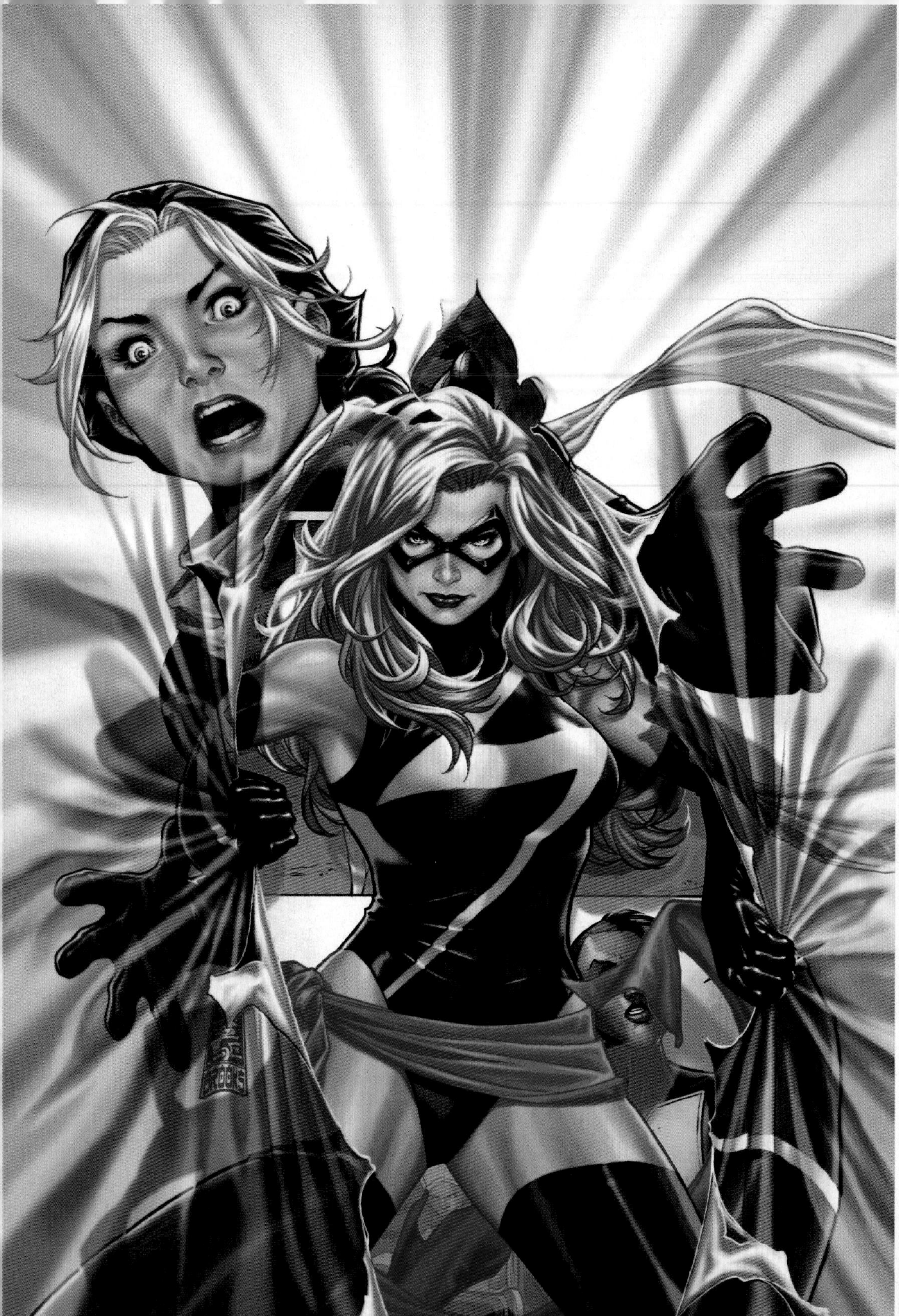

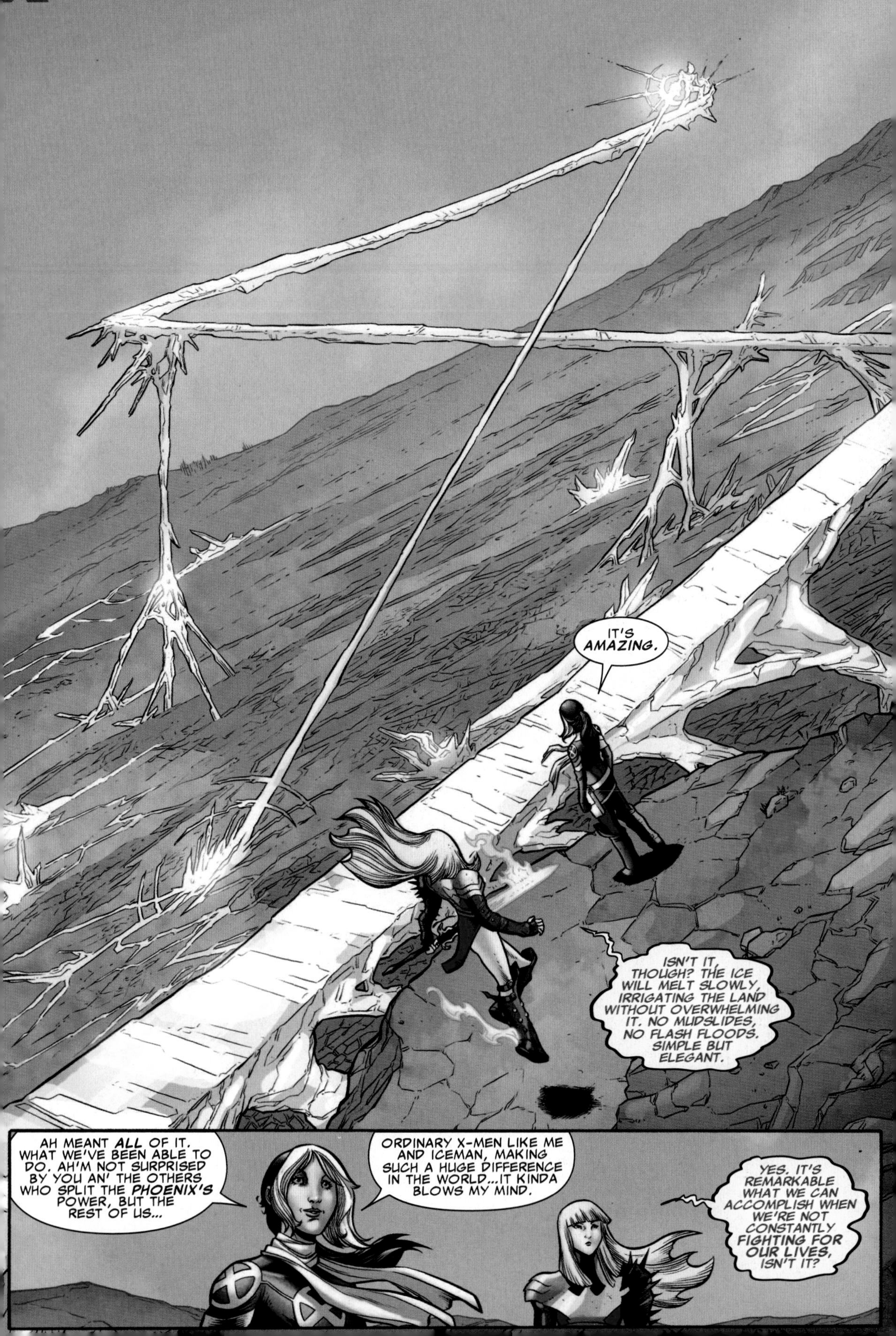
IT'S AMAZING.
ISN'T IT, THOUGH? THE ICE WILL MELT SLOWLY, IRRIGATING THE LAND WITHOUT OVERWHELMING IT. NO MUDSLIDES, NO FLASH FLOODS. SIMPLE BUT ELEGANT.
AH MEANT ALL OF IT. WHAT WE'VE BEEN ABLE TO DO. AH'M NOT SURPRISED BY YOU AN' THE OTHERS WHO SPLIT THE PHOENIX'S POWER, BUT THE REST OF US...
ORDINARY X-MEN LIKE ME AND ICEMAN, MAKING SUCH A HUGE DIFFERENCE IN THE WORLD...IT KINDA BLOWS MY MIND.
YES. IT'S REMARKABLE WHAT WE CAN ACCOMPLISH WHEN WE'RE NOT CONSTANTLY FIGHTING FOR OUR LIVES, ISN'T IT?

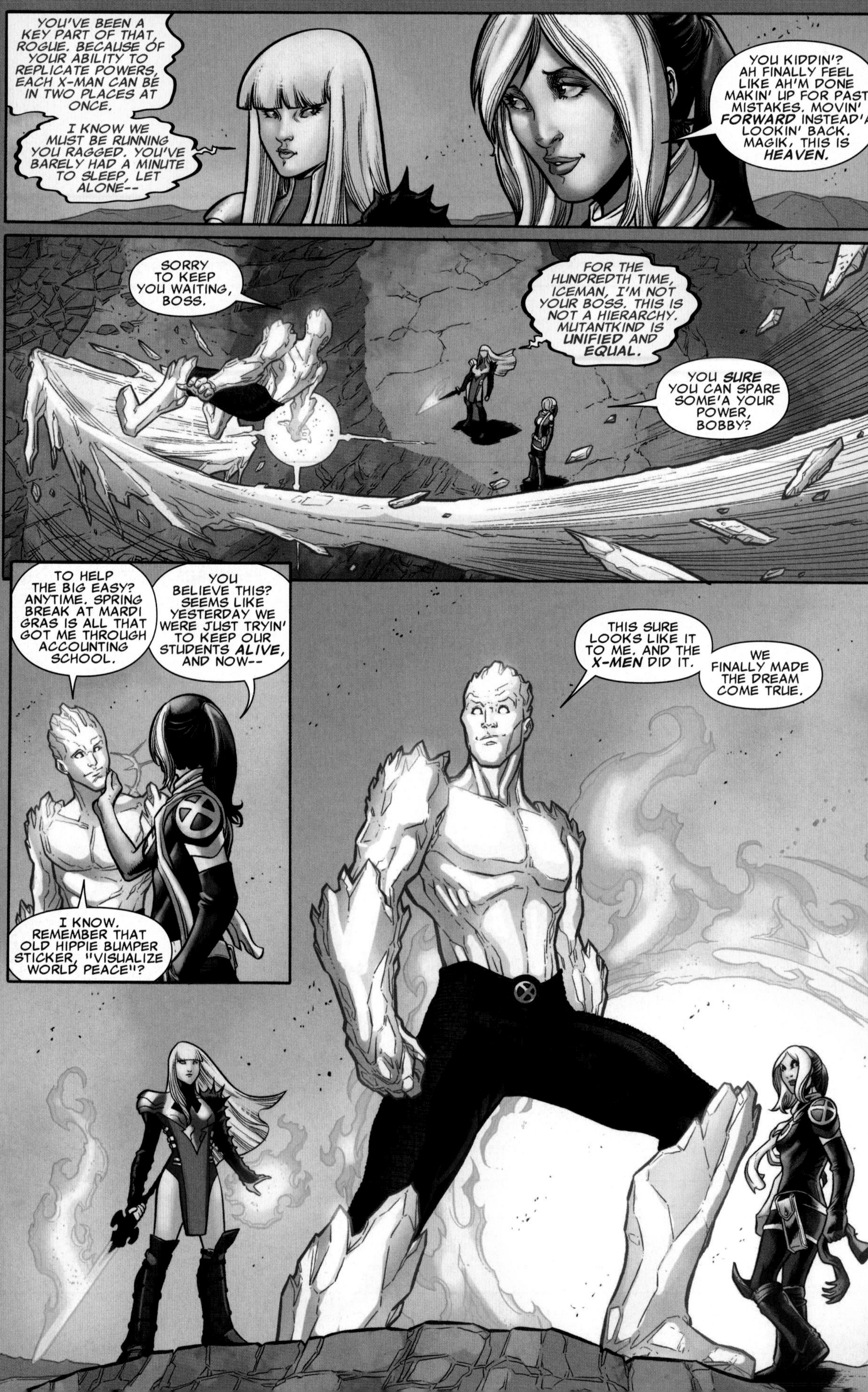
YOU'VE BEEN A KEY PART OF THAT, ROGUE. BECAUSE OF YOUR ABILITY TO REPLICATE POWERS, EACH X-MAN CAN BE IN TWO PLACES AT ONCE.
I KNOW WE MUST BE RUNNING YOU RAGGED. YOU'VE BARELY HAD A MINUTE TO SLEEP, LET ALONE--
YOU KIDDIN'? AH FINALLY FEEL LIKE AH'M DONE MAKIN' UP FOR PAST MISTAKES. MOVIN' FORWARD INSTEAD'A LOOKIN' BACK. MAGIK, THIS IS HEAVEN.
SORRY TO KEEP YOU WAITING, BOSS.
FOR THE HUNDREDTH TIME, ICEMAN, I'M NOT YOUR BOSS. THIS IS NOT A HIERARCHY. MUTANTKIND IS UNIFIED AND EQUAL.
YOU SURE YOU CAN SPARE SOME'A YOUR POWER, BOBBY?
TO HELP THE BIG EASY? ANYTIME. SPRING BREAK AT MARDI GRAS IS ALL THAT GOT ME THROUGH ACCOUNTING SCHOOL.
YOU BELIEVE THIS? SEEMS LIKE YESTERDAY WE WERE JUST TRYIN' TO KEEP OUR STUDENTS ALIVE, AND NOW--
I KNOW. REMEMBER THAT OLD HIPPIE BUMPER STICKER, "VISUALIZE WORLD PEACE"?
THIS SURE LOOKS LIKE IT TO ME. AND THE X-MEN DID IT.
WE FINALLY MADE THE DREAM COME TRUE.

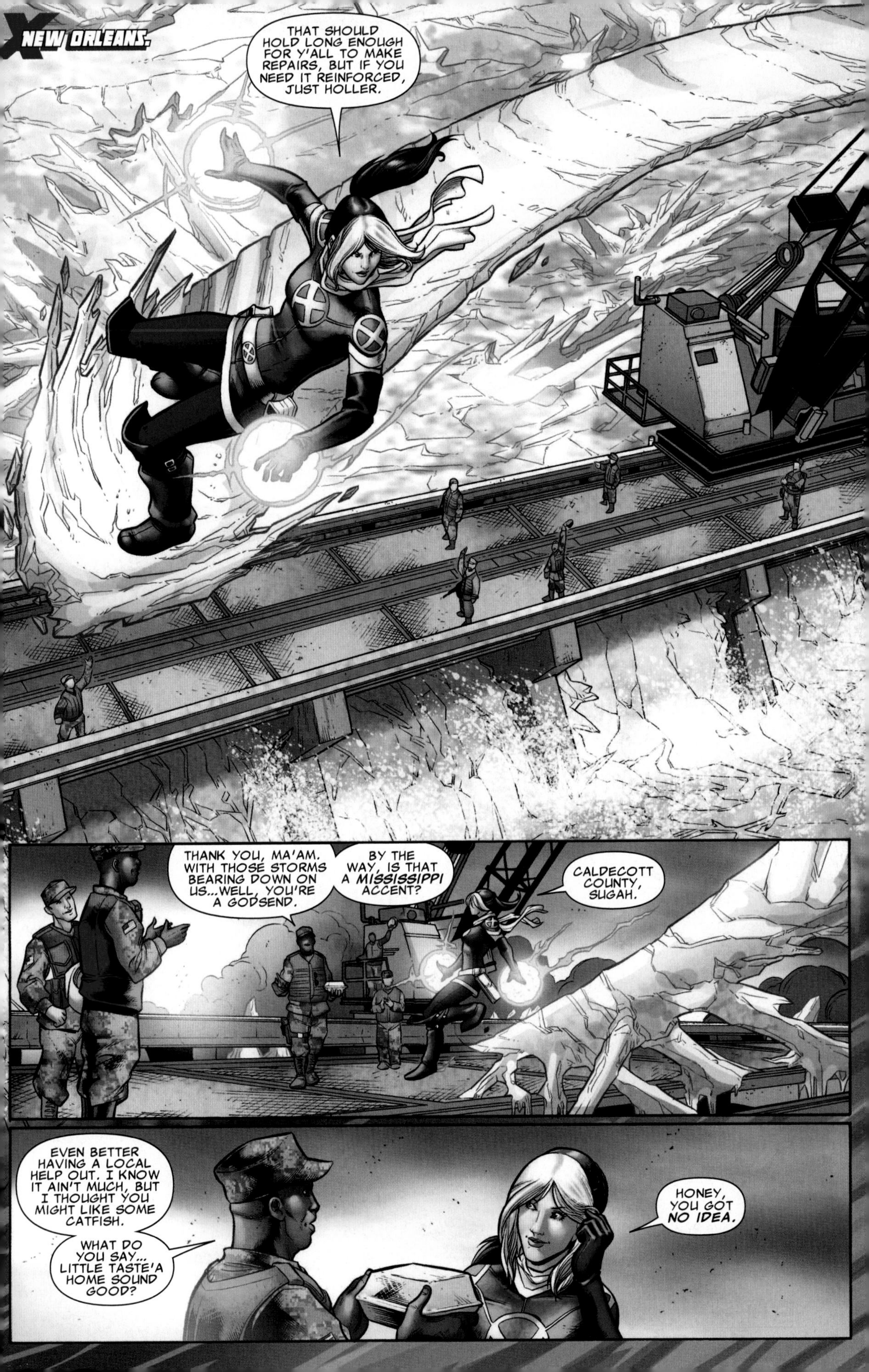
X NEW ORLEANS.
THAT SHOULD HOLD LONG ENOUGH FOR Y'ALL TO MAKE REPAIRS, BUT IF YOU NEED IT REINFORCED, JUST HOLLER.
THANK YOU, MA'AM. WITH THOSE STORMS BEARING DOWN ON US...WELL, YOU'RE A GODSEND.
BY THE WAY, IS THAT A MISSISSIPPI ACCENT?
CALDECOTT COUNTY, SUGAH.
EVEN BETTER HAVING A LOCAL HELP OUT. I KNOW IT AIN'T MUCH, BUT I THOUGHT YOU MIGHT LIKE SOME CATFISH.
WHAT DO YOU SAY... LITTLE TASTE'A HOME SOUND GOOD?
HONEY, YOU GOT NO IDEA.

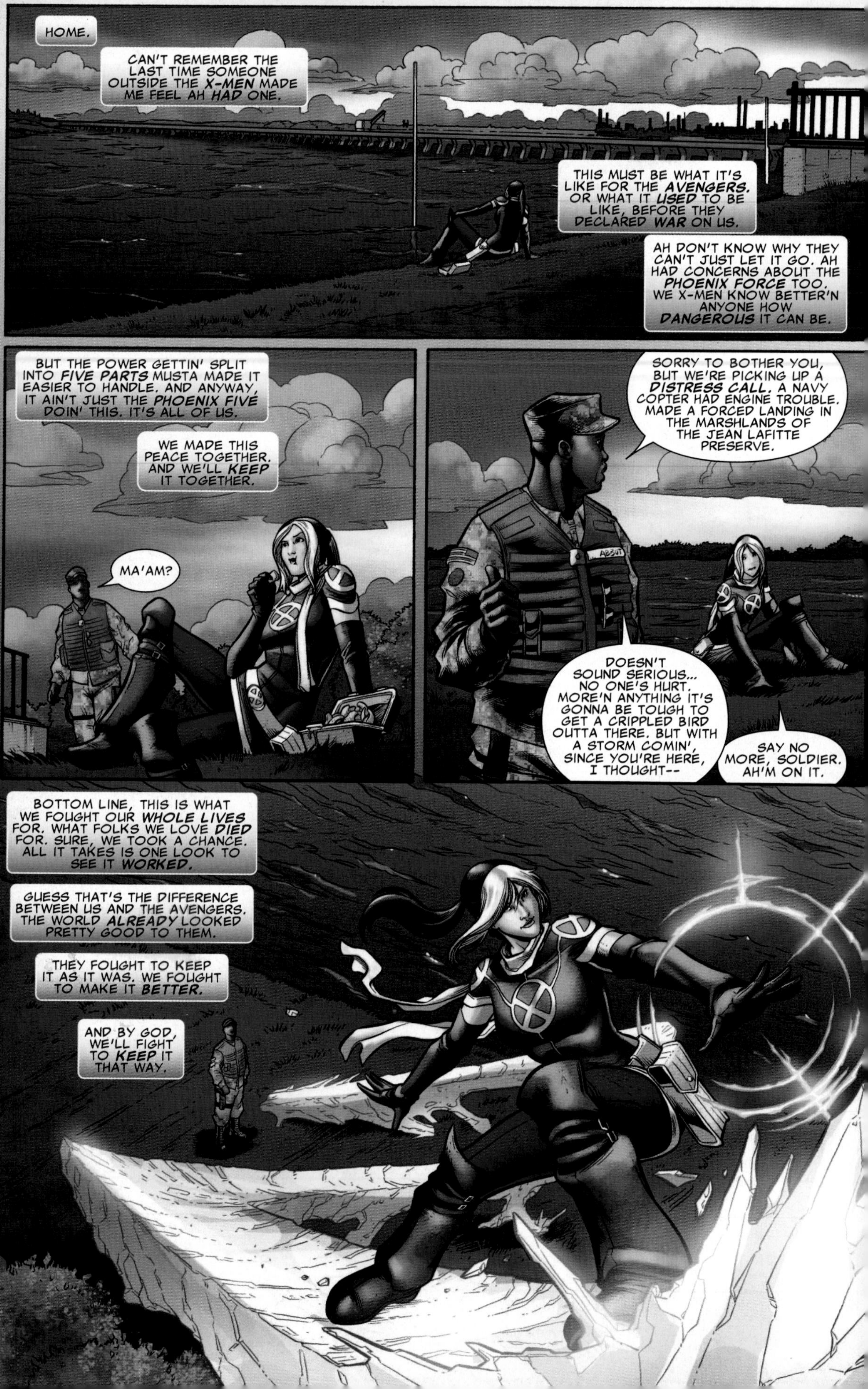
HOME.
CAN'T REMEMBER THE LAST TIME SOMEONE OUTSIDE THE X-MEN MADE ME FEEL AH HAD ONE.
THIS MUST BE WHAT IT'S LIKE FOR THE AVENGERS. OR WHAT IT USED TO BE LIKE, BEFORE THEY DECLARED WAR ON US.
AH DON'T KNOW WHY THEY CAN'T JUST LET IT GO. AH HAD CONCERNS ABOUT THE PHOENIX FORCE TOO. WE X-MEN KNOW BETTER'N ANYONE HOW DANGEROUS IT CAN BE.
BUT THE POWER GETTIN' SPLIT INTO FIVE PARTS MUSTA MADE IT EASIER TO HANDLE. AND ANYWAY, IT AIN'T JUST THE PHOENIX FIVE DOIN' THIS. IT'S ALL OF US.
WE MADE THIS PEACE TOGETHER. AND WE'LL KEEP IT TOGETHER.
MA'AM?
SORRY TO BOTHER YOU, BUT WE'RE PICKING UP A DISTRESS CALL. A NAVY COPTER HAD ENGINE TROUBLE. MADE A FORCED LANDING IN THE MARSHLANDS OF THE JEAN LAFITTE PRESERVE.
DOESN'T SOUND SERIOUS... NO ONE'S HURT. MORE'N ANYTHING IT'S GONNA BE TOUGH TO GET A CRIPPLED BIRD OUTTA THERE. BUT WITH A STORM COMIN', SINCE YOU'RE HERE, I THOUGHT--
SAY NO MORE, SOLDIER. AH'M ON IT.
BOTTOM LINE, THIS IS WHAT WE FOUGHT OUR WHOLE LIVES FOR. WHAT FOLKS WE LOVE DIED FOR. SURE, WE TOOK A CHANCE. ALL IT TAKES IS ONE LOOK TO SEE IT WORKED.
GUESS THAT'S THE DIFFERENCE BETWEEN US AND THE AVENGERS. THE WORLD ALREADY LOOKED PRETTY GOOD TO THEM.
THEY FOUGHT TO KEEP IT AS IT WAS. WE FOUGHT TO MAKE IT BETTER.
AND BY GOD, WE'LL FIGHT TO KEEP IT THAT WAY.

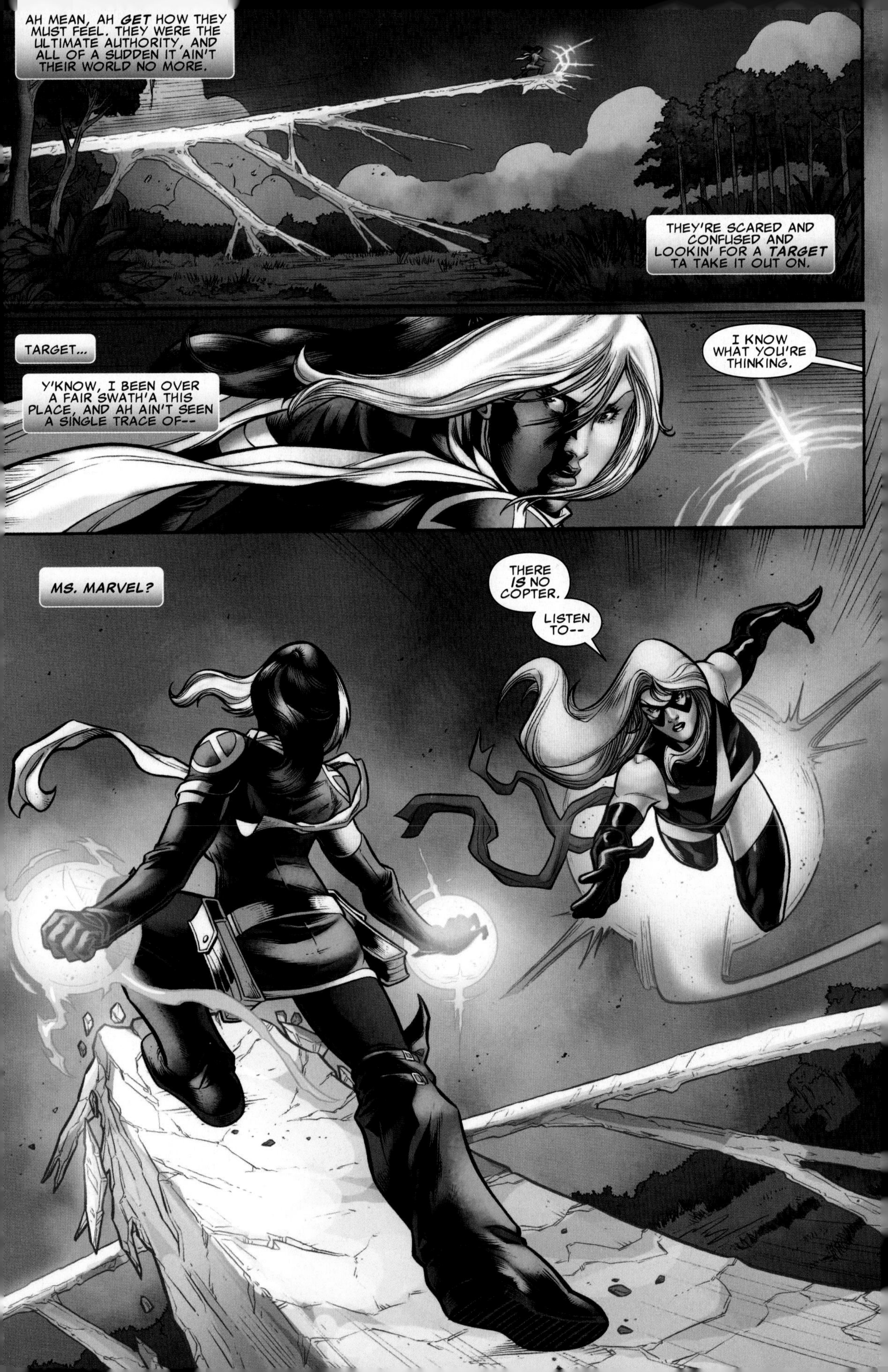
AH MEAN, AH GET HOW THEY MUST FEEL. THEY WERE THE ULTIMATE AUTHORITY, AND ALL OF A SUDDEN IT AIN'T THEIR WORLD NO MORE.
THEY'RE SCARED AND CONFUSED AND LOOKIN' FOR A TARGET TA TAKE IT OUT ON.
TARGET...
Y'KNOW, I BEEN OVER A FAIR SWATH'A THIS PLACE, AND AH AIN'T SEEN A SINGLE TRACE OF--
I KNOW WHAT YOU'RE THINKING.
MS. MARVEL?
THERE IS NO COPTER.
LISTEN TO--

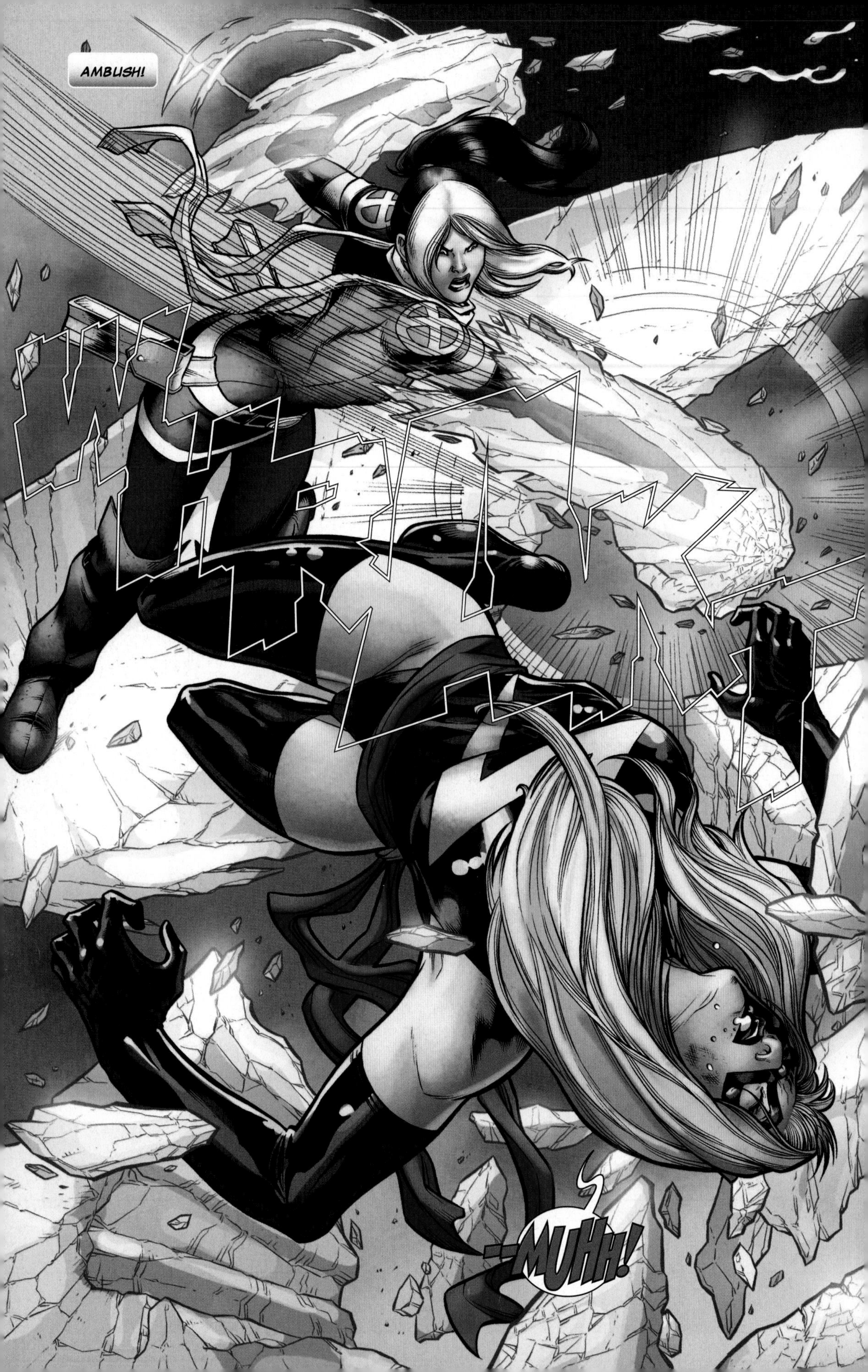
AMBUSH!
--MUHH!

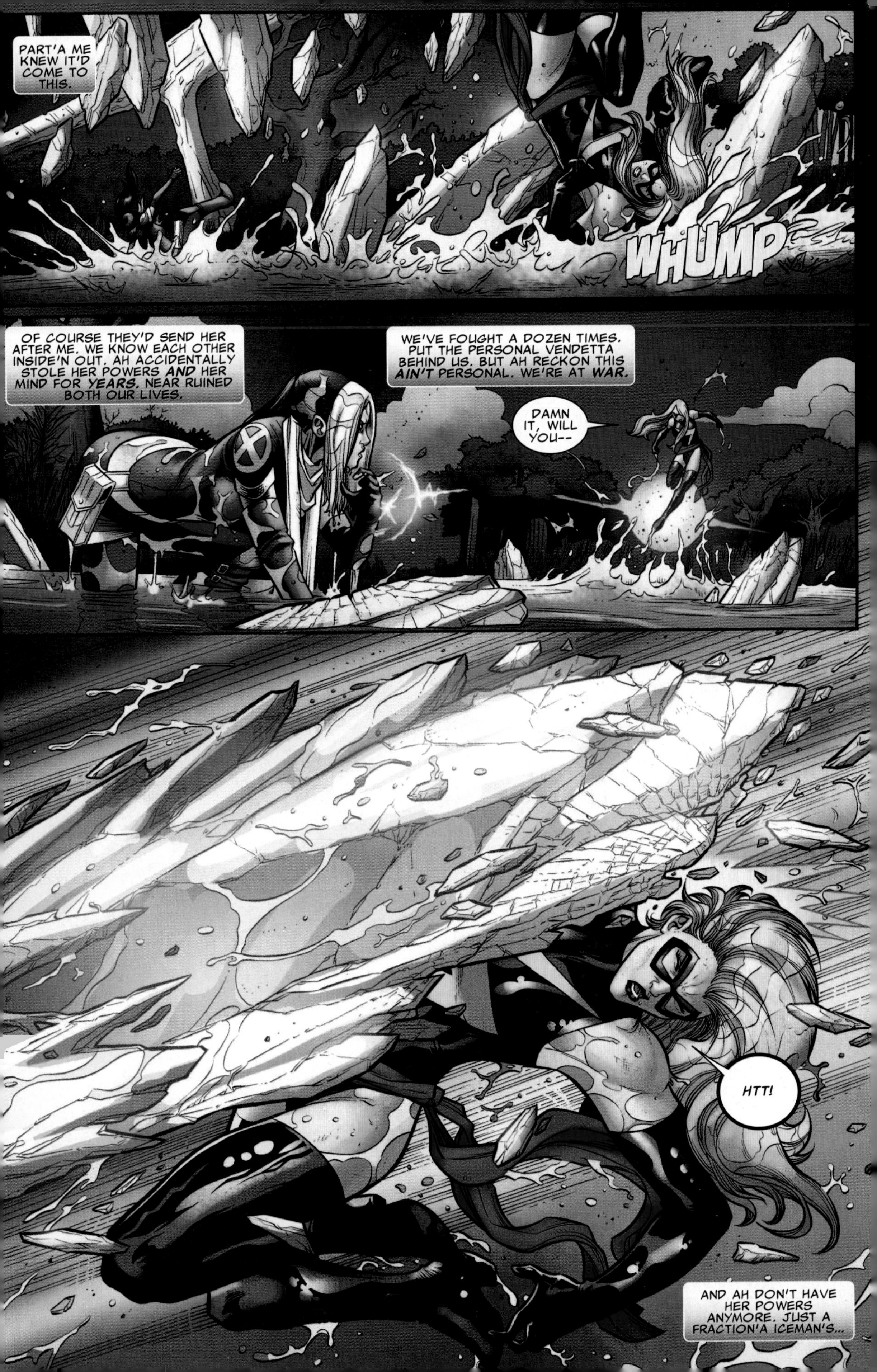
PART'A ME KNEW IT'D COME TO THIS.
WHUMP
OF COURSE THEY'D SEND HER AFTER ME. WE KNOW EACH OTHER INSIDE'N OUT. AH ACCIDENTALLY STOLE HER POWERS AND HER MIND FOR YEARS. NEAR RUINED BOTH OUR LIVES.
WE'VE FOUGHT A DOZEN TIMES. PUT THE PERSONAL VENDETTA BEHIND US. BUT AH RECKON THIS AIN'T PERSONAL. WE'RE AT WAR.
DAMN IT, WILL YOU--
HTT!
AND AH DON'T HAVE HER POWERS ANYMORE. JUST A FRACTION'A ICEMAN'S...

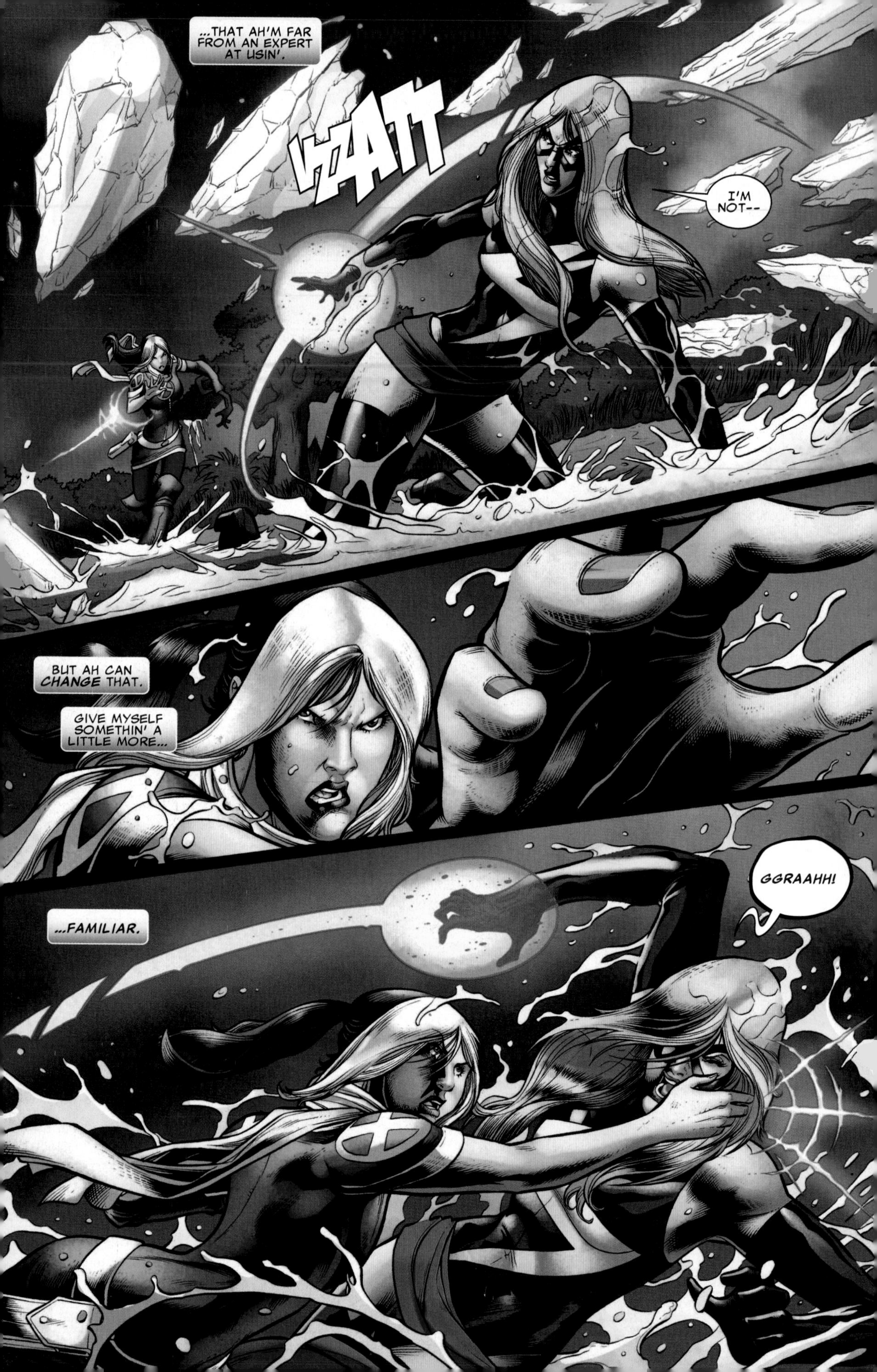
...THAT AH'M FAR FROM AN EXPERT AT USIN'.
VZZATT
I'M NOT--
BUT AH CAN CHANGE THAT.
GIVE MYSELF SOMETHIN' A LITTLE MORE...
...FAMILIAR.
GGRAAHH!

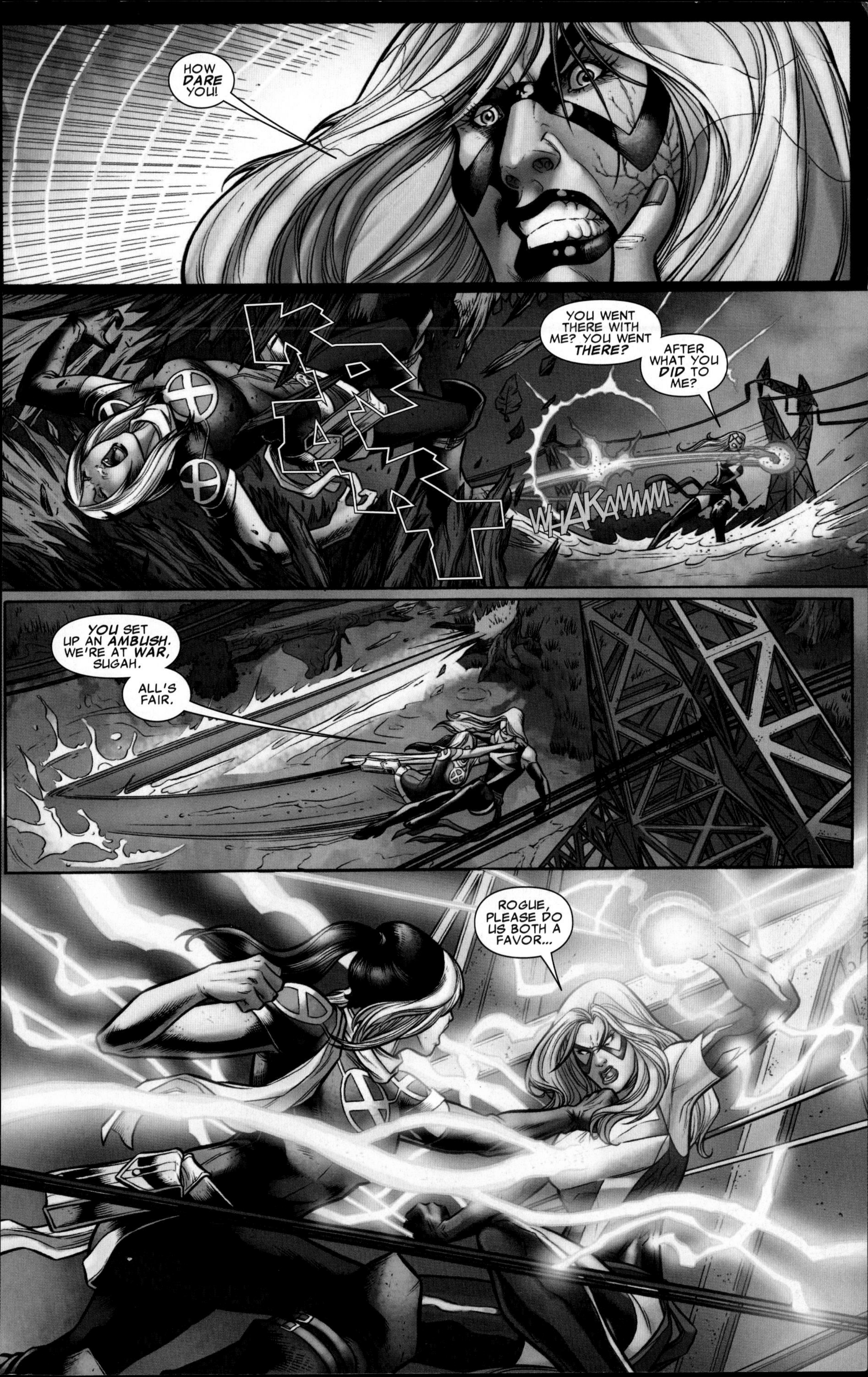
HOW DARE YOU!
YOU WENT THERE WITH ME? YOU WENT THERE?
AFTER WHAT YOU DID TO ME?
WHAKAMMMM
YOU SET UP AN AMBUSH. WE'RE AT WAR, SUGAH.
ALL'S FAIR.
ROGUE, PLEASE DO US BOTH A FAVOR...

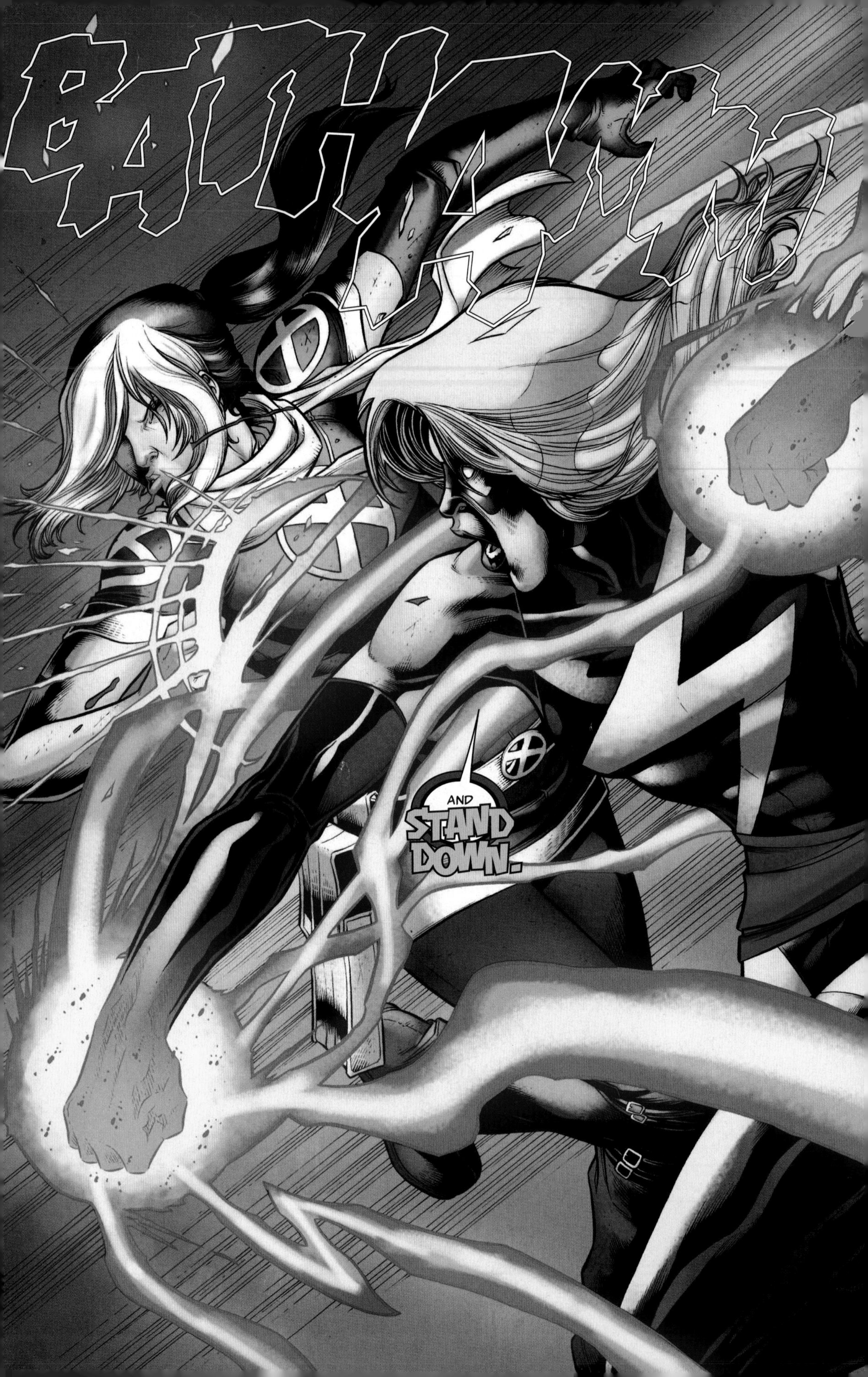
AND STAND DOWN.

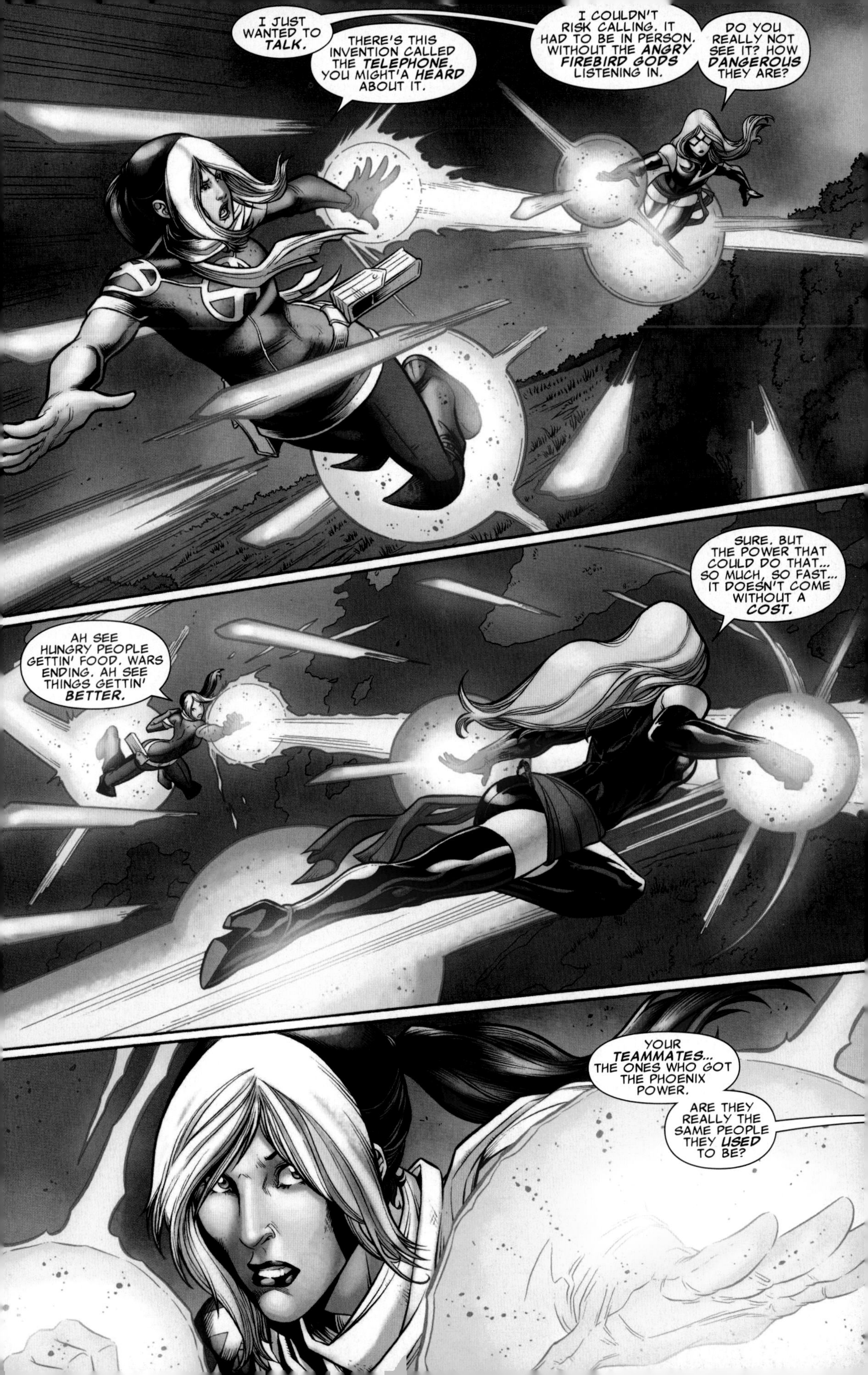
I JUST WANTED TO TALK.
THERE'S THIS INVENTION CALLED THE TELEPHONE. YOU MIGHT'A HEARD ABOUT IT.
I COULDN'T RISK CALLING. IT HAD TO BE IN PERSON. WITHOUT THE ANGRY FIREBIRD GODS LISTENING IN.
DO YOU REALLY NOT SEE IT? HOW DANGEROUS THEY ARE?
AH SEE HUNGRY PEOPLE GETTIN' FOOD. WARS ENDING. AH SEE THINGS GETTIN' BETTER.
SURE. BUT THE POWER THAT COULD DO THAT... SO MUCH, SO FAST... IT DOESN'T COME WITHOUT A COST.
YOUR TEAMMATES... THE ONES WHO GOT THE PHOENIX POWER.
ARE THEY REALLY THE SAME PEOPLE THEY USED TO BE?

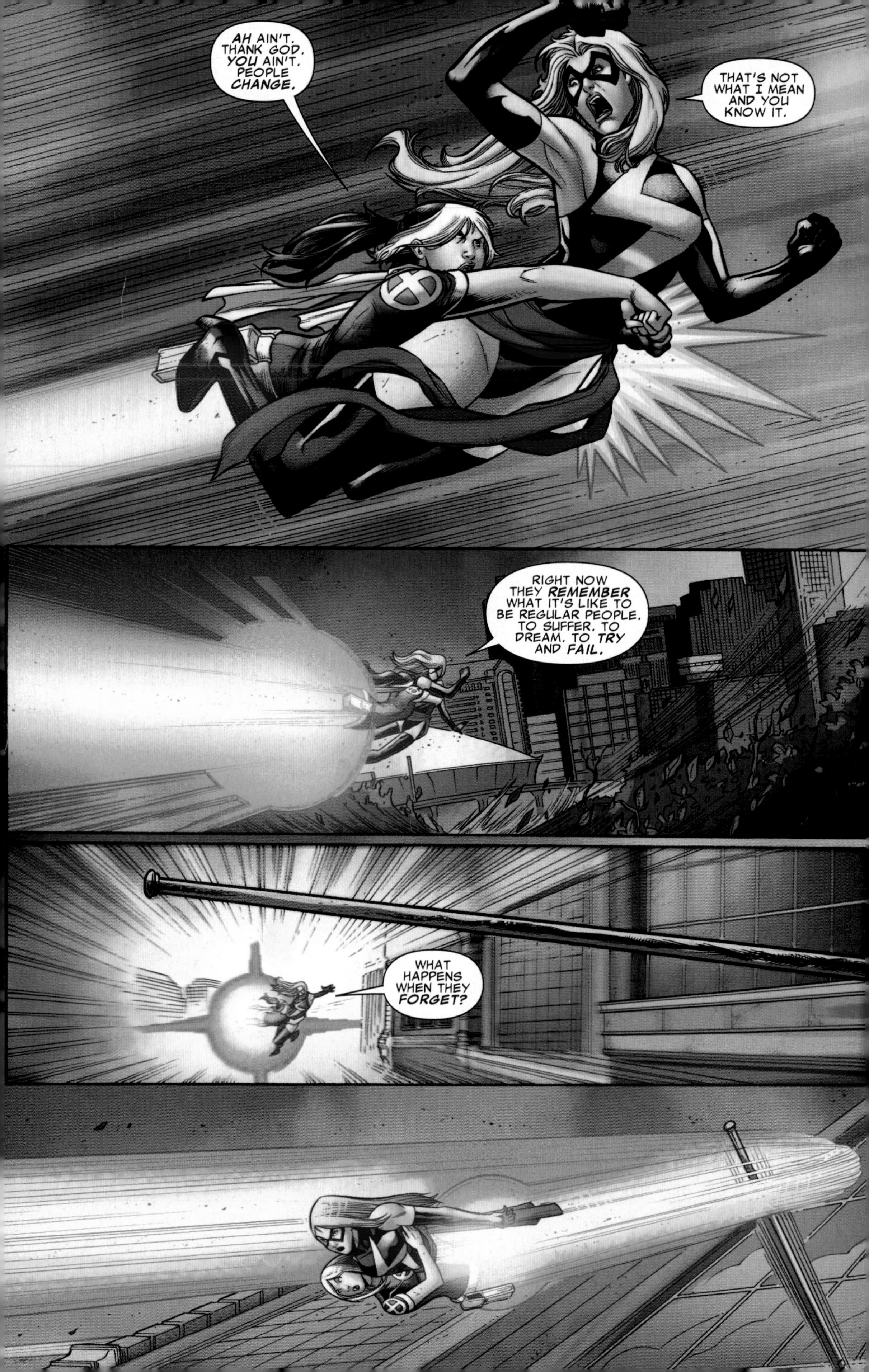
AH AIN'T. THANK GOD. YOU AIN'T. PEOPLE CHANGE.
THAT'S NOT WHAT I MEAN AND YOU KNOW IT.
RIGHT NOW THEY REMEMBER WHAT IT'S LIKE TO BE REGULAR PEOPLE. TO SUFFER. TO DREAM. TO TRY AND FAIL.
WHAT HAPPENS WHEN THEY FORGET?

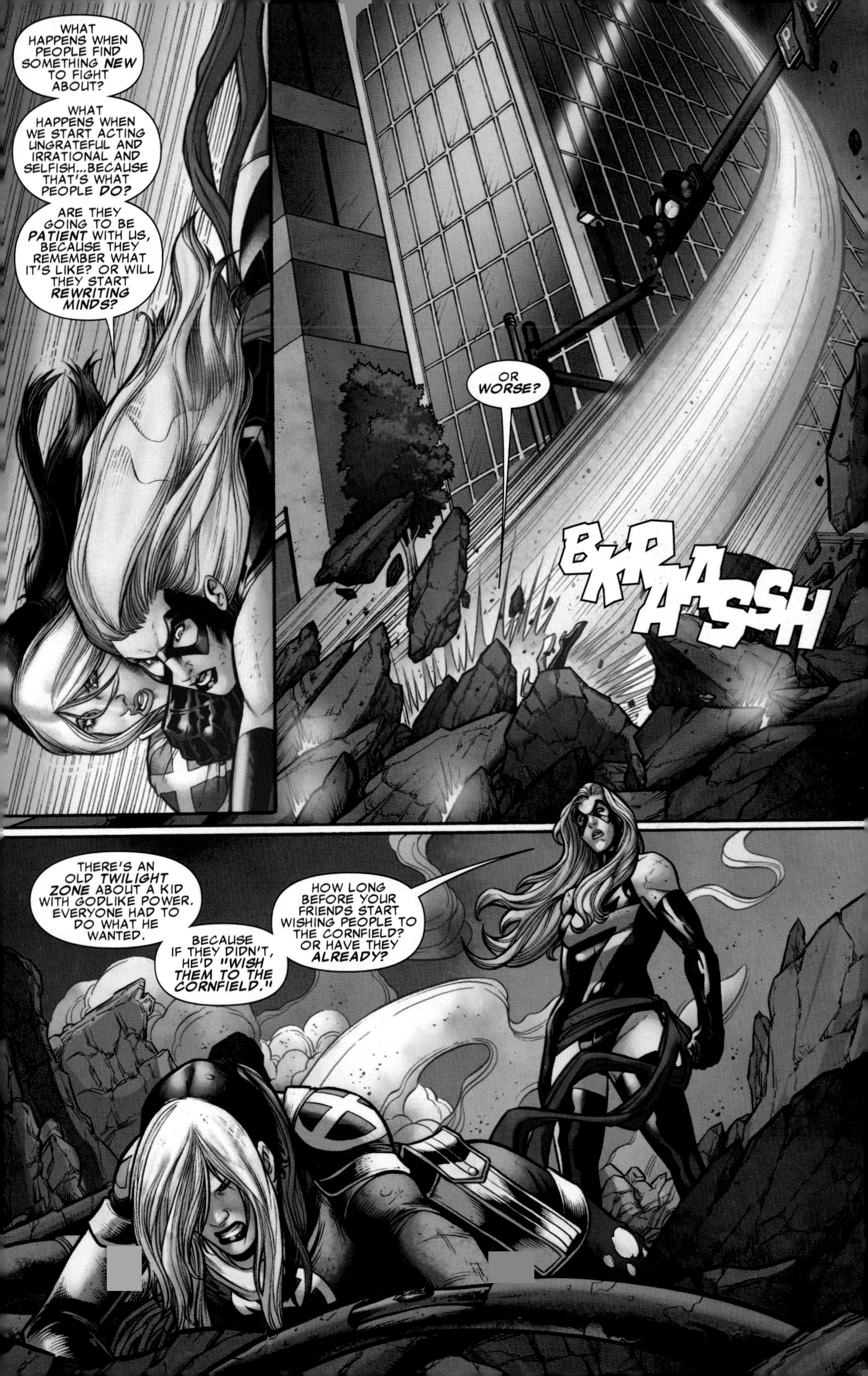

WHAT HAPPENS WHEN PEOPLE FIND SOMETHING **NEW** TO FIGHT ABOUT?
WHAT HAPPENS WHEN WE START ACTING UNGRATEFUL AND IRRATIONAL AND SELFISH...BECAUSE THAT'S WHAT PEOPLE **DO?**
ARE THEY GOING TO BE **PATIENT** WITH US, BECAUSE THEY REMEMBER WHAT IT'S LIKE? OR WILL THEY START **REWRITING MINDS?**
OR **WORSE?**
BKRAASSH
THERE'S AN OLD **TWILIGHT ZONE** ABOUT A KID WITH GODLIKE POWER. EVERYONE HAD TO DO WHAT HE WANTED.
BECAUSE IF THEY DIDN'T, HE'D **"WISH THEM TO THE CORNFIELD."**
HOW LONG BEFORE YOUR FRIENDS START WISHING PEOPLE TO THE CORNFIELD? OR HAVE THEY **ALREADY?**

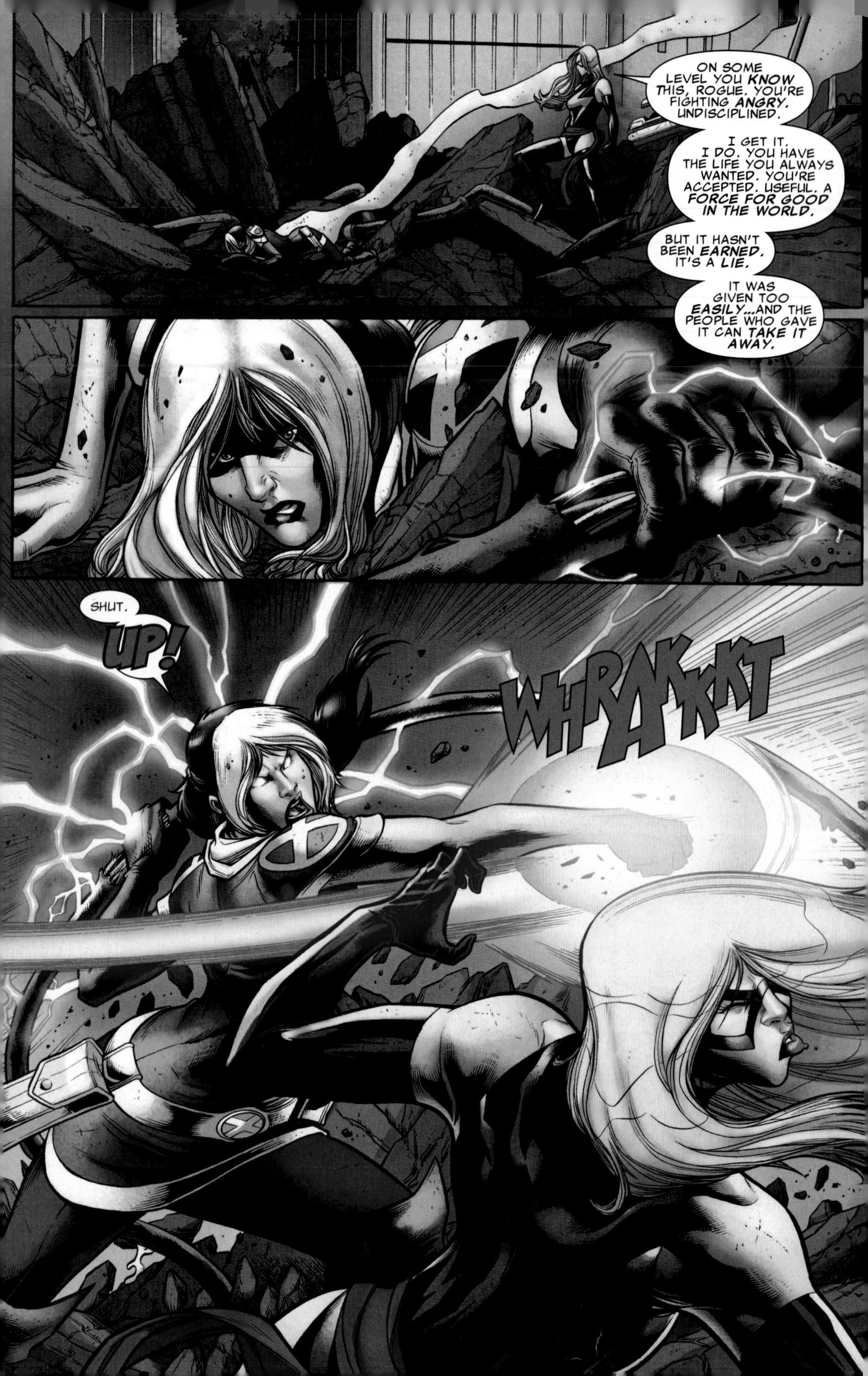
ON SOME LEVEL YOU KNOW THIS, ROGUE. YOU'RE FIGHTING ANGRY. UNDISCIPLINED.
I GET IT. I DO. YOU HAVE THE LIFE YOU ALWAYS WANTED. YOU'RE ACCEPTED. USEFUL. A FORCE FOR GOOD IN THE WORLD.
BUT IT HASN'T BEEN EARNED. IT'S A LIE.
IT WAS GIVEN TOO EASILY...AND THE PEOPLE WHO GAVE IT CAN TAKE IT AWAY.
SHUT. UP!
WHRAKKKT

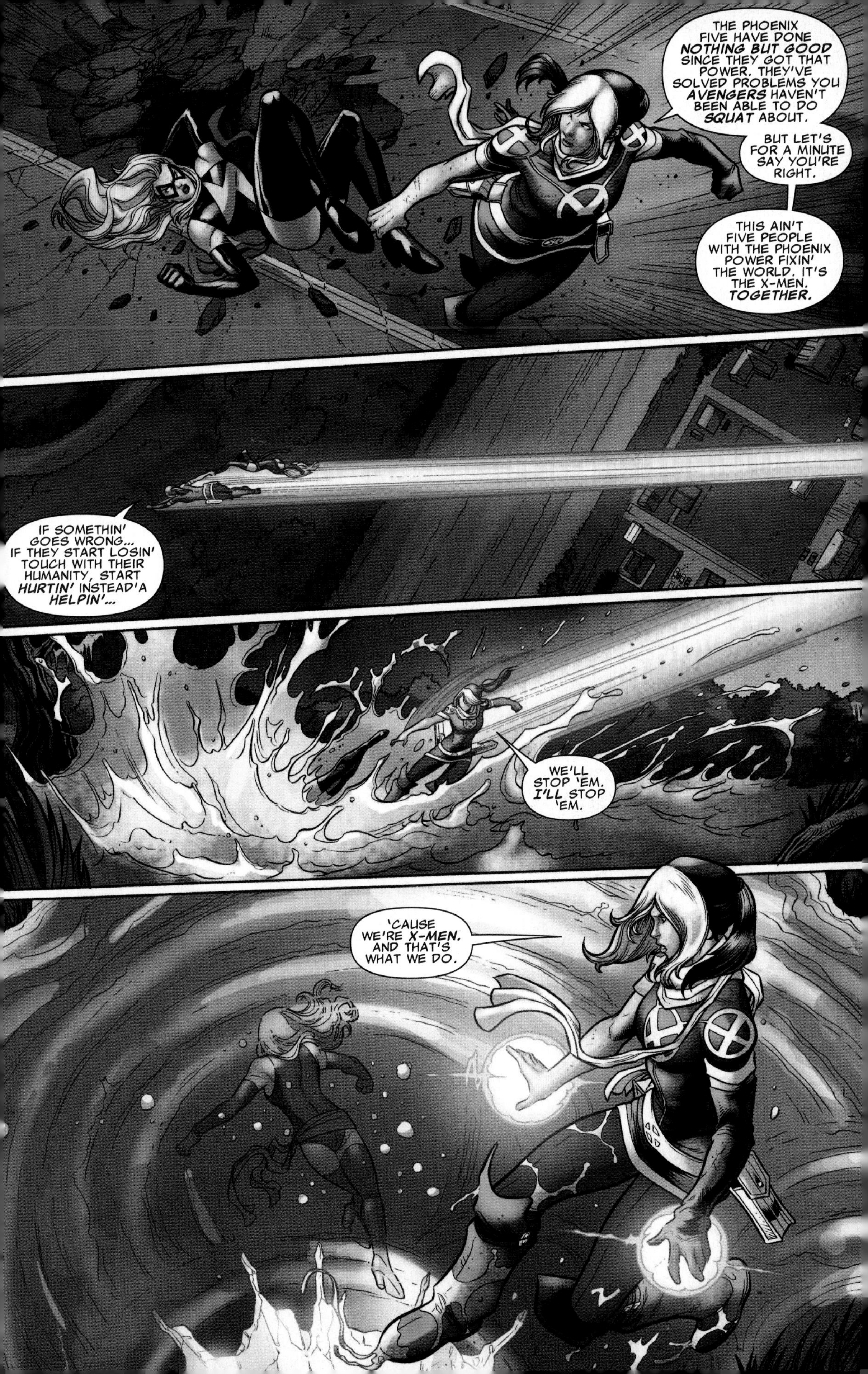
THE PHOENIX FIVE HAVE DONE NOTHING BUT GOOD SINCE THEY GOT THAT POWER. THEY'VE SOLVED PROBLEMS YOU AVENGERS HAVEN'T BEEN ABLE TO DO SQUAT ABOUT.
BUT LET'S FOR A MINUTE SAY YOU'RE RIGHT.
THIS AIN'T FIVE PEOPLE WITH THE PHOENIX POWER FIXIN' THE WORLD. IT'S THE X-MEN. TOGETHER.
IF SOMETHIN' GOES WRONG... IF THEY START LOSIN' TOUCH WITH THEIR HUMANITY, START HURTIN' INSTEAD'A HELPIN'...
WE'LL STOP 'EM. I'LL STOP 'EM.
'CAUSE WE'RE X-MEN. AND THAT'S WHAT WE DO.

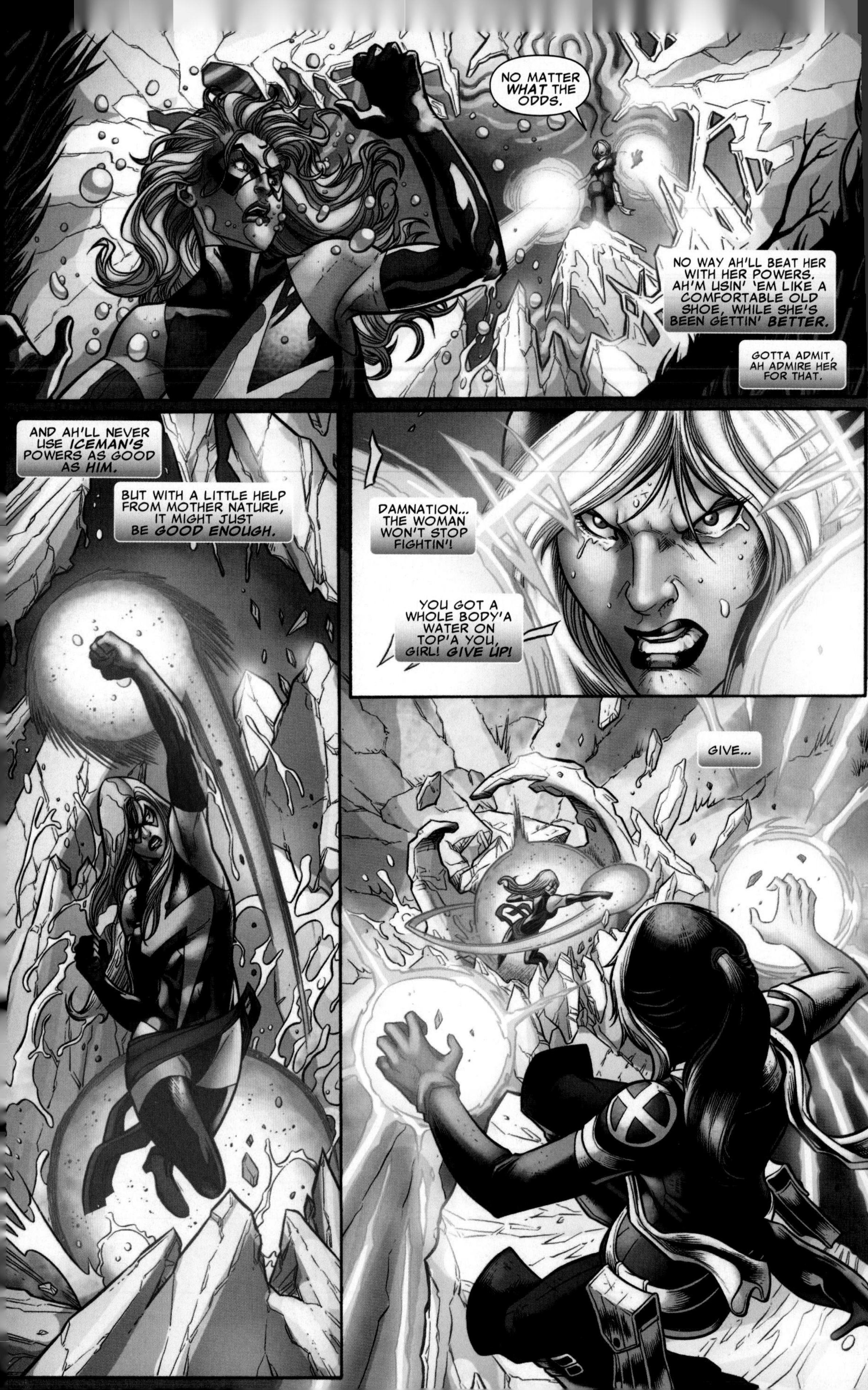
NO MATTER WHAT THE ODDS.
NO WAY AH'LL BEAT HER WITH HER POWERS. AH'M USIN' 'EM LIKE A COMFORTABLE OLD SHOE, WHILE SHE'S BEEN GETTIN' BETTER.
GOTTA ADMIT, AH ADMIRE HER FOR THAT.
AND AH'LL NEVER USE ICEMAN'S POWERS AS GOOD AS HIM.
BUT WITH A LITTLE HELP FROM MOTHER NATURE, IT MIGHT JUST BE GOOD ENOUGH.
DAMNATION... THE WOMAN WON'T STOP FIGHTIN'!
YOU GOT A WHOLE BODY'A WATER ON TOP'A YOU, GIRL! GIVE UP!
GIVE...

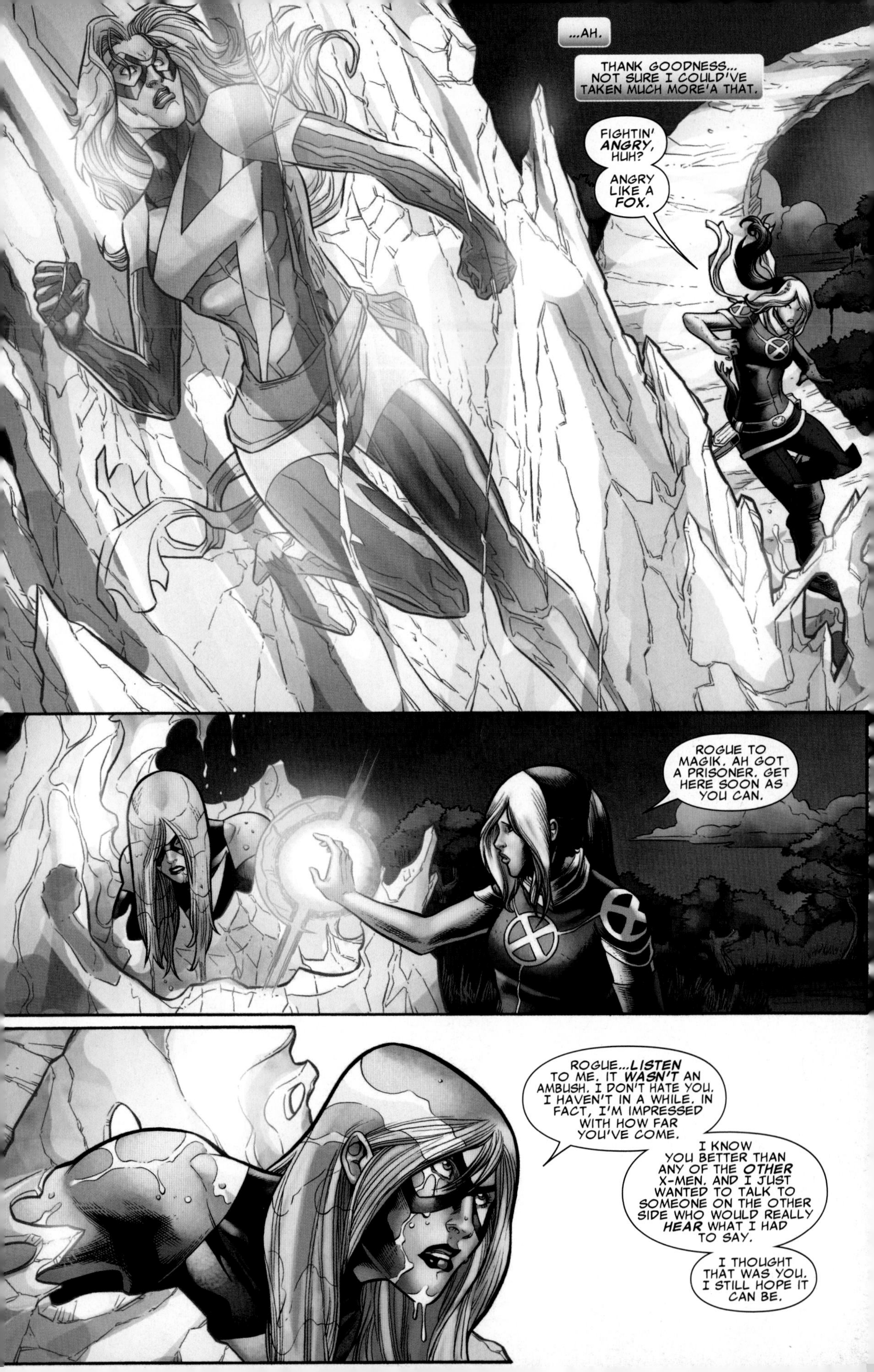
...AH.
THANK GOODNESS... NOT SURE I COULD'VE TAKEN MUCH MORE'A THAT.
FIGHTIN' ANGRY, HUH?
ANGRY LIKE A FOX.
ROGUE TO MAGIK. AH GOT A PRISONER. GET HERE SOON AS YOU CAN.
ROGUE...LISTEN TO ME. IT WASN'T AN AMBUSH. I DON'T HATE YOU. I HAVEN'T IN A WHILE. IN FACT, I'M IMPRESSED WITH HOW FAR YOU'VE COME.
I KNOW YOU BETTER THAN ANY OF THE OTHER X-MEN. AND I JUST WANTED TO TALK TO SOMEONE ON THE OTHER SIDE WHO WOULD REALLY HEAR WHAT I HAD TO SAY.
I THOUGHT THAT WAS YOU. I STILL HOPE IT CAN BE.

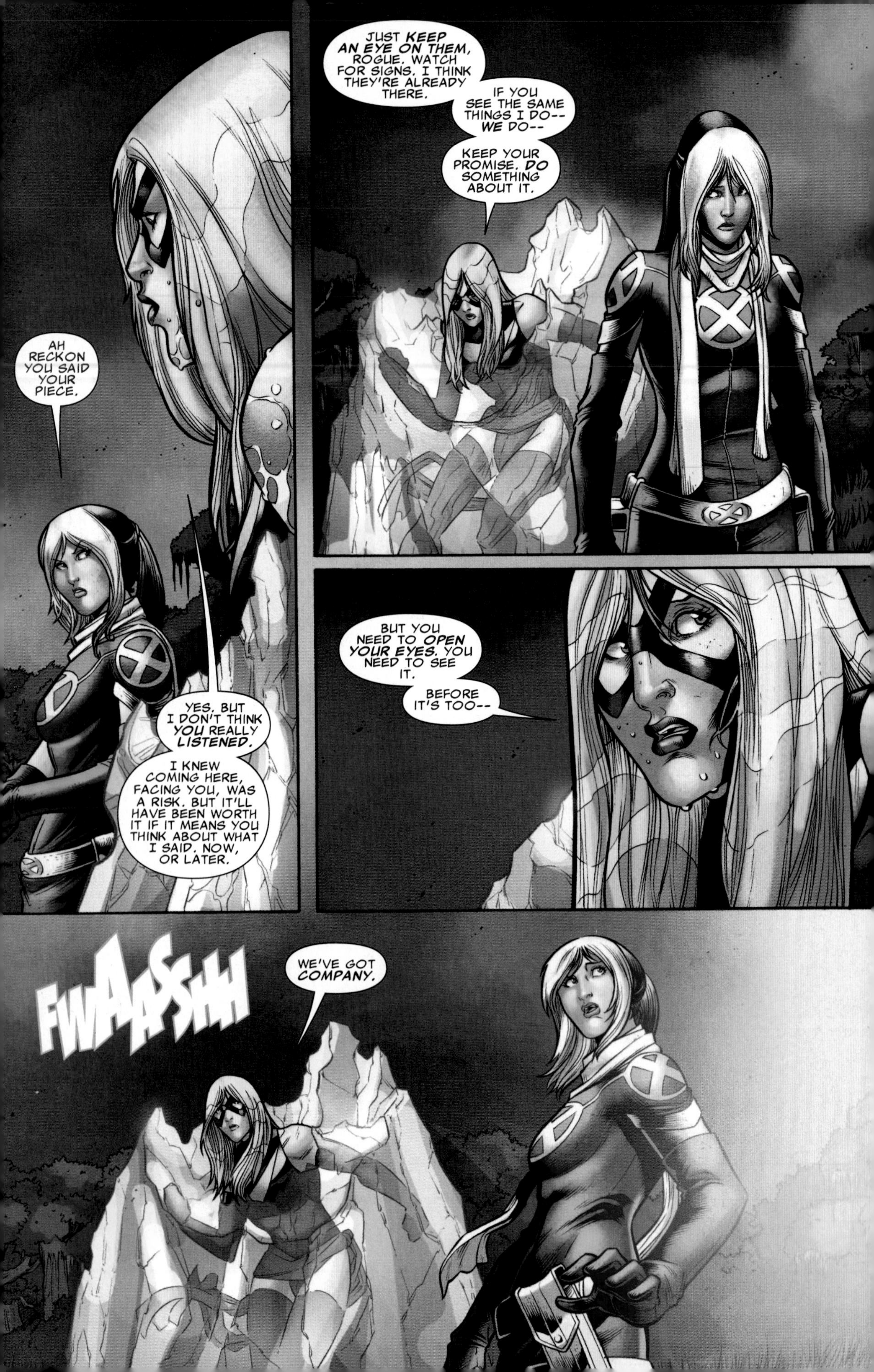
AH RECKON YOU SAID YOUR PIECE.
YES. BUT I DON'T THINK YOU REALLY LISTENED.
I KNEW COMING HERE, FACING YOU, WAS A RISK. BUT IT'LL HAVE BEEN WORTH IT IF IT MEANS YOU THINK ABOUT WHAT I SAID. NOW, OR LATER.
JUST KEEP AN EYE ON THEM, ROGUE. WATCH FOR SIGNS. I THINK THEY'RE ALREADY THERE.
IF YOU SEE THE SAME THINGS I DO-- WE DO--
KEEP YOUR PROMISE. DO SOMETHING ABOUT IT.
BUT YOU NEED TO OPEN YOUR EYES. YOU NEED TO SEE IT.
BEFORE IT'S TOO--
FWAASHH
WE'VE GOT COMPANY.

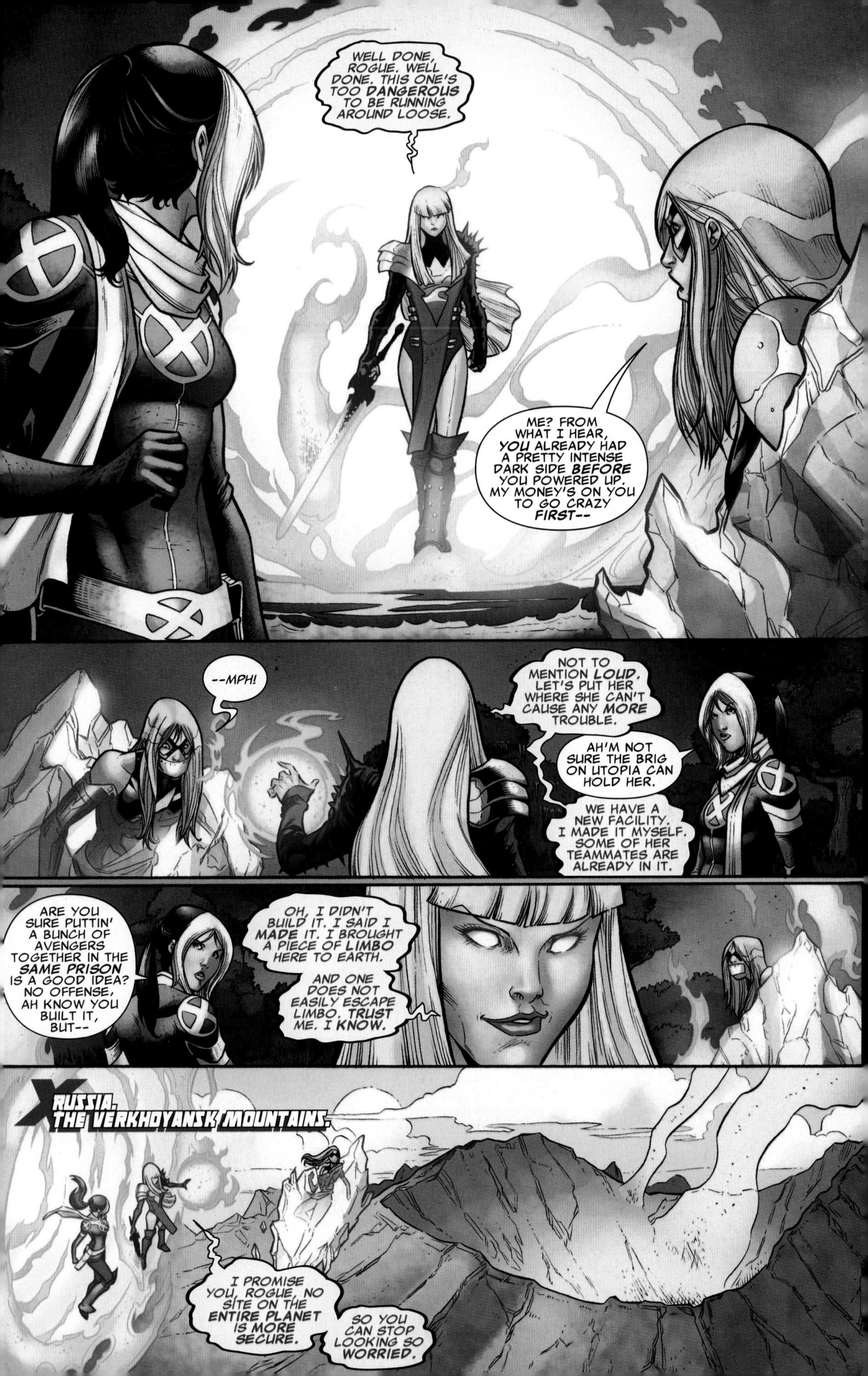
WELL DONE, ROGUE. WELL DONE. THIS ONE'S TOO DANGEROUS TO BE RUNNING AROUND LOOSE.
ME? FROM WHAT I HEAR, YOU ALREADY HAD A PRETTY INTENSE DARK SIDE BEFORE YOU POWERED UP. MY MONEY'S ON YOU TO GO CRAZY FIRST--
--MPH!
NOT TO MENTION LOUD. LET'S PUT HER WHERE SHE CAN'T CAUSE ANY MORE TROUBLE.
AH'M NOT SURE THE BRIG ON UTOPIA CAN HOLD HER.
WE HAVE A NEW FACILITY. I MADE IT MYSELF. SOME OF HER TEAMMATES ARE ALREADY IN IT.
ARE YOU SURE PUTTIN' A BUNCH OF AVENGERS TOGETHER IN THE SAME PRISON IS A GOOD IDEA? NO OFFENSE, AH KNOW YOU BUILT IT, BUT--
OH, I DIDN'T BUILD IT. I SAID I MADE IT. I BROUGHT A PIECE OF LIMBO HERE TO EARTH.
AND ONE DOES NOT EASILY ESCAPE LIMBO. TRUST ME. I KNOW.
RUSSIA. THE VERKHOYANSK MOUNTAINS.
I PROMISE YOU, ROGUE, NO SITE ON THE ENTIRE PLANET IS MORE SECURE.
SO YOU CAN STOP LOOKING SO WORRIED.

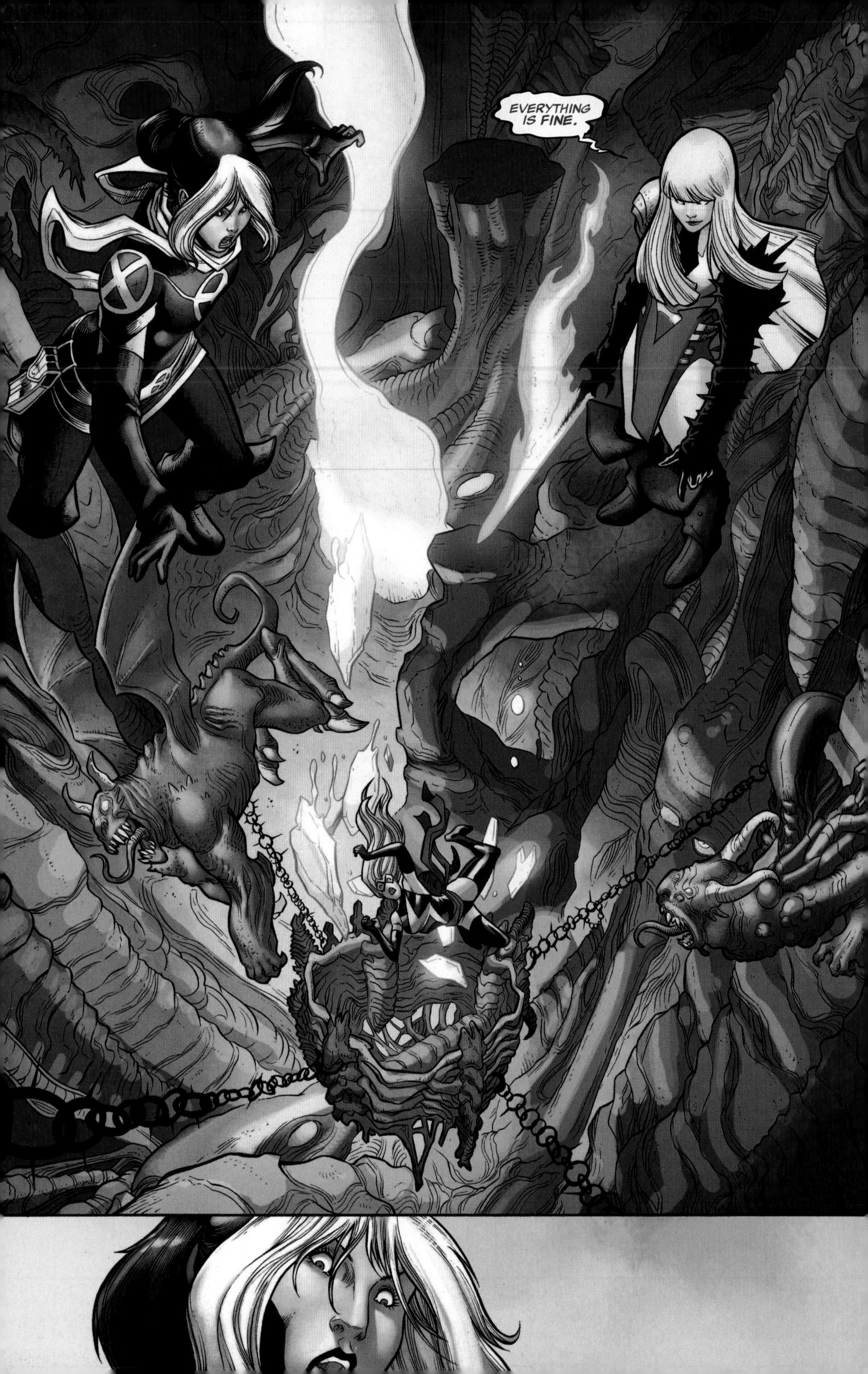
EVERYTHING IS FINE.

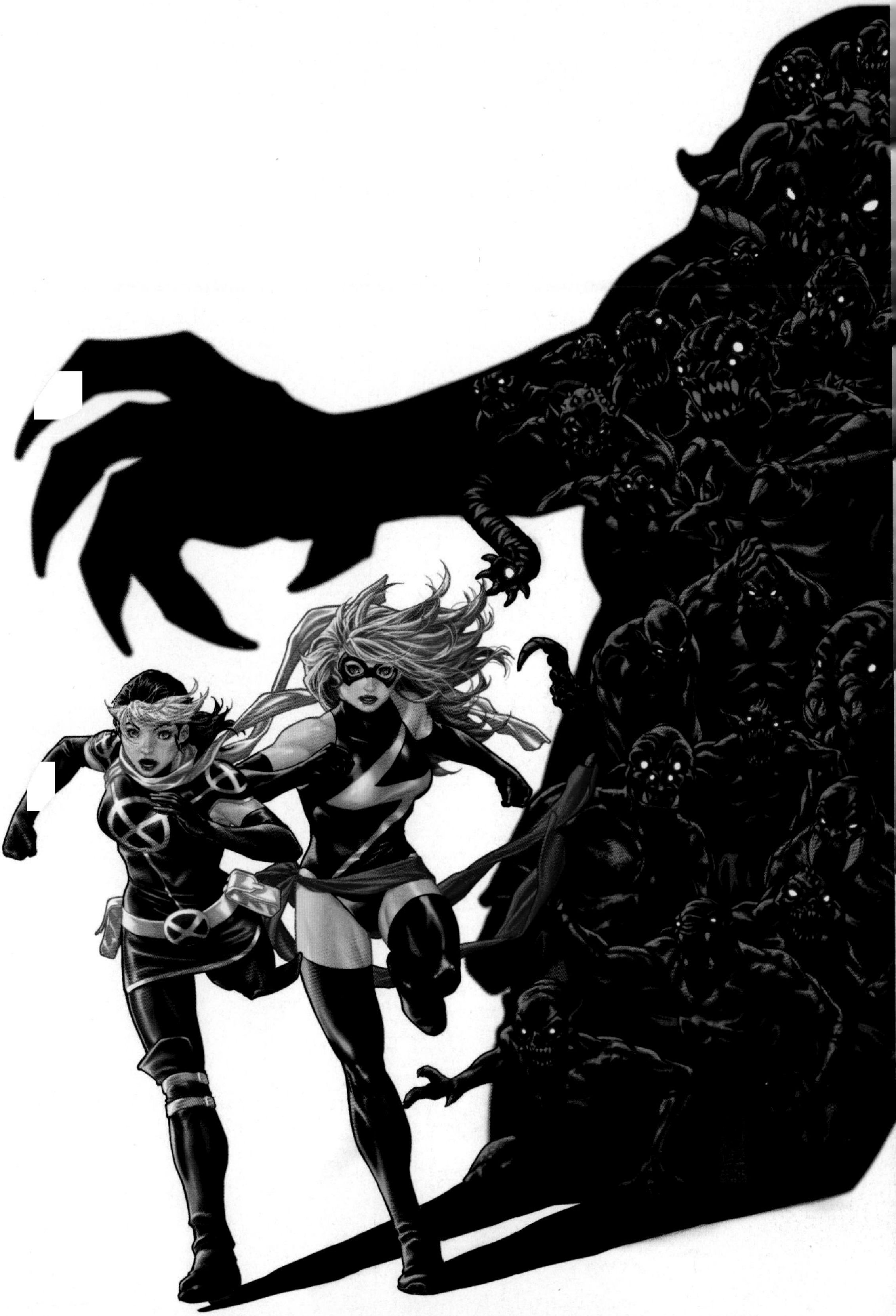

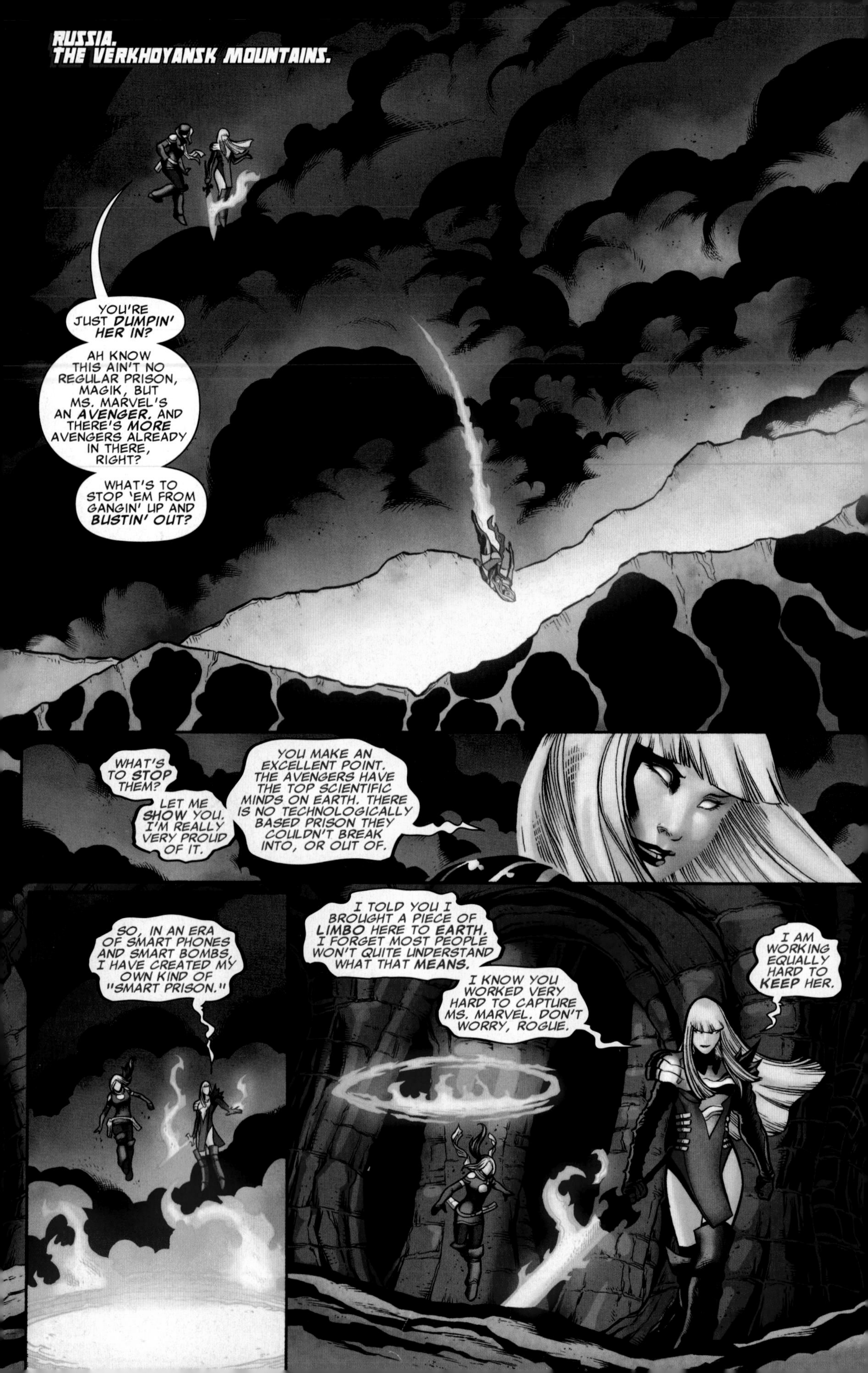
RUSSIA.
THE VERKHOYANSK MOUNTAINS.
YOU'RE JUST DUMPIN' HER IN?
AH KNOW THIS AIN'T NO REGULAR PRISON, MAGIK, BUT MS. MARVEL'S AN AVENGER. AND THERE'S MORE AVENGERS ALREADY IN THERE, RIGHT?
WHAT'S TO STOP 'EM FROM GANGIN' UP AND BUSTIN' OUT?
WHAT'S TO STOP THEM?
LET ME SHOW YOU. I'M REALLY VERY PROUD OF IT.
YOU MAKE AN EXCELLENT POINT. THE AVENGERS HAVE THE TOP SCIENTIFIC MINDS ON EARTH. THERE IS NO TECHNOLOGICALLY BASED PRISON THEY COULDN'T BREAK INTO, OR OUT OF.
SO, IN AN ERA OF SMART PHONES AND SMART BOMBS, I HAVE CREATED MY OWN KIND OF "SMART PRISON."
I TOLD YOU I BROUGHT A PIECE OF LIMBO HERE TO EARTH. I FORGET MOST PEOPLE WON'T QUITE UNDERSTAND WHAT THAT MEANS.
I KNOW YOU WORKED VERY HARD TO CAPTURE MS. MARVEL. DON'T WORRY, ROGUE.
I AM WORKING EQUALLY HARD TO KEEP HER.

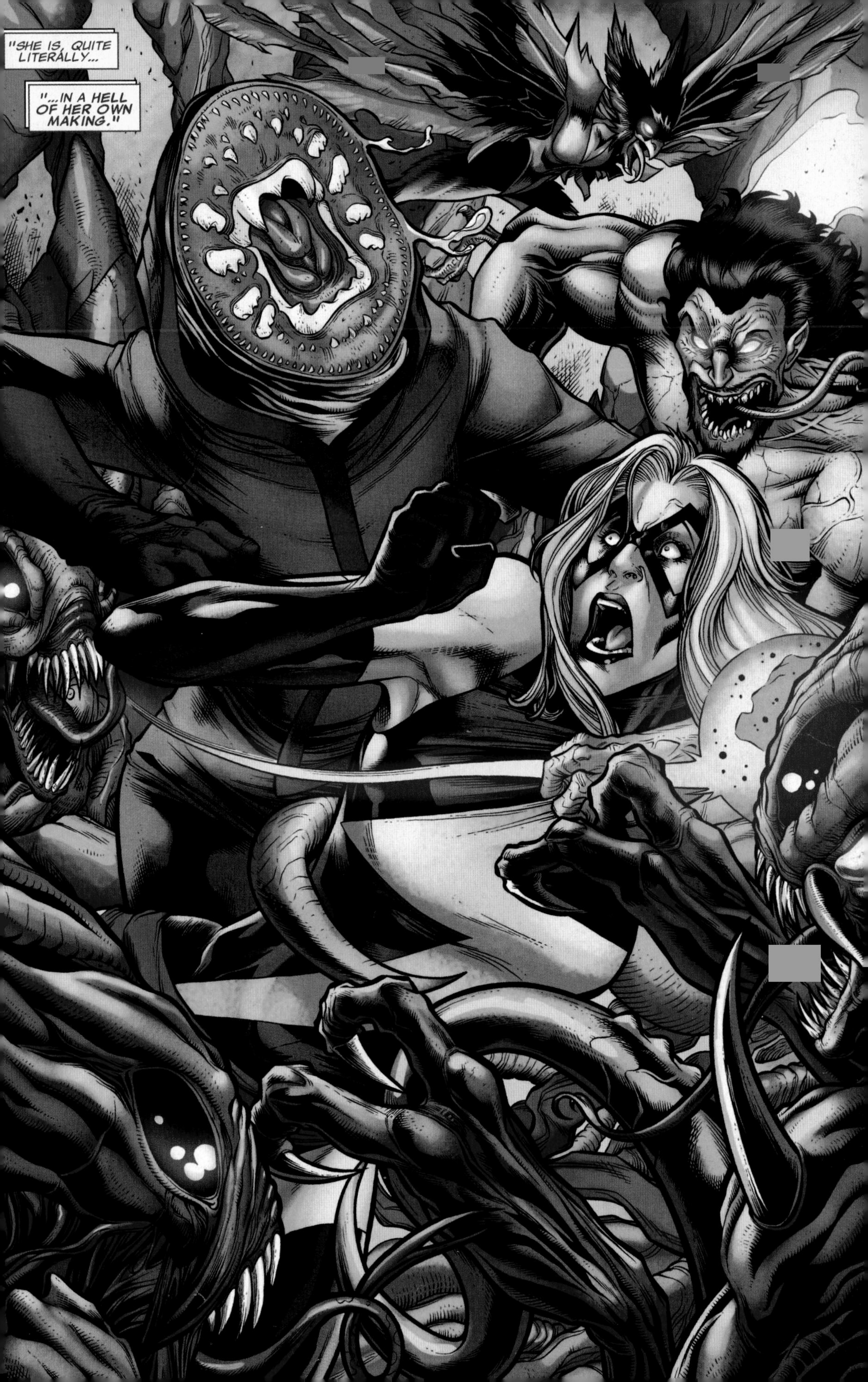
"SHE IS, QUITE LITERALLY...
"...IN A HELL OF HER OWN MAKING."

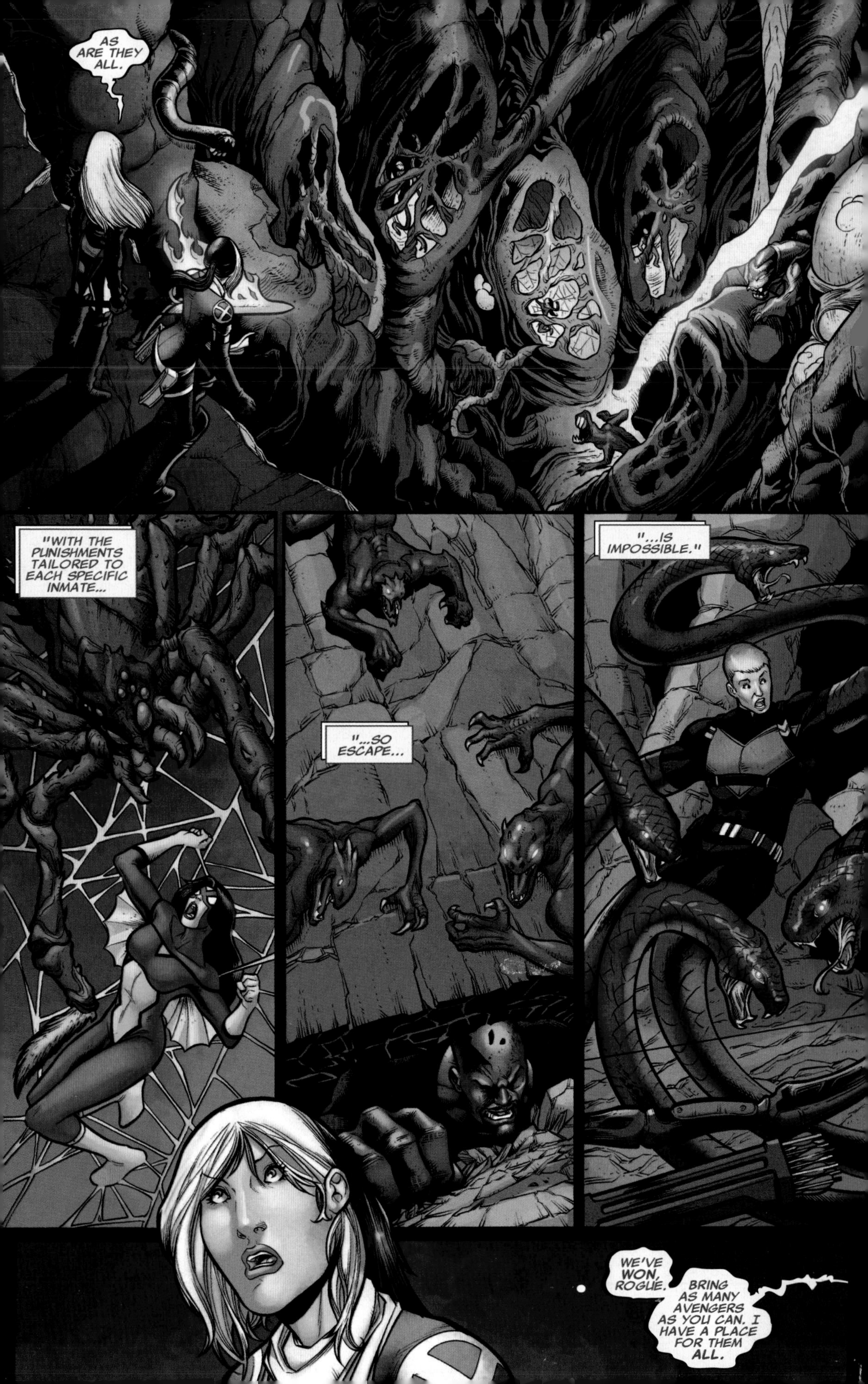

AS ARE THEY ALL.
"WITH THE PUNISHMENTS TAILORED TO EACH SPECIFIC INMATE...
"...SO ESCAPE...
"...IS IMPOSSIBLE."
WE'VE WON, ROGUE.
BRING AS MANY AVENGERS AS YOU CAN. I HAVE A PLACE FOR THEM ALL.

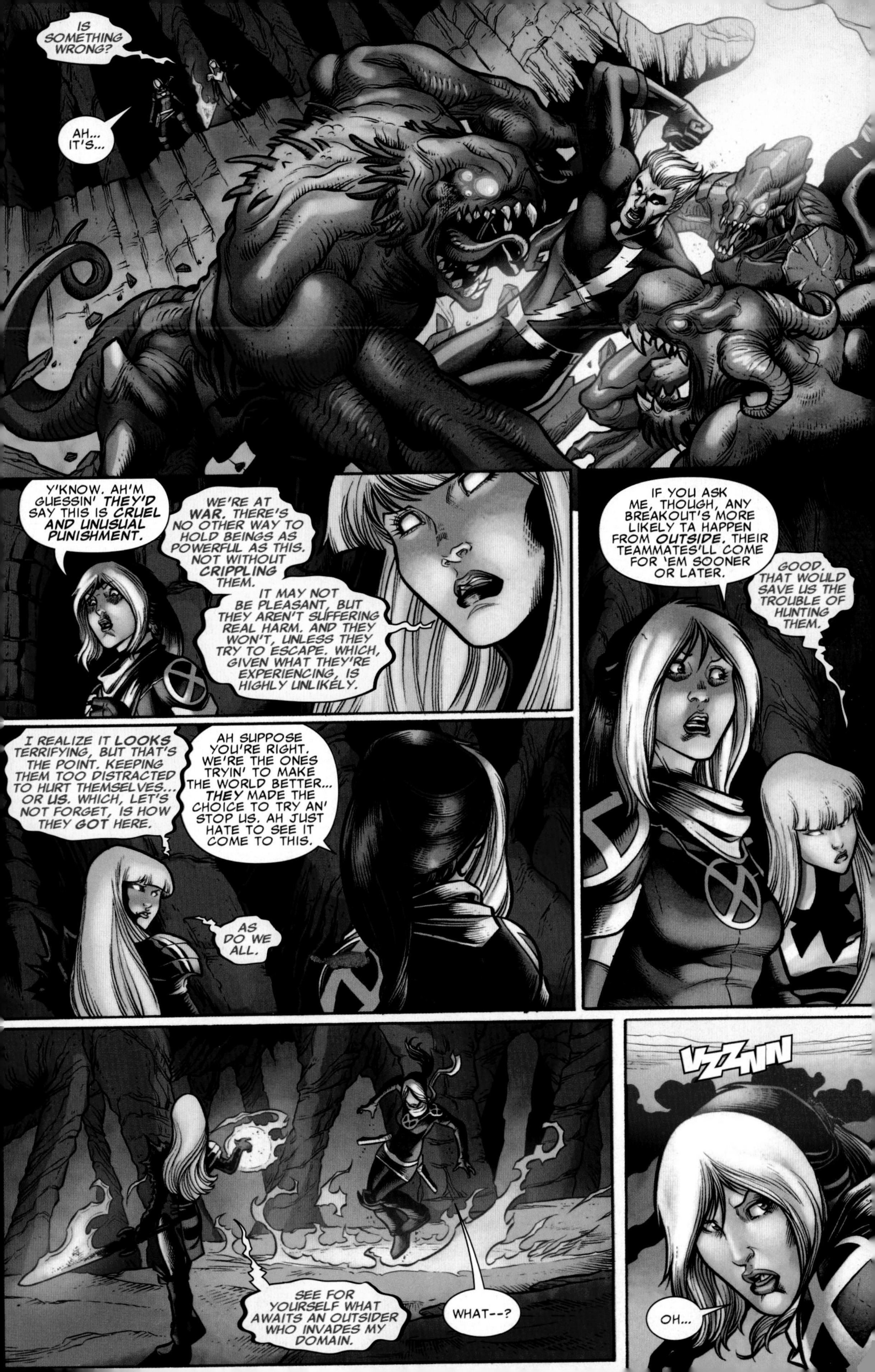
IS SOMETHING WRONG?
AH... IT'S...
Y'KNOW. AH'M GUESSIN' THEY'D SAY THIS IS CRUEL AND UNUSUAL PUNISHMENT.
WE'RE AT WAR. THERE'S NO OTHER WAY TO HOLD BEINGS AS POWERFUL AS THIS. NOT WITHOUT CRIPPLING THEM.
IT MAY NOT BE PLEASANT, BUT THEY AREN'T SUFFERING REAL HARM. AND THEY WON'T, UNLESS THEY TRY TO ESCAPE. WHICH, GIVEN WHAT THEY'RE EXPERIENCING, IS HIGHLY UNLIKELY.
I REALIZE IT LOOKS TERRIFYING, BUT THAT'S THE POINT. KEEPING THEM TOO DISTRACTED TO HURT THEMSELVES... OR US. WHICH, LET'S NOT FORGET, IS HOW THEY GOT HERE.
AH SUPPOSE YOU'RE RIGHT. WE'RE THE ONES TRYIN' TO MAKE THE WORLD BETTER... THEY MADE THE CHOICE TO TRY AN' STOP US. AH JUST HATE TO SEE IT COME TO THIS.
AS DO WE ALL.
IF YOU ASK ME, THOUGH, ANY BREAKOUT'S MORE LIKELY TA HAPPEN FROM OUTSIDE. THEIR TEAMMATES'LL COME FOR 'EM SOONER OR LATER.
GOOD. THAT WOULD SAVE US THE TROUBLE OF HUNTING THEM.
SEE FOR YOURSELF WHAT AWAITS AN OUTSIDER WHO INVADES MY DOMAIN.
WHAT--?
VZZNN
OH...

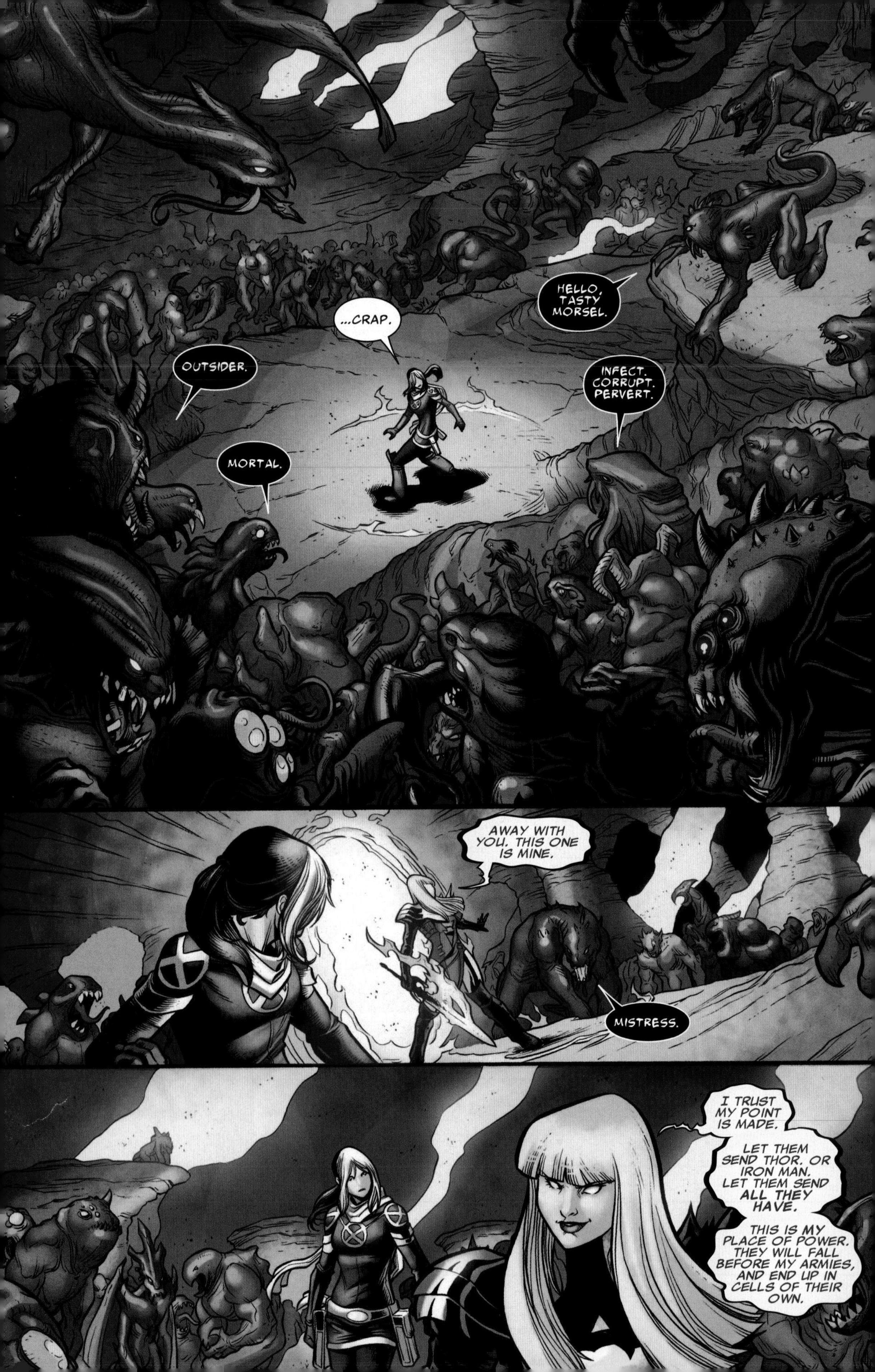
...CRAP.
HELLO, TASTY MORSEL.
OUTSIDER.
INFECT. CORRUPT. PERVERT.
MORTAL.
AWAY WITH YOU. THIS ONE IS MINE.
MISTRESS.
I TRUST MY POINT IS MADE.
LET THEM SEND THOR. OR IRON MAN. LET THEM SEND ALL THEY HAVE.
THIS IS MY PLACE OF POWER. THEY WILL FALL BEFORE MY ARMIES, AND END UP IN CELLS OF THEIR OWN.

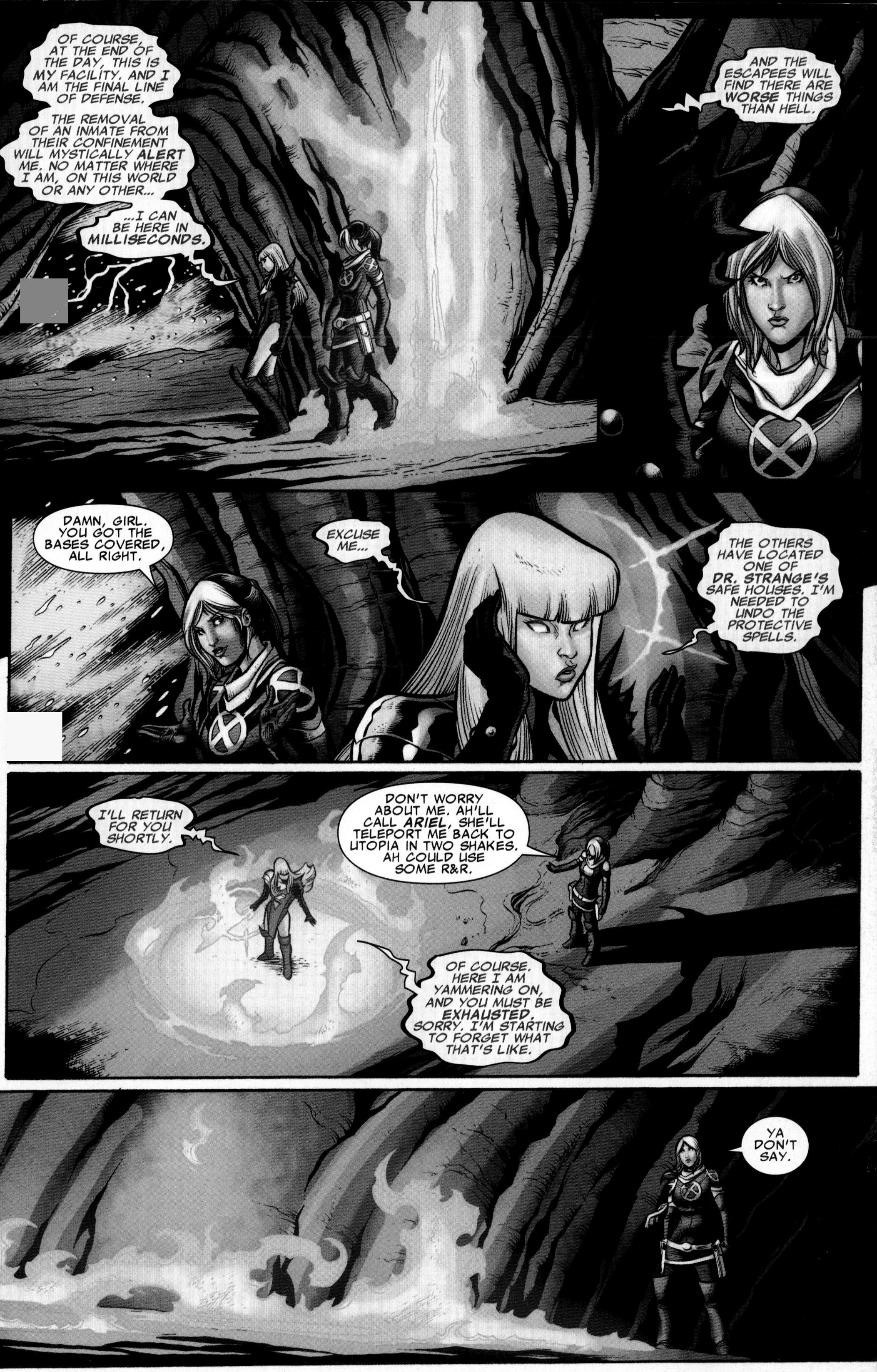
OF COURSE, AT THE END OF THE DAY, THIS IS MY FACILITY, AND I AM THE FINAL LINE OF DEFENSE.
THE REMOVAL OF AN INMATE FROM THEIR CONFINEMENT WILL MYSTICALLY ALERT ME, NO MATTER WHERE I AM, ON THIS WORLD OR ANY OTHER...
...I CAN BE HERE IN MILLISECONDS.
AND THE ESCAPEES WILL FIND THERE ARE WORSE THINGS THAN HELL.
DAMN, GIRL. YOU GOT THE BASES COVERED, ALL RIGHT.
EXCUSE ME...
THE OTHERS HAVE LOCATED ONE OF DR. STRANGE'S SAFE HOUSES. I'M NEEDED TO UNDO THE PROTECTIVE SPELLS.
I'LL RETURN FOR YOU SHORTLY.
DON'T WORRY ABOUT ME. AH'LL CALL ARIEL, SHE'LL TELEPORT ME BACK TO UTOPIA IN TWO SHAKES. AH COULD USE SOME R&R.
OF COURSE. HERE I AM YAMMERING ON, AND YOU MUST BE EXHAUSTED. SORRY. I'M STARTING TO FORGET WHAT THAT'S LIKE.
YA DON'T SAY.

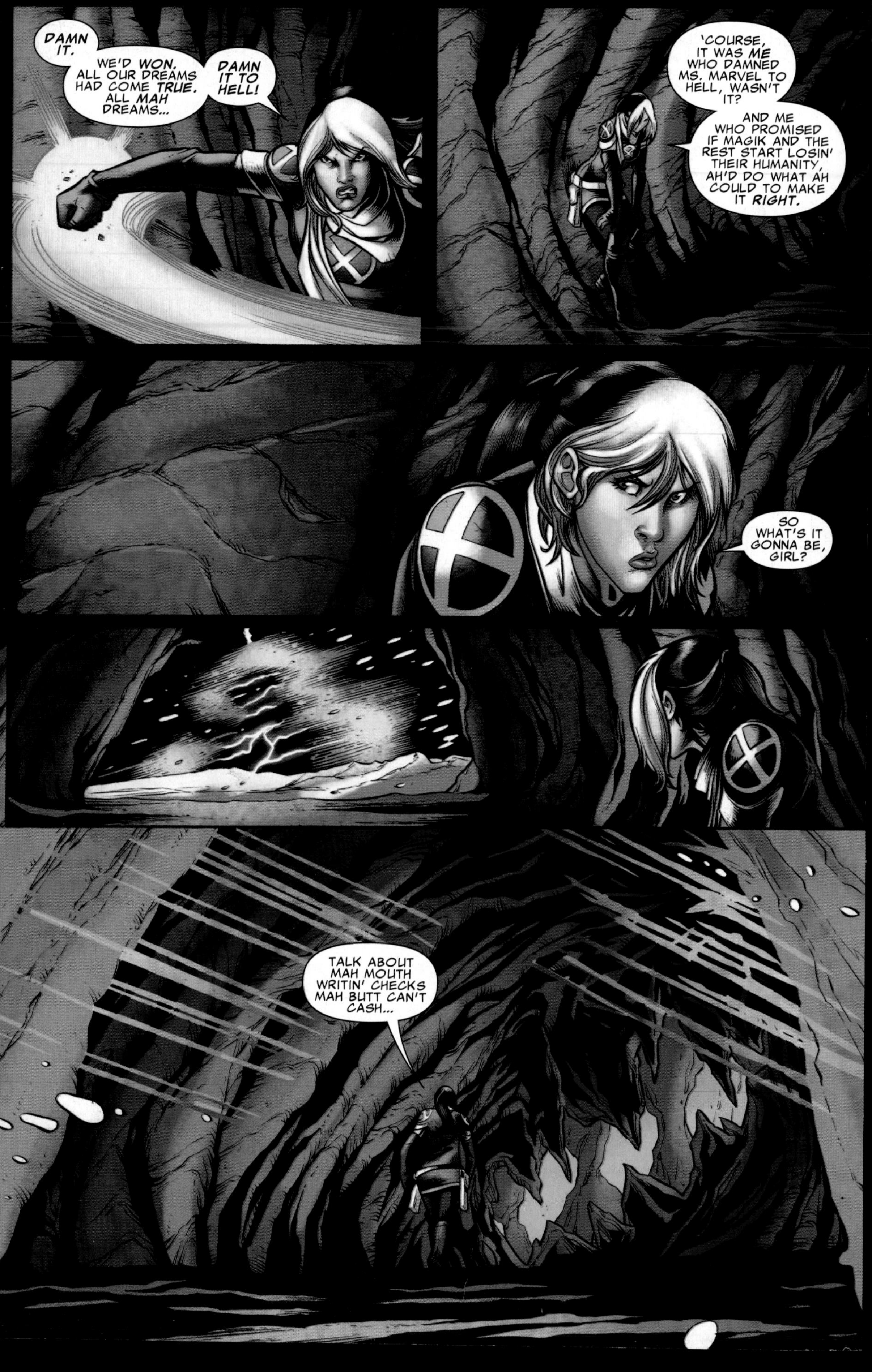
DAMN IT.
WE'D WON. ALL OUR DREAMS HAD COME TRUE. ALL MAH DREAMS...
DAMN IT TO HELL!
'COURSE, IT WAS ME WHO DAMNED MS. MARVEL TO HELL, WASN'T IT?
AND ME WHO PROMISED IF MAGIK AND THE REST START LOSIN' THEIR HUMANITY, AH'D DO WHAT AH COULD TO MAKE IT RIGHT.
SO WHAT'S IT GONNA BE, GIRL?
TALK ABOUT MAH MOUTH WRITIN' CHECKS MAH BUTT CAN'T CASH...

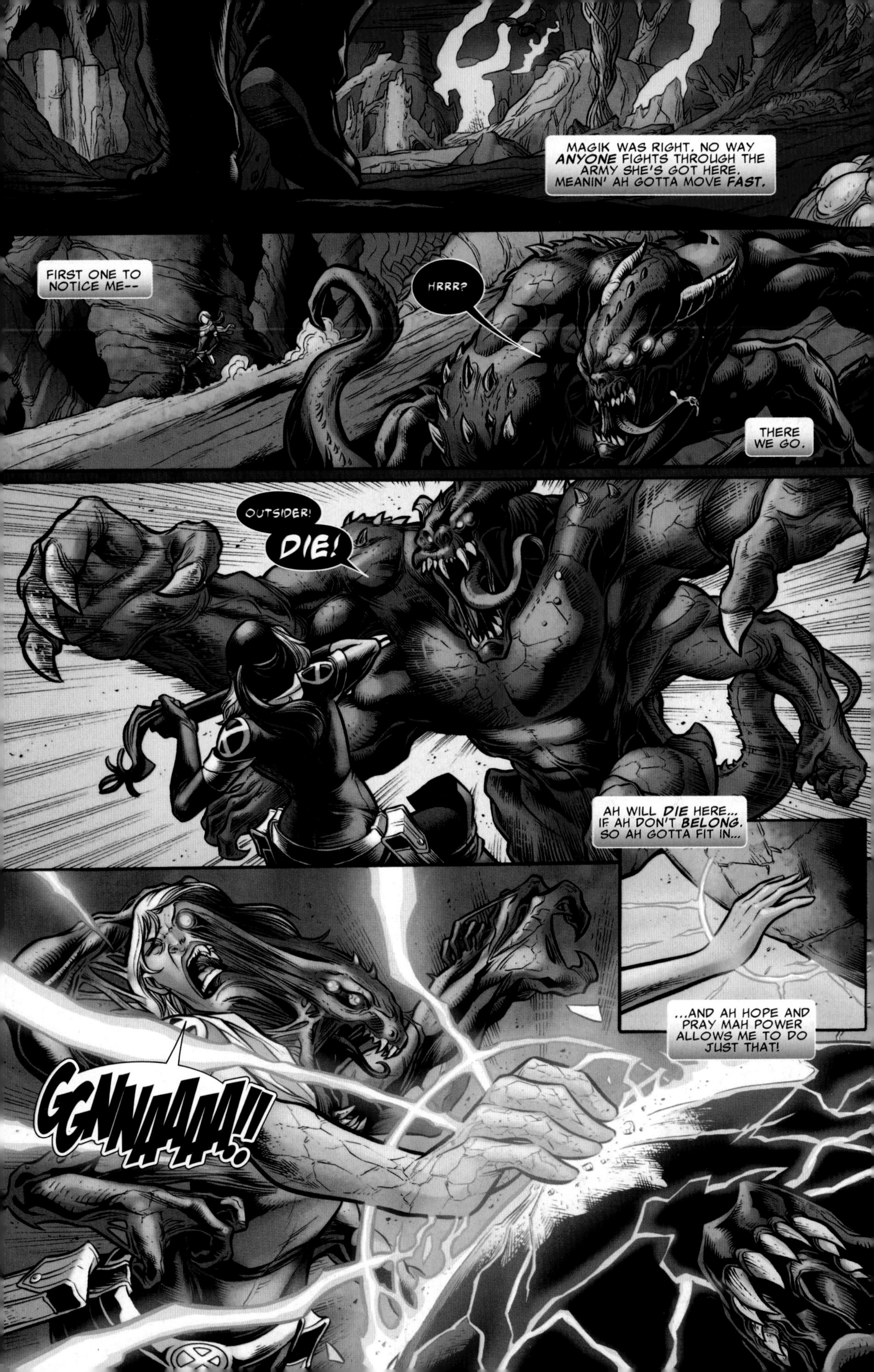
MAGIK WAS RIGHT. NO WAY ANYONE FIGHTS THROUGH THE ARMY SHE'S GOT HERE. MEANIN' AH GOTTA MOVE FAST.
FIRST ONE TO NOTICE ME--
HRRR?
THERE WE GO.
OUTSIDER! DIE!
AH WILL DIE HERE... IF AH DON'T BELONG. SO AH GOTTA FIT IN...
...AND AH HOPE AND PRAY MAH POWER ALLOWS ME TO DO JUST THAT!
GGNNAAAA!!

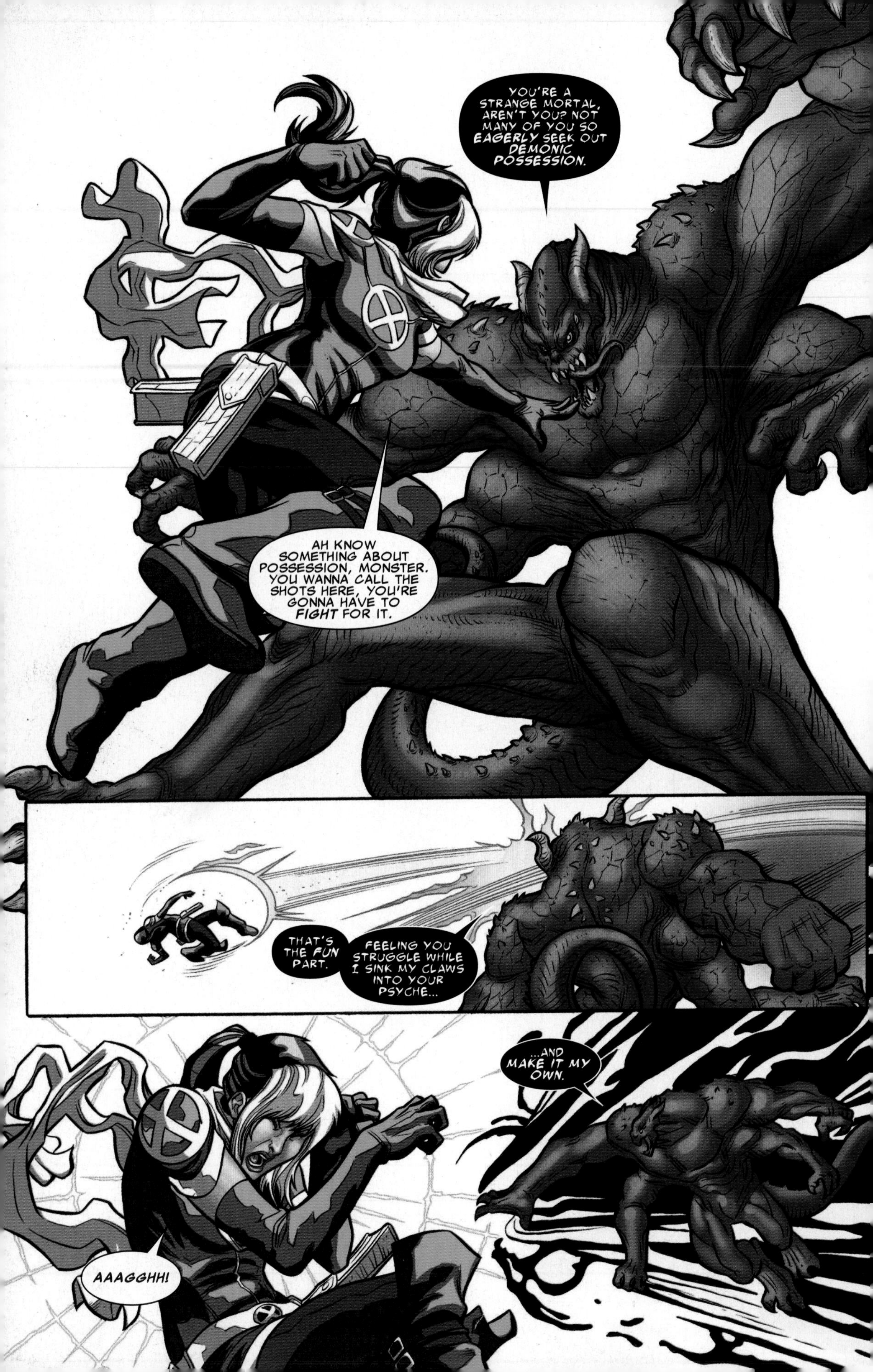
YOU'RE A STRANGE MORTAL, AREN'T YOU? NOT MANY OF YOU SO EAGERLY SEEK OUT DEMONIC POSSESSION.
AH KNOW SOMETHING ABOUT POSSESSION, MONSTER. YOU WANNA CALL THE SHOTS HERE, YOU'RE GONNA HAVE TO FIGHT FOR IT.
THAT'S THE FUN PART.
FEELING YOU STRUGGLE WHILE I SINK MY CLAWS INTO YOUR PSYCHE...
...AND MAKE IT MY OWN.
AAAGGHH!

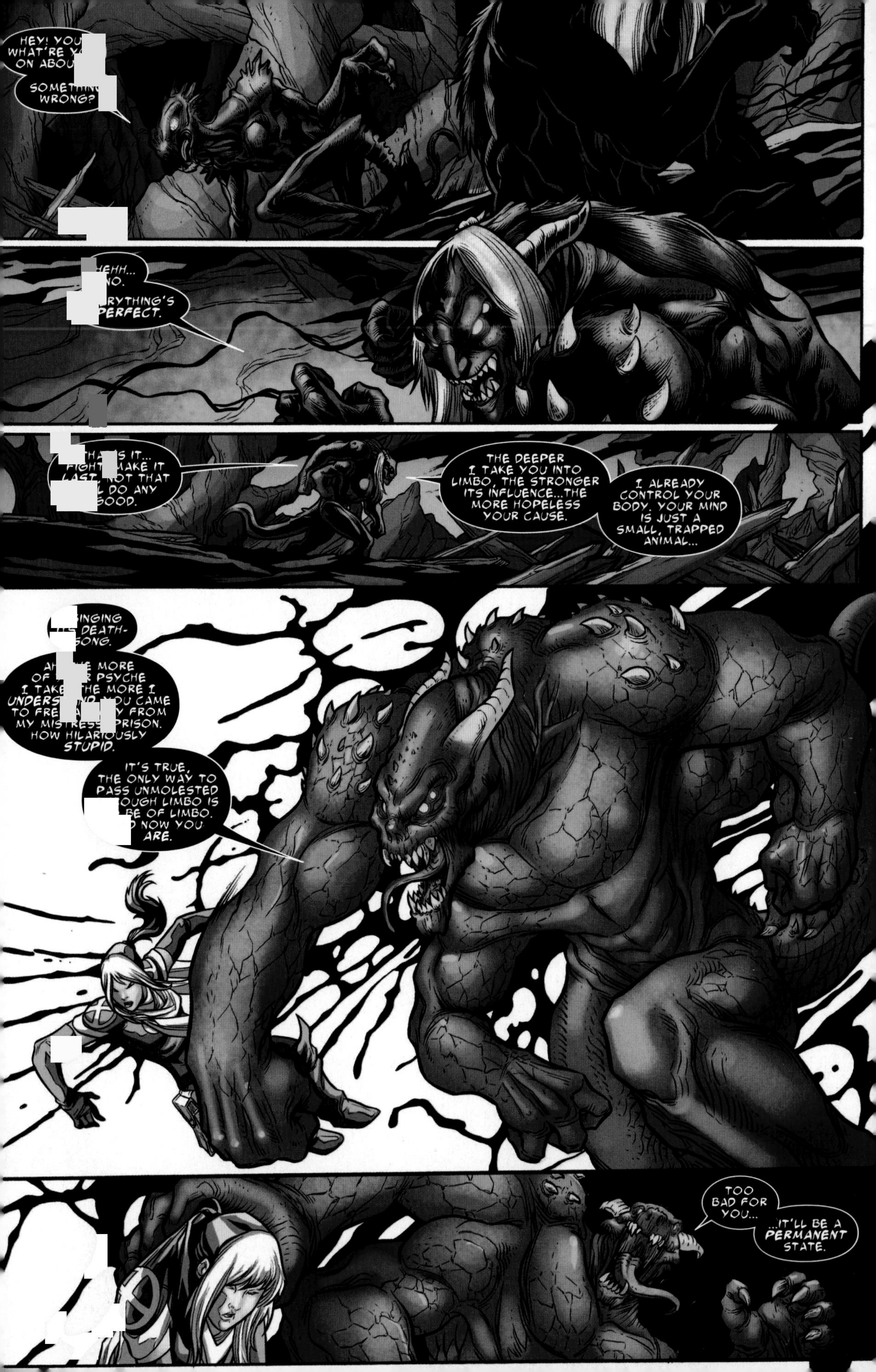

HEY! YOU WHAT'RE YO ON ABOU
SOMETHI WRONG?
HEHH... NO. RYTHING'S PERFECT.
THAT S IT... FIGHT MAKE IT LAST, NOT THAT DO ANY GOOD.
THE DEEPER I TAKE YOU INTO LIMBO, THE STRONGER ITS INFLUENCE...THE MORE HOPELESS YOUR CAUSE.
I ALREADY CONTROL YOUR BODY. YOUR MIND IS JUST A SMALL, TRAPPED ANIMAL...
SINGING DEATH- SONG.
AH E MORE OF R PSYCHE I TAKE THE MORE I UNDERS YOU CAME TO FRE Y FROM MY MISTRESS PRISON. HOW HILARIOUSLY STUPID.
IT'S TRUE, THE ONLY WAY TO PASS UNMOLESTED OUGH LIMBO IS BE OF LIMBO. D NOW YOU ARE.
TOO BAD FOR YOU...
...IT'LL BE A PERMANENT STATE.

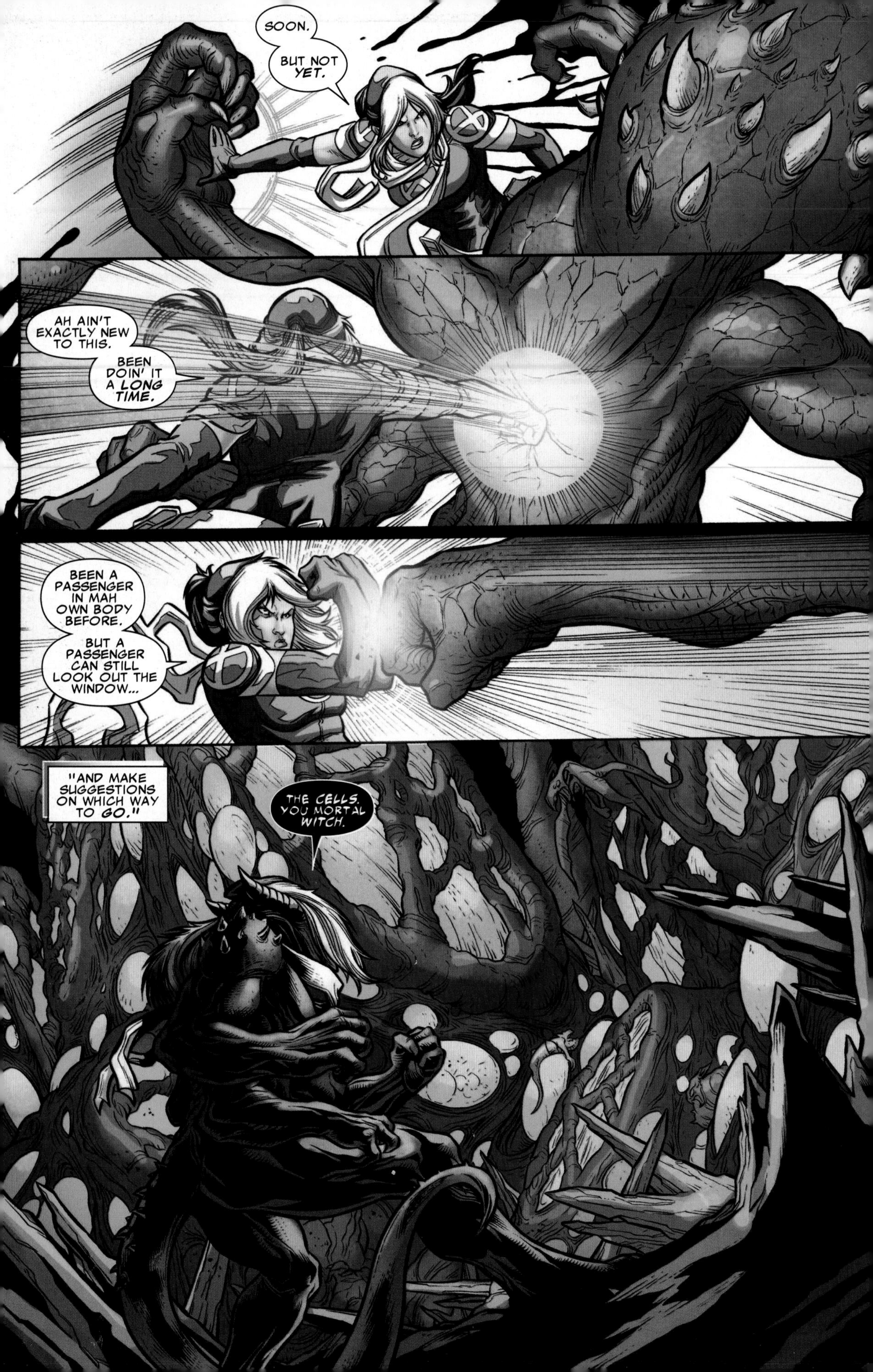
SOON.
BUT NOT YET.
AH AIN'T EXACTLY NEW TO THIS.
BEEN DOIN' IT A LONG TIME.
BEEN A PASSENGER IN MAH OWN BODY BEFORE.
BUT A PASSENGER CAN STILL LOOK OUT THE WINDOW...
"AND MAKE SUGGESTIONS ON WHICH WAY TO GO."
THE CELLS. YOU MORTAL WITCH.

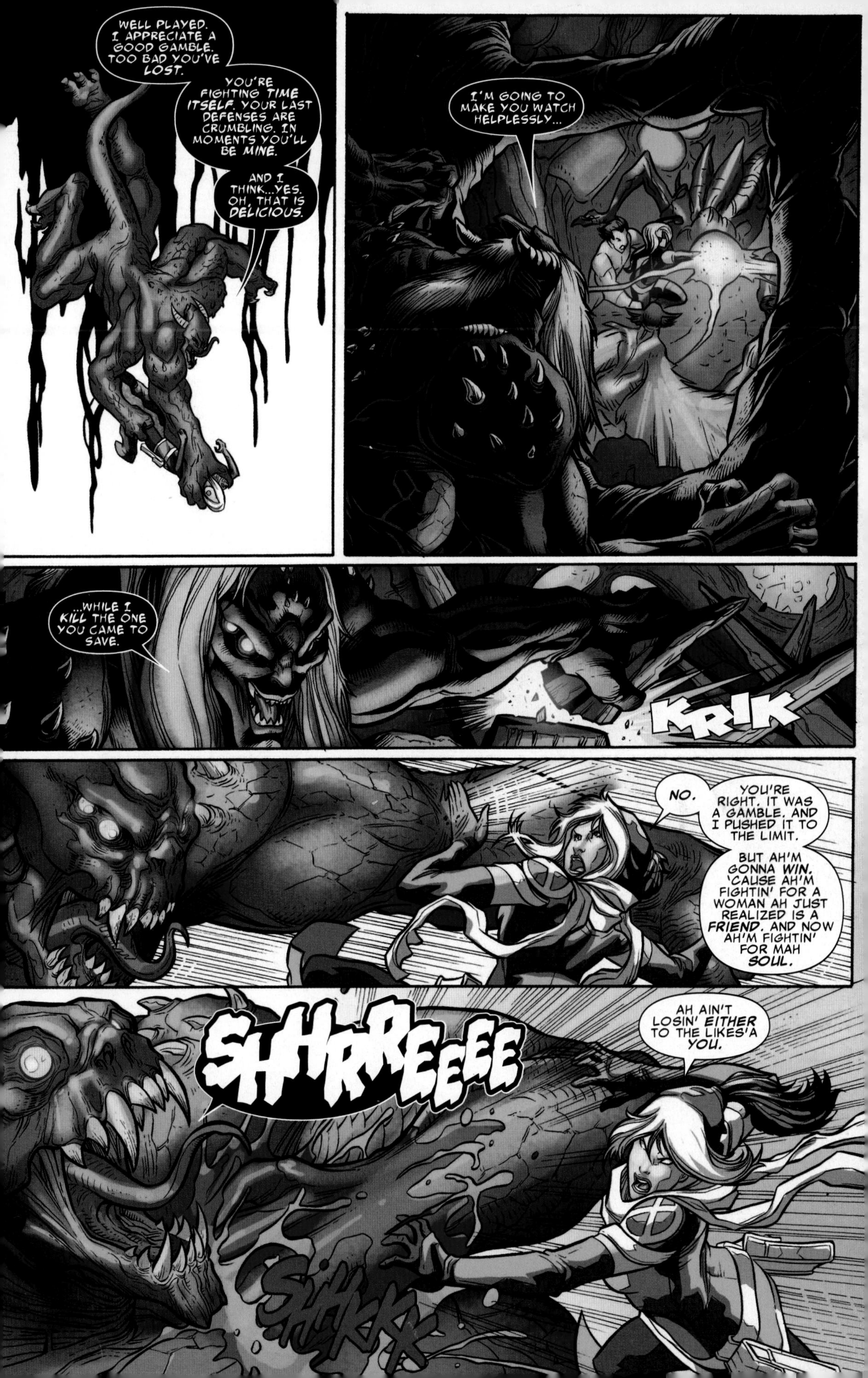
WELL PLAYED. I APPRECIATE A GOOD GAMBLE. TOO BAD YOU'VE LOST.
YOU'RE FIGHTING TIME ITSELF. YOUR LAST DEFENSES ARE CRUMBLING. IN MOMENTS YOU'LL BE MINE.
AND I THINK...YES. OH, THAT IS DELICIOUS.
I'M GOING TO MAKE YOU WATCH HELPLESSLY...
...WHILE I KILL THE ONE YOU CAME TO SAVE.
KRIK
NO.
YOU'RE RIGHT. IT WAS A GAMBLE, AND I PUSHED IT TO THE LIMIT.
BUT AH'M GONNA WIN, 'CAUSE AH'M FIGHTIN' FOR A WOMAN AH JUST REALIZED IS A FRIEND. AND NOW AH'M FIGHTIN' FOR MAH SOUL.
SHHRREEEE
AH AIN'T LOSIN' EITHER TO THE LIKES'A YOU.
SHKKK

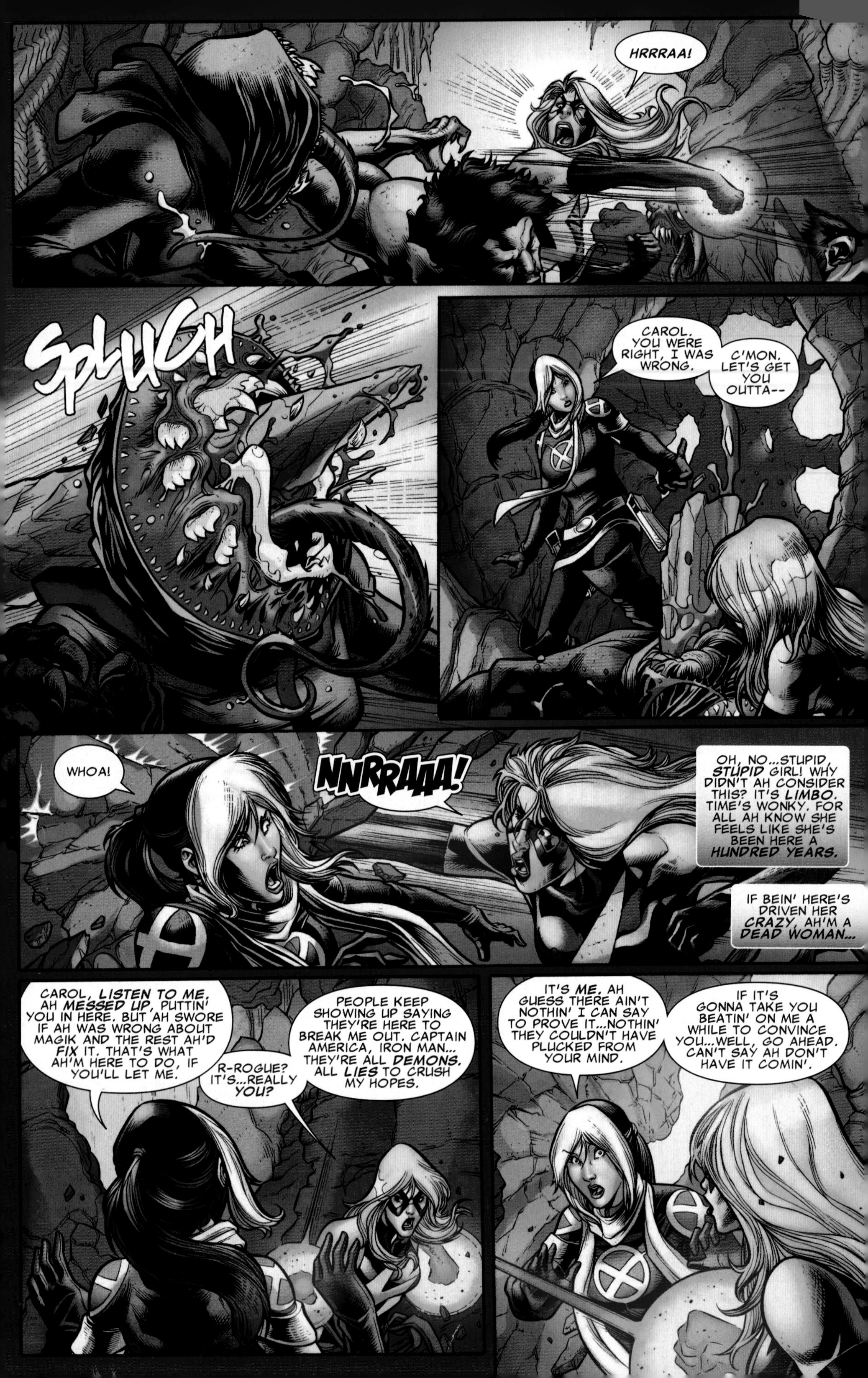
HRRRAA!
SPLUCH
CAROL. YOU WERE RIGHT, I WAS WRONG.
C'MON. LET'S GET YOU OUTTA--
WHOA!
NNRRAAA!
OH, NO...STUPID, STUPID GIRL! WHY DIDN'T AH CONSIDER THIS? IT'S LIMBO. TIME'S WONKY. FOR ALL AH KNOW SHE FEELS LIKE SHE'S BEEN HERE A HUNDRED YEARS.
IF BEIN' HERE'S DRIVEN HER CRAZY, AH'M A DEAD WOMAN...
CAROL, LISTEN TO ME. AH MESSED UP, PUTTIN' YOU IN HERE. BUT AH SWORE IF AH WAS WRONG ABOUT MAGIK AND THE REST AH'D FIX IT. THAT'S WHAT AH'M HERE TO DO, IF YOU'LL LET ME.
R-ROGUE? IT'S...REALLY YOU?
PEOPLE KEEP SHOWING UP SAYING THEY'RE HERE TO BREAK ME OUT. CAPTAIN AMERICA, IRON MAN... THEY'RE ALL DEMONS. ALL LIES TO CRUSH MY HOPES.
IT'S ME. AH GUESS THERE AIN'T NOTHIN' I CAN SAY TO PROVE IT...NOTHIN' THEY COULDN'T HAVE PLUCKED FROM YOUR MIND.
IF IT'S GONNA TAKE YOU A WHILE TO CONVINCE YOU...WELL, GO AHEAD. CAN'T SAY AH DON'T HAVE IT COMIN'.

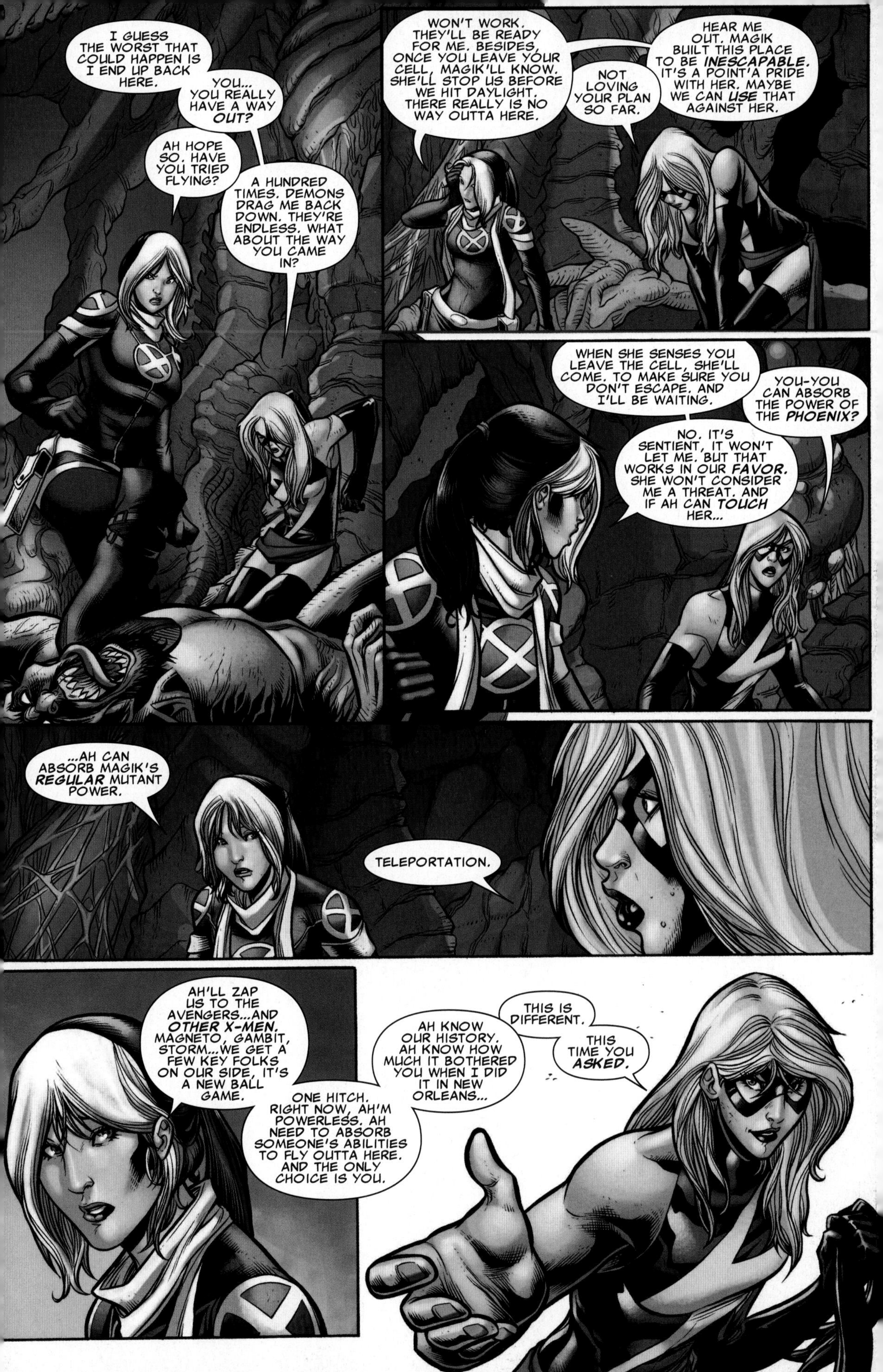

I GUESS THE WORST THAT COULD HAPPEN IS I END UP BACK HERE.
YOU... YOU REALLY HAVE A WAY OUT?
AH HOPE SO. HAVE YOU TRIED FLYING?
A HUNDRED TIMES. DEMONS DRAG ME BACK DOWN. THEY'RE ENDLESS. WHAT ABOUT THE WAY YOU CAME IN?
WON'T WORK. THEY'LL BE READY FOR ME. BESIDES, ONCE YOU LEAVE YOUR CELL, MAGIK'LL KNOW. SHE'LL STOP US BEFORE WE HIT DAYLIGHT. THERE REALLY IS NO WAY OUTTA HERE.
NOT LOVING YOUR PLAN SO FAR.
HEAR ME OUT. MAGIK BUILT THIS PLACE TO BE INESCAPABLE. IT'S A POINT'A PRIDE WITH HER. MAYBE WE CAN USE THAT AGAINST HER.
WHEN SHE SENSES YOU LEAVE THE CELL, SHE'LL COME, TO MAKE SURE YOU DON'T ESCAPE. AND I'LL BE WAITING.
YOU-YOU CAN ABSORB THE POWER OF THE PHOENIX?
NO. IT'S SENTIENT, IT WON'T LET ME. BUT THAT WORKS IN OUR FAVOR. SHE WON'T CONSIDER ME A THREAT. AND IF AH CAN TOUCH HER...
...AH CAN ABSORB MAGIK'S REGULAR MUTANT POWER.
TELEPORTATION.
AH'LL ZAP US TO THE AVENGERS...AND OTHER X-MEN. MAGNETO, GAMBIT, STORM...WE GET A FEW KEY FOLKS ON OUR SIDE, IT'S A NEW BALL GAME.
ONE HITCH. RIGHT NOW, AH'M POWERLESS. AH NEED TO ABSORB SOMEONE'S ABILITIES TO FLY OUTTA HERE. AND THE ONLY CHOICE IS YOU.
AH KNOW OUR HISTORY. AH KNOW HOW MUCH IT BOTHERED YOU WHEN I DID IT IN NEW ORLEANS...
THIS IS DIFFERENT.
THIS TIME YOU ASKED.

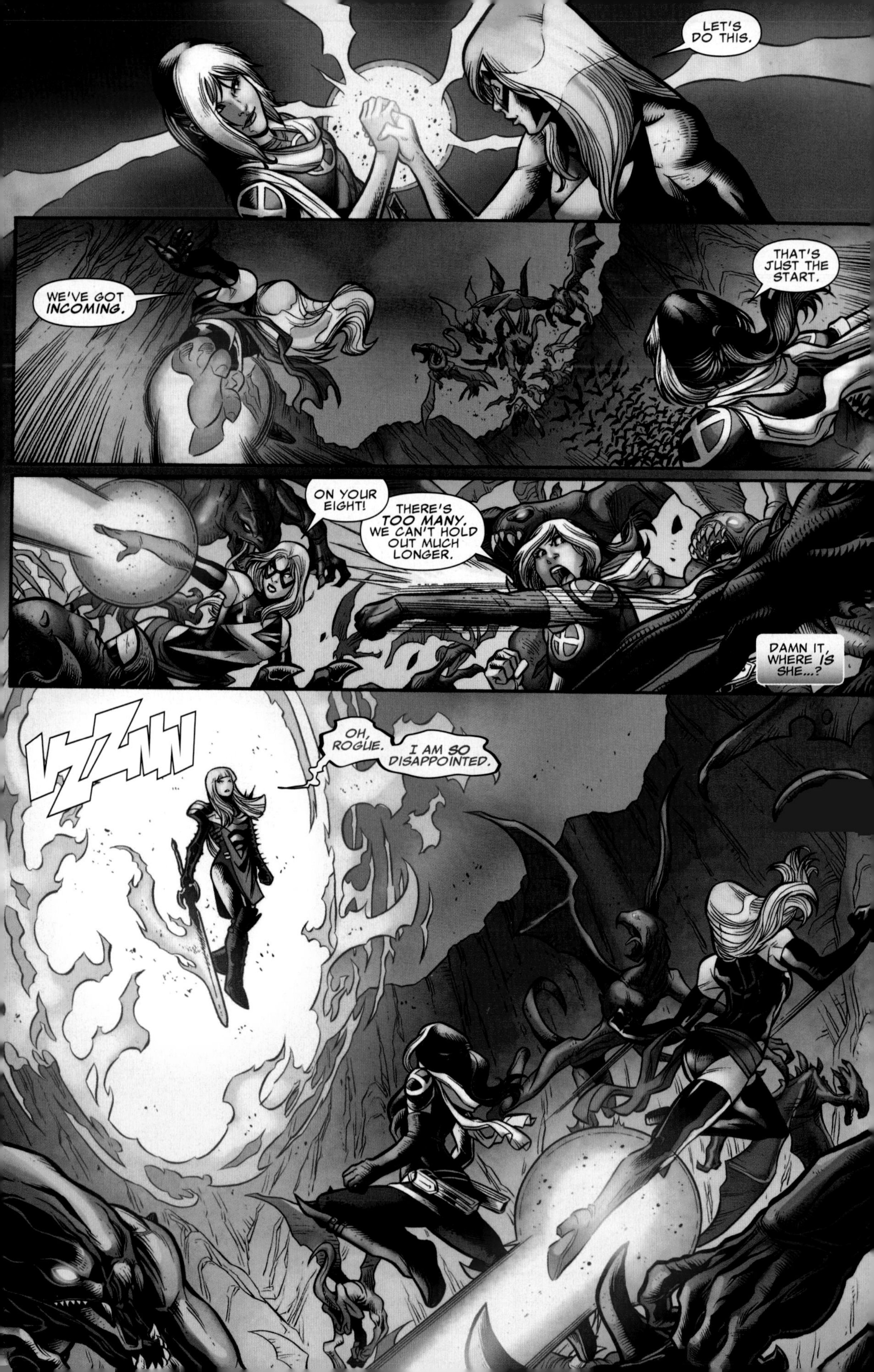
LET'S DO THIS.
WE'VE GOT INCOMING.
THAT'S JUST THE START.
ON YOUR EIGHT!
THERE'S TOO MANY. WE CAN'T HOLD OUT MUCH LONGER.
DAMN IT, WHERE IS SHE...?
VZZNN
OH, ROGUE.
I AM SO DISAPPOINTED.

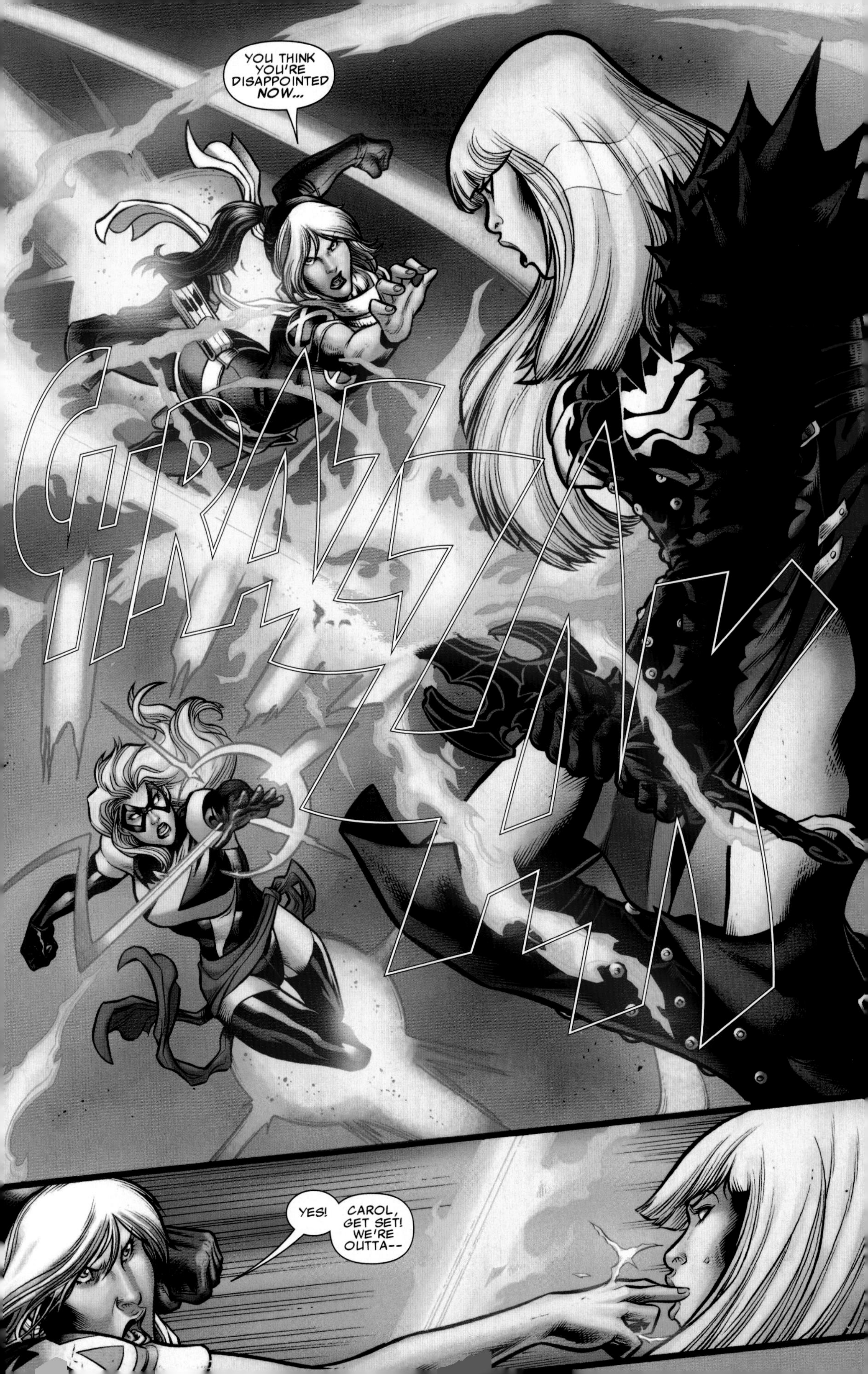
YOU THINK YOU'RE DISAPPOINTED NOW...
YES!
CAROL, GET SET! WE'RE OUTTA--

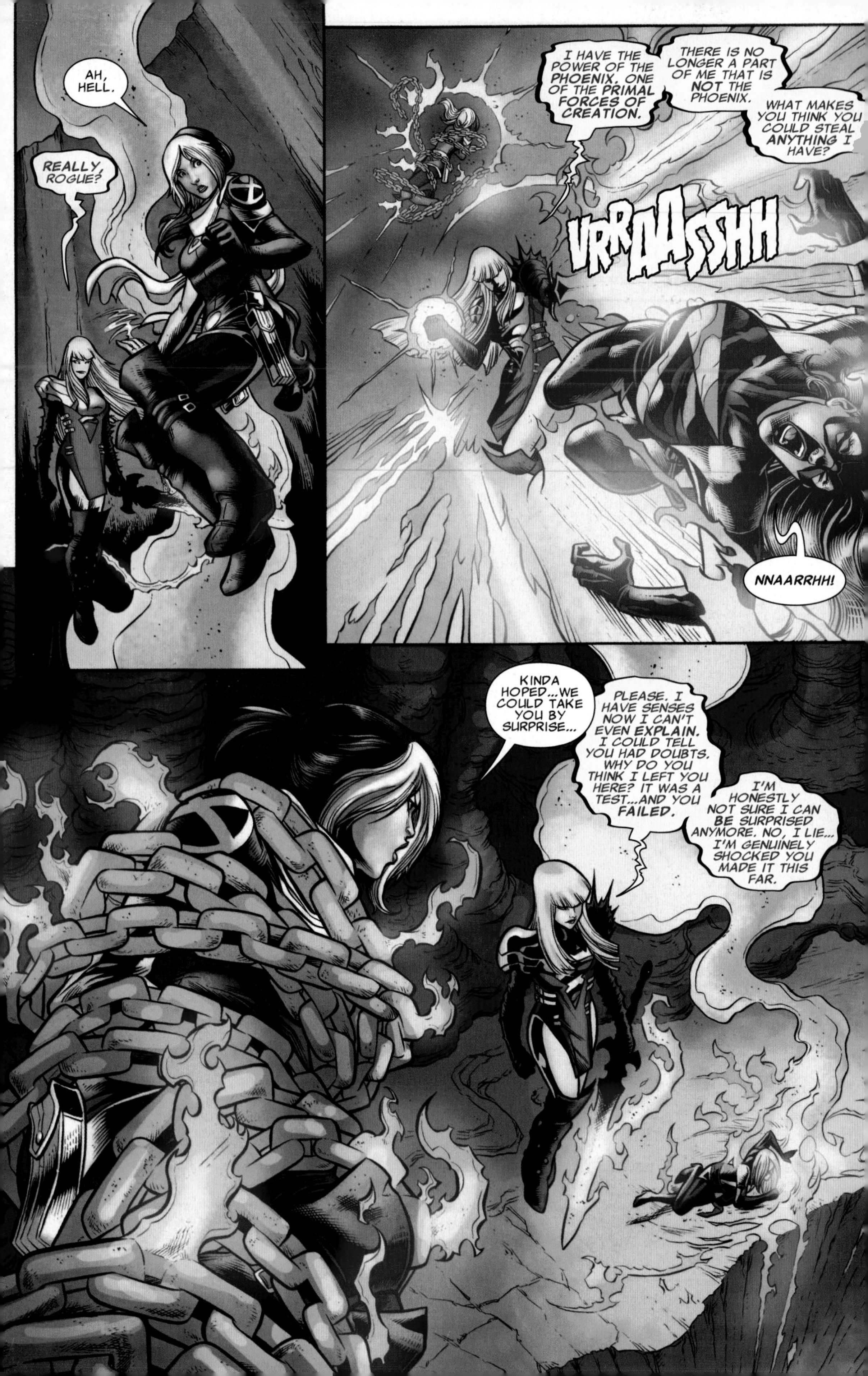
AH, HELL.
REALLY, ROGUE?
I HAVE THE POWER OF THE PHOENIX, ONE OF THE PRIMAL FORCES OF CREATION.
THERE IS NO LONGER A PART OF ME THAT IS NOT THE PHOENIX.
WHAT MAKES YOU THINK YOU COULD STEAL ANYTHING I HAVE?
VRRAASSHH
NNAARRHH!
KINDA HOPED...WE COULD TAKE YOU BY SURPRISE...
PLEASE. I HAVE SENSES NOW I CAN'T EVEN EXPLAIN. I COULD TELL YOU HAD DOUBTS. WHY DO YOU THINK I LEFT YOU HERE? IT WAS A TEST...AND YOU FAILED.
I'M HONESTLY NOT SURE I CAN BE SURPRISED ANYMORE. NO, I LIE... I'M GENUINELY SHOCKED YOU MADE IT THIS FAR.

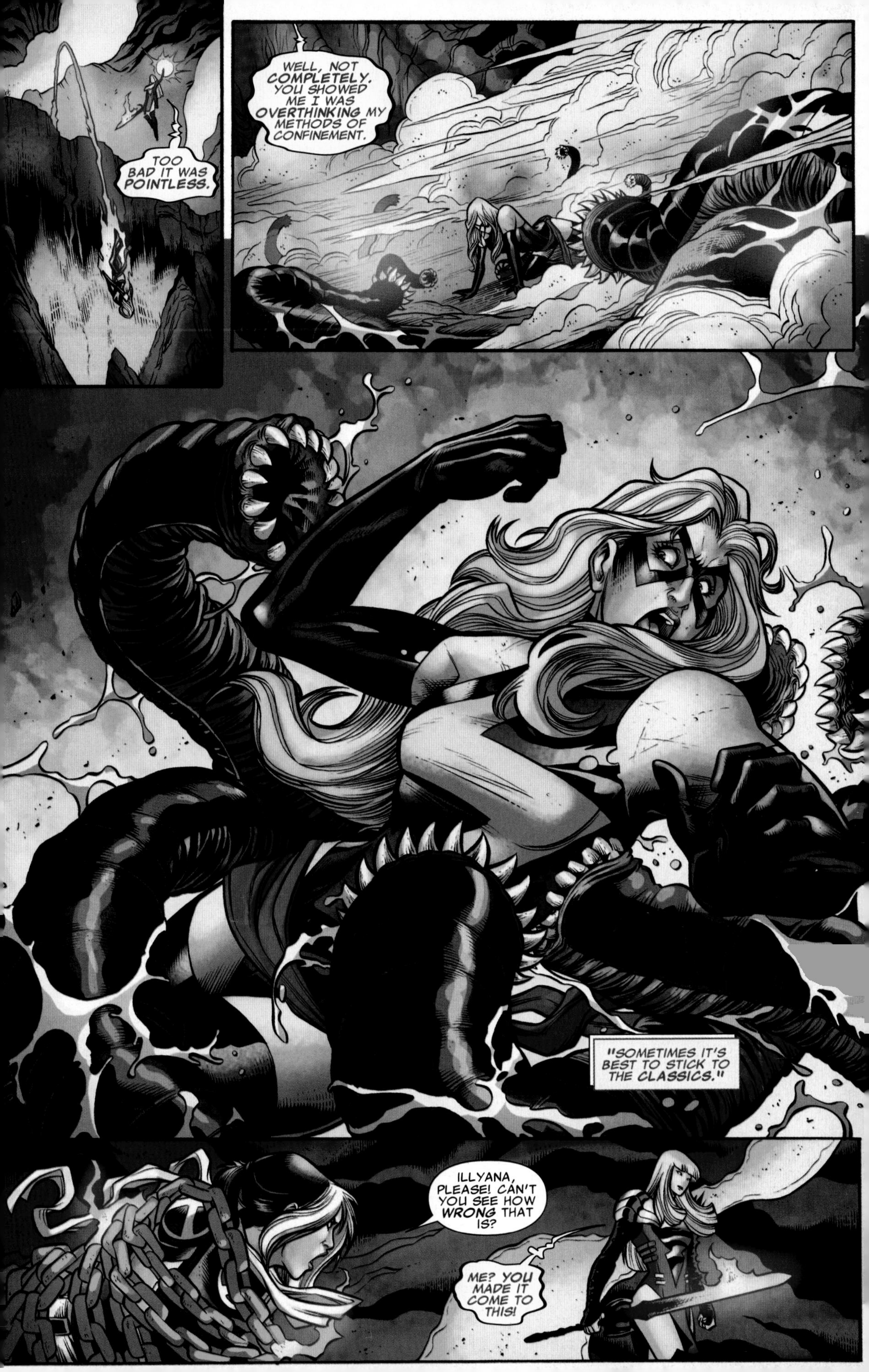
TOO BAD IT WAS POINTLESS.
WELL, NOT COMPLETELY. YOU SHOWED ME I WAS OVERTHINKING MY METHODS OF CONFINEMENT.
"SOMETIMES IT'S BEST TO STICK TO THE CLASSICS."
ILLYANA, PLEASE! CAN'T YOU SEE HOW WRONG THAT IS?
ME? YOU MADE IT COME TO THIS!

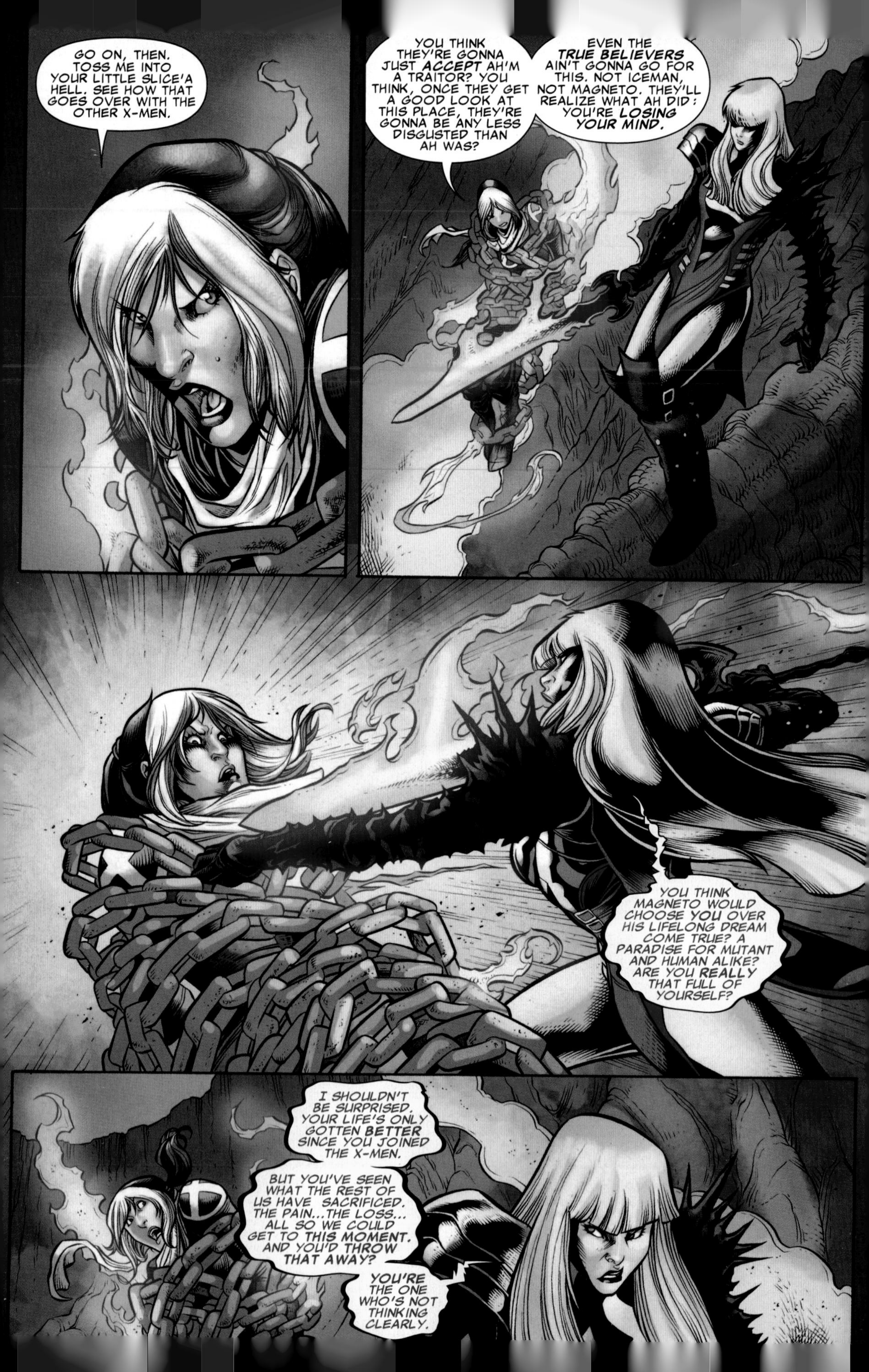
GO ON, THEN. TOSS ME INTO YOUR LITTLE SLICE'A HELL. SEE HOW THAT GOES OVER WITH THE OTHER X-MEN.
YOU THINK THEY'RE GONNA JUST ACCEPT AH'M A TRAITOR? YOU THINK, ONCE THEY GET A GOOD LOOK AT THIS PLACE, THEY'RE GONNA BE ANY LESS DISGUSTED THAN AH WAS?
EVEN THE TRUE BELIEVERS AIN'T GONNA GO FOR THIS. NOT ICEMAN, NOT MAGNETO. THEY'LL REALIZE WHAT AH DID: YOU'RE LOSING YOUR MIND.
YOU THINK MAGNETO WOULD CHOOSE YOU OVER HIS LIFELONG DREAM COME TRUE? A PARADISE FOR MUTANT AND HUMAN ALIKE? ARE YOU REALLY THAT FULL OF YOURSELF?
I SHOULDN'T BE SURPRISED. YOUR LIFE'S ONLY GOTTEN BETTER SINCE YOU JOINED THE X-MEN.
BUT YOU'VE SEEN WHAT THE REST OF US HAVE SACRIFICED. THE PAIN...THE LOSS... ALL SO WE COULD GET TO THIS MOMENT. AND YOU'D THROW THAT AWAY?
YOU'RE THE ONE WHO'S NOT THINKING CLEARLY.

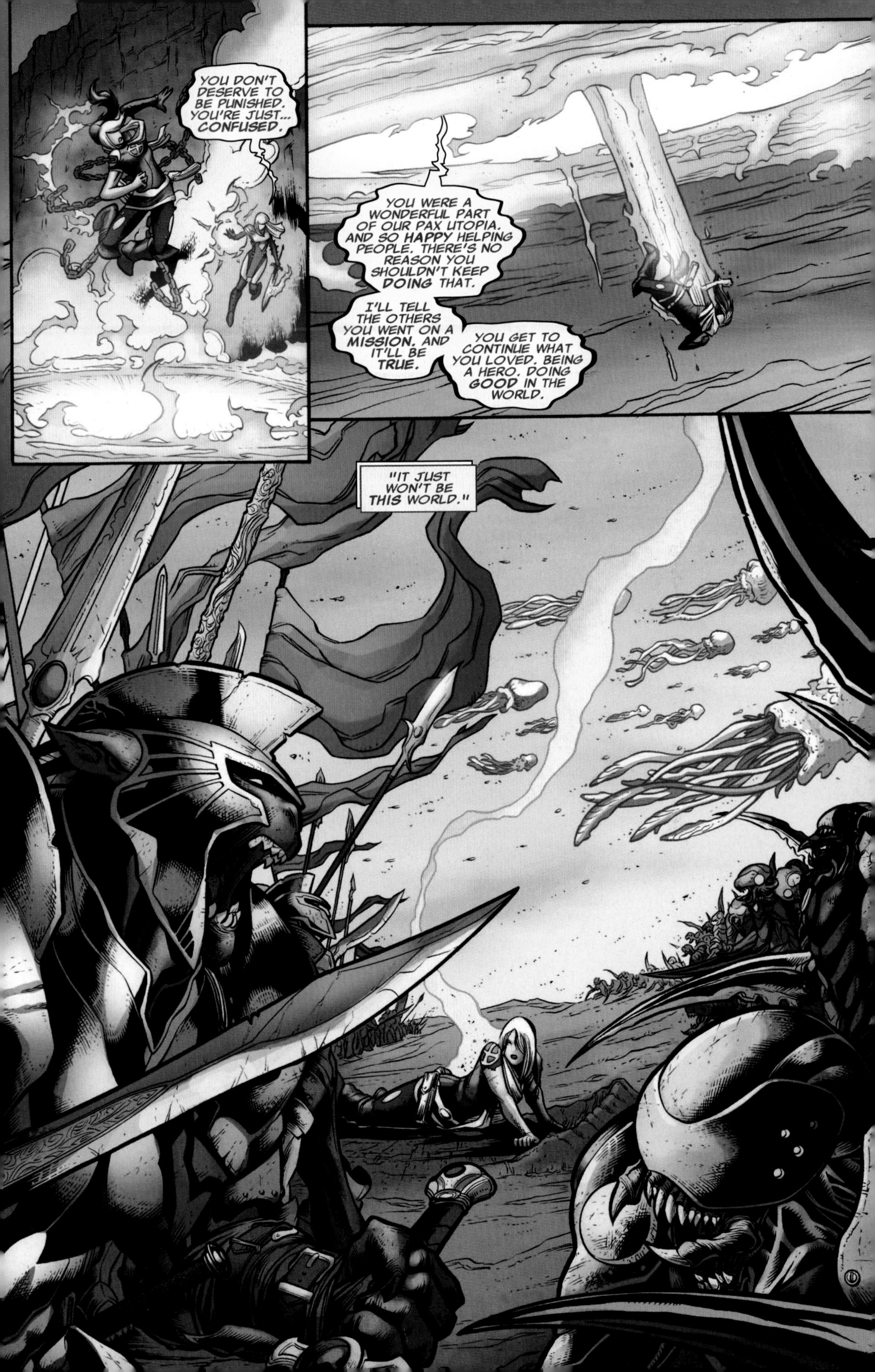
YOU DON'T DESERVE TO BE PUNISHED. YOU'RE JUST... CONFUSED.
YOU WERE A WONDERFUL PART OF OUR PAX UTOPIA. AND SO HAPPY HELPING PEOPLE. THERE'S NO REASON YOU SHOULDN'T KEEP DOING THAT.
I'LL TELL THE OTHERS YOU WENT ON A MISSION. AND IT'LL BE TRUE.
YOU GET TO CONTINUE WHAT YOU LOVED. BEING A HERO. DOING GOOD IN THE WORLD.
"IT JUST WON'T BE THIS WORLD."

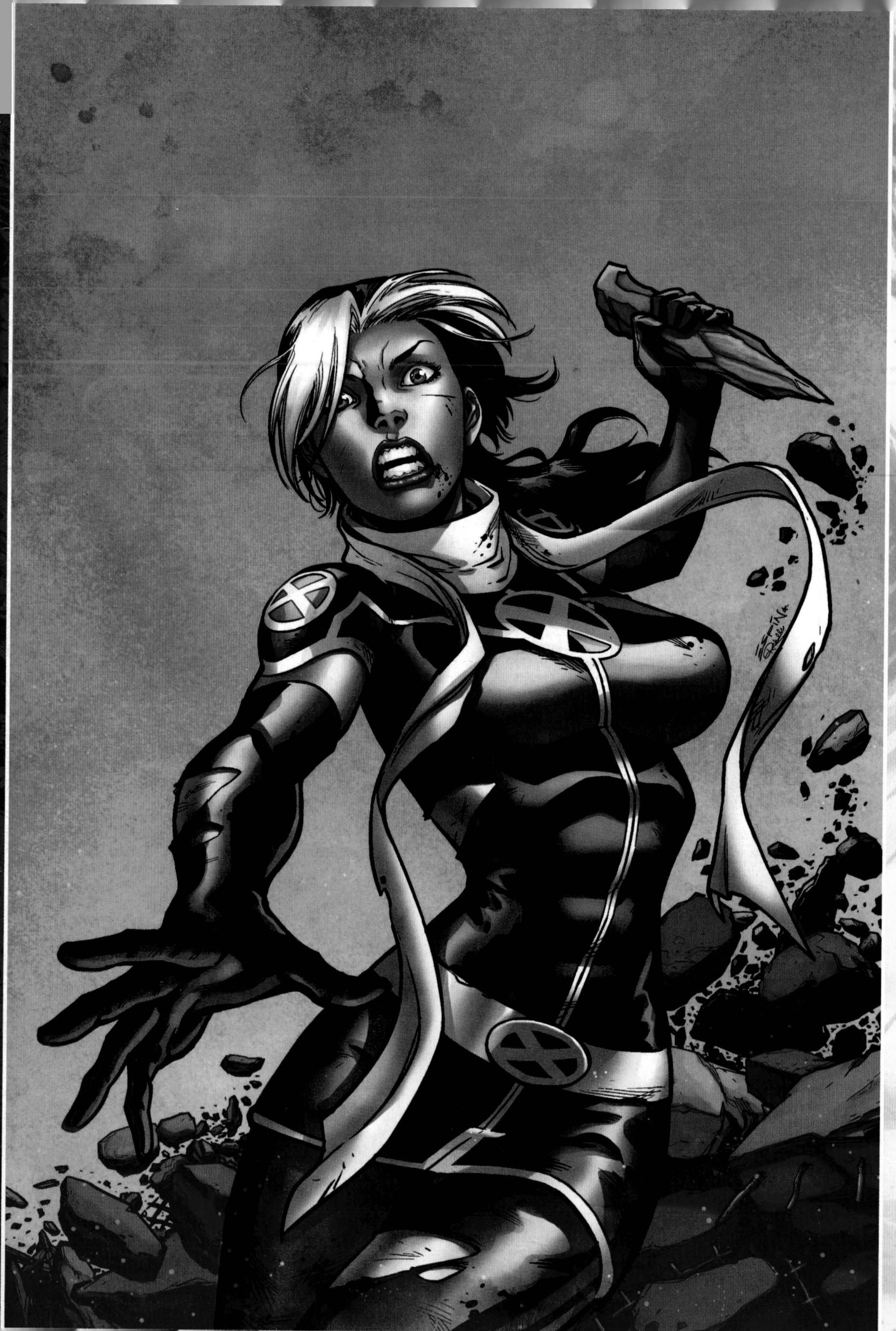

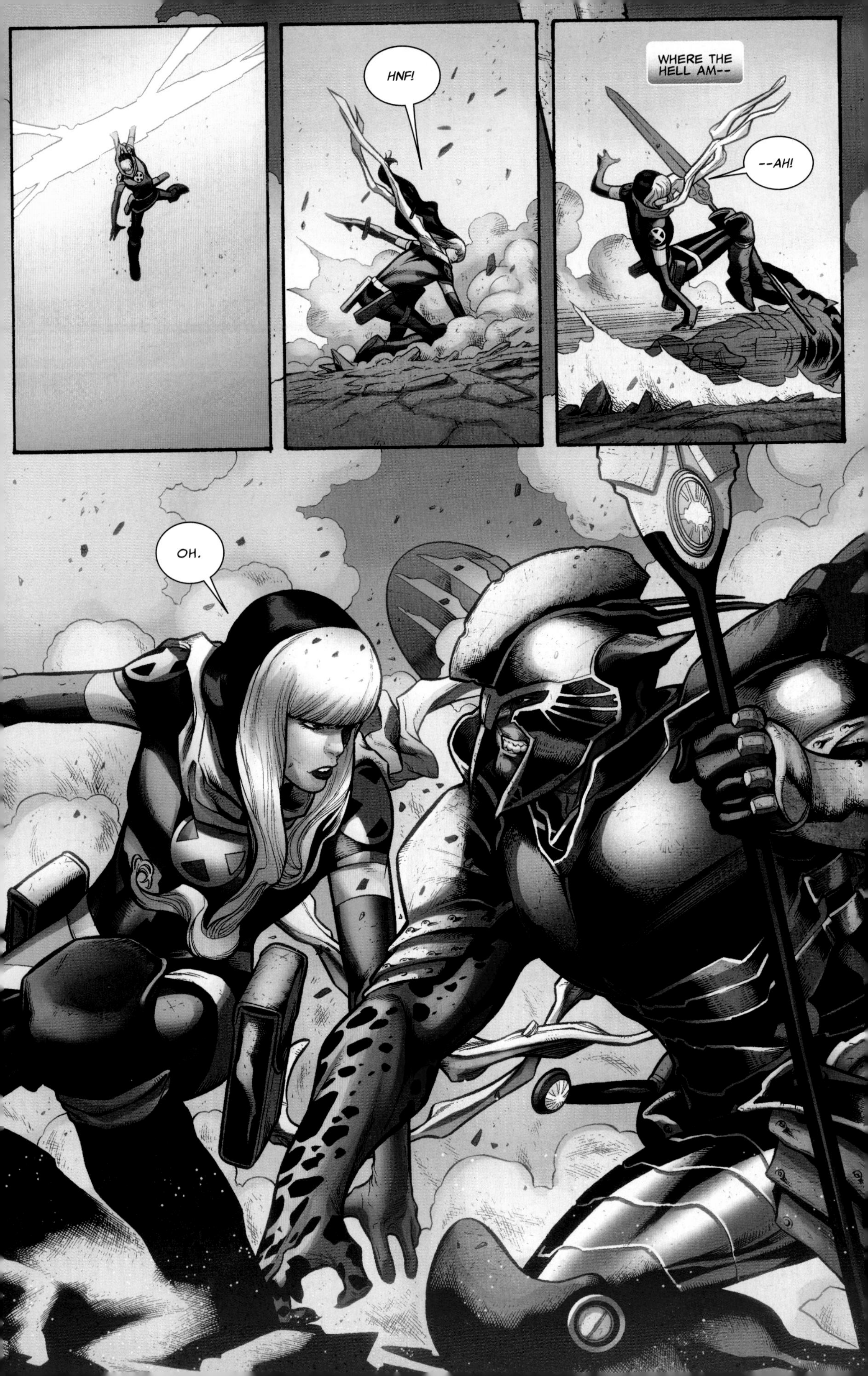
HNF!
WHERE THE HELL AM--
--AH!
OH.

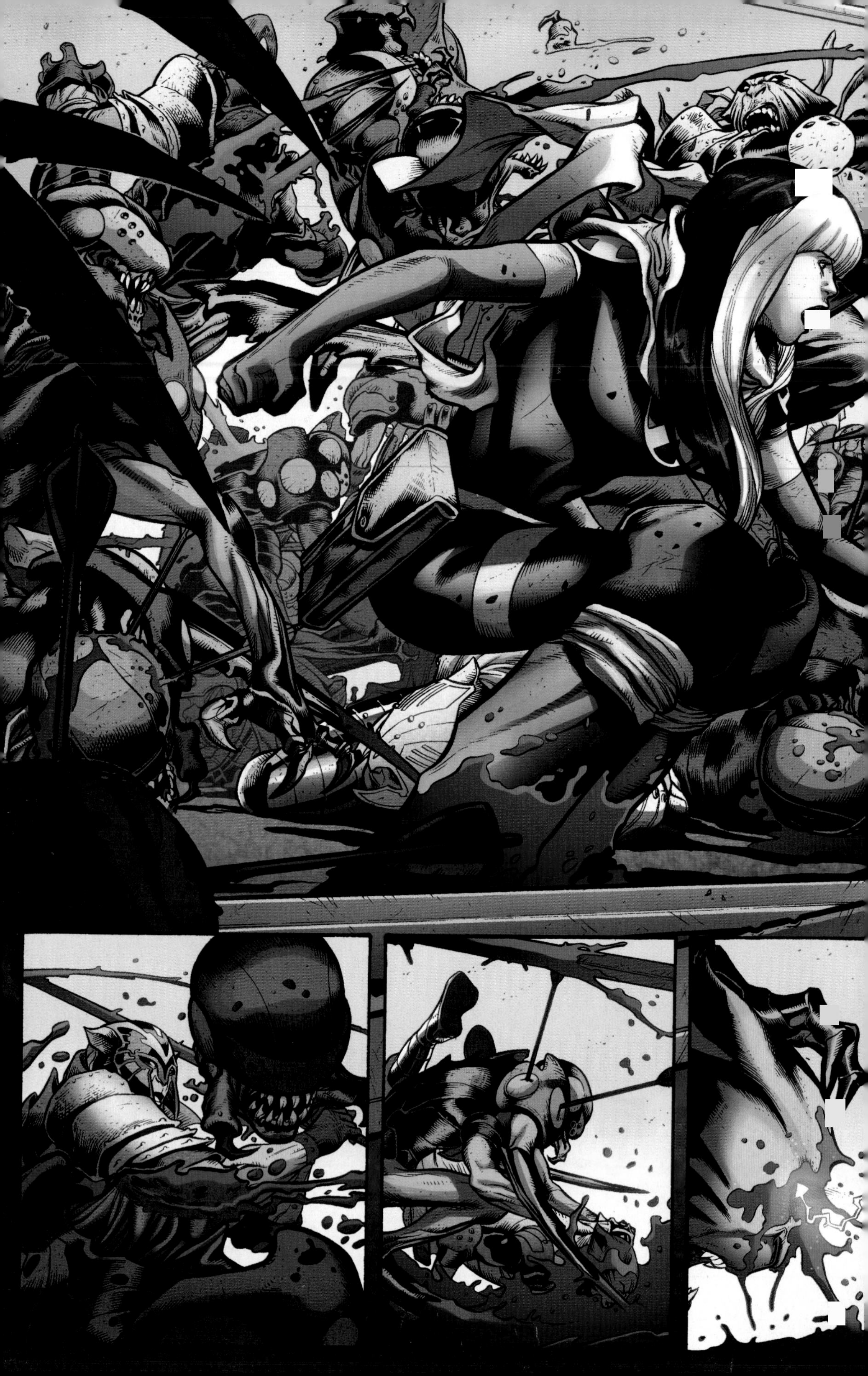

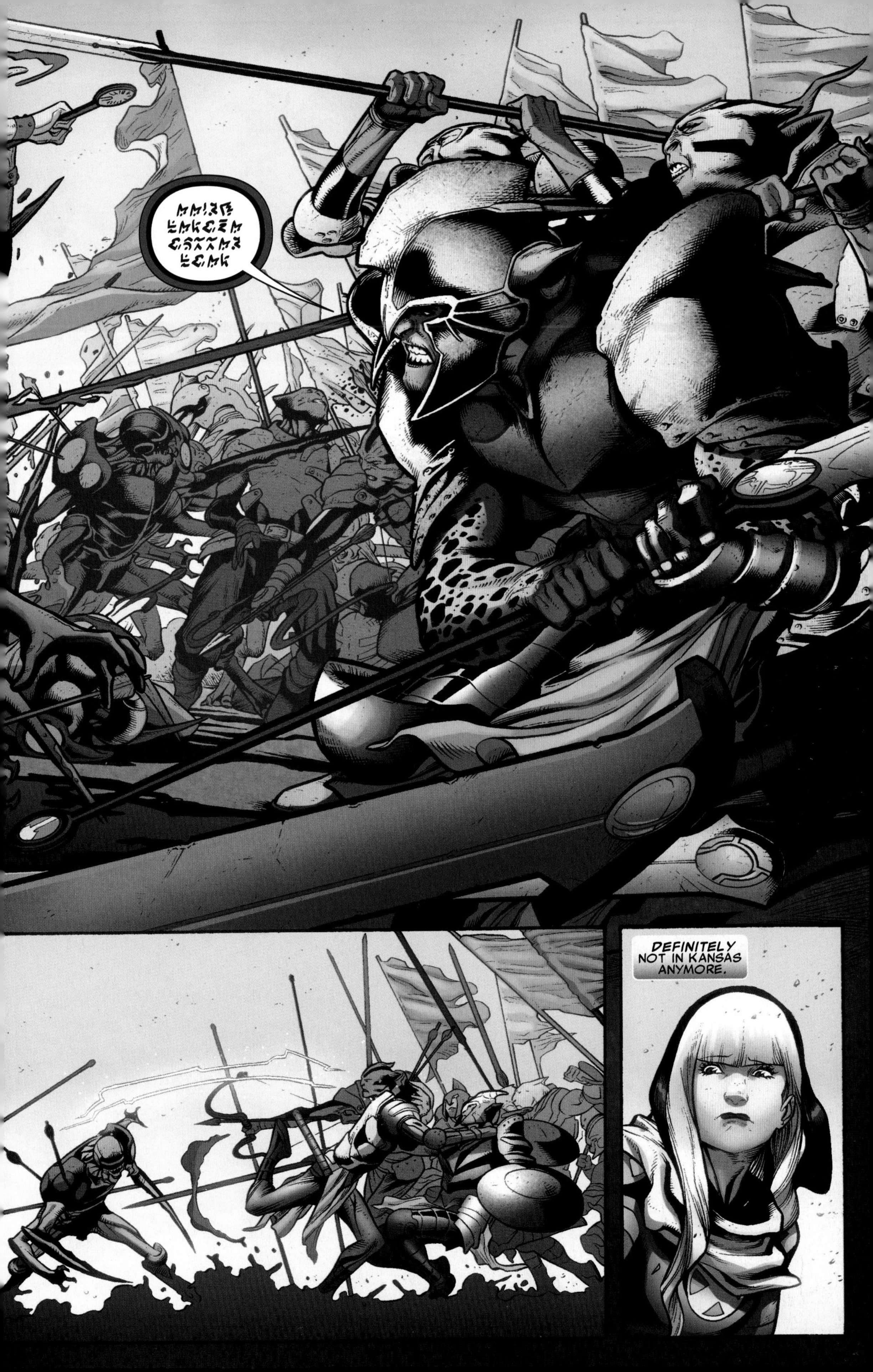
DEFINITELY NOT IN KANSAS ANYMORE.

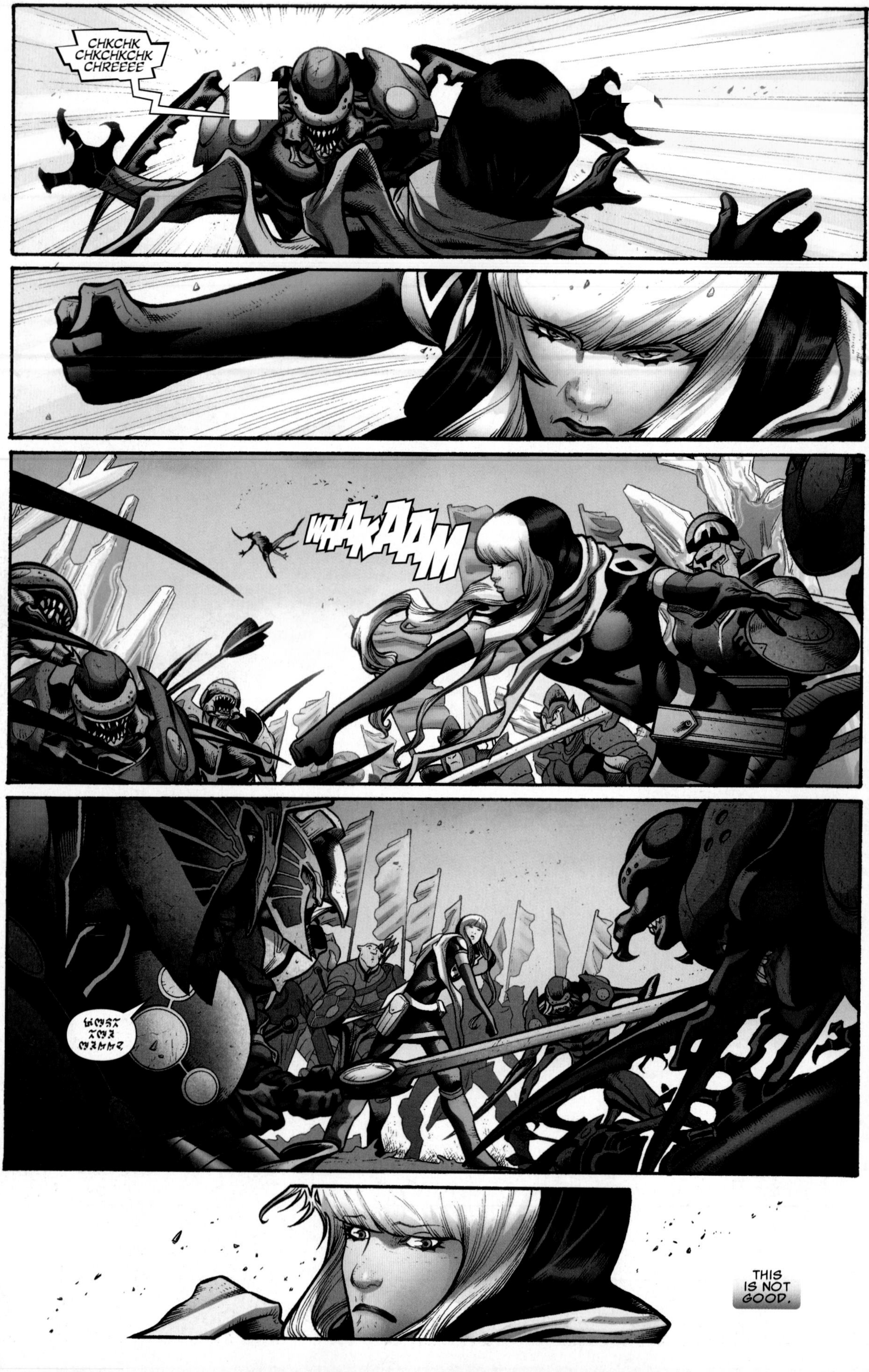
CHKCHK CHKCHKCHK CHREEEE
WHAKAAM
THIS IS NOT GOOD.

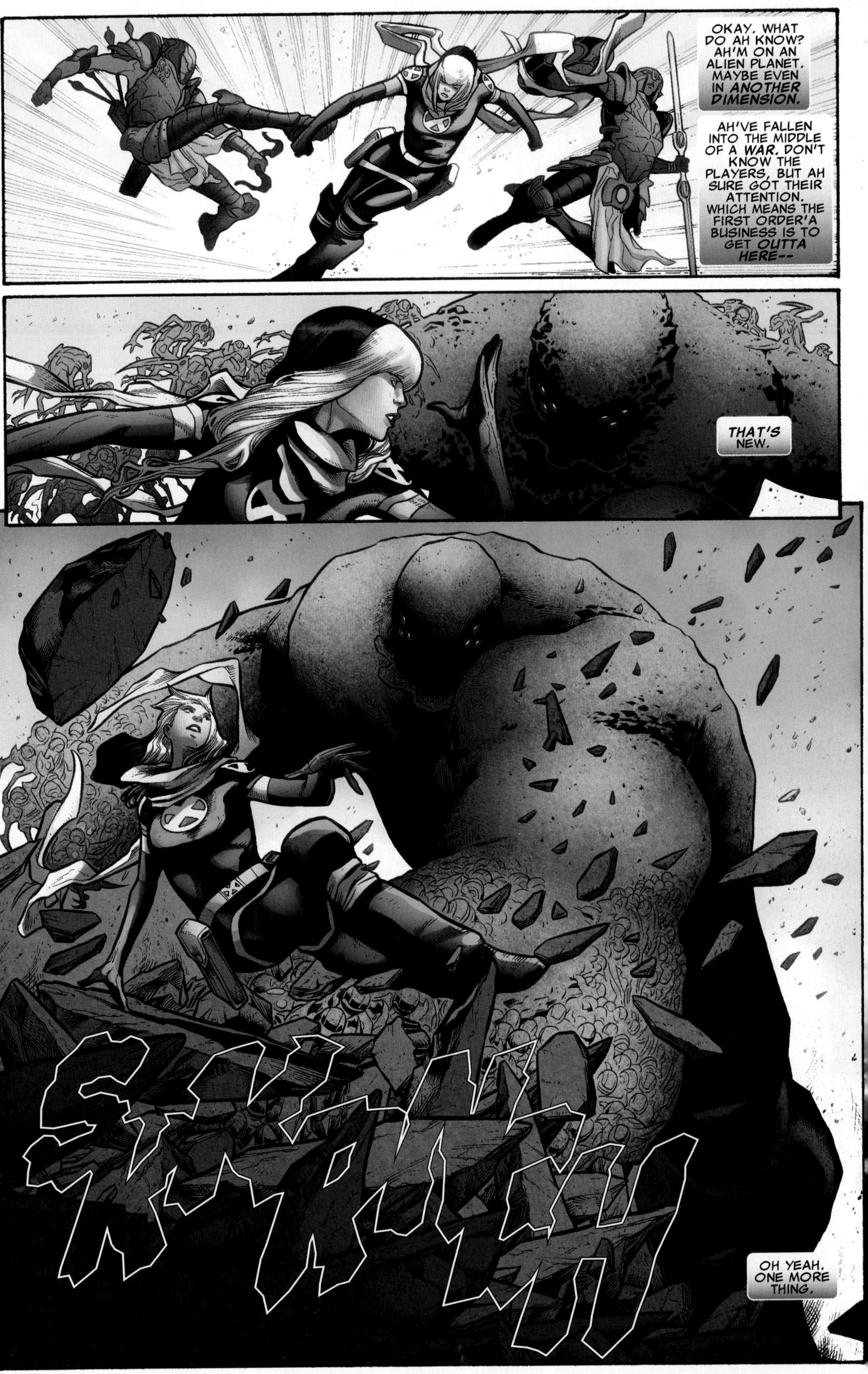
OKAY. WHAT DO AH KNOW? AH'M ON AN ALIEN PLANET. MAYBE EVEN IN ANOTHER DIMENSION.
AH'VE FALLEN INTO THE MIDDLE OF A WAR. DON'T KNOW THE PLAYERS, BUT AH SURE GOT THEIR ATTENTION. WHICH MEANS THE FIRST ORDER'A BUSINESS IS TO GET OUTTA HERE--
THAT'S NEW.
OH YEAH. ONE MORE THING.

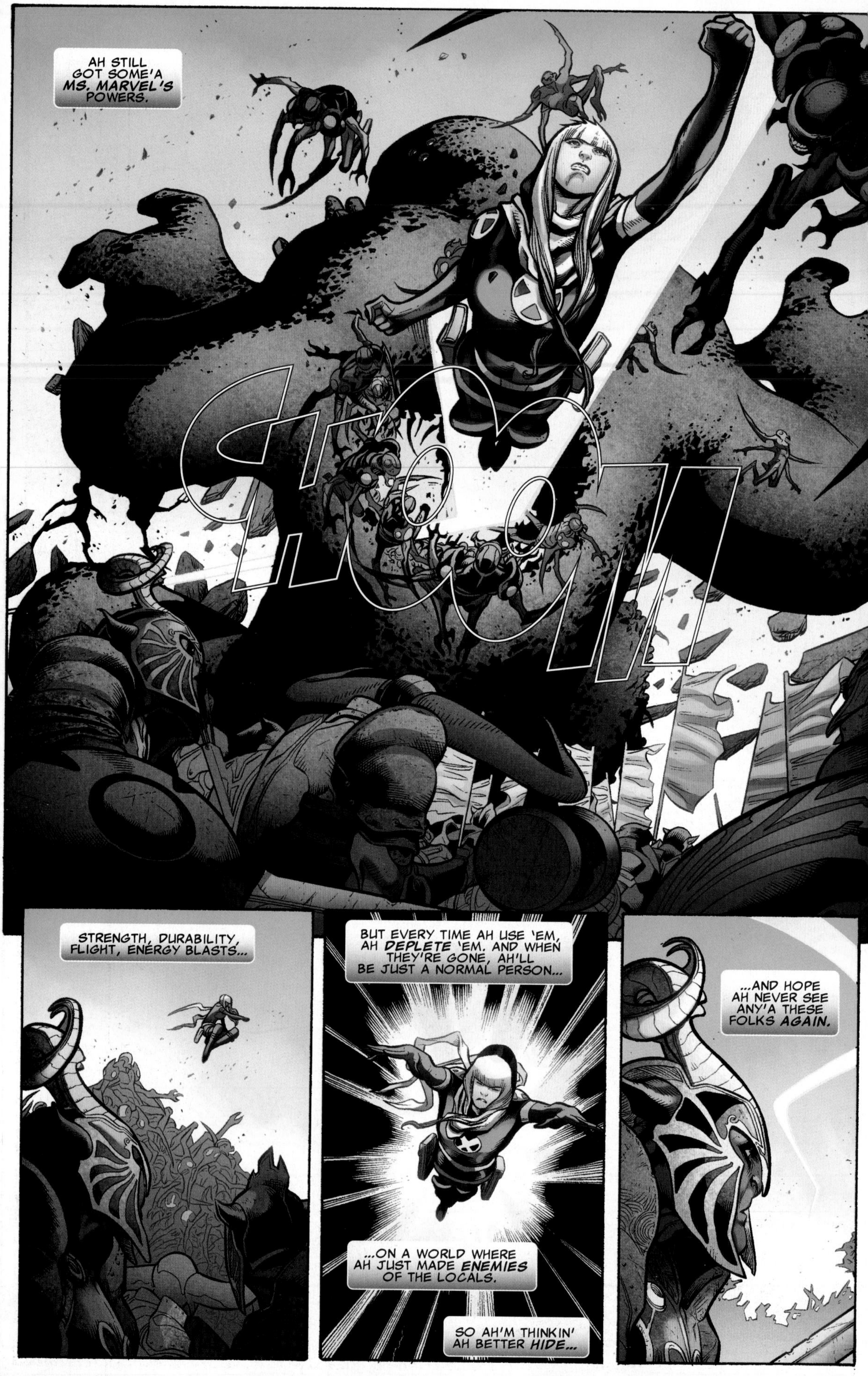
AH STILL GOT SOME'A MS. MARVEL'S POWERS.
STRENGTH, DURABILITY, FLIGHT, ENERGY BLASTS...
BUT EVERY TIME AH USE 'EM, AH DEPLETE 'EM. AND WHEN THEY'RE GONE, AH'LL BE JUST A NORMAL PERSON...
...ON A WORLD WHERE AH JUST MADE ENEMIES OF THE LOCALS.
SO AH'M THINKIN' AH BETTER HIDE...
...AND HOPE AH NEVER SEE ANY'A THESE FOLKS AGAIN.

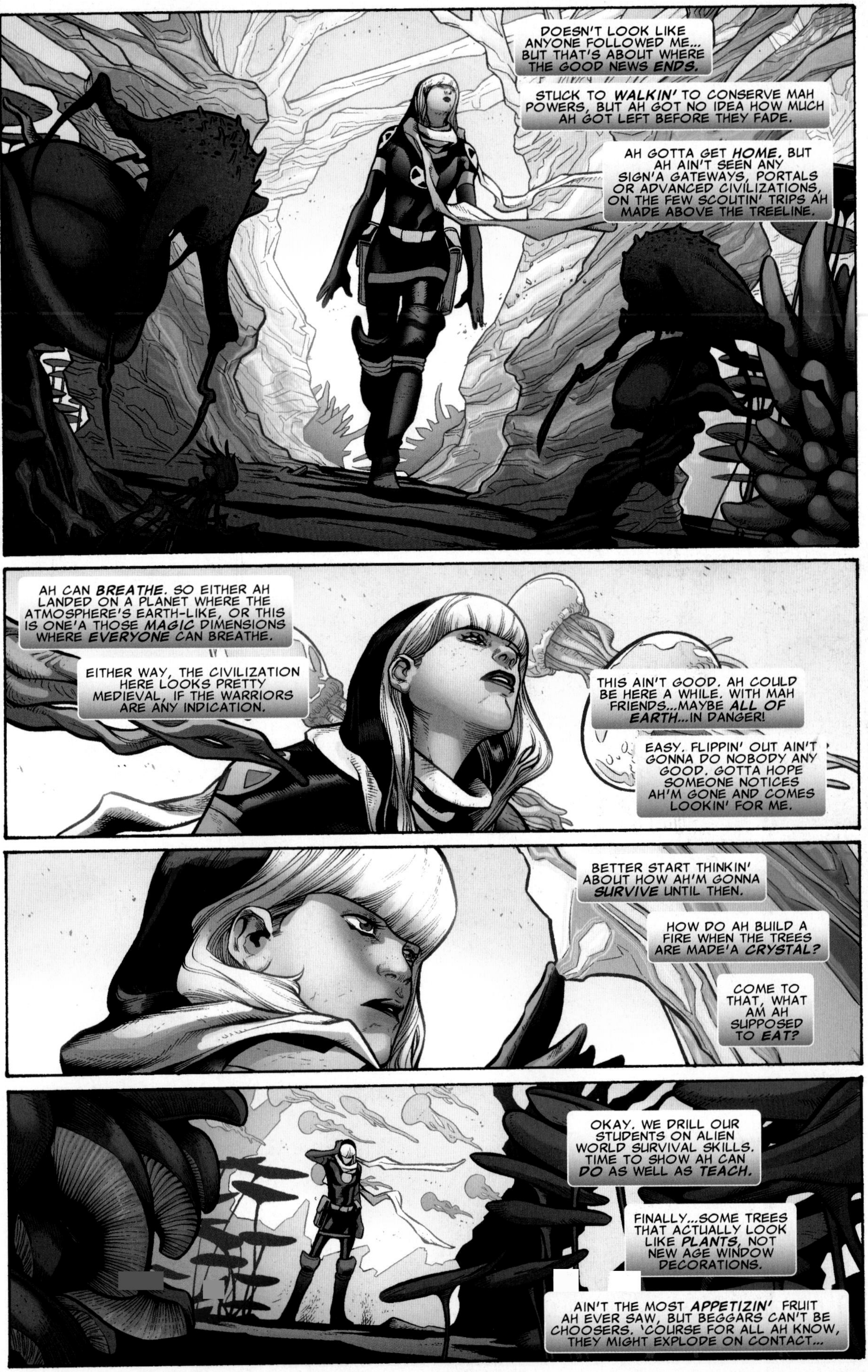
DOESN'T LOOK LIKE ANYONE FOLLOWED ME... BUT THAT'S ABOUT WHERE THE GOOD NEWS ENDS.
STUCK TO WALKIN' TO CONSERVE MAH POWERS, BUT AH GOT NO IDEA HOW MUCH AH GOT LEFT BEFORE THEY FADE.
AH GOTTA GET HOME. BUT AH AIN'T SEEN ANY SIGN'A GATEWAYS, PORTALS OR ADVANCED CIVILIZATIONS, ON THE FEW SCOUTIN' TRIPS AH MADE ABOVE THE TREELINE.
AH CAN BREATHE. SO EITHER AH LANDED ON A PLANET WHERE THE ATMOSPHERE'S EARTH-LIKE, OR THIS IS ONE'A THOSE MAGIC DIMENSIONS WHERE EVERYONE CAN BREATHE.
EITHER WAY, THE CIVILIZATION HERE LOOKS PRETTY MEDIEVAL, IF THE WARRIORS ARE ANY INDICATION.
THIS AIN'T GOOD. AH COULD BE HERE A WHILE. WITH MAH FRIENDS...MAYBE ALL OF EARTH...IN DANGER!
EASY. FLIPPIN' OUT AIN'T GONNA DO NOBODY ANY GOOD. GOTTA HOPE SOMEONE NOTICES AH'M GONE AND COMES LOOKIN' FOR ME.
BETTER START THINKIN' ABOUT HOW AH'M GONNA SURVIVE UNTIL THEN.
HOW DO AH BUILD A FIRE WHEN THE TREES ARE MADE'A CRYSTAL?
COME TO THAT, WHAT AM AH SUPPOSED TO EAT?
OKAY. WE DRILL OUR STUDENTS ON ALIEN WORLD SURVIVAL SKILLS. TIME TO SHOW AH CAN DO AS WELL AS TEACH.
FINALLY...SOME TREES THAT ACTUALLY LOOK LIKE PLANTS, NOT NEW AGE WINDOW DECORATIONS.
AIN'T THE MOST APPETIZIN' FRUIT AH EVER SAW, BUT BEGGARS CAN'T BE CHOOSERS. 'COURSE FOR ALL AH KNOW, THEY MIGHT EXPLODE ON CONTACT...

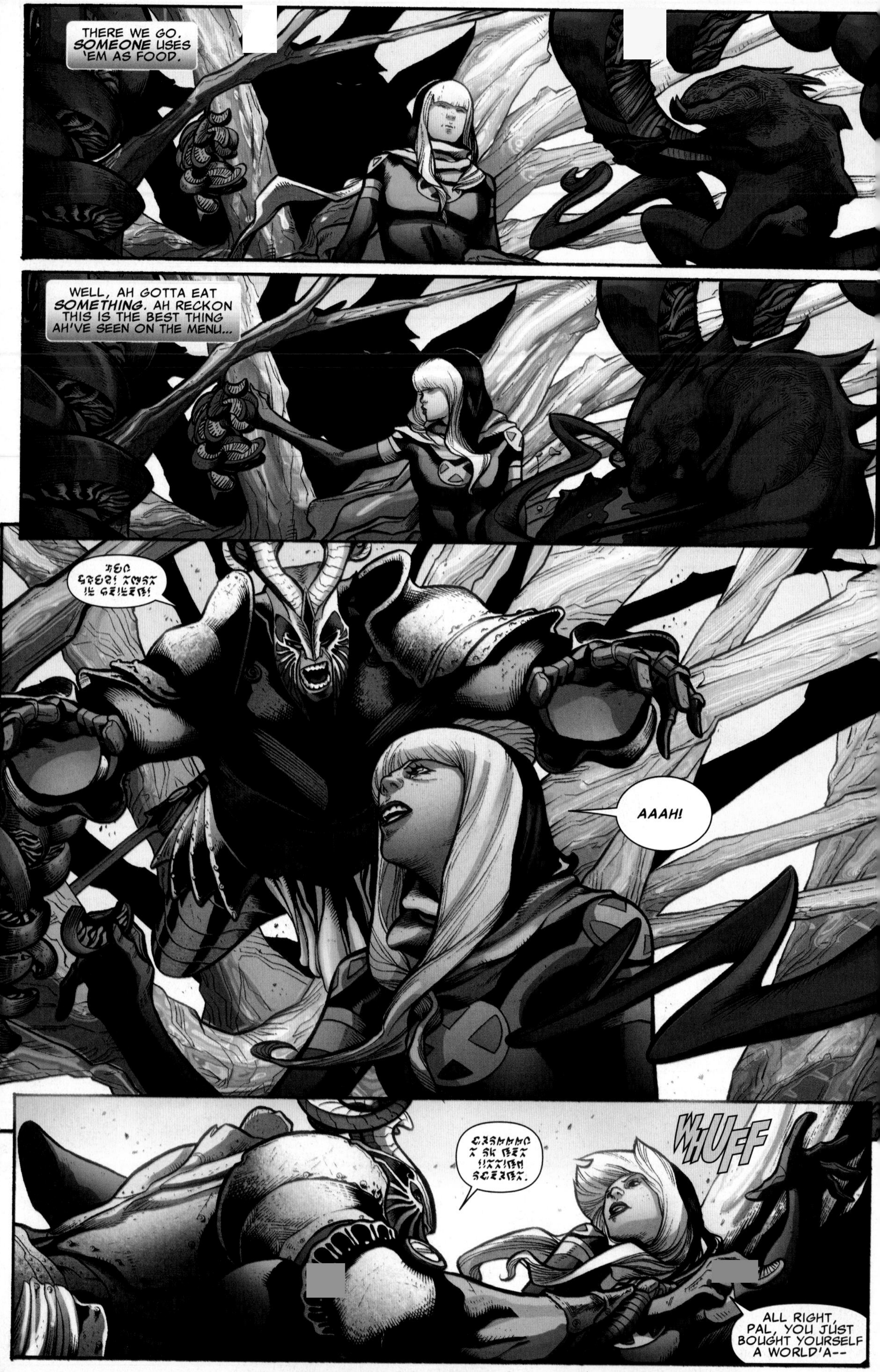
THERE WE GO. SOMEONE USES 'EM AS FOOD.
WELL, AH GOTTA EAT SOMETHING. AH RECKON THIS IS THE BEST THING AH'VE SEEN ON THE MENU...
AAAH!
WHUFF
ALL RIGHT, PAL, YOU JUST BOUGHT YOURSELF A WORLD'A--

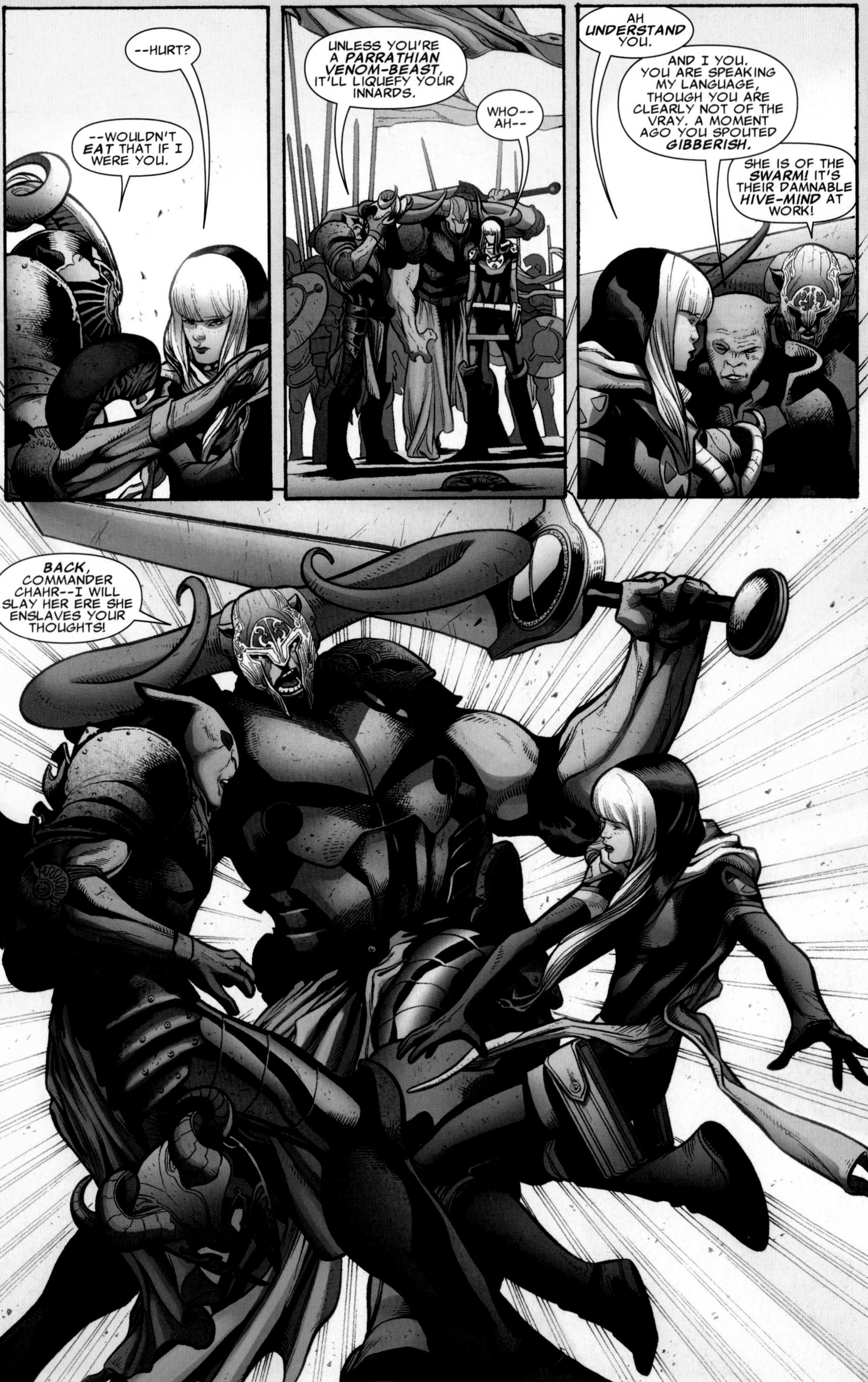
--HURT?
--WOULDN'T EAT THAT IF I WERE YOU.
UNLESS YOU'RE A PARRATHIAN VENOM-BEAST, IT'LL LIQUEFY YOUR INNARDS.
WHO-- AH--
AH UNDERSTAND YOU.
AND I YOU. YOU ARE SPEAKING MY LANGUAGE, THOUGH YOU ARE CLEARLY NOT OF THE VRAY. A MOMENT AGO YOU SPOUTED GIBBERISH.
SHE IS OF THE SWARM! IT'S THEIR DAMNABLE HIVE-MIND AT WORK!
BACK, COMMANDER CHAHR--I WILL SLAY HER ERE SHE ENSLAVES YOUR THOUGHTS!

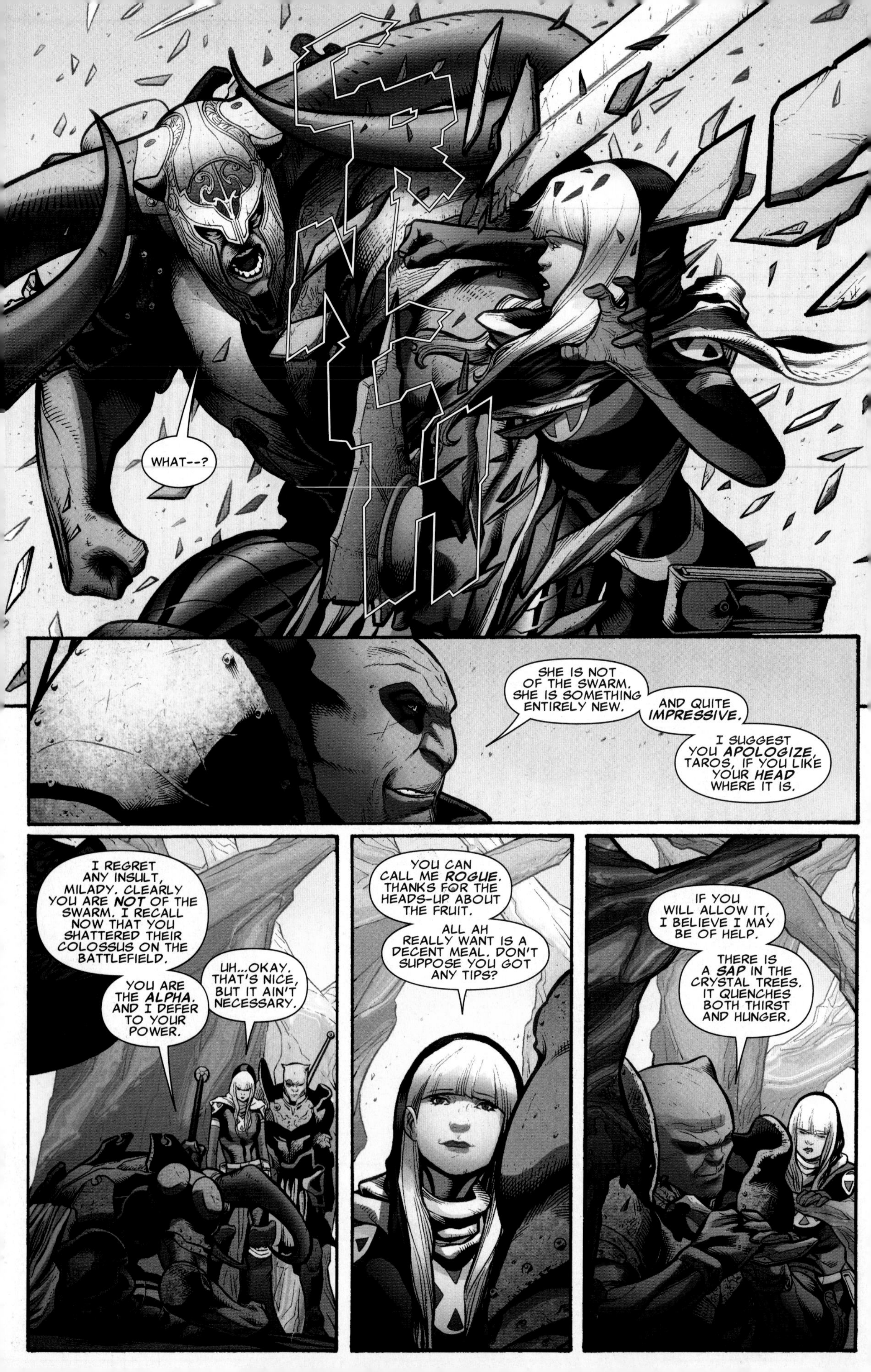
WHAT--?
SHE IS NOT OF THE SWARM. SHE IS SOMETHING ENTIRELY NEW.
AND QUITE IMPRESSIVE.
I SUGGEST YOU APOLOGIZE, TAROS, IF YOU LIKE YOUR HEAD WHERE IT IS.
I REGRET ANY INSULT, MILADY. CLEARLY YOU ARE NOT OF THE SWARM. I RECALL NOW THAT YOU SHATTERED THEIR COLOSSUS ON THE BATTLEFIELD.
YOU ARE THE ALPHA. AND I DEFER TO YOUR POWER.
UH...OKAY. THAT'S NICE, BUT IT AIN'T NECESSARY.
YOU CAN CALL ME ROGUE. THANKS FOR THE HEADS-UP ABOUT THE FRUIT.
ALL AH REALLY WANT IS A DECENT MEAL. DON'T SUPPOSE YOU GOT ANY TIPS?
IF YOU WILL ALLOW IT, I BELIEVE I MAY BE OF HELP.
THERE IS A SAP IN THE CRYSTAL TREES. IT QUENCHES BOTH THIRST AND HUNGER.

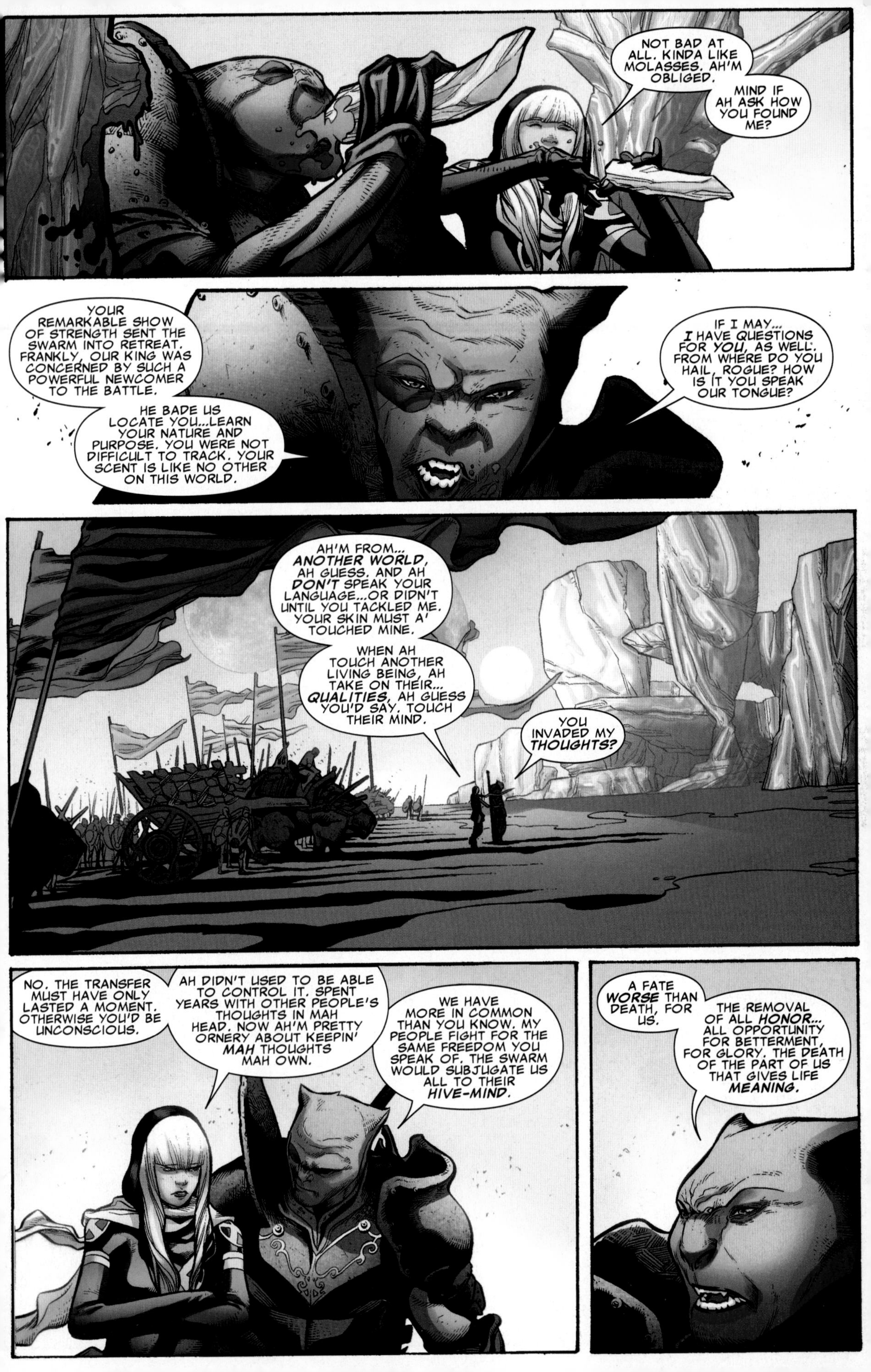
NOT BAD AT ALL. KINDA LIKE MOLASSES. AH'M OBLIGED.
MIND IF AH ASK HOW YOU FOUND ME?
YOUR REMARKABLE SHOW OF STRENGTH SENT THE SWARM INTO RETREAT. FRANKLY, OUR KING WAS CONCERNED BY SUCH A POWERFUL NEWCOMER TO THE BATTLE.
HE BADE US LOCATE YOU...LEARN YOUR NATURE AND PURPOSE. YOU WERE NOT DIFFICULT TO TRACK. YOUR SCENT IS LIKE NO OTHER ON THIS WORLD.
IF I MAY... I HAVE QUESTIONS FOR YOU, AS WELL. FROM WHERE DO YOU HAIL, ROGUE? HOW IS IT YOU SPEAK OUR TONGUE?
AH'M FROM... ANOTHER WORLD, AH GUESS. AND AH DON'T SPEAK YOUR LANGUAGE...OR DIDN'T UNTIL YOU TACKLED ME. YOUR SKIN MUST A' TOUCHED MINE.
WHEN AH TOUCH ANOTHER LIVING BEING, AH TAKE ON THEIR... QUALITIES, AH GUESS YOU'D SAY. TOUCH THEIR MIND.
YOU INVADED MY THOUGHTS?
NO. THE TRANSFER MUST HAVE ONLY LASTED A MOMENT. OTHERWISE YOU'D BE UNCONSCIOUS.
AH DIDN'T USED TO BE ABLE TO CONTROL IT. SPENT YEARS WITH OTHER PEOPLE'S THOUGHTS IN MAH HEAD. NOW AH'M PRETTY ORNERY ABOUT KEEPIN' MAH THOUGHTS MAH OWN.
WE HAVE MORE IN COMMON THAN YOU KNOW. MY PEOPLE FIGHT FOR THE SAME FREEDOM YOU SPEAK OF. THE SWARM WOULD SUBJUGATE US ALL TO THEIR HIVE-MIND.
A FATE WORSE THAN DEATH, FOR US.
THE REMOVAL OF ALL HONOR... ALL OPPORTUNITY FOR BETTERMENT, FOR GLORY. THE DEATH OF THE PART OF US THAT GIVES LIFE MEANING.

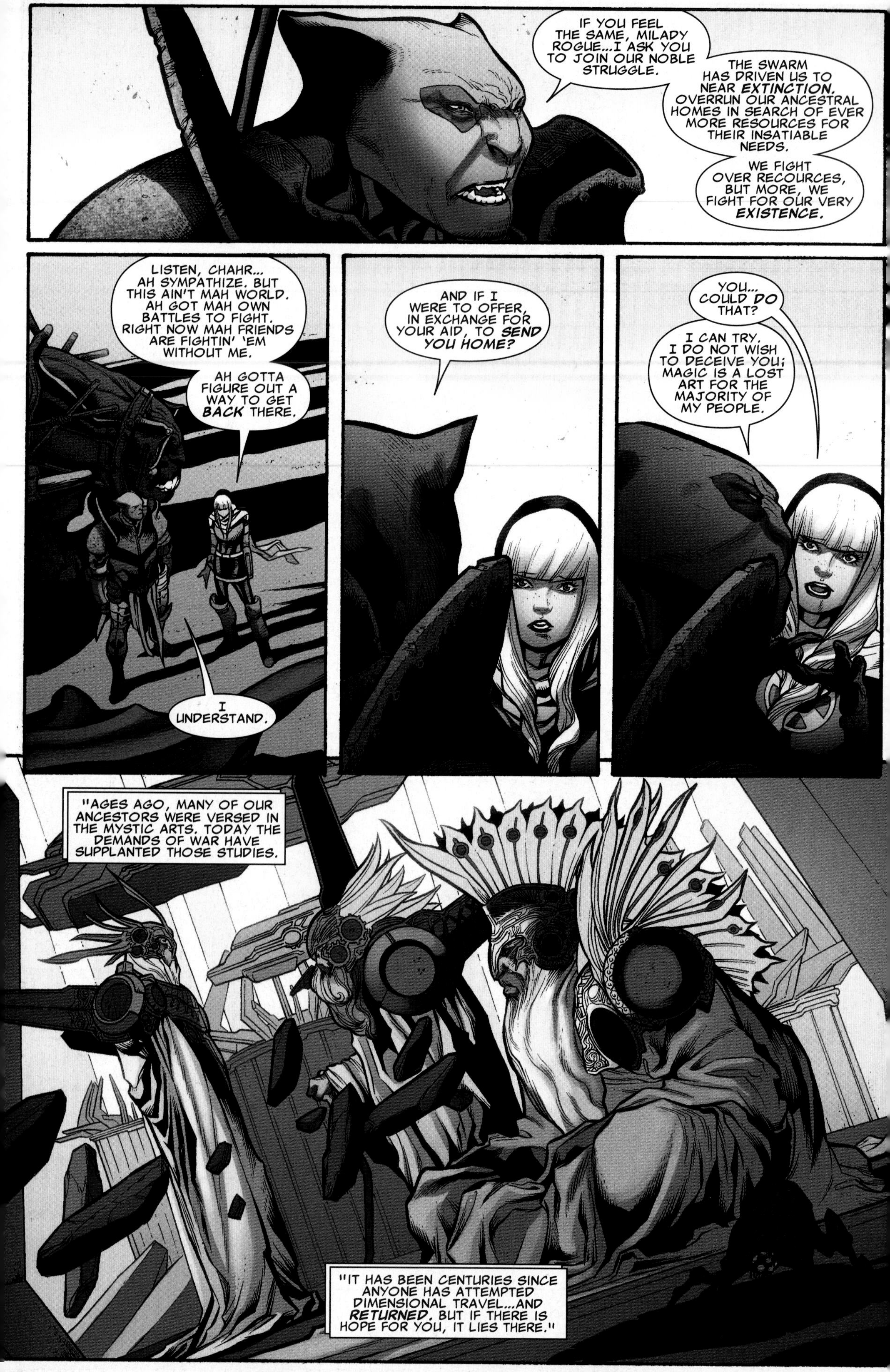
IF YOU FEEL THE SAME, MILADY ROGUE...I ASK YOU TO JOIN OUR NOBLE STRUGGLE.
THE SWARM HAS DRIVEN US TO NEAR EXTINCTION. OVERRUN OUR ANCESTRAL HOMES IN SEARCH OF EVER MORE RESOURCES FOR THEIR INSATIABLE NEEDS.
WE FIGHT OVER RECOURCES, BUT MORE, WE FIGHT FOR OUR VERY EXISTENCE.
LISTEN, CHAHR... AH SYMPATHIZE. BUT THIS AIN'T MAH WORLD. AH GOT MAH OWN BATTLES TO FIGHT. RIGHT NOW MAH FRIENDS ARE FIGHTIN' 'EM WITHOUT ME.
AH GOTTA FIGURE OUT A WAY TO GET BACK THERE.
I UNDERSTAND.
AND IF I WERE TO OFFER, IN EXCHANGE FOR YOUR AID, TO SEND YOU HOME?
YOU... COULD DO THAT?
I CAN TRY. I DO NOT WISH TO DECEIVE YOU; MAGIC IS A LOST ART FOR THE MAJORITY OF MY PEOPLE.
"AGES AGO, MANY OF OUR ANCESTORS WERE VERSED IN THE MYSTIC ARTS. TODAY THE DEMANDS OF WAR HAVE SUPPLANTED THOSE STUDIES.
"IT HAS BEEN CENTURIES SINCE ANYONE HAS ATTEMPTED DIMENSIONAL TRAVEL...AND RETURNED. BUT IF THERE IS HOPE FOR YOU, IT LIES THERE."

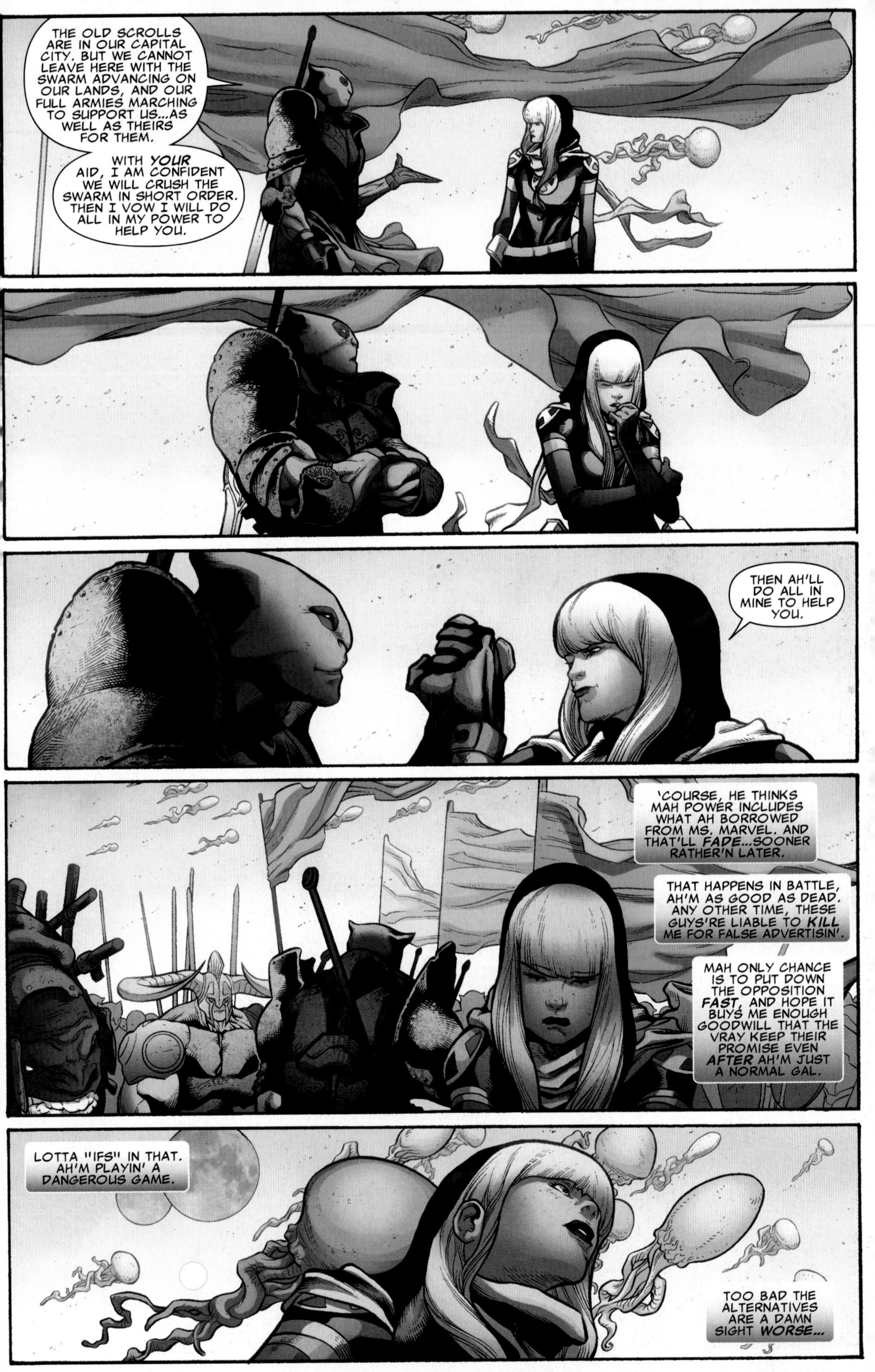

THE OLD SCROLLS ARE IN OUR CAPITAL CITY. BUT WE CANNOT LEAVE HERE WITH THE SWARM ADVANCING ON OUR LANDS, AND OUR FULL ARMIES MARCHING TO SUPPORT US...AS WELL AS THEIRS FOR THEM.
WITH YOUR AID, I AM CONFIDENT WE WILL CRUSH THE SWARM IN SHORT ORDER. THEN I VOW I WILL DO ALL IN MY POWER TO HELP YOU.
THEN AH'LL DO ALL IN MINE TO HELP YOU.
'COURSE, HE THINKS MAH POWER INCLUDES WHAT AH BORROWED FROM MS. MARVEL. AND THAT'LL FADE...SOONER RATHER'N LATER.
THAT HAPPENS IN BATTLE, AH'M AS GOOD AS DEAD. ANY OTHER TIME, THESE GUYS'RE LIABLE TO KILL ME FOR FALSE ADVERTISIN'.
MAH ONLY CHANCE IS TO PUT DOWN THE OPPOSITION FAST, AND HOPE IT BUYS ME ENOUGH GOODWILL THAT THE VRAY KEEP THEIR PROMISE EVEN AFTER AH'M JUST A NORMAL GAL.
LOTTA "IFS" IN THAT. AH'M PLAYIN' A DANGEROUS GAME.
TOO BAD THE ALTERNATIVES ARE A DAMN SIGHT WORSE...

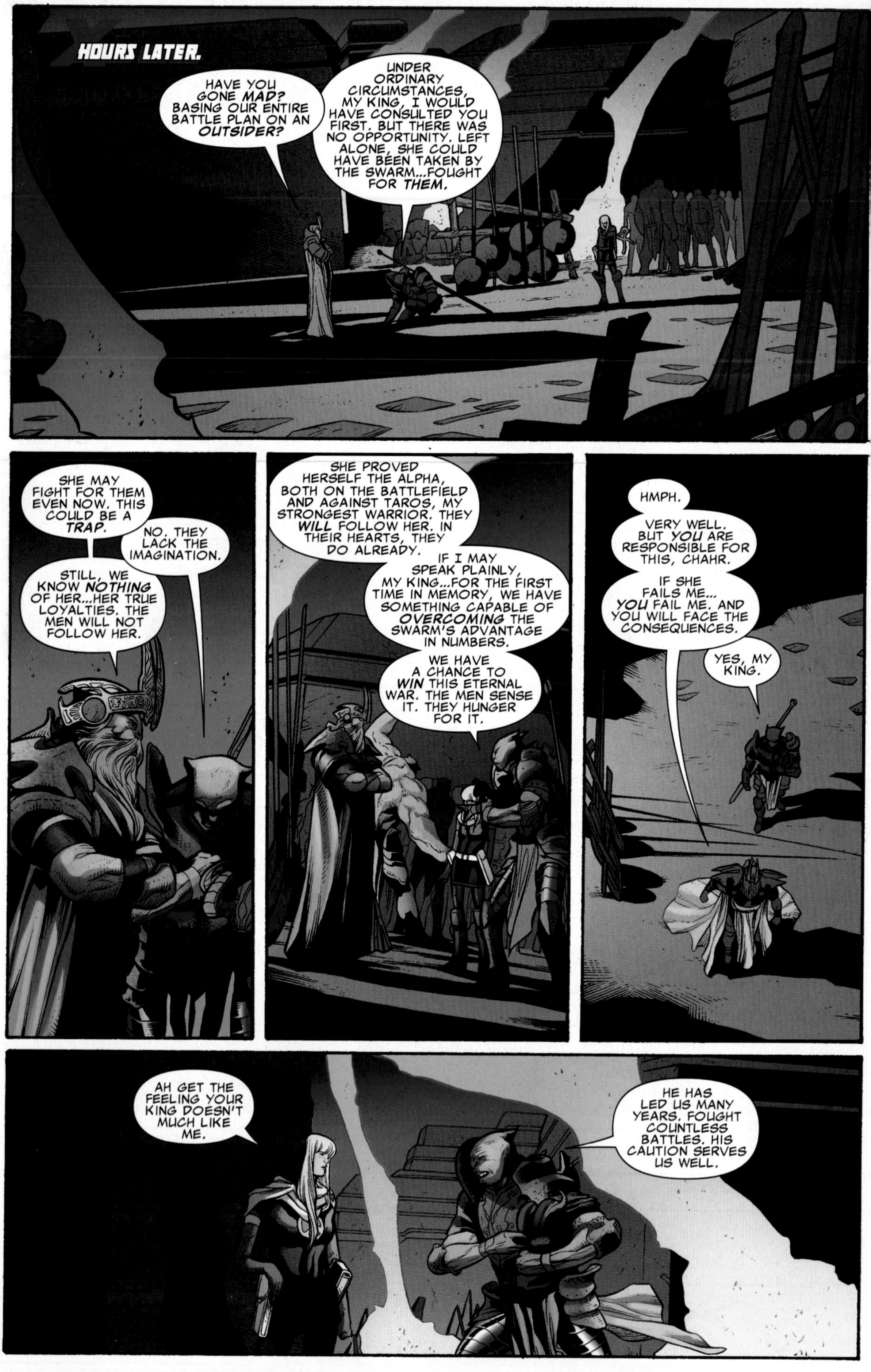
HOURS LATER.
HAVE YOU GONE MAD? BASING OUR ENTIRE BATTLE PLAN ON AN OUTSIDER?
UNDER ORDINARY CIRCUMSTANCES, MY KING, I WOULD HAVE CONSULTED YOU FIRST. BUT THERE WAS NO OPPORTUNITY. LEFT ALONE, SHE COULD HAVE BEEN TAKEN BY THE SWARM...FOUGHT FOR THEM.
SHE MAY FIGHT FOR THEM EVEN NOW. THIS COULD BE A TRAP.
NO. THEY LACK THE IMAGINATION.
STILL, WE KNOW NOTHING OF HER...HER TRUE LOYALTIES. THE MEN WILL NOT FOLLOW HER.
SHE PROVED HERSELF THE ALPHA, BOTH ON THE BATTLEFIELD AND AGAINST TAROS, MY STRONGEST WARRIOR. THEY WILL FOLLOW HER. IN THEIR HEARTS, THEY DO ALREADY.
IF I MAY SPEAK PLAINLY, MY KING...FOR THE FIRST TIME IN MEMORY, WE HAVE SOMETHING CAPABLE OF OVERCOMING THE SWARM'S ADVANTAGE IN NUMBERS.
WE HAVE A CHANCE TO WIN THIS ETERNAL WAR. THE MEN SENSE IT. THEY HUNGER FOR IT.
HMPH.
VERY WELL. BUT YOU ARE RESPONSIBLE FOR THIS, CHAHR.
IF SHE FAILS ME... YOU FAIL ME. AND YOU WILL FACE THE CONSEQUENCES.
YES, MY KING.
AH GET THE FEELING YOUR KING DOESN'T MUCH LIKE ME.
HE HAS LED US MANY YEARS. FOUGHT COUNTLESS BATTLES. HIS CAUTION SERVES US WELL.

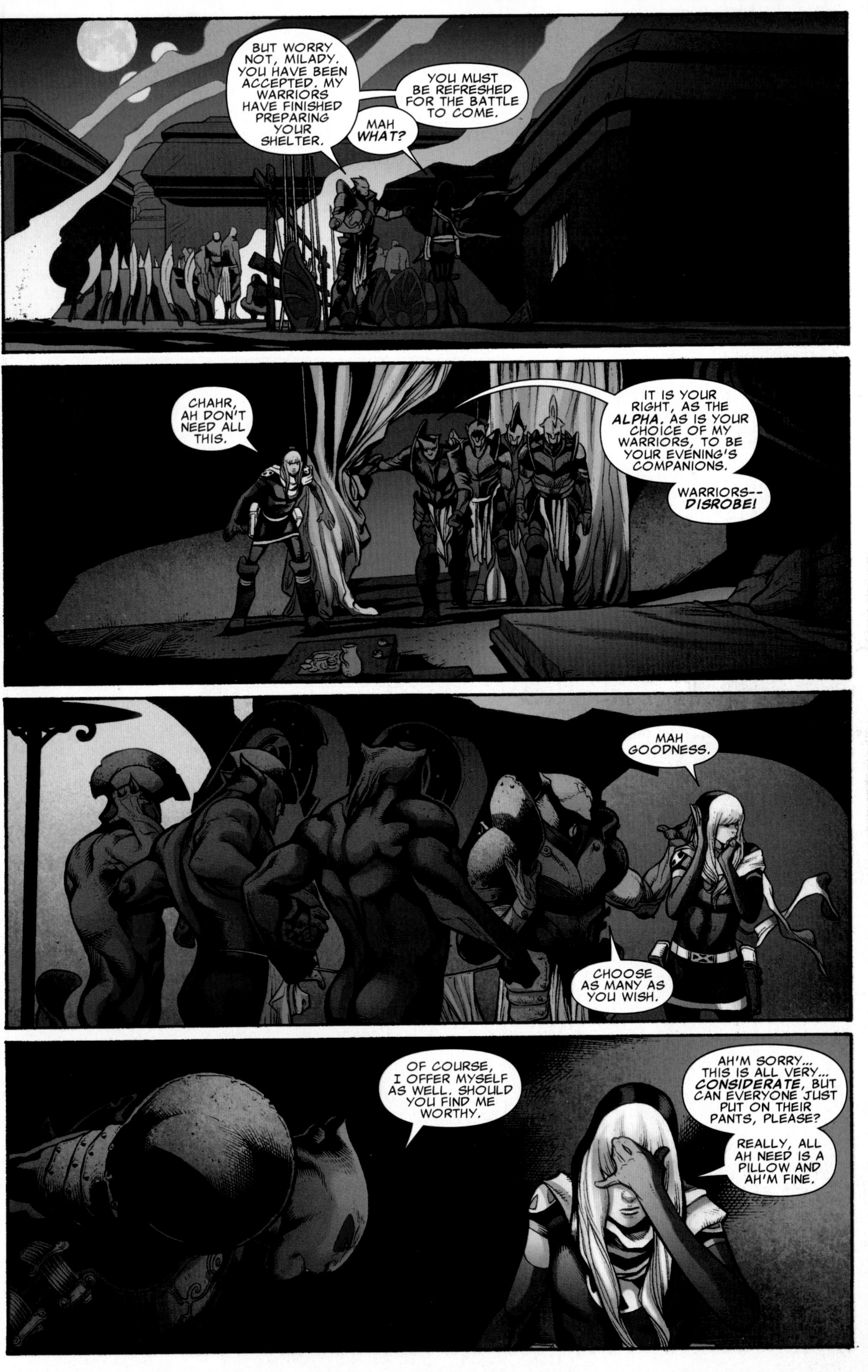
BUT WORRY NOT, MILADY. YOU HAVE BEEN ACCEPTED. MY WARRIORS HAVE FINISHED PREPARING YOUR SHELTER.
YOU MUST BE REFRESHED FOR THE BATTLE TO COME.
MAH WHAT?
CHAHR, AH DON'T NEED ALL THIS.
IT IS YOUR RIGHT, AS THE ALPHA. AS IS YOUR CHOICE OF MY WARRIORS, TO BE YOUR EVENING'S COMPANIONS.
WARRIORS-- DISROBE!
MAH GOODNESS.
CHOOSE AS MANY AS YOU WISH.
OF COURSE, I OFFER MYSELF AS WELL. SHOULD YOU FIND ME WORTHY.
AH'M SORRY... THIS IS ALL VERY... CONSIDERATE, BUT CAN EVERYONE JUST PUT ON THEIR PANTS, PLEASE?
REALLY, ALL AH NEED IS A PILLOW AND AH'M FINE.

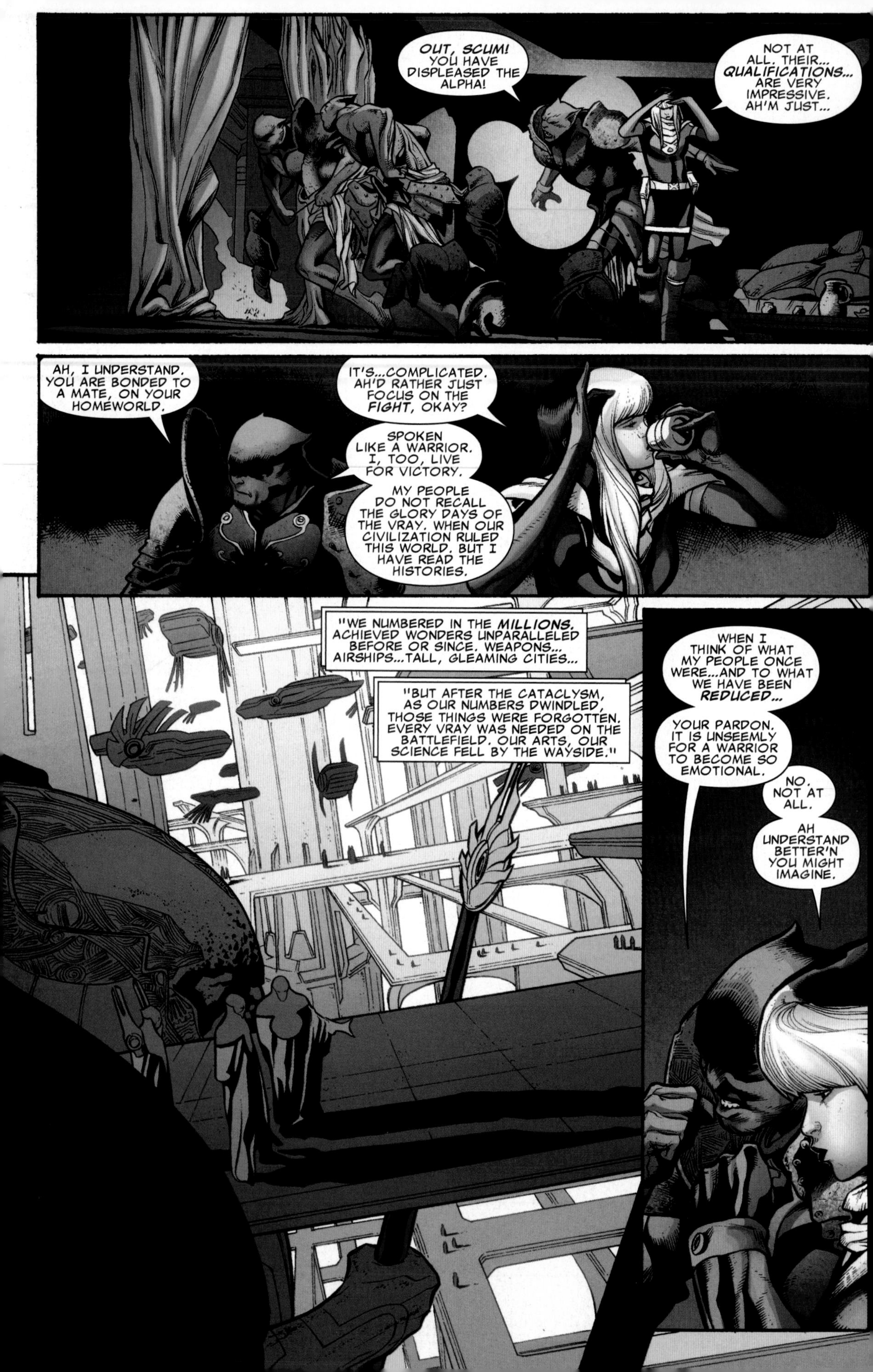
OUT, SCUM! YOU HAVE DISPLEASED THE ALPHA!
NOT AT ALL. THEIR... QUALIFICATIONS... ARE VERY IMPRESSIVE. AH'M JUST...
AH, I UNDERSTAND. YOU ARE BONDED TO A MATE, ON YOUR HOMEWORLD.
IT'S...COMPLICATED. AH'D RATHER JUST FOCUS ON THE FIGHT, OKAY?
SPOKEN LIKE A WARRIOR. I, TOO, LIVE FOR VICTORY.
MY PEOPLE DO NOT RECALL THE GLORY DAYS OF THE VRAY. WHEN OUR CIVILIZATION RULED THIS WORLD. BUT I HAVE READ THE HISTORIES.
"WE NUMBERED IN THE MILLIONS. ACHIEVED WONDERS UNPARALLELED BEFORE OR SINCE. WEAPONS... AIRSHIPS...TALL, GLEAMING CITIES...
"BUT AFTER THE CATACLYSM, AS OUR NUMBERS DWINDLED, THOSE THINGS WERE FORGOTTEN. EVERY VRAY WAS NEEDED ON THE BATTLEFIELD. OUR ARTS, OUR SCIENCE FELL BY THE WAYSIDE."
WHEN I THINK OF WHAT MY PEOPLE ONCE WERE...AND TO WHAT WE HAVE BEEN REDUCED...
YOUR PARDON. IT IS UNSEEMLY FOR A WARRIOR TO BECOME SO EMOTIONAL.
NO. NOT AT ALL.
AH UNDERSTAND BETTER'N YOU MIGHT IMAGINE.

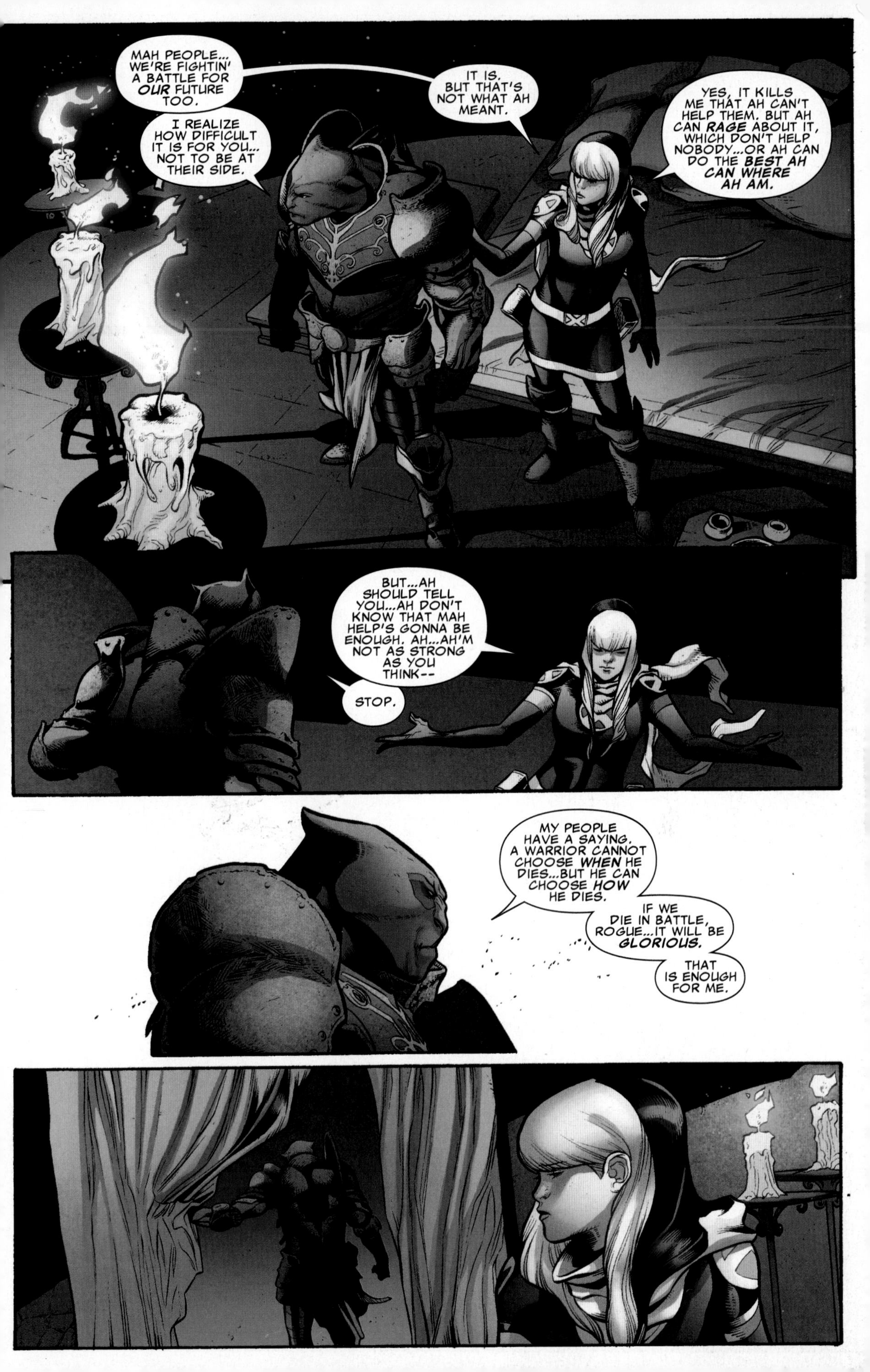
MAH PEOPLE... WE'RE FIGHTIN' A BATTLE FOR OUR FUTURE TOO.
I REALIZE HOW DIFFICULT IT IS FOR YOU... NOT TO BE AT THEIR SIDE.
IT IS. BUT THAT'S NOT WHAT AH MEANT.
YES, IT KILLS ME THAT AH CAN'T HELP THEM. BUT AH CAN RAGE ABOUT IT, WHICH DON'T HELP NOBODY...OR AH CAN DO THE BEST AH CAN WHERE AH AM.
BUT...AH SHOULD TELL YOU...AH DON'T KNOW THAT MAH HELP'S GONNA BE ENOUGH. AH...AH'M NOT AS STRONG AS YOU THINK--
STOP.
MY PEOPLE HAVE A SAYING. A WARRIOR CANNOT CHOOSE WHEN HE DIES...BUT HE CAN CHOOSE HOW HE DIES.
IF WE DIE IN BATTLE, ROGUE...IT WILL BE GLORIOUS.
THAT IS ENOUGH FOR ME.

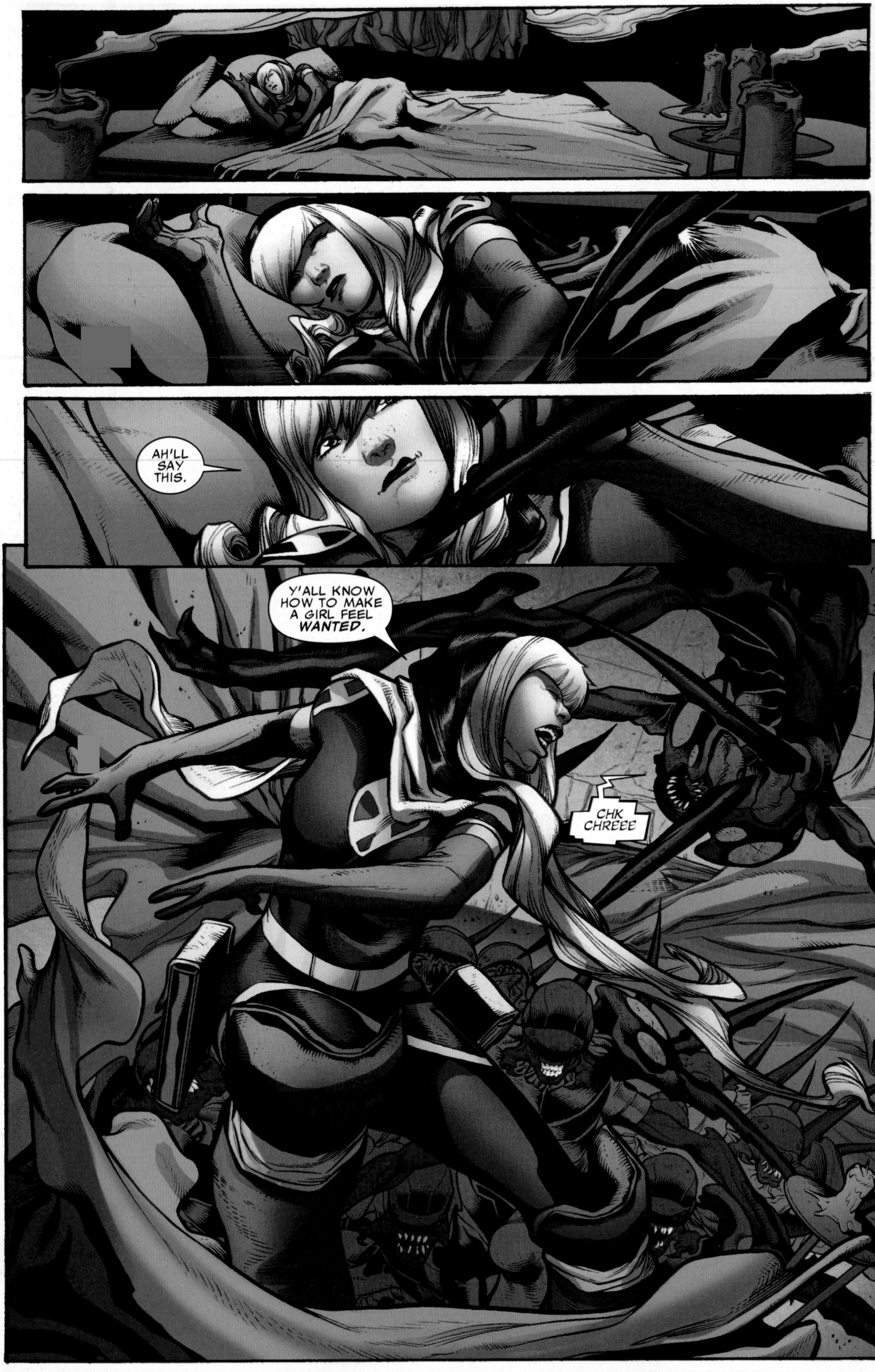
AH'LL SAY THIS.
Y'ALL KNOW HOW TO MAKE A GIRL FEEL WANTED.
CHK CHREEE

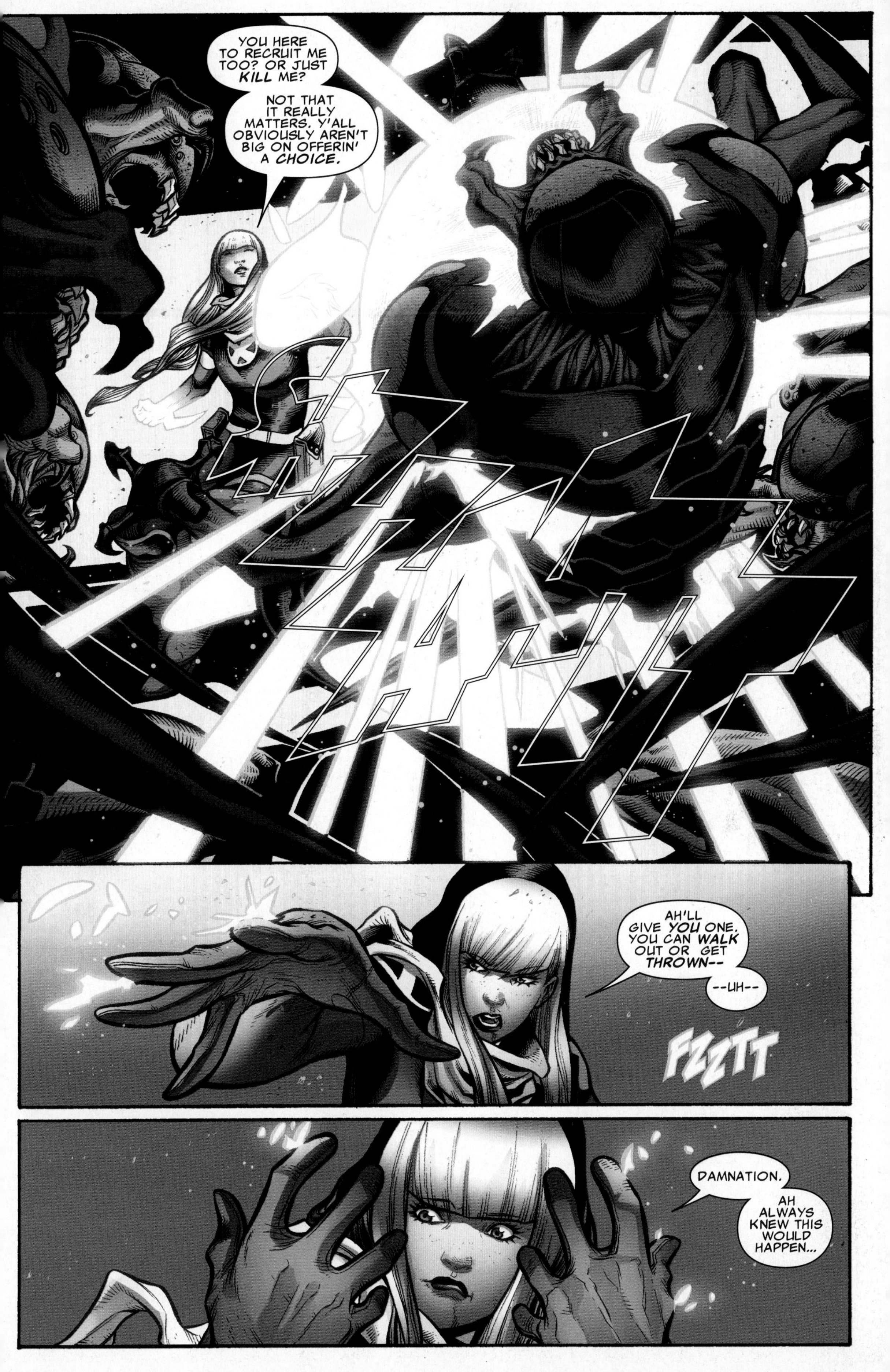
YOU HERE TO RECRUIT ME TOO? OR JUST KILL ME?
NOT THAT IT REALLY MATTERS. Y'ALL OBVIOUSLY AREN'T BIG ON OFFERIN' A CHOICE.
AH'LL GIVE YOU ONE. YOU CAN WALK OUT OR GET THROWN--
--UH--
FZZTT
DAMNATION.
AH ALWAYS KNEW THIS WOULD HAPPEN...

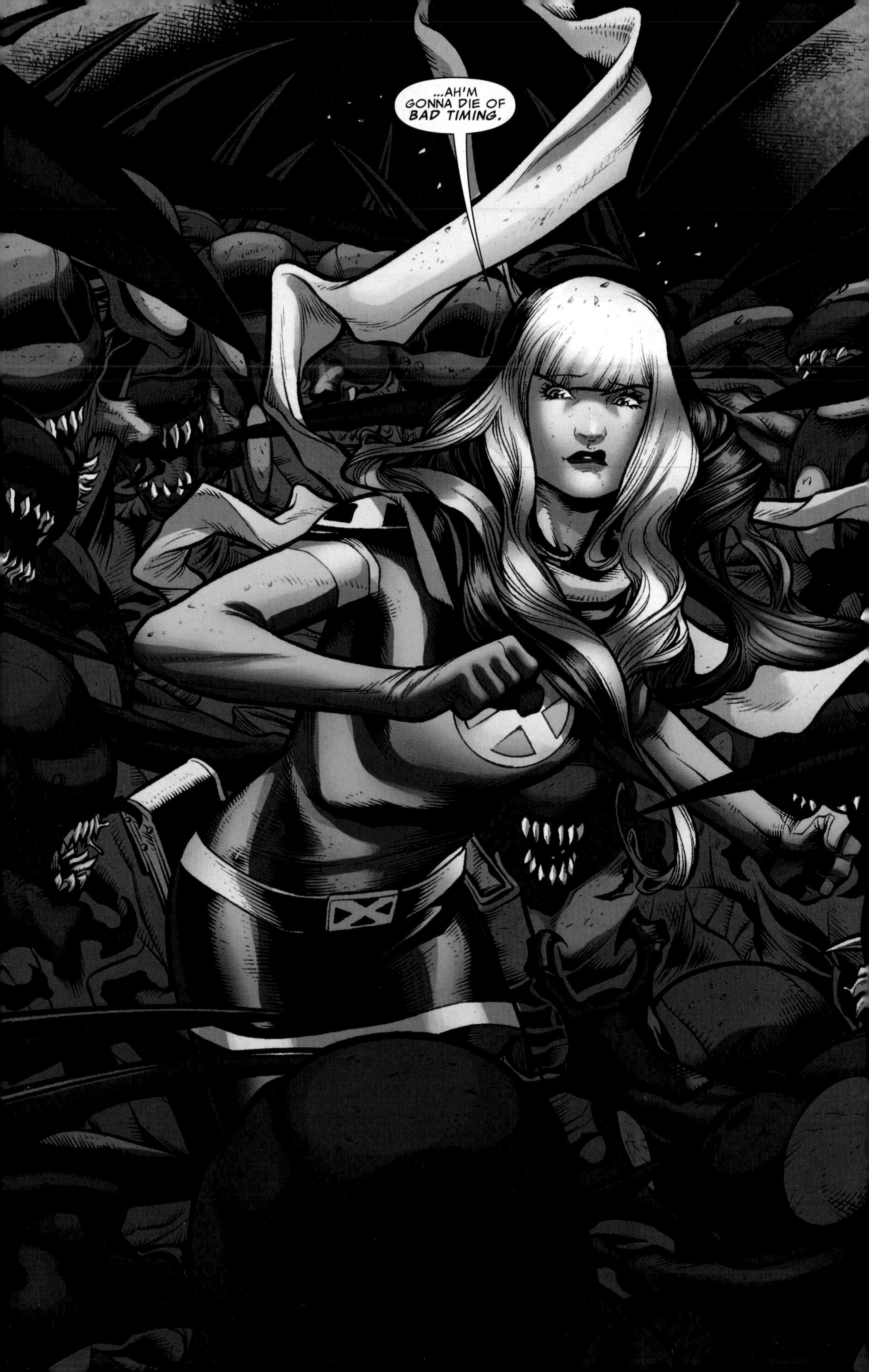
...AH'M GONNA DIE OF BAD TIMING.

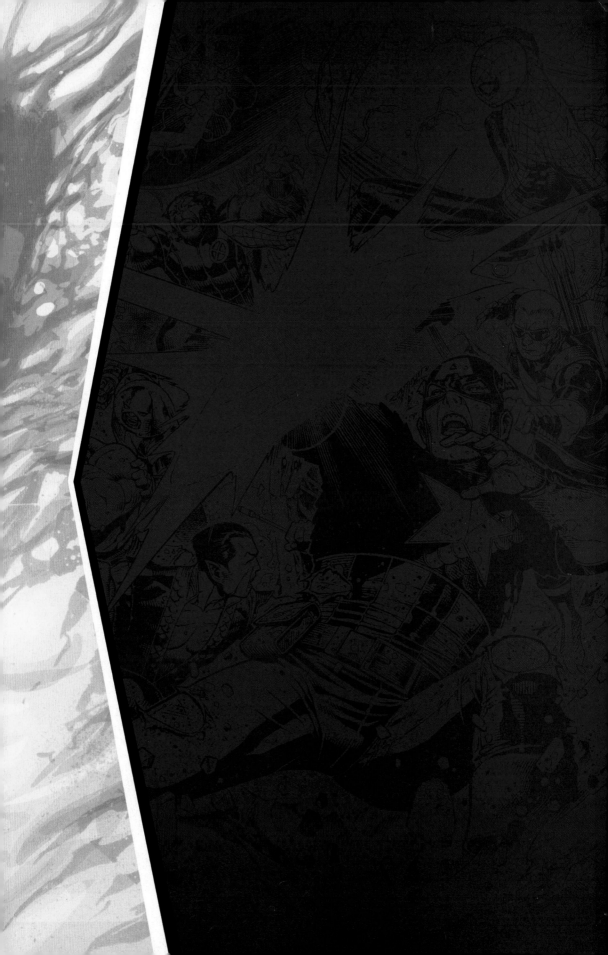

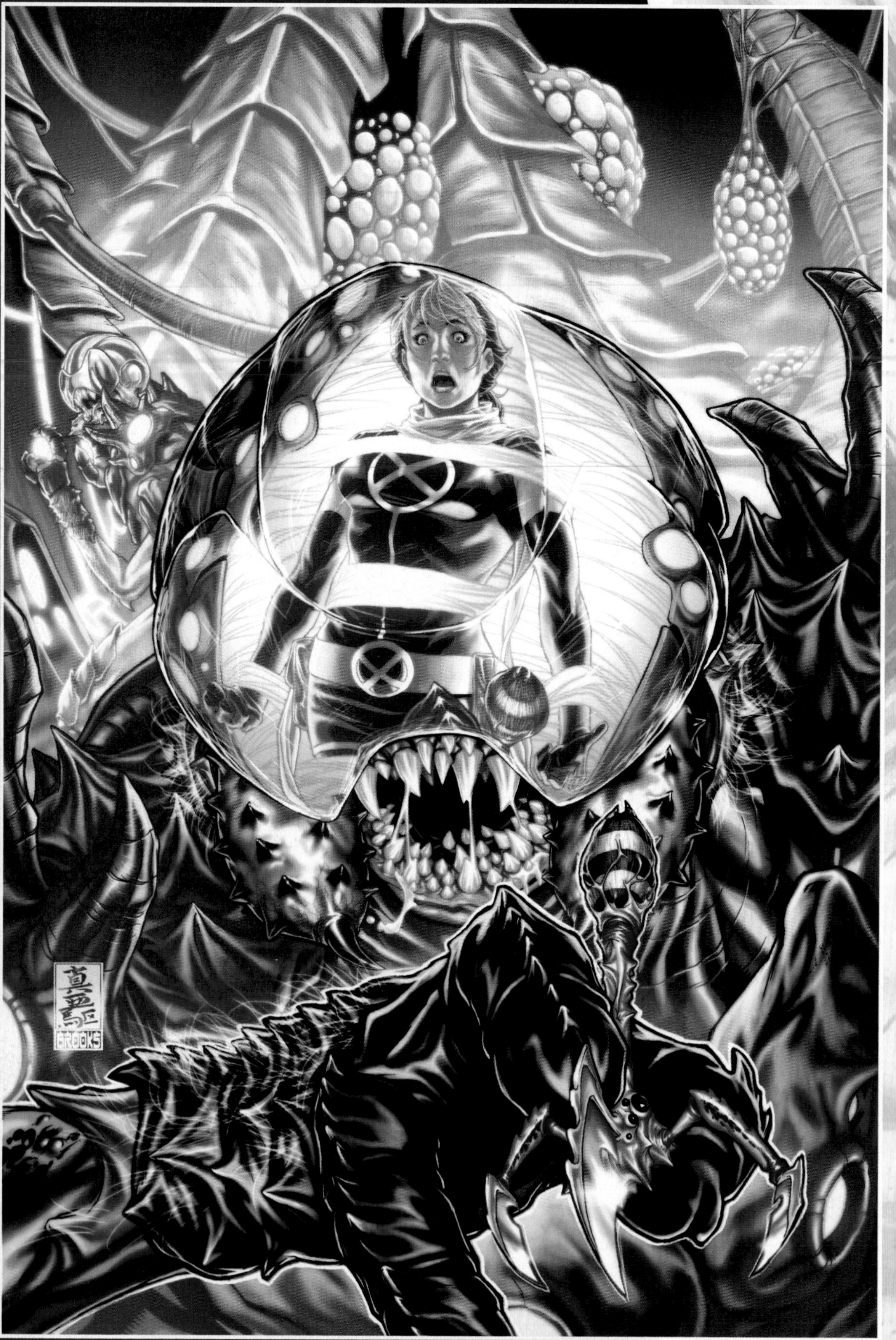
BROOKS

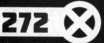

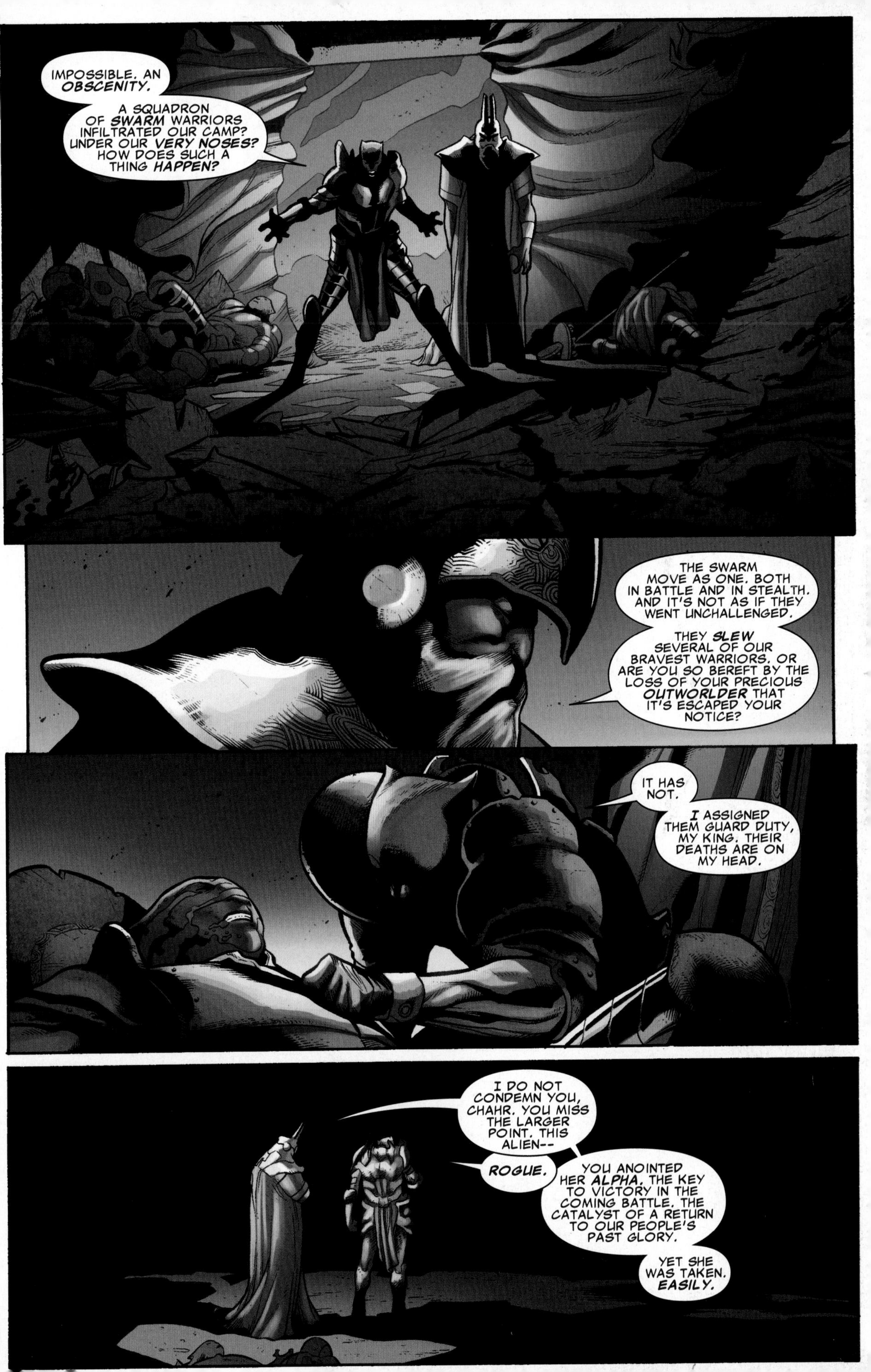
IMPOSSIBLE. AN OBSCENITY.
A SQUADRON OF SWARM WARRIORS INFILTRATED OUR CAMP? UNDER OUR VERY NOSES? HOW DOES SUCH A THING HAPPEN?
THE SWARM MOVE AS ONE. BOTH IN BATTLE AND IN STEALTH. AND IT'S NOT AS IF THEY WENT UNCHALLENGED.
THEY SLEW SEVERAL OF OUR BRAVEST WARRIORS. OR ARE YOU SO BEREFT BY THE LOSS OF YOUR PRECIOUS OUTWORLDER THAT IT'S ESCAPED YOUR NOTICE?
IT HAS NOT.
I ASSIGNED THEM GUARD DUTY, MY KING. THEIR DEATHS ARE ON MY HEAD.
I DO NOT CONDEMN YOU, CHAHR. YOU MISS THE LARGER POINT. THIS ALIEN--
ROGUE.
YOU ANOINTED HER ALPHA. THE KEY TO VICTORY IN THE COMING BATTLE. THE CATALYST OF A RETURN TO OUR PEOPLE'S PAST GLORY.
YET SHE WAS TAKEN. EASILY.

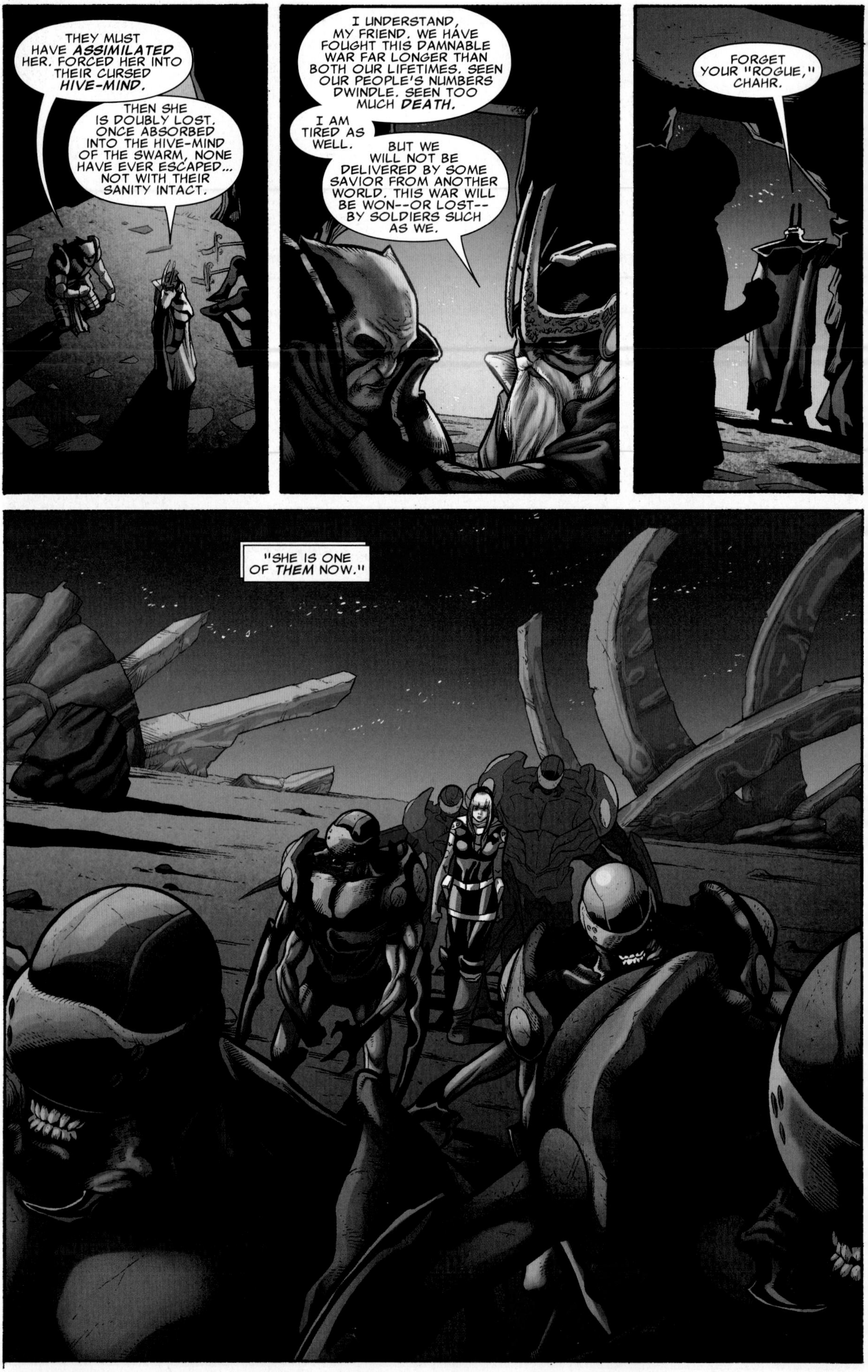
THEY MUST HAVE ASSIMILATED HER. FORCED HER INTO THEIR CURSED HIVE-MIND.
THEN SHE IS DOUBLY LOST. ONCE ABSORBED INTO THE HIVE-MIND OF THE SWARM, NONE HAVE EVER ESCAPED... NOT WITH THEIR SANITY INTACT.
I UNDERSTAND, MY FRIEND. WE HAVE FOUGHT THIS DAMNABLE WAR FAR LONGER THAN BOTH OUR LIFETIMES. SEEN OUR PEOPLE'S NUMBERS DWINDLE. SEEN TOO MUCH DEATH.
I AM TIRED AS WELL.
BUT WE WILL NOT BE DELIVERED BY SOME SAVIOR FROM ANOTHER WORLD. THIS WAR WILL BE WON--OR LOST--BY SOLDIERS SUCH AS WE.
FORGET YOUR "ROGUE," CHAHR.
"SHE IS ONE OF THEM NOW."

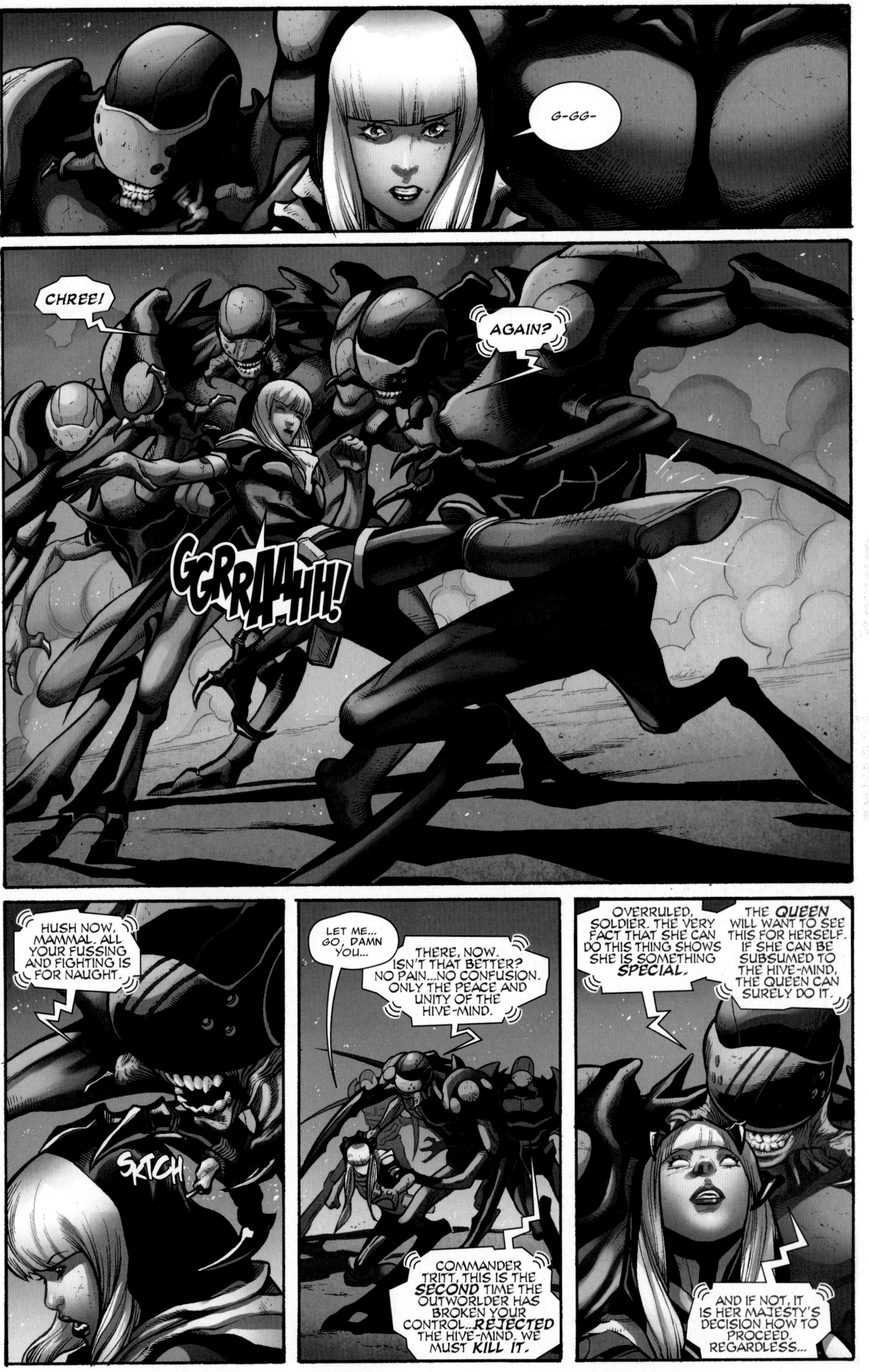
G-GG-
CHREE!
AGAIN?
GGRRAAHH!
HUSH NOW, MAMMAL. ALL YOUR FUSSING AND FIGHTING IS FOR NAUGHT.
SKTCH
LET ME... GO, DAMN YOU...
THERE, NOW. ISN'T THAT BETTER? NO PAIN... NO CONFUSION. ONLY THE PEACE AND UNITY OF THE HIVE-MIND.
COMMANDER TRITT, THIS IS THE SECOND TIME THE OUTWORLDER HAS BROKEN YOUR CONTROL... REJECTED THE HIVE-MIND. WE MUST KILL IT.
OVERRULED, SOLDIER. THE VERY FACT THAT SHE CAN DO THIS THING SHOWS SHE IS SOMETHING SPECIAL.
THE QUEEN WILL WANT TO SEE THIS FOR HERSELF. IF SHE CAN BE SUBSUMED TO THE HIVE-MIND, THE QUEEN CAN SURELY DO IT.
AND IF NOT, IT IS HER MAJESTY'S DECISION HOW TO PROCEED. REGARDLESS...

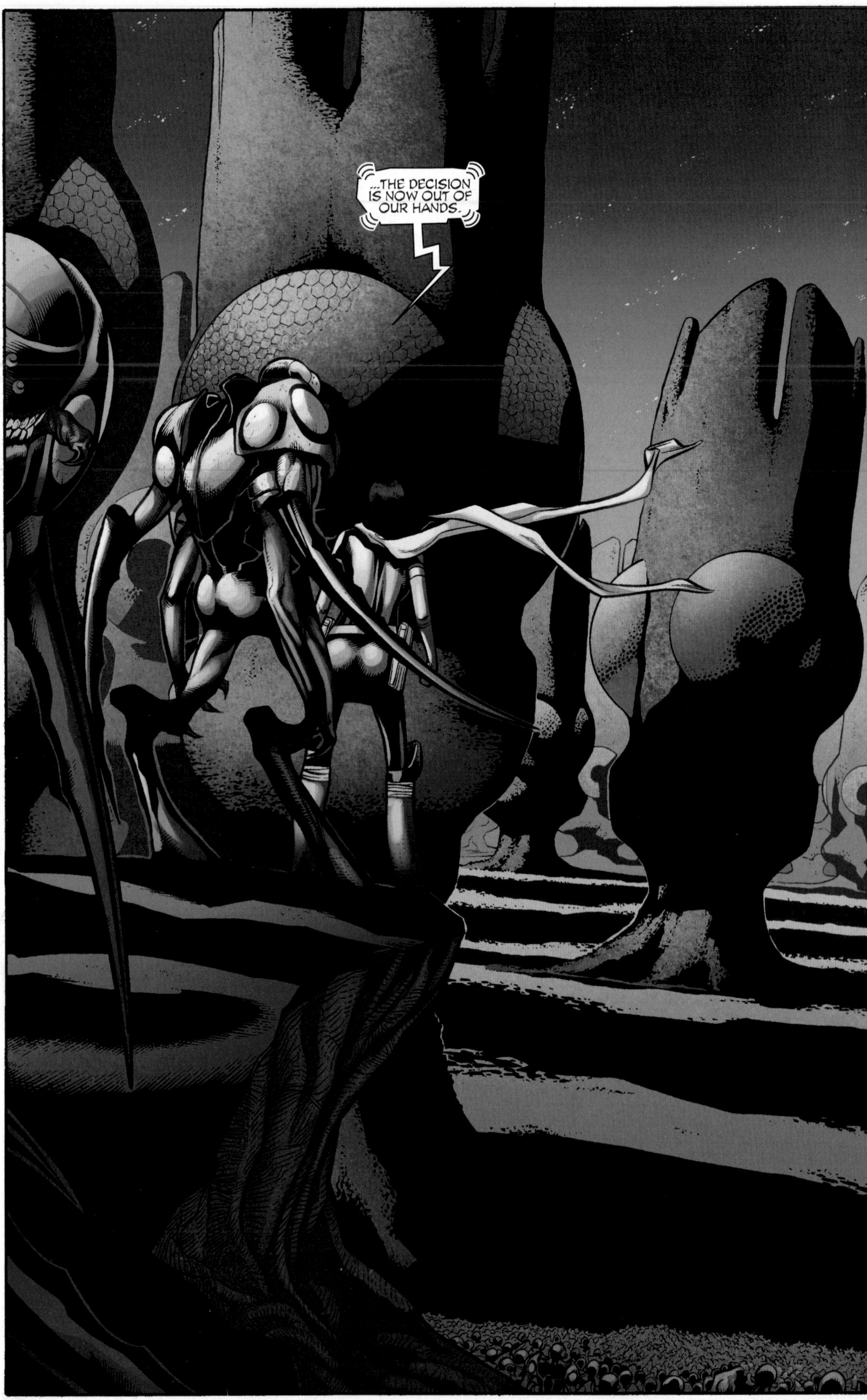
...THE DECISION IS NOW OUT OF OUR HANDS.

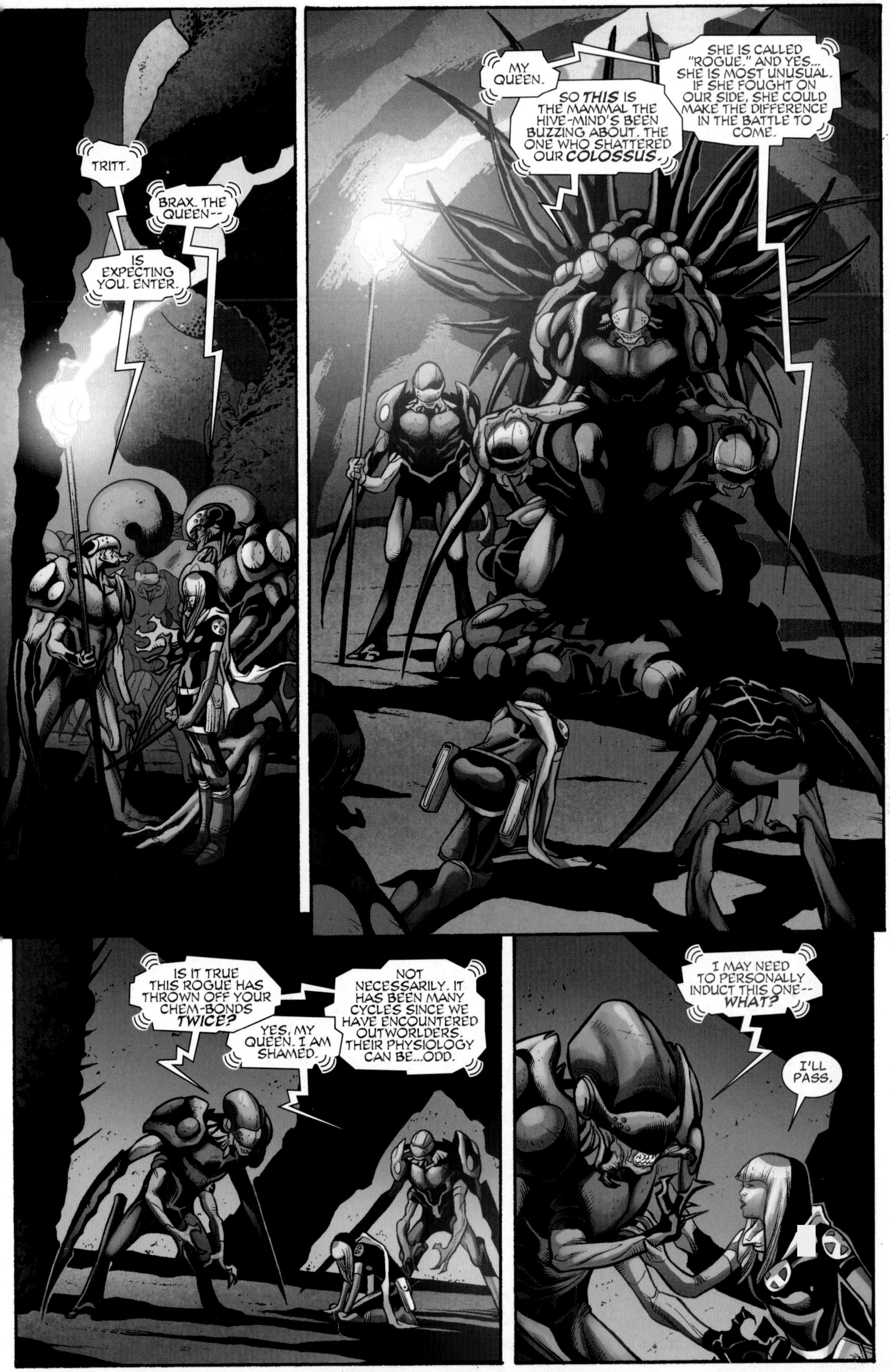
TRITT.
BRAX. THE QUEEN--
IS EXPECTING YOU. ENTER.
MY QUEEN.
SO THIS IS THE MAMMAL THE HIVE-MIND'S BEEN BUZZING ABOUT. THE ONE WHO SHATTERED OUR COLOSSUS.
SHE IS CALLED "ROGUE." AND YES... SHE IS MOST UNUSUAL. IF SHE FOUGHT ON OUR SIDE, SHE COULD MAKE THE DIFFERENCE IN THE BATTLE TO COME.
IS IT TRUE THIS ROGUE HAS THROWN OFF YOUR CHEM-BONDS TWICE?
YES, MY QUEEN. I AM SHAMED.
NOT NECESSARILY. IT HAS BEEN MANY CYCLES SINCE WE HAVE ENCOUNTERED OUTWORLDERS. THEIR PHYSIOLOGY CAN BE...ODD.
I MAY NEED TO PERSONALLY INDUCT THIS ONE-- WHAT?
I'LL PASS.

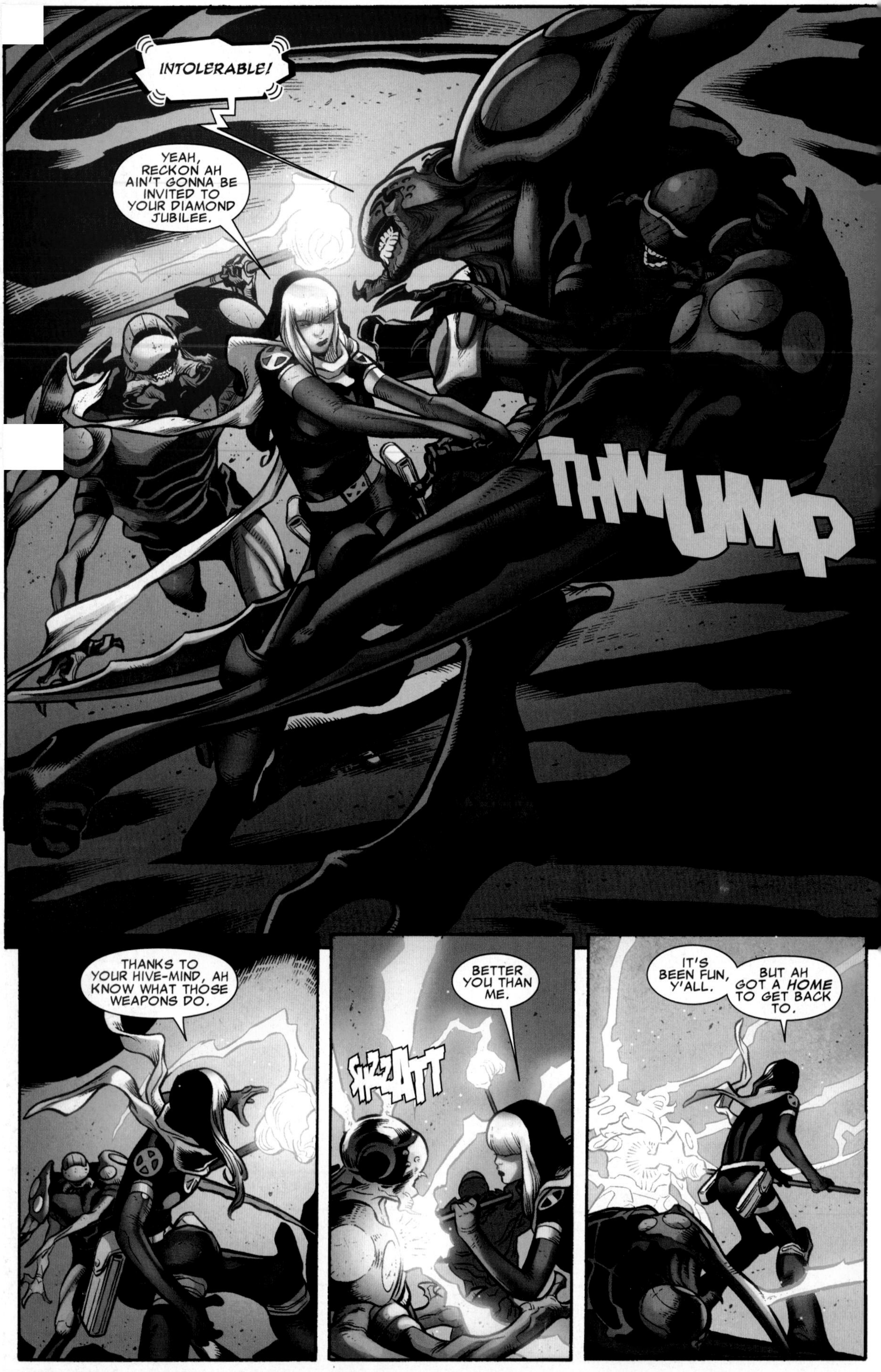
INTOLERABLE!
YEAH, RECKON AH AIN'T GONNA BE INVITED TO YOUR DIAMOND JUBILEE.
THWUMP
THANKS TO YOUR HIVE-MIND, AH KNOW WHAT THOSE WEAPONS DO.
SHZZATT
BETTER YOU THAN ME.
IT'S BEEN FUN, Y'ALL.
BUT AH GOT A HOME TO GET BACK TO.

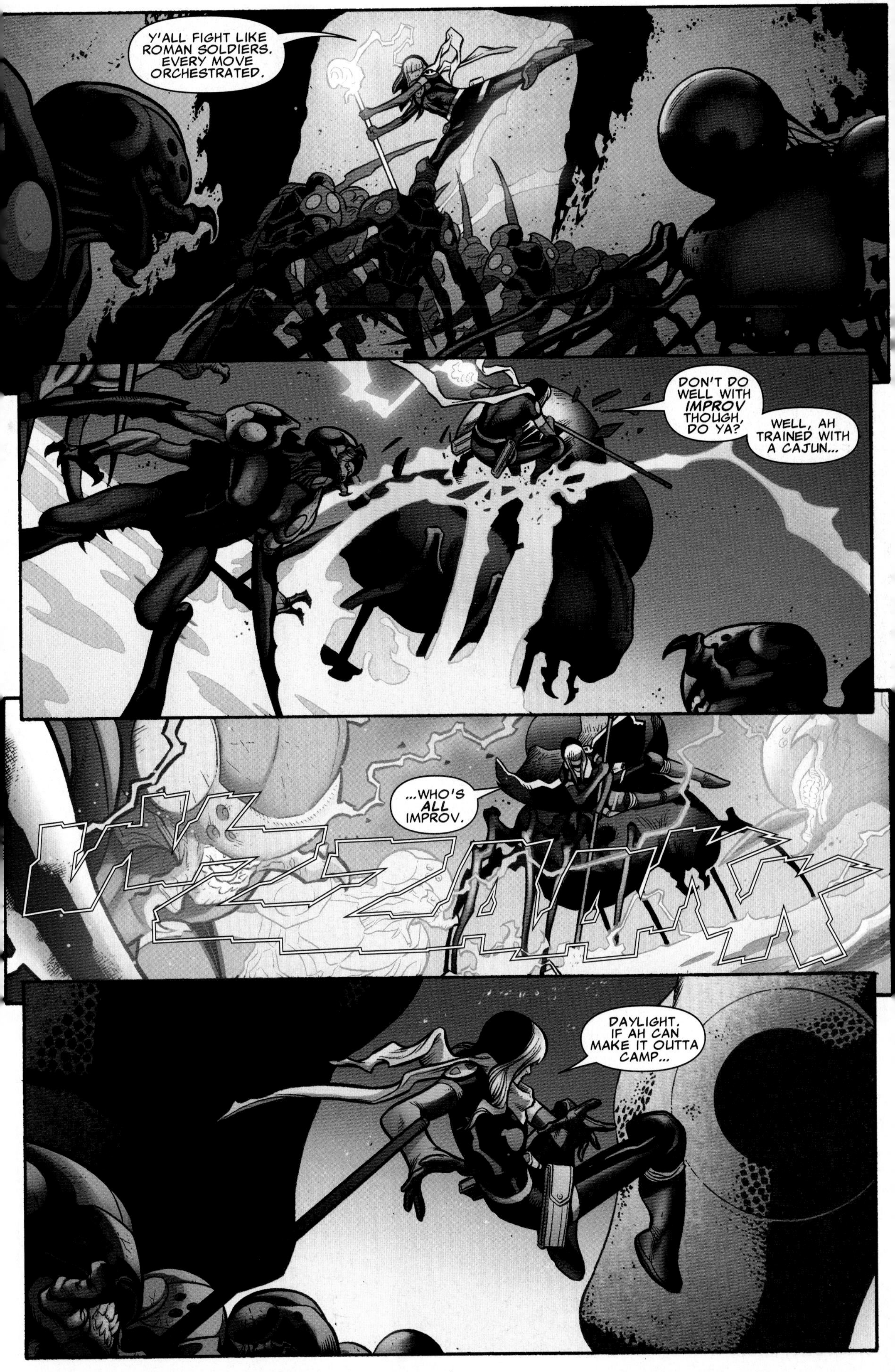
Y'ALL FIGHT LIKE ROMAN SOLDIERS. EVERY MOVE ORCHESTRATED.
DON'T DO WELL WITH IMPROV THOUGH, DO YA?
WELL, AH TRAINED WITH A CAJUN...
...WHO'S ALL IMPROV.
DAYLIGHT. IF AH CAN MAKE IT OUTTA CAMP...

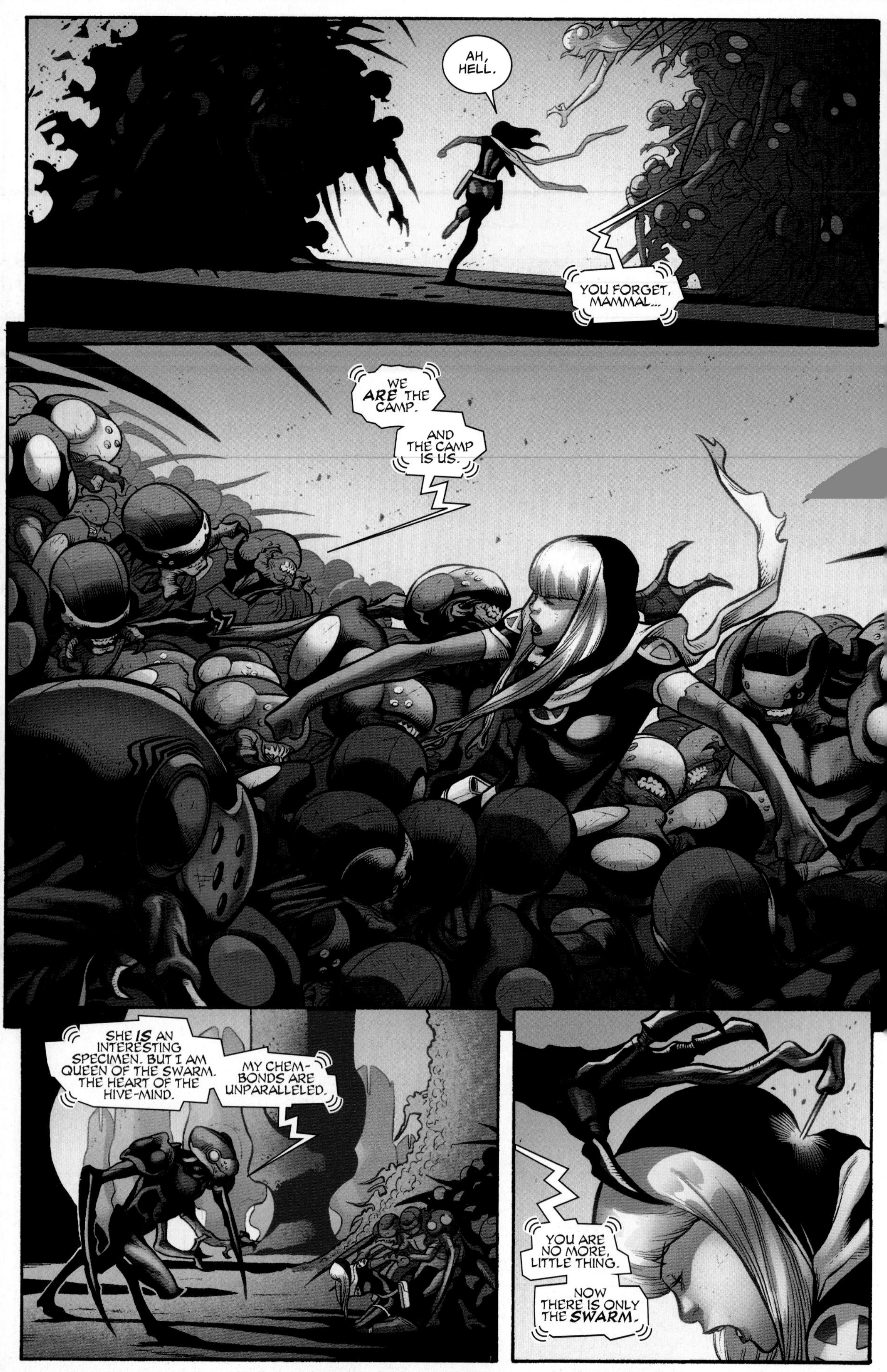
AH, HELL.
YOU FORGET, MAMMAL...
WE ARE THE CAMP.
AND THE CAMP IS US.
SHE IS AN INTERESTING SPECIMEN. BUT I AM QUEEN OF THE SWARM. THE HEART OF THE HIVE-MIND.
MY CHEM-BONDS ARE UNPARALLELED.
YOU ARE NO MORE, LITTLE THING.
NOW THERE IS ONLY THE SWARM.

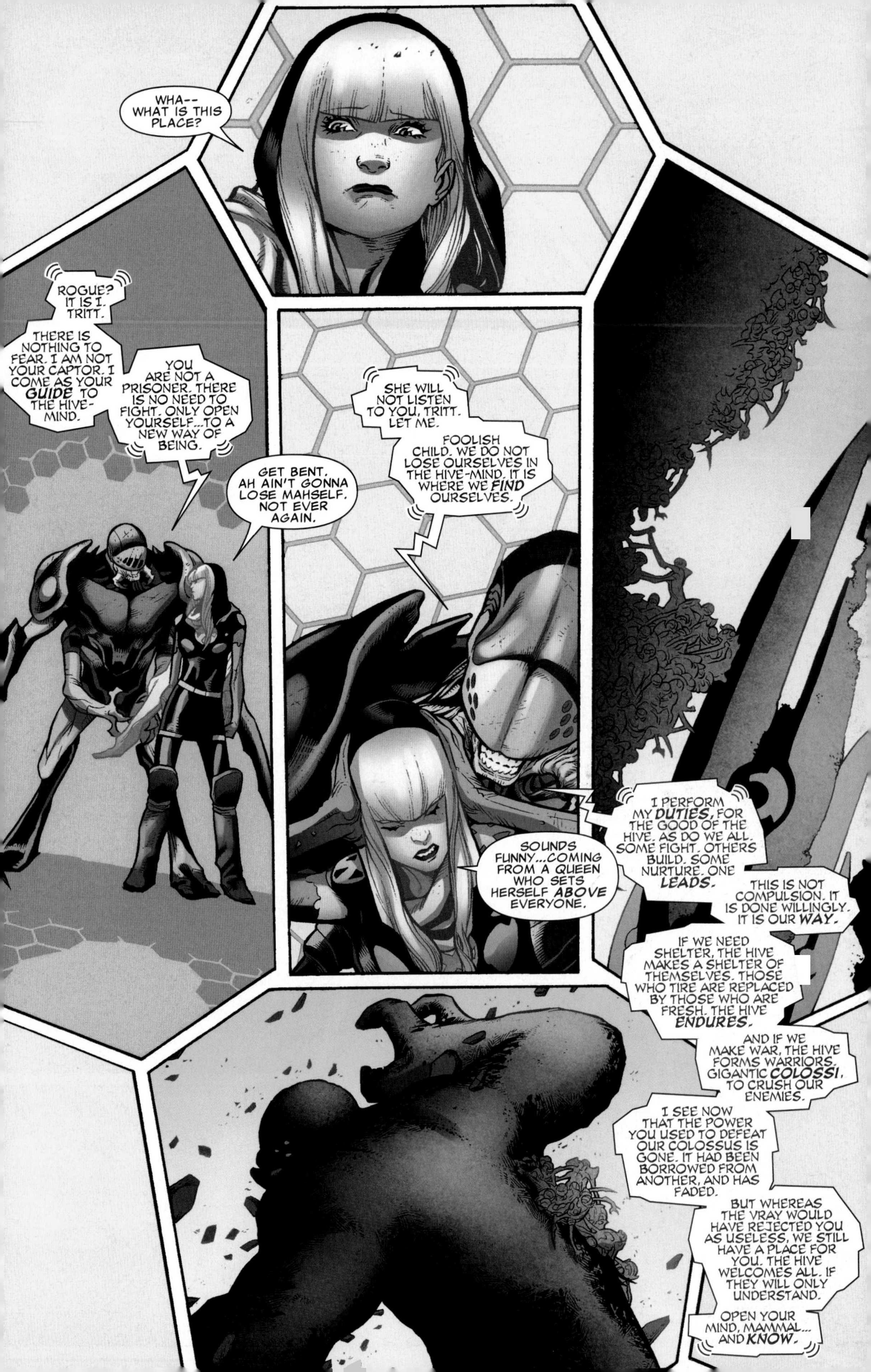
WHA-- WHAT IS THIS PLACE?
ROGUE? IT IS I. TRITT.
THERE IS NOTHING TO FEAR. I AM NOT YOUR CAPTOR. I COME AS YOUR GUIDE TO THE HIVE-MIND.
YOU ARE NOT A PRISONER. THERE IS NO NEED TO FIGHT. ONLY OPEN YOURSELF...TO A NEW WAY OF BEING.
GET BENT. AH AIN'T GONNA LOSE MAHSELF. NOT EVER AGAIN.
SHE WILL NOT LISTEN TO YOU, TRITT. LET ME.
FOOLISH CHILD. WE DO NOT LOSE OURSELVES IN THE HIVE-MIND. IT IS WHERE WE FIND OURSELVES.
SOUNDS FUNNY...COMING FROM A QUEEN WHO SETS HERSELF ABOVE EVERYONE.
I PERFORM MY DUTIES, FOR THE GOOD OF THE HIVE. AS DO WE ALL. SOME FIGHT. OTHERS BUILD. SOME NURTURE. ONE LEADS.
THIS IS NOT COMPULSION. IT IS DONE WILLINGLY. IT IS OUR WAY.
IF WE NEED SHELTER, THE HIVE MAKES A SHELTER OF THEMSELVES. THOSE WHO TIRE ARE REPLACED BY THOSE WHO ARE FRESH. THE HIVE ENDURES.
AND IF WE MAKE WAR, THE HIVE FORMS WARRIORS. GIGANTIC COLOSSI, TO CRUSH OUR ENEMIES.
I SEE NOW THAT THE POWER YOU USED TO DEFEAT OUR COLOSSUS IS GONE. IT HAD BEEN BORROWED FROM ANOTHER, AND HAS FADED.
BUT WHEREAS THE VRAY WOULD HAVE REJECTED YOU AS USELESS, WE STILL HAVE A PLACE FOR YOU. THE HIVE WELCOMES ALL. IF THEY WILL ONLY UNDERSTAND.
OPEN YOUR MIND, MAMMAL... AND KNOW.

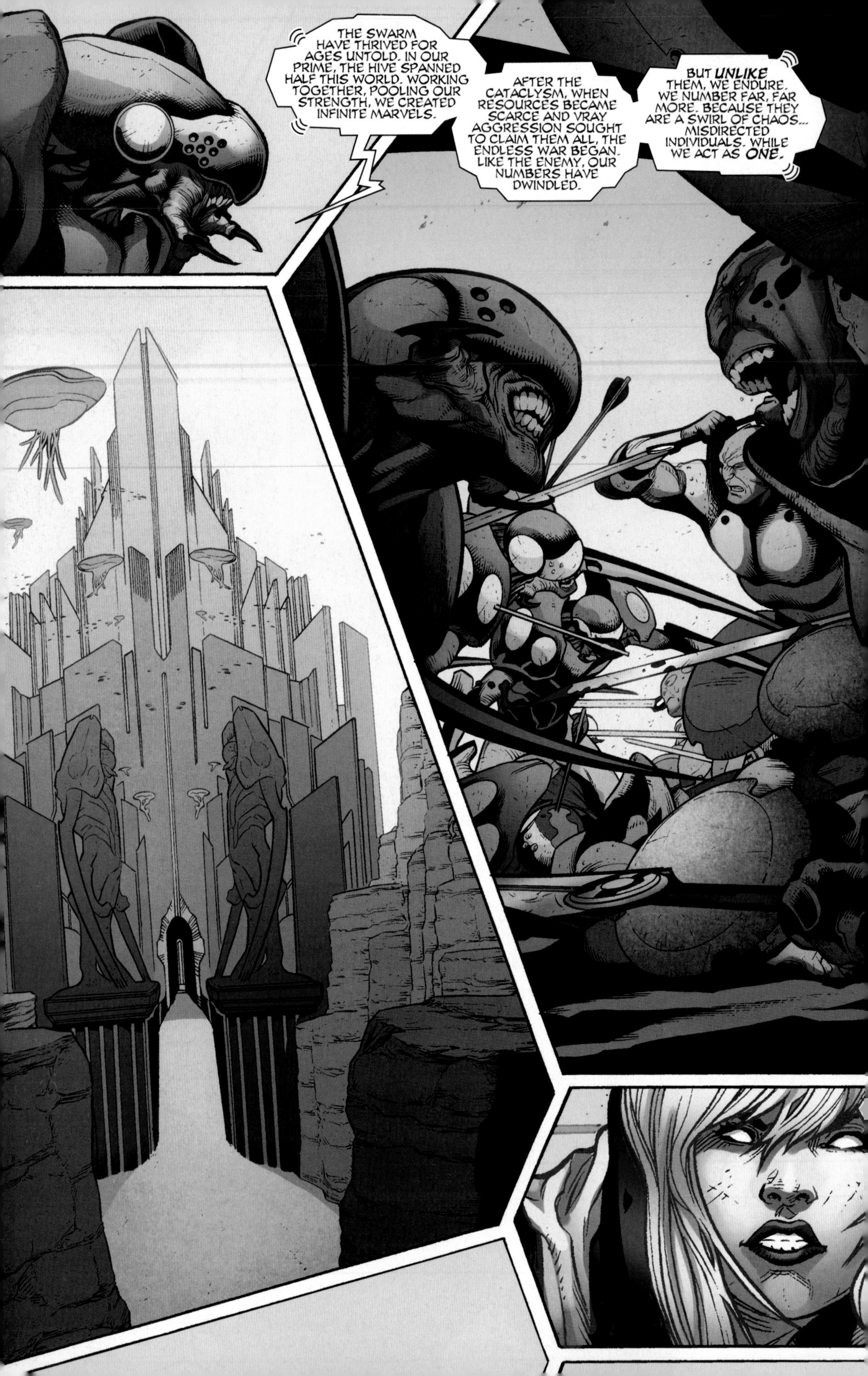
THE SWARM HAVE THRIVED FOR AGES UNTOLD. IN OUR PRIME, THE HIVE SPANNED HALF THIS WORLD. WORKING TOGETHER, POOLING OUR STRENGTH, WE CREATED INFINITE MARVELS.
AFTER THE CATACLYSM, WHEN RESOURCES BECAME SCARCE AND VRAY AGGRESSION SOUGHT TO CLAIM THEM ALL, THE ENDLESS WAR BEGAN. LIKE THE ENEMY, OUR NUMBERS HAVE DWINDLED.
BUT UNLIKE THEM, WE ENDURE. WE NUMBER FAR, FAR MORE. BECAUSE THEY ARE A SWIRL OF CHAOS... MISDIRECTED INDIVIDUALS. WHILE WE ACT AS ONE.

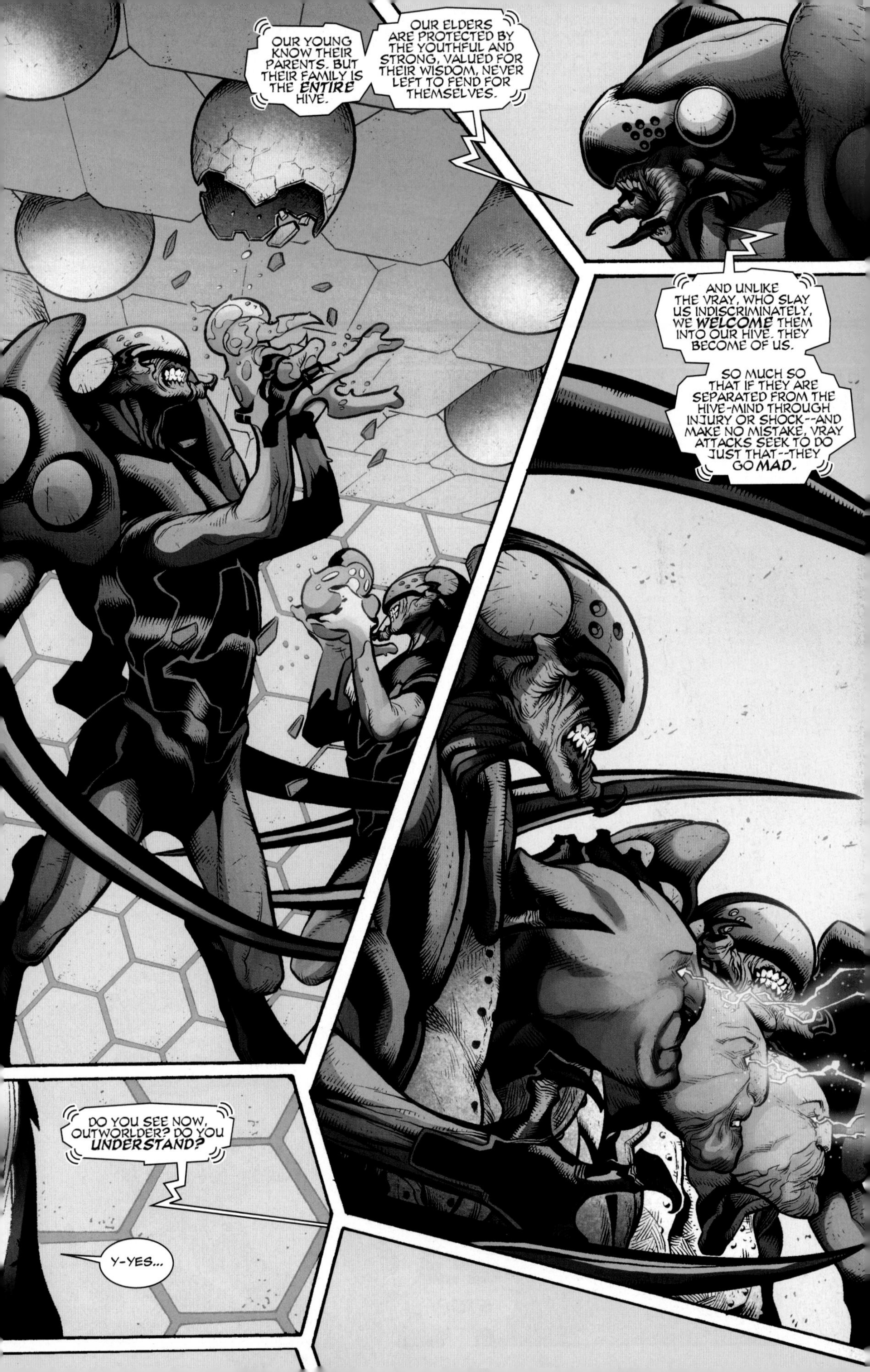
OUR YOUNG KNOW THEIR PARENTS. BUT THEIR FAMILY IS THE ENTIRE HIVE.
OUR ELDERS ARE PROTECTED BY THE YOUTHFUL AND STRONG, VALUED FOR THEIR WISDOM, NEVER LEFT TO FEND FOR THEMSELVES.
AND UNLIKE THE VRAY, WHO SLAY US INDISCRIMINATELY, WE WELCOME THEM INTO OUR HIVE. THEY BECOME OF US.
SO MUCH SO THAT IF THEY ARE SEPARATED FROM THE HIVE-MIND THROUGH INJURY OR SHOCK--AND MAKE NO MISTAKE, VRAY ATTACKS SEEK TO DO JUST THAT--THEY GO MAD.
DO YOU SEE NOW, OUTWORLDER? DO YOU UNDERSTAND?
Y-YES...

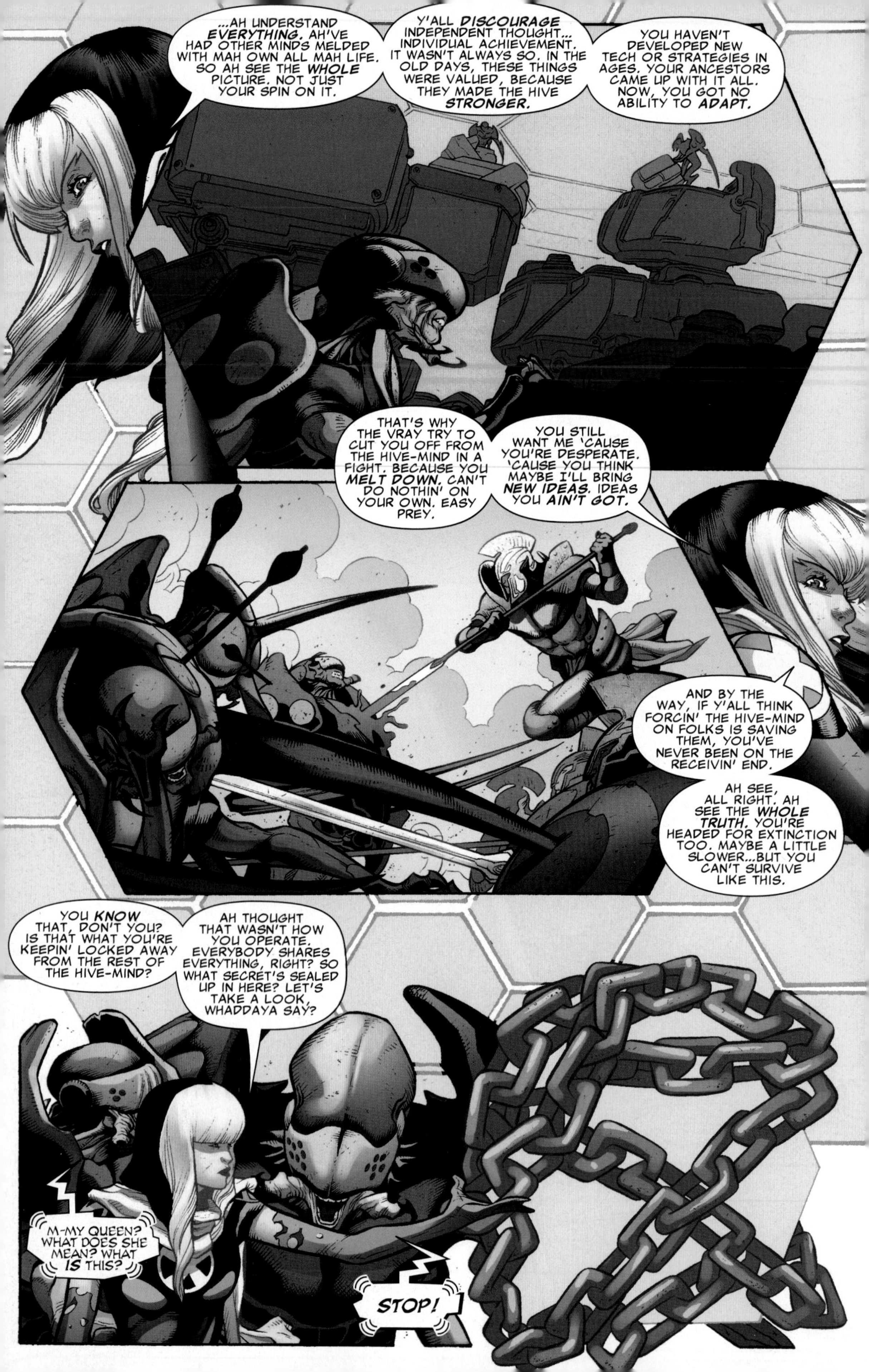
...AH UNDERSTAND EVERYTHING. AH'VE HAD OTHER MINDS MELDED WITH MAH OWN ALL MAH LIFE. SO AH SEE THE WHOLE PICTURE. NOT JUST YOUR SPIN ON IT.
Y'ALL DISCOURAGE INDEPENDENT THOUGHT... INDIVIDUAL ACHIEVEMENT. IT WASN'T ALWAYS SO. IN THE OLD DAYS, THESE THINGS WERE VALUED, BECAUSE THEY MADE THE HIVE STRONGER.
YOU HAVEN'T DEVELOPED NEW TECH OR STRATEGIES IN AGES. YOUR ANCESTORS CAME UP WITH IT ALL. NOW, YOU GOT NO ABILITY TO ADAPT.
THAT'S WHY THE VRAY TRY TO CUT YOU OFF FROM THE HIVE-MIND IN A FIGHT. BECAUSE YOU MELT DOWN. CAN'T DO NOTHIN' ON YOUR OWN. EASY PREY.
YOU STILL WANT ME 'CAUSE YOU'RE DESPERATE. 'CAUSE YOU THINK MAYBE I'LL BRING NEW IDEAS. IDEAS YOU AIN'T GOT.
AND BY THE WAY, IF Y'ALL THINK FORCIN' THE HIVE-MIND ON FOLKS IS SAVING THEM, YOU'VE NEVER BEEN ON THE RECEIVIN' END.
AH SEE, ALL RIGHT. AH SEE THE WHOLE TRUTH. YOU'RE HEADED FOR EXTINCTION TOO. MAYBE A LITTLE SLOWER...BUT YOU CAN'T SURVIVE LIKE THIS.
YOU KNOW THAT, DON'T YOU? IS THAT WHAT YOU'RE KEEPIN' LOCKED AWAY FROM THE REST OF THE HIVE-MIND?
AH THOUGHT THAT WASN'T HOW YOU OPERATE. EVERYBODY SHARES EVERYTHING, RIGHT? SO WHAT SECRET'S SEALED UP IN HERE? LET'S TAKE A LOOK, WHADDAYA SAY?
M-MY QUEEN? WHAT DOES SHE MEAN? WHAT IS THIS?
STOP!

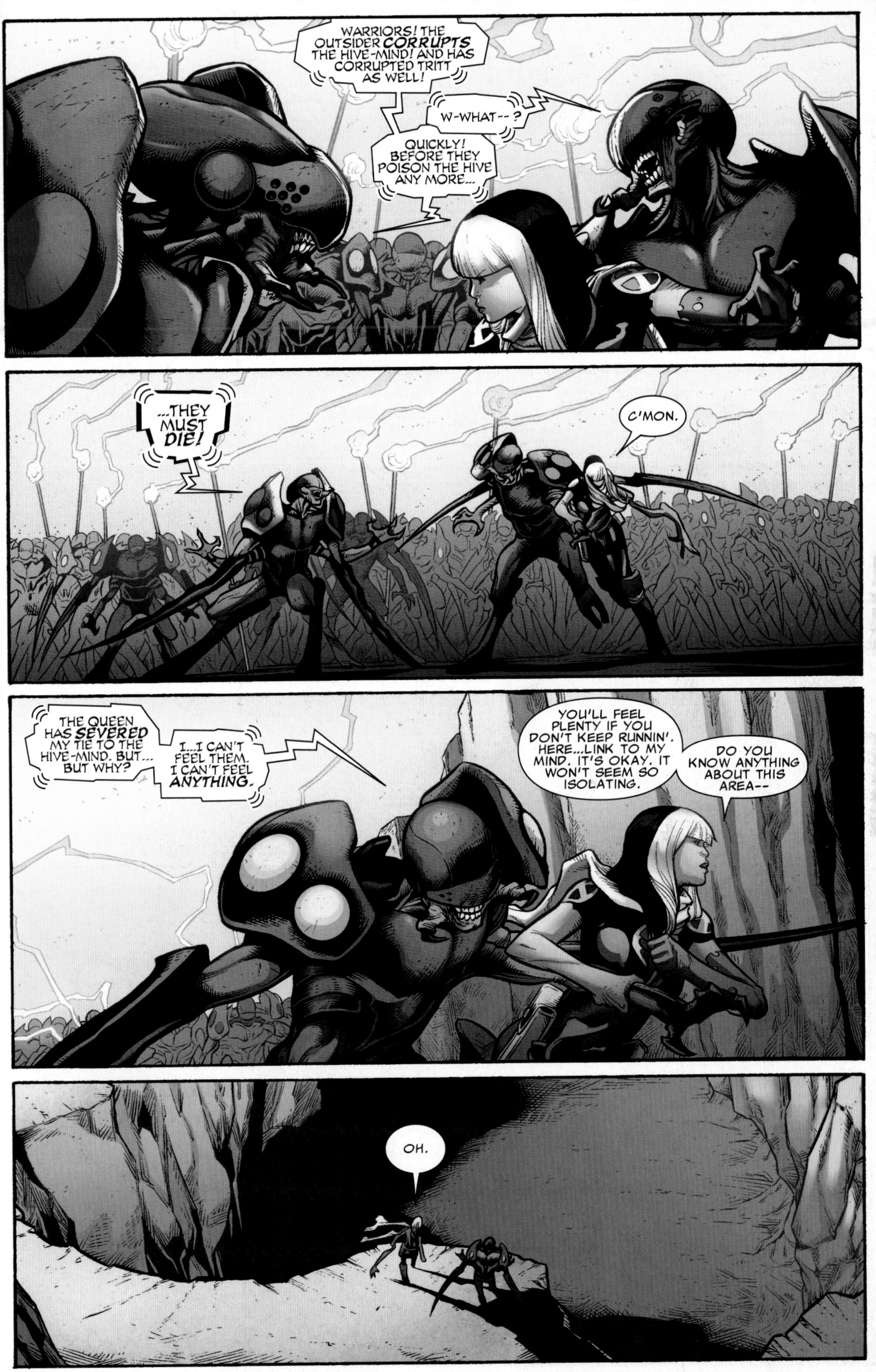
WARRIORS! THE OUTSIDER CORRUPTS THE HIVE-MIND! AND HAS CORRUPTED TRITT AS WELL!
W-WHAT-- ?
QUICKLY! BEFORE THEY POISON THE HIVE ANY MORE...
...THEY MUST DIE!
C'MON.
THE QUEEN HAS SEVERED MY TIE TO THE HIVE-MIND. BUT... BUT WHY?
I...I CAN'T FEEL THEM. I CAN'T FEEL ANYTHING.
YOU'LL FEEL PLENTY IF YOU DON'T KEEP RUNNIN'. HERE...LINK TO MY MIND. IT'S OKAY. IT WON'T SEEM SO ISOLATING.
DO YOU KNOW ANYTHING ABOUT THIS AREA--
OH.

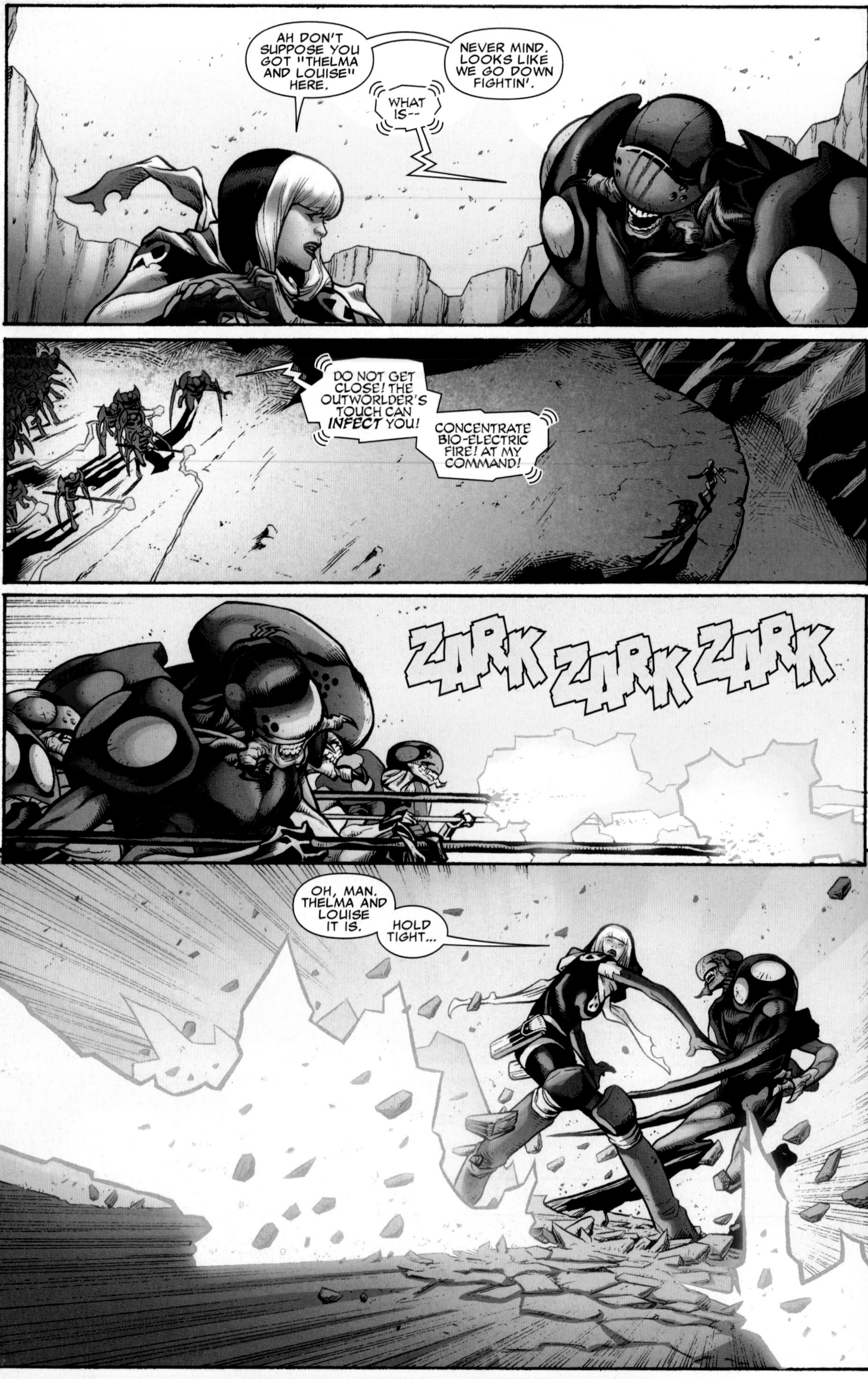
AH DON'T SUPPOSE YOU GOT "THELMA AND LOUISE" HERE.
WHAT IS--
NEVER MIND. LOOKS LIKE WE GO DOWN FIGHTIN'.
DO NOT GET CLOSE! THE OUTWORLDER'S TOUCH CAN INFECT YOU!
CONCENTRATE BIO-ELECTRIC FIRE! AT MY COMMAND!
ZARK ZARK ZARK
OH, MAN. THELMA AND LOUISE IT IS.
HOLD TIGHT...

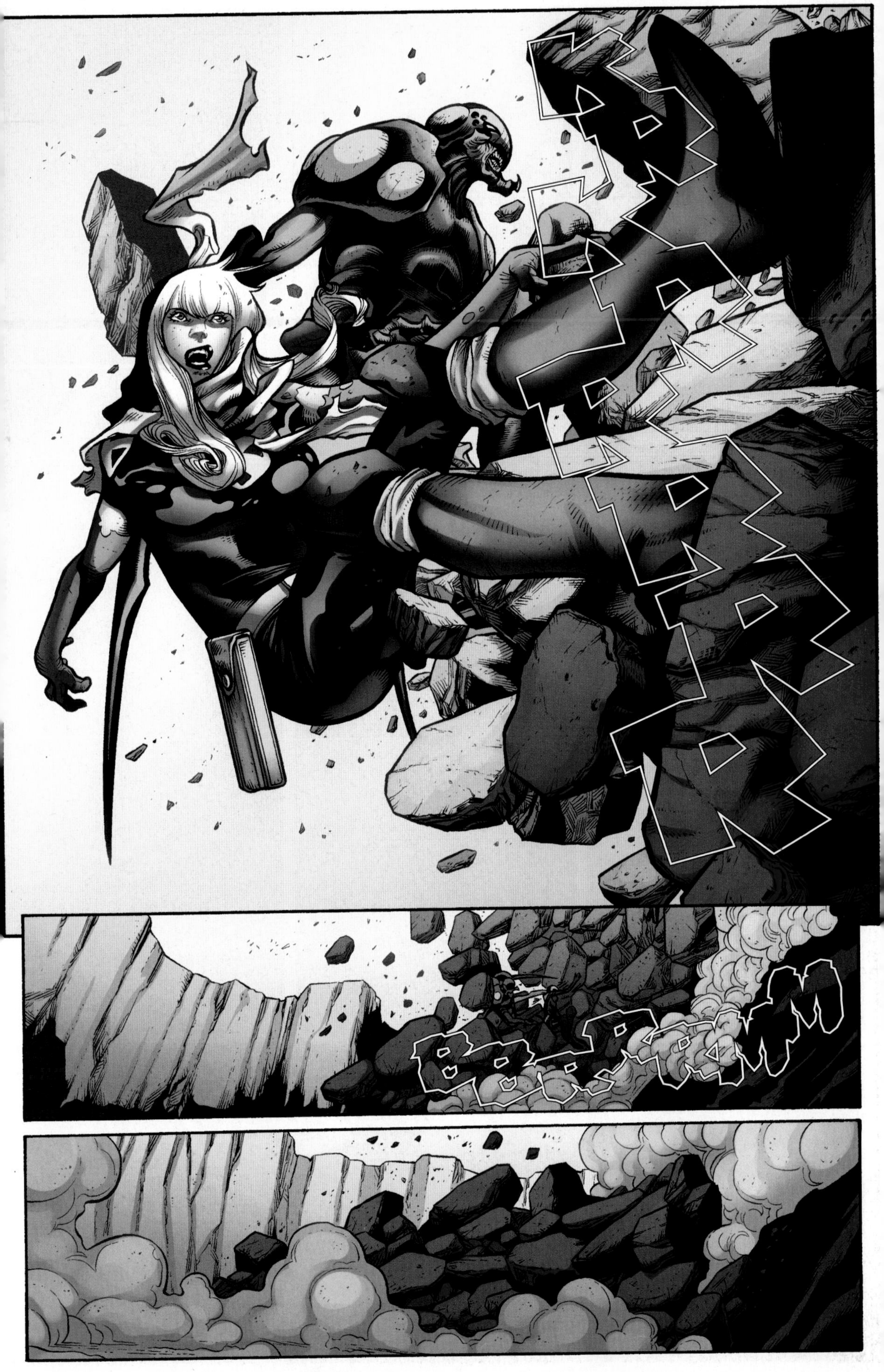

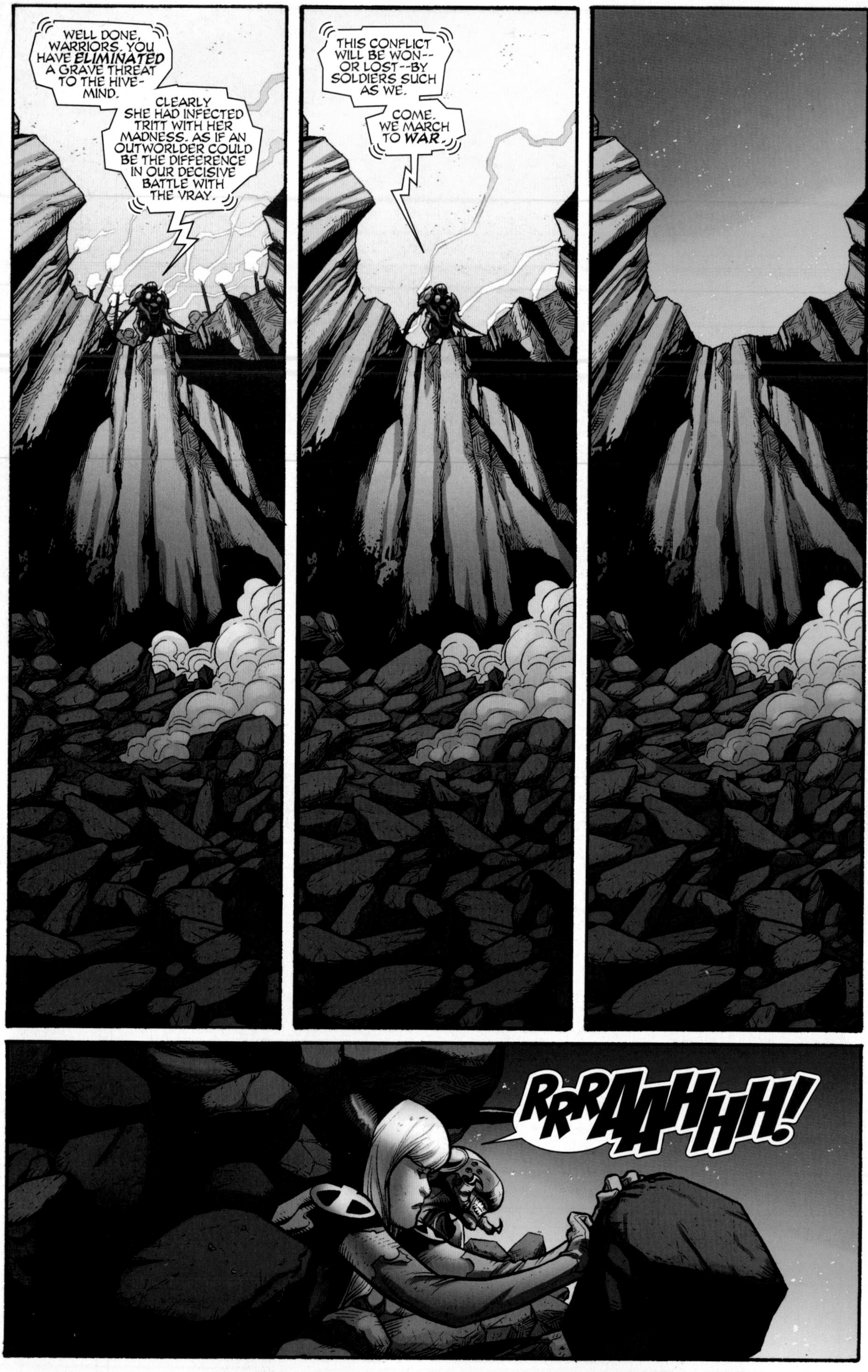
WELL DONE, WARRIORS. YOU HAVE ELIMINATED A GRAVE THREAT TO THE HIVE-MIND.
CLEARLY SHE HAD INFECTED TRITT WITH HER MADNESS. AS IF AN OUTWORLDER COULD BE THE DIFFERENCE IN OUR DECISIVE BATTLE WITH THE VRAY.
THIS CONFLICT WILL BE WON--OR LOST--BY SOLDIERS SUCH AS WE.
COME. WE MARCH TO WAR.
RRRAAHHHH!

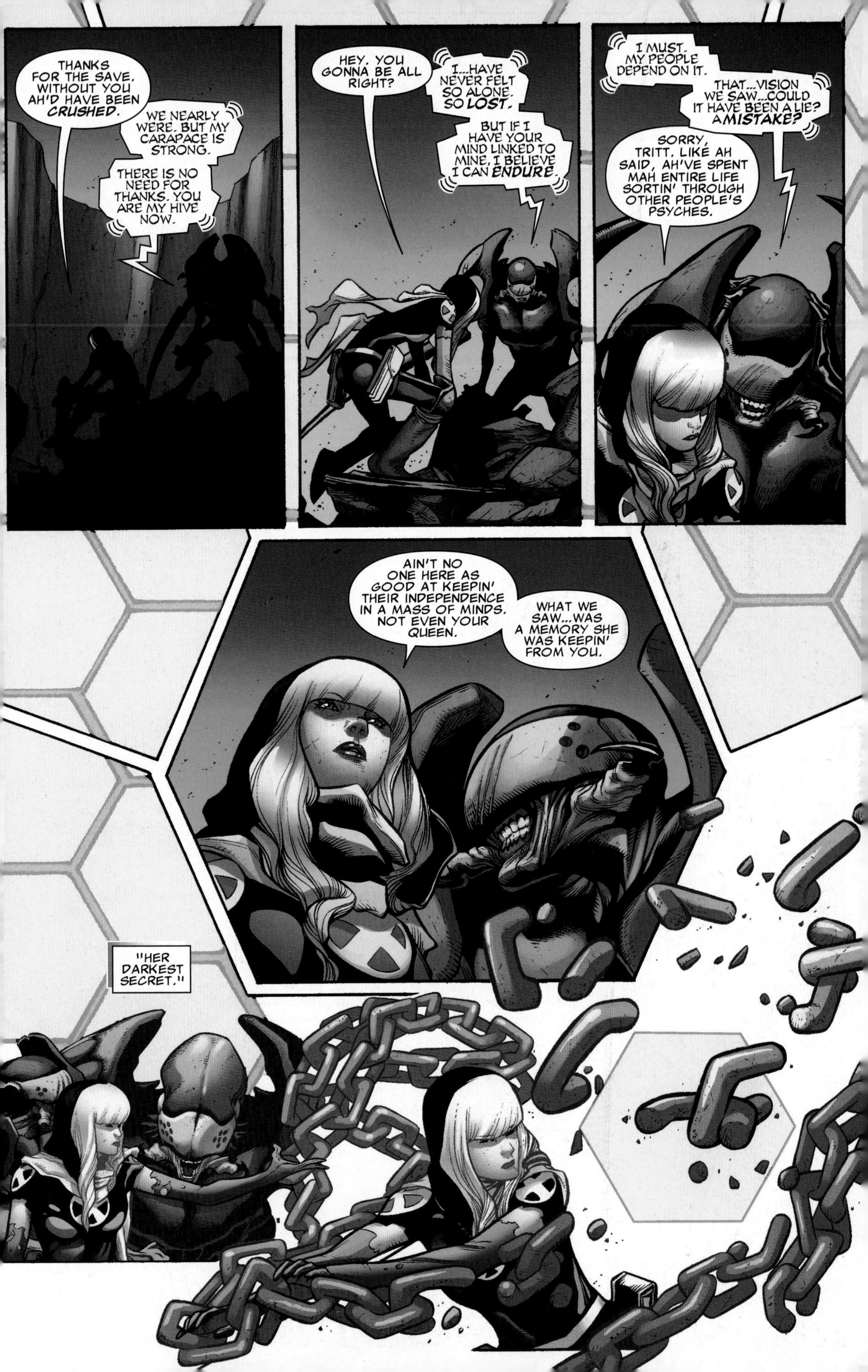
THANKS FOR THE SAVE. WITHOUT YOU AH'D HAVE BEEN CRUSHED.
WE NEARLY WERE. BUT MY CARAPACE IS STRONG.
THERE IS NO NEED FOR THANKS. YOU ARE MY HIVE NOW.
HEY. YOU GONNA BE ALL RIGHT?
I...HAVE NEVER FELT SO ALONE. SO LOST.
BUT IF I HAVE YOUR MIND LINKED TO MINE, I BELIEVE I CAN ENDURE.
I MUST. MY PEOPLE DEPEND ON IT.
THAT...VISION WE SAW...COULD IT HAVE BEEN A LIE? A MISTAKE?
SORRY, TRITT. LIKE AH SAID, AH'VE SPENT MAH ENTIRE LIFE SORTIN' THROUGH OTHER PEOPLE'S PSYCHES.
AIN'T NO ONE HERE AS GOOD AT KEEPIN' THEIR INDEPENDENCE IN A MASS OF MINDS. NOT EVEN YOUR QUEEN.
WHAT WE SAW...WAS A MEMORY SHE WAS KEEPIN' FROM YOU.
"HER DARKEST SECRET."

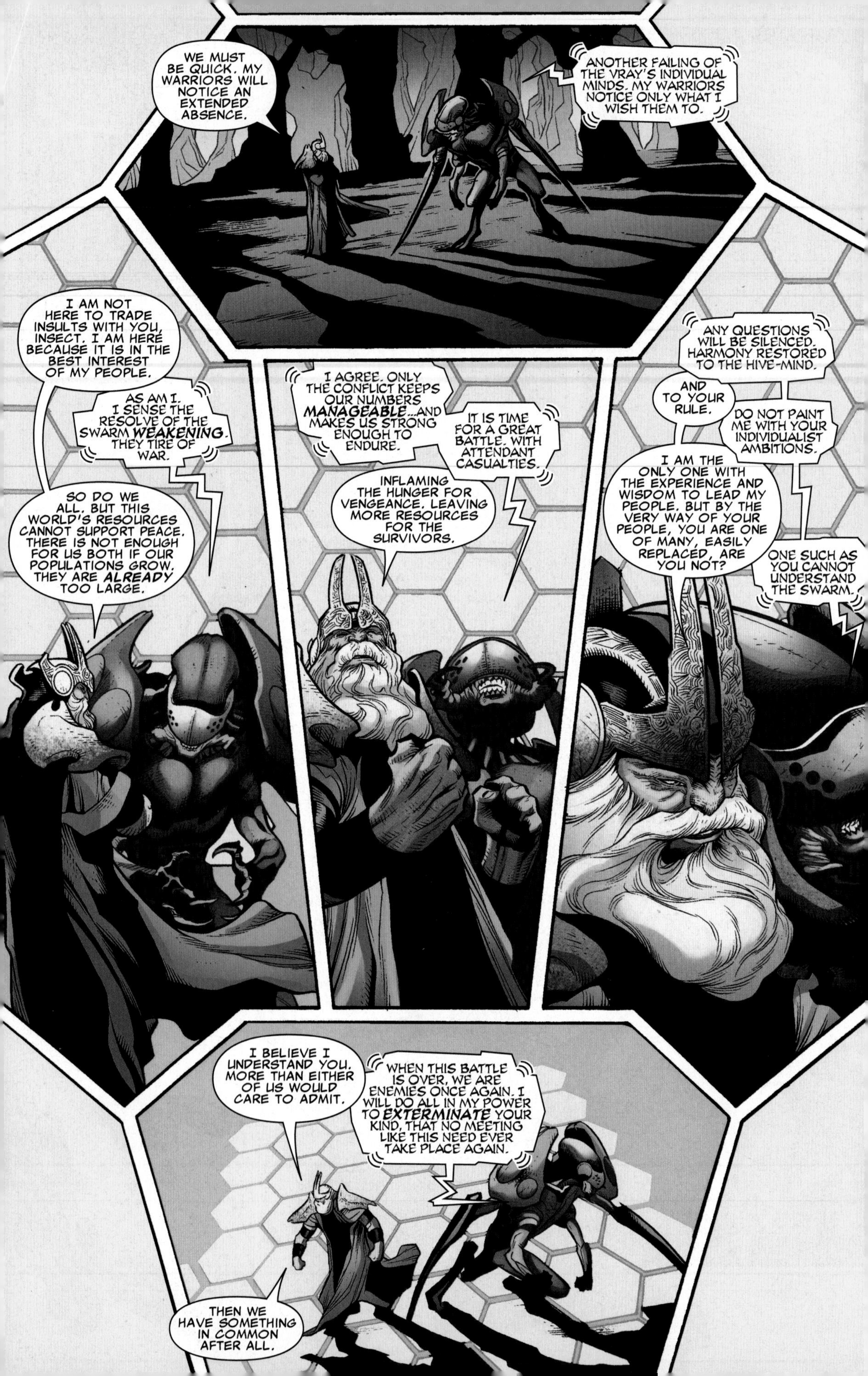
WE MUST BE QUICK. MY WARRIORS WILL NOTICE AN EXTENDED ABSENCE.
ANOTHER FAILING OF THE VRAY'S INDIVIDUAL MINDS. MY WARRIORS NOTICE ONLY WHAT I WISH THEM TO.
I AM NOT HERE TO TRADE INSULTS WITH YOU, INSECT. I AM HERE BECAUSE IT IS IN THE BEST INTEREST OF MY PEOPLE.
AS AM I. I SENSE THE RESOLVE OF THE SWARM WEAKENING. THEY TIRE OF WAR.
SO DO WE ALL. BUT THIS WORLD'S RESOURCES CANNOT SUPPORT PEACE. THERE IS NOT ENOUGH FOR US BOTH IF OUR POPULATIONS GROW. THEY ARE ALREADY TOO LARGE.
I AGREE. ONLY THE CONFLICT KEEPS OUR NUMBERS MANAGEABLE...AND MAKES US STRONG ENOUGH TO ENDURE.
IT IS TIME FOR A GREAT BATTLE. WITH ATTENDANT CASUALTIES.
INFLAMING THE HUNGER FOR VENGEANCE. LEAVING MORE RESOURCES FOR THE SURVIVORS.
ANY QUESTIONS WILL BE SILENCED. HARMONY RESTORED TO THE HIVE-MIND.
AND TO YOUR RULE.
DO NOT PAINT ME WITH YOUR INDIVIDUALIST AMBITIONS.
I AM THE ONLY ONE WITH THE EXPERIENCE AND WISDOM TO LEAD MY PEOPLE. BUT BY THE VERY WAY OF YOUR PEOPLE, YOU ARE ONE OF MANY, EASILY REPLACED, ARE YOU NOT?
ONE SUCH AS YOU CANNOT UNDERSTAND THE SWARM.
I BELIEVE I UNDERSTAND YOU. MORE THAN EITHER OF US WOULD CARE TO ADMIT.
WHEN THIS BATTLE IS OVER, WE ARE ENEMIES ONCE AGAIN. I WILL DO ALL IN MY POWER TO EXTERMINATE YOUR KIND, THAT NO MEETING LIKE THIS NEED EVER TAKE PLACE AGAIN.
THEN WE HAVE SOMETHING IN COMMON AFTER ALL.

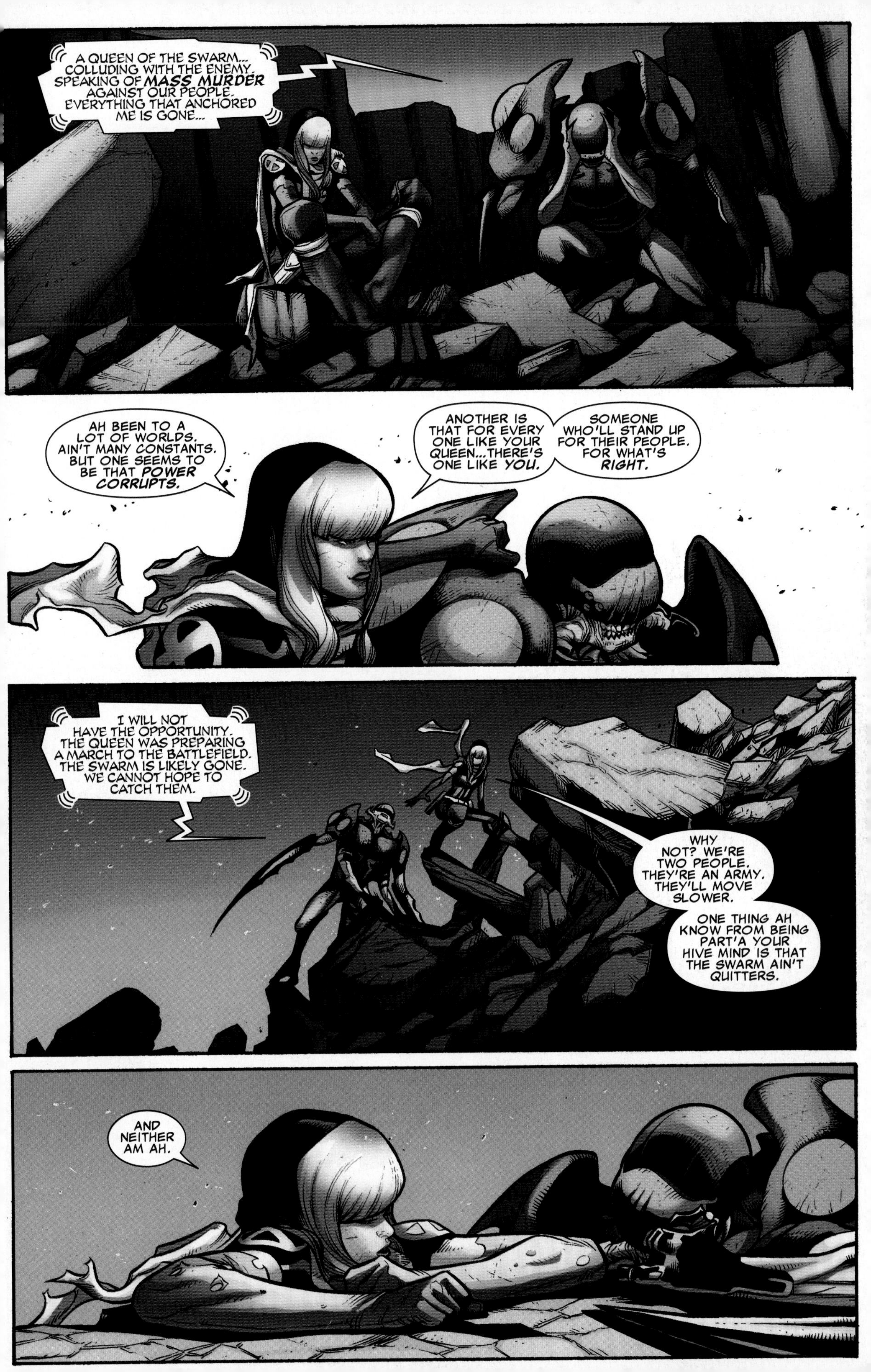
A QUEEN OF THE SWARM... COLLUDING WITH THE ENEMY. SPEAKING OF MASS MURDER AGAINST OUR PEOPLE. EVERYTHING THAT ANCHORED ME IS GONE...
AH BEEN TO A LOT OF WORLDS. AIN'T MANY CONSTANTS. BUT ONE SEEMS TO BE THAT POWER CORRUPTS.
ANOTHER IS THAT FOR EVERY ONE LIKE YOUR QUEEN...THERE'S ONE LIKE YOU.
SOMEONE WHO'LL STAND UP FOR THEIR PEOPLE. FOR WHAT'S RIGHT.
I WILL NOT HAVE THE OPPORTUNITY. THE QUEEN WAS PREPARING A MARCH TO THE BATTLEFIELD. THE SWARM IS LIKELY GONE. WE CANNOT HOPE TO CATCH THEM.
WHY NOT? WE'RE TWO PEOPLE. THEY'RE AN ARMY. THEY'LL MOVE SLOWER.
ONE THING AH KNOW FROM BEING PART'A YOUR HIVE MIND IS THAT THE SWARM AIN'T QUITTERS.
AND NEITHER AM AH.

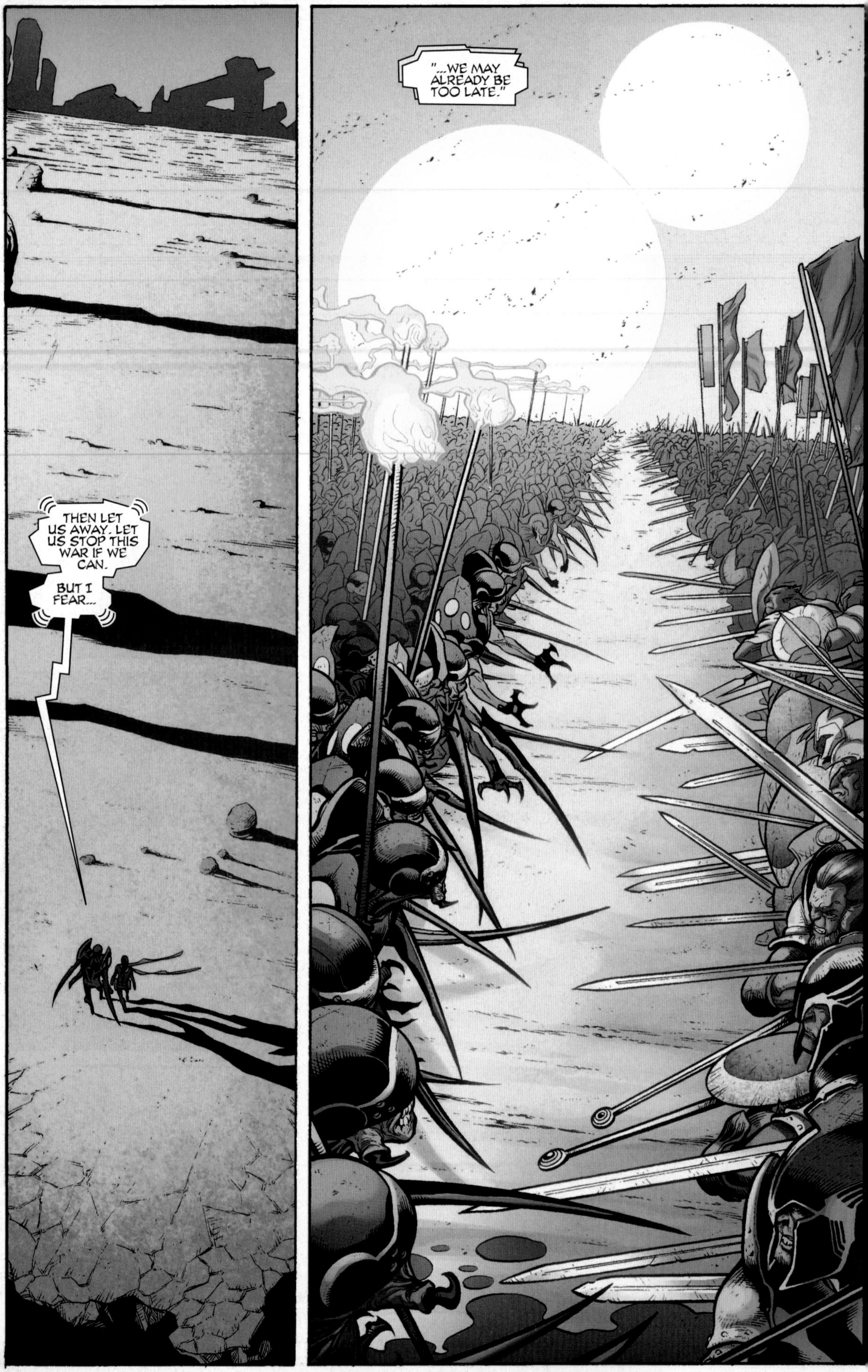
THEN LET US AWAY. LET US STOP THIS WAR IF WE CAN.
BUT I FEAR...
"...WE MAY ALREADY BE TOO LATE."

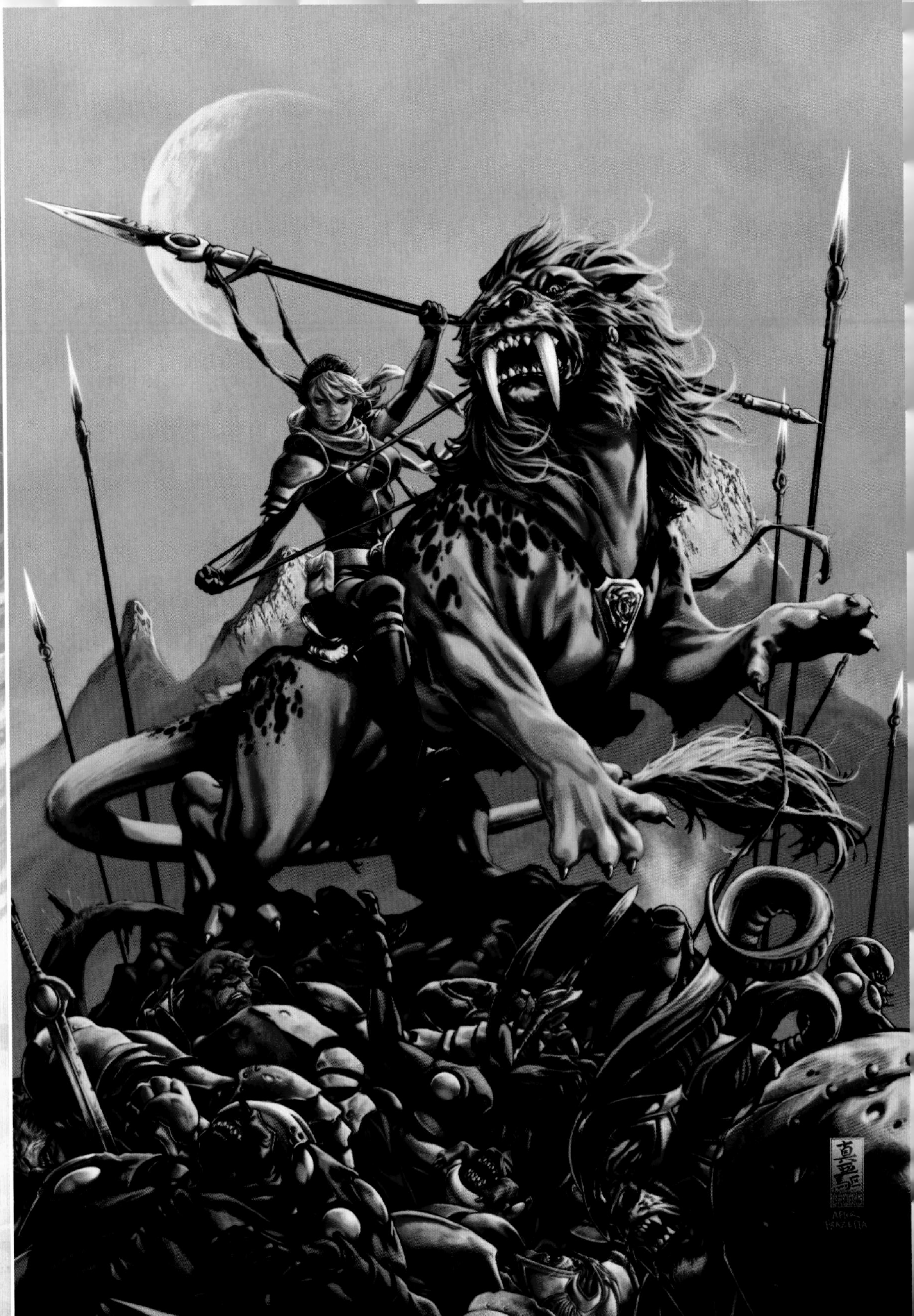

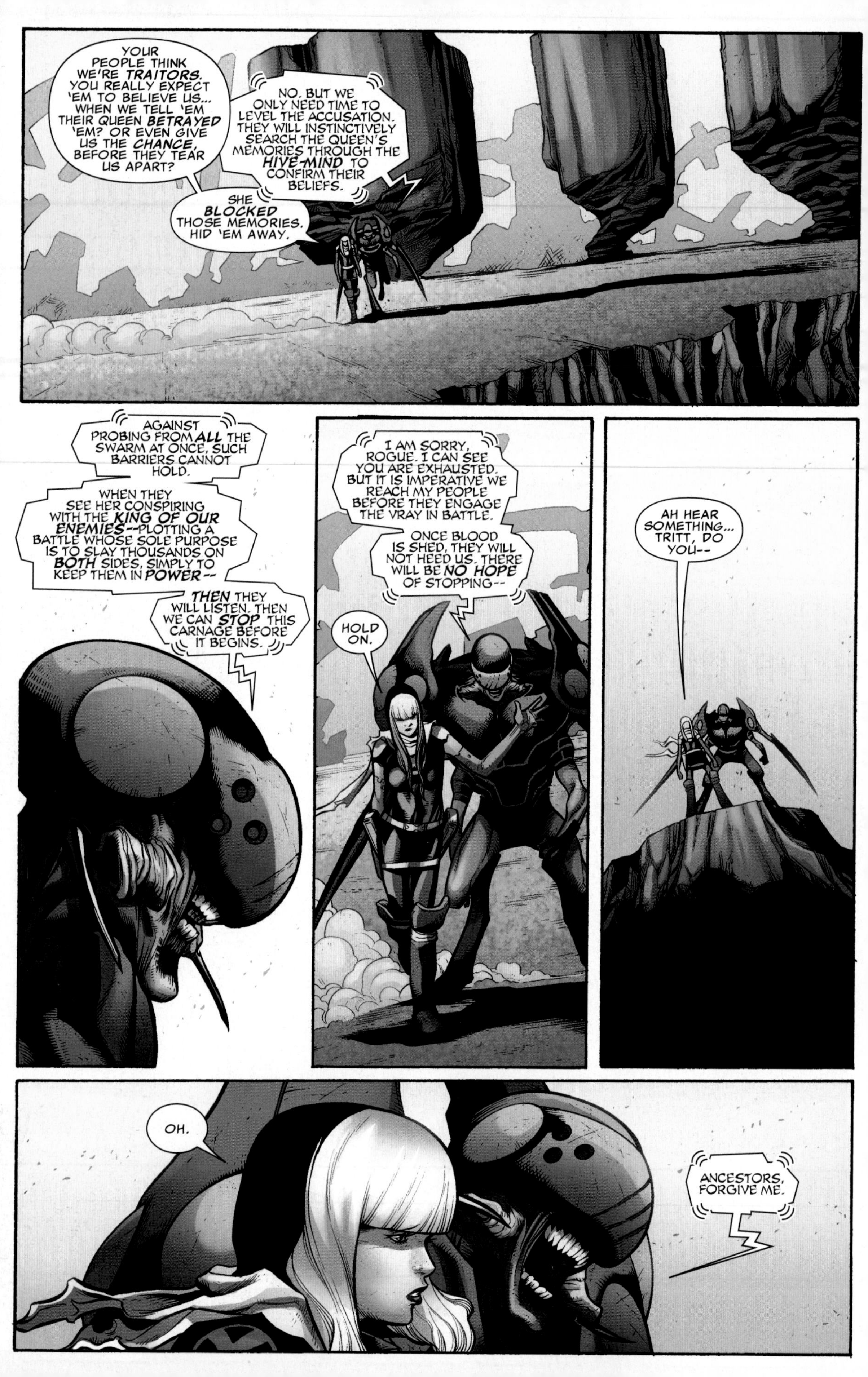
YOUR PEOPLE THINK WE'RE TRAITORS. YOU REALLY EXPECT 'EM TO BELIEVE US... WHEN WE TELL 'EM THEIR QUEEN BETRAYED 'EM? OR EVEN GIVE US THE CHANCE, BEFORE THEY TEAR US APART?
NO. BUT WE ONLY NEED TIME TO LEVEL THE ACCUSATION. THEY WILL INSTINCTIVELY SEARCH THE QUEEN'S MEMORIES THROUGH THE HIVE-MIND TO CONFIRM THEIR BELIEFS.
SHE BLOCKED THOSE MEMORIES. HID 'EM AWAY.
AGAINST PROBING FROM ALL THE SWARM AT ONCE, SUCH BARRIERS CANNOT HOLD.
WHEN THEY SEE HER CONSPIRING WITH THE KING OF OUR ENEMIES--PLOTTING A BATTLE WHOSE SOLE PURPOSE IS TO SLAY THOUSANDS ON BOTH SIDES, SIMPLY TO KEEP THEM IN POWER--
THEN THEY WILL LISTEN. THEN WE CAN STOP THIS CARNAGE BEFORE IT BEGINS.
I AM SORRY, ROGUE. I CAN SEE YOU ARE EXHAUSTED. BUT IT IS IMPERATIVE WE REACH MY PEOPLE BEFORE THEY ENGAGE THE VRAY IN BATTLE.
ONCE BLOOD IS SHED, THEY WILL NOT HEED US. THERE WILL BE NO HOPE OF STOPPING--
HOLD ON.
AH HEAR SOMETHING... TRITT, DO YOU--
OH.
ANCESTORS, FORGIVE ME.

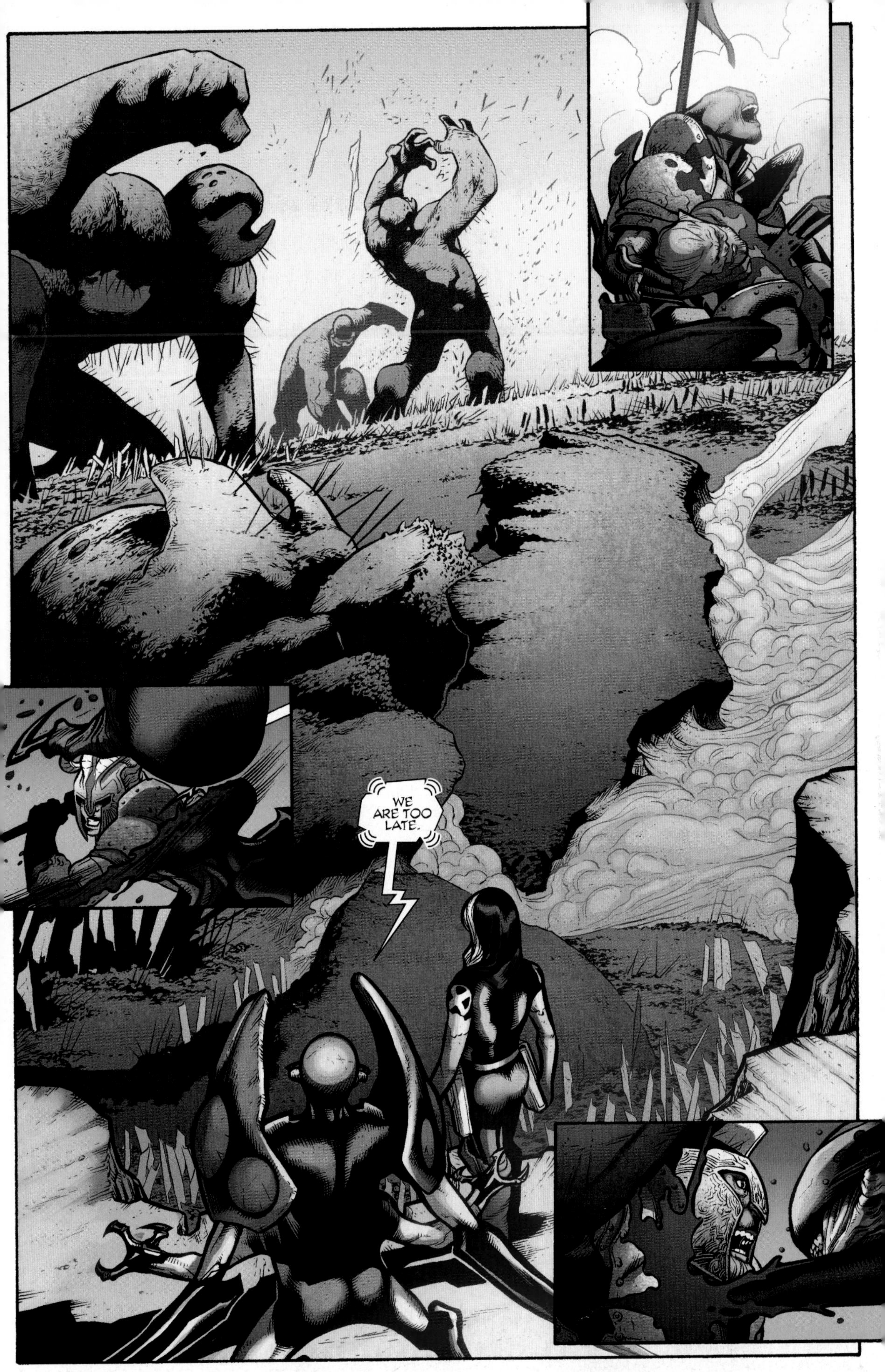
WE ARE TOO LATE.

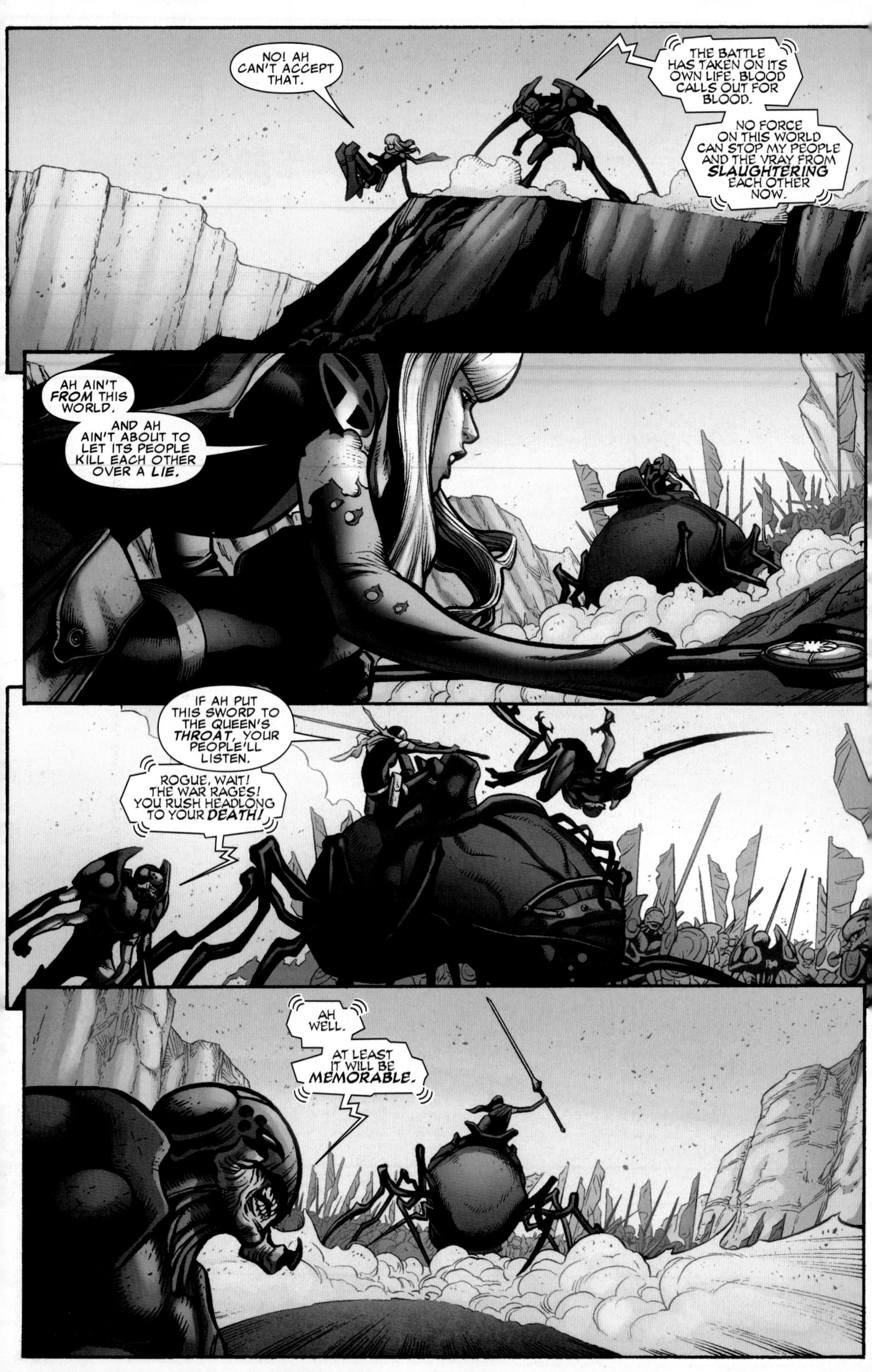
NO! AH CAN'T ACCEPT THAT.
THE BATTLE HAS TAKEN ON ITS OWN LIFE. BLOOD CALLS OUT FOR BLOOD.
NO FORCE ON THIS WORLD CAN STOP MY PEOPLE AND THE VRAY FROM SLAUGHTERING EACH OTHER NOW.
AH AIN'T FROM THIS WORLD.
AND AH AIN'T ABOUT TO LET ITS PEOPLE KILL EACH OTHER OVER A LIE.
IF AH PUT THIS SWORD TO THE QUEEN'S THROAT, YOUR PEOPLE'LL LISTEN.
ROGUE, WAIT! THE WAR RAGES! YOU RUSH HEADLONG TO YOUR DEATH!
AH WELL.
AT LEAST IT WILL BE MEMORABLE.

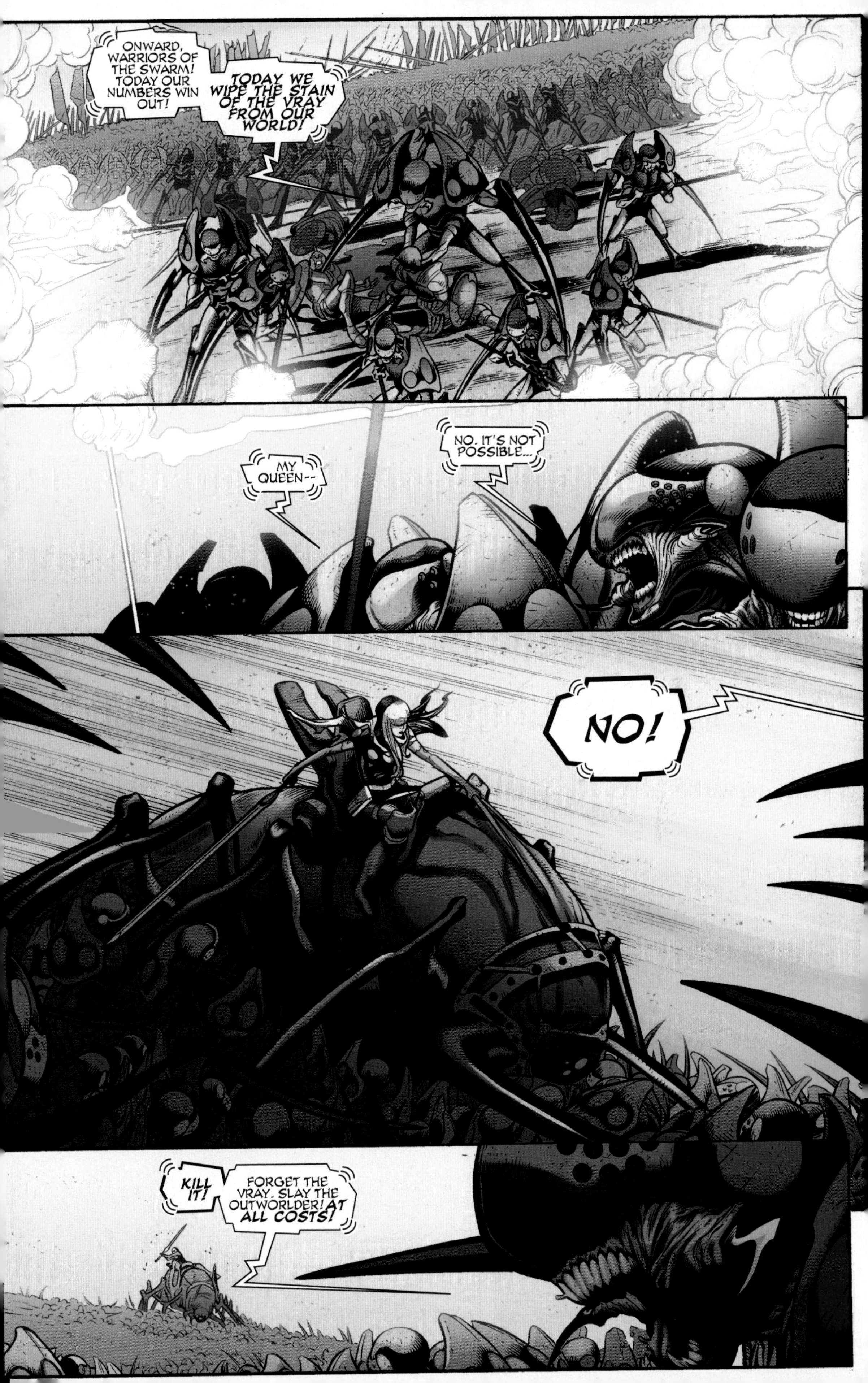
ONWARD, WARRIORS OF THE SWARM! TODAY OUR NUMBERS WIN OUT!
TODAY WE WIPE THE STAIN OF THE VRAY FROM OUR WORLD!
MY QUEEN--
NO. IT'S NOT POSSIBLE...
NO!
KILL IT!
FORGET THE VRAY. SLAY THE OUTWORLDER! AT ALL COSTS!

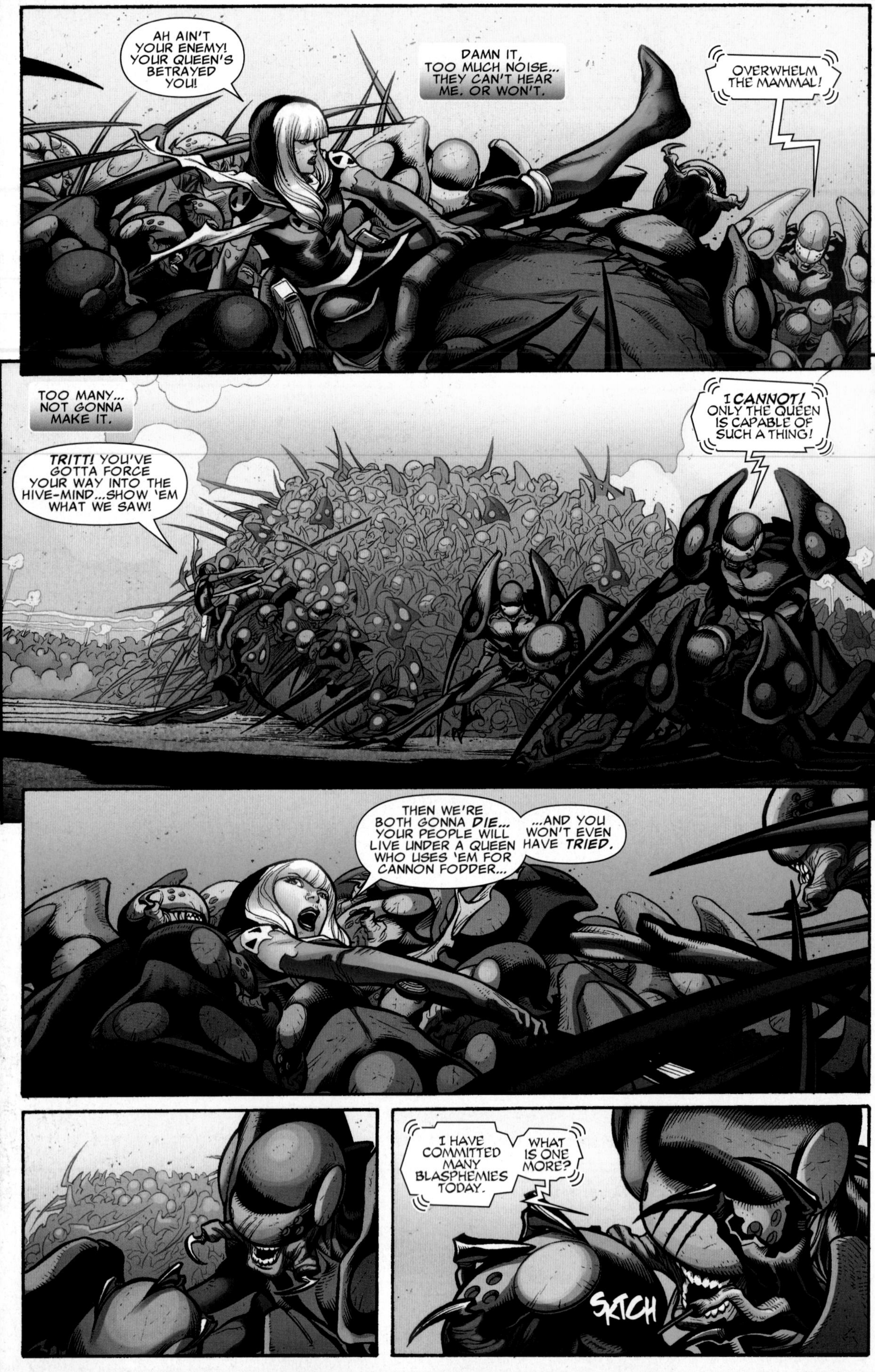
AH AIN'T YOUR ENEMY! YOUR QUEEN'S BETRAYED YOU!
DAMN IT, TOO MUCH NOISE... THEY CAN'T HEAR ME. OR WON'T.
OVERWHELM THE MAMMAL!
TOO MANY... NOT GONNA MAKE IT.
TRITT! YOU'VE GOTTA FORCE YOUR WAY INTO THE HIVE-MIND...SHOW 'EM WHAT WE SAW!
I CANNOT! ONLY THE QUEEN IS CAPABLE OF SUCH A THING!
THEN WE'RE BOTH GONNA DIE... YOUR PEOPLE WILL LIVE UNDER A QUEEN WHO USES 'EM FOR CANNON FODDER...
...AND YOU WON'T EVEN HAVE TRIED.
I HAVE COMMITTED MANY BLASPHEMIES TODAY.
WHAT IS ONE MORE?
SKTCH

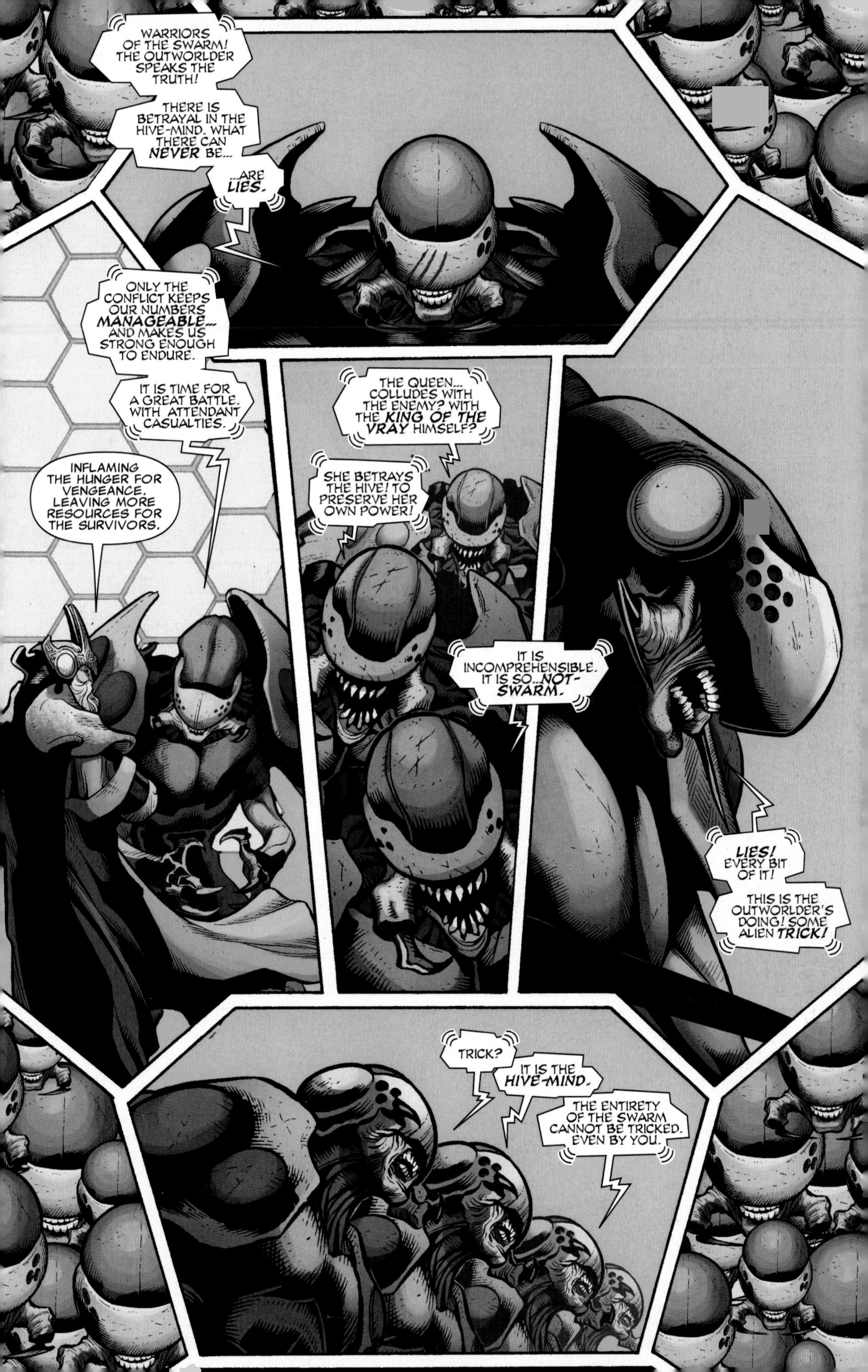
WARRIORS OF THE SWARM! THE OUTWORLDER SPEAKS THE TRUTH!
THERE IS BETRAYAL IN THE HIVE-MIND. WHAT THERE CAN NEVER BE...
...ARE LIES.
ONLY THE CONFLICT KEEPS OUR NUMBERS MANAGEABLE... AND MAKES US STRONG ENOUGH TO ENDURE.
IT IS TIME FOR A GREAT BATTLE. WITH ATTENDANT CASUALTIES.
INFLAMING THE HUNGER FOR VENGEANCE. LEAVING MORE RESOURCES FOR THE SURVIVORS.
THE QUEEN... COLLUDES WITH THE ENEMY? WITH THE KING OF THE VRAY HIMSELF?
SHE BETRAYS THE HIVE! TO PRESERVE HER OWN POWER!
IT IS INCOMPREHENSIBLE. IT IS SO...NOT-SWARM.
LIES! EVERY BIT OF IT!
THIS IS THE OUTWORLDER'S DOING! SOME ALIEN TRICK!
TRICK?
IT IS THE HIVE-MIND.
THE ENTIRETY OF THE SWARM CANNOT BE TRICKED. EVEN BY YOU.

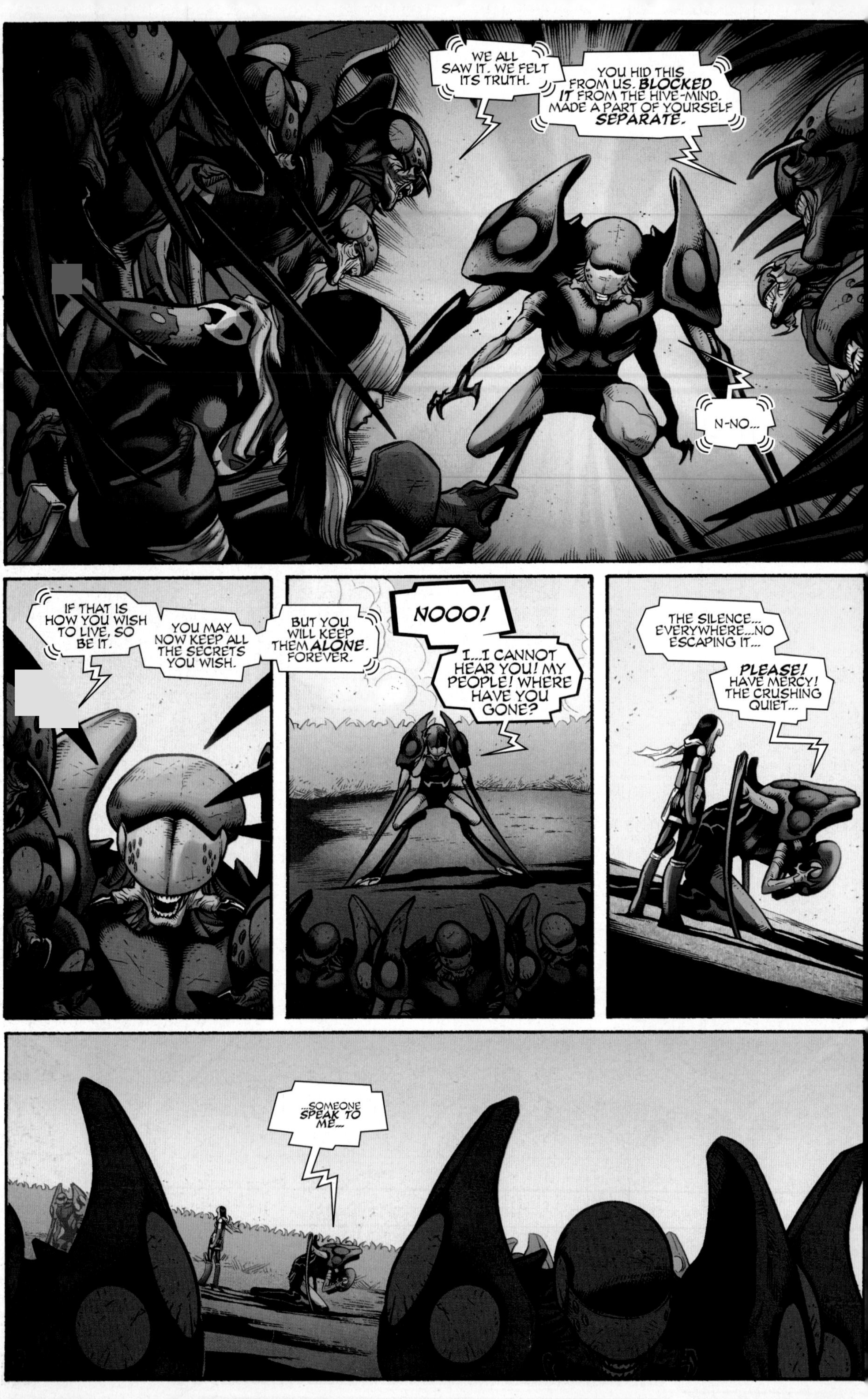
WE ALL SAW IT. WE FELT ITS TRUTH.
YOU HID THIS FROM US. BLOCKED IT FROM THE HIVE-MIND. MADE A PART OF YOURSELF SEPARATE.
N-NO...
IF THAT IS HOW YOU WISH TO LIVE, SO BE IT.
YOU MAY NOW KEEP ALL THE SECRETS YOU WISH.
BUT YOU WILL KEEP THEM ALONE. FOREVER.
NOOO!
I...I CANNOT HEAR YOU! MY PEOPLE! WHERE HAVE YOU GONE?
THE SILENCE... EVERYWHERE...NO ESCAPING IT...
PLEASE! HAVE MERCY! THE CRUSHING QUIET...
...SOMEONE SPEAK TO ME...

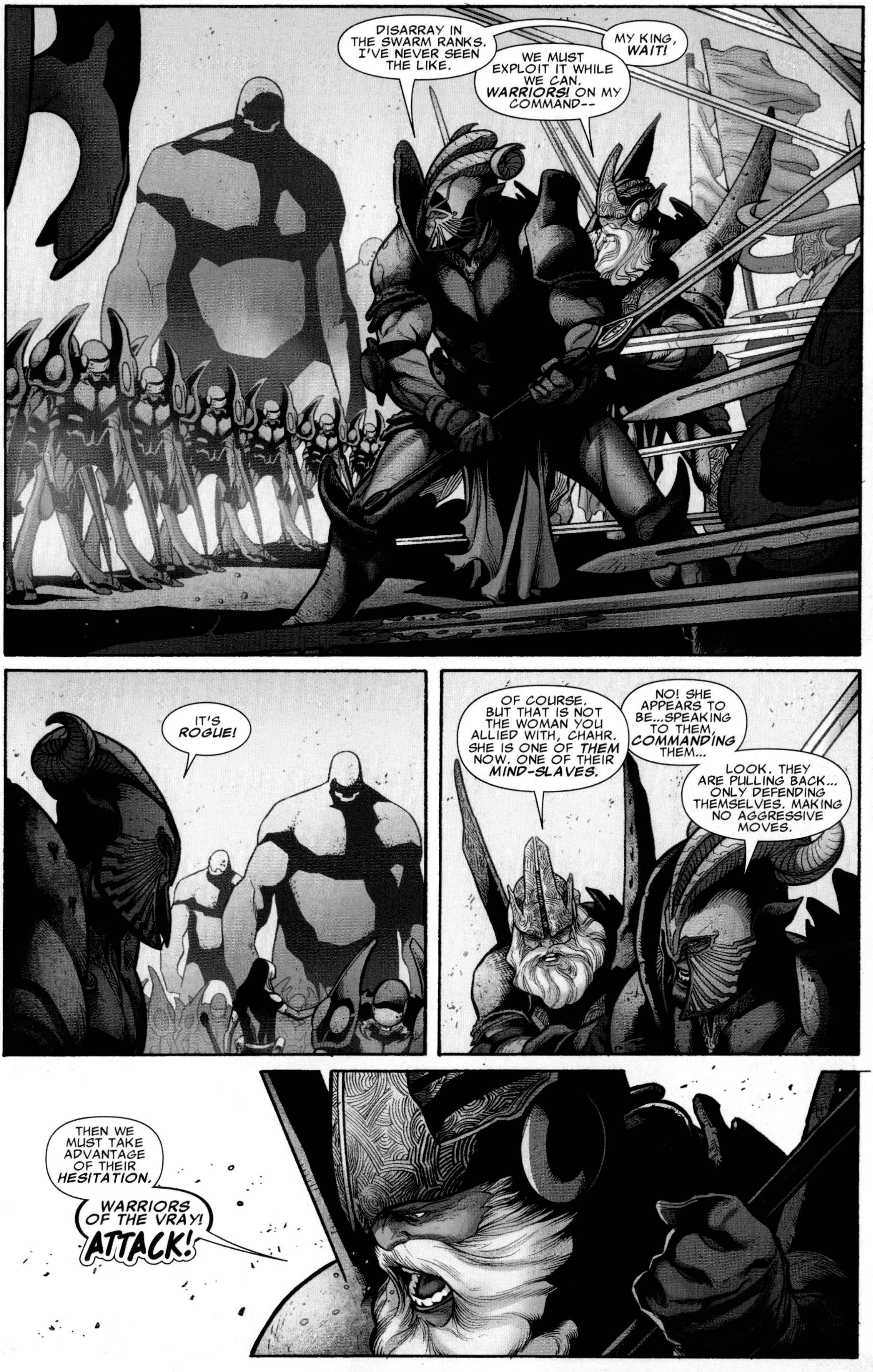
DISARRAY IN THE SWARM RANKS. I'VE NEVER SEEN THE LIKE.
MY KING, WAIT!
WE MUST EXPLOIT IT WHILE WE CAN. WARRIORS! ON MY COMMAND--
IT'S ROGUE!
OF COURSE. BUT THAT IS NOT THE WOMAN YOU ALLIED WITH, CHAHR. SHE IS ONE OF THEM NOW. ONE OF THEIR MIND-SLAVES.
NO! SHE APPEARS TO BE...SPEAKING TO THEM, COMMANDING THEM...
LOOK. THEY ARE PULLING BACK... ONLY DEFENDING THEMSELVES. MAKING NO AGGRESSIVE MOVES.
THEN WE MUST TAKE ADVANTAGE OF THEIR HESITATION.
WARRIORS OF THE VRAY! ATTACK!

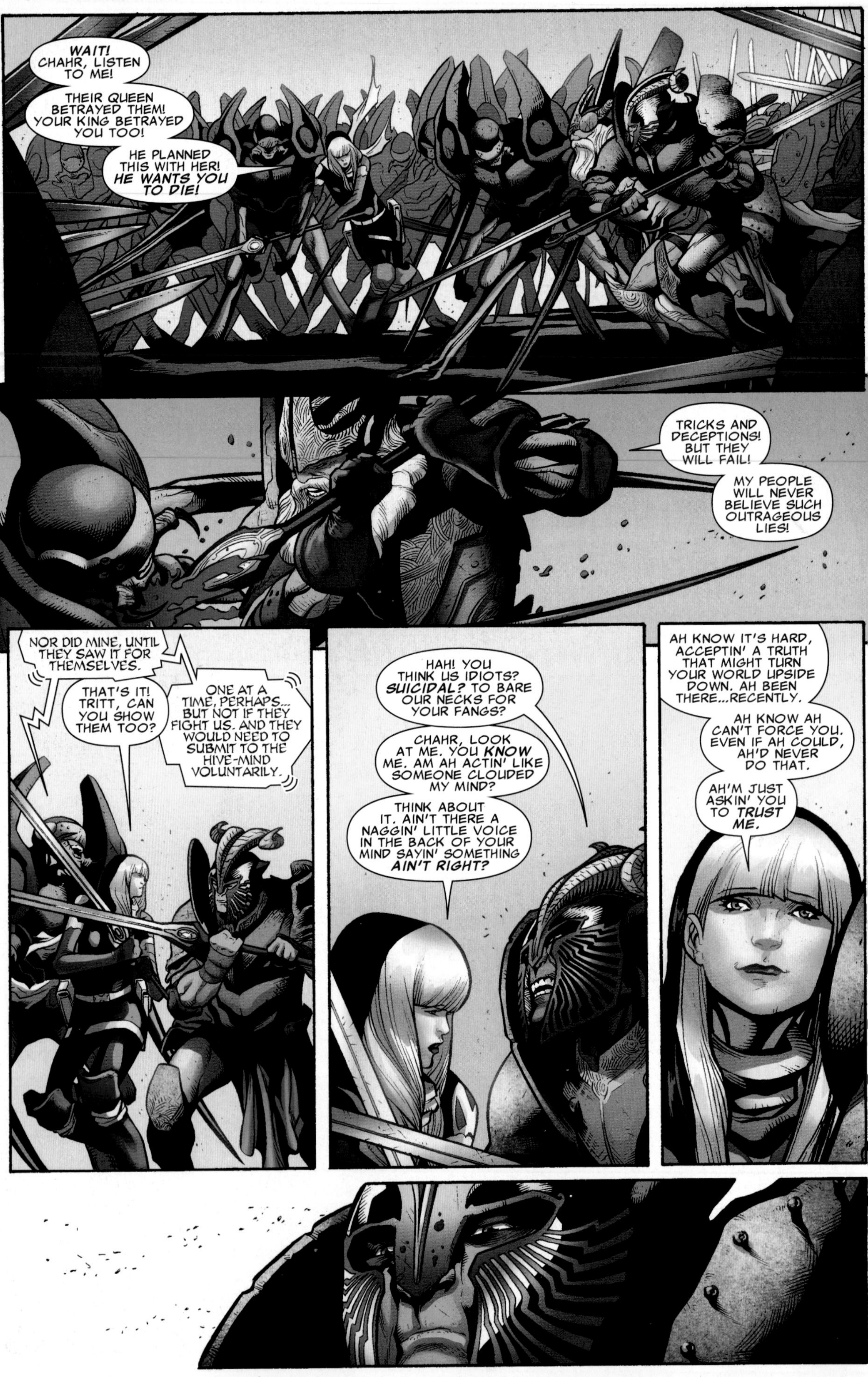
WAIT! CHAHR, LISTEN TO ME!
THEIR QUEEN BETRAYED THEM! YOUR KING BETRAYED YOU TOO!
HE PLANNED THIS WITH HER! HE WANTS YOU TO DIE!
TRICKS AND DECEPTIONS! BUT THEY WILL FAIL!
MY PEOPLE WILL NEVER BELIEVE SUCH OUTRAGEOUS LIES!
NOR DID MINE, UNTIL THEY SAW IT FOR THEMSELVES.
THAT'S IT! TRITT, CAN YOU SHOW THEM TOO?
ONE AT A TIME, PERHAPS... BUT NOT IF THEY FIGHT US. AND THEY WOULD NEED TO SUBMIT TO THE HIVE-MIND VOLUNTARILY.
HAH! YOU THINK US IDIOTS? SUICIDAL? TO BARE OUR NECKS FOR YOUR FANGS?
CHAHR, LOOK AT ME. YOU KNOW ME. AM AH ACTIN' LIKE SOMEONE CLOUDED MY MIND?
THINK ABOUT IT. AIN'T THERE A NAGGIN' LITTLE VOICE IN THE BACK OF YOUR MIND SAYIN' SOMETHING AIN'T RIGHT?
AH KNOW IT'S HARD, ACCEPTIN' A TRUTH THAT MIGHT TURN YOUR WORLD UPSIDE DOWN. AH BEEN THERE...RECENTLY.
AH KNOW AH CAN'T FORCE YOU. EVEN IF AH COULD, AH'D NEVER DO THAT.
AH'M JUST ASKIN' YOU TO TRUST ME.

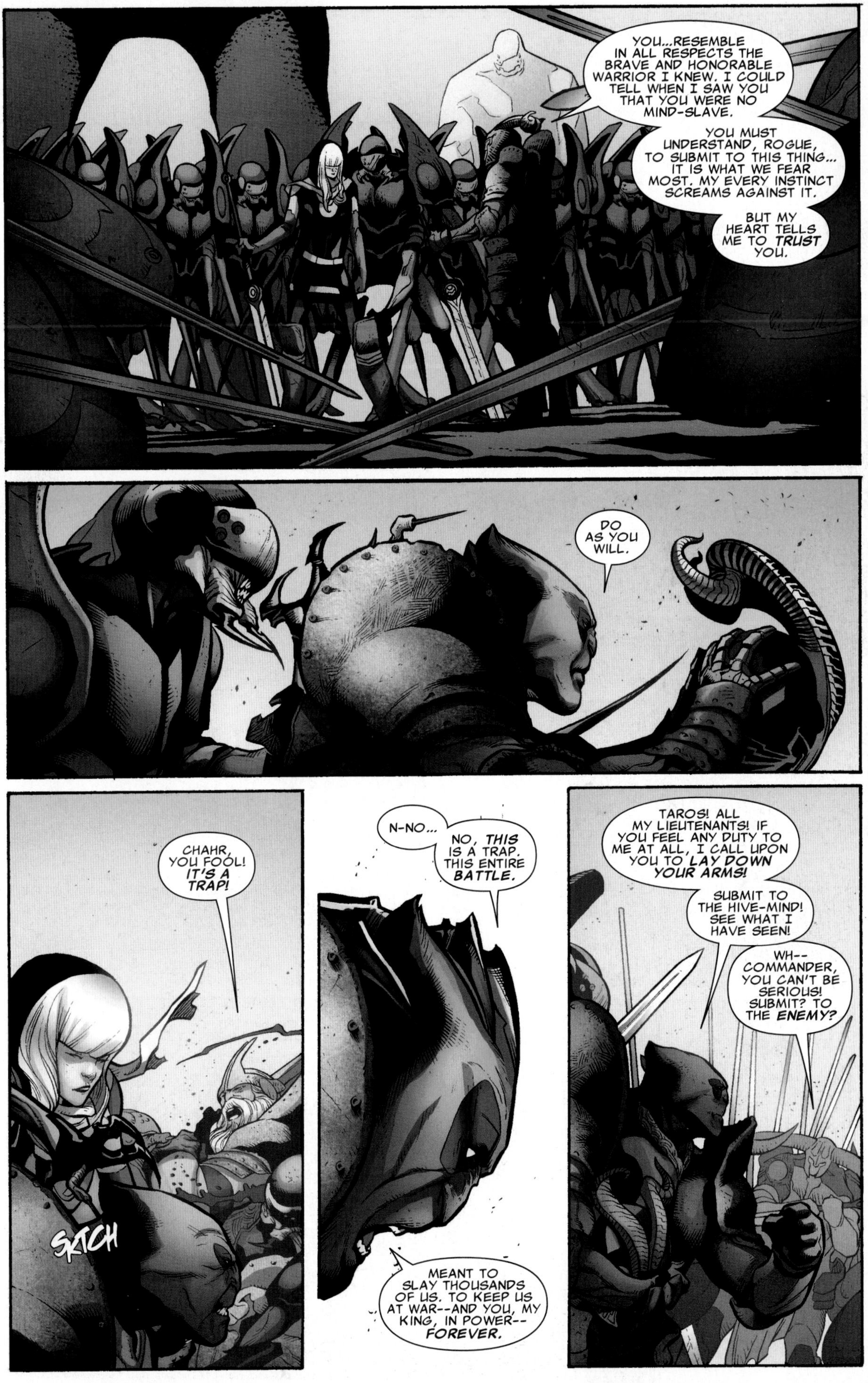
YOU...RESEMBLE IN ALL RESPECTS THE BRAVE AND HONORABLE WARRIOR I KNEW. I COULD TELL WHEN I SAW YOU THAT YOU WERE NO MIND-SLAVE.
YOU MUST UNDERSTAND, ROGUE, TO SUBMIT TO THIS THING... IT IS WHAT WE FEAR MOST. MY EVERY INSTINCT SCREAMS AGAINST IT.
BUT MY HEART TELLS ME TO TRUST YOU.
DO AS YOU WILL.
CHAHR, YOU FOOL! IT'S A TRAP!
SKTCH
N-NO...
NO, THIS IS A TRAP. THIS ENTIRE BATTLE.
MEANT TO SLAY THOUSANDS OF US. TO KEEP US AT WAR--AND YOU, MY KING, IN POWER--FOREVER.
TAROS! ALL MY LIEUTENANTS! IF YOU FEEL ANY DUTY TO ME AT ALL, I CALL UPON YOU TO LAY DOWN YOUR ARMS!
SUBMIT TO THE HIVE-MIND! SEE WHAT I HAVE SEEN!
WH-- COMMANDER, YOU CAN'T BE SERIOUS! SUBMIT? TO THE ENEMY?

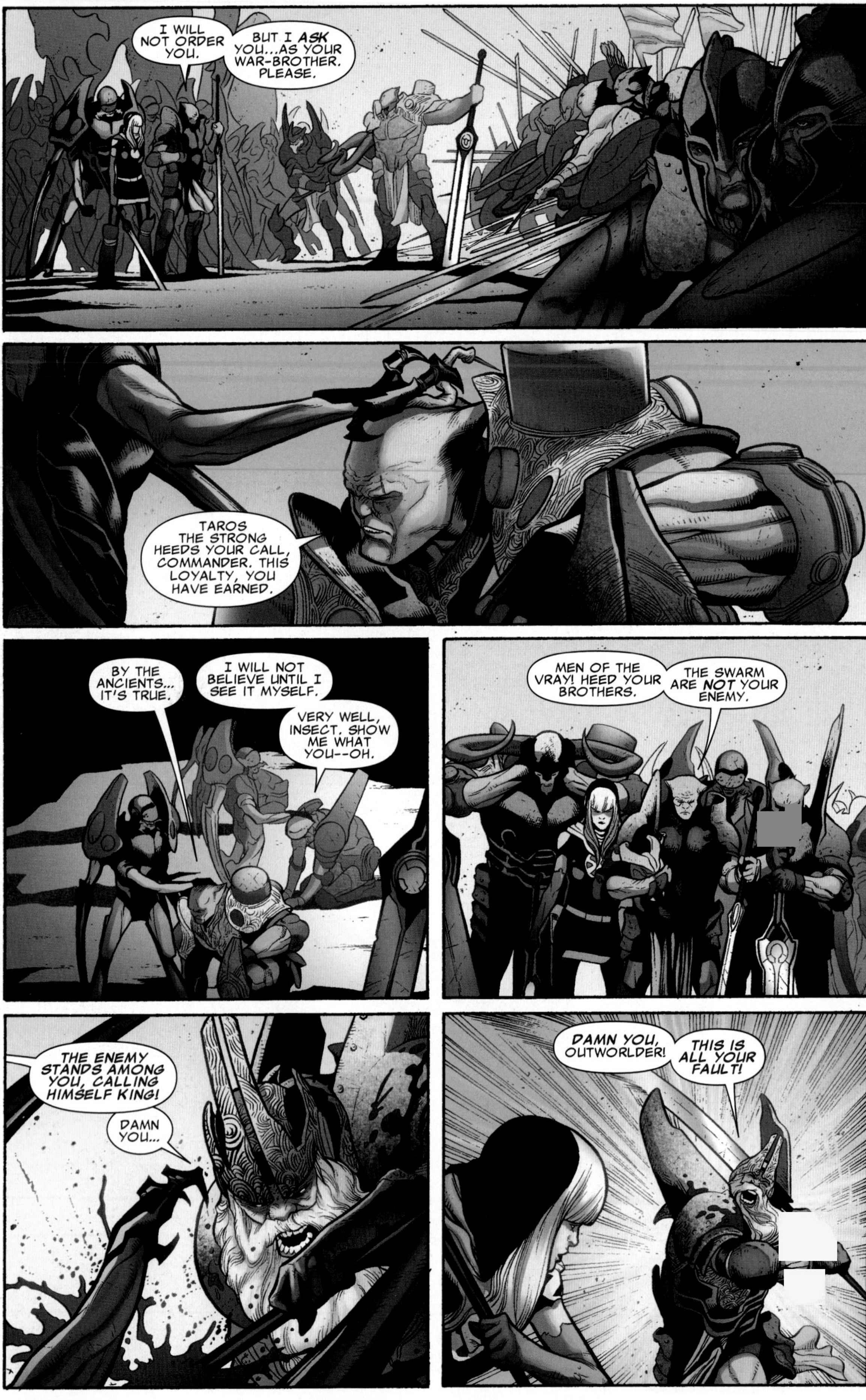
I WILL NOT ORDER YOU.
BUT I ASK YOU...AS YOUR WAR-BROTHER. PLEASE.
TAROS THE STRONG HEEDS YOUR CALL, COMMANDER. THIS LOYALTY, YOU HAVE EARNED.
BY THE ANCIENTS... IT'S TRUE.
I WILL NOT BELIEVE UNTIL I SEE IT MYSELF.
VERY WELL, INSECT. SHOW ME WHAT YOU--OH.
MEN OF THE VRAY! HEED YOUR BROTHERS.
THE SWARM ARE NOT YOUR ENEMY.
THE ENEMY STANDS AMONG YOU, CALLING HIMSELF KING!
DAMN YOU...
DAMN YOU, OUTWORLDER!
THIS IS ALL YOUR FAULT!

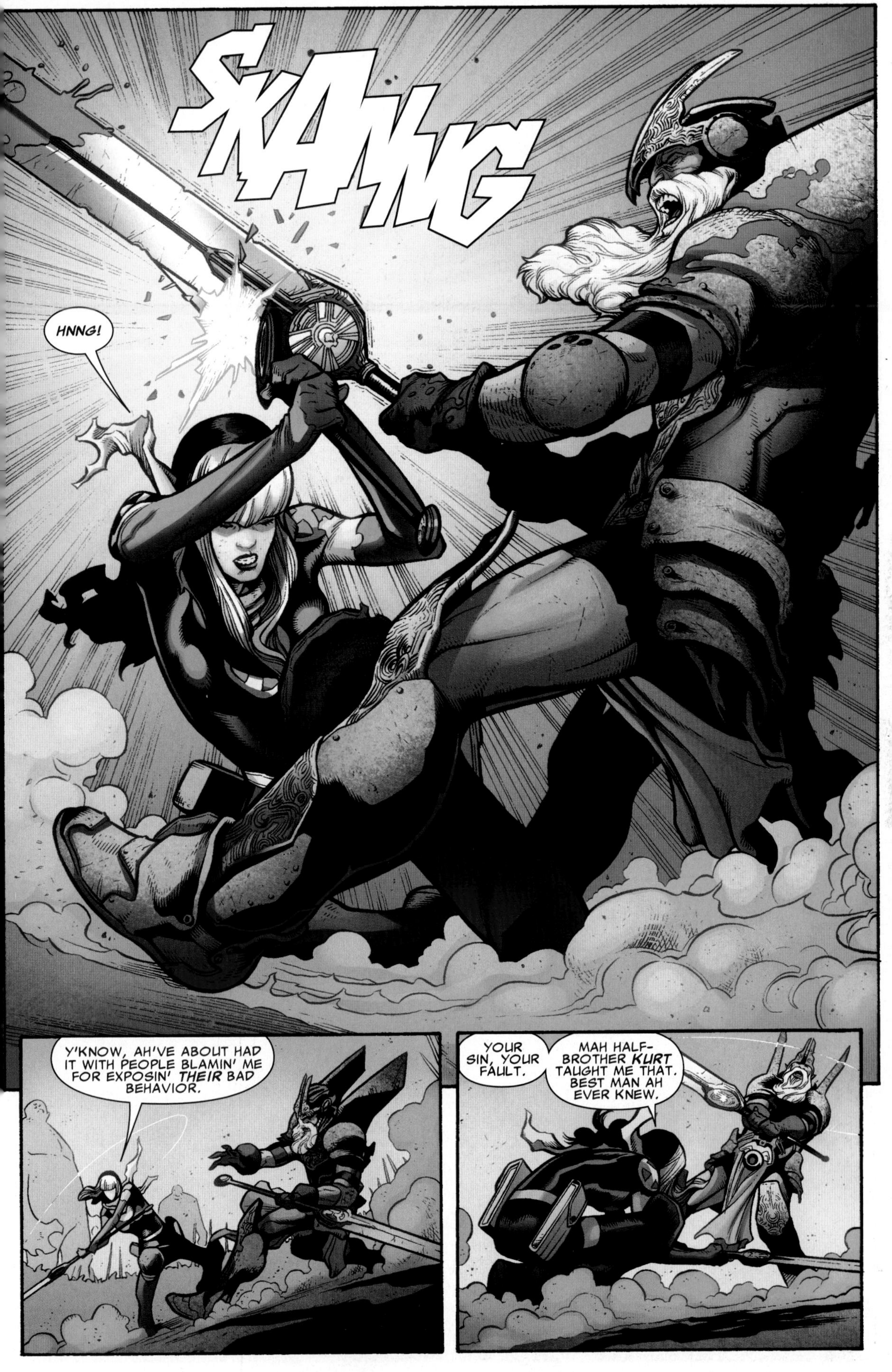
SKANNG
HNNG!
Y'KNOW, AH'VE ABOUT HAD IT WITH PEOPLE BLAMIN' ME FOR EXPOSIN' THEIR BAD BEHAVIOR.
YOUR SIN, YOUR FAULT.
MAH HALF-BROTHER KURT TAUGHT ME THAT. BEST MAN AH EVER KNEW.

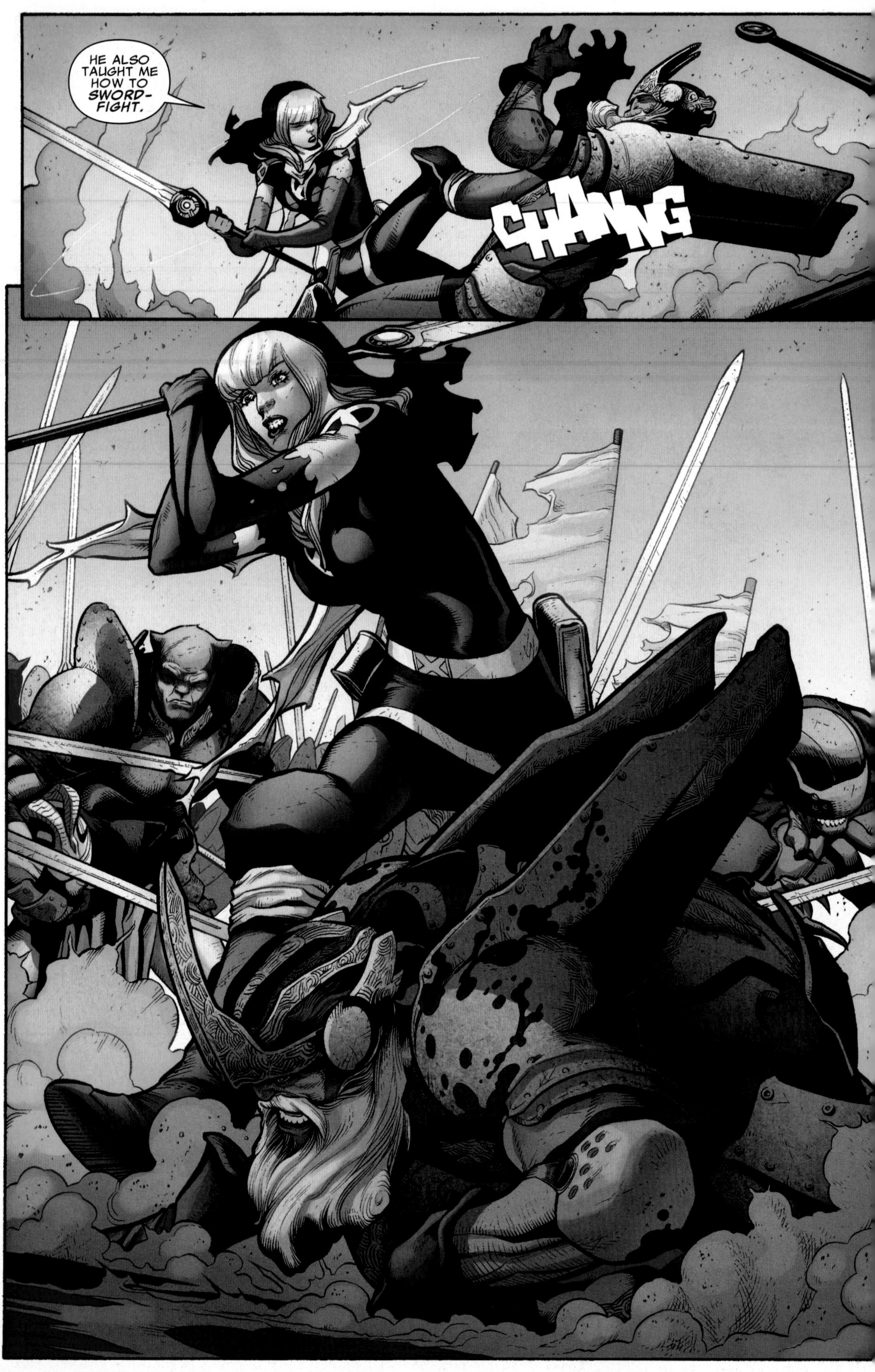
HE ALSO TAUGHT ME HOW TO SWORD-FIGHT.
CHANNG

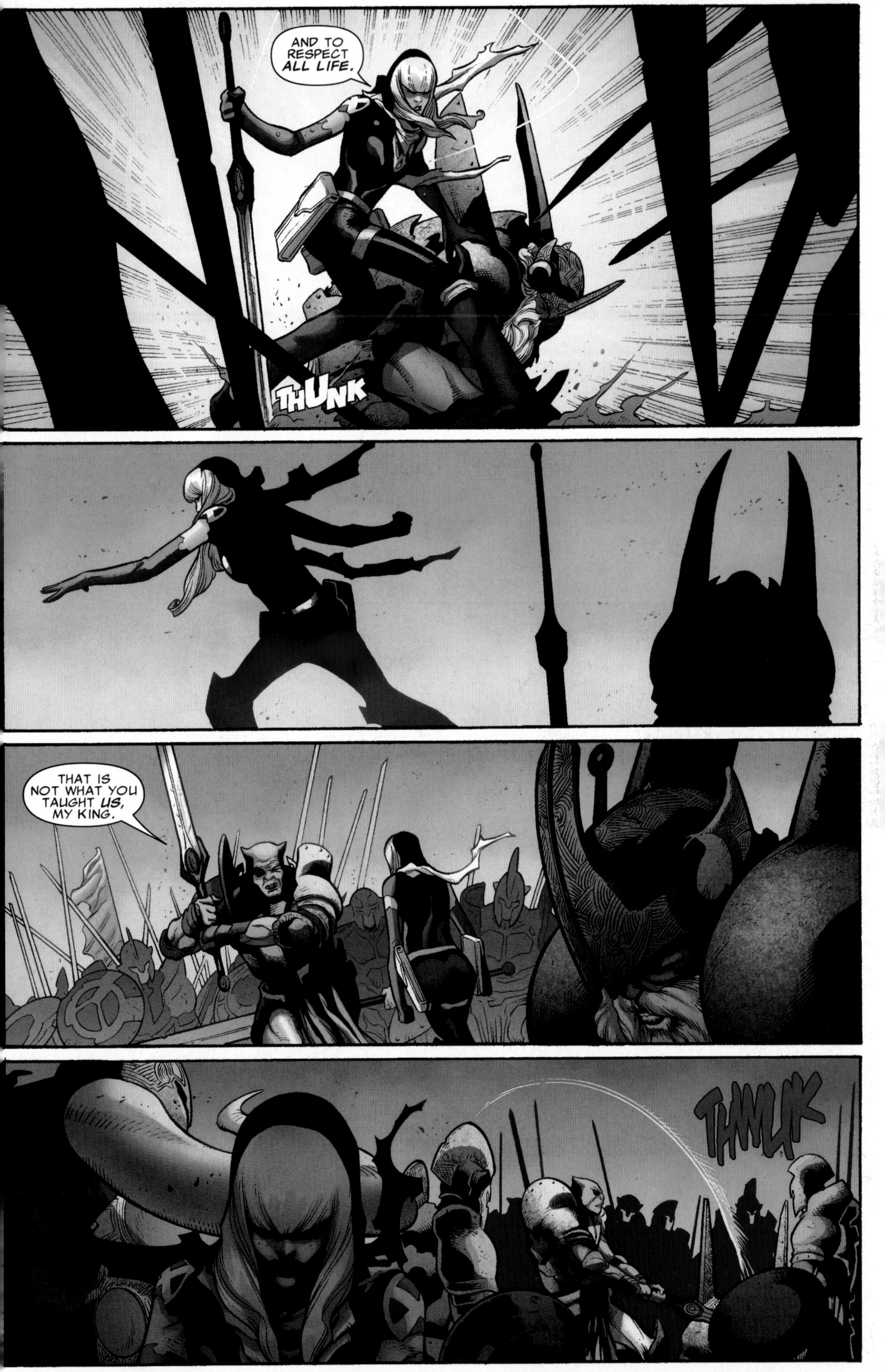
AND TO RESPECT ALL LIFE.
THUNK
THAT IS NOT WHAT YOU TAUGHT US, MY KING.
THWUK

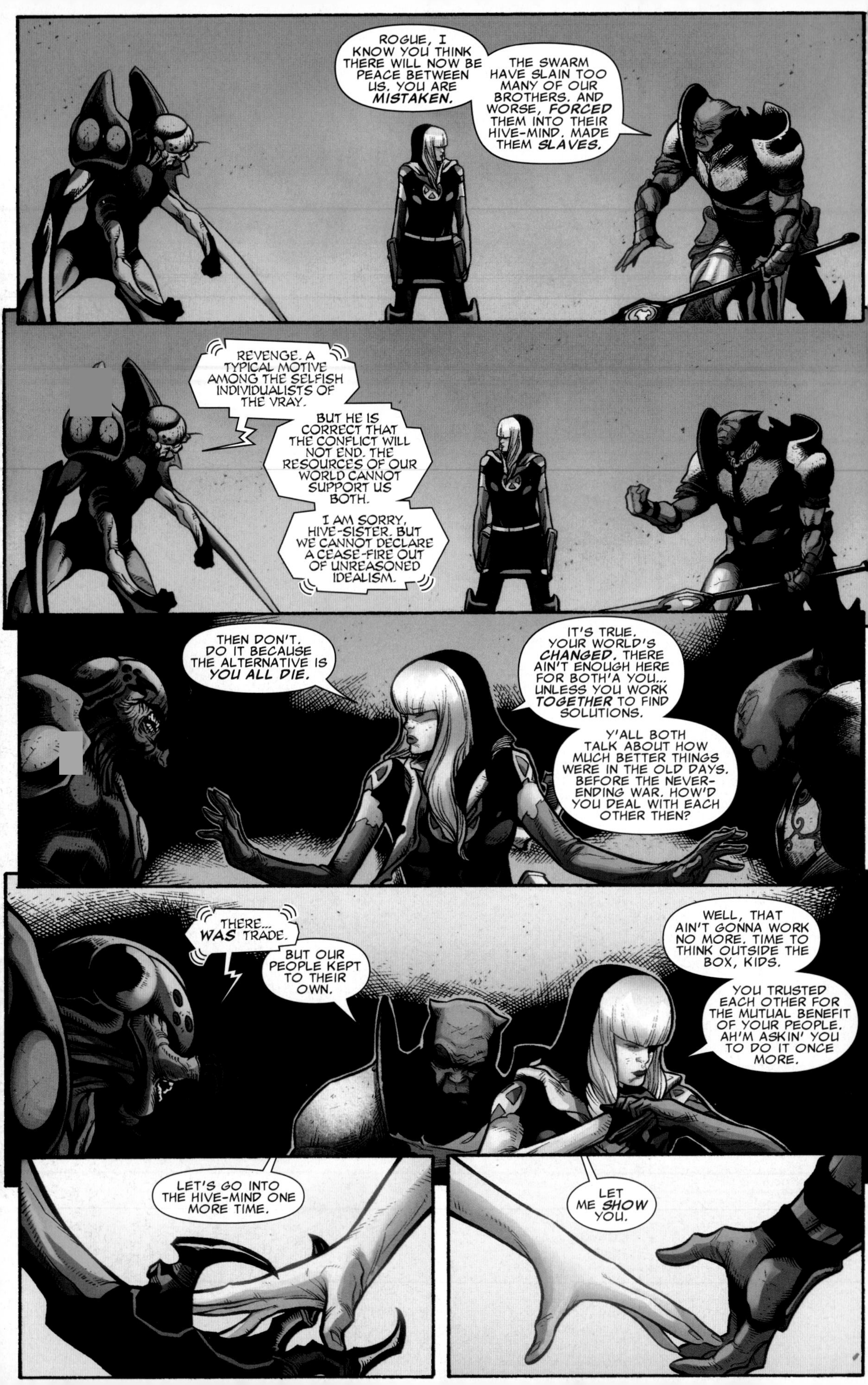
ROGUE, I KNOW YOU THINK THERE WILL NOW BE PEACE BETWEEN US. YOU ARE MISTAKEN.
THE SWARM HAVE SLAIN TOO MANY OF OUR BROTHERS. AND WORSE, FORCED THEM INTO THEIR HIVE-MIND. MADE THEM SLAVES.
REVENGE. A TYPICAL MOTIVE AMONG THE SELFISH INDIVIDUALISTS OF THE VRAY.
BUT HE IS CORRECT THAT THE CONFLICT WILL NOT END. THE RESOURCES OF OUR WORLD CANNOT SUPPORT US BOTH.
I AM SORRY, HIVE-SISTER. BUT WE CANNOT DECLARE A CEASE-FIRE OUT OF UNREASONED IDEALISM.
THEN DON'T. DO IT BECAUSE THE ALTERNATIVE IS YOU ALL DIE.
IT'S TRUE. YOUR WORLD'S CHANGED. THERE AIN'T ENOUGH HERE FOR BOTH'A YOU... UNLESS YOU WORK TOGETHER TO FIND SOLUTIONS.
Y'ALL BOTH TALK ABOUT HOW MUCH BETTER THINGS WERE IN THE OLD DAYS. BEFORE THE NEVER-ENDING WAR. HOW'D YOU DEAL WITH EACH OTHER THEN?
THERE... WAS TRADE.
BUT OUR PEOPLE KEPT TO THEIR OWN.
WELL, THAT AIN'T GONNA WORK NO MORE. TIME TO THINK OUTSIDE THE BOX, KIDS.
YOU TRUSTED EACH OTHER FOR THE MUTUAL BENEFIT OF YOUR PEOPLE. AH'M ASKIN' YOU TO DO IT ONCE MORE.
LET'S GO INTO THE HIVE-MIND ONE MORE TIME.
LET ME SHOW YOU.

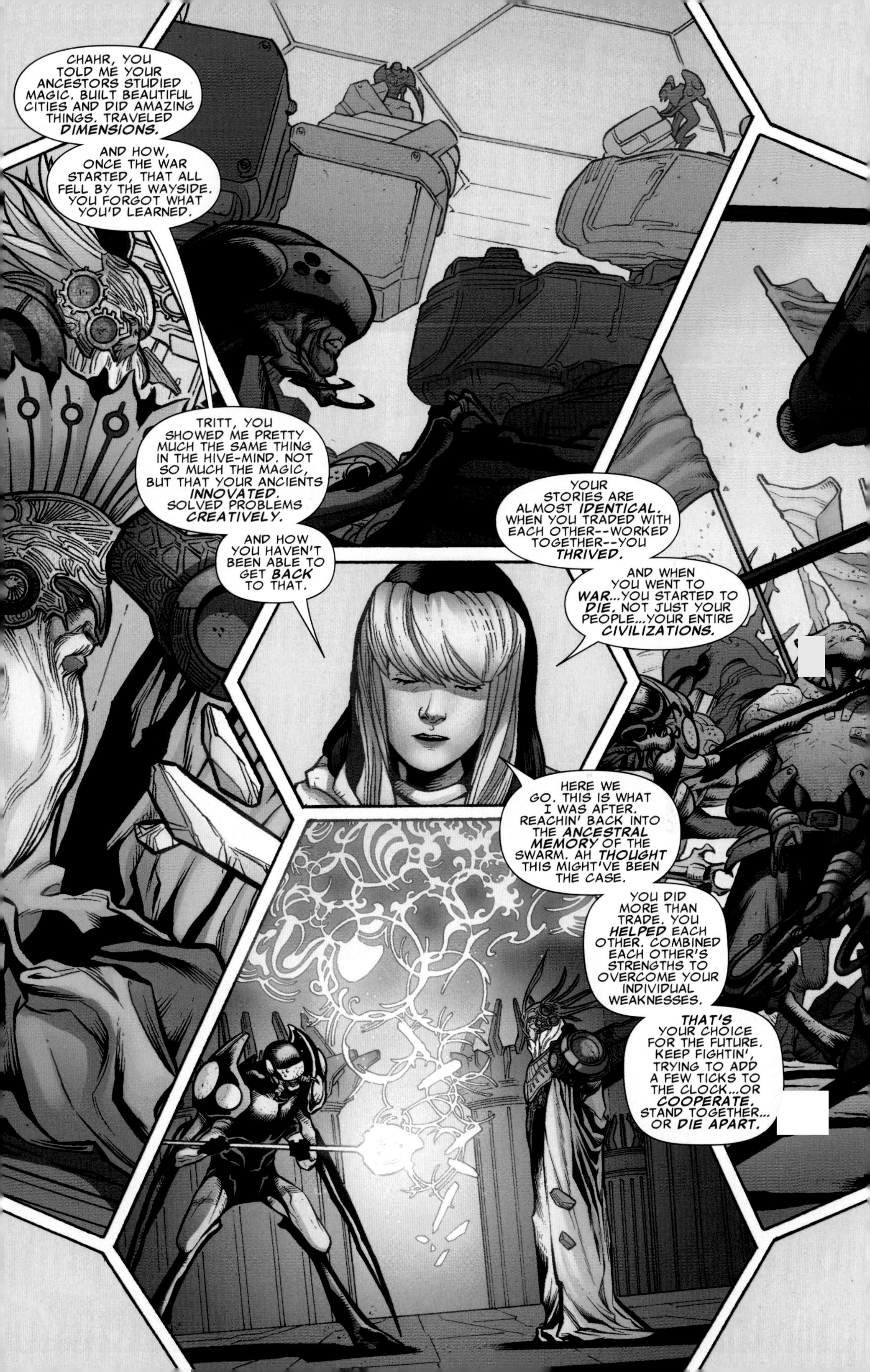
CHAHR, YOU TOLD ME YOUR ANCESTORS STUDIED MAGIC. BUILT BEAUTIFUL CITIES AND DID AMAZING THINGS. TRAVELED DIMENSIONS.
AND HOW, ONCE THE WAR STARTED, THAT ALL FELL BY THE WAYSIDE. YOU FORGOT WHAT YOU'D LEARNED.
TRITT, YOU SHOWED ME PRETTY MUCH THE SAME THING IN THE HIVE-MIND. NOT SO MUCH THE MAGIC, BUT THAT YOUR ANCIENTS INNOVATED. SOLVED PROBLEMS CREATIVELY.
AND HOW YOU HAVEN'T BEEN ABLE TO GET BACK TO THAT.
YOUR STORIES ARE ALMOST IDENTICAL. WHEN YOU TRADED WITH EACH OTHER--WORKED TOGETHER--YOU THRIVED.
AND WHEN YOU WENT TO WAR...YOU STARTED TO DIE. NOT JUST YOUR PEOPLE...YOUR ENTIRE CIVILIZATIONS.
HERE WE GO. THIS IS WHAT I WAS AFTER. REACHIN' BACK INTO THE ANCESTRAL MEMORY OF THE SWARM. AH THOUGHT THIS MIGHT'VE BEEN THE CASE.
YOU DID MORE THAN TRADE. YOU HELPED EACH OTHER. COMBINED EACH OTHER'S STRENGTHS TO OVERCOME YOUR INDIVIDUAL WEAKNESSES.
THAT'S YOUR CHOICE FOR THE FUTURE. KEEP FIGHTIN', TRYING TO ADD A FEW TICKS TO THE CLOCK...OR COOPERATE. STAND TOGETHER... OR DIE APART.

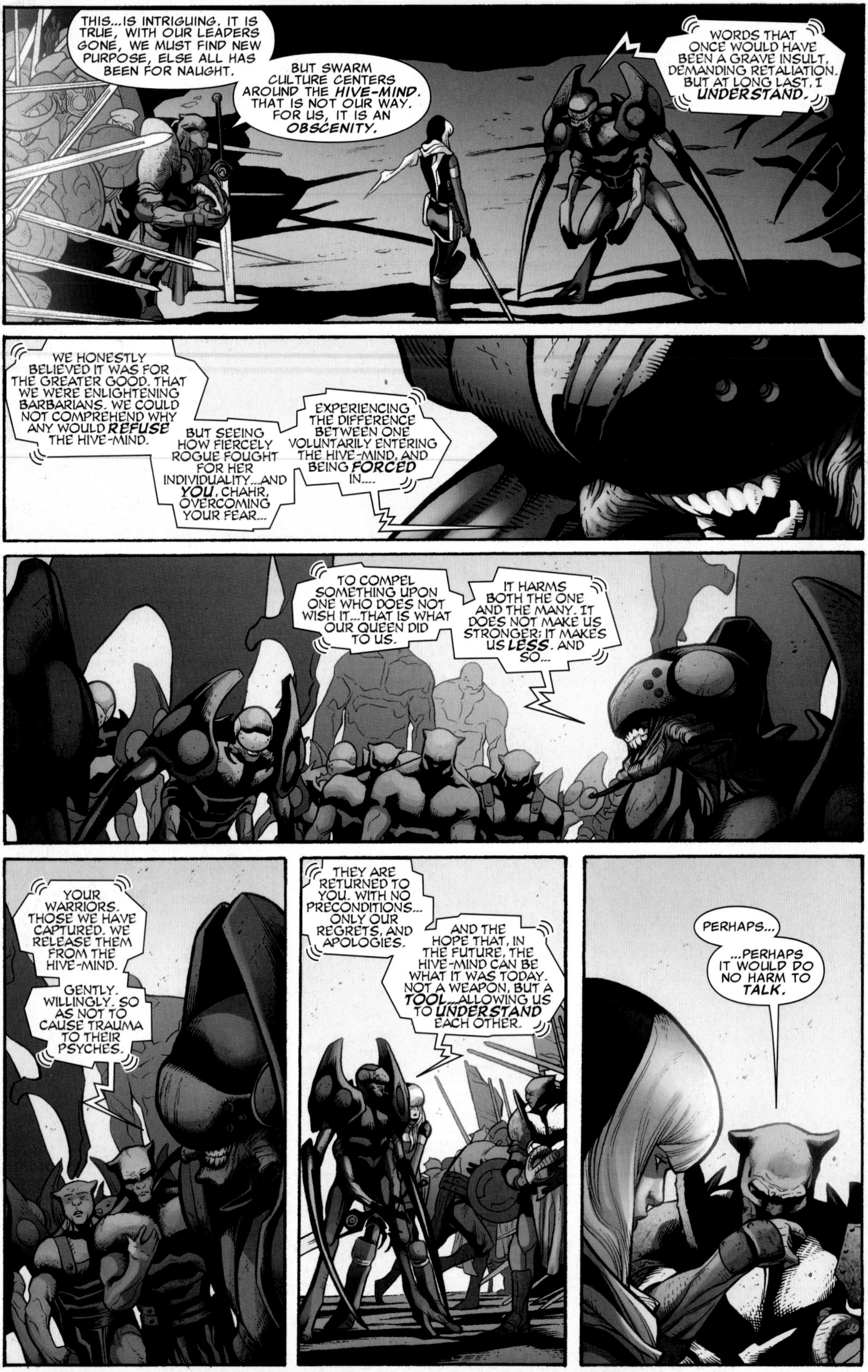

THIS...IS INTRIGUING. IT IS TRUE, WITH OUR LEADERS GONE, WE MUST FIND NEW PURPOSE, ELSE ALL HAS BEEN FOR NAUGHT.
BUT SWARM CULTURE CENTERS AROUND THE HIVE-MIND. THAT IS NOT OUR WAY. FOR US, IT IS AN OBSCENITY.
WORDS THAT ONCE WOULD HAVE BEEN A GRAVE INSULT, DEMANDING RETALIATION. BUT AT LONG LAST, I UNDERSTAND.
WE HONESTLY BELIEVED IT WAS FOR THE GREATER GOOD. THAT WE WERE ENLIGHTENING BARBARIANS. WE COULD NOT COMPREHEND WHY ANY WOULD REFUSE THE HIVE-MIND.
BUT SEEING HOW FIERCELY ROGUE FOUGHT FOR HER INDIVIDUALITY...AND YOU, CHAHR, OVERCOMING YOUR FEAR...
EXPERIENCING THE DIFFERENCE BETWEEN ONE VOLUNTARILY ENTERING THE HIVE-MIND, AND BEING FORCED IN....
TO COMPEL SOMETHING UPON ONE WHO DOES NOT WISH IT...THAT IS WHAT OUR QUEEN DID TO US.
IT HARMS BOTH THE ONE AND THE MANY. IT DOES NOT MAKE US STRONGER; IT MAKES US LESS. AND SO...
YOUR WARRIORS. THOSE WE HAVE CAPTURED. WE RELEASE THEM FROM THE HIVE-MIND.
GENTLY. WILLINGLY. SO AS NOT TO CAUSE TRAUMA TO THEIR PSYCHES.
THEY ARE RETURNED TO YOU. WITH NO PRECONDITIONS... ONLY OUR REGRETS, AND APOLOGIES.
AND THE HOPE THAT, IN THE FUTURE, THE HIVE-MIND CAN BE WHAT IT WAS TODAY. NOT A WEAPON, BUT A TOOL...ALLOWING US TO UNDERSTAND EACH OTHER.
PERHAPS...
...PERHAPS IT WOULD DO NO HARM TO TALK.

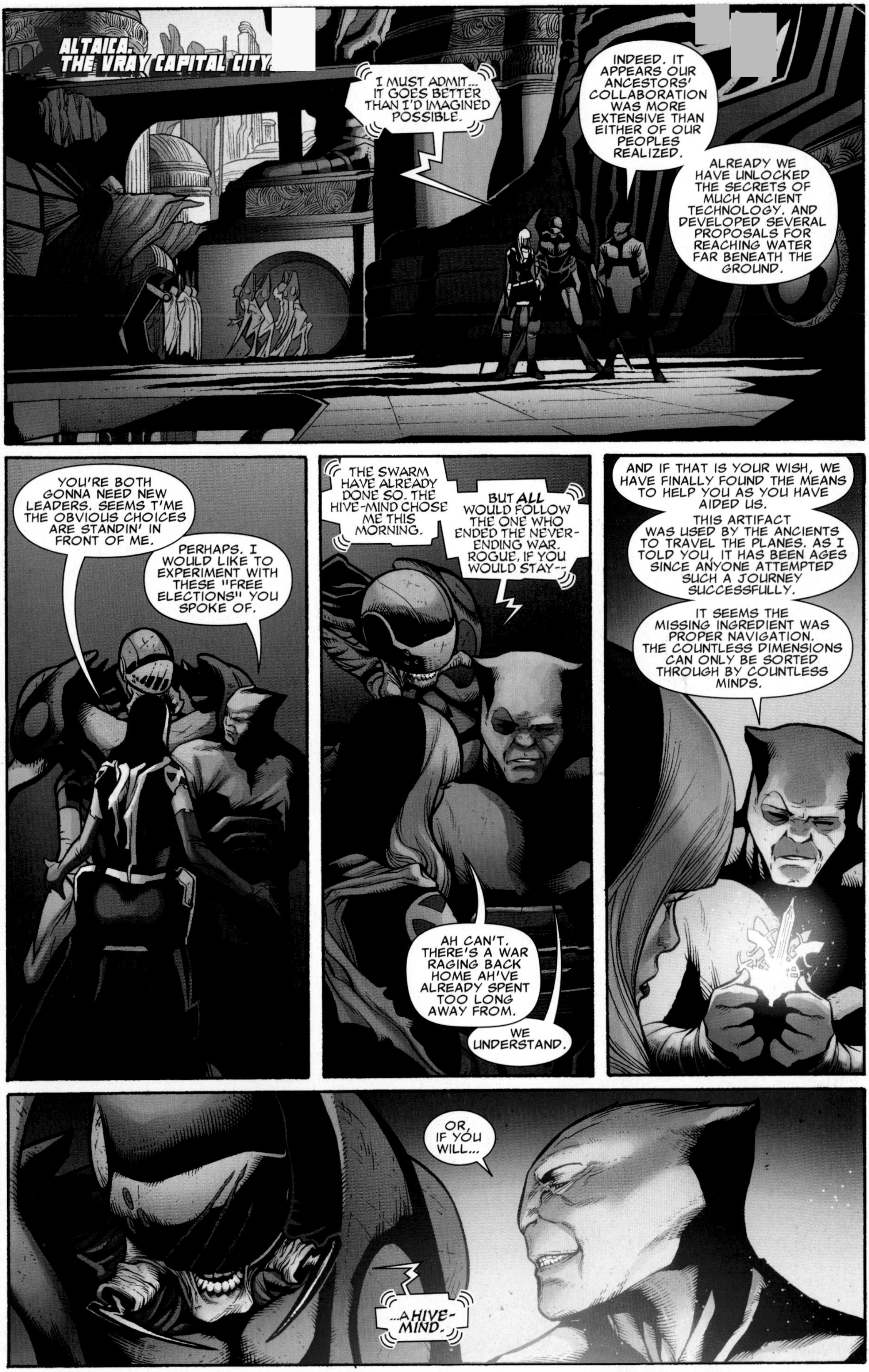
ALTAICA. THE VRAY CAPITAL CITY.
I MUST ADMIT... IT GOES BETTER THAN I'D IMAGINED POSSIBLE.
INDEED. IT APPEARS OUR ANCESTORS' COLLABORATION WAS MORE EXTENSIVE THAN EITHER OF OUR PEOPLES REALIZED.
ALREADY WE HAVE UNLOCKED THE SECRETS OF MUCH ANCIENT TECHNOLOGY. AND DEVELOPED SEVERAL PROPOSALS FOR REACHING WATER FAR BENEATH THE GROUND.
YOU'RE BOTH GONNA NEED NEW LEADERS. SEEMS T'ME THE OBVIOUS CHOICES ARE STANDIN' IN FRONT OF ME.
PERHAPS. I WOULD LIKE TO EXPERIMENT WITH THESE "FREE ELECTIONS" YOU SPOKE OF.
THE SWARM HAVE ALREADY DONE SO. THE HIVE-MIND CHOSE ME THIS MORNING.
BUT ALL WOULD FOLLOW THE ONE WHO ENDED THE NEVER-ENDING WAR. ROGUE, IF YOU WOULD STAY--
AH CAN'T. THERE'S A WAR RAGING BACK HOME AH'VE ALREADY SPENT TOO LONG AWAY FROM.
WE UNDERSTAND.
AND IF THAT IS YOUR WISH, WE HAVE FINALLY FOUND THE MEANS TO HELP YOU AS YOU HAVE AIDED US.
THIS ARTIFACT WAS USED BY THE ANCIENTS TO TRAVEL THE PLANES. AS I TOLD YOU, IT HAS BEEN AGES SINCE ANYONE ATTEMPTED SUCH A JOURNEY SUCCESSFULLY.
IT SEEMS THE MISSING INGREDIENT WAS PROPER NAVIGATION. THE COUNTLESS DIMENSIONS CAN ONLY BE SORTED THROUGH BY COUNTLESS MINDS.
OR, IF YOU WILL...
...A HIVE-MIND.

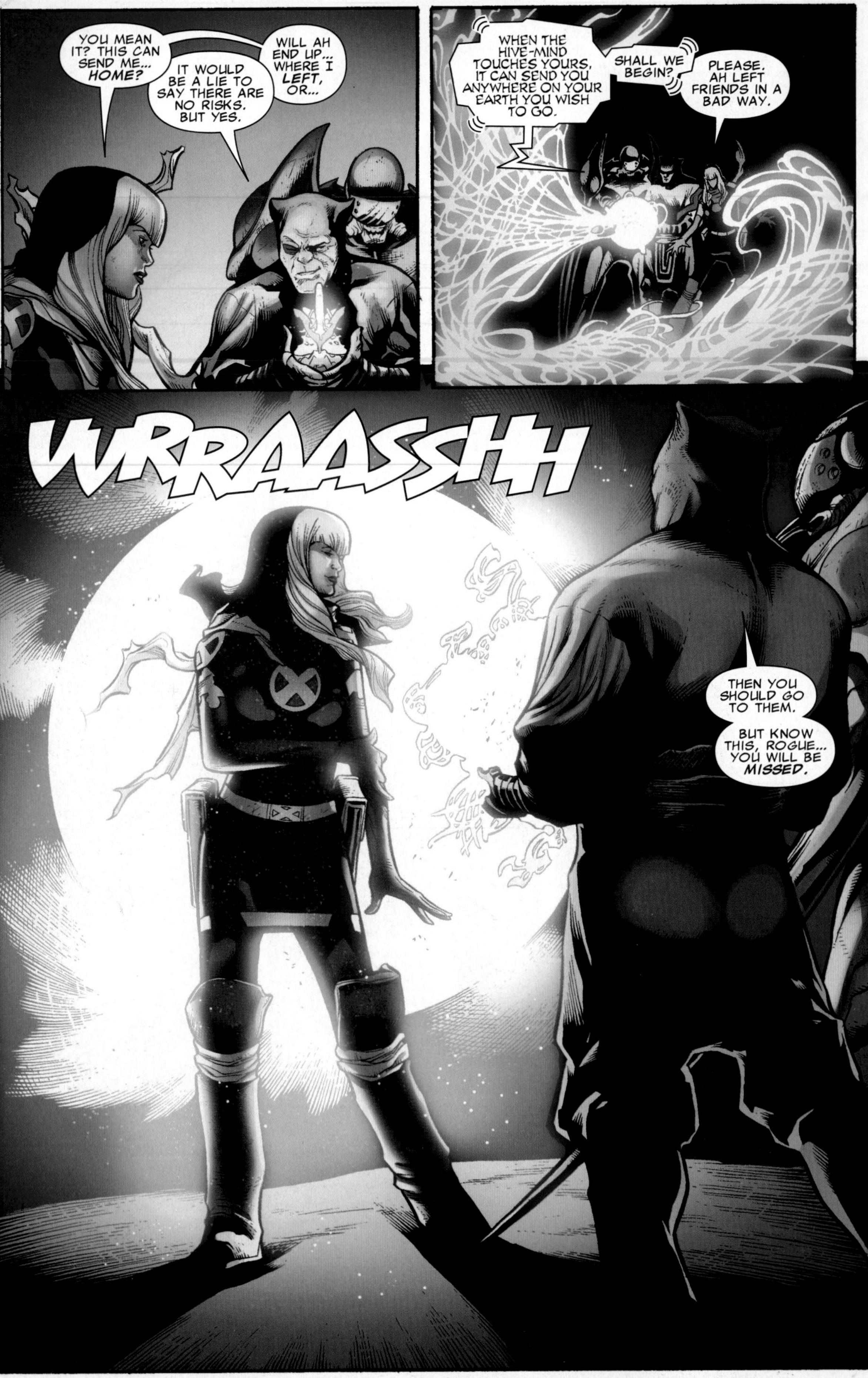
YOU MEAN IT? THIS CAN SEND ME... HOME?
IT WOULD BE A LIE TO SAY THERE ARE NO RISKS. BUT YES.
WILL AH END UP... WHERE I LEFT, OR...
WHEN THE HIVE-MIND TOUCHES YOURS, IT CAN SEND YOU ANYWHERE ON YOUR EARTH YOU WISH TO GO.
SHALL WE BEGIN?
PLEASE. AH LEFT FRIENDS IN A BAD WAY.
WRRAASSHH
THEN YOU SHOULD GO TO THEM.
BUT KNOW THIS, ROGUE... YOU WILL BE MISSED.

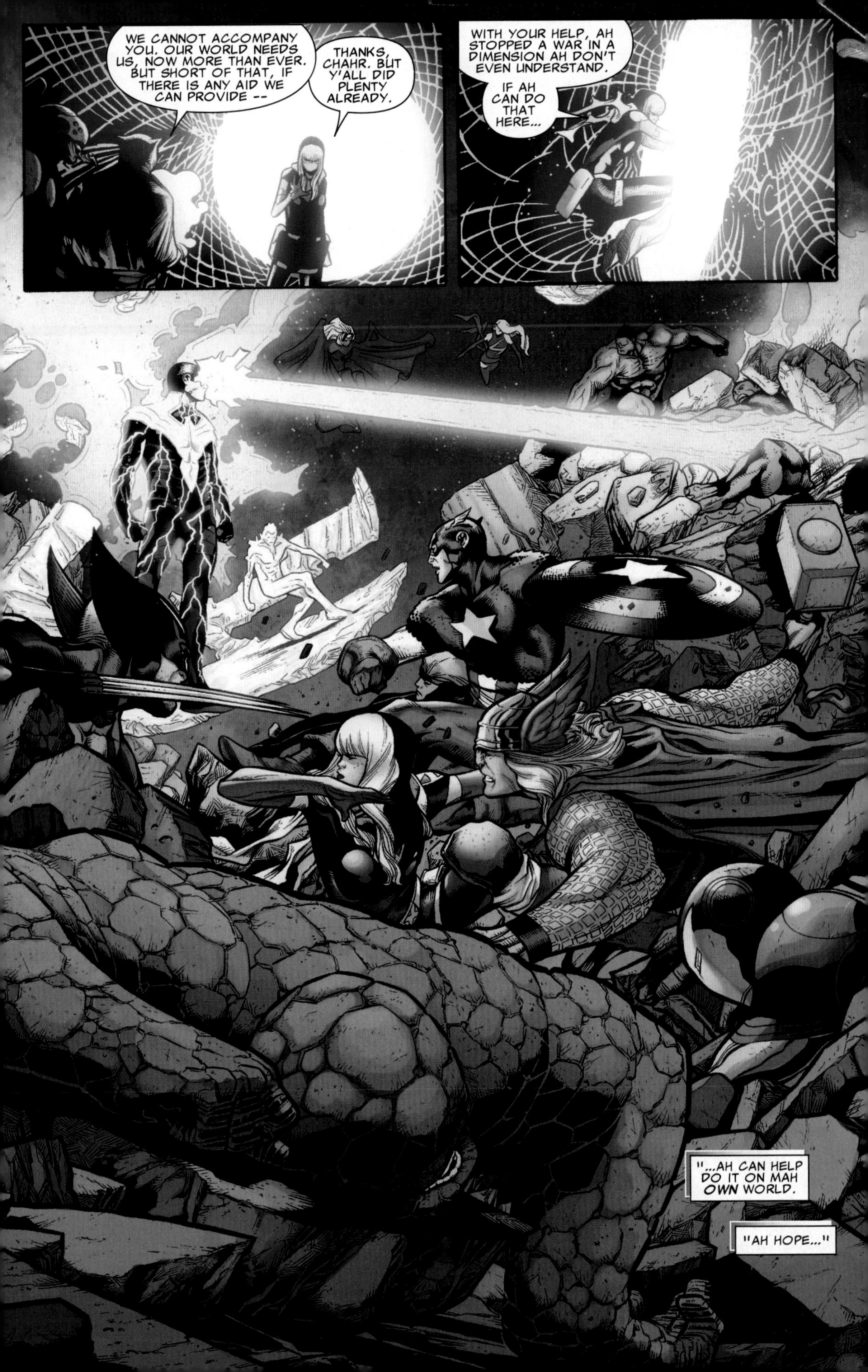
WE CANNOT ACCOMPANY YOU. OUR WORLD NEEDS US, NOW MORE THAN EVER. BUT SHORT OF THAT, IF THERE IS ANY AID WE CAN PROVIDE --
THANKS, CHAHR. BUT Y'ALL DID PLENTY ALREADY.
WITH YOUR HELP, AH STOPPED A WAR IN A DIMENSION AH DON'T EVEN UNDERSTAND.
IF AH CAN DO THAT HERE...
"...AH CAN HELP DO IT ON MAH OWN WORLD.
"AH HOPE..."

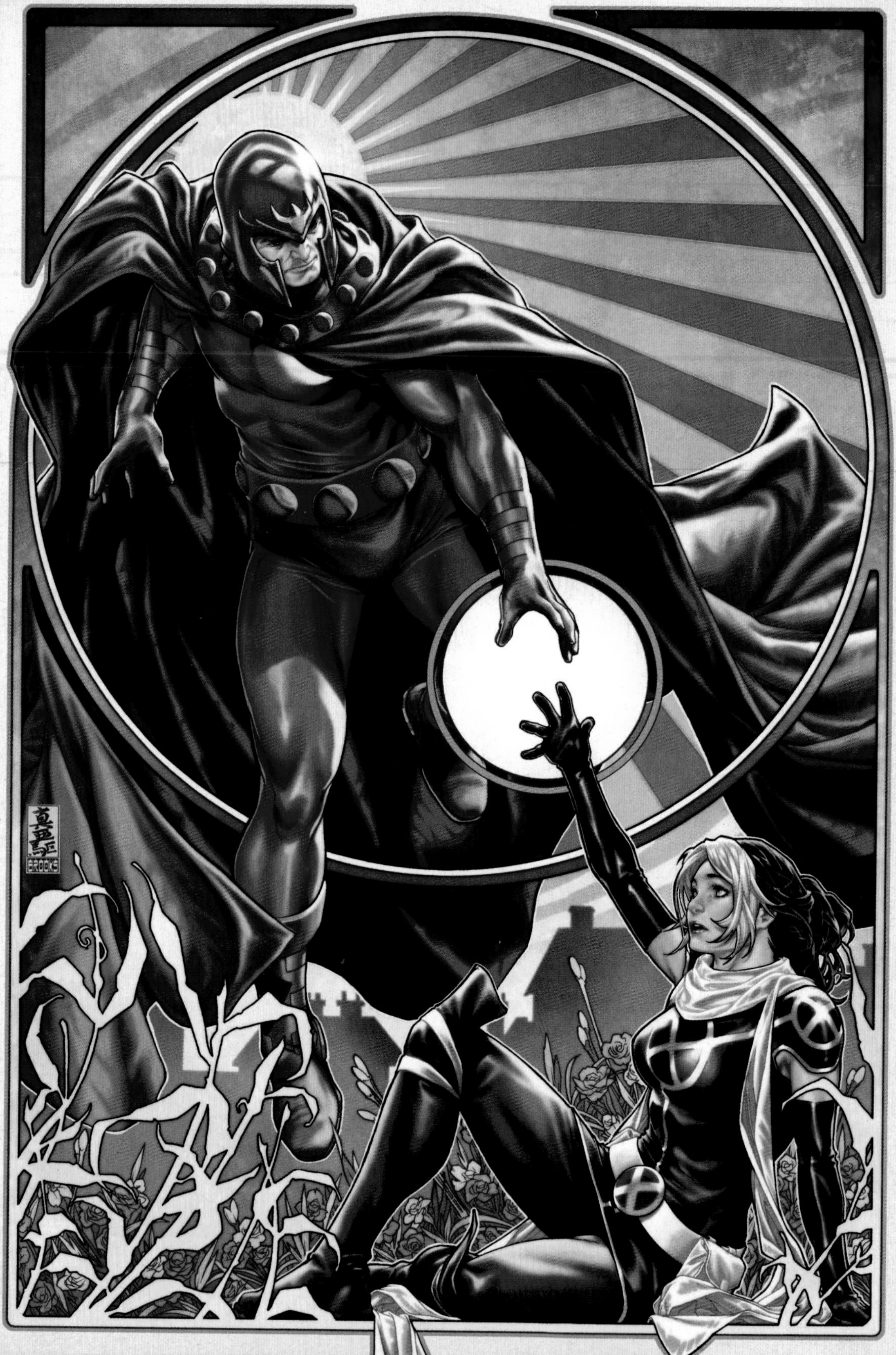
BROOKS

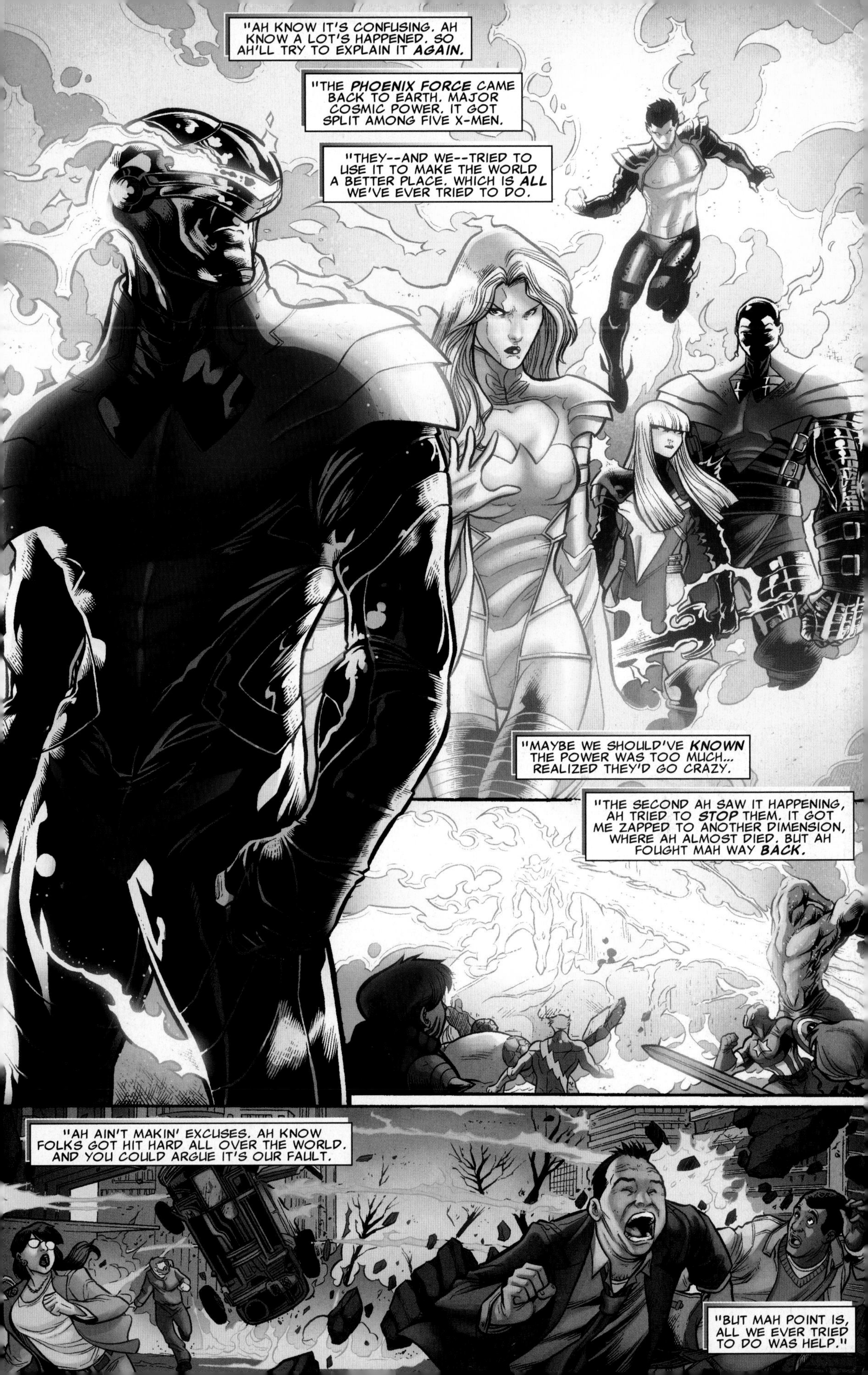
"AH KNOW IT'S CONFUSING. AH KNOW A LOT'S HAPPENED. SO AH'LL TRY TO EXPLAIN IT AGAIN.
"THE PHOENIX FORCE CAME BACK TO EARTH. MAJOR COSMIC POWER. IT GOT SPLIT AMONG FIVE X-MEN.
"THEY--AND WE--TRIED TO USE IT TO MAKE THE WORLD A BETTER PLACE. WHICH IS ALL WE'VE EVER TRIED TO DO.
"MAYBE WE SHOULD'VE KNOWN THE POWER WAS TOO MUCH... REALIZED THEY'D GO CRAZY.
"THE SECOND AH SAW IT HAPPENING, AH TRIED TO STOP THEM. IT GOT ME ZAPPED TO ANOTHER DIMENSION, WHERE AH ALMOST DIED. BUT AH FOUGHT MAH WAY BACK.
"AH AIN'T MAKIN' EXCUSES. AH KNOW FOLKS GOT HIT HARD ALL OVER THE WORLD. AND YOU COULD ARGUE IT'S OUR FAULT.
"BUT MAH POINT IS, ALL WE EVER TRIED TO DO WAS HELP."

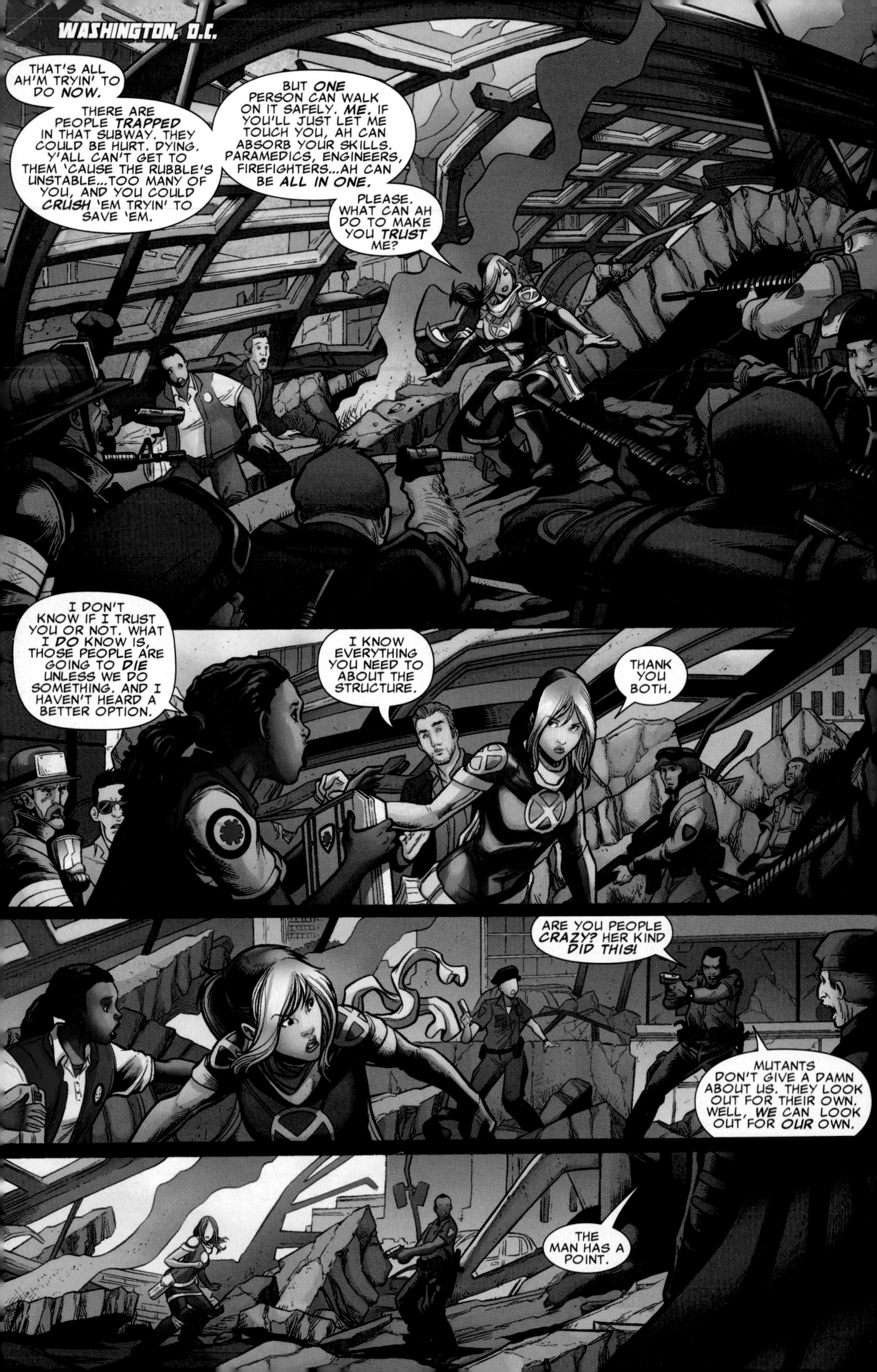
WASHINGTON, D.C.
THAT'S ALL AH'M TRYIN' TO DO NOW.
THERE ARE PEOPLE TRAPPED IN THAT SUBWAY. THEY COULD BE HURT. DYING. Y'ALL CAN'T GET TO THEM 'CAUSE THE RUBBLE'S UNSTABLE...TOO MANY OF YOU, AND YOU COULD CRUSH 'EM TRYIN' TO SAVE 'EM.
BUT ONE PERSON CAN WALK ON IT SAFELY. ME. IF YOU'LL JUST LET ME TOUCH YOU, AH CAN ABSORB YOUR SKILLS. PARAMEDICS, ENGINEERS, FIREFIGHTERS...AH CAN BE ALL IN ONE.
PLEASE. WHAT CAN AH DO TO MAKE YOU TRUST ME?
I DON'T KNOW IF I TRUST YOU OR NOT. WHAT I DO KNOW IS, THOSE PEOPLE ARE GOING TO DIE UNLESS WE DO SOMETHING. AND I HAVEN'T HEARD A BETTER OPTION.
I KNOW EVERYTHING YOU NEED TO ABOUT THE STRUCTURE.
THANK YOU BOTH.
ARE YOU PEOPLE CRAZY? HER KIND DID THIS!
MUTANTS DON'T GIVE A DAMN ABOUT US. THEY LOOK OUT FOR THEIR OWN. WELL, WE CAN LOOK OUT FOR OUR OWN.
THE MAN HAS A POINT.

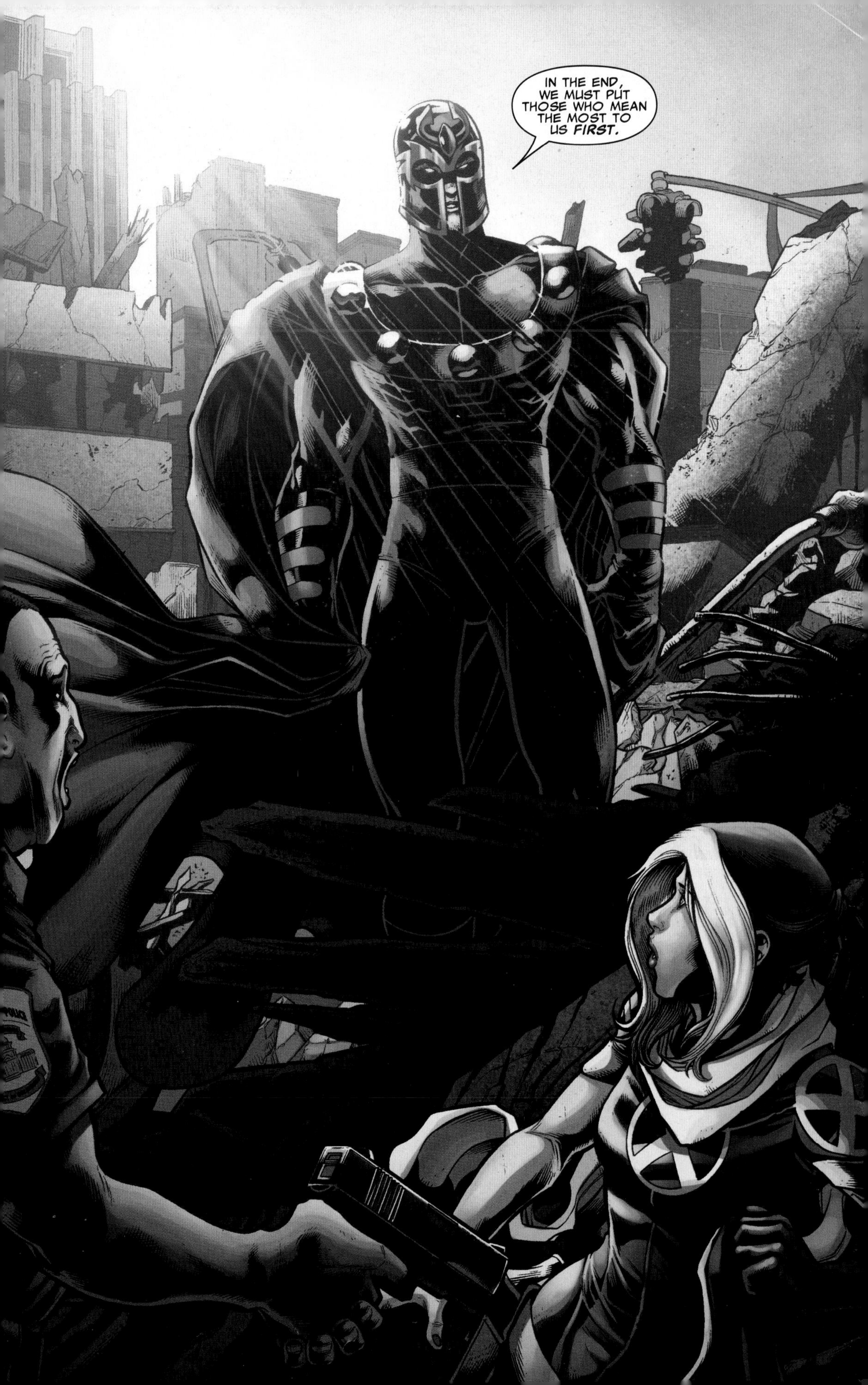
IN THE END, WE MUST PUT THOSE WHO MEAN THE MOST TO US FIRST.

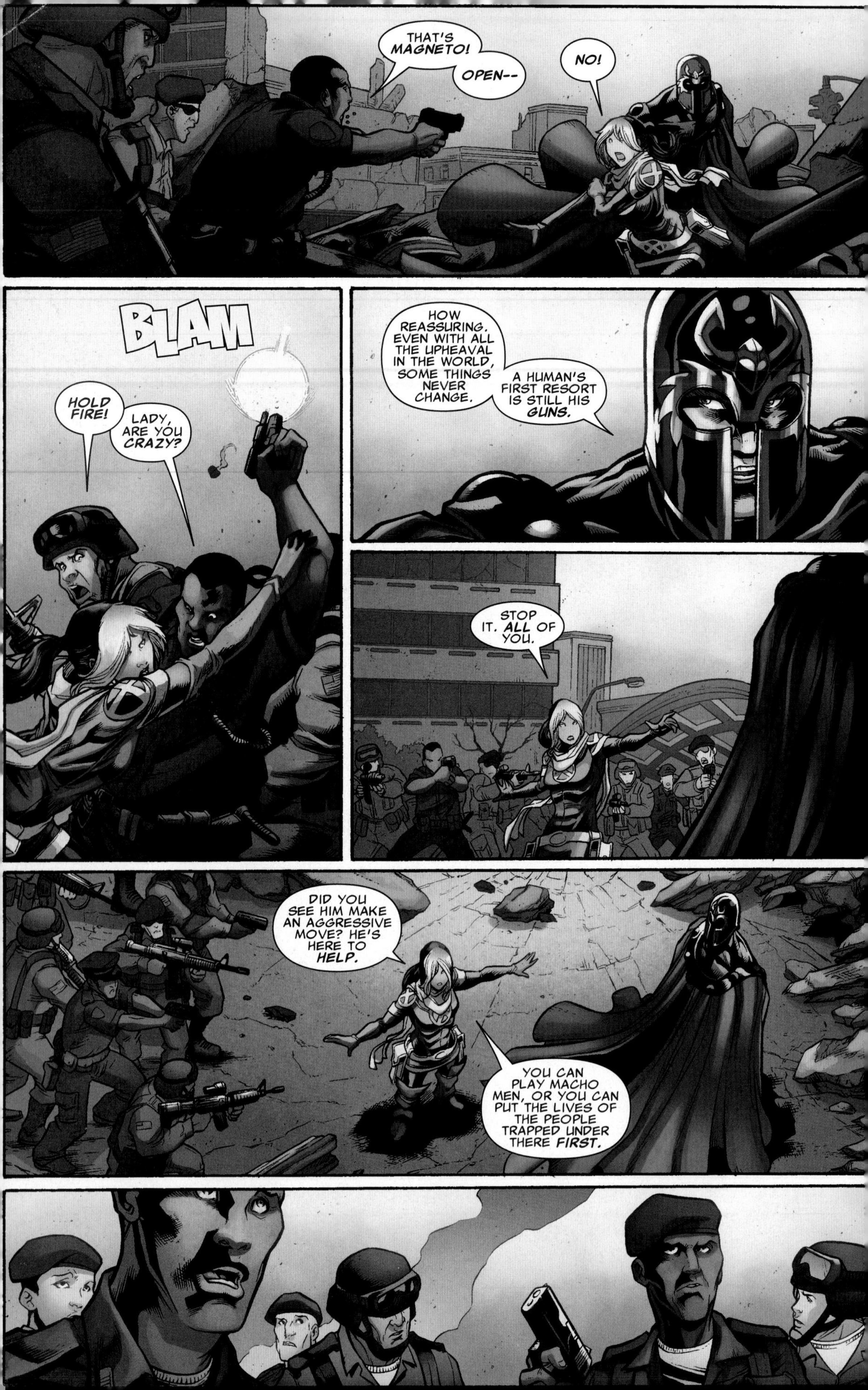
THAT'S MAGNETO!
OPEN--
NO!
BLAM
HOLD FIRE!
LADY, ARE YOU CRAZY?
HOW REASSURING. EVEN WITH ALL THE UPHEAVAL IN THE WORLD, SOME THINGS NEVER CHANGE.
A HUMAN'S FIRST RESORT IS STILL HIS GUNS.
STOP IT. ALL OF YOU.
DID YOU SEE HIM MAKE AN AGGRESSIVE MOVE? HE'S HERE TO HELP.
YOU CAN PLAY MACHO MEN, OR YOU CAN PUT THE LIVES OF THE PEOPLE TRAPPED UNDER THERE FIRST.

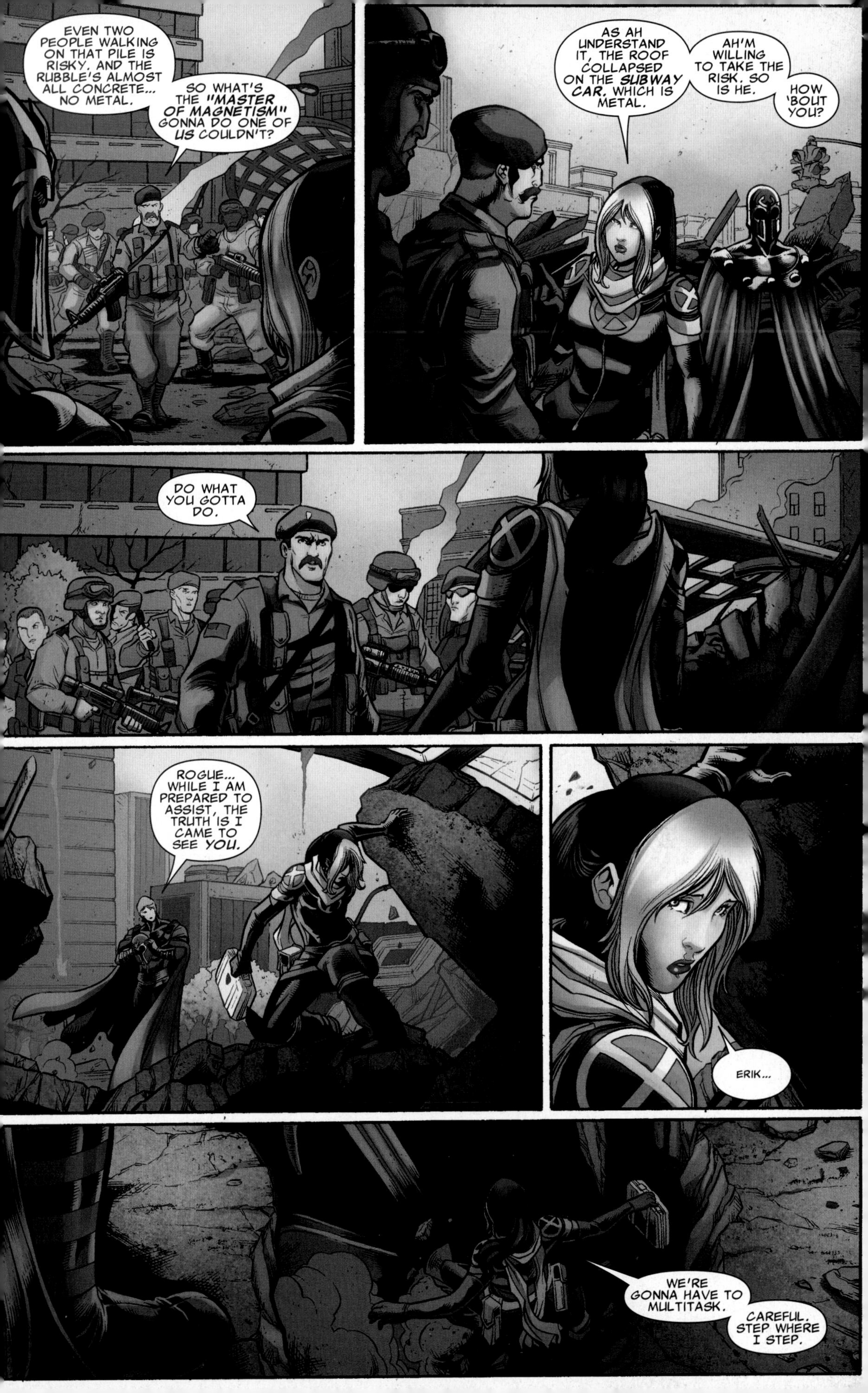
EVEN TWO PEOPLE WALKING ON THAT PILE IS RISKY, AND THE RUBBLE'S ALMOST ALL CONCRETE... NO METAL.
SO WHAT'S THE "MASTER OF MAGNETISM" GONNA DO ONE OF US COULDN'T?
AS AH UNDERSTAND IT, THE ROOF COLLAPSED ON THE SUBWAY CAR, WHICH IS METAL.
AH'M WILLING TO TAKE THE RISK. SO IS HE.
HOW 'BOUT YOU?
DO WHAT YOU GOTTA DO.
ROGUE... WHILE I AM PREPARED TO ASSIST, THE TRUTH IS I CAME TO SEE YOU.
ERIK...
WE'RE GONNA HAVE TO MULTITASK.
CAREFUL. STEP WHERE I STEP.

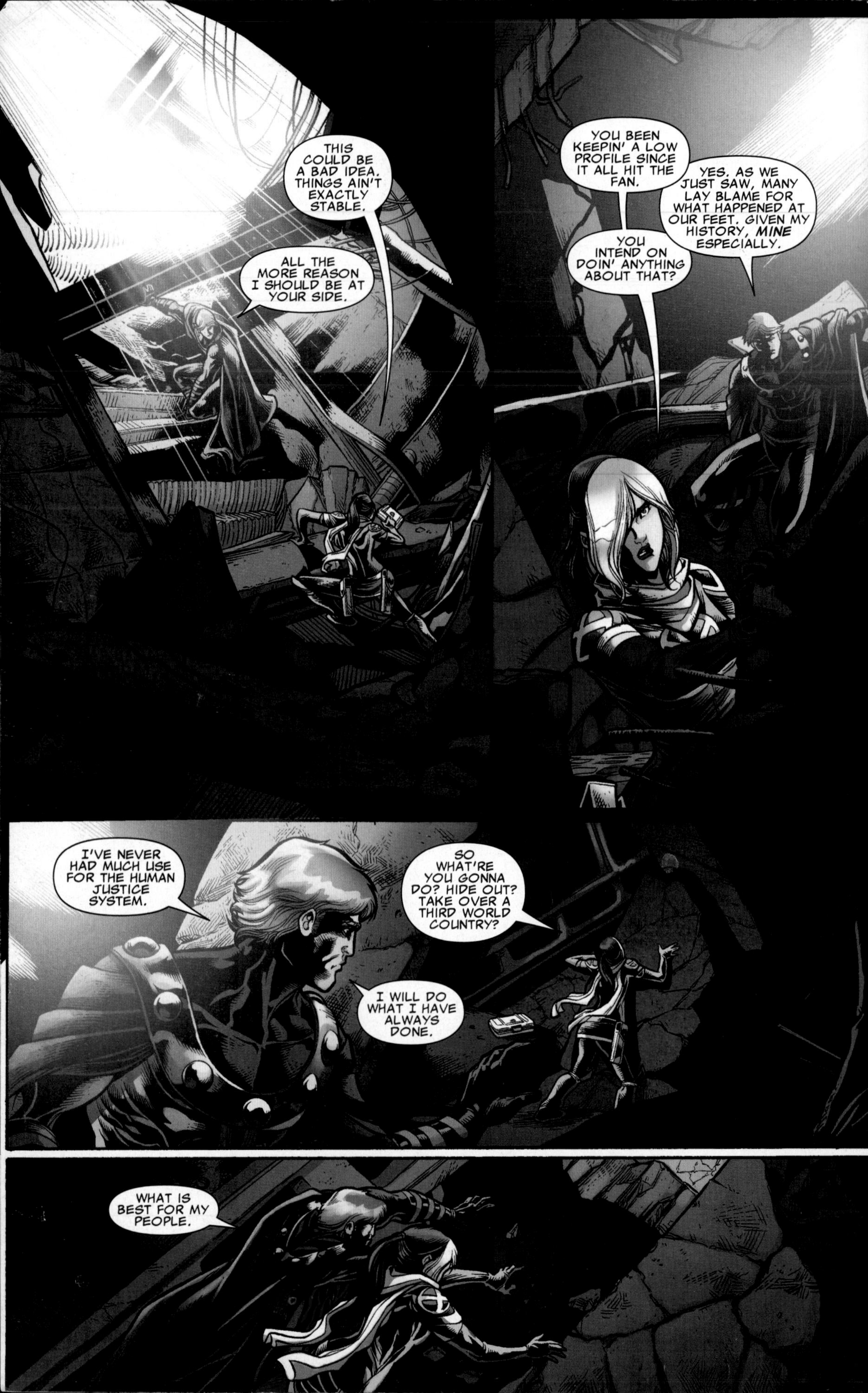
THIS COULD BE A BAD IDEA. THINGS AIN'T EXACTLY STABLE.
ALL THE MORE REASON I SHOULD BE AT YOUR SIDE.
YOU BEEN KEEPIN' A LOW PROFILE SINCE IT ALL HIT THE FAN.
YOU INTEND ON DOIN' ANYTHING ABOUT THAT?
YES. AS WE JUST SAW, MANY LAY BLAME FOR WHAT HAPPENED AT OUR FEET. GIVEN MY HISTORY, MINE ESPECIALLY.
I'VE NEVER HAD MUCH USE FOR THE HUMAN JUSTICE SYSTEM.
SO WHAT'RE YOU GONNA DO? HIDE OUT? TAKE OVER A THIRD WORLD COUNTRY?
I WILL DO WHAT I HAVE ALWAYS DONE.
WHAT IS BEST FOR MY PEOPLE.

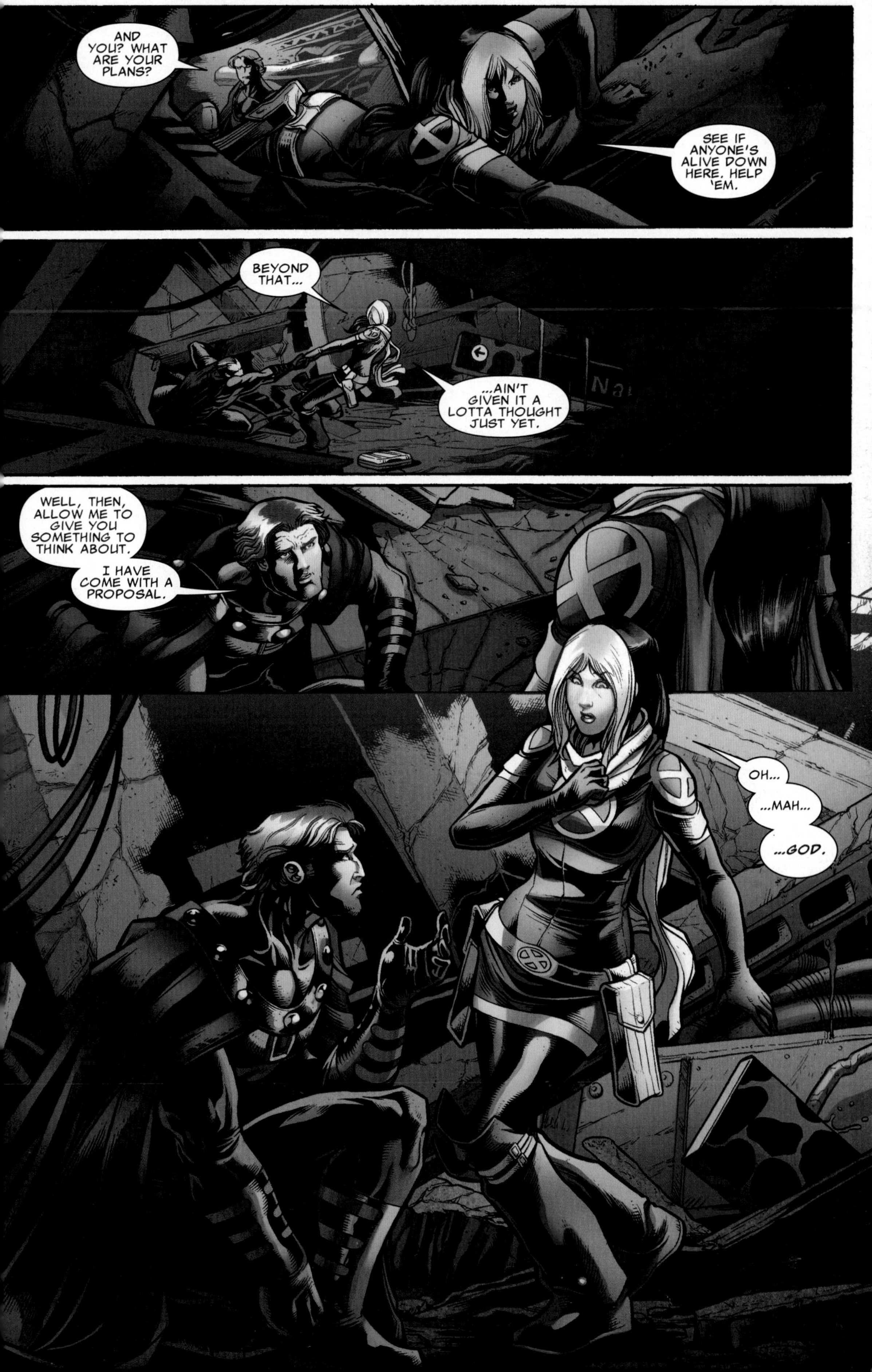
AND YOU? WHAT ARE YOUR PLANS?
SEE IF ANYONE'S ALIVE DOWN HERE. HELP 'EM.
BEYOND THAT...
...AIN'T GIVEN IT A LOTTA THOUGHT JUST YET.
WELL, THEN, ALLOW ME TO GIVE YOU SOMETHING TO THINK ABOUT.
I HAVE COME WITH A PROPOSAL.
OH...
...MAH...
...GOD.

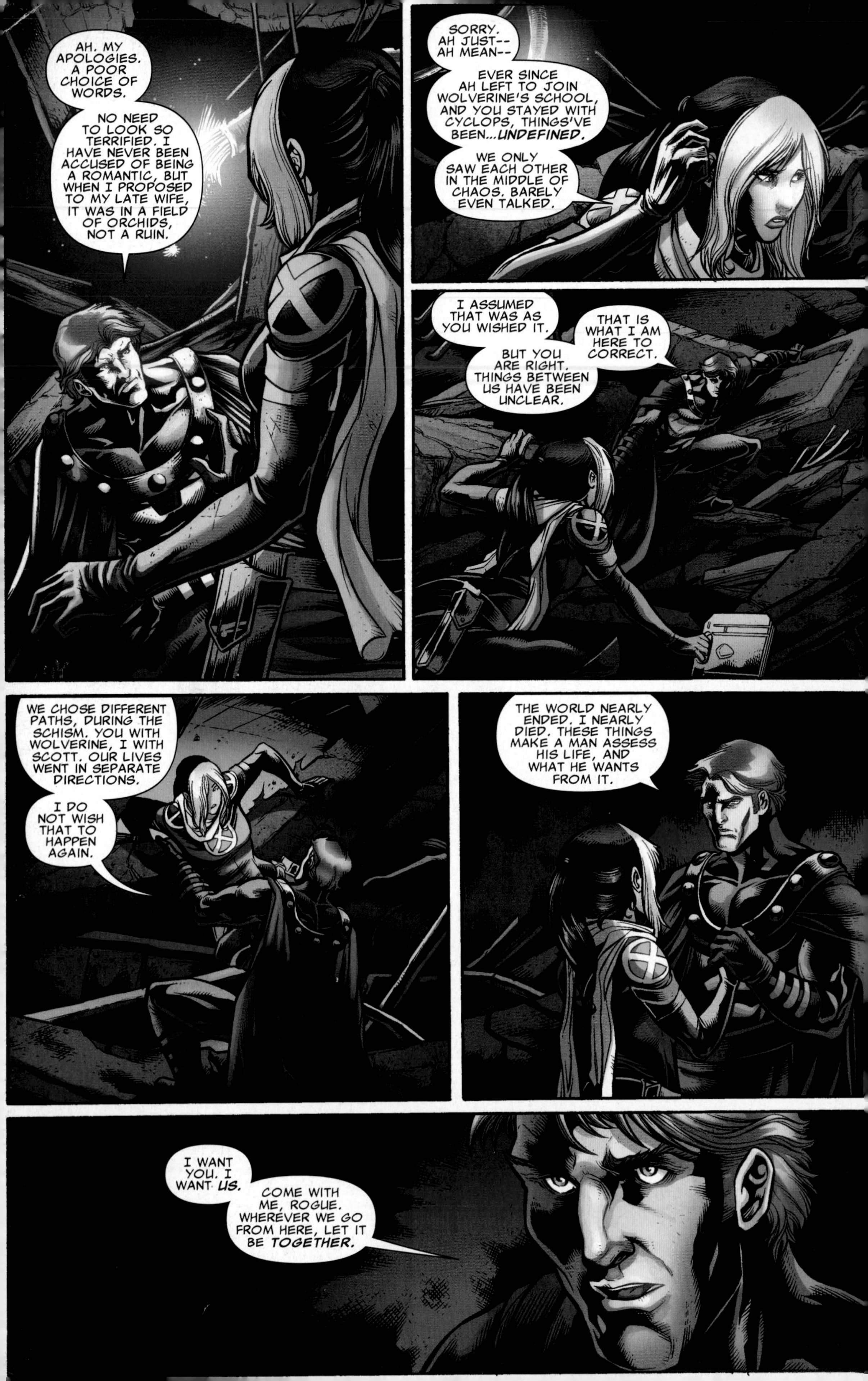
AH. MY APOLOGIES. A POOR CHOICE OF WORDS.
NO NEED TO LOOK SO TERRIFIED. I HAVE NEVER BEEN ACCUSED OF BEING A ROMANTIC, BUT WHEN I PROPOSED TO MY LATE WIFE, IT WAS IN A FIELD OF ORCHIDS, NOT A RUIN.
SORRY. AH JUST-- AH MEAN--
EVER SINCE AH LEFT TO JOIN WOLVERINE'S SCHOOL, AND YOU STAYED WITH CYCLOPS, THINGS'VE BEEN...UNDEFINED.
WE ONLY SAW EACH OTHER IN THE MIDDLE OF CHAOS. BARELY EVEN TALKED.
I ASSUMED THAT WAS AS YOU WISHED IT.
THAT IS WHAT I AM HERE TO CORRECT.
BUT YOU ARE RIGHT. THINGS BETWEEN US HAVE BEEN UNCLEAR.
WE CHOSE DIFFERENT PATHS, DURING THE SCHISM. YOU WITH WOLVERINE, I WITH SCOTT. OUR LIVES WENT IN SEPARATE DIRECTIONS.
I DO NOT WISH THAT TO HAPPEN AGAIN.
THE WORLD NEARLY ENDED. I NEARLY DIED. THESE THINGS MAKE A MAN ASSESS HIS LIFE, AND WHAT HE WANTS FROM IT.
I WANT YOU. I WANT US.
COME WITH ME, ROGUE. WHEREVER WE GO FROM HERE, LET IT BE TOGETHER.

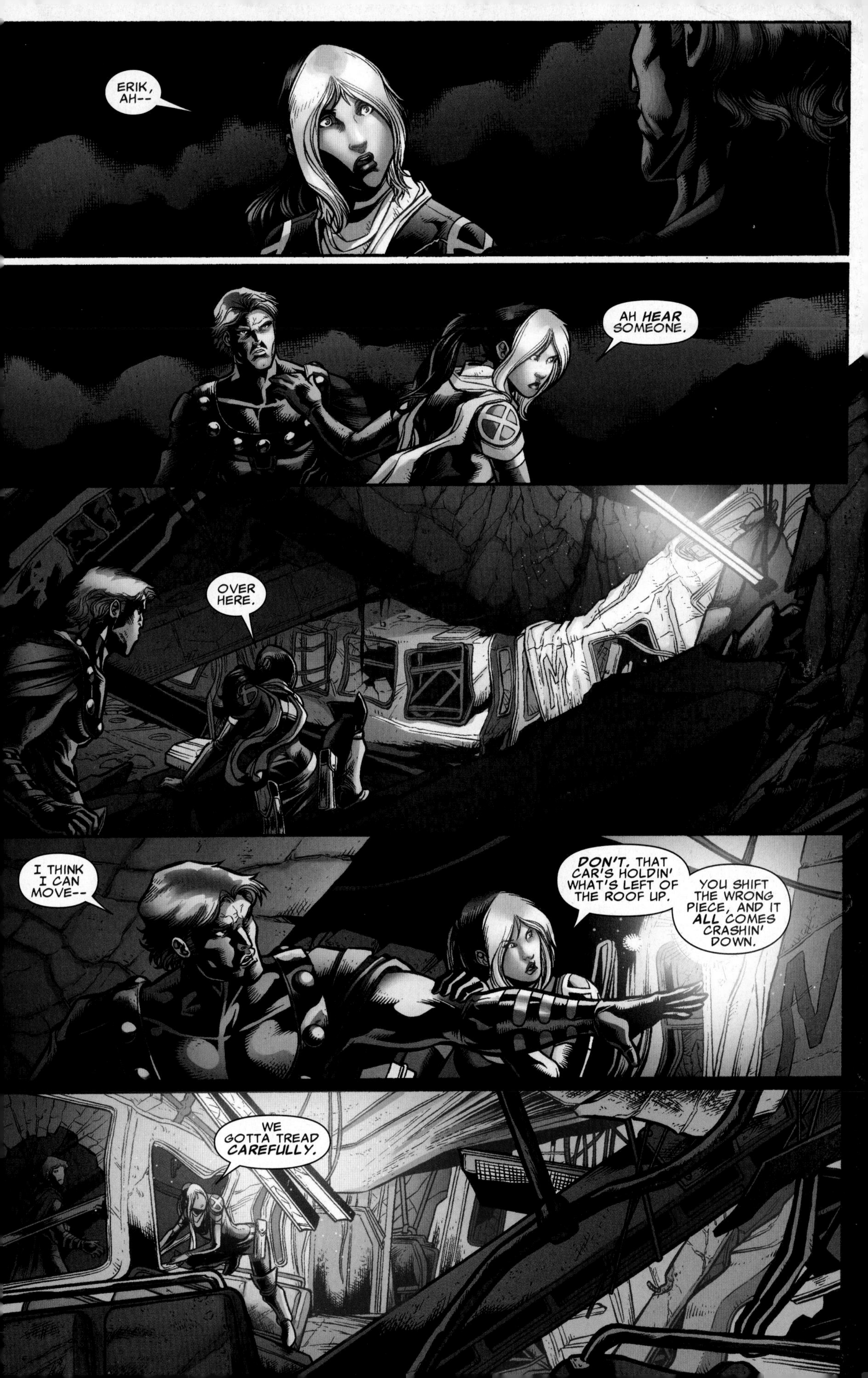
ERIK, AH--
AH HEAR SOMEONE.
OVER HERE.
I THINK I CAN MOVE--
DON'T. THAT CAR'S HOLDIN' WHAT'S LEFT OF THE ROOF UP.
YOU SHIFT THE WRONG PIECE, AND IT ALL COMES CRASHIN' DOWN.
WE GOTTA TREAD CAREFULLY.

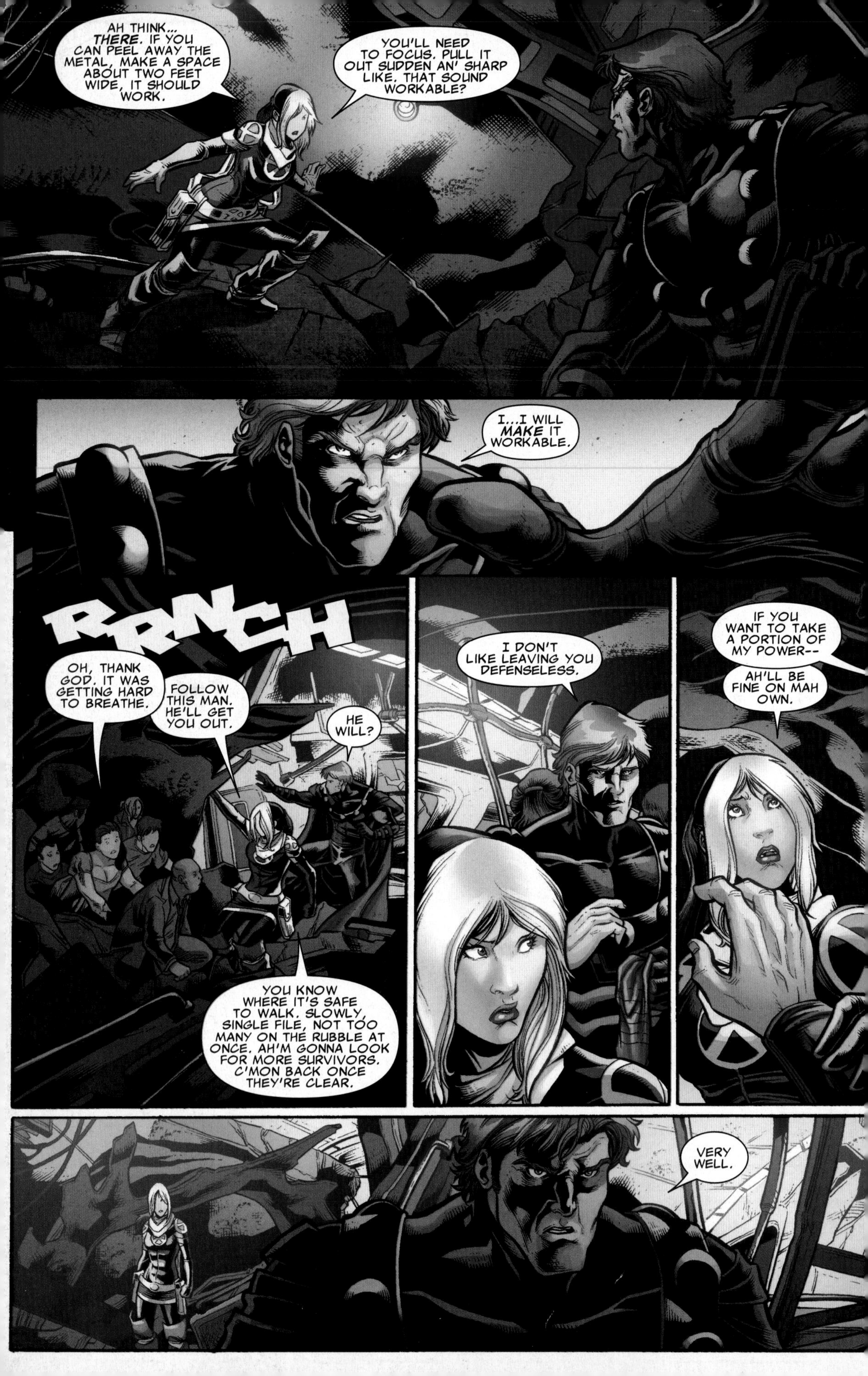
AH THINK... THERE. IF YOU CAN PEEL AWAY THE METAL, MAKE A SPACE ABOUT TWO FEET WIDE, IT SHOULD WORK.
YOU'LL NEED TO FOCUS. PULL IT OUT SUDDEN AN' SHARP LIKE. THAT SOUND WORKABLE?
I...I WILL MAKE IT WORKABLE.
RRNCH
OH, THANK GOD. IT WAS GETTING HARD TO BREATHE.
FOLLOW THIS MAN. HE'LL GET YOU OUT.
HE WILL?
YOU KNOW WHERE IT'S SAFE TO WALK. SLOWLY, SINGLE FILE, NOT TOO MANY ON THE RUBBLE AT ONCE. AH'M GONNA LOOK FOR MORE SURVIVORS. C'MON BACK ONCE THEY'RE CLEAR.
I DON'T LIKE LEAVING YOU DEFENSELESS.
IF YOU WANT TO TAKE A PORTION OF MY POWER--
AH'LL BE FINE ON MAH OWN.
VERY WELL.

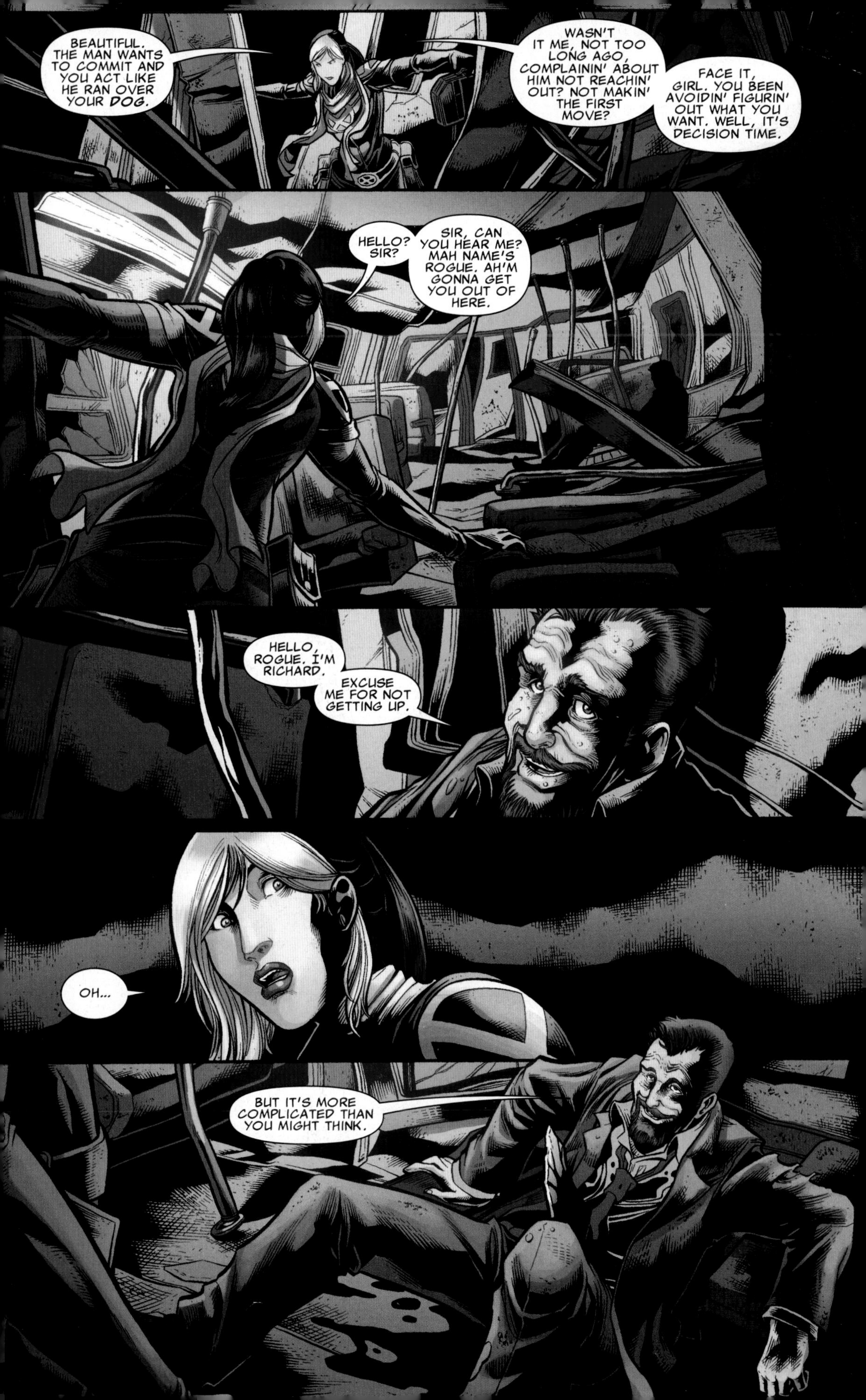
BEAUTIFUL. THE MAN WANTS TO COMMIT AND YOU ACT LIKE HE RAN OVER YOUR **DOG**.
WASN'T IT ME, NOT TOO LONG AGO, COMPLAININ' ABOUT HIM NOT REACHIN' OUT? NOT MAKIN' THE FIRST MOVE?
FACE IT, GIRL. YOU BEEN AVOIDIN' FIGURIN' OUT WHAT YOU WANT. WELL, IT'S DECISION TIME.
HELLO? SIR?
SIR, CAN YOU HEAR ME? MAH NAME'S ROGUE. AH'M GONNA GET YOU OUT OF HERE.
HELLO, ROGUE. I'M RICHARD.
EXCUSE ME FOR NOT GETTING UP.
OH...
BUT IT'S MORE COMPLICATED THAN YOU MIGHT THINK.

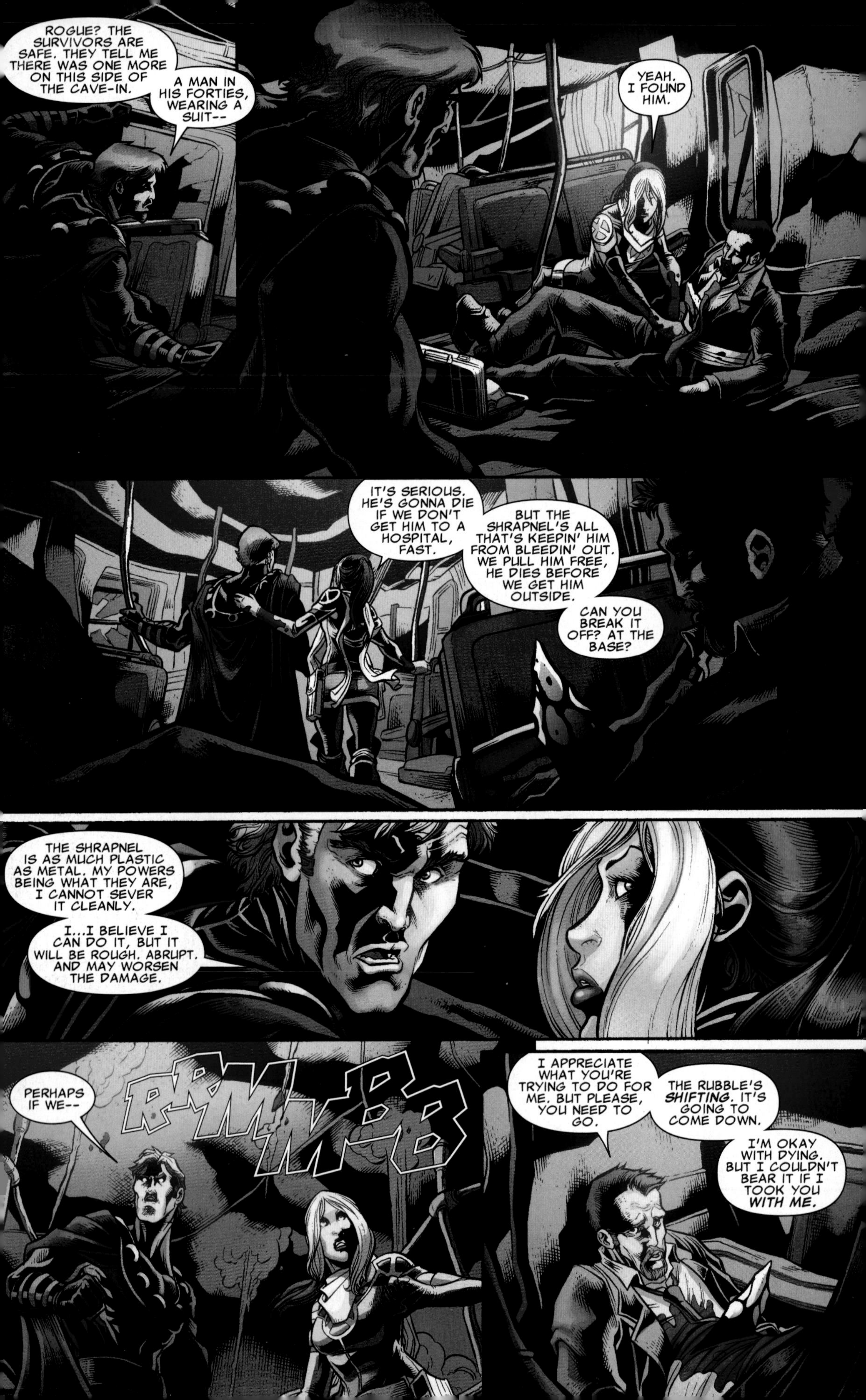
ROGUE? THE SURVIVORS ARE SAFE. THEY TELL ME THERE WAS ONE MORE ON THIS SIDE OF THE CAVE-IN.
A MAN IN HIS FORTIES, WEARING A SUIT--
YEAH. I FOUND HIM.
IT'S SERIOUS. HE'S GONNA DIE IF WE DON'T GET HIM TO A HOSPITAL, FAST.
BUT THE SHRAPNEL'S ALL THAT'S KEEPIN' HIM FROM BLEEDIN' OUT. WE PULL HIM FREE, HE DIES BEFORE WE GET HIM OUTSIDE.
CAN YOU BREAK IT OFF? AT THE BASE?
THE SHRAPNEL IS AS MUCH PLASTIC AS METAL. MY POWERS BEING WHAT THEY ARE, I CANNOT SEVER IT CLEANLY.
I...I BELIEVE I CAN DO IT, BUT IT WILL BE ROUGH. ABRUPT. AND MAY WORSEN THE DAMAGE.
PERHAPS IF WE--
RMMBB
I APPRECIATE WHAT YOU'RE TRYING TO DO FOR ME. BUT PLEASE, YOU NEED TO GO.
THE RUBBLE'S *SHIFTING*. IT'S GOING TO COME DOWN.
I'M OKAY WITH DYING. BUT I COULDN'T BEAR IT IF I TOOK YOU *WITH ME*.

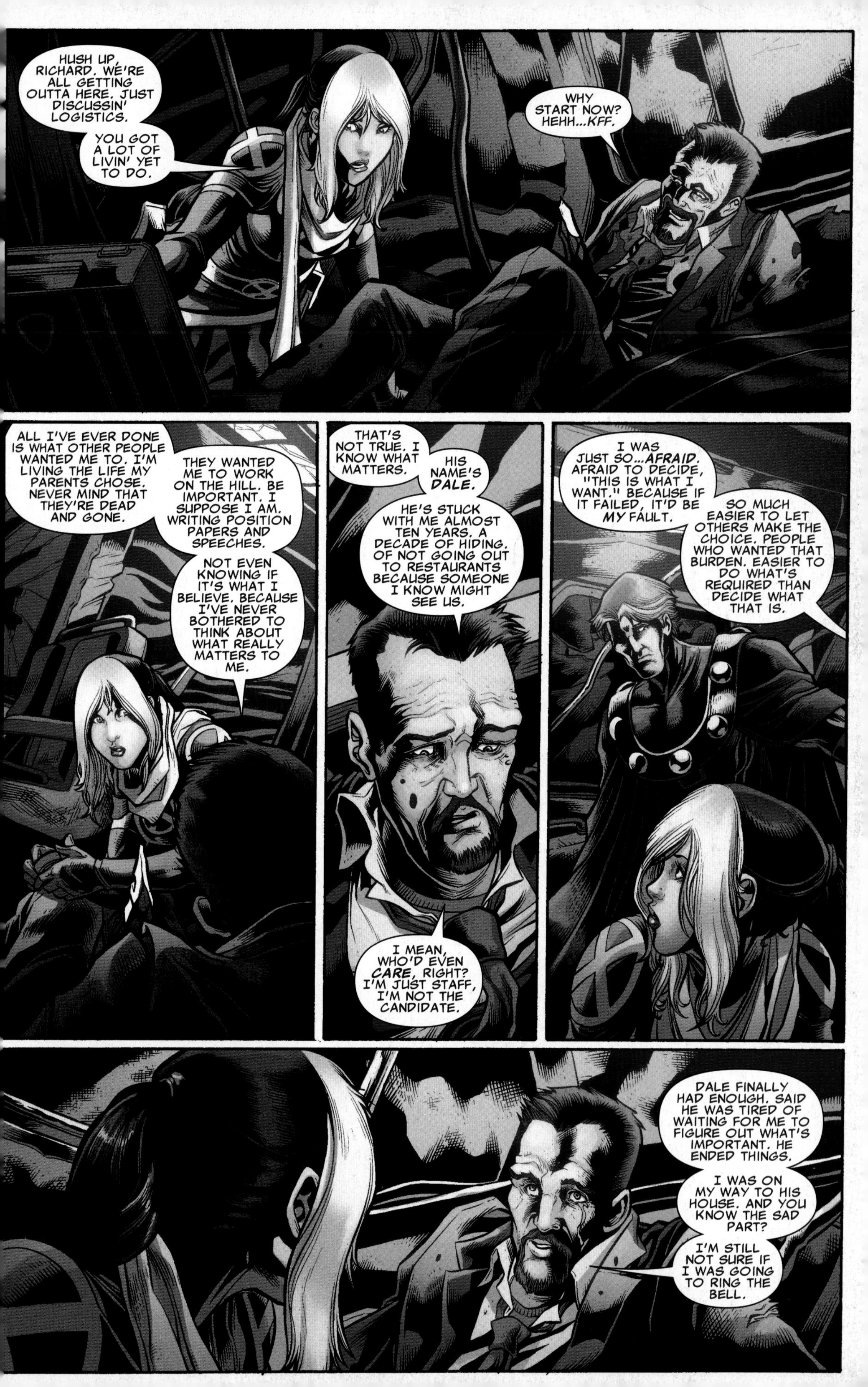

HUSH UP, RICHARD. WE'RE ALL GETTING OUTTA HERE. JUST DISCUSSIN' LOGISTICS.
YOU GOT A LOT OF LIVIN' YET TO DO.
WHY START NOW? HEHH...KFF.
ALL I'VE EVER DONE IS WHAT OTHER PEOPLE WANTED ME TO. I'M LIVING THE LIFE MY PARENTS CHOSE. NEVER MIND THAT THEY'RE DEAD AND GONE.
THEY WANTED ME TO WORK ON THE HILL. BE IMPORTANT. I SUPPOSE I AM. WRITING POSITION PAPERS AND SPEECHES.
NOT EVEN KNOWING IF IT'S WHAT I BELIEVE. BECAUSE I'VE NEVER BOTHERED TO THINK ABOUT WHAT REALLY MATTERS TO ME.
THAT'S NOT TRUE. I KNOW WHAT MATTERS.
HIS NAME'S *DALE.*
HE'S STUCK WITH ME ALMOST TEN YEARS. A DECADE OF HIDING. OF NOT GOING OUT TO RESTAURANTS BECAUSE SOMEONE I KNOW MIGHT SEE US.
I MEAN, WHO'D EVEN *CARE*, RIGHT? I'M JUST STAFF, I'M NOT THE CANDIDATE.
I WAS JUST SO...*AFRAID.* AFRAID TO DECIDE, "THIS IS WHAT I WANT." BECAUSE IF IT FAILED, IT'D BE *MY* FAULT.
SO MUCH EASIER TO LET OTHERS MAKE THE CHOICE. PEOPLE WHO WANTED THAT BURDEN. EASIER TO DO WHAT'S REQUIRED THAN DECIDE WHAT THAT IS.
DALE FINALLY HAD ENOUGH. SAID HE WAS TIRED OF WAITING FOR ME TO FIGURE OUT WHAT'S IMPORTANT. HE ENDED THINGS.
I WAS ON MY WAY TO HIS HOUSE. AND YOU KNOW THE SAD PART?
I'M STILL NOT SURE IF I WAS GOING TO RING THE BELL.

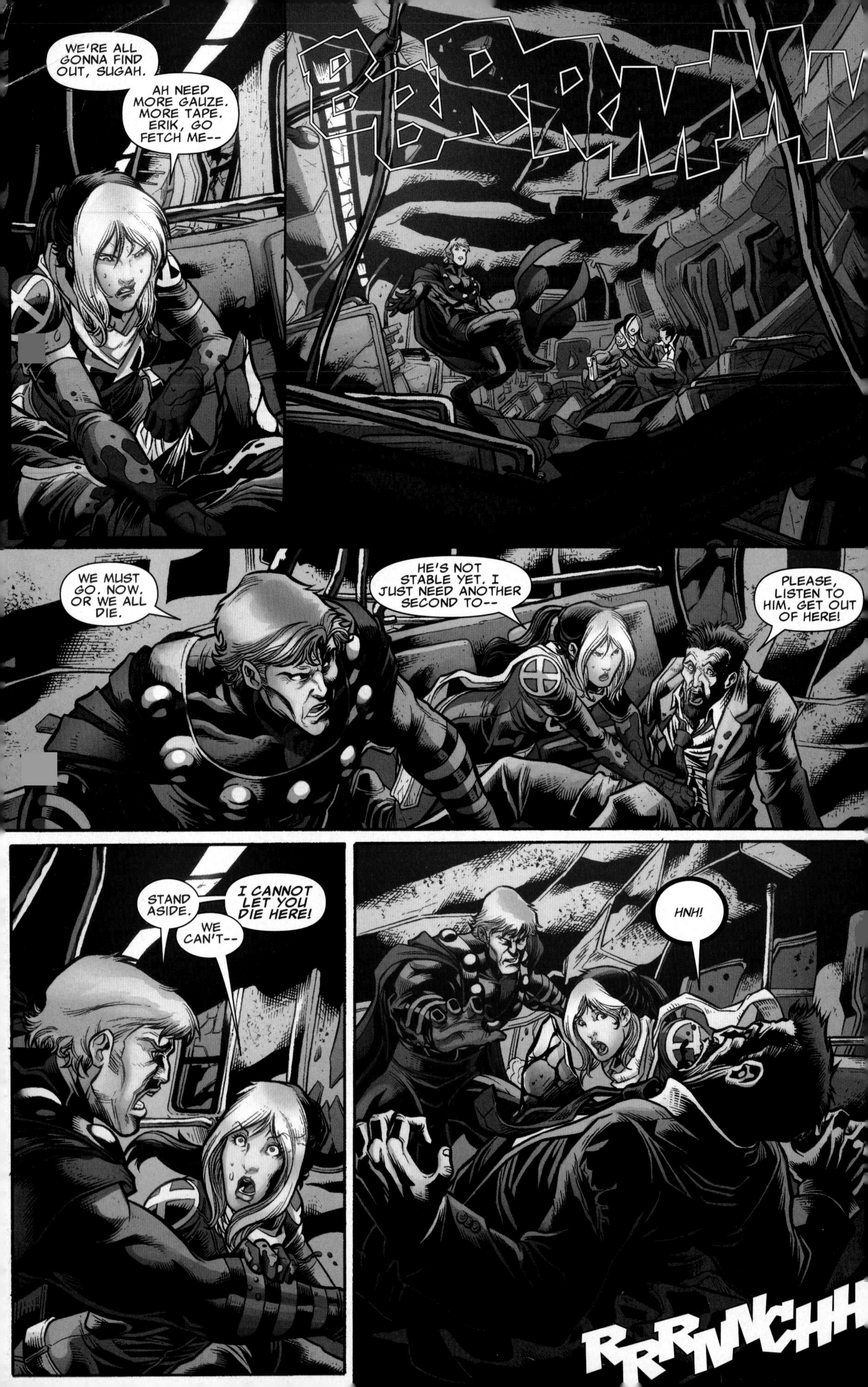
WE'RE ALL GONNA FIND OUT, SUGAH.
AH NEED MORE GAUZE. MORE TAPE. ERIK, GO FETCH ME--
WE MUST GO. NOW. OR WE ALL DIE.
HE'S NOT STABLE YET. I JUST NEED ANOTHER SECOND TO--
PLEASE, LISTEN TO HIM. GET OUT OF HERE!
STAND ASIDE.
WE CAN'T--
I CANNOT LET YOU DIE HERE!
HNH!
RRRNNCHH

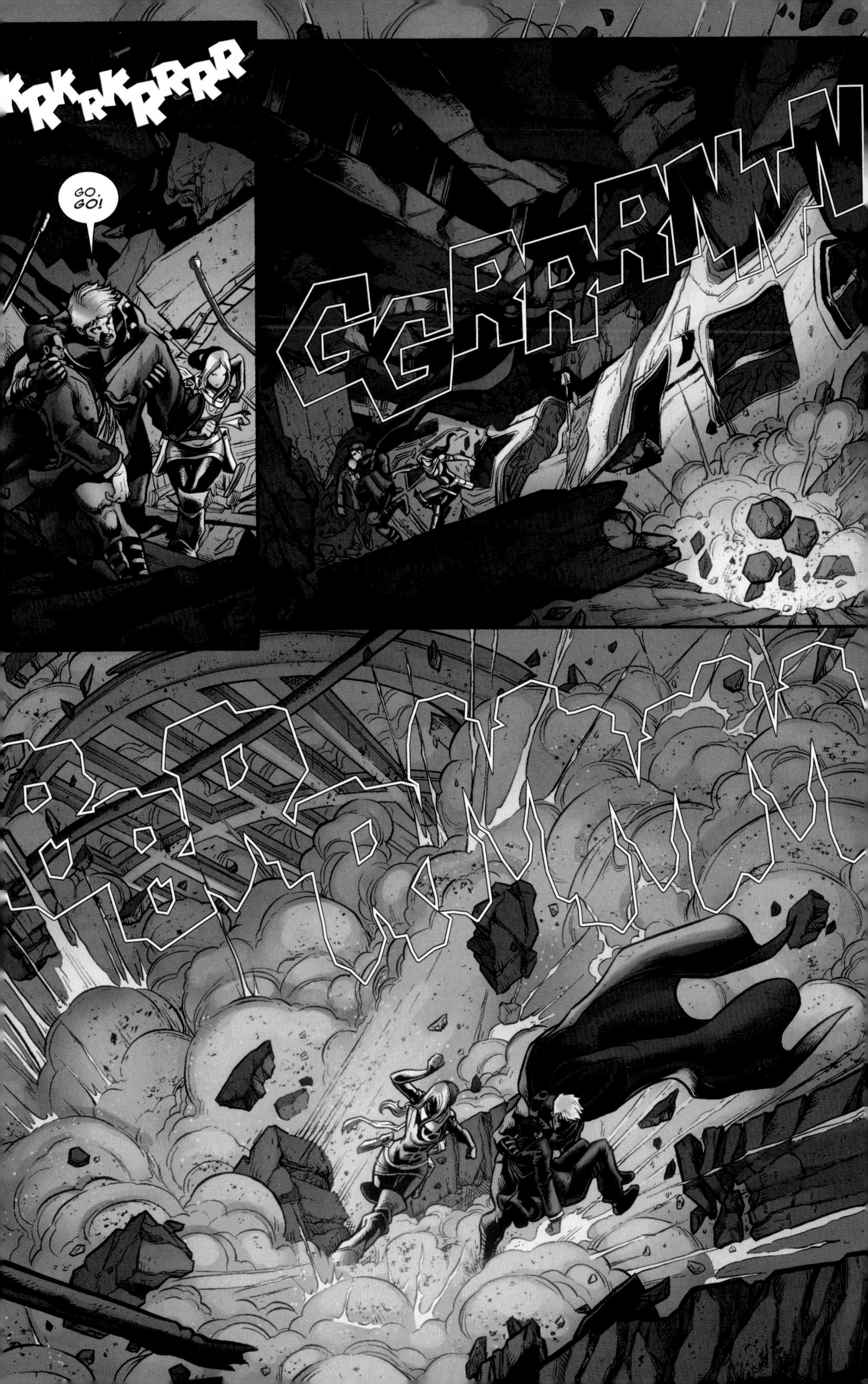

KRKRKRRRR
GO, GO!
GGRRRMMM

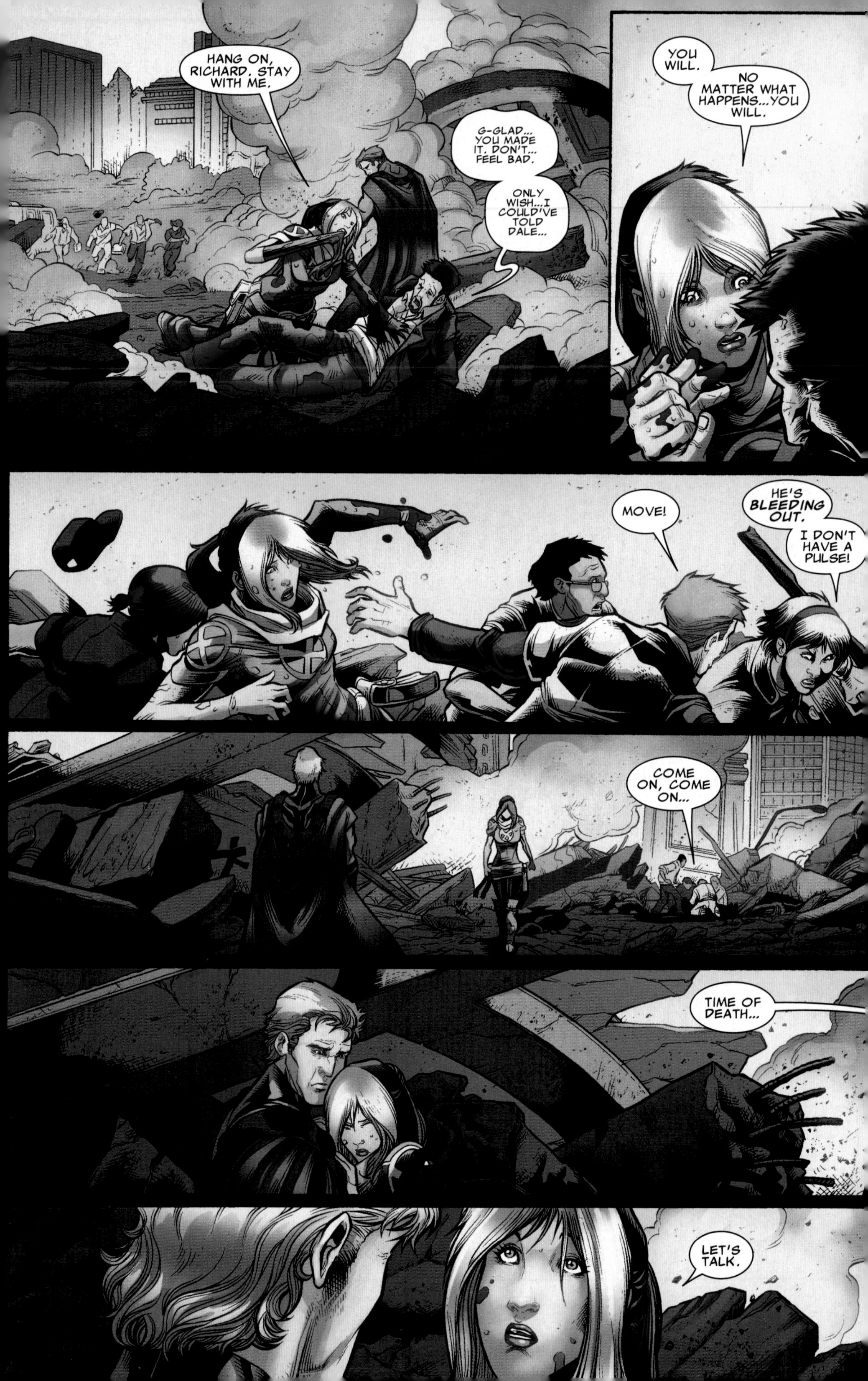
HANG ON, RICHARD. STAY WITH ME.
G-GLAD... YOU MADE IT. DON'T... FEEL BAD.
ONLY WISH... I COULD'VE TOLD DALE...
YOU WILL.
NO MATTER WHAT HAPPENS... YOU WILL.
MOVE!
HE'S BLEEDING OUT.
I DON'T HAVE A PULSE!
COME ON, COME ON...
TIME OF DEATH...
LET'S TALK.

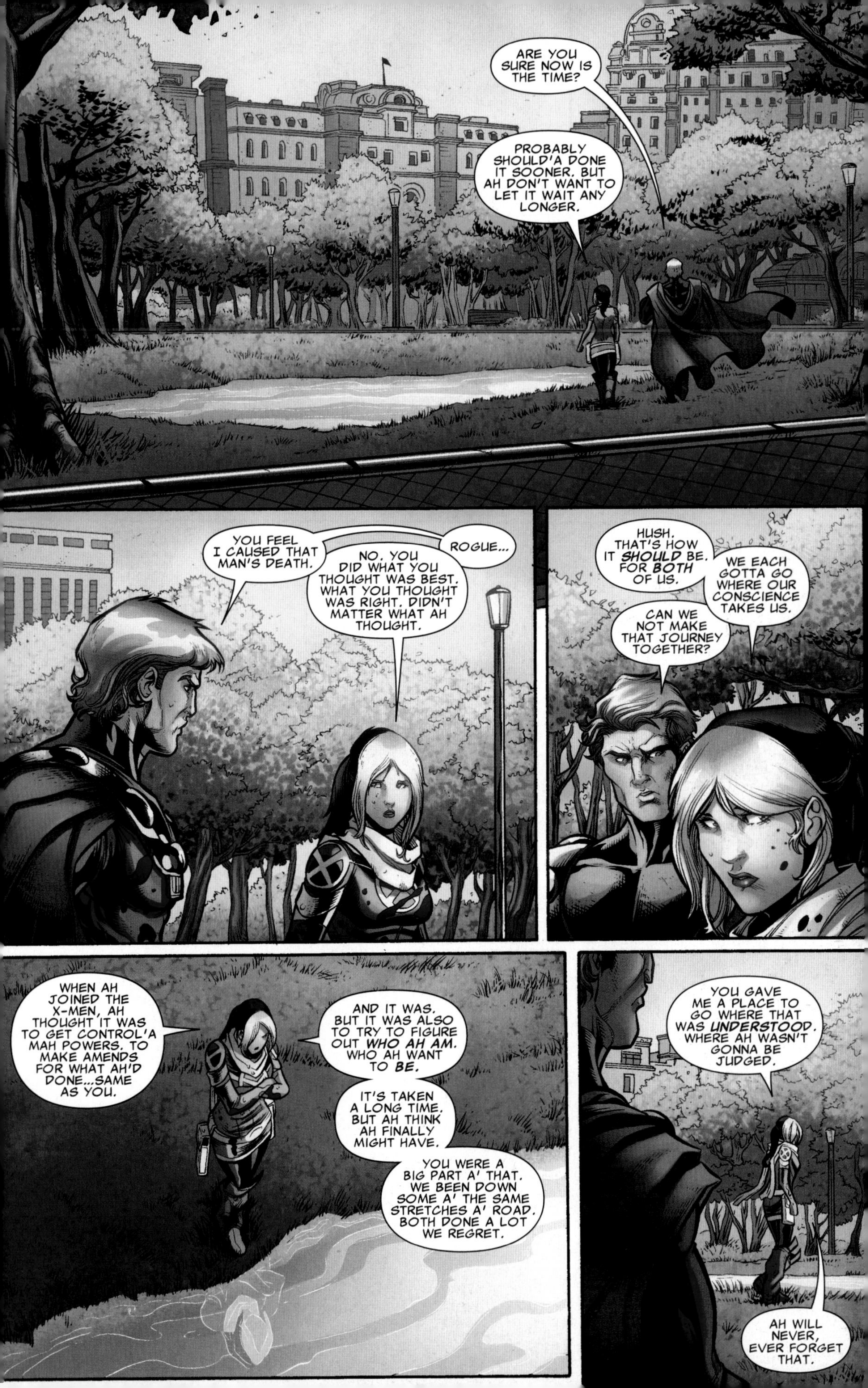

ARE YOU SURE NOW IS THE TIME?
PROBABLY SHOULD'A DONE IT SOONER. BUT AH DON'T WANT TO LET IT WAIT ANY LONGER.
YOU FEEL I CAUSED THAT MAN'S DEATH.
ROGUE...
NO. YOU DID WHAT YOU THOUGHT WAS BEST. WHAT YOU THOUGHT WAS RIGHT. DIDN'T MATTER WHAT AH THOUGHT.
HUSH. THAT'S HOW IT SHOULD BE. FOR BOTH OF US.
WE EACH GOTTA GO WHERE OUR CONSCIENCE TAKES US.
CAN WE NOT MAKE THAT JOURNEY TOGETHER?
WHEN AH JOINED THE X-MEN, AH THOUGHT IT WAS TO GET CONTROL'A MAH POWERS. TO MAKE AMENDS FOR WHAT AH'D DONE...SAME AS YOU.
AND IT WAS. BUT IT WAS ALSO TO TRY TO FIGURE OUT WHO AH AM. WHO AH WANT TO BE.
IT'S TAKEN A LONG TIME. BUT AH THINK AH FINALLY MIGHT HAVE.
YOU WERE A BIG PART A' THAT. WE BEEN DOWN SOME A' THE SAME STRETCHES A' ROAD. BOTH DONE A LOT WE REGRET.
YOU GAVE ME A PLACE TO GO WHERE THAT WAS UNDERSTOOD. WHERE AH WASN'T GONNA BE JUDGED.
AH WILL NEVER, EVER FORGET THAT.

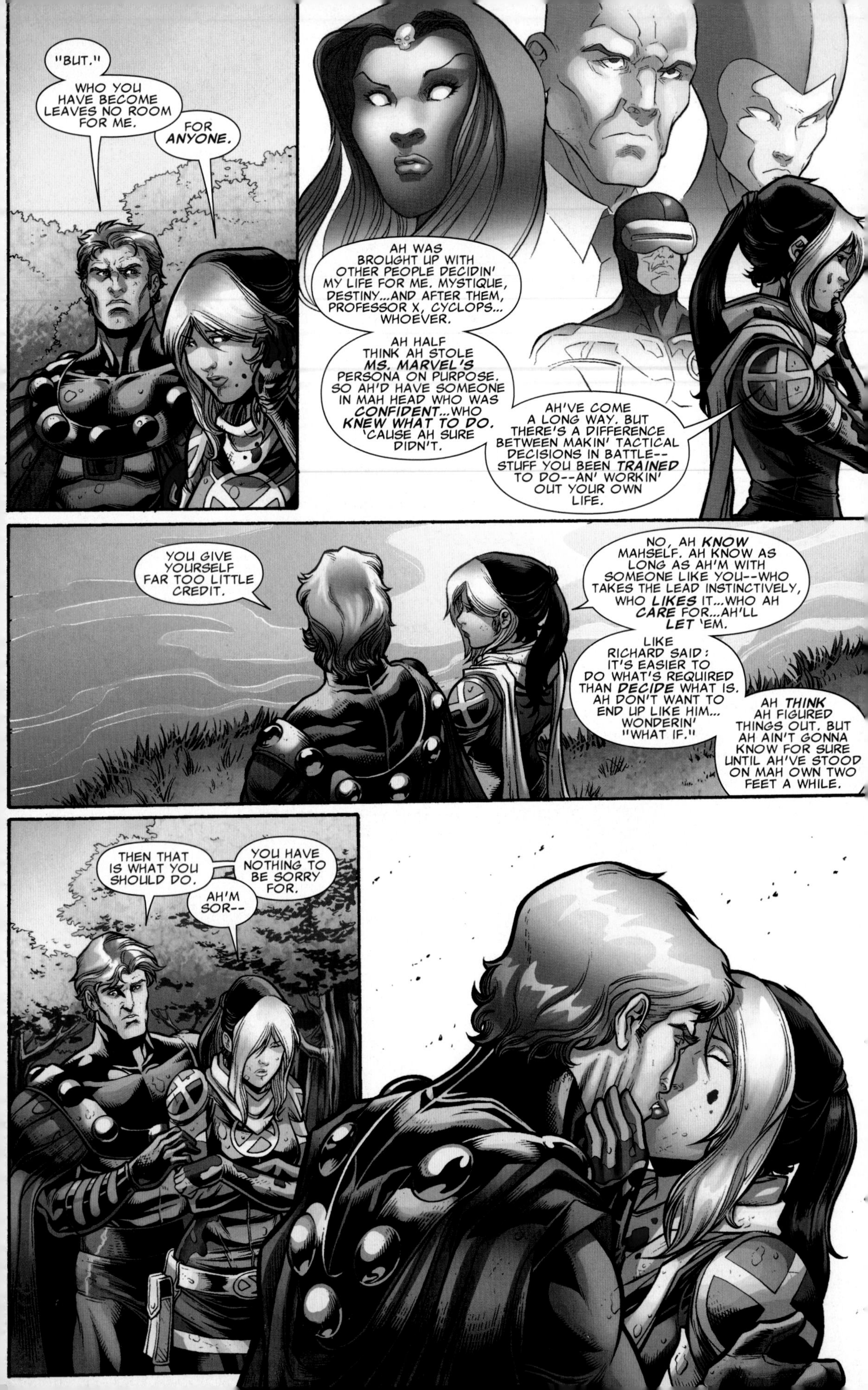
"BUT."
WHO YOU HAVE BECOME LEAVES NO ROOM FOR ME.
FOR ANYONE.
AH WAS BROUGHT UP WITH OTHER PEOPLE DECIDIN' MY LIFE FOR ME. MYSTIQUE, DESTINY...AND AFTER THEM, PROFESSOR X, CYCLOPS... WHOEVER.
AH HALF THINK AH STOLE MS. MARVEL'S PERSONA ON PURPOSE. SO AH'D HAVE SOMEONE IN MAH HEAD WHO WAS CONFIDENT...WHO KNEW WHAT TO DO. 'CAUSE AH SURE DIDN'T.
AH'VE COME A LONG WAY. BUT THERE'S A DIFFERENCE BETWEEN MAKIN' TACTICAL DECISIONS IN BATTLE--STUFF YOU BEEN TRAINED TO DO--AN' WORKIN' OUT YOUR OWN LIFE.
YOU GIVE YOURSELF FAR TOO LITTLE CREDIT.
NO, AH KNOW MAHSELF. AH KNOW AS LONG AS AH'M WITH SOMEONE LIKE YOU--WHO TAKES THE LEAD INSTINCTIVELY, WHO LIKES IT...WHO AH CARE FOR...AH'LL LET 'EM.
LIKE RICHARD SAID: IT'S EASIER TO DO WHAT'S REQUIRED THAN DECIDE WHAT IS. AH DON'T WANT TO END UP LIKE HIM... WONDERIN' "WHAT IF."
AH THINK AH FIGURED THINGS OUT. BUT AH AIN'T GONNA KNOW FOR SURE UNTIL AH'VE STOOD ON MAH OWN TWO FEET A WHILE.
THEN THAT IS WHAT YOU SHOULD DO.
AH'M SOR--
YOU HAVE NOTHING TO BE SORRY FOR.

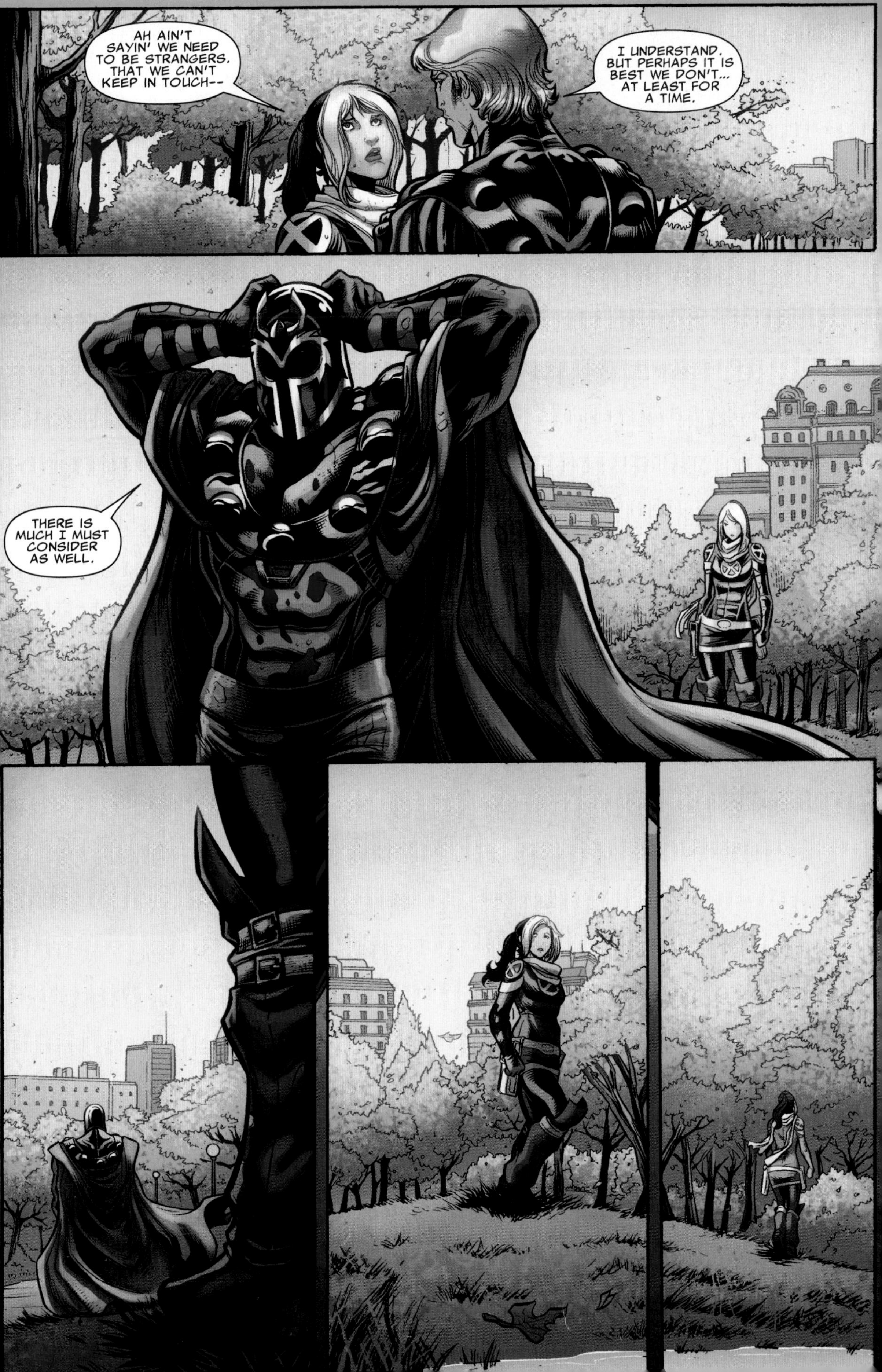
AH AIN'T SAYIN' WE NEED TO BE STRANGERS. THAT WE CAN'T KEEP IN TOUCH--
I UNDERSTAND. BUT PERHAPS IT IS BEST WE DON'T... AT LEAST FOR A TIME.
THERE IS MUCH I MUST CONSIDER AS WELL.

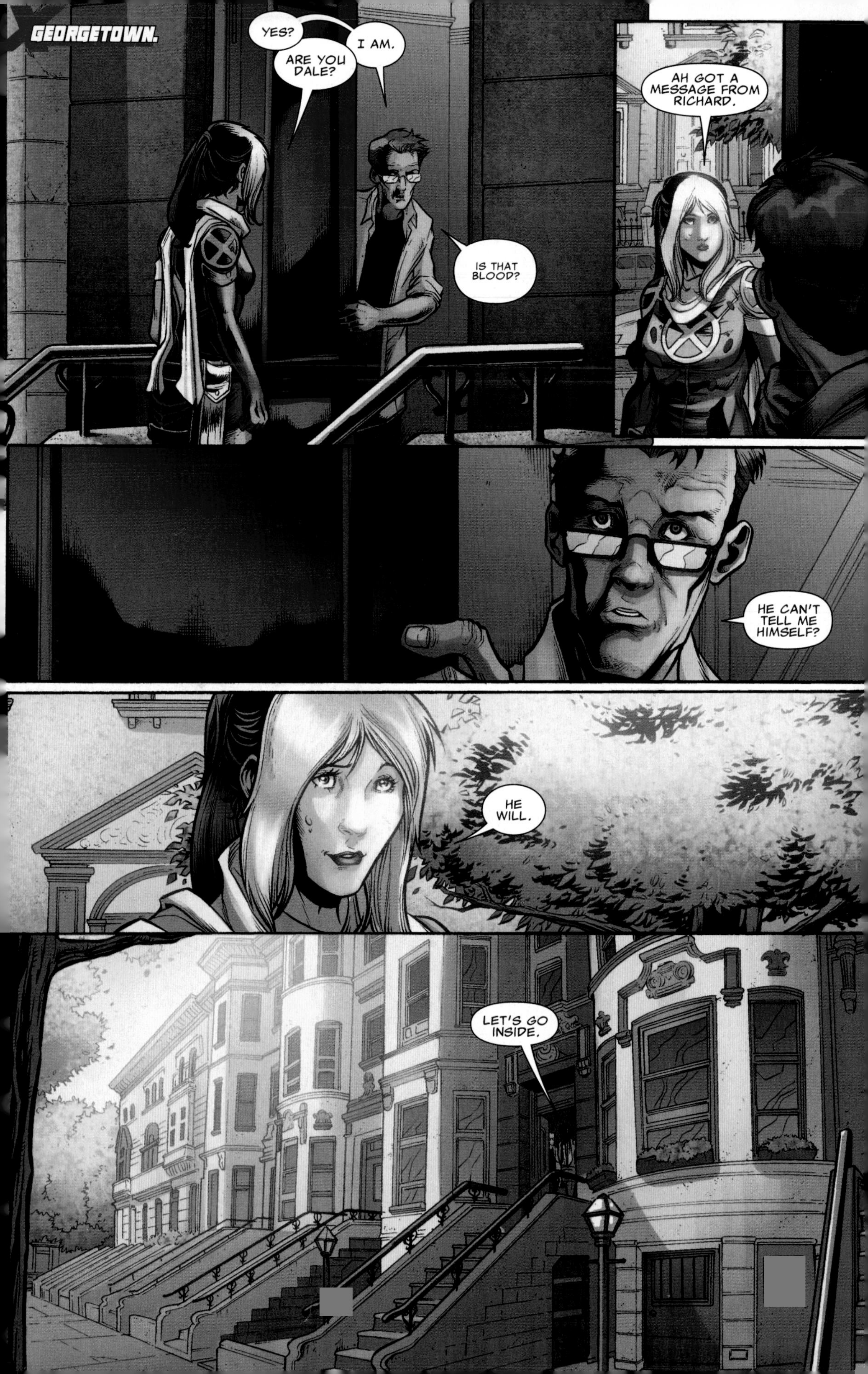
GEORGETOWN.
YES?
I AM.
ARE YOU DALE?
IS THAT BLOOD?
AH GOT A MESSAGE FROM RICHARD.
HE CAN'T TELL ME HIMSELF?
HE WILL.
LET'S GO INSIDE.

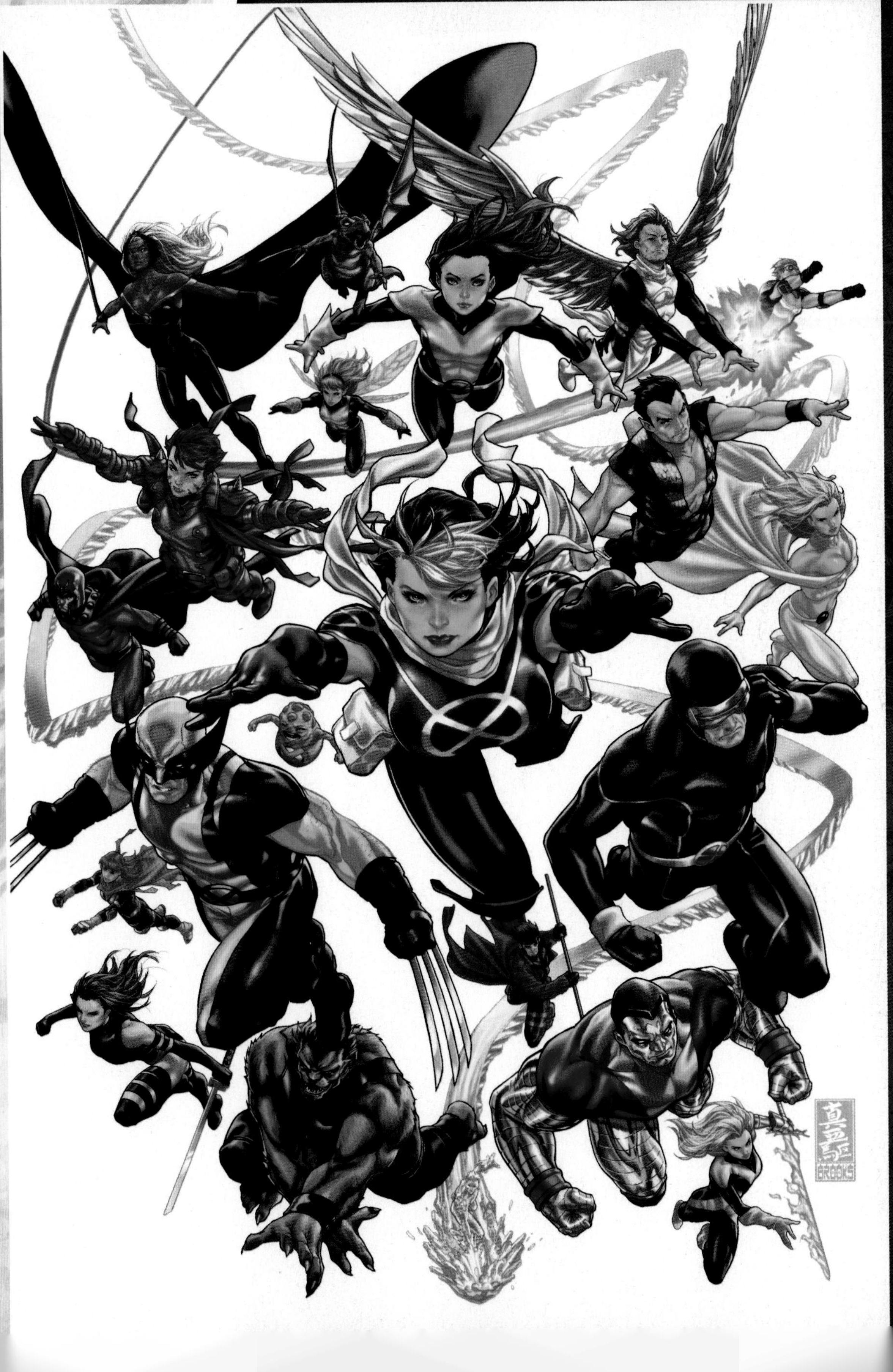
BROOKS

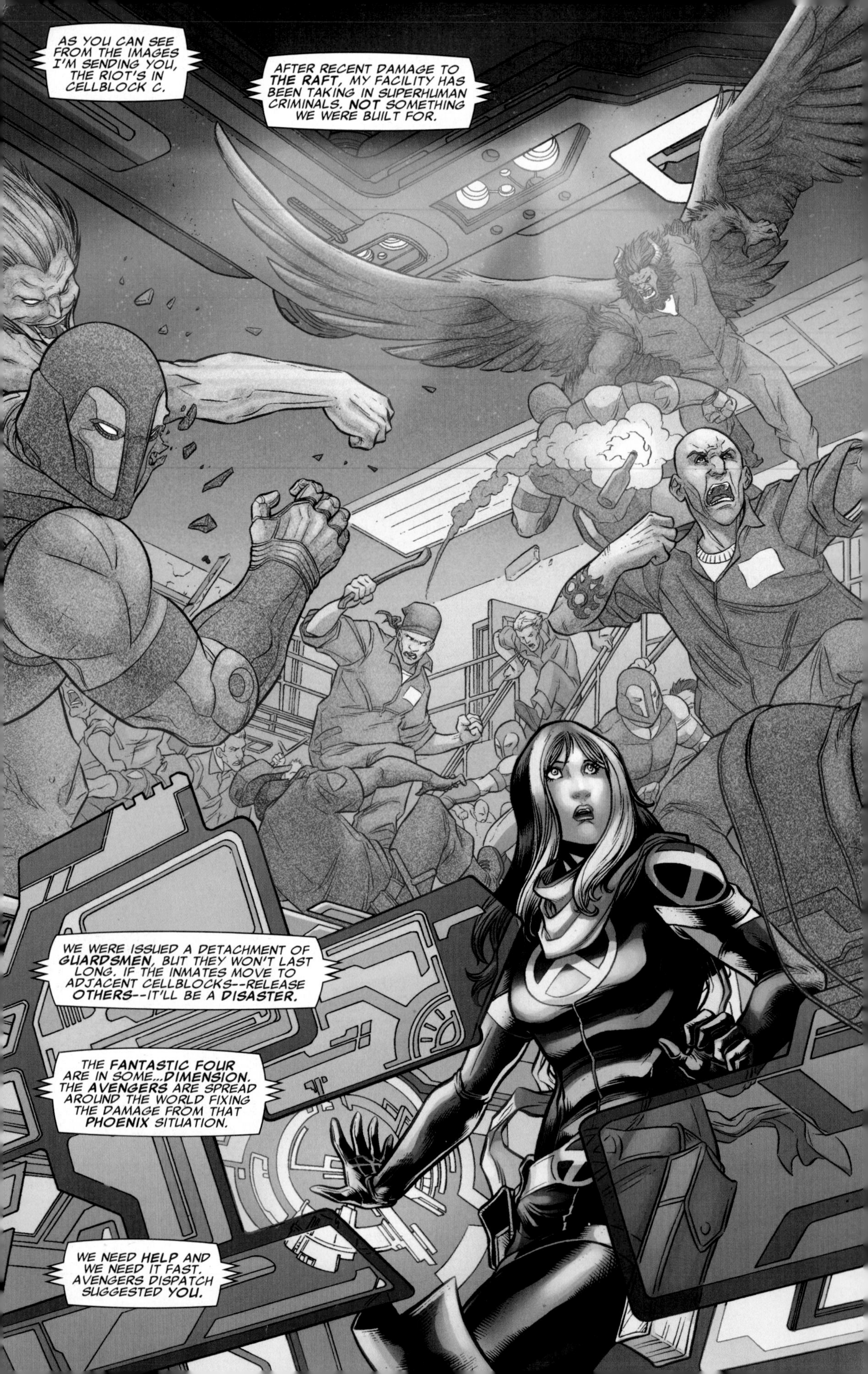
AS YOU CAN SEE FROM THE IMAGES I'M SENDING YOU, THE RIOT'S IN CELLBLOCK C.
AFTER RECENT DAMAGE TO THE RAFT, MY FACILITY HAS BEEN TAKING IN SUPERHUMAN CRIMINALS. NOT SOMETHING WE WERE BUILT FOR.
WE WERE ISSUED A DETACHMENT OF GUARDSMEN, BUT THEY WON'T LAST LONG. IF THE INMATES MOVE TO ADJACENT CELLBLOCKS--RELEASE OTHERS--IT'LL BE A DISASTER.
THE FANTASTIC FOUR ARE IN SOME...DIMENSION. THE AVENGERS ARE SPREAD AROUND THE WORLD FIXING THE DAMAGE FROM THAT PHOENIX SITUATION.
WE NEED HELP AND WE NEED IT FAST. AVENGERS DISPATCH SUGGESTED YOU.

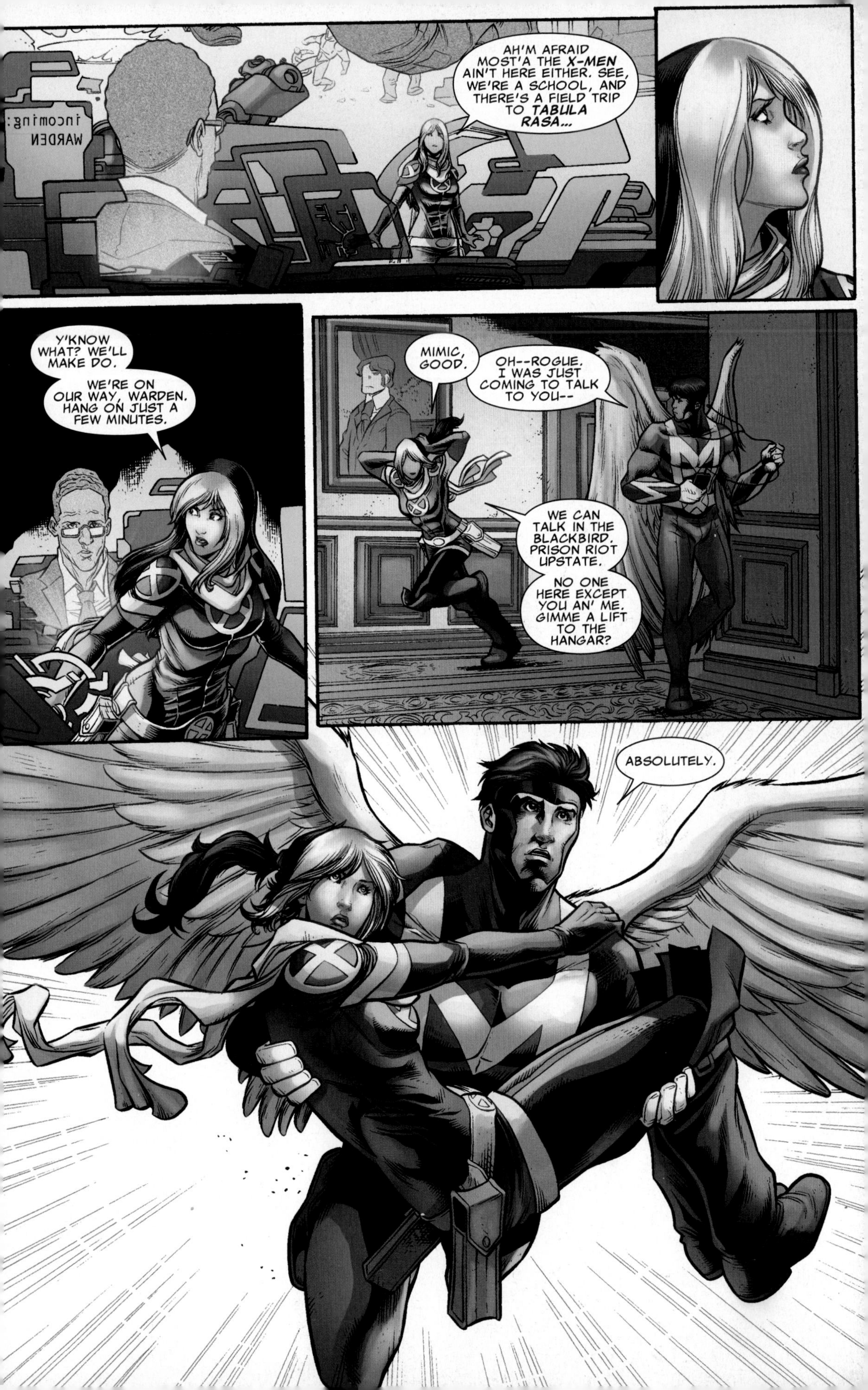
incoming:
WARDEN
AH'M AFRAID MOST'A THE X-MEN AIN'T HERE EITHER. SEE, WE'RE A SCHOOL, AND THERE'S A FIELD TRIP TO TABULA RASA...
Y'KNOW WHAT? WE'LL MAKE DO.
WE'RE ON OUR WAY, WARDEN. HANG ON JUST A FEW MINUTES.
MIMIC, GOOD.
OH--ROGUE. I WAS JUST COMING TO TALK TO YOU--
WE CAN TALK IN THE BLACKBIRD. PRISON RIOT UPSTATE.
NO ONE HERE EXCEPT YOU AN' ME. GIMME A LIFT TO THE HANGAR?
ABSOLUTELY.

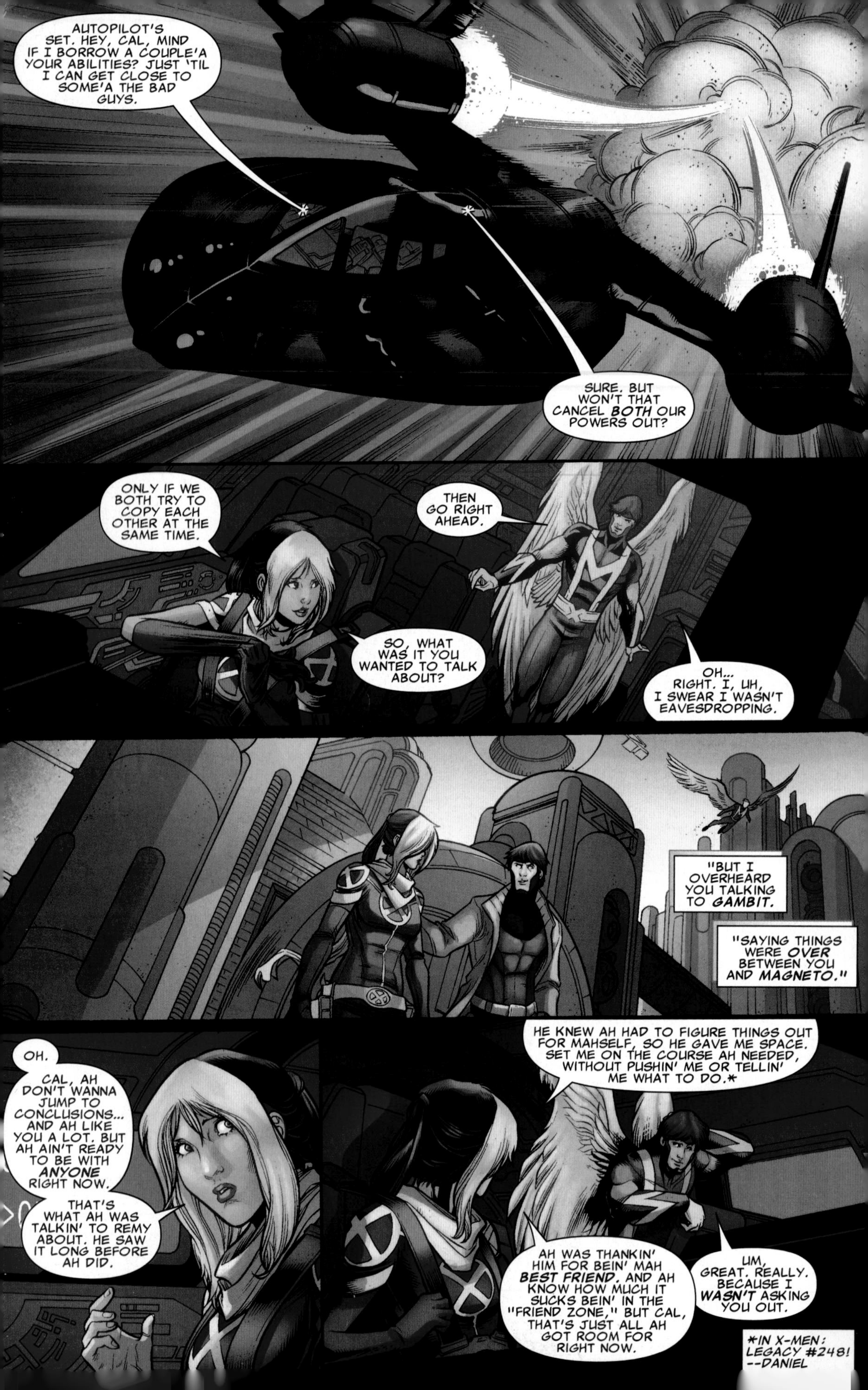
AUTOPILOT'S SET. HEY, CAL, MIND IF I BORROW A COUPLE'A YOUR ABILITIES? JUST 'TIL I CAN GET CLOSE TO SOME'A THE BAD GUYS.
SURE. BUT WON'T THAT CANCEL BOTH OUR POWERS OUT?
ONLY IF WE BOTH TRY TO COPY EACH OTHER AT THE SAME TIME.
THEN GO RIGHT AHEAD.
SO, WHAT WAS IT YOU WANTED TO TALK ABOUT?
OH... RIGHT. I, UH, I SWEAR I WASN'T EAVESDROPPING.
"BUT I OVERHEARD YOU TALKING TO GAMBIT.
"SAYING THINGS WERE OVER BETWEEN YOU AND MAGNETO."
OH.
CAL, AH DON'T WANNA JUMP TO CONCLUSIONS... AND AH LIKE YOU A LOT. BUT AH AIN'T READY TO BE WITH ANYONE RIGHT NOW.
THAT'S WHAT AH WAS TALKIN' TO REMY ABOUT. HE SAW IT LONG BEFORE AH DID.
HE KNEW AH HAD TO FIGURE THINGS OUT FOR MAHSELF, SO HE GAVE ME SPACE. SET ME ON THE COURSE AH NEEDED, WITHOUT PUSHIN' ME OR TELLIN' ME WHAT TO DO.*
AH WAS THANKIN' HIM FOR BEIN' MAH BEST FRIEND. AND AH KNOW HOW MUCH IT SUCKS BEIN' IN THE "FRIEND ZONE," BUT CAL, THAT'S JUST ALL AH GOT ROOM FOR RIGHT NOW.
UM, GREAT. REALLY. BECAUSE I WASN'T ASKING YOU OUT.
*IN X-MEN: LEGACY #248! --DANIEL

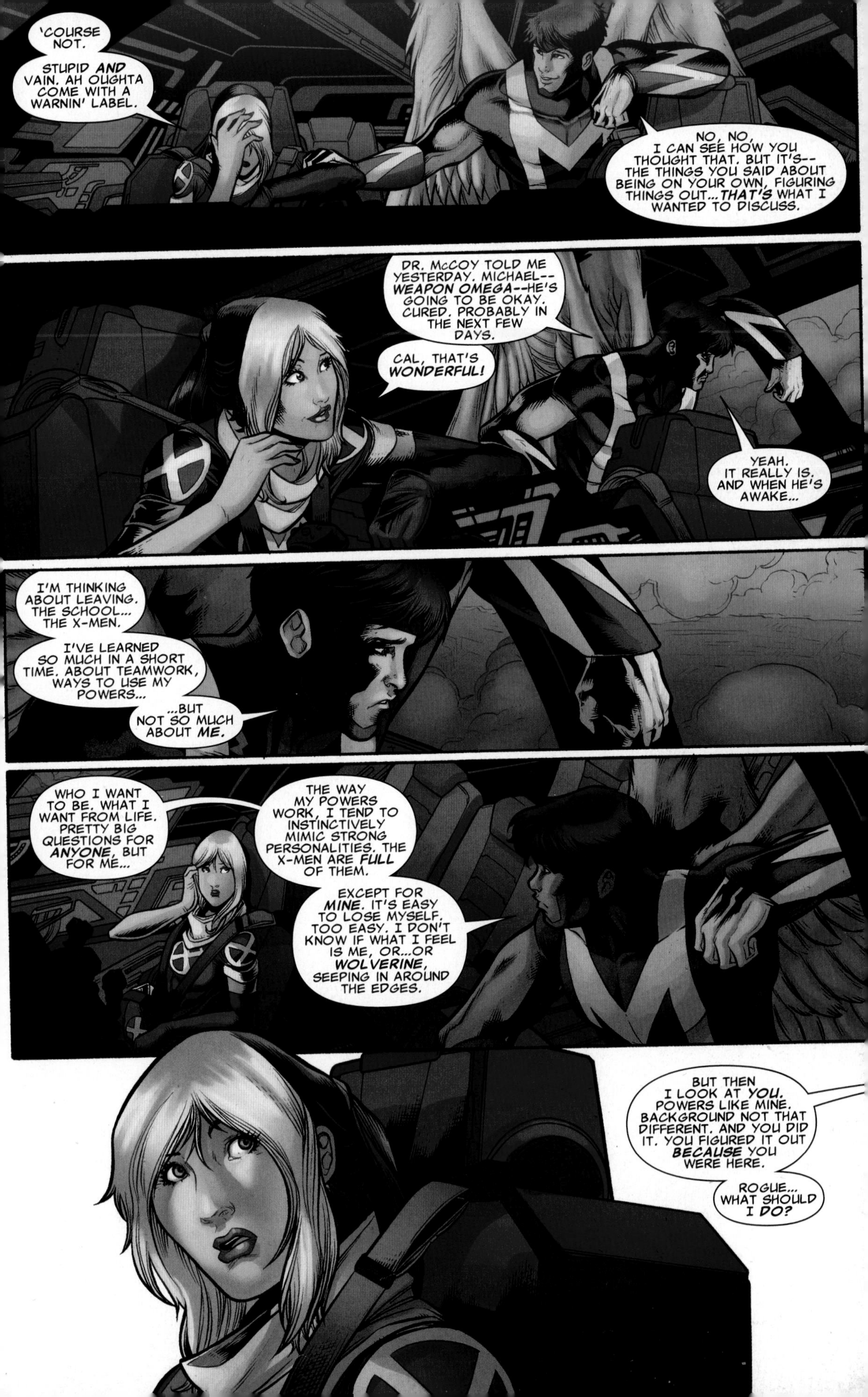
'COURSE NOT.
STUPID AND VAIN. AH OUGHTA COME WITH A WARNIN' LABEL.
NO, NO, I CAN SEE HOW YOU THOUGHT THAT. BUT IT'S-- THE THINGS YOU SAID ABOUT BEING ON YOUR OWN, FIGURING THINGS OUT...THAT'S WHAT I WANTED TO DISCUSS.
DR. McCOY TOLD ME YESTERDAY. MICHAEL-- WEAPON OMEGA--HE'S GOING TO BE OKAY. CURED. PROBABLY IN THE NEXT FEW DAYS.
CAL, THAT'S WONDERFUL!
YEAH. IT REALLY IS. AND WHEN HE'S AWAKE...
I'M THINKING ABOUT LEAVING. THE SCHOOL... THE X-MEN.
I'VE LEARNED SO MUCH IN A SHORT TIME. ABOUT TEAMWORK, WAYS TO USE MY POWERS...
...BUT NOT SO MUCH ABOUT ME.
WHO I WANT TO BE. WHAT I WANT FROM LIFE. PRETTY BIG QUESTIONS FOR ANYONE, BUT FOR ME...
THE WAY MY POWERS WORK, I TEND TO INSTINCTIVELY MIMIC STRONG PERSONALITIES. THE X-MEN ARE FULL OF THEM.
EXCEPT FOR MINE. IT'S EASY TO LOSE MYSELF. TOO EASY. I DON'T KNOW IF WHAT I FEEL IS ME, OR...OR WOLVERINE, SEEPING IN AROUND THE EDGES.
BUT THEN I LOOK AT YOU. POWERS LIKE MINE. BACKGROUND NOT THAT DIFFERENT. AND YOU DID IT. YOU FIGURED IT OUT BECAUSE YOU WERE HERE.
ROGUE... WHAT SHOULD I DO?

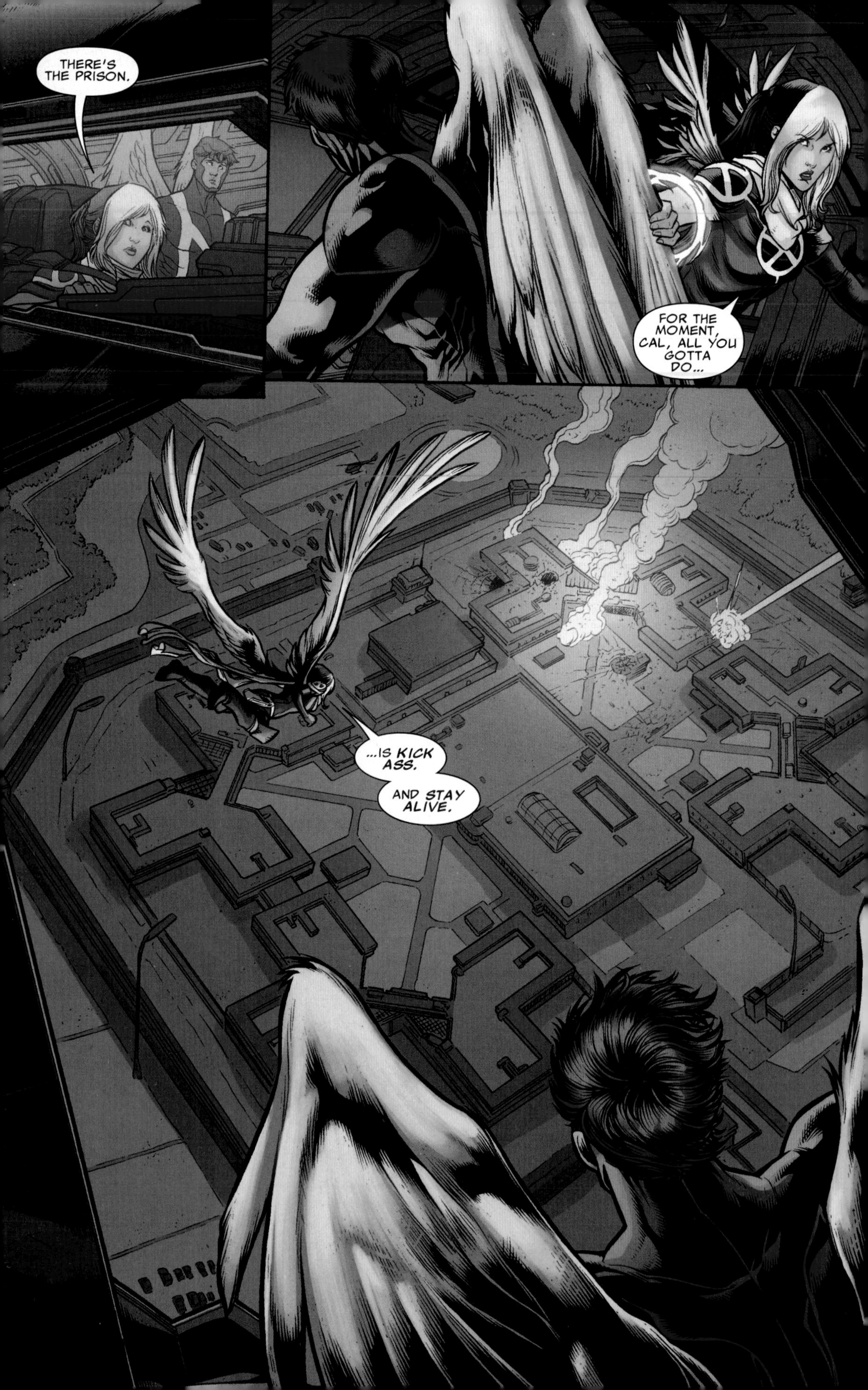
THERE'S THE PRISON.
FOR THE MOMENT, CAL, ALL YOU GOTTA DO...
...IS KICK ASS.
AND STAY ALIVE.

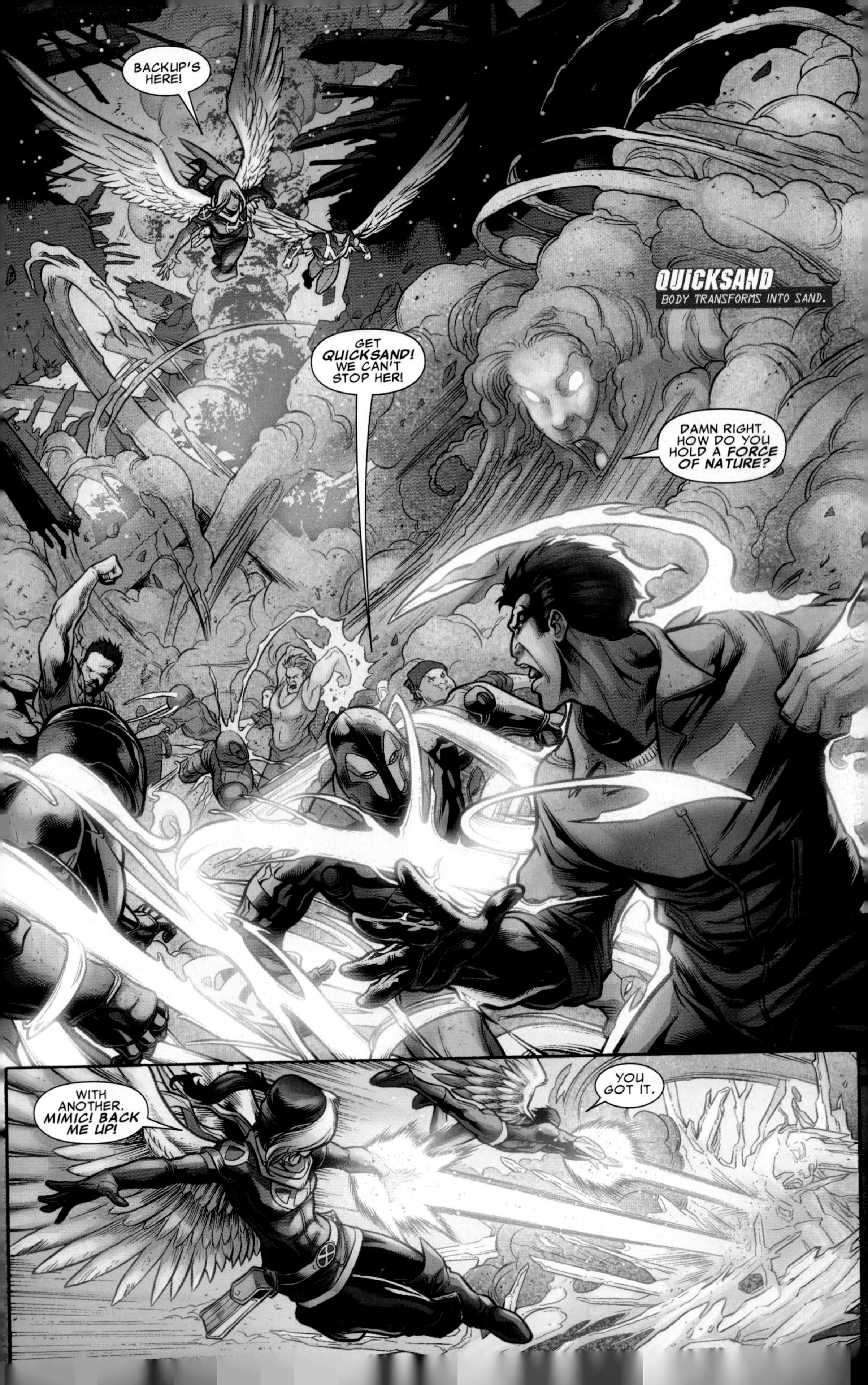
BACKUP'S HERE!
QUICKSAND
BODY TRANSFORMS INTO SAND.
GET QUICKSAND! WE CAN'T STOP HER!
DAMN RIGHT. HOW DO YOU HOLD A FORCE OF NATURE?
WITH ANOTHER. MIMIC! BACK ME UP!
YOU GOT IT.

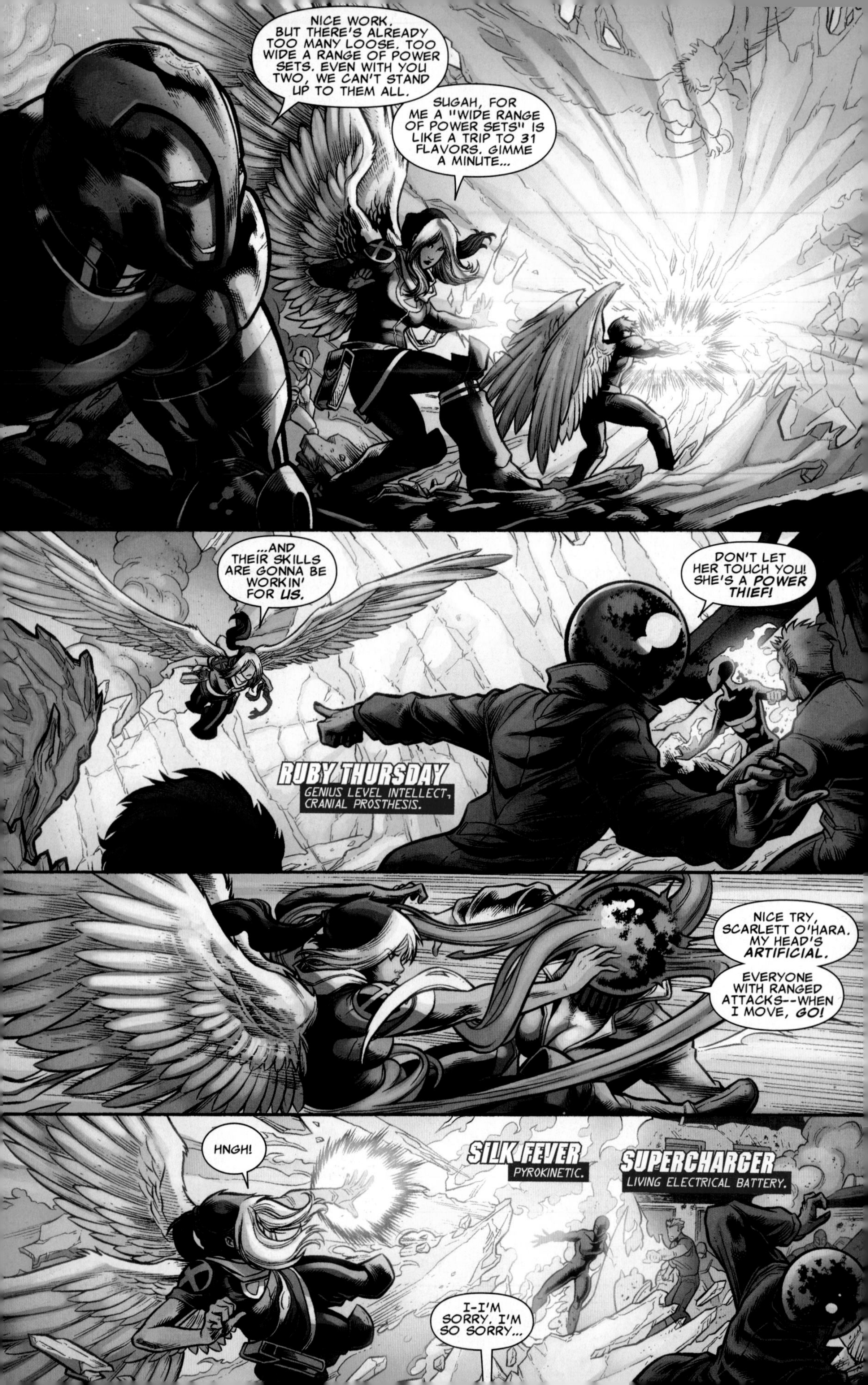
NICE WORK. BUT THERE'S ALREADY TOO MANY LOOSE. TOO WIDE A RANGE OF POWER SETS. EVEN WITH YOU TWO, WE CAN'T STAND UP TO THEM ALL.
SUGAH, FOR ME A "WIDE RANGE OF POWER SETS" IS LIKE A TRIP TO 31 FLAVORS. GIMME A MINUTE...
...AND THEIR SKILLS ARE GONNA BE WORKIN' FOR US.
DON'T LET HER TOUCH YOU! SHE'S A POWER THIEF!
RUBY THURSDAY
GENIUS LEVEL INTELLECT, CRANIAL PROSTHESIS.
NICE TRY, SCARLETT O'HARA. MY HEAD'S ARTIFICIAL.
EVERYONE WITH RANGED ATTACKS--WHEN I MOVE, GO!
HNGH!
SILK FEVER
PYROKINETIC.
SUPERCHARGER
LIVING ELECTRICAL BATTERY.
I-I'M SORRY. I'M SO SORRY...

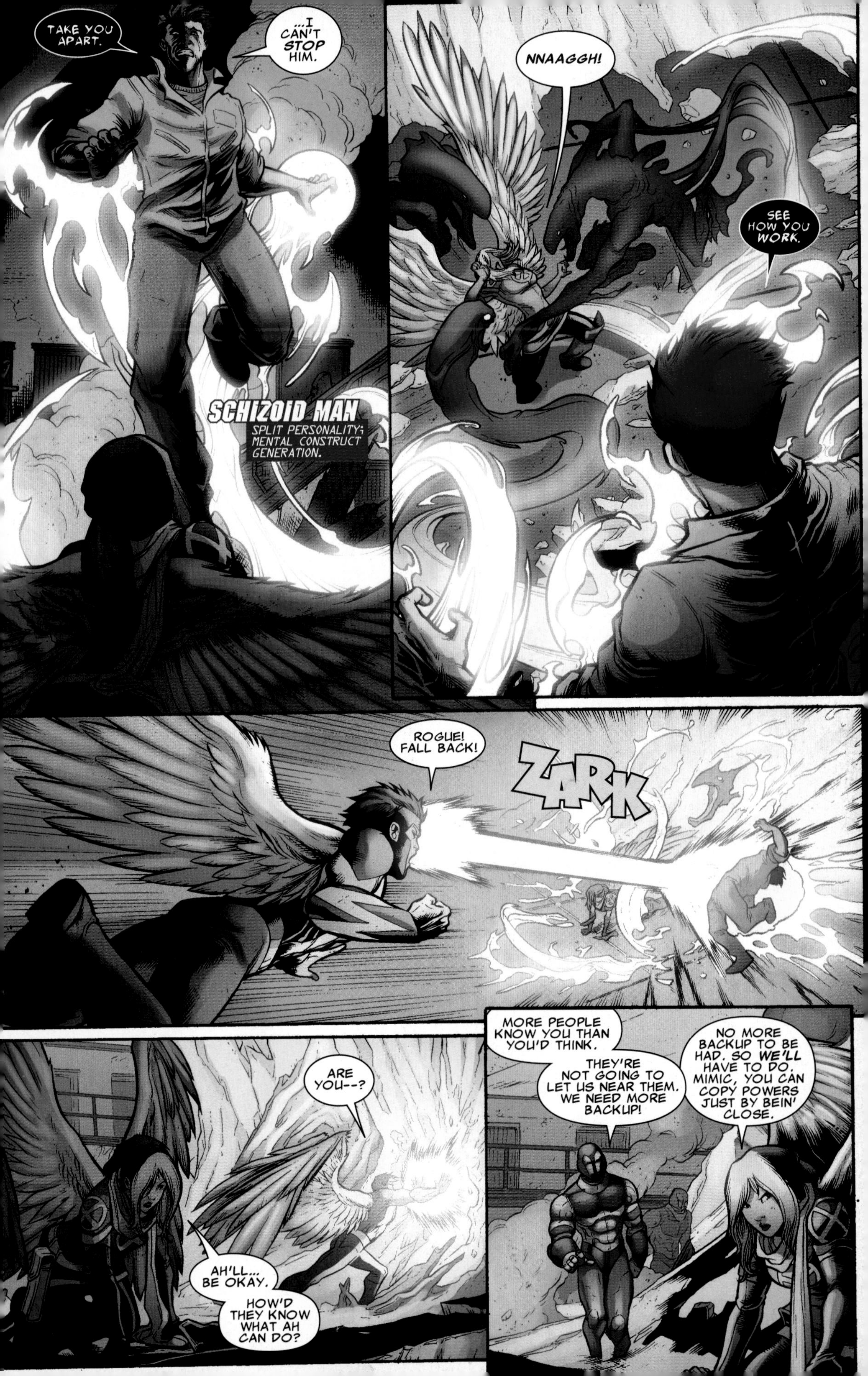
TAKE YOU APART.
...I CAN'T STOP HIM.
SCHIZOID MAN
SPLIT PERSONALITY; MENTAL CONSTRUCT GENERATION.
NNAAGGH!
SEE HOW YOU WORK.
ROGUE! FALL BACK!
ZARK
ARE YOU--?
AH'LL... BE OKAY.
HOW'D THEY KNOW WHAT AH CAN DO?
MORE PEOPLE KNOW YOU THAN YOU'D THINK.
THEY'RE NOT GOING TO LET US NEAR THEM. WE NEED MORE BACKUP!
NO MORE BACKUP TO BE HAD. SO WE'LL HAVE TO DO. MIMIC, YOU CAN COPY POWERS JUST BY BEIN' CLOSE.

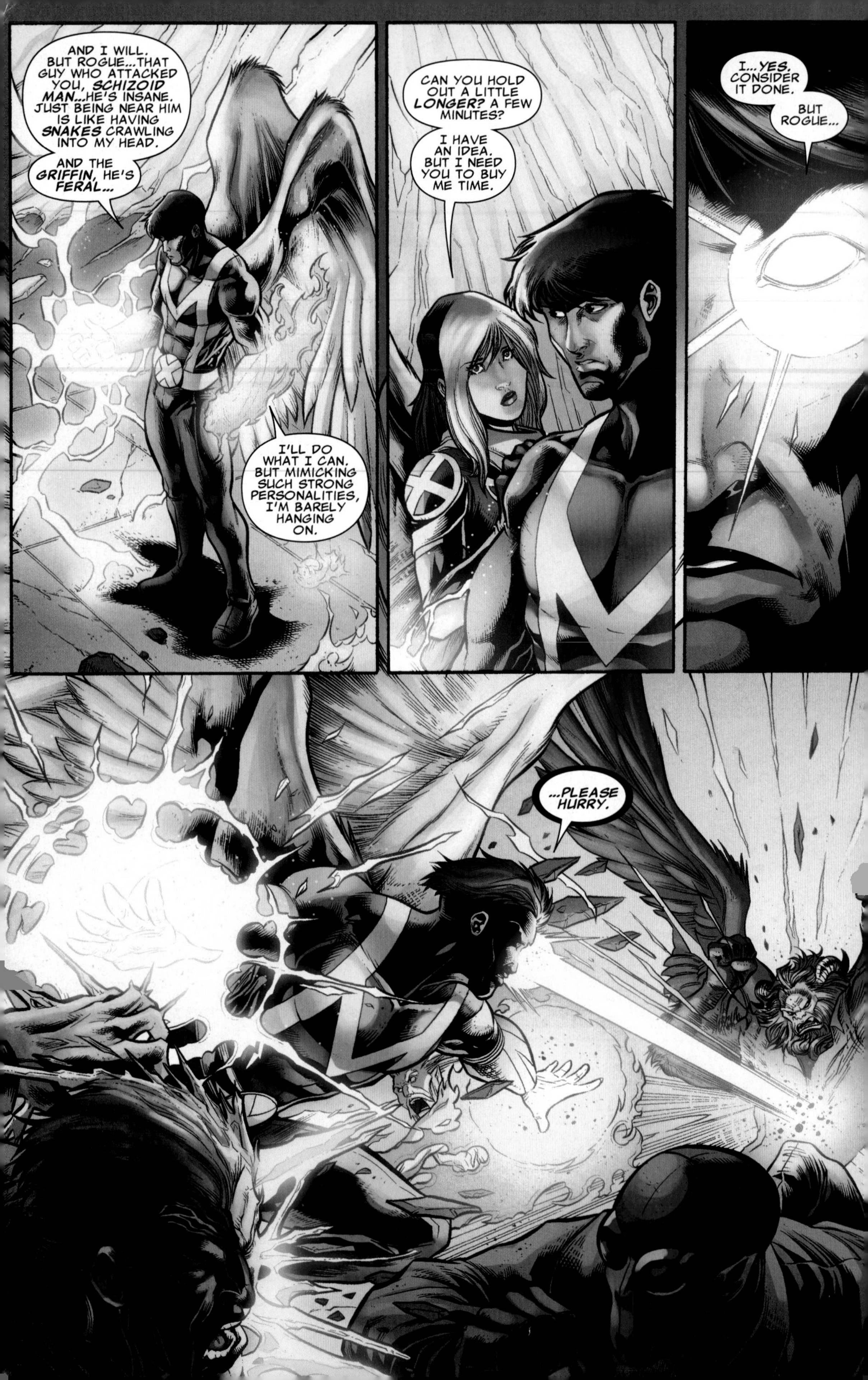
AND I WILL. BUT ROGUE...THAT GUY WHO ATTACKED YOU, SCHIZOID MAN...HE'S INSANE. JUST BEING NEAR HIM IS LIKE HAVING SNAKES CRAWLING INTO MY HEAD.
AND THE GRIFFIN, HE'S FERAL...
I'LL DO WHAT I CAN. BUT MIMICKING SUCH STRONG PERSONALITIES, I'M BARELY HANGING ON.
CAN YOU HOLD OUT A LITTLE LONGER? A FEW MINUTES?
I HAVE AN IDEA. BUT I NEED YOU TO BUY ME TIME.
I...YES. CONSIDER IT DONE.
BUT ROGUE...
...PLEASE HURRY.

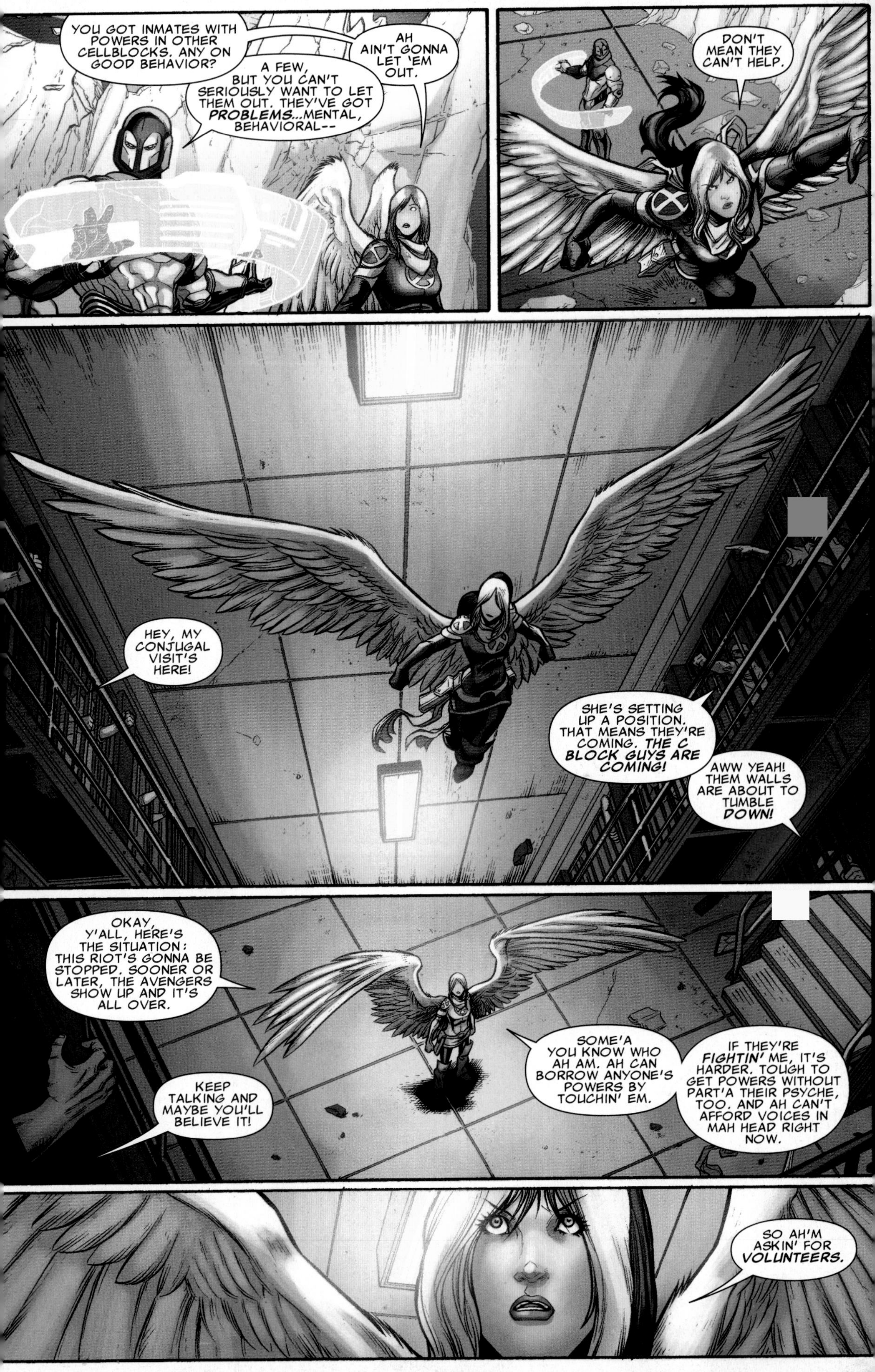
YOU GOT INMATES WITH POWERS IN OTHER CELLBLOCKS. ANY ON GOOD BEHAVIOR?
A FEW, BUT YOU CAN'T SERIOUSLY WANT TO LET THEM OUT. THEY'VE GOT PROBLEMS...MENTAL, BEHAVIORAL--
AH AIN'T GONNA LET 'EM OUT.
DON'T MEAN THEY CAN'T HELP.
HEY, MY CONJUGAL VISIT'S HERE!
SHE'S SETTING UP A POSITION. THAT MEANS THEY'RE COMING. THE C BLOCK GUYS ARE COMING!
AWW YEAH! THEM WALLS ARE ABOUT TO TUMBLE DOWN!
OKAY, Y'ALL, HERE'S THE SITUATION: THIS RIOT'S GONNA BE STOPPED. SOONER OR LATER, THE AVENGERS SHOW UP AND IT'S ALL OVER.
KEEP TALKING AND MAYBE YOU'LL BELIEVE IT!
SOME'A YOU KNOW WHO AH AM. AH CAN BORROW ANYONE'S POWERS BY TOUCHIN' EM.
IF THEY'RE FIGHTIN' ME, IT'S HARDER. TOUGH TO GET POWERS WITHOUT PART'A THEIR PSYCHE, TOO. AND AH CAN'T AFFORD VOICES IN MAH HEAD RIGHT NOW.
SO AH'M ASKIN' FOR VOLUNTEERS.

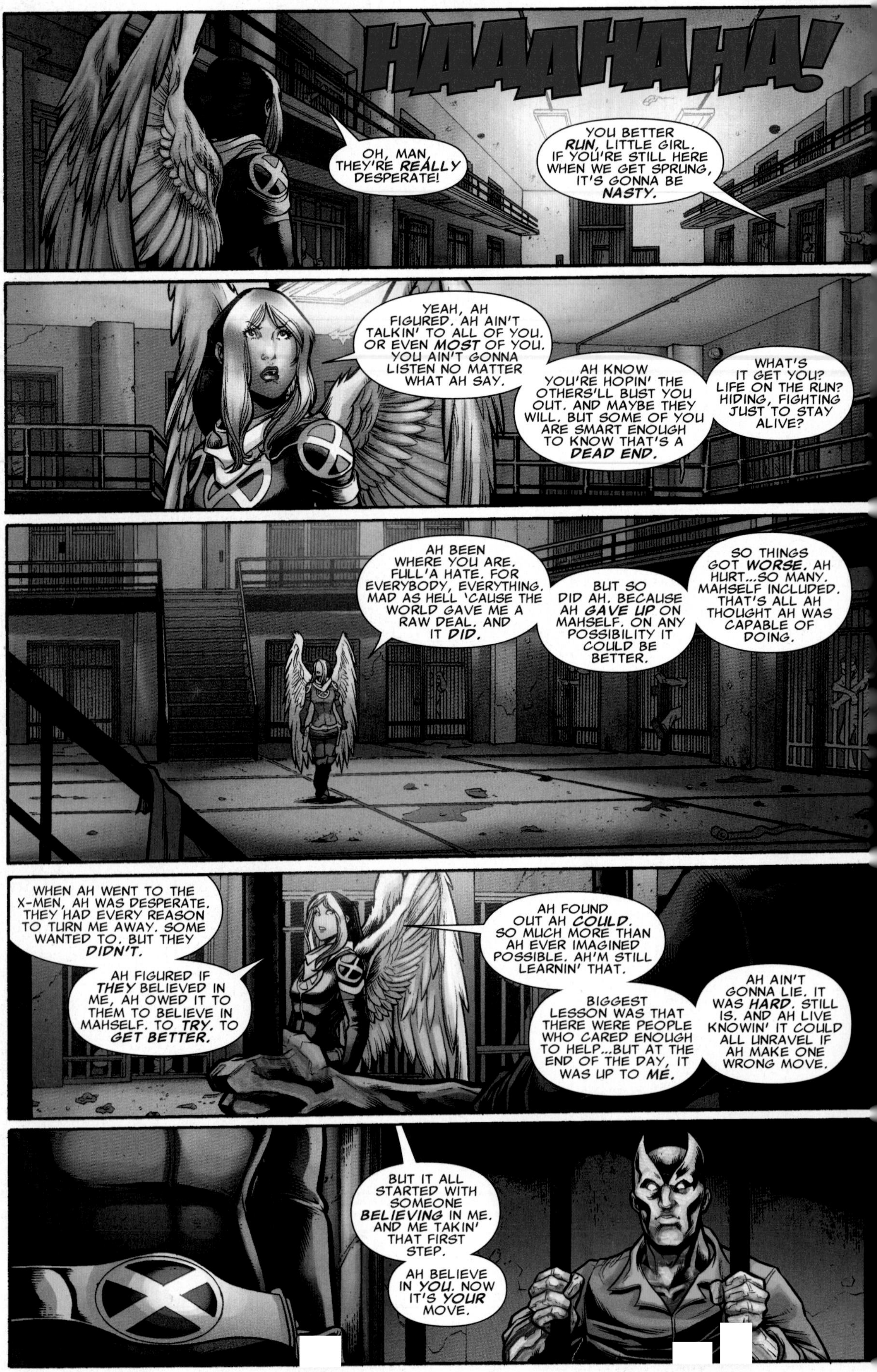
HAAAAHAHA!
OH, MAN, THEY'RE REALLY DESPERATE!
YOU BETTER RUN, LITTLE GIRL. IF YOU'RE STILL HERE WHEN WE GET SPRUNG, IT'S GONNA BE NASTY.
YEAH, AH FIGURED. AH AIN'T TALKIN' TO ALL OF YOU. OR EVEN MOST OF YOU. YOU AIN'T GONNA LISTEN NO MATTER WHAT AH SAY.
AH KNOW YOU'RE HOPIN' THE OTHERS'LL BUST YOU OUT. AND MAYBE THEY WILL. BUT SOME OF YOU ARE SMART ENOUGH TO KNOW THAT'S A DEAD END.
WHAT'S IT GET YOU? LIFE ON THE RUN? HIDING, FIGHTING JUST TO STAY ALIVE?
AH BEEN WHERE YOU ARE. FULL'A HATE. FOR EVERYBODY, EVERYTHING. MAD AS HELL 'CAUSE THE WORLD GAVE ME A RAW DEAL. AND IT DID.
BUT SO DID AH. BECAUSE AH GAVE UP ON MAHSELF. ON ANY POSSIBILITY IT COULD BE BETTER.
SO THINGS GOT WORSE. AH HURT...SO MANY. MAHSELF INCLUDED. THAT'S ALL AH THOUGHT AH WAS CAPABLE OF DOING.
WHEN AH WENT TO THE X-MEN, AH WAS DESPERATE. THEY HAD EVERY REASON TO TURN ME AWAY. SOME WANTED TO. BUT THEY DIDN'T.
AH FIGURED IF THEY BELIEVED IN ME, AH OWED IT TO THEM TO BELIEVE IN MAHSELF. TO TRY. TO GET BETTER.
AH FOUND OUT AH COULD. SO MUCH MORE THAN AH EVER IMAGINED POSSIBLE. AH'M STILL LEARNIN' THAT.
BIGGEST LESSON WAS THAT THERE WERE PEOPLE WHO CARED ENOUGH TO HELP...BUT AT THE END OF THE DAY, IT WAS UP TO ME.
AH AIN'T GONNA LIE. IT WAS HARD. STILL IS. AND AH LIVE KNOWIN' IT COULD ALL UNRAVEL IF AH MAKE ONE WRONG MOVE.
BUT IT ALL STARTED WITH SOMEONE BELIEVING IN ME. AND ME TAKIN' THAT FIRST STEP.
AH BELIEVE IN YOU. NOW IT'S YOUR MOVE.

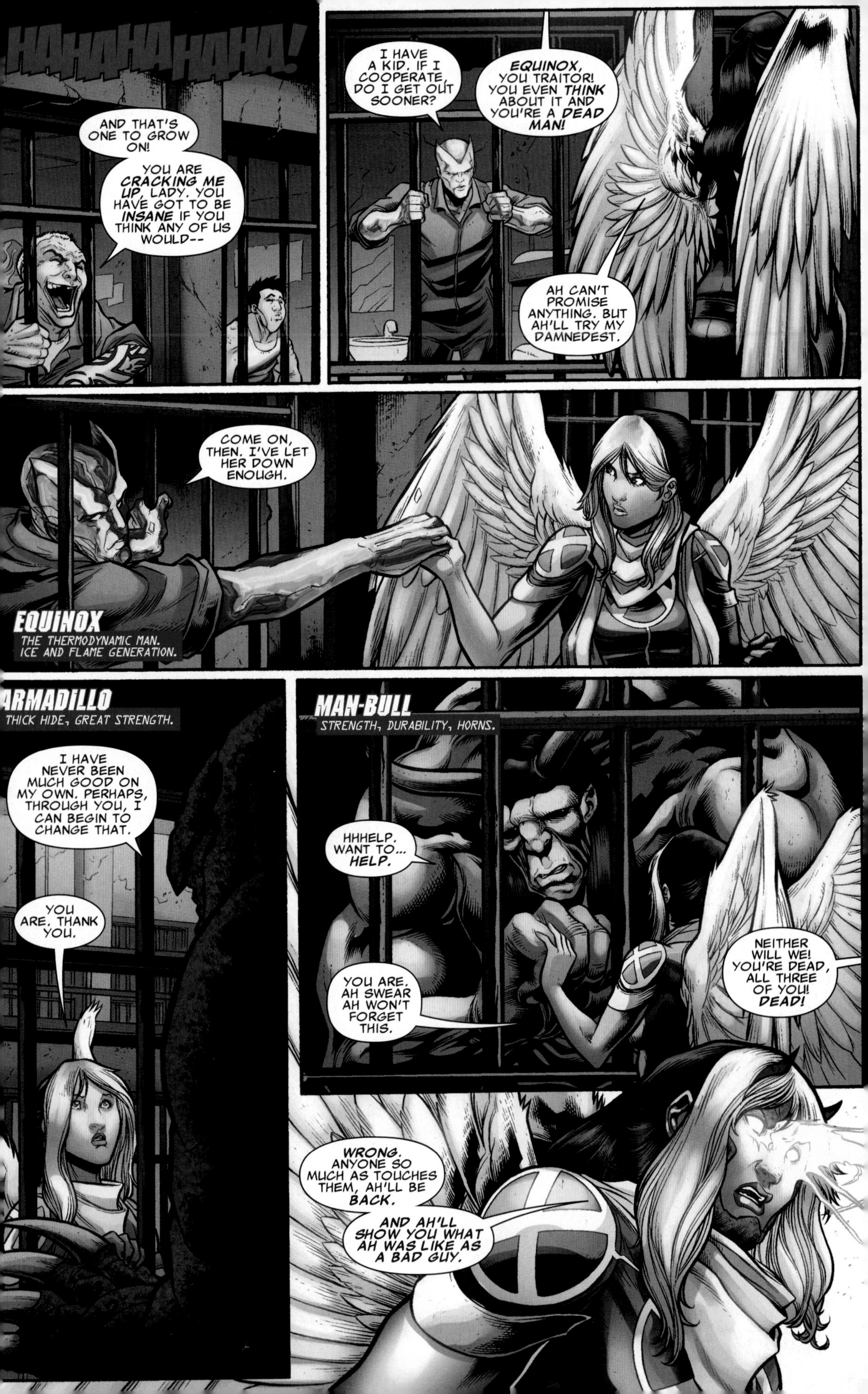
HAHAHAHAHAHA!
AND THAT'S ONE TO GROW ON!
YOU ARE CRACKING ME UP, LADY. YOU HAVE GOT TO BE INSANE IF YOU THINK ANY OF US WOULD--
I HAVE A KID. IF I COOPERATE, DO I GET OUT SOONER?
EQUINOX, YOU TRAITOR! YOU EVEN THINK ABOUT IT AND YOU'RE A DEAD MAN!
AH CAN'T PROMISE ANYTHING. BUT AH'LL TRY MY DAMNEDEST.
COME ON, THEN. I'VE LET HER DOWN ENOUGH.
EQUINOX
THE THERMODYNAMIC MAN. ICE AND FLAME GENERATION.
ARMADILLO
THICK HIDE, GREAT STRENGTH.
I HAVE NEVER BEEN MUCH GOOD ON MY OWN. PERHAPS, THROUGH YOU, I CAN BEGIN TO CHANGE THAT.
YOU ARE. THANK YOU.
MAN-BULL
STRENGTH, DURABILITY, HORNS.
HHHELP. WANT TO... HELP.
YOU ARE. AH SWEAR AH WON'T FORGET THIS.
NEITHER WILL WE! YOU'RE DEAD, ALL THREE OF YOU! DEAD!
WRONG. ANYONE SO MUCH AS TOUCHES THEM, AH'LL BE BACK.
AND AH'LL SHOW YOU WHAT AH WAS LIKE AS A BAD GUY.

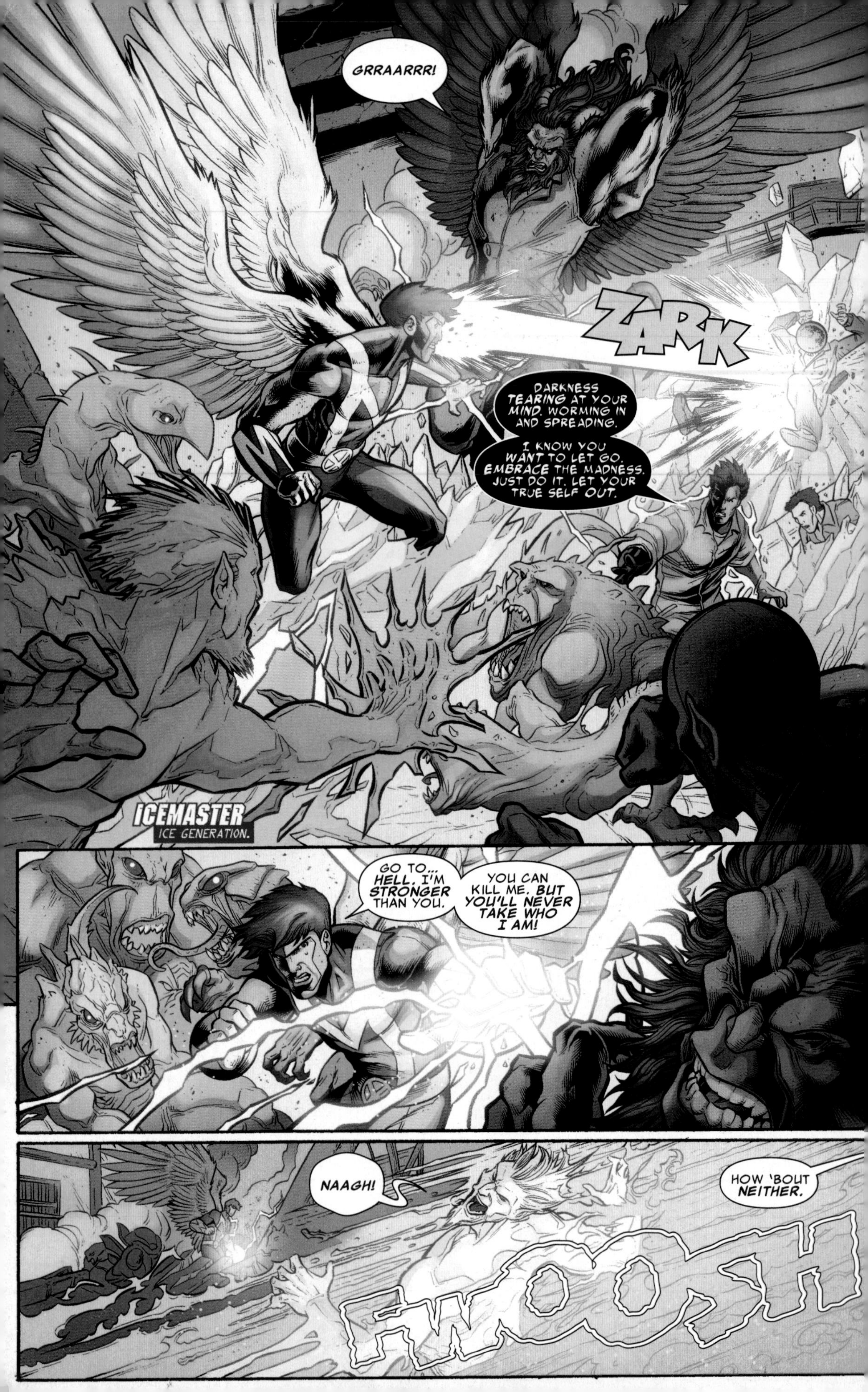
GRRAARRR!
ZARK
DARKNESS TEARING AT YOUR MIND. WORMING IN AND SPREADING.
I KNOW YOU WANT TO LET GO. EMBRACE THE MADNESS. JUST DO IT. LET YOUR TRUE SELF OUT.
ICEMASTER
ICE GENERATION.
GO TO... HELL. I'M STRONGER THAN YOU.
YOU CAN KILL ME. BUT YOU'LL NEVER TAKE WHO I AM!
NAAGH!
HOW 'BOUT NEITHER.
FWOOOSH

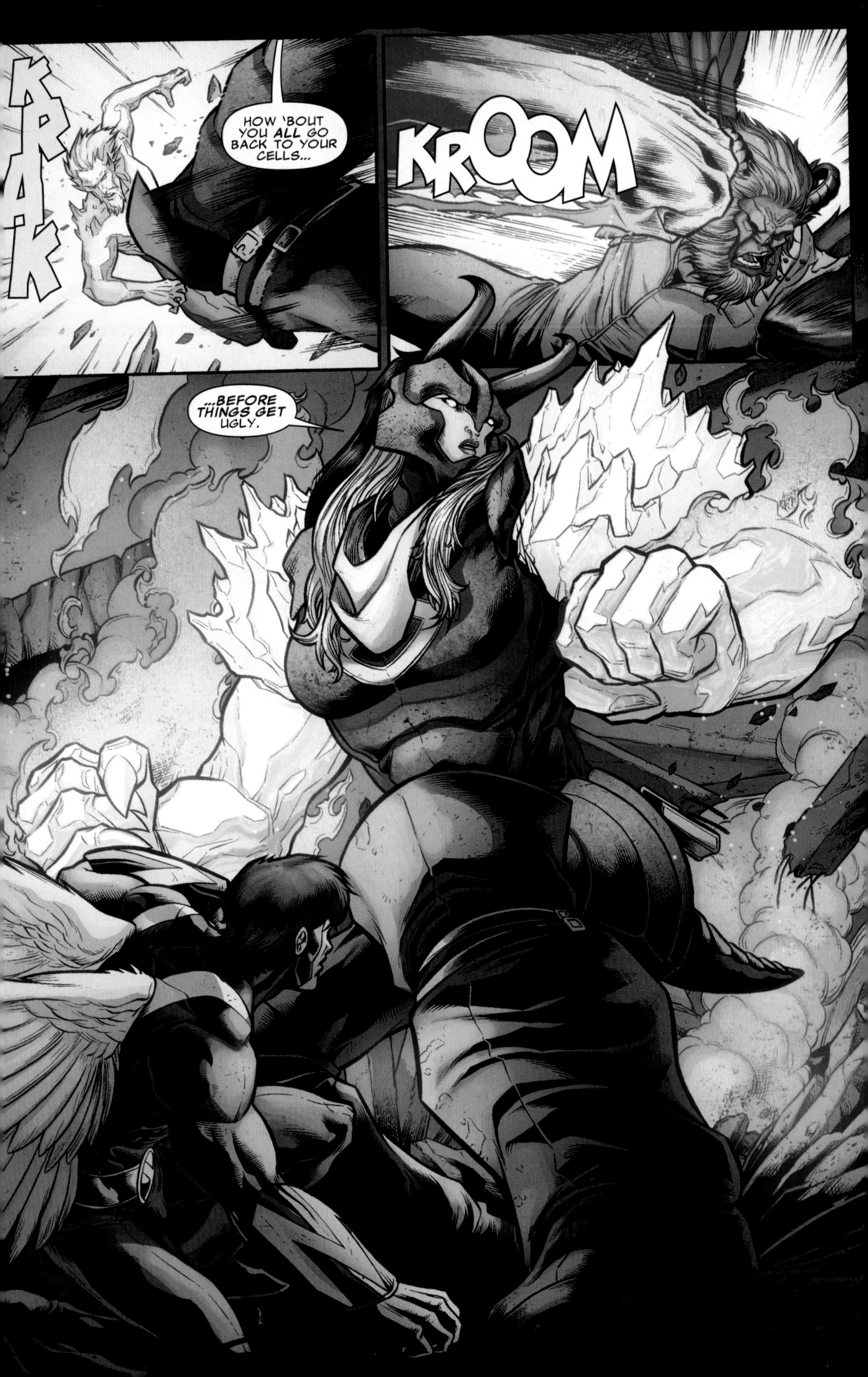
KRAK
HOW 'BOUT YOU ALL GO BACK TO YOUR CELLS...
KROOM
...BEFORE THINGS GET UGLY.

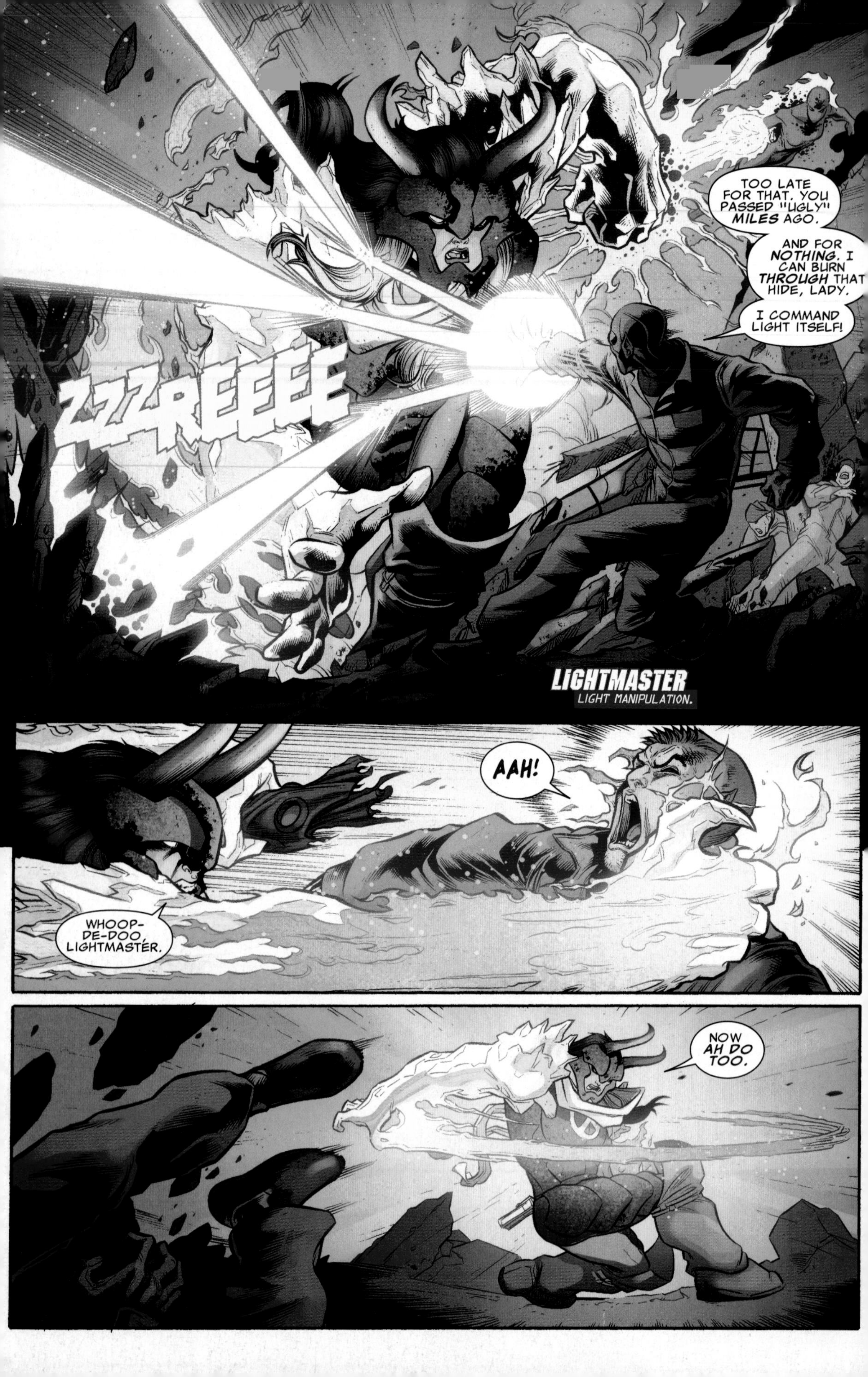
TOO LATE FOR THAT. YOU PASSED "UGLY" MILES AGO.
AND FOR NOTHING. I CAN BURN THROUGH THAT HIDE, LADY.
I COMMAND LIGHT ITSELF!
ZZZREEEE
LIGHTMASTER
LIGHT MANIPULATION.
AAH!
WHOOP-DE-DOO, LIGHTMASTER.
NOW AH DO TOO.

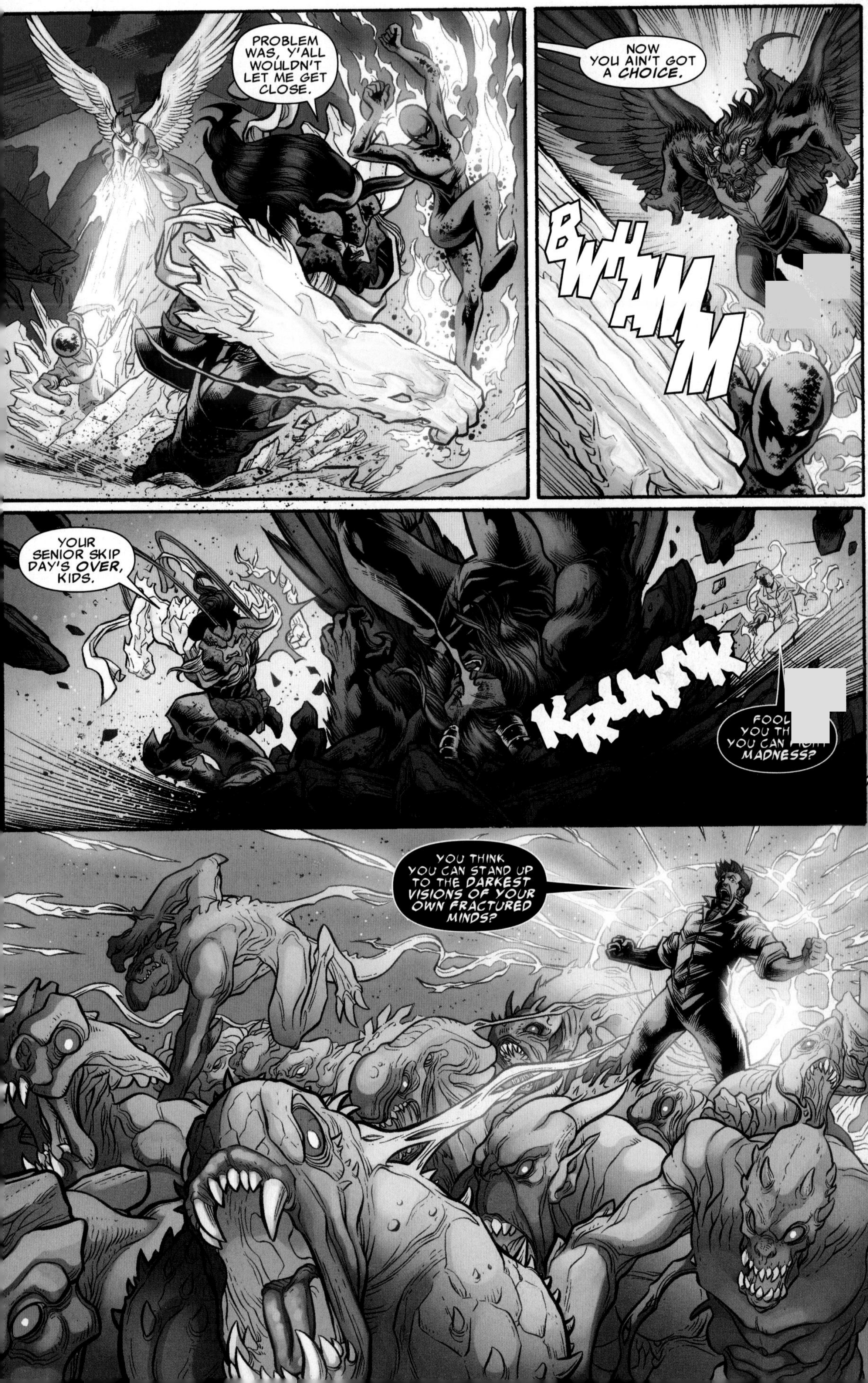
PROBLEM WAS, Y'ALL WOULDN'T LET ME GET CLOSE.
NOW YOU AIN'T GOT A CHOICE.
BWHAMM
YOUR SENIOR SKIP DAY'S OVER, KIDS.
KRUNK
FOOL
YOU TH
YOU CAN
MADNESS?
YOU THINK YOU CAN STAND UP TO THE DARKEST VISIONS OF YOUR OWN FRACTURED MINDS?

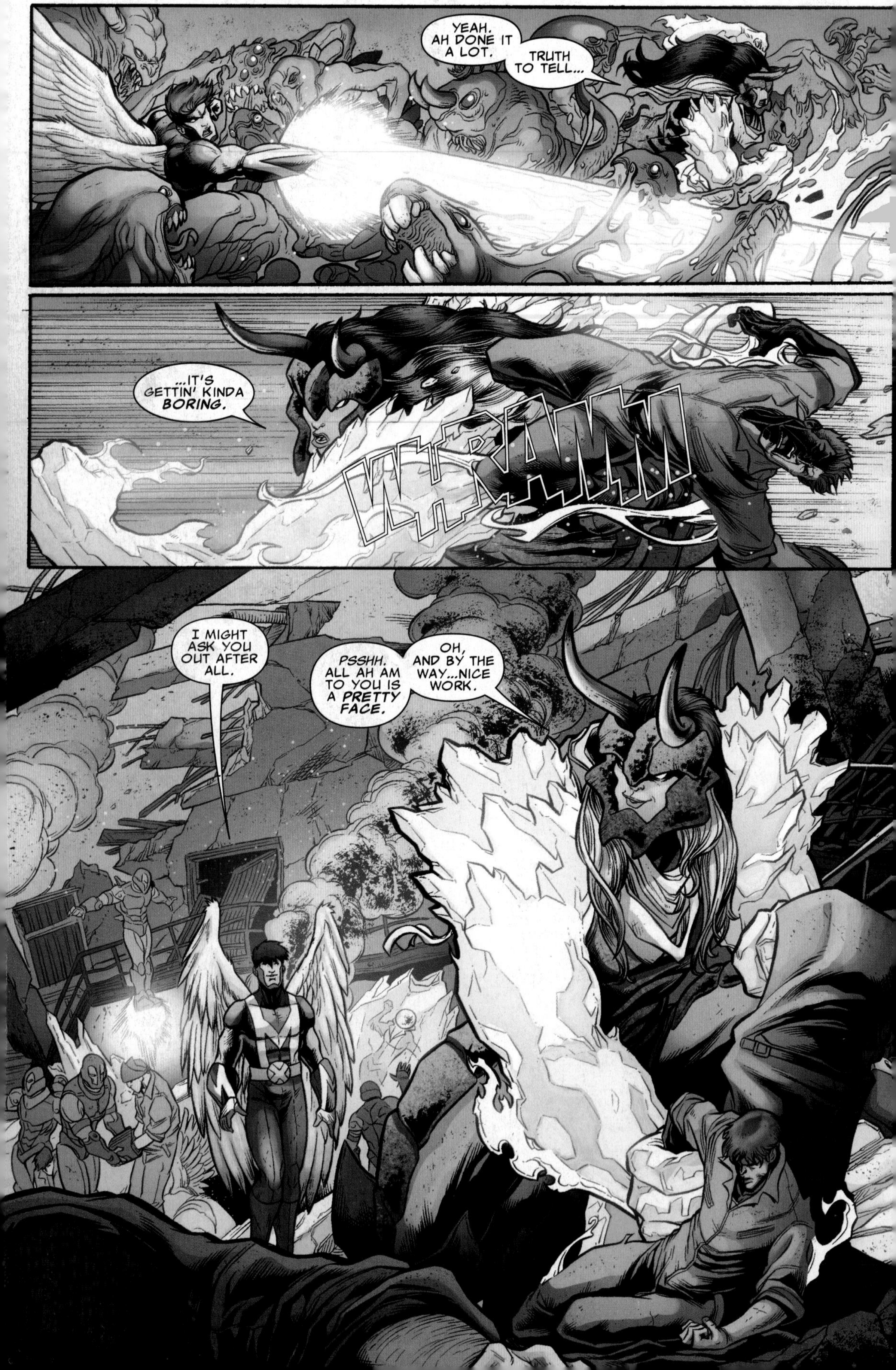
YEAH. AH DONE IT A LOT.
TRUTH TO TELL...
...IT'S GETTIN' KINDA BORING.
WHRAMM
I MIGHT ASK YOU OUT AFTER ALL.
PSSHH. ALL AH AM TO YOU IS A PRETTY FACE.
OH, AND BY THE WAY...NICE WORK.

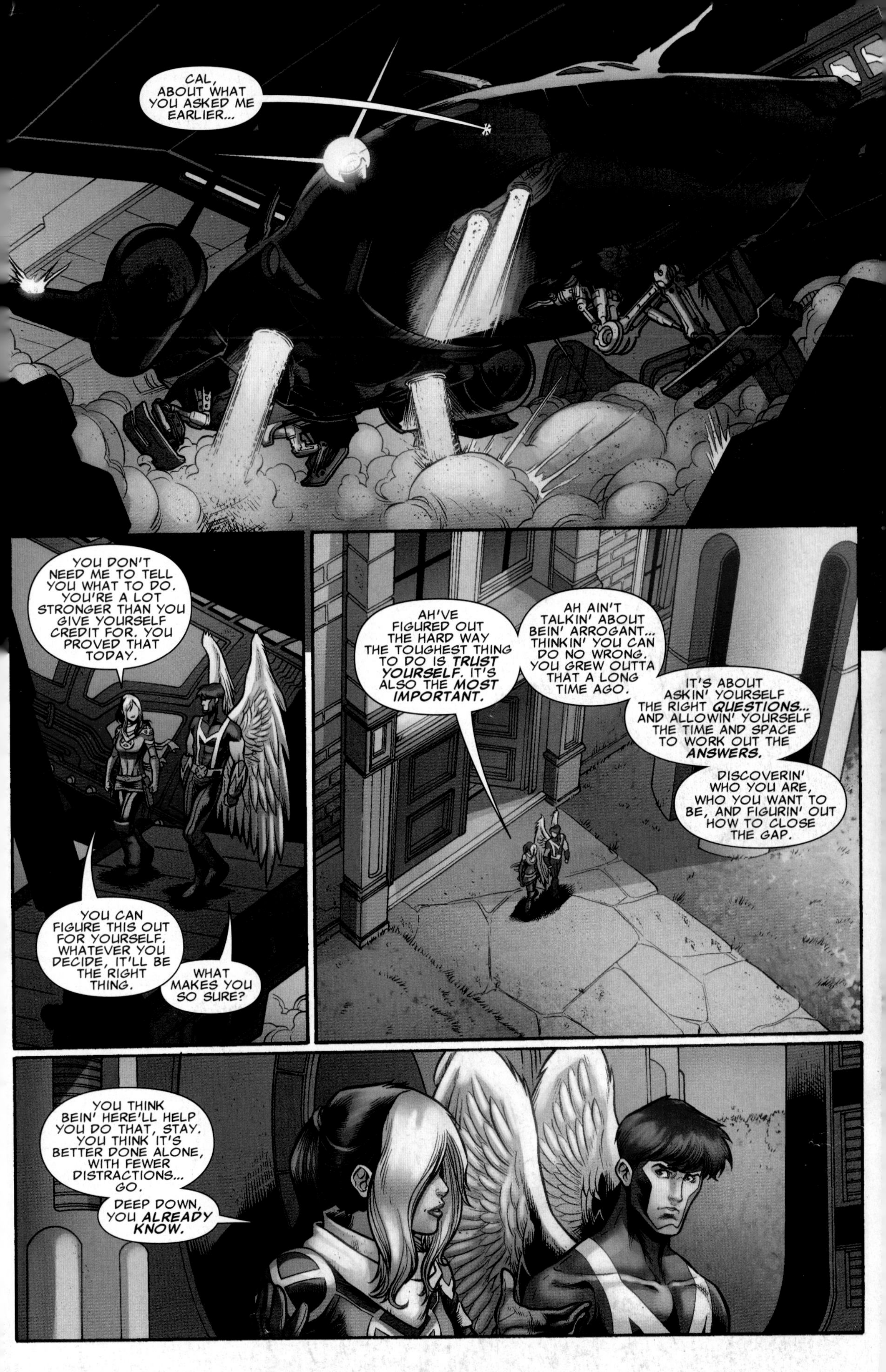
CAL, ABOUT WHAT YOU ASKED ME EARLIER...
YOU DON'T NEED ME TO TELL YOU WHAT TO DO. YOU'RE A LOT STRONGER THAN YOU GIVE YOURSELF CREDIT FOR. YOU PROVED THAT TODAY.
YOU CAN FIGURE THIS OUT FOR YOURSELF. WHATEVER YOU DECIDE, IT'LL BE THE RIGHT THING.
WHAT MAKES YOU SO SURE?
AH'VE FIGURED OUT THE HARD WAY THE TOUGHEST THING TO DO IS **TRUST YOURSELF.** IT'S ALSO THE **MOST IMPORTANT.**
AH AIN'T TALKIN' ABOUT BEIN' ARROGANT... THINKIN' YOU CAN DO NO WRONG. YOU GREW OUTTA THAT A LONG TIME AGO.
IT'S ABOUT ASKIN' YOURSELF THE RIGHT **QUESTIONS...** AND ALLOWIN' YOURSELF THE TIME AND SPACE TO WORK OUT THE **ANSWERS.**
DISCOVERIN' WHO YOU ARE, WHO YOU WANT TO BE, AND FIGURIN' OUT HOW TO CLOSE THE GAP.
YOU THINK BEIN' HERE'LL HELP YOU DO THAT, STAY. YOU THINK IT'S BETTER DONE ALONE, WITH FEWER DISTRACTIONS... GO.
DEEP DOWN, YOU **ALREADY KNOW.**

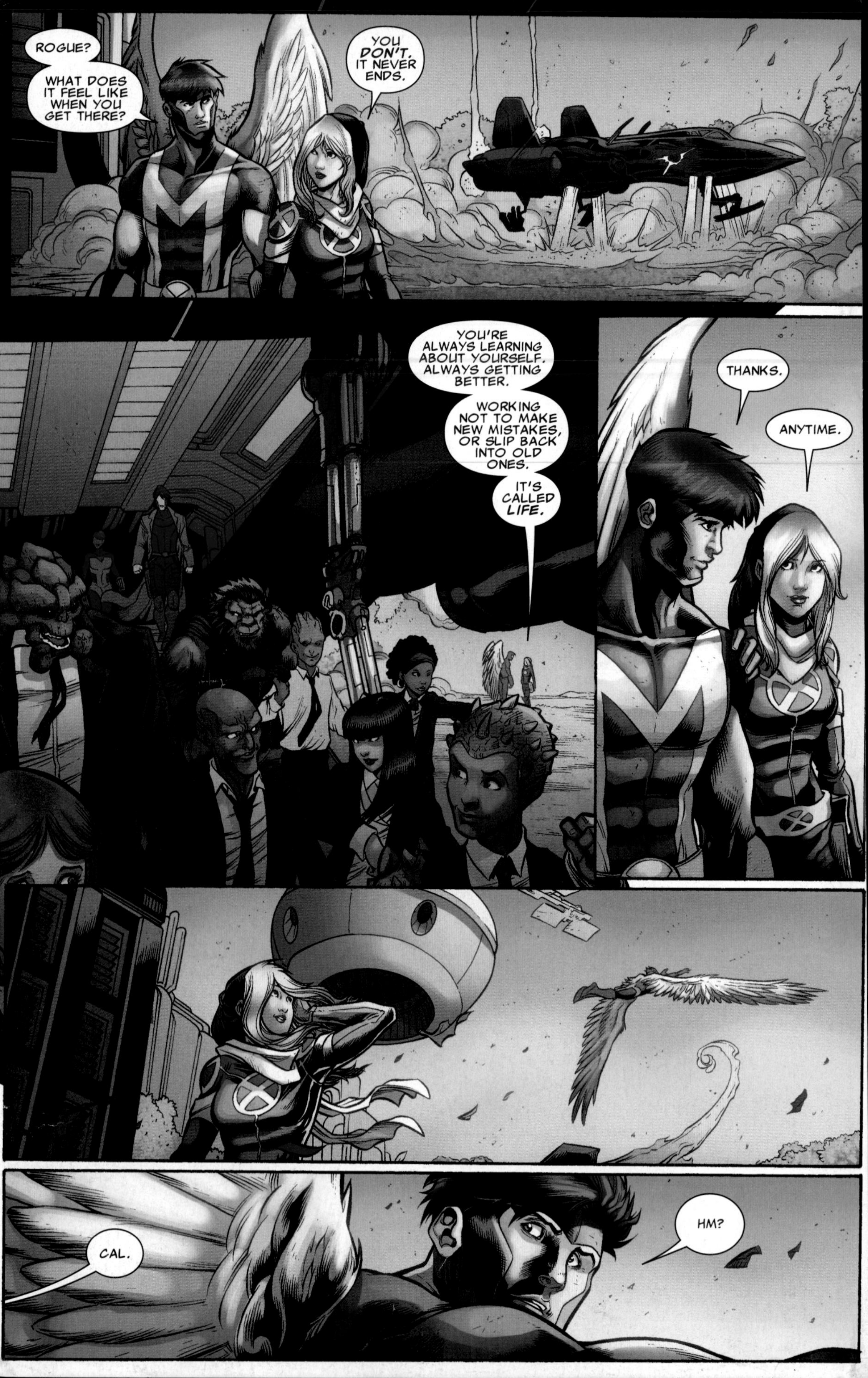
ROGUE?
WHAT DOES IT FEEL LIKE WHEN YOU GET THERE?
YOU DON'T. IT NEVER ENDS.
YOU'RE ALWAYS LEARNING ABOUT YOURSELF. ALWAYS GETTING BETTER.
WORKING NOT TO MAKE NEW MISTAKES, OR SLIP BACK INTO OLD ONES.
IT'S CALLED LIFE.
THANKS.
ANYTIME.
CAL.
HM?

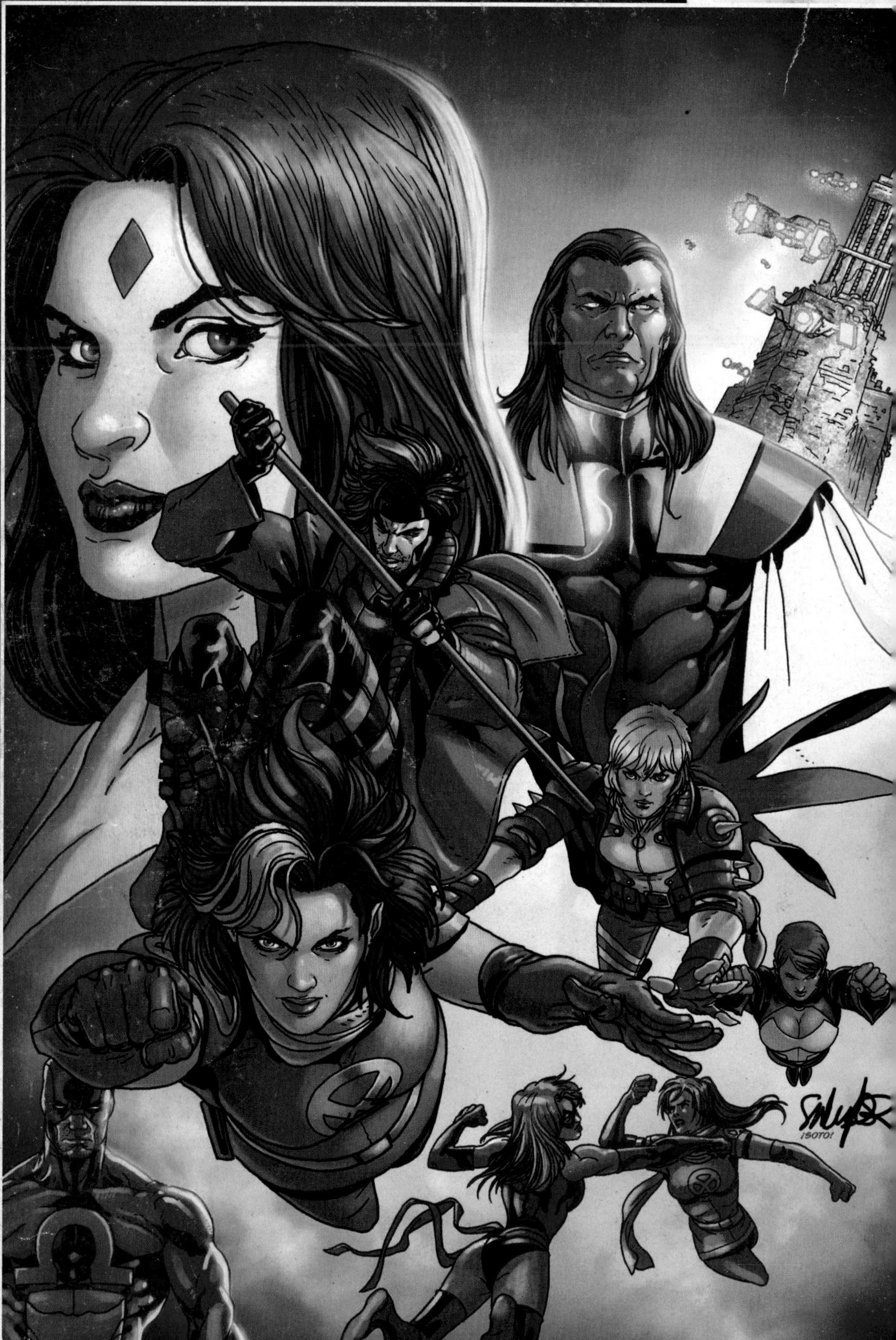

#275 VARIANT

BY **SALAVDOR LARROCA & CHRIS SOTOMAYOR**

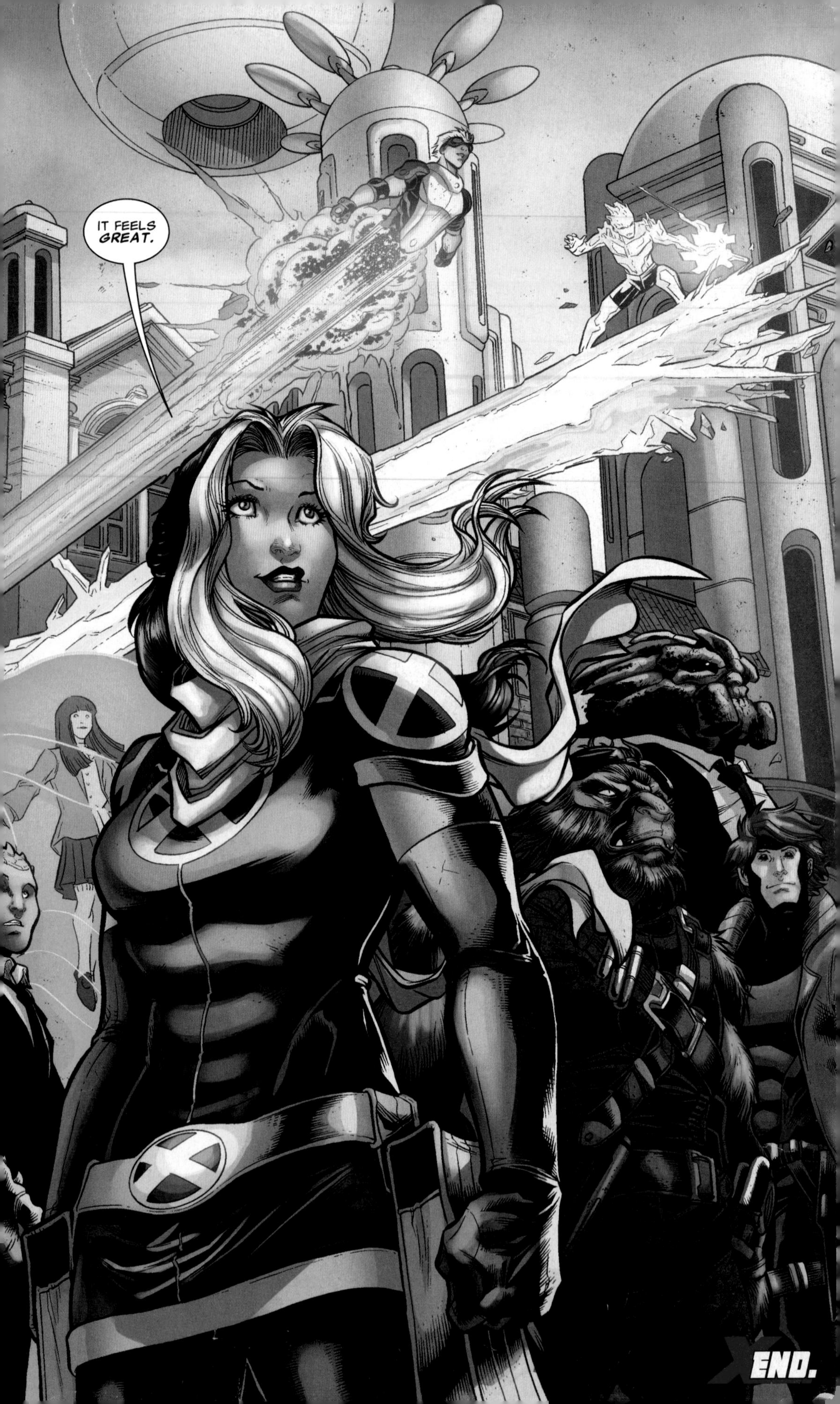
IT FEELS GREAT.
END.